MICROECONOMICS

Principles and Analysis

MICROECONOMICS

Principles and Analysis

Frank A. Cowell

STICERD and Department of Economics

London School of Economics

September 2005

OXFORD
UNIVERSITY PRESS

OXFORD
UNIVERSITY PRESS

Great Clarendon Street, Oxford OX2 6DP

Oxford University Press is a department of the University of Oxford.
It furthers the University's objective of excellence in research, scholarship,
and education by publishing worldwide in

Oxford New York

Auckland Cape Town Dar es Salaam Hong Kong Karachi
Kuala Lumpur Madrid Melbourne Mexico City Nairobi
New Delhi Shanghai Taipei Toronto

With offices in

Argentina Austria Brazil Chile Czech Republic France Greece
Guatemala Hungary Italy Japan Poland Portugal Singapore
South Korea Switzerland Thailand Turkey Ukraine Vietnam

Oxford is a registered trademark of Oxford University Press
in the UK and in certain other countries

Published in the United States
by Oxford University Press Inc., New York

First published 2006

British Library Cataloguing in Publication Data
Data available

Library of Congress Cataloging in Publication Data
Data available

Typeset by Laserwords Private Limited, Chennai, India
Printed and bound by
CPI Group (UK) Ltd,
Croydon, CR0 4YY

ISBN 978-0-19-926777-4

10

To Isabella who, if she becomes an economist like her dad and her granddad, will find that the methods will be different and that the answers will be different, but that the questions will remain the same.

PREFACE

In a book project of this sort one incurs many debts. My biggest debt is to the hundreds of students who took the courses on which this book is based: without them there would have been nothing. But also there would have been nothing without supportive colleagues, teaching assistants, and friends in the profession. Many provided suggestions on the teaching material from which the chapters derived; many more raised thought-provoking questions that led to changes or innovations. All provided continuous help and encouragement. I also am aware that I owe friends and family a considerable amount because of the way that writing this has dominated my time.

When the moment came to prepare the final draft I found that I had received sackfuls of helpful comments from many people, some of whom had spent a lot of their time warding me off errors or infelicities. I would particularly like to mention Guillermo Cruces, Michael Fessel, Maitreesh Ghatak, Jim Hines, Barbara Luppi, Rocco Macchiavello, Inés Macho-Stadler, François Maniquet, David Pérez-Castrillo, Andrew Potticary, Alberto Salvo-Farre, and Miguel Sanchez. My apologies to any whose special insights and ideas did not make it into the finished work, either through my forgetfulness or my pig-headedness.

I am very grateful to two indefatigable young colleagues, Alberto Galasso and Zhong Sheng, who provided further comments and suggestions, who bullied me daily (in the nicest possible way) to make sure that I did the corrections properly, and who carefully checked the emerging versions of the final text, and also to Silva Ule who provided me with assistance on sources far beyond that of many professional libraries.

CONTENTS

LIST OF FIGURES

LIST OF TABLES

ABBREVIATIONS

CARA	constant absolute risk aversion
CE	competitive equilibrium
CRRA	constant relative risk aversion
CRTS	constant returns to scale
CS	consumer's surplus
CV	compensating variation
DRTS	decreasing returns to scale
EV	equivalent variation
FOC	first-order condition
IRTS	increasing returns to scale
LHS	left-hand side
MRS	marginal rate of substitution
MRT	marginal rate of transformation
MRTS	marginal rate of technical substitution
RHS	right-hand side
WARP	weak axiom of revealed preference

1 Introduction

> ...the greater part of human actions have their origin not in logical reasoning but in sentiment. This is particularly true for actions that are not motivated economically...Man, although impelled to act by nonlogical motives, likes to tie his actions logically to certain principles; he therefore invents these a posteriori in order to justify his actions.
>
> Vilfredo Pareto, '*The Rise and Fall of Elites*' (1991).

1.1 The rôle of microeconomic principles

Why *principles* in microeconomics? Principles take you further than pure economic theory; principles show you the reasons underlying good practice in applied economics; principles help you tie together issues in microeconomics that might otherwise remain as isolated topics.

This book aims to introduce these principles: it does not try to cover everything in the field of microeconomics nor to explore all the ramifications of standard abstract models. Rather its purpose is to conduct you through an account of the central canon of microeconomics, showing you how it can assist in understanding everyday economic phenomena and helping you to develop a flair for economic reasoning. If you grasp some basic principles in theoretical and applied economics, you can often make considerable headway through a mixture of technical expertise and healthy common sense. There are a lot of rules of thumb, standard analytical procedures, and simple theorems that can be applied again and again to apparently dissimilar economic problems. The student of microeconomics can exploit the fact that many basic problems have a common structure and that they can be analysed using the same insights and methods. I hope that this book will help students to do just that.

1.2 Microeconomic models

Modern microeconomics focuses on the use of abstract models as a means of pursuing the inner truth of key issues. What are they for? What makes a good model?

1.2.1 Purpose

Apart from claims to intrinsic intellectual beauty—and some models do have an inherent attractiveness all of their own—the quality of a model depends upon such things as its power to explain the reasons underlying observed economic phenomena, to make precise the insights born of common sense and to expose erroneous reasoning. It is almost meaningless to describe a microeconomic model as 'good' or 'bad' without further qualification. Whether or not a particular model is good depends on the purpose for which it is designed—unless the model is actually so bad that it violates some fundamental economic principle or is valid only in circumstances so special that they are almost vacuous (the equivalent, say, of assuming that water can flow uphill).

So, to assess the worth of an economic model we need a specific context in which to place its abstract components and mechanisms. Different circumstances—but apparently the same economic problem—may demand a different type of model. This does not mean that microeconomics is inconsistent or ambiguous, just that we have to be careful to pause and rethink the objectives of the model, the context in which it is set and the way the model components are to be implemented. The essential components of a microeconomic model can be summarised under the following headings:

- The economic actors
- Motivation
- The economic environment
- Assumptions and axioms.

1.2.2 The economic actors

At the heart of the model is the economic actor or agent—someone or something that is taking economic decisions. It is common practice to speak as though this entity is just an isolated person—a solitary John Doe acting or reacting in the artificial world of the economic model. However, often the same principles apply whether this actor is considered to be an isolated consumer, a worker, a representative member of a group, or the embodiment of a corporation.

1.2.3 Motivation

Cynics may say that economics is about greed. In a sense cynics are right: most microeconomic models assume that somewhere deep in the mechanism is the driving force of self-interest. Are there useful alternatives? Certainly it is possible to imagine many cases where self-interest is not well defined because the 'self' may be a difficult concept—we shall briefly encounter this in chapter 9 where we consider what is meant by 'social' choices among alternatives. It is also possible to consider cases where individuals care about others' consumption or others' welfare. But in a sense even this can be seen as an extension of the standard paradigm of selfishness—I get personal satisfaction from observing a friend's consumption increase. So, we settle for greed; but at least it is *rational* greed: for now we will take on trust the idea of rationality, but we will examine it in more detail when we consider the formal modelling of consumers' motivation in chapter 4 (page 73).

The assumption of selfishness is not essential to economics, but it gets us a long way in formulating problems precisely and, even though it may go against the grain of the public-spirited people who study microeconomics, it can be useful in specifying a well-crafted model.

Where the topic of motivation runs into difficulty is in characterising the content and structure of these selfish aspirations. In the matter of specifying agents' preferences the model builder usually has to fall back on assertion based on extrapolation from one's own preferences and principles or, sometimes, on mathematical convenience. A special example of this difficulty lies in the representation of people's preferences under uncertainty (chapter 8): here strong far-reaching results can be obtained on the basis of a few elementary assumptions about preference structure, but it is not at all clear that they are in fact a suitable way of encapsulating individuals' motivation when faced with choices under uncertainty.

1.2.4 The economic environment

The economic environment may take a variety of forms. The principal form relevant to our discussion is some sort of market. The market itself could be represented in a number of ways: obviously it consists of a collection of other economic actors, but in order to complete its description as the economic environment we need to specify the 'rules of the game'. The rules of the game could refer literally to a game (see chapter 10) but, even in models where game theory makes no formal appearance, the assumptions about the forms of action and interaction that are admissible in the model are crucial in specifying clearly how a model is supposed to work and what it can tell us about human behaviour.

This can be illustrated even without using a formal model. We could imagine three levels of interaction of an individual economic agent with the environment, in ascending order of complexity:

- Agents may just accept the economic environment like we accept the weather. Just as you cannot change the weather so no agent is large or influential enough to manipulate the economic environment, so the argument goes.
- Maybe agents do not have to accept the economic environment as a given. Just as some human activities may indeed be big enough to affect the weather, so some agents' economic activities may be big enough to influence the market price of a product. However, interaction with the environment is limited: even if you can change the weather it doesn't try to anticipate your actions.
- A third view is that the environment in which agents operate is not like the weather at all. Everyone has to take into consideration the explicit interaction with everyone else. This interaction will include possible anticipation by one agent of what another agent may do.

Which view of the environment is appropriate clearly depends on the type of microeconomic model and its purpose.

1.2.5 Assumptions and axioms

Some of the basic ideas about the elements of a model—the nature of preferences, the structure of organisations, the physical nature of production possibilities—have to be modelled from scratch. The free hand enjoyed by the model builder should be used in a way that well represents the modeller's craft. The principal way that this craft is exercised in scratch modelling is known as the axiomatic method.

Axioms are just formally stated assumptions. They cannot be right or wrong, although they could be woefully inappropriate, judged by the purpose of the economic model.

What is the purpose of this formalisation? Axioms can help us:

- carefully develop the flow of an argument,
- concentrate on the individual components of key results,
- debug a wonky theory.

But they can never substitute for clear thinking about the purpose and essential functioning of the parent model and about the rôle of the specific model components for which axioms are to be introduced.

1.2.6 'Testing' a model

What is the criterion of 'relevance' of an economic model? Clearly it is advantageous if the predictions of the model do not immediately fall over when confronted with facts. However, this does not mean that all features of a model should be or could be subjected to rigorous empirical test. The standard methods of quantitative investigation can reveal a lot about the detail of agents' behavioural responses to the market environment and yet miss the central point of a model. In some cases, what may be more promising is to turn this connection between theory and empirics around; if the theory predicts a certain pattern of behaviour by economic agents then use the theoretical predictions as restrictions on relevant econometric models in order to provide more useful estimates.

Testing the quality of a theoretical model is a more subtle process than just confronting it with empirical testing. The model's quality also depends on such factors as simplicity of form, clarity of prediction, and the absence of 'blind-alley' assumptions (those that leave you with nowhere to go when you try to relax them).

1.3 Equilibrium analysis

The importance of economic equilibrium in understanding and applying economic principles cannot be overstated. An equilibrium can be regarded as an artificial construct that allows one to examine the properties of the model in a situation where every agent's choices and activities are consistent with each other and no agent would have an incentive to change its choices or activities. We can visualise an equilibrium as a posed picture of how a particular piece of the economic mechanism works.

1.3.1 Equilibrium and economic context

The equilibrium has to be defined relative to the economic environment. So if we make the environment more complicated within the economic model it should not come as a surprise that we need a more carefully specified definition of what an equilibrium state is. We can imagine this by analogy with a mechanical model: the more intricate the system of levers, wheels, and pulleys, the more you add on extra subsystems, the more carefully you will need to specify the conditions for the whole contraption to be in balance.

1.3.2 The comparative statics method

How do things in the model change as things in the environment around it change? The comparative statics method provides a way of dealing with this issue. It is built on the concept of equilibrium and focuses on the relationship between the equilibrium itself and one or more key parameters. It is not a description of a process but is more like a set of snapshots of different instances of equilibrium that leave a trace of a process.

The comparative statics method is sometimes incorporated into specific relationships that are used as a shorthand to characterise the behaviour of an economic agent. The prime example of this is demand and supply functions—collectively referred to as response functions. A second example is the reaction function in the analysis of game-theoretic models (chapter 10)—how one player responds to the actions of another on the assumption of a specific form of the rules of the game.

We use the comparative statics method time and again to get some insight on where the economic machine might move if certain levers were pulled. *How* the machine moves from point to point requires an explicit model of dynamic processes.

1.3.3 Dynamics and stability

With very few exceptions this book does not examine behaviour out of equilibrium. Some of the main issues of disequilibrium arise in the brief discussion of the stability of a general equilibrium system (subsection 7.4.4). It is important to distinguish between equilibrium itself and the stability of equilibrium.[1] We need this notion of stability in order to have some idea of whether the equilibrium states on which we spend so much intellectual energy are likely to prove no more than an ephemeral distraction.

1.4 Background to this book

This book assumes that you are not coming to the subject with a completely clean slate. Here is a brief overview of the background that is assumed in order to pursue the argument.

1.4.1 Economics

The opening chapters assume that you have mastered an introductory university course in economics, so that you will already have some familiarity with production functions,

? Mini Problems

1 Take an ordinary pencil with a sharpened point and place it on a flat table. How many equilibria does it have? Which of them are stable?

utility, demand and supply curves, the operation of the market, and the nature of equilibrium. However, we will reinforce and deepen understanding of these essential concepts by putting them on a formal basis. Later developments build on this foundation to introduce more advanced ideas.

1.4.2 Mathematics

This is not a book about mathematical economics nor about mathematics in economics. But it does not shy away from mathematics. Where a mathematical explanation could help to make an argument concise, or to give an additional economic insight that could be lost in the fog of words, we use it. As far as possible algebraic arguments are backed up with diagrams to present the underlying intuition.

The mathematical level does not get harder as the argument of the book progresses; nor is it the case that the harder economic problems are typically associated with harder mathematics. The material in Appendix A is intended to be a statement of fair dealing concerning the technical requirements of the main text: there are no mathematical surprises in the book that are not briefly covered in that material. Dipping into Appendix A is a way of reassuring yourself of how far you are expected to go with the mathematics as well as brushing up on particular technical points.

1.5 Using the book

The argument on each topic proceeds by a mixture of narrative and practice. The narrative is designed to take you briskly through the main themes of modern microeconomics. The material has been organised in a way that both has an inner logic to it and permits extensive reuse of techniques as you progress through the chapters. To achieve this, I have tried to minimise the interruption to the flow of narrative by relegating some formal proofs to appendices or to guided exercises. The practice involves a mixture of examples, exercises, and quick discussion points that you are encouraged to use in order to provide depth on particular points within the main themes and to develop familiarity with important solution techniques.

1.5.1 A route map

We begin with each of the two main economic actors—the firm and the household—and their relationships to the market. Understanding how these relationships work is the key to a lot of other interesting microeconomic problems.

The argument naturally moves on to consider how the economic system works as a whole. This addresses the key question on the rôle of the market in delivering goods to individual consumers and calling forth resources to produce the goods. The background message here is 'the market works' and can be used as a method of achieving desirable allocations of goods and services in the economy. But the discussion moves on to economic reasons why the argument does not work and why the paradigm of price taking may be too restrictive. There is no magic bullet to blow away the market as an institution, but an understanding of microeconomic principles can help in appraising the various possibilities for modifying market mechanisms and piecemeal solutions for overriding or replacing particular markets.

1.5.2 Some tips

- You will probably find it useful to check through the brief summary of mathematics in Appendix A. There you will also find some suggestions for further reading if you are a bit rusty on certain techniques. You should be certain to check carefully the list of symbol conventions used throughout the book—see page 483.
- The proof of some of the results are hived off to Appendix C. This is not because the results are not interesting, but because the method of proof is not particularly illuminating or is rather technical.
- Throughout each chapter there are Mini Problems that focus on detailed points of the argument. These take the form of one-liners that have suggested answers or outline solutions in Appendix B.
- Each chapter has several practical illustrative examples drawn from the relevant applied economics literature.
- The bibliographic references for the examples and for further reading are collected together on page 474 onwards.
- At the end of each chapter there are exercises that are designed to give you a more serious mental workout than the Mini Problems scattered throughout the chapters. Outline answers for these are on the Online Resource Centre—go to **www.oxfordtextbooks.co.uk/orc/cowell/**.
- Also on the website are several PowerPoint slide shows to accompany the material in chapters 2–13. They can be useful in understanding many of the key results and in isolating the economic relationships underlying many of the diagrams in the book.

2 The Firm

I think business is very simple. Profit. Loss. Take the sales, subtract the costs and you get this big positive number. The math is quite straightforward.

Bill Gates, *US News and World Report*, 15 February 1993.

2.1 Basic setting

We begin with the economic problem of the firm, partly because an understanding of this subject provides a good basis for several other topics that arise later in the book, partly because the formal analysis of this problem is quite straightforward and can usually be tied into everyday experience and observation.

We will tackle the issues that arise in the microeconomic analysis of the firm in seven stages. The first four of these are as follows:

- We analyse the structure of production and introduce some basic concepts that are useful in solving the firm's optimisation problem.
- We solve the optimisation problem of the price-taking, profit-maximising firm. Along the way we look at the problem of cost minimisation.
- The solution functions from the optimisation are used to characterise the firm's responses to market stimuli in the long and the short run.
- The analysis is extended to consider the problems confronting a multiproduct firm.

The remaining three topics focus on the firm's relationship with the market and are dealt with in chapter 3.

In this chapter we will find in part a review of some standard results that you may have already encountered in introductory treatments of microeconomics, and in part introduce a framework for future analysis. I shall give a brief account of the behaviour of a firm under very special assumptions; we then build on this by relaxing some of the assumptions and by showing how the main results carry over to other interesting issues. This follows a strategy that is used throughout the later chapters—set out the principles in simple cases and then move on to consider the way the principles need to be modified for more challenging situations and for other economic settings that lend themselves to the same type of treatment.

The firm: basic notation

z_i	amount used of input i
q	amount of output
ϕ	production function
w_i	price of input i
p	price of output

2.1.1 The firm: basic ingredients

Let us introduce the three main components of the problem, the technology, the environment, and economic motivation.

Technology

You may well be familiar with the idea of a production function. Perhaps the form you have seen it in before is as a simple one-output, two-input equation: $q = F(K, L)$ ('quantity of output = a function of capital and labour'), which is a convenient way of picking up some of the features that are essential to analysing the behaviour of the firm.

However, we shall express the technological possibilities for a firm in terms of a fundamental *in*equality specifying the relationship between a single output and a vector of m inputs:

$$q \leq \phi(\mathbf{z}) \tag{2.1}$$

Expression (2.1) allows for a generalisation of the idea of the production relation. Essentially the function ϕ tells us the maximum amount of output q that can be obtained from the list of inputs $\mathbf{z} := (z_1, z_2, \ldots, z_m)$; putting the specification of technological possibilities given in the form (2.1) allows us to:

- handle multiple inputs,
- consider the possibility of inefficient production.

On the second point note that if the '=' part of (2.1) holds we shall call production *technically efficient*—you cannot get any more output for the given list of inputs $\mathbf{z}$.

The particular properties of the function ϕ incorporate our assumptions about the 'facts of life' concerning the production technology of the firm. Working with the single-product firm makes description of the 'direction of production' easy. However, sometimes we have to represent multiple outputs, where this specification will not do—see section 2.5 below where we go further still in generalising the concept of the production function.

Environment

We assume that the firm operates in a market in which there is pure competition. The meaning of this in the present context is simply that the firm takes as given a price p for its output and a list of prices $\mathbf{w} := (w_1, w_2, \ldots, w_m)$ for each of the m inputs respectively (mnemonic—think of w_i as the 'wage' of input i).

Of course it may be interesting to consider forms of economic organisation other than the market, and it may also be reasonable to introduce other constraints in addition to those imposed by a simple specification of market conditions—for example the problem of 'short-run' optimisation, or of rationing. However, the standard competitive, price-taking model provides a solid analytical basis for a careful discussion of these other possibilities for the firm and for situations where a firm has some control over the price of output p or of some of the input prices w_i.

Motivation

Almost without exception we shall assume that the objective of the firm is to *maximise profits*: this assumes either that the firm is run by owner-managers or that the firm correctly interprets shareholders' interests.[1]

Within the context of our simplified model we can write down profits in schematic terms as follows:

firm's profits = sales revenue − purchases of inputs

More formally, we define the expression for profits as

$$\Pi := pq - \sum_{i=1}^{m} w_i z_i. \tag{2.2}$$

Before we go any further let us note that it seems reasonable to assume that ϕ in (2.1) has the property:

$$\phi(0) = 0 \tag{2.3}$$

which in plain language means both that the firm cannot make something for nothing and that it can always decide to shut up shop, use no inputs, produce no output, and thus make zero profits. Therefore we do not need to concern ourselves with the possibility of firms making negative profits (tactful name for losses) in the profit-maximisation problem.[2]

2.1.2 Properties of the production function

Let us examine more closely the production function given in (2.1) above. We will call a particular vector of inputs a *technique*. It is useful to introduce two concepts relating to the techniques available for a particular output level q:

? Mini Problems

1 What alternative to profit-maximisation might it be reasonable to consider?

2 In real life we come across firms reporting losses. In what ways would our simplified model need to be extended in order to account for this phenomenon?

1. Pick some arbitrary level of output q: then the *input-requirement set* for the specified value q is the following set of techniques:

$$Z(q) := \{\mathbf{z} : \phi(\mathbf{z}) \geq q\}. \tag{2.4}$$

2. The *q-isoquant* of the production function ϕ is the contour of ϕ in the space of inputs

$$\{\mathbf{z} : \phi(\mathbf{z}) = q\}. \tag{2.5}$$

Clearly the q-isoquant is just the boundary of $Z(q)$. Although you may be familiar with the isoquant and the input-requirement set Z may seem to be a novelty, the set Z is, in fact, useful for characterising the fundamental properties of the production function and the consequences for the behaviour of the optimising firm. Certain features of shape of Z will dictate the general way in which the firm responds to market signals as we will see in section 2.3 below.

In a two-input version of the model Figure 2.1 illustrates four possible shapes of $Z(q)$ corresponding to different assumptions about the production function. Note the following:

- An isoquant can touch the axis if one input is not essential.

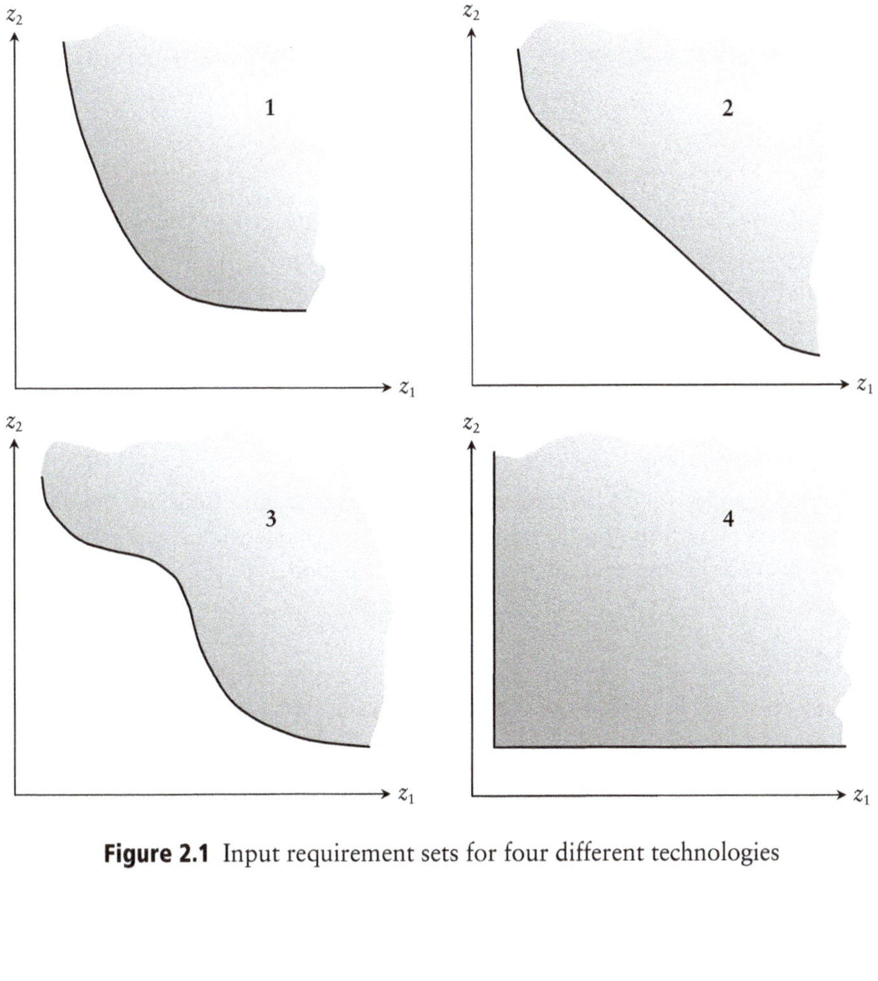

Figure 2.1 Input requirement sets for four different technologies

- An isoquant may have flat segments (case 2 in Figure 2.1). We can interpret this as locally perfect substitutes in production.
- The convexity of $Z(q)$ implies that production processes are, in some sense, divisible. To see this, do the following with cases 1, 2, or 4 in Figure 2.1: take any two vectors $\mathbf{z}'$ and $\mathbf{z}''$ that lie in $Z(q)$; draw the straight line between them; any point on this line clearly also belongs to $Z(q)$ and such a point can be expressed as $t\mathbf{z}' + [1 - t]\mathbf{z}''$ where $0 < t < 1$; what you have established is that if the production techniques $\mathbf{z}'$ and $\mathbf{z}''$ are feasible for q, then so too is a mixture of them (half one and half the other, say).[3] However, this does not work everywhere in case 3 (check the part of Z where there is a 'dent'). Here a mixture of two feasible techniques may lie outside Z: non-convexity implies that there is some indivisibility in the production process.
- An isoquant may have 'kinks' or corners: (case 4).

Marginal rate of technical substitution

Where ϕ is differentiable (i.e. at points on the isoquant other than kinks) we shall often find it convenient to work with the slope of the isoquant, which is formally defined as follows:

Definition 2.1

The *marginal rate of technical substitution* of input i for input j is given by

$$\text{MRTS}_{ij} := \frac{\phi_j(\mathbf{z})}{\phi_i(\mathbf{z})}.$$

In this definition and elsewhere we use subscripts as a shorthand for the appropriate partial derivative. In this case $\phi_i(\mathbf{z})$ means $\partial\phi(\mathbf{z})/\partial z_i$.

The MRTS reflects the 'relative value' of one input in terms of another from the firm's point of view. The particular value of the MRTS for inputs (z_1^0, z_2^0) is represented in Figure 2.2 by the slope at point $\mathbf{z}^\circ$; the slope of the ray through $\mathbf{z}^\circ$ represents the corresponding *input ratio* z_2/z_1 at this point.

Elasticity of substitution

We can use this idea to characterise the shape of the isoquant. Consider the question: how responsive is the firm's production technology to a change in this relative valuation? This may be made precise by using the following definition.

? Mini Problems

3 A firm has offices in London and New York. Fractional units of labour can be employed in each place (part-timers can be hired) and the headquarters could be in either city. The minimum viable office staff is one full-time employee and the minimum size of headquarters is three full-timers. Sketch the isoquants in this case and explain why $Z(q)$ is not convex.

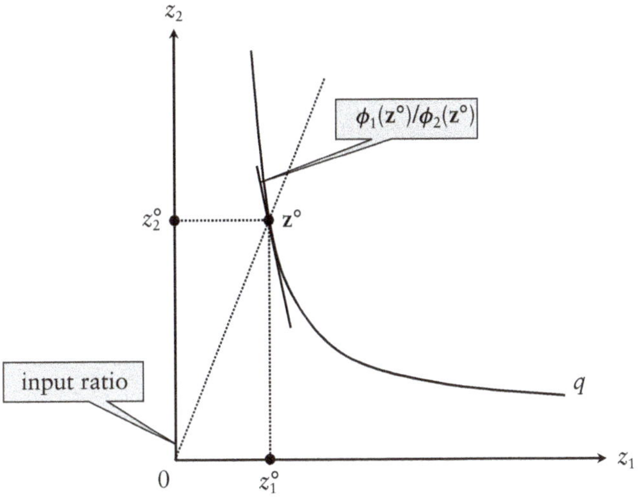

Figure 2.2 Marginal rate of technical substitution

Definition 2.2

The *elasticity of substitution* is

$$\sigma_{ij} := -\frac{\partial \log\left(z_j/z_i\right)}{\partial \log\left(\phi_j(\mathbf{z})/\phi_i(\mathbf{z})\right)}. \tag{2.6}$$

Notice that $\sigma_{ij} \geq 0$ and that (2.6) has the simple interpretation

$$\frac{\text{proportional change in input ratio}}{\text{proportional change in MRTS}}$$

(in absolute terms).[4] Higher values of σ mean that the production function is more 'flexible' in that there is a proportionately larger change in the production technique in response to a given proportionate change in the implicit relative valuation of the factors: Figure 2.3 illustrates isoquant maps for two cases, where σ is low (large changes in the MRTS are associated with small changes in the input ratio) and where σ is high (small changes in the MRTS are associated with large changes in the input ratio).

We can build up an entire family of isoquants corresponding to all the possible values of q and there may be a wide variety of potentially interesting forms that the resulting map might take.[5]

? Mini Problems

4 Show that $\sigma_{ij} = \sigma_{ji}$. You may find the material on page 494 useful.

5 (a) Two firms have differentiable production functions $\phi(\cdot)$ and $\hat{\phi}(\cdot)$ where both $\phi_1(\mathbf{z}) > 0$ and $\hat{\phi}_1(\mathbf{z}) > 0$. Suppose it is true that, for all $\mathbf{z}$:

$$\hat{\phi}(\mathbf{z}) = \Psi(\phi(\mathbf{z}))$$

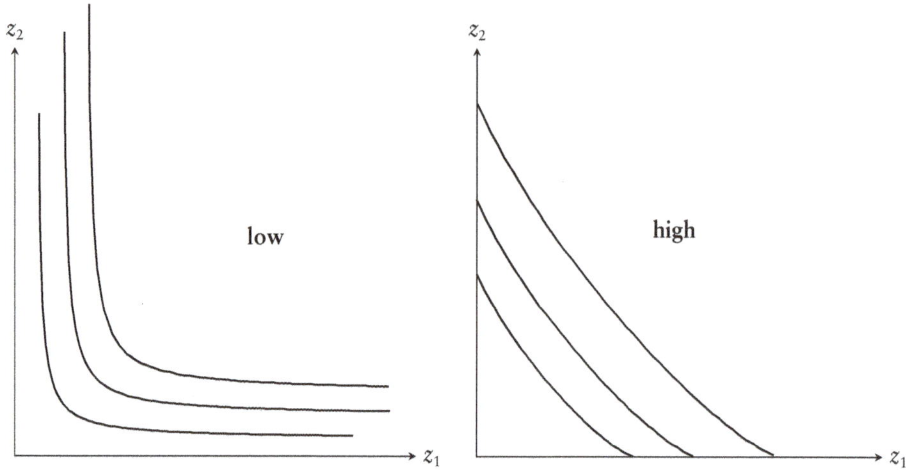

Figure 2.3 Low and high elasticity of substitution

Homothetic and homogeneous production functions

For many purposes it is worth considering further restrictions on the function ϕ that have convenient interpretations. The left-hand half of Figure 2.4 illustrates the case of *homothetic* contours: each isoquant appears like a photocopied enlargement; along any ray through the origin all the tangents have the same slope so that the MRTS depends only on the relative proportions of the inputs used in the production process. The right-hand half of Figure 2.4 illustrates an important subcase of this family—*homogeneous* production functions—for which the map looks the same but where the labelling of the contours has to satisfy the following rule: for any scalar $t > 0$ and any input vector $\mathbf{z} \geq 0$:

$$\phi(t\mathbf{z}) = t^r \phi(\mathbf{z}), \tag{2.7}$$

where r is a positive scalar. If $\phi(\cdot)$ satisfies the property in (2.7) then it is said to be homogeneous of degree r. Clearly the parameter r carries important information about the way

? Mini Problems

where Ψ is a differentiable, strictly increasing function. Show that for any given $\mathbf{z}$ the firms have the same MRTS_{1i} for all inputs $2, \ldots, m$. (b) Suppose $\mathbf{z}$ is an m-vector of inputs, that $\mathbf{z}^{\circ}$ denotes the first k components and $\mathbf{z}'$ denotes the remaining $m-k$ components of $\mathbf{z}$, so that

$$\mathbf{z} = \left[\mathbf{z}^{\circ}, \mathbf{z}'\right].$$

Show that if there exist functions ψ and Ψ such that

$$\phi(\mathbf{z}) = \Psi\left(\psi\left(\mathbf{z}^{\circ}\right), \mathbf{z}'\right)$$

and $\phi(\cdot)$ is everywhere differentiable with $\phi_1(\mathbf{z}) > 0$ then MRTS_{1i} is independent of $\mathbf{z}'$ for all $i = 2, \ldots, k$.

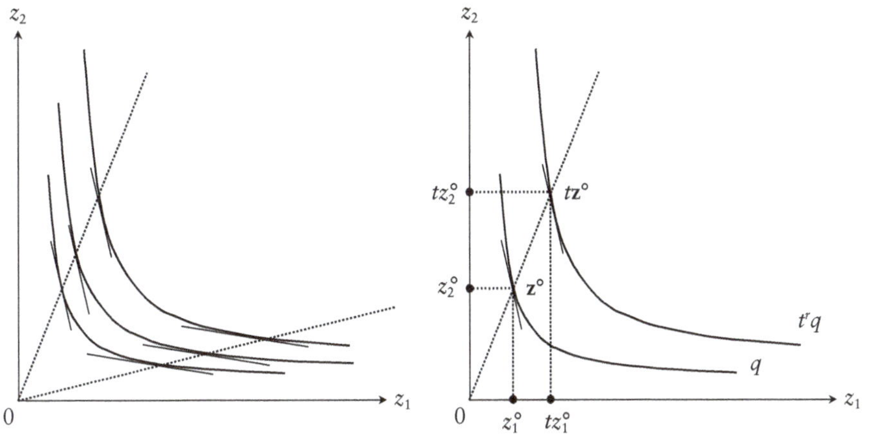

Figure 2.4 Homothetic and homogeneous functions

output responds to a proportionate change in all inputs together: if $r > 1$, for example, then doubling more inputs will more than double output.[6]

Returns to scale

However, homogeneous functions, although very convenient analytically, are obviously rather special. It is helpful to be able to classify the effect of changing the scale of production more generally. This is done using the following definition:

Definition 2.3

The production function ϕ exhibits

1. *increasing returns to scale (IRTS)* if, for any scalar $t > 1$:

$$\phi(t\mathbf{z}) > t\phi(\mathbf{z}). \tag{2.8}$$

? Mini Problems

6 Which of the following production functions are homothetic? Which are homogeneous? Briefly explain. [Hint: use definitions A.13 and A.14 in Appendix A.]

1. $\phi(\mathbf{z}) = z_1^{0.1} z_2^{0.2}$
2. $\phi(\mathbf{z}) = \log z_1 + 2 \log z_2$
3. $\phi(\mathbf{z}) = z_1^{0.5} + 2z_2^{0.5}$
4. $\phi(\mathbf{z}) = \exp\left(z_1^{0.5} z_2^{0.5}\right)$
5. $\phi(\mathbf{z}) = [z_1 - k]^{0.5} + [z_2 - k]^{0.5}, z_1 \geq k, z_2 \geq k, \phi(\mathbf{z}) = 0$ otherwise.
6. $\phi(\mathbf{z}) = z_1^{0.1} + z_2^{0.2}$

In two of these six cases the pattern of the isoquant map is exactly the same—which two?

2. *decreasing returns to scale (DRTS)* if, for any scalar $t > 1$:

$$\phi(t\mathbf{z}) < t\phi(\mathbf{z}). \tag{2.9}$$

3. *constant returns to scale (CRTS)* if, for any positive scalar t:

$$\phi(t\mathbf{z}) = t\phi(\mathbf{z}). \tag{2.10}$$

Figures 2.5 to 2.7 illustrate production functions with two inputs and a single output corresponding to each of these three cases. In each case the set of points on or 'underneath' the tent-like shape represents feasible input-output combinations. Take a point on the surface such as the one marked in each of the three figures:

- Its vertical coordinate gives the maximum amount of output that can be produced from the input quantities represented by its (z_1, z_2) coordinates.
- The dotted path through this point in each figure is the *expansion path*; this gives the output and input combinations as (z_1, z_2) are varied in the same proportion (for example variations along the ray through the origin in the two-dimensional Figure 2.2).[7] In the simple constant returns to scale production function the expansion path is itself a ray through the origin (Figure 2.7); in the IRTS and DRTS cases this path is clearly curved.

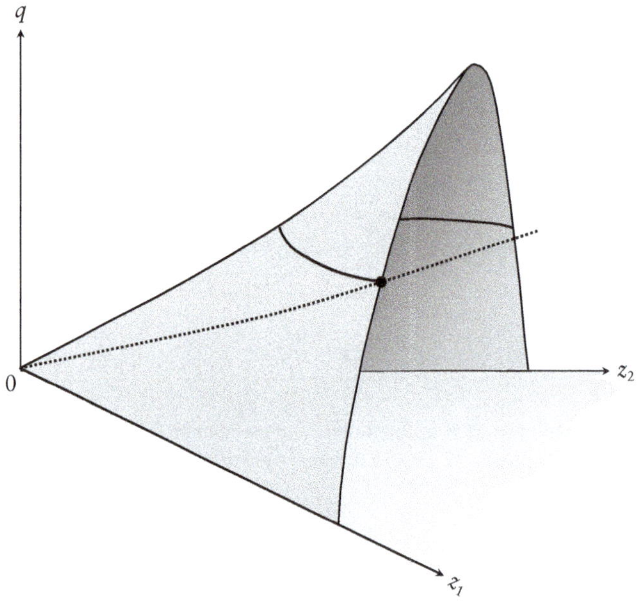

Figure 2.5 An IRTS production function

? Mini Problems

7 In the special case of homogeneous production functions what are the values of r that correspond to increasing/constant/decreasing returns to scale?

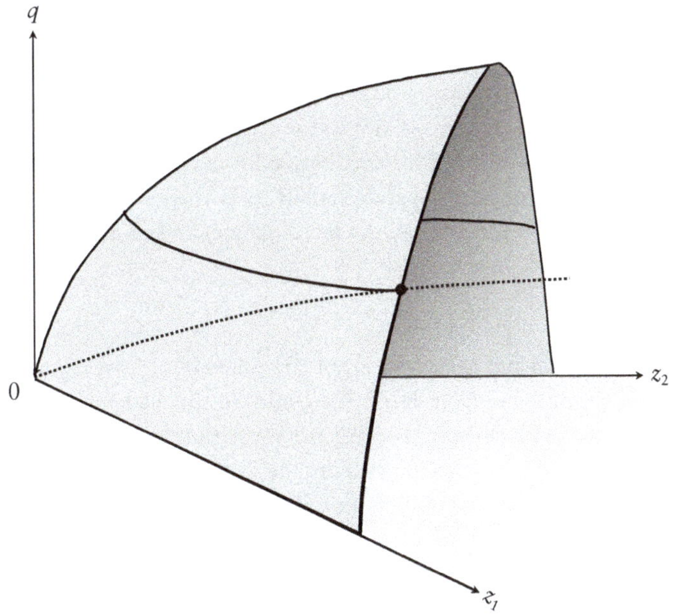

Figure 2.6 A DRTS production function

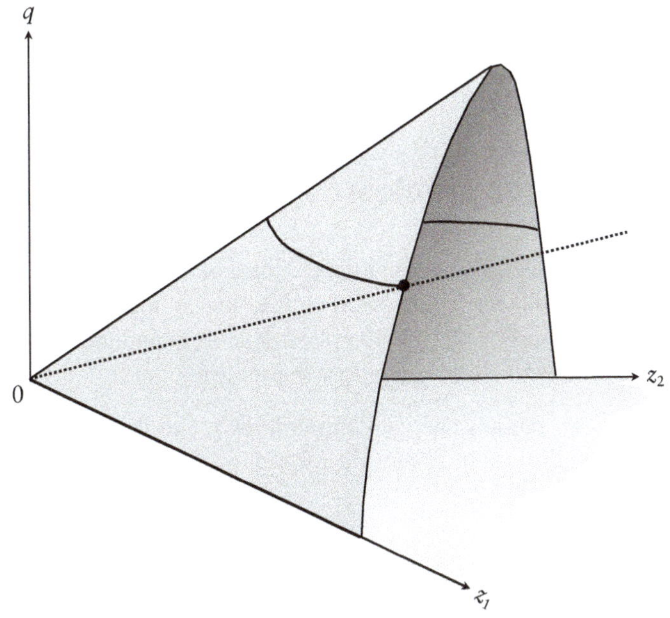

Figure 2.7 A CRTS production function

- The solid curve through this point in each figure is a *contour* of ϕ; project this contour down into the (z_1, z_2)-plane (the 'floor' of the diagram) and you get the isoquant.

Of course one could specify localised increasing returns to scale by limiting the range of values of t for which (2.8) is true—likewise for decreasing or constant returns to scale; quite a common assumption is that for small-scale production (low values of z_1 and z_2) IRTS is true while for large-scale operations DRTS is true. Furthermore, it is easy to check that if ϕ is a concave function all the sets $Z(q)$ are convex and returns to scale are constant or decreasing everywhere.[8]

Marginal product

Now consider the relationship between output and one input (z_1 let us say) whilst all the other inputs are kept at some fixed level. We could do this in Figure 2.7, for example, by picking an arbitrary z_2 value and then slicing through the tent-shape in a plane parallel to $q0z_1$. This would give a shape such as the Case 1 in Figure 2.8.[9] Cases 2–4 in Figure 2.8 illustrate the same type of diagram for three other production functions.[10] We can use this view of the production function to depict another very useful concept, shown in Figure 2.9.

Definition 2.4

The *marginal product* of input i is the derivative (where it is defined) of the production function with respect to z_i.

Of course the concept of marginal product was already implicit in the Definition 2.1 earlier: it represents the 'value' to the firm of an input—measured in terms of output.

2.2 The optimisation problem

We could now set out the firm's objectives in the form of a standard constrained optimisation problem. To do this we would specify a Lagrangean incorporating profits (2.2), and the production constraint (2.1). However, it is more illuminating to adopt a two-stage approach to solving the firm's optimisation problem:

1. *Cost Minimisation.* For any specified output level q, find the combination of inputs that will minimise the cost of producing q for known input prices **w**.

? Mini Problems

8 What are returns to scale exhibited by each of the production functions in Mini Problem 6?

9 Sketch 3-D diagrams like the one above that will correspond to Cases 2 to 4 in Figure 2.8.

10 Assume constant returns to scale: then two of the four cases in Figure 2.1 correspond to two of the four cases in Figure 2.8. Which are they? Suggest a simple formula for each of the two production functions that would yield these forms.

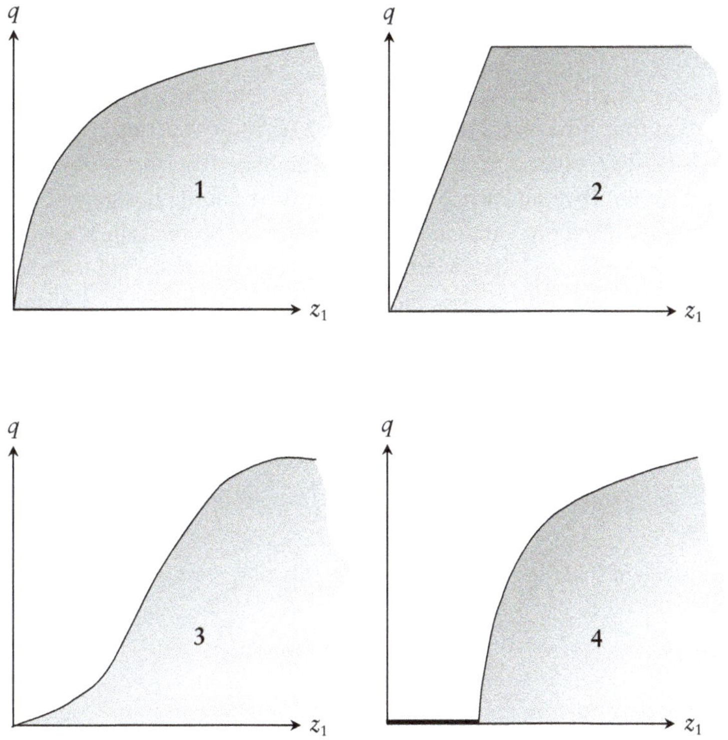

Figure 2.8 Four different technologies

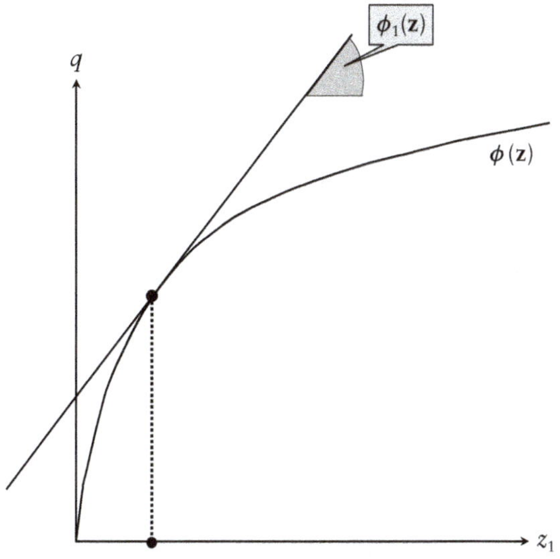

Figure 2.9 The marginal product

2. *Output Optimisation*. Once the appropriate input policy conditional upon an arbitrary output level is known, choose the appropriate output level.

In stage 1 we notionally *fix* the output level at some arbitrary level q as in Figure 2.1; in stage 2 the output level becomes endogenous. Why go via this roundabout route? There are two reasons. First, it neatly compartmentalises two aspects of the firm's activities that have an intuitive independent rationale; for example the stage-2 problem is a self-contained topic often presented in introductory texts. Second, the stage-1 problem is highly 'portable': we will see later examples of this approach to the solution of microeconomic problems that are in effect just a simple translation of the firm's cost-minimisation problem.

2.2.1 Optimisation stage 1: cost minimisation

The essence of the problem can be set out simply in terms of just two inputs: we can represent it diagrammatically as in Figure 2.10. There are two important points to note about this diagram:

- Consider a line drawn with slope w_1/w_2 in this diagram. By definition this has the equation:

$$w_1 z_2 + w_2 z_2 = \textbf{constant} \tag{2.11}$$

  In other words, all the points lying on such a line represent input combinations that require the same financial outlay by the firm. For this reason such a line is known as an *isocost* line.

- Shift an isocost line up and cost goes up: you just change the constant on the right-hand side of (2.11).

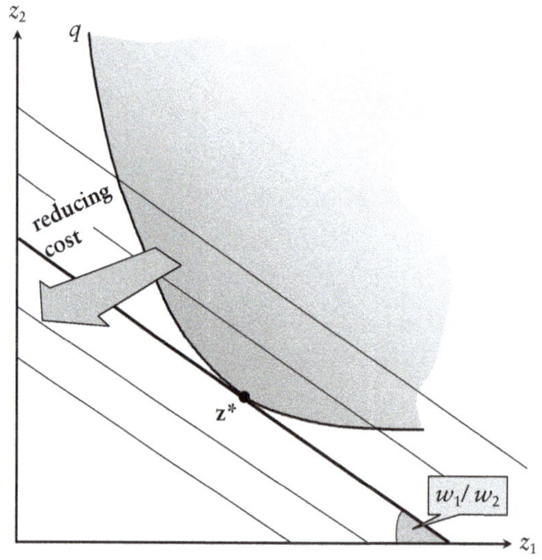

Figure 2.10 Cost minimisation

Intuitively the cost-minimisation problem for a given output q involves reaching the lowest isocost line subject to staying within the input-requirement set $Z(q)$. Formally we can represent the cost-minimisation problem as that of minimising the Lagrangean:

$$\mathcal{L}(\mathbf{z}, \lambda; \mathbf{w}, q) := \sum_{i=1}^{m} w_i z_i + \lambda [q - \phi(\mathbf{z})] \tag{2.12}$$

for some specified output level q, and for given input prices $\mathbf{w}$, subject to the restrictions that $z_i \geq 0$ for every input i, where λ is the Lagrange multiplier associated with the constraint (2.1).

Differentiating (2.12) with respect to z_i we can derive the first-order conditions (FOCs) for a minimum. Let $\mathbf{z}^*$ denote the vector of cost-minimising inputs that emerges in the solution to (2.12); if input i is used in strictly positive amounts at the optimum then the FOC implies:

$$\lambda^* \phi_i(\mathbf{z}^*) = w_i. \tag{2.13}$$

More generally we have:[11]

$$\lambda^* \phi_i(\mathbf{z}^*) \leq w_i \tag{2.14}$$

for every i where the '$<$' part applies only if $z_i^* = 0$. Likewise, differentiating (2.12) with respect to λ, we would find

$$q = \phi(\mathbf{z}^*). \tag{2.15}$$

The general condition for an optimum is actually

$$q \leq \phi(\mathbf{z}^*) \tag{2.16}$$

where the '$<$' part applies only if $\lambda^* = 0$. However, conditions (2.13, 2.14) imply that the Lagrange multiplier λ^* must be positive at the optimum,[12] and so we actually do have (2.15)—production must be technically efficient.[13] From all of this we can deduce that if cost minimisation requires a positive amount of input i then for any other input j:[14]

$$\frac{\phi_j(\mathbf{z}^*)}{\phi_i(\mathbf{z}^*)} \leq \frac{w_j}{w_i} \tag{2.17}$$

? Mini Problems

11 [Exercise for the mathematically inclined] Formally the case where one allows for corner solutions is a standard example of a non-linear programming problem. Use the Kuhn–Tucker conditions (A.50)–(A.53) for an optimum (page 509) to set out the solution to the problem in detail and to verify the statements made in the text.

12 Explain why this implies that λ^* must be positive in non-trivial cases.

13 Provide an intuitive argument to show (2.15). Hint: Suppose that at $\mathbf{z}^*$ the strict *inequality* part of (2.1) were true; show that you could then find a feasible input vector that is cheaper for the firm.

14 (a) Draw a figure illustrating the corner solution in (2.17). (b) Interpret this first-order condition using the concept of the firm's 'relative value' of one input in terms of another from the firm's point of view (see page 12) (i) in the case where '$<$' holds in (2.17), (ii) in the case where '$=$' holds in (2.17).

with equality in (2.17) if input j is also used in positive amounts. So in the case where cost-minimising amounts of both inputs are positive we have:

MRTS	=	input price ratio

Drawing all these remarks together we have established the following result:

Theorem 2.1 (Properties of the minimum-cost solution)

(a) The cost-minimising output under perfect competition is technically efficient. (b) For any two inputs i, j purchased in positive amounts, MRTS_{ij} must equal the input price ratio w_j/w_i. (c) If i is an input that is purchased, and j is an input that is not purchased then MRTS_{ij} will be less than or equal to the input price ratio w_j/w_i.

As the earlier discussion implies, the solution may be at a corner, and it may not be unique: this all depends on the shape of the input-requirement set $Z(q)$, as we will see later.

We can express the inputs that satisfy (2.15) and (2.17) in terms of the specified output level q and the input-price vector $\mathbf{w}$. We shall write this solution as follows:

$$z_i^* = H^i(\mathbf{w}, q) \tag{2.18}$$

for inputs $i = 1, \ldots, m$. Think of the relationship H^i as *the conditional demand* for input i—demand that is conditional upon the level q. We shall discuss a number of aspects of this relationship—in particular the conditions under which H^i is a genuine single-valued function—after we have considered some other important features of the optimum (but you have to wait until chapter 4 on the consumer to see why the letter H is used...).

2.2.2 The cost function

We can also write the minimised cost that is the solution to (2.12) as a function of q and $\mathbf{w}$. This will prove to be a valuable concept that has applications not only throughout the rest of our discussion of the theory of the firm, but also in other areas of economic theory, such as consumer optimisation.

Definition 2.5

The firm's *cost function* is a real-valued function C of input prices and the output level such that:

$$C(\mathbf{w}, q) := \min_{\{\mathbf{z}\geq 0, \phi(\mathbf{z})\geq q\}} \sum_{i=1}^{m} w_i z_i \tag{2.19}$$

$$= \sum_{i=1}^{m} w_i H^i(\mathbf{w}, q) \tag{2.20}$$

The meaning of the cost function is as follows. Given a specified value for the price of each input and for the level of output, what is the minimum outlay that the firm requires in order to purchase the inputs?[15] Because the function C is derived from a process of cost minimisation, it possesses a number of very useful properties.

First, C must be *strictly increasing* in at least one of the input prices and, if the production function is continuous, C must be strictly increasing in output too: if this were not so then you could either use less of all inputs to get the same level of output, or get

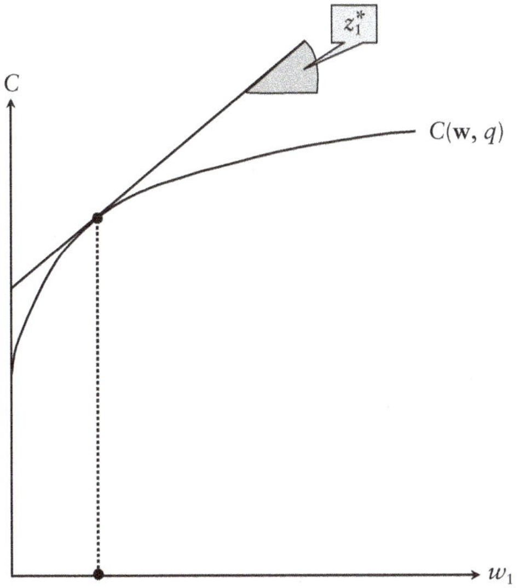

Figure 2.11 Cost and input price

? Mini Problems

15 Suppose the production function is given in logarithmic form as

$$\log q \leq \frac{1}{4}\log z_1 + \frac{3}{4}\log z_2$$

(a) Write down the Lagrangean for the cost-minimisation problem. (b) Explain why we can be sure that the cost-minimisation problem will not have a corner solution. (c) Find the FOCs for a minimum. (d) What are the cost-minimising values of the inputs z_1 and z_2? (e) What is the cost function?.

more output for the same expenditure on inputs; either way, you clearly would not be at a cost-minimising point. For much the same sort of reason we can see that C cannot be decreasing in any of the w_i.[16]

Second, we can see from (2.17) that a 10 per cent increase in both input prices w_1 and w_2 would not change the optimal input levels z_1^* and z_2^*; so by how much would the minimised cost, $w_1 z_1^* + w_2 z_2^*$ have increased? Obviously 10 per cent. The argument easily extends to m inputs and an arbitrary rescaling of all input prices.

Third, the cost function must be *concave in prices*, as illustrated by the one-input snapshot that is illustrated in Figure 2.11: note that this is a general result and does not depend on any special properties of the production function ϕ.[17]

Fourth, imagine that you are employing a thousand hours of labour at the cost-minimising point: by how much would your firm's costs increase if there were an infinitesimal increase in the wage paid to labour (say one penny an hour)? By how much would your costs have gone up had you been employing 1200 hundred units of labour at the cost-minimising point? 1200 pence? If your intuition is sharp you should have spotted that the rate of increase of cost with respect to input price equals the amount of units of that input that you employ at the optimum—a property of the cost function that is known as *Shephard's Lemma*.[18]

All these features can be summarised as follows (a proof is provided in Appendix C):

Theorem 2.2 Properties of the cost function

The competitive firm's cost function C in (2.19) is nondecreasing and continuous in $\mathbf{w}$, homogeneous of degree one in $\mathbf{w}$ and concave in $\mathbf{w}$. It is strictly increasing in at least one w_i. If the production function is continuous then C is strictly increasing in q. At every point where the differential is defined

$$\frac{\partial C(\mathbf{w}, q)}{\partial w_i} = z_i^* \tag{2.21}$$

the optimal demand for input i.

For a couple of further points of interest we introduce the concepts of *average cost* $C(\mathbf{w}, q)/q$, and of *marginal cost* $C_q(\mathbf{w}, q)$. There is a neat and very useful relationship between the 'returns-to-scale' property of the production function ϕ and the behaviour of average cost: decreasing returns to scale imply rising average cost[19] and vice versa; constant returns to scale imply constant average cost. Also rising average cost implies

? Mini Problems

16 C could be constant in some of the w_i. Why?

17 Show that the cost function must be concave using Remark A.4 in Appendix A.

18 Prove this in the special case where $\mathbf{z}^*$ is unique and strictly positive. [Hint: differentiate (2.20) with respect to w_i and use the first-order conditions.]

19 Prove this. Hint: draw a pair of isoquants at $\bar{q}$ and $t\bar{q}$; for a given input-price ratio mark in the cost-minimising input combination on the $t\bar{q}$-isoquant and draw a ray through this point; find

that marginal cost is above average cost; falling average cost implies that marginal cost is below average cost.[20] Furthermore, consider the impact of an increase in the specified level of output on the cost-minimisation problem. Noting that (2.15) holds at the optimum, we must have

$$C(\mathbf{w},q) = \sum_{i=1}^{m} w_i z_i^* + \lambda^* [q - \phi(\mathbf{z}^*)] . \tag{2.22}$$

Equation (2.22) leads to the following very useful general result on marginal cost (see Appendix C):[21]

$$C_q(\mathbf{w}, q) = \lambda^* . \tag{2.23}$$

To see why we get this result, put the question: 'how much would the firm be prepared to pay for an infinitesimal relaxation of the output target in (2.12) from q to $q - \Delta q$?' The intuitive answer to this is: 'an amount that is just equal to the extra cost of producing Δq.' In other words, in the neighbourhood of the optimum, the appropriate 'value' of the constraint in (2.12)—the Lagrange multiplier—is the marginal cost of output at q.

Example 2.1

The analysis can be immediately applied empirically. Consider production conditions in the electricity-supply industry. A classic paper (Nerlove 1963) models the problem in terms of three key inputs: labour (input 1), capital (input 2), and fuel (input 3). If the technology can be appropriately represented by a Cobb–Douglas production function

$$\phi(\mathbf{z}) = A z_1^{\alpha_1} z_2^{\alpha_2} z_3^{\alpha_3}$$

then the following equation for the logarithm of total costs will hold:

$$\log C = \gamma + \beta_0 \log q + \beta_1 \log w_1 + \beta_2 \log w_2 + \beta_3 \log w_3 \tag{2.24}$$

where $\beta_0, \ldots, \beta_3, \gamma$ are parameters and

$$\beta_1 + \beta_2 + \beta_3 = 1. \tag{2.25}$$

There will be increasing returns to scale if $\beta_0 < 1$. [If you do not immediately see why these things are true then check Mini Problem 15 and Exercise 2.4.] Equation (2.24) yields the econometric specification

$$\log C_i = \gamma + \beta_0 \log q_i + \beta_1 \log w_{1i} + \beta_2 \log w_{2i} + \beta_3 \log w_{3i} + \varepsilon_i \tag{2.26}$$

continued...

? Mini Problems

the point where this ray intersects $\overline{q}$-isoquant and work out the input bill at this point; then use the definition of the cost function.

20 Show this.

21 Show this in the special case where $\mathbf{z}^*$ is unique and strictly positive [Hint: differentiate (2.12) or (2.20) with respect to q and use the first-order conditions. Also check the results on page 512.]

...continued

where the i index refers to observation on individual firm i and ε_i is a disturbance term. Nerlove estimates (2.26) using data on 145 US firms in 1955. Are the data consistent with the homogeneity restriction (2.25)? Are there increasing returns to scale in the electricity industry? The answers to these questions are yes and yes. For more on the econometric issues concerning this model see Hayashi (2000: 60–8).

2.2.3 Optimisation stage 2: choosing output

Using the cost function we can now set out the problem of finding optimal output. What we do is simply substitute $C(\mathbf{w}, q)$ back into (2.2). Then the problem becomes:

$$\max_{\{q \geq 0\}} pq - C(\mathbf{w}, q). \tag{2.27}$$

The first-order condition for this maximisation problem yields an optimum quantity q^* where

$$\left.\begin{aligned} p &= C_q(\mathbf{w}, q^*) \text{ if } q^* > 0, \\ p &\leq C_q(\mathbf{w}, q^*) \text{ if } q^* = 0. \end{aligned}\right\} \tag{2.28}$$

In other words product price is less than or equal to marginal cost at the optimum.

A necessary condition for a maximum of (2.27) is that its second derivative with respect to q should be negative or zero in the neighbourhood of q^*. Working this out we find that this implies:

$$C_{qq}(\mathbf{w}, q) \geq 0. \tag{2.29}$$

So the optimum must be on a constant or rising portion of the marginal cost curve. However, we must also take into account the obvious restriction that no firm will stay in business if it makes a loss.[22] Clearly this requires

$$pq - C(\mathbf{w}, q) \geq 0, \tag{2.30}$$

which we may rewrite as

$$\frac{C(\mathbf{w}, q)}{q} \leq p, \tag{2.31}$$

which in plain language says that average cost must not exceed product price at the optimum.

Once again we can, in principle, express the optimal supply of output as a function of the exogenously given variables in the problem by solving for q^* from the first-order condition (2.28); let us think for a moment about this supply relationship. Suppose that there is some value of output $\underline{q}$ at which marginal cost equals average cost. If marginal cost is

? Mini Problems

22 We have ruled out $\Pi < 0$, but what would be likely to happen in a market if $\Pi > 0$? See page 58.

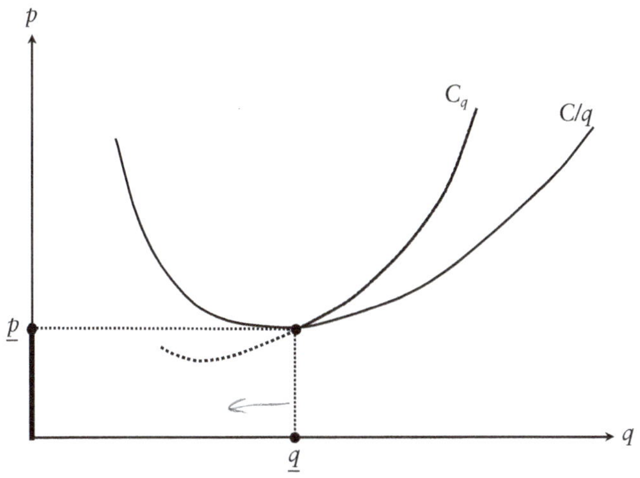

Figure 2.12 Optimal output may be multivalued

strictly greater than average cost (to the right of $\underline{q}$),[23] and if marginal cost is rising then there is a one-to-one relationship between price p and optimal output; if marginal cost is less than average cost (to the left of $\underline{q}$), then the firm will produce no output; if marginal cost equals average cost then the firm is indifferent between producing $\underline{q}$ and producing nothing at all—see Figure 2.12. So there may be more than one profit-maximising output level for a single value of $p = \underline{p}$. We shall develop this point later, but for the moment, let us set it aside and return to the overall optimisation problem of the firm.

2.2.4 Assembling the solution

Let us now see what we get when we put together the solutions to the two component problems, cost minimisation and output optimisation. The main result is as follows:

Theorem 2.3 Marginal products and input prices

At the profit-maximising technique, for any input the value of the marginal product of the input must be no greater than the price of that input. If the input is purchased in positive amounts, the value of its marginal product must equal its price.

The proof of this result requires no more than gathering together some points that we already know: from expression (2.14) in the cost-minimisation problem we know that λ times the marginal product of i must be less than or equal to w_i; our discussion of the cost function revealed that λ must be marginal cost; from the optimisation of output problem we know that marginal cost equals price.

? Mini Problems

23 What must be true about the production function ϕ for such a $\underline{q}$ to exist?

Of course, now that we have obtained the solution of the combined problem in terms of market prices p and $\mathbf{w}$ it would be interesting to know how the solution might be affected if those prices were to change.

2.3 The firm as a 'black box'

We shall now see how we can put the firm's cost function to work: we use it to characterise the equilibrium of the firm in a simple way, and to analyse how the profit-maximising firm will react to changes in its market environment. We can imagine the firm to be like an electronic black box that accepts incoming signals from the market in the form of prices and, as the result of some predetermined inner workings, processes them and emits other signals in the form of quantities of input demands and output supply. Our task is to characterise the inner workings of the black box.

To do this we shall make use of the method of *comparative statics*, which basically means that we see how the solution to the optimisation problem would change if some of the market data were to be altered a little. This can do more than just provide a simple mechanical response; it can reveal information about the structure of the solution as well. We shall then extend our analysis of the elementary model of the firm to cover two important developments: its reaction to 'short-run' constraints, and the possibility of acting as a price maker rather than as a price taker.

As a simple example of the basic comparative statics method let us go back to a point that we made earlier, that the nature of the solution to the firm's cost-minimisation problem would depend on the shape of the input-requirement set $Z(q)$. To examine the implications of alternative possible shapes for $Z(q)$ try the following four-part experiment:

- Take the case where $Z(q)$ is *strictly convex*—case 1 in Figure 2.13—and use a straight edge to represent the isocost line on the figure. Then, on a separate piece of paper, plot the cost-minimising value of z_1 against w_1/w_2, the slope of the isocost line; you should get a continuous, downward-sloping curve. The shading of the boundary indicates the optimal $\mathbf{z}$-values that you pick up as you do the experiment.
- If you conduct the same experiment for the case where $Z(q)$ is convex but not strictly convex (case 2), you should find that you get a similar graph, but that there will be at least one point at which a single value of w_1/w_2 corresponds to an *interval* of values of z_1.
- Thirdly, try it for the case where $Z(q)$ is non-convex (case 3): you should find a point at which a single value of w_1/w_2 corresponds to exactly two values of z_1: between these two z_1-values there is a discontinuity in the relationship you are plotting.
- Fourthly, try it for the 'kinked case': you will find that at a kink there is a range of w_1/w_2-values for which the optimal z_1 remains unchanged. However, although there

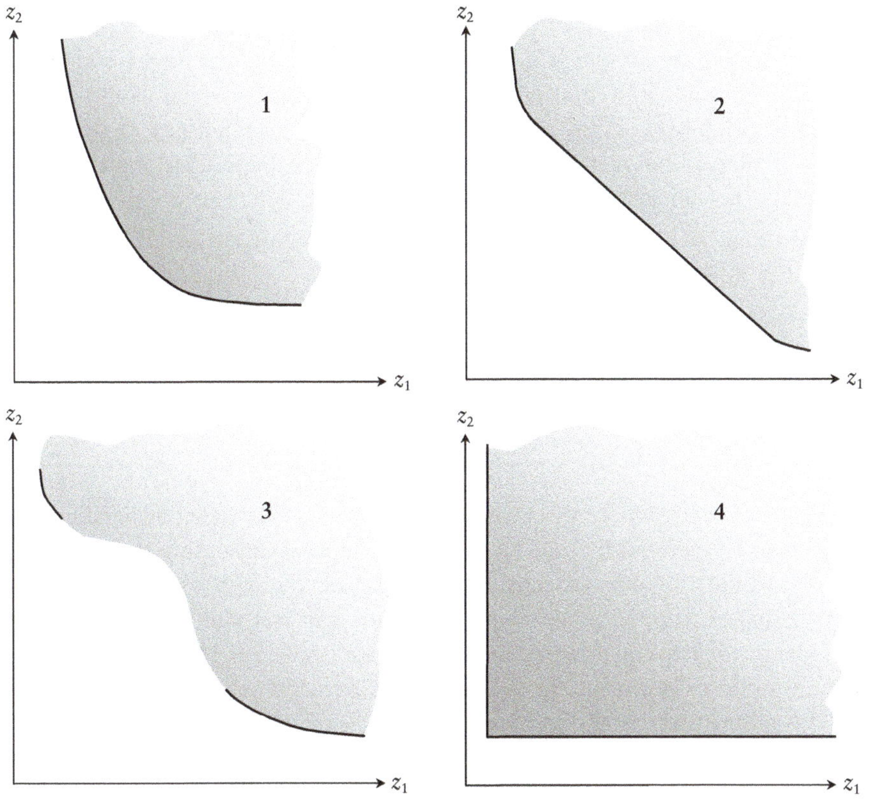

Figure 2.13 Convexity and input demands

is a unique input demand for a given w_1/w_2 value at the kinks, you will find a range of (w_1/w_2)-values which yield the same input demand.[24]

It is useful to compare Figures 2.1 and 2.13: note that not all the boundary points of $Z(q)$ (Figure 2.1) emerge as possible solution points in the cost-minimisation exercise (Figure 2.13) if $Z(q)$ is non-convex. The experiment shows that the issue of convexity of the input-requirement set is central to the relationship between market prices and input demands. Also kinkedness of the boundary may destroy the uniqueness of the relationship between input demands and input prices. This will be put on a more formal basis in a moment; we will find that these insights apply in other aspects of economic optimisation.

? Mini Problems

24 Draw a case where $Z(q)$ is strictly convex *and* for which the boundary has multiple kinks. Draw the relationship between input price and conditional input demand and check that input demands are always uniquely defined.

2.3.1 Demand and supply functions of the firm

Let us follow up the point that emerged from the experiment, that for a suitably shaped $Z(q)$—in other words a 'well-behaved' production function ϕ—you would get a one-to-one relationship between the input price ratio and the demand for an input, but that for other production functions multiple solutions might emerge. This point—proved in Appendix C—is summarised more formally as:

Theorem 2.4 Firm's demand and supply functions

(a) If all input-requirement sets are strictly convex, conditional input demand functions are always well defined and continuous for all positive input prices. (b) If the production function is strictly concave, the supply function and input demand functions are always well defined and continuous for all positive input prices.

The conditions required for the second half of this result are rather demanding. To see why this is so let us recall that the 'conventional' supply relationship that we sketched in Figure 2.12 does not actually satisfy the requirements of part (b). If the average cost curve is U-shaped then the firm's supply of output is in fact multivalued at one point: this is point $\underline{q}$, where p equals minimum average cost (given $p = \underline{p}$ the firm does not care whether it produces at $\underline{q}$ or produces nothing at all because it makes zero profits either way). This means that, strictly speaking, we have a supply *correspondence* rather than a supply function (see page 485 in Appendix A for this important technical distinction). The firm's supply curve is discontinuous at $\underline{p}$: there is a jump from 0 to $\underline{q}$ as the market price increases from a level just below $\underline{p}$ to just above $\underline{p}$. The reason for this is simple: the left-hand branch of the U-shape (to the left of $\underline{q}$) is a region where there is increasing returns to scale: the production function is not concave in this region.

Having thought about this, let us promptly ignore it for the moment and introduce three key concepts that we shall use frequently from now on. The first two are:

Definition 2.6

The *conditional demand functions* for inputs $i = 1, 2, \ldots, m$ are a set of real-valued functions H^i of input prices and an output level such that

$$z_i^* = H^i(\mathbf{w}, q) \tag{2.32}$$

where $(z_1^*, z_2^*, \ldots, z_m^*)$ are the cost-minimising inputs for $\mathbf{w}$ and q.

Definition 2.7

The *supply function* of the competitive firm is a real-valued function S of prices such that

$$q^* = S(\mathbf{w}, p) \tag{2.33}$$

where q^* is the profit-maximising output for $\mathbf{w}$ and p.

Notice that H^i must be homogeneous of degree zero in input prices $\mathbf{w}$, and that S is homogeneous of degree zero in $(\mathbf{w}, p)$.[25] Next, stick together these two principal solution functions that we have introduced. This then gives us the third key concept:

Definition 2.8

The *unconditional demand function* for input i is a real-valued function D^i of input prices and the output price such that:

$$z_i^* = D^i(\mathbf{w}, p), \tag{2.34}$$

where

$$D^i(\mathbf{w}, p) := H^i(\mathbf{w}, S(\mathbf{w}, p)). \tag{2.35}$$

Equation (2.35) emphasises that conditional and unconditional demands are just two different ways of tying down the same basic concept: in the first case we write the solution to the input-optimisation problem as a function of input prices and output; in the second we write it as a function of input prices and the output price. Both versions are useful, as we shall see.

2.3.2 Comparative statics: the general case

Working with the supply curve is a simple example of comparative statics: we can show how q^* responds to p given the assumption of profit maximisation.

Suppose that we are in the interesting part of the problem where the firm is producing a strictly positive output. Then the points on the supply curve must also satisfy the standard first-order condition 'price = marginal cost'. Substituting in for q^* from (2.33), we may thus write:

$$p = C_q(\mathbf{w}, S(\mathbf{w}, p)) \tag{2.36}$$

where we have again used the subscript notation to represent the partial derivative. Differentiate (2.36) with respect to p and rearrange it to get:[26]

$$S_p(\mathbf{w}, p) = \frac{1}{C_{qq}(\mathbf{w}, q^*)}. \tag{2.37}$$

The left-hand side of (2.37) is the slope of the supply curve. The right-hand side depends on the way marginal cost C_q increases with output q. Since we know from the

? Mini Problems

25 Use the properties of the cost function to explain why this is so.

26 Do the differentiation and show this. You may find a review of the 'function-of-a-function' rule helpful—see section A.4.3 (page 491).

second-order conditions that C_{qq} must be positive at the optimum, we see immediately from this that the competitive firm must have a rising supply curve.

Now consider input demands using the same sort of approach. Suppose the market price of output rises: as we know, output goes up, but what happens to input usage? Will a shift in the demand for the product also increase demand for, say, labour? Let us use the fundamental relationship between the two ways of writing input demands given in equation (2.35). Differentiating (2.35) with respect to p we get

$$D^i_p(\mathbf{w}, p) = H^i_q(\mathbf{w}, q^*)S_p(\mathbf{w}, p). \tag{2.38}$$

So the answer to our question is not quite straightforward: a rise in p will increase the demand for labour if and only if the term H^i_q is positive: this term is an 'output effect' describing what would happen to conditional input demand if the specified level of output q were to be increased; the conventional assumption is that it is positive, so that z^*_i would go up as output level is increased (a 'normal input'); but there are odd cases (so-called inferior inputs) where this does not happen. We can get further insight on this if we use Shephard's Lemma which, using (2.21) and (2.32), we may write as:

$$C_i(\mathbf{w}, q) = H^i(\mathbf{w}, q). \tag{2.39}$$

Then we find that (2.38) can be rewritten[27]

$$D^i_p(\mathbf{w}, p) = \frac{\partial C_q(\mathbf{w}, q^*)}{\partial w_i} S_p(\mathbf{w}, p). \tag{2.40}$$

So, if the cost structure is such that an increase in the wage rate would have raised marginal cost, then we may deduce that an increase in product price would increase the employment of labour.

Now, what would happen to the demand for input i if the market price of input j were to alter? If the cost of paper (w_j) goes up do you employ fewer secretaries (z^*_i)? To address this issue, differentiate equation (2.35) again, this time with respect to w_j:

$$D^i_j(\mathbf{w}, p) = H^i_j(\mathbf{w}, q^*) + H^i_q(\mathbf{w}, q^*)S_j(\mathbf{w}, p). \tag{2.41}$$

We can simplify the second term on the right-hand side of this expression using the same sort of tricks as we have employed for earlier comparative-statics exercises. Using Shephard's Lemma the term H^i_q can be put in terms of the second derivative of the cost function; and differentiating (2.36) with respect to w_j we can get an expression for the required derivative of the supply function.[28] Substituting into (2.41) we find:

$$D^i_j(\mathbf{w}, p) = H^i_j(\mathbf{w}, q^*) - \frac{C_{iq}(\mathbf{w}, q^*)C_{jq}(\mathbf{w}, q^*)}{C_{qq}(\mathbf{w}, q^*)}. \tag{2.42}$$

? Mini Problems

27 Show this, using the basic theorem on the properties of the cost function and the fact that the second partial differentials of C commute.

28 Do all this and derive (2.42).

This fundamental decomposition formula for the effect of a price change can be expressed as follows:

total effect	=	substitution effect	+	output effect

The first component, the substitution effect, is the response that a firm would make to the input-price change if it were constrained to meet a fixed output target. The second component, the output effect, gives the change in input demand that is induced by a change in optimal output. Two nice results follow from the decomposition formula (2.42).

First, consider the substitution term H_j^i. Because of (2.39) we can write this term as C_{ij}, the cross-partial derivative of the cost function; and because $C_{ij} = C_{ji}$ (if the function is well behaved, the order of differentiation does not matter) we see immediately that $H_j^i = H_i^j$ wherever the derivatives are well defined. In other words all the substitution terms must be symmetric.

Second, have a look at the output effect term in (2.42). Clearly this too is symmetric in i and j. So since both this and the substitution term are symmetric we must also have $D_j^i = D_i^j$ for the uncompensated demands too: the overall cross-price effects are symmetric. So a rise in the price of paper would have the same effect on the (ordinary) demand for secretarial hours as would a rise in the wages of secretaries on the demand for paper.

Now let us think about the important special case where goods i and j happen to be the same, in other words the demand-response of input i to its own price, w_i. Because C is concave in **w**, we must have $C_{ii} \leq 0$ and hence $H_i^i \leq 0$.[29] In fact we can show that if ϕ were everywhere smooth and concave contoured then, for all strictly positive input price vectors, we would have $H_i^i < 0$: the conditional demand for input i must be a decreasing function of its own price. Furthermore, a quick check on the decomposition formula (2.42) reveals that in the own-price case we have:

$$D_i^i(\mathbf{w}, p) = H_i^i(\mathbf{w}, q^*) - \frac{C_{iq}(\mathbf{w}, q^*)^2}{C_{qq}(\mathbf{w}, q^*)}. \tag{2.43}$$

We have just seen that the substitution effect in (2.43) is negative; so too, evidently, is the output effect (the squared term and C_{qq} are both positive); hence we have $D_i^i(\mathbf{w}, p) \leq 0$.[30]

? Mini Problems

29 [For the mathematically inclined.] Show this by using the result that a differentiable concave function must have a negative-semidefinite matrix of second partial derivatives—see page 505.

30 Will the downward-sloping demand-curve also apply to consumer demand?

We can pull all this together in the following statement:[31]

Theorem 2.5 Input prices and demands

(a) The effect of an increase in the price of input *j* on the conditional demand for input *i* equals the effect of an increase in the price of input *i* on the conditional demand for input *j*; (b) the same result holds for the unconditional input demands; (c) the effect of an increase in the price of input *i* on the conditional demand for input *i* must be non-positive; (d) the effect of an increase in the price of input *i* on the unconditional demand for input *i* must be non-positive and greater in absolute size than the effect in (c).

We can use this information to sketch the shape of the demand curves for an input:—Figure 2.14 depicts the demand for input 1, conditional on a particular output level q. It must be downward sloping, because $H_1^1 < 0$ (Theorem 2.5): if the price of input 1 were to fall as shown in Figure 2.14 and the output level were held fixed at q then demand for input 1 would rise from z_1^* to z_1°. We also know that $H^1(\mathbf{w}, q)$ gives the marginal change in cost $C(\mathbf{w}, q)$ as w_1 changes (Shephard's Lemma): so the change in cost (for a fixed output q) resulting from a change in w_1 is given by the integral of H^1, which is depicted by the shaded area in Figure 2.14.

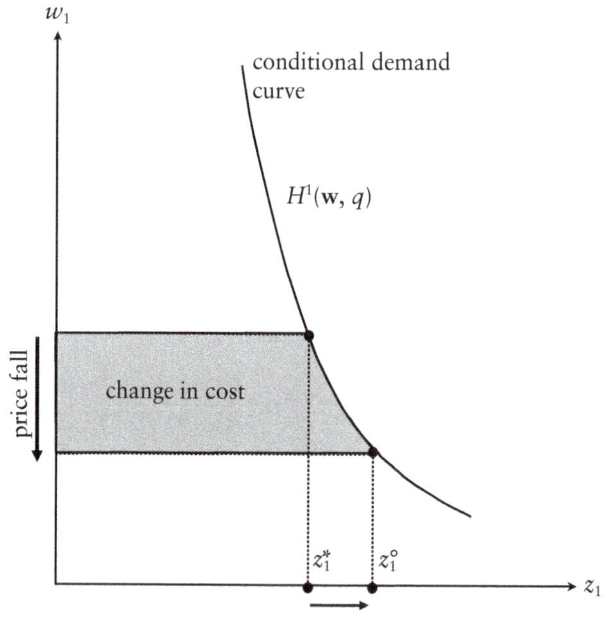

Figure 2.14 The substitution effect of a fall in price

? Mini Problems

31 Take the production function in Mini Problem 15. Find the conditioned demand functions and verify the results of Theorem 2.5 parts (a) and (c).

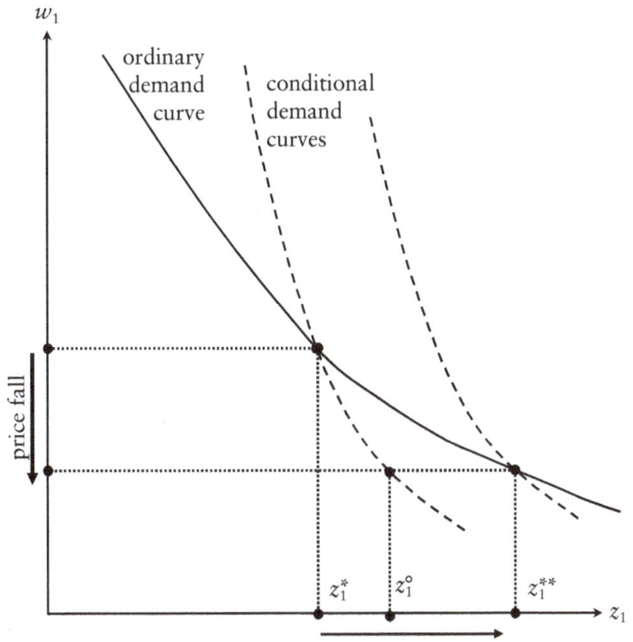

Figure 2.15 Input-price fall: total effect

Let us consider the full effect of such a fall in w_1 such as that shown in Figure 2.14. It is obvious from Figure 2.14 that z_1 must increase, but that is purely a substitution effect. As we saw in equation (2.43) there is also an output effect; let us suppose that as w_1 falls the marginal cost curve in Figure 2.12 shifts downward so that output rises (the case of a normal input). It is clear that the total impact of the fall in input price is as shown in Figure 2.15 so that the output effect makes the firm's response more sensitive to the price fall than if we were to consider the substitution effect alone—if q is adjusted optimally by the firm then demand for input 1 rises from z_1^* to z_1^{**}, not just to z_1°.[32]

Finally there is in this diagram a separate conditional demand curve for each level of output: that is why *two* conditional demand curves are drawn in—one for q^* (the original output level) and one for q^{**} (the output level after the price fall).

2.4 The short run

The short run is a notional period in which one or more inputs are assumed to be fixed. We introduce it to our model by taking input m to be fixed in the short run although, of course, it is variable in the long run.

? Mini Problems

32 This reasoning implies that, for normal inputs, the ordinary demand curve is flatter than the conditional demand curve. Does the same apply to inferior inputs?

The firm: solution functions

LONG RUN	
C	Cost function
D^i	Unconditional demand for input i
H^i	Conditional demand for input i
S	Supply function
SHORT RUN	
$\tilde{C}$	Cost function
$\tilde{H}^i$	Conditional demand for input i

- *Example 1: capital equipment.*[33] Take input m to be a mainframe computer. At some stage the firm has to decide how large a computer to install. The short-run curves are then derived on the assumption of a given size of computer, varying other inputs such as programmers' hours, secretarial hours, consumables.
- *Example 2: employment protection.* Some types of workers may be able to negotiate long-term contracts with an employer. This section of staff in effect becomes a quasi-fixed factor.

To see the impact of this short-run fixity of an input, think of the behaviour of the profit-maximising firm as a mechanism, converting market data (prices) into supplies of output and demands for inputs. We have seen how this mechanism works in the comparative statics manipulations that we performed earlier on. Now suppose you tie down part of the system by imposing short-run constraints: what would we expect to happen? Presumably this will make the mechanism more sluggish—it will be less flexible in its response to changes in the market environment. This is in fact exactly what occurs.

To see this, let us introduce a proper definition of what we mean by the short run. Suppose that the conventional cost-minimisation problem has been solved for some specified output level $\bar{q}$ by setting input demands to $\bar{z}_1, \bar{z}_2, \ldots, \bar{z}_m$. By definition we have:

$$\left.\begin{aligned} \bar{z}_1 &= H^1(\mathbf{w}, \bar{q}), \\ \bar{z}_2 &= H^2(\mathbf{w}, \bar{q}), \\ &\ldots \ldots \\ \bar{z}_m &= H^m(\mathbf{w}, \bar{q}). \end{aligned}\right\} \tag{2.44}$$

Now suppose that the specified output level is changed to some other value of q, but that the firm is constrained to keep its usage of the mth input fixed. Clearly it may want to alter its usage of the remaining $m - 1$ variables; we will find the following concept useful:

? Mini Problems

33 In what way might this be useful in representing firms' activities in a macroeconomic model?

Definition 2.9

The firm's *short-run cost function* is a real-valued function $\tilde{C}$ of input prices, the output level, and an amount of input m such that:

$$\tilde{C}(\mathbf{w}, q, \bar{z}_m) := \min_{\{z_i \geq 0, \phi(\mathbf{z}) \geq q, z_m = \bar{z}_m\}} \sum_{i=1}^{m} w_i z_i \tag{2.45}$$

The idea of these short-run costs is that they are the best that you can do given that you are committed to an input level of $\bar{z}_m$ for the mth input.[34] Check this definition, term by term, against the definition of the firm's cost function in (2.19); in fact this function inherits—with very simple modifications—most of the conventional cost function's properties. In particular, we have:

$$\tilde{C}_i(\mathbf{w}, q, \bar{z}_m) = \tilde{H}^i(\mathbf{w}, q, \bar{z}_m), \tag{2.46}$$

where $\tilde{H}^i (i = 1, \ldots, m-1)$ is the short-run demand for input i, conditional on output q, which emerges from the solution of the problem in (2.45).

By definition of the cost function, we must have

$$\tilde{C}(\mathbf{w}, q, \bar{z}_m) \geq C(\mathbf{w}, q). \tag{2.47}$$

Dividing both sides of (2.47) by q, we see immediately that long-run average cost must be less than or equal to short-run average cost. Of course, exactly at the point $q = \bar{q}$ it is true that:

$$\tilde{C}(\mathbf{w}, \bar{q}, \bar{z}_m) = C(\mathbf{w}, \bar{q}). \tag{2.48}$$

and therefore, at this point, $\partial\tilde{C}(\mathbf{w}, \bar{q}, \bar{z}_m)/\partial\bar{z}_m = 0$.

Let us look at the behaviour of long-run and short-run costs. What would have happened were we to have started from a different output level $\bar{q}$? Use (2.44) to write (2.48) as

$$\tilde{C}(\mathbf{w}, \bar{q}, H^m(\mathbf{w}, \bar{q})) = C(\mathbf{w}, \bar{q}) \tag{2.49}$$

and then differentiate this with respect to $\bar{q}$ so as to obtain, on simplification:[35]

$$\tilde{C}_q(\mathbf{w}, \bar{q}, \bar{z}_m) = C_q(\mathbf{w}, \bar{q}). \tag{2.50}$$

? Mini Problems

34 It is sometimes convenient to work with the concepts of short-run variable costs (the first $m-1$ terms of the sum in the above definition) and of *fixed costs*, which are simply $w_m\bar{z}_m$. Show that the results which follow also work for short-run variable costs, rather than $\tilde{C}$, as defined.

35 Explain why $\partial\tilde{C}/\partial\bar{z}_m = 0$ at $q = \bar{q}$, and prove (2.50).

Thus, when output is at the level that is optimal for the fixed input level $\bar{z}_m$, long-run marginal costs (C_q) equal short-run marginal costs ($\tilde{C}_q$).[36] Hence at $\bar{q}$ the slope of the long-run average cost curve must equal the slope of the short-run average cost curve. Using the same general method we can differentiate (2.48) with respect to w_i so as to obtain

$$\tilde{C}_i(\mathbf{w}, \bar{q}, \bar{z}_m) = C_i(\mathbf{w}, \bar{q}), \tag{2.51}$$

which implies

$$\tilde{H}^i(\mathbf{w}, \bar{q}, \bar{z}_m) = H^i(\mathbf{w}, \bar{q}). \tag{2.52}$$

So, in the neighbourhood of $\bar{q}$, short-run and long-run conditional input demands are identical.

Now let us look at the second-order conditions. Using the conditional input demand function for input m (see equation (2.44) above) differentiate (2.50) with respect to $\bar{q}$:

$$\tilde{C}_{qq}(\mathbf{w}, \bar{q}, \bar{z}_m) + \tilde{C}_{q\bar{z}_m}(\mathbf{w}, \bar{q}, \bar{z}_m) H^m_q(\mathbf{w}, \bar{q}) = C_{qq}(\mathbf{w}, \bar{q}). \tag{2.53}$$

Rearranging (2.53) we get:[37]

$$C_{qq}(\mathbf{w}, \bar{q}) = \tilde{C}_{qq}(\mathbf{w}, \bar{q}, \bar{z}_m) + \frac{H^m_q(\mathbf{w}, \bar{q})^2}{H^m_m(\mathbf{w}, \bar{q})}. \tag{2.54}$$

But we know that the own-price substitution effect H^m_m must be non-positive (and if the production function is smooth it must be strictly negative). Hence for a locally smooth production function we find:

$$C_{qq}(\mathbf{w}, \bar{q}) < \tilde{C}_{qq}(\mathbf{w}, \bar{q}, \bar{z}_m). \tag{2.55}$$

In other words short-run marginal cost is steeper than long-run marginal cost.

In like manner by differentiating (2.52) with respect to $w_i (i = 1, 2, \ldots, m-1)$ we can derive[38]

$$H^i_i(\mathbf{w}, \bar{q}) > \tilde{H}^i_i(\mathbf{w}, \bar{q}, \bar{z}_m), \tag{2.56}$$

so that short-run input demand is less elastic (to its own price) than long-run input demand.

We can summarise the above results thus:

Theorem 2.6 Short-run demand and supply

(a) Where output is at the optimal level for the fixed input, short-run and long-run total costs are equal. (b) At this output level, short- and long-run marginal costs are equal.

? Mini Problems

36 Show this using the envelope theorem—Theorem A.13. [Hint: show that it is possible to write long-run costs as $\tilde{C}(\mathbf{w}, q, H^m(\mathbf{w}, q))$.]

37 Show this. [Hint: substitute the conditional demand function for $\bar{z}_m$ in (2.50) and differentiate (2.50) with respect to w_m, noting that $\partial\tilde{C}_q/\partial w_m = 0$ [Why?]; you then find an expression for $\tilde{C}_{q\bar{z}_m}$ to substitute in (2.53).]

38 Show this by following through the same steps as for short-run marginal costs, using Shephard's Lemma and the fact that the second derivatives of C commute.

(c) At this output level, short- and long-run input demands are equal. (d) The short-run marginal cost curve is at least as steep as the long-run marginal cost curve. (e) Long-run input demands are at least as elastic as short-run demands.

Figure 2.16 illustrates these results in the case where long-run marginal costs are rising. Take the example where input m represents the computer the firm has just installed: technological change may have shifted the production function so that the firm now wishes it had a larger computer, but for now it is committed to the installation ($z_m = \bar{z}_m$). The output level marked $\bar{q}$ on the diagram—where (2.48) is satisfied—is clearly crucial. The broken cost curve represents the situation with the existing computer (allowing programmers' hours and materials to be varied in the short run);[39] the solid curve represents average costs given that computer installation can itself be taken as a variable input.

The results may be easily generalised. Instead of just one constraint, $z_m = \bar{z}_m$, let a further input be constrained, and then another and then another. Then we have the following for this sequential exercise:

$$\left.\frac{\partial z_i^*}{\partial w_i}\right|_{\text{no constraints}} \leq \left.\frac{\partial z_i^*}{\partial w_i}\right|_{\text{one constraint}} \leq \left.\frac{\partial z_i^*}{\partial w_i}\right|_{\text{two constraints}} \leq \cdots \tag{2.57}$$

a result which makes the 'short run' as short as you like.

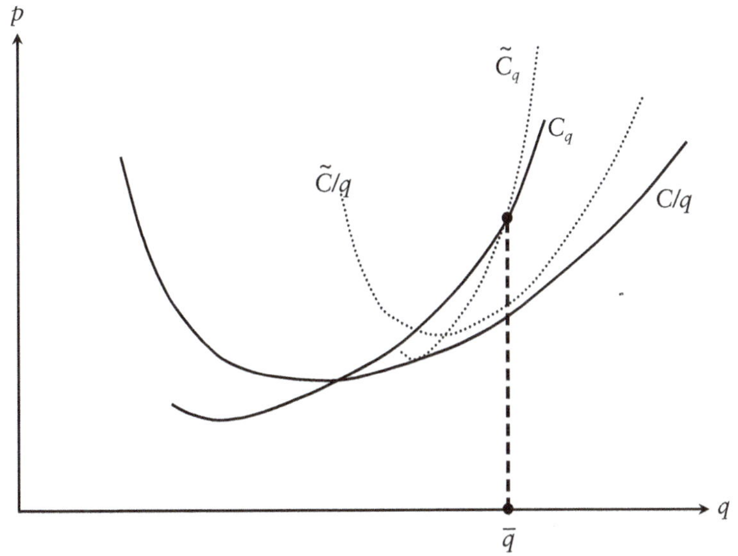

Figure 2.16 Marginal and average costs in the short and long run

? Mini Problems

39 Draw in on this diagram the short-run cost curves given that a computer system of ideal size had been installed.

Example 2.2

A classic study of US airlines (Eads et al. 1969) modelled long run costs as

$$C(\mathbf{w}, q) = C_f + kq^{\frac{1}{\gamma}} w_1^{\frac{\alpha_1}{\gamma}} w_2^{\frac{\alpha_2}{\gamma}} \tag{2.58}$$

where q is an index of airline output, C_f is the cost of fuel (separately estimated), w_1 is the price of labour other than pilots and co-pilots and w_2 is the price of pilots and co-pilots: the αs are parameters to be estimated econometrically, $\gamma = \alpha_1 + \alpha_2$, and k is also a function of the αs. Differentiate (2.58) with respect to w_1 we get

$$z_i^* = H^1(\mathbf{w}, q) = \frac{\alpha_1 k}{\gamma} q^{\frac{1}{\gamma}} w_1^{\frac{\alpha_1}{\gamma}-1} w_2^{\frac{\alpha_2}{\gamma}}. \tag{2.59}$$

In other words the (long-run) conditional demand for labour of type 1 is given by the log-linear equation:

$$\log(z_i^*) = \beta_0 + \beta_1 \log(w_1) + \beta_2 \log(w_2) - \gamma \log(q). \tag{2.60}$$

Eads et al. (1969) assumed that in the short run pilots and co-pilots are a fixed factor (try sacking them!). The short-run cost function is then

$$\tilde{C}(\mathbf{w}, q, z_2) = C_f + kq^{\frac{1}{\alpha_1}} w_1 z_2^{-\alpha_2/\alpha_1}. \tag{2.61}$$

Differentiating this with respect to w_1 we get the short-run demand for non-pilot labour which will also be log-linear. Try it.

2.5 The multiproduct firm

Clearly the assumption that the firm produces but a single output is rather limiting. To try to put this matter right we need another way of representing production possibilities. A method that is particularly convenient in the multiproduct case involves introducing one new concept—that of *net output*. Net outputs subsume both inputs and outputs using a natural sign convention under which outputs are measured in the positive direction ($q_i > 0$), and inputs negatively ($q_i < 0$).

Suppose there are n goods in the economy: the net output vector $\mathbf{q} := (q_1, \ldots, q_n)$ for the firm summarises all the firms' activities in the outside world. The firm's non-zero amounts of output or input for each good can be described according to the above sign convention; irrelevant goods, or pure intermediate goods can be ignored ($q_i = 0$). The production constraint[40] corresponding to (2.1) can be written

$$\Phi(\mathbf{q}) \leq 0 \tag{2.62}$$

? Mini Problems

40 Express the single-output production function (2.1) in this notation.

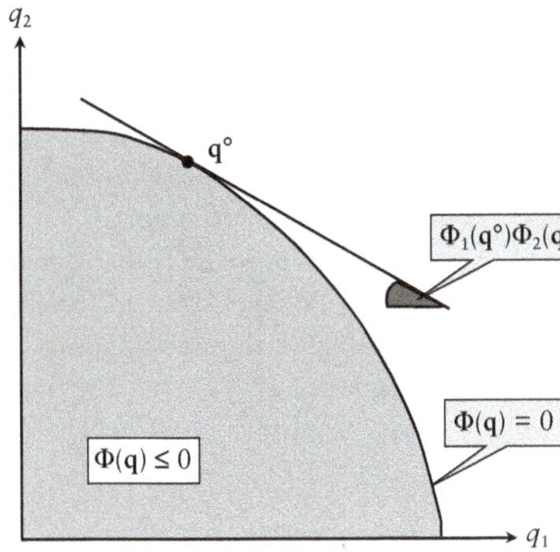

Figure 2.17 Firm's transformation curve

where the function Φ is non-decreasing[41] in each of the q_i. A sectional snapshot of the multiproduct firm's production function is given in Figure 2.17: this shows the production possibilities of two outputs that are potentially produced by the firm (of course the exact form of this snapshot depends on the values of the other components of the net-output vector—dimensions $3, 4, \ldots, n$). The shaded set depicts the net-output vectors that satisfy (2.62); the boundary of this set is known as the *transformation curve.*

There are obvious counterparts of assumptions about the single-output production function (see section 2.1.2 above) that can be easily established for Φ. Many of the standard concepts such as MRTS, marginal products, and returns to scale[42] carry over straightforwardly to the multiproduct case: for the first two of these concepts the trick is usually to identify the appropriate contour of Φ. Obviously we have skated over these issues rather rapidly: we will have much more to say about them in chapter 6.

One important new concept can be defined wherever the production function is differentiable:

Definition 2.10

The *marginal rate of transformation* of (net) output i into (net) output j is given by

$$\text{MRT}_{ij} := \frac{\Phi_j(\mathbf{q})}{\Phi_i(\mathbf{q})}.$$

? Mini Problems

41 Explain why it makes economic sense for Φ to be a non-decreasing function in each component, whether it be an input or an output.

42 How would constant returns to scale be expressed in terms of the multi-output production function $\Phi(\cdot)$?

The MRT is the firm's tradeoff or marginal valuation of a pair of goods—for example, the rate at which the firm would have to give up on one output in order to produce more of another. It has a central rôle to play in characterising market equilibrium (this is dealt with in chapters 6 and 7) and the efficiency of the allocation of goods and resources in an economy (chapter 9). Notice that the MRTS in Definition 2.1 can be seen as a special case of Definition 2.10 where goods i and j are both inputs.

One of the advantages of the net-output approach is that one has a particularly convenient expression for profits. To see this, imagine that for a particular firm the goods are labelled so that $1, \ldots, m$ are unambiguously inputs, goods $m+1, \ldots, r$ are either intermediate goods or irrelevant, and goods $r+1, \ldots, n$ are unambiguously outputs (the labelling of goods is arbitrary, so we can always do this). The total value of inputs is given by:

$$\text{COST} = \sum_{i=1}^{m} p_i \left[-q_i\right] \tag{2.63}$$

where the term $-q_i$ is a positive number (because q_i is negative for inputs, under the convention); this is the absolute amount used of input i. The value of the outputs from the firm is obviously

$$\text{REVENUE} = \sum_{i=r+1}^{n} p_i q_i. \tag{2.64}$$

So, subtracting (2.63) from (2.64) and noting that the valuation of goods $m+1, \ldots, r$ is zero (because here all the q_i values are zero) we find that

$$\text{PROFITS} = \sum_{i=1}^{n} p_i q_i. \tag{2.65}$$

The diagrammatic representation of profits works in just the same way as the diagrammatic representation of costs in Figure 2.10, but in the opposite direction—see the set of parallel *isoprofit* lines with slope $-p_1/p_2$ in Figure 2.18 that are the counterparts to the isocost lines in Figure 2.10. The firm's optimisation problem[43] then requires a solution to the constrained-maximum problem 'maximise (2.65) subject to the feasibility condition (2.62)'. Intuitively this involves reaching the highest isoprofit line in Figure 2.18 subject to remaining in the technologically feasible set (shaded in the figure). The method for solving this is in effect a modification of the cost-minimisation problem that we carried out for a fixed single output and a vector of m variable inputs in section 2.2.1. Formally we can represent this problem as that of maximising the Lagrangean:

$$\mathcal{L}(\mathbf{q}, \lambda; \mathbf{p}) := \sum_{i=1}^{n} p_i q_i - \lambda \Phi(\mathbf{q}) \tag{2.66}$$

for given prices $\mathbf{p}$, where λ is the Lagrange multiplier associated with the constraint (2.62). Differentiating (2.66) with respect to q_i we can derive a set of first-order conditions that are the counterparts of the FOC in section 2.2.1. The result is a set of n

? Mini Problems

43 Re-express condition (2.30) for the multiproduct case.

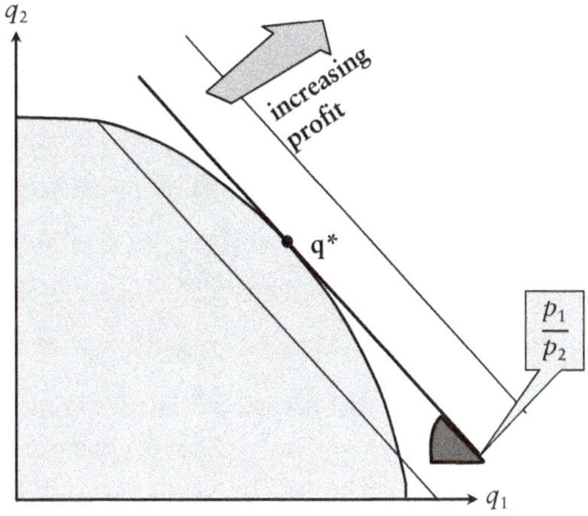

Figure 2.18 Profit maximisation: multiproduct firm

profit-maximising net outputs $(q_1^*, \ldots, q_n^*)$ that satisfy the set of FOCs. In a manner similar to section 2.2.1 we then find:

- If net output i is produced in non-zero amounts at the optimum then

$$\lambda^* \Phi_i(\mathbf{q}^*) = p_i. \tag{2.67}$$

- For any pair of outputs i and j where output i is produced in positive amounts at the optimum the FOCs imply:

$$\frac{\Phi_j(\mathbf{q}^*)}{\Phi_i(\mathbf{q}^*)} \leq \frac{p_j}{p_i} \tag{2.68}$$

  with equality in (2.68) if input i is also used in positive amounts.[44]

- At the vector of optimal net outputs:

$$\Phi(\mathbf{q}^*) = 0. \tag{2.69}$$

So, once again we find that production is technically efficient and, in the case where profit-maximising amounts of both outputs are positive, we have the rule of thumb:

MRT	=	output price ratio

? Mini Problems

44 Draw a diagram to illustrate the case where '<' holds in (2.68). Give a brief verbal interpretation of the optimum.

Furthermore, the result of this optimisation process is another solution function as follows:

Definition 2.11

The firm's *profit function* is a real-valued function Π of net output prices such that:

$$\Pi(\mathbf{p}) := \max_{\{\Phi(\mathbf{z})\leq 0\}} \sum_{i=1}^{n} p_i q_i \tag{2.70}$$

Clearly the profit function Π is the 'twin' of the cost function C for the cost-minimisation problem in sections 2.2.1 and 2.2.2. So it is not surprising to find that there is a theorem characterising the properties of the profit function that is very similar to Theorem 2.2 for the cost function:

Theorem 2.7 Properties of profit function

The competitive firm's profit function Π is non-decreasing, continuous, homogeneous of degree one, and concave in $\mathbf{p}$. At every point where the differential is defined

$$\frac{\partial \Pi(\mathbf{p})}{\partial p_i} = q_i^* \tag{2.71}$$

the optimal value of net output i.

For proof see Appendix C. Equation (2.71) is usually known as Hotelling's Lemma and is established in the same way as Shephard's Lemma. In particular, we can see that the part of the theorem about the slope of the profit function in equation (2.71) is obviously just Shephard's Lemma 'turned around' in the case where i is an input. Other parts of the theorem are proved in the same way as for Theorem 2.2.

We can push the analogy between the analysis of the multiproduct firm and the single product firm in sections 2.2 and 2.3 one stage further. Clearly the optimal net output value in (2.71) can be expressed as a function (or as a correspondence) of the price vector:

$$q_i^* = q_i(\mathbf{p}). \tag{2.72}$$

The properties of the net-output function $q_i(\cdot)$ in (2.72) follow from those of the single-output firm's demand and supply functions (see for example Theorems 2.4 and 2.5 and the associated discussion). So we find that $q_i(\cdot)$ is homogeneous of degree zero, is non-decreasing in its own price p_i and that, for any i and j:

$$\frac{\partial q_i(\mathbf{p})}{\partial p_j} = \frac{\partial q_j(\mathbf{p})}{\partial p_i}. \tag{2.73}$$

The analysis in terms of the profit function and net outputs has an attractive elegance. However, it is not for the sake of elegance that we have introduced it on top of the more pedestrian output-as-a-function-of-input approach. We will find that this approach has special advantages when we come to model the economic system as a whole.

Summary

The elementary microeconomic model of the firm can be constructed rigorously and informatively with rather few ingredients. Perhaps the hardest part is to decide what the appropriate assumptions are that should be imposed on the production function that determines the firm's technological constraints.

The fundamental economic problem of the competitive firm can be usefully broken down into two subproblems: that of minimising the cost of inputs for a given output and that of finding the profit-maximising output, given that input combinations have already been optimally selected for each output level. Each of these subproblems gives rise to some intuitively appealing rules of thumb such as 'MRTS = input price ratio' for the first subproblem and 'price = marginal cos' for the second subproblem.

Changing the model by introducing side constraints enables us to derive a modified solution function (the short-run cost function) and a collection of modified response functions. We get the common-sense result that the more of these side constraints there are, the less flexible is the firm's response to changes in signals from the market.

The elementary model of the firm can usefully be generalised by what amounts to little more than a relabelling trick. Outputs and inputs are replaced by the concept of *net output*. This trick is an important step for the future development of the production model in chapters 6 and onwards.

Reading notes

On the mathematical modelling of production see Fuss and McFadden (1980). The classic references that introduced the cost function and the profit function are Hotelling (1932) and Shephard (1953). See also Samuelson (1983) chapters III and IV.

The separation or aggregation result noted in Mini Problem 5 is of fundamental importance not only in the theory of production but also in the analysis of consumer preferences—see chapters 5 and 8—and is due to Leontief (1947a, 1947b). See also Fisher and Monz (1992), pp. ix-xvi on which Lemma C.1 and Theorem C.1 in Appendix C are based.

Exercises

2.1 Suppose that a unit of output q can be produced by any of the following combinations of inputs

$$\mathbf{z}^1 = \begin{bmatrix} 0.2 \\ 0.5 \end{bmatrix}, \mathbf{z}^2 = \begin{bmatrix} 0.3 \\ 0.2 \end{bmatrix}, \mathbf{z}^3 = \begin{bmatrix} 0.5 \\ 0.1 \end{bmatrix}.$$

1. Construct the isoquant for $q = 1$.
2. Assuming constant returns to scale, construct the isoquant for $q = 2$.

3. If the technique $\mathbf{z}^4 = [0.25, 0.5]$ were also available would it be included in the isoquant for $q = 1$?

2.2 A firm uses two inputs in the production of a single good. The input requirements per unit of output for a number of alternative techniques are given by the following table:

Process	1	2	3	4	5	6
Input 1	9	15	7	1	3	4
Input 2	4	2	6	10	9	7

The firm has exactly 140 units of input 1 and 410 units of input 2 at its disposal.

1. Discuss the concepts of technological and economic efficiency with reference to this example.
2. Describe the optimal production plan for the firm.
3. Would the firm prefer 10 extra units of input 1 or 20 extra units of input 2?

2.3 Consider the following structure of the cost function: $C(\mathbf{w}, 0) = 0, C_q(\mathbf{w}, q) = \text{int}(q)$ where $\text{int}(x)$ is the smallest integer greater than or equal to x. Sketch total, average, and marginal cost curves.

2.4 Suppose a firm's production function has the *Cobb–Douglas* form

$$q = z_1^{\alpha_1} z_2^{\alpha_2}$$

where z_1 and z_2 are inputs, q is output, and α_1, α_2 are positive parameters.

1. Draw the isoquants. Do they touch the axes?
2. What is the elasticity of substitution in this case?
3. Using the Lagrangean method find the cost-minimising values of the inputs and the cost function.
4. Under what circumstances will the production function exhibit (a) decreasing (b) constant (c) increasing returns to scale? Explain this using first the production function and then the cost function. [Hint: check the result on page 24 to verify your answers.]
5. Find the conditional demand curve for input 1.

2.5 Suppose a firm's production function has the *Leontief* form

$$q = \min\left\{\frac{z_1}{\alpha_1}, \frac{z_2}{\alpha_2}\right\}$$

where the notation is the same as in Exercise 2.4 .

1. Draw the isoquants.
2. For a given level of output identify the cost-minimising input combination(s) on the diagram.
3. Hence write down the cost function in this case. Why would the Lagrangean method of Exercise 2.4 be inappropriate here?
4. What is the conditional input demand curve for input 1?

5. Repeat parts 1-4 for each of the two production functions

$$q = a_1 z_1 + a_2 z_2$$

$$q = a_1 z_1^2 + a_2 z_2^2.$$

Explain carefully how the solution to the cost-minimisation problem differs in these two cases.

2.6 Assume the production function

$$\phi(\mathbf{z}) = \left[a_1 z_1^\beta + a_2 z_2^\beta\right]^{\frac{1}{\beta}}$$

where z_i is the quantity of input i and $a_i \geq 0$, $-\infty < \beta \leq 1$ are parameters. This is an example of the CES (Constant Elasticity of Substitution) production function.

1. Show that the elasticity of substitution is $\frac{1}{1-\beta}$.
2. Explain what happens to the form of the production function and the elasticity of substitution in each of the following three cases: $\beta \to -\infty$, $\beta \to 0$, $\beta \to 1$.
3. Relate your answer to the answers to Exercises 2.4 and 2.4.

2.7 For the CES function in Exercise 2.6 find $H^1(\mathbf{w}, q)$, the conditional demand for good 1, for the case where $\beta \neq 0, 1$. Verify that it is decreasing in w_1 and homogeneous of degree 0 in (w_1,w_2).

2.8 For any homothetic production function show that the cost function must be expressible in the form

$$C(\mathbf{w}, q) = a(\mathbf{w})\, b(q).$$

2.9 Consider the production function

$$q = \left[a_1 z_1^{-1} + a_2 z_2^{-1} + a_3 z_3^{-1}\right]^{-1}.$$

1. Find the long-run cost function and sketch the long-run and short-run marginal and average cost curves and comment on their form.
2. Suppose input 3 is fixed in the short run. Repeat the analysis for the short-run case.
3. What is the elasticity of supply in the short and the long run?

2.10 A competitive firm's output q is determined by

$$q = z_1^{a_1} z_2^{a_2} \cdots z_m^{a_m}$$

where z_i is its usage of input i and $a_i > 0$ is a parameter $i = 1, 2, \ldots, m$. Assume that in the short run only k of the m inputs are variable.

1. Find the long-run average and marginal cost functions for this firm. Under what conditions will marginal cost rise with output?
2. Find the short-run marginal cost function.
3. Find the firm's short-run elasticity of supply. What would happen to this elasticity if k were reduced?

2.11 A firm produces goods 1 and 2 using goods 3, ..., 5 as inputs. The production of one unit of good i ($i = 1, 2$) requires at least a_{ij} units of good j, ($j = 3, 4, 5$).

1. Assuming constant returns to scale, how much of resource j will be needed to produce q_i units of commodity 1?
2. For given values of q_3, q_4, q_5 sketch the set of technologically feasible outputs of goods 1 and 2.

2.12 Suppose a firm's production function has the *Cobb–Douglas* form

$$q = z_1^{\alpha_1} z_2^{\alpha_2}$$

where z_1 and z_2 are inputs, q is output, and α_1, α_2 are positive parameters.

1. Draw the isoquants. Do they touch the axes?
2. What is the elasticity of substitution in this case?
3. Using the Lagrangean method find the cost-minimising values of the inputs and the cost function.
4. Under what circumstances will the production function exhibit (a) decreasing (b) constant (c) increasing returns to scale? Explain this using first the production function and then the cost function. [Hint: check the result on page 24 to verify your answers.]
5. Find the conditional demand curve for input 1.

2.13 An agricultural producer raises sheep to produce wool (good 1) and meat (good 2). There is a choice of four breeds (A, B, C, D) that can be used to stock the farm; each breed can be considered as a separate input to the production process. The yield of wool and of meat per 1000 sheep (in arbitrary units) for each breed is given in Table 2.1.

1. On a diagram show the production possibilities if the producer stocks exactly 1000 sheep using just one breed from the set $\{A, B, C, D\}$.
2. Using this diagram show the production possibilities if the producer's 1000 sheep are a mixture of breeds A and B. Do the same for a mixture of breeds B and C; and again for a mixture of breeds C and D. Hence draw the (wool, meat) transformation curve for 1000 sheep. What would be the transformation curve for 2000 sheep?
3. What is the MRT of meat into wool if a combination of breeds A and B are used? What is the MRT if a combination of breeds B and C are used? And if breeds C and D are used?

	A	B	C	D
wool	20	65	85	90
meat	70	50	20	10

Table 2.1 Yield per 1000 sheep for breeds A, ..., D

4. Why will the producer not find it necessary to use more than two breeds?
5. A new breed E becomes available that has a (wool, meat) yield per 1000 sheep of (50,50). Explain why the producer would never be interested in stocking breed E if breeds A,...,D are still available and why the transformation curve remains unaffected.
6. Another new breed F becomes available that has a (wool, meat) yield per 1000 sheep of (50,50). Explain how this will alter the transformation curve.

2.14 A firm that produces goods 1 and 2 uses labour (good 3) as input subject to the production constraint

$$[q_1]^2 + [q_2]^2 + Aq_3 \leq 0$$

where q_i is net output of good i and A is a positive constant. Draw the transformation curve for goods 1 and 2. What would happen to this transformation curve if the constant A had a larger value?

3 The Firm and the Market

...the struggle for survival tends to make those organisations prevail, which are best fitted to thrive in their environment, but not necessarily those best fitted to benefit their environment, unless it happens that they are duly rewarded for all the benefits which they confer, whether direct or indirect.

Alfred Marshall, *Principles of Economics*, 8th edition (1920), 596–7.

3.1 Introduction

Chapter 2 considered the economic problem of the firm in splendid isolation. The firm received signals (prices of inputs, prices of outputs) from the outside world and responded blindly with perfectly calculated optimal quantities. The demand for inputs and the supply of output pertained only to the behaviour of this single economic actor.

It is now time to extend this to consider more fully the rôle of the firm in the market. We could perhaps go a stage further and characterise the market as 'the industry', although this arguably sidesteps the issue because the definition of the industry presupposes the definition of specific commodities. To pursue this route we need to examine the joint effect of several firms responding to price signals together. What we shall not be doing at this stage of the argument is considering the possibility of strategic game-theoretic interplay amongst firms; this needs new analytical tools and so comes after the discussion in chapter 10.

We extend our discussion of the firm by introducing three further developments:

- We consider the market equilibrium of many independent price-taking firms producing either an identical product or closely related products.
- We look at problems raised by interactions amongst firms in their production process.
- We extend the price-taking paradigm to analyse situations where the firm can control market prices to some extent. What are these? One of the simplest cases—but in some ways a rather unusual one—is that discussed in section 3.6 where there is but a single firm in the market. However, this special case of monopoly provides a useful general framework of analysis into which other forms of 'monopolistic competition' can be fitted (see section 3.7).

We shall build upon the analysis of the individual competitive firm's supply function, as discussed on page 30 above, and we will briefly examine difficulties in the concept of market equilibrium. The crucial assumption that we shall make is that each firm faces determinate demand conditions: either they take known market prices as given or they face a known demand function such as (3.7)—we defer until chapter 10 deeper questions raised by the possibility that one firm's demand may depend on the assumed behaviour of other firms.

3.2 The market supply curve

How is the overall supply of product to the market related to the story about the supply of the individual firm sketched in section 2.3.1 of chapter 2?

We begin with an overly simplified version of the supply curve. Suppose we have a market with just two potential producers—low-cost firm 1 and high-cost firm 2, each of which has zero fixed costs and rising marginal costs. Let us write q^f for the amount of the single, homogeneous output produced by firm f (for the moment f can take just the values 1 or 2). The supply curve for each firm is equal to the marginal cost curve—see the first two panels in Figure 3.1. To construct the supply curve to the market (on the assumption that both firms continue to act as price takers) pick a price on the vertical axis; read off the value of q^1 from the first panel, the value of q^2 from the second panel; in the third panel plot $q^1 + q^2$ at that price; continuing in this way for all other prices you get the market supply curve depicted in the third panel. It is clear that the aggregation of individual supply curves involves a kind of 'horizontal sum' process.

However, there are at least three features of this story that strike one immediately as unsatisfactory: (1) the fact that each firm just carries on as a price taker even though it (presumably) knows that there is just one other firm in the market; (2) the fixed number of firms and (3) the fact that each firm's supply curve is rather different from that which we sketched in chapter 2. Point 1 is a big one and going to be dealt with in chapter 10; point 2 comes up later in this chapter (section 3.5). But point 3 is dealt with right away.

The problem is that we have assumed away a feature of the supply function that is evident in Figure 2.12. So, instead of the case in Figure 3.1, imagine a case where the two firms have different fixed costs and marginal costs that rise everywhere at the same

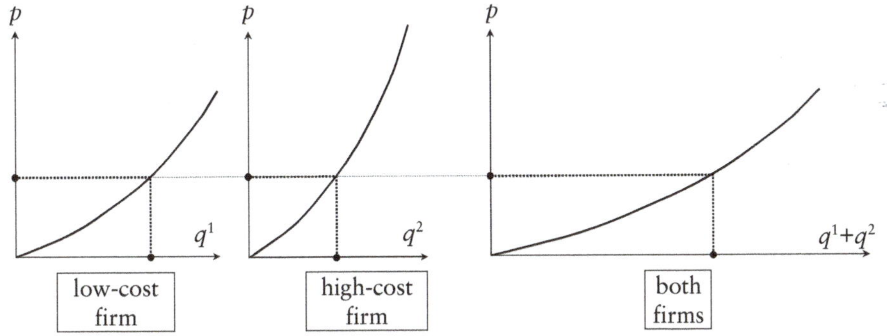

Figure 3.1 A market with two firms

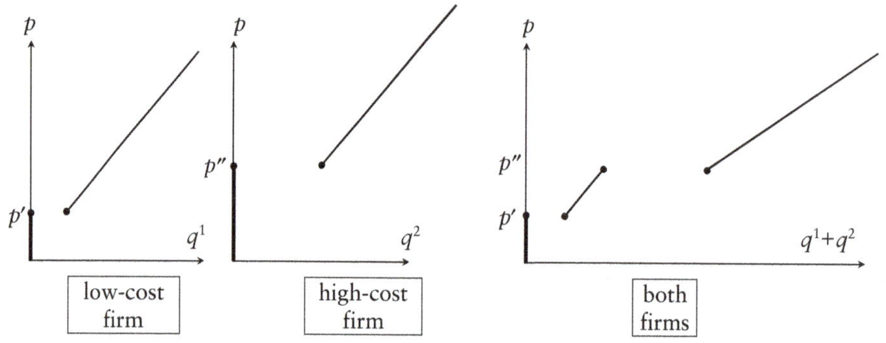

Figure 3.2 Another market with two firms

rate. The situation is now as in Figure 3.2. Consider what happens as the price of output rises from 0. Initially only firm 1 is in the market for prices in the range $p' \leq p < p''$ (left-hand panel). Once the price hits p'' firm 2 enters the market (second panel): the combined behaviour of the two firms is depicted in the third panel. Notice the following features of Figure 3.2.

- Even though each firm's supply curve has the same slope, the aggregate supply curve is flatter—in our example it is exactly half the slope. (This feature was already present in the earlier case)
- There is a discontinuity in aggregate supply as each firm enters the market.

A discontinuous supply curve in the aggregate might seem to be rather problematic—how do you find the equilibrium in one market if the demand curve goes through one of the 'holes' in the supply curve? This situation is illustrated in Figure 3.3. Here it appears that there is no market equilibrium at all: above price p'' the market will supply more than consumers demand of the product, below p'' there will be the reverse problem (at a given price p people want to consume more than is being produced); and exactly at p'' it is not self-evident what will happen; given the way that the demand curve has been drawn you will never get an exact match between demand and supply.

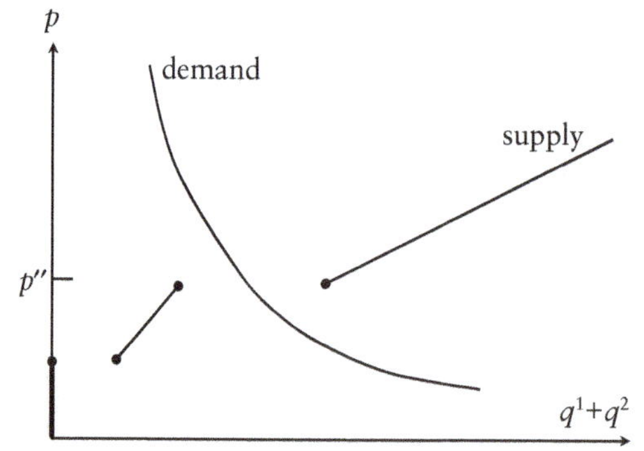

Figure 3.3 Absence of market equilibrium

These simple exercises suggests a number of directions in which the analysis of the firm in the market might be pursued.

- *Market size and equilibrium.* We shall investigate how the problem of the existence of equilibrium depends on the number of firms in the market.
- *Interactions amongst firms.* We have assumed that each firm's supply curve is in effect independent of any other firm's actions. How would such interactions affect aggregate market behaviour?
- *The number of firms.* We have supposed that there was some arbitrarily given number of firms n_f in the market—as though there were just n_f licences for potential producers. In principle we ought to allow for the possibility that new firms can set up in business, in which case n_f becomes *endogenous*.
- *Product differentiation.* We have supposed that for every commodity $i = 1, 2, \ldots, n$ there is a large number of firms supplying the market with indistinguishable units of that commodity. In reality there may be only a few suppliers of any one narrowly defined commodity type although there is still effective competition amongst firms because of substitution in consumption amongst the product types. Instead of supplying identical packets of tea to the market, firms may sell packets that are distinguished by brand name, flavour or size, or they may sell them in locations that distinguish them as being particularly convenient for particular groups of consumers.

Let us deal with each of these issues in turn.

3.3 Large numbers and the supply curve

Actually, this problem of non-existence may not be such a problem in practice. To see why consider again the second example of section 3.2 where each firm had a straight-line marginal cost curve. Take firm 1 as a standard case and imagine the effect of there being potentially many small firms just like firm 1: if there were a huge number of firms waiting in the wings which would enter the market as p hit p' what would the aggregate supply curve look like? To answer this question consider first of all a market in which there are just two identical firms. Suppose that each firm has the supply curve illustrated in either of the first two panels of Figure 3.4. Using the notation of section 3.2 the equation of either firm's supply curve is given by:[1]

$$q^f = \begin{cases} 0, & \text{if } p < p' \\ 16 + a[p - p'], & \text{if } p \geq p'. \end{cases} \tag{3.1}$$

? Mini Problems

1 Write down a cost function consistent with this supply curve.

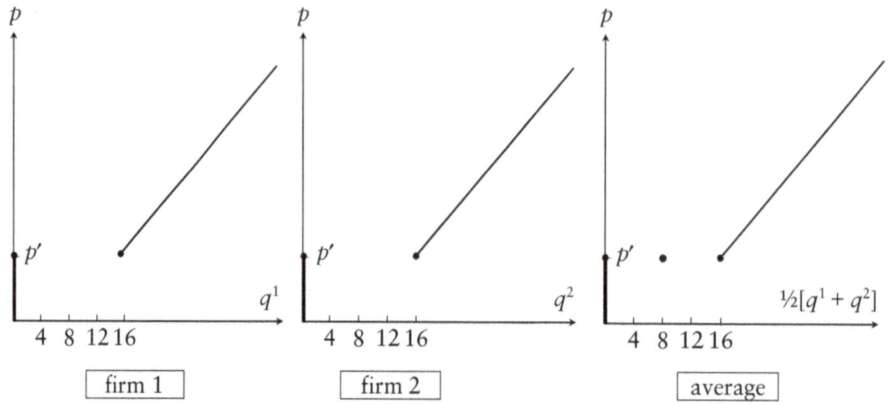

Figure 3.4 Average supply of two identical firms

Clearly for $p > p'$ total output is given by

$$q^1 + q^2 = 32 + 2a[p - p'] \tag{3.2}$$

and so for $p > p'$ *average* output is given by

$$\frac{1}{2}[q^1 + q^2] = 16 + a[p - p']. \tag{3.3}$$

Obviously for $p < p'$ total—and hence average—output is zero. But what happens exactly at $p = p'$? Clearly either we must have either $(q^1 = 0, q^2 = 0)$ or $(q^1 = 0, q^2 = 16)$, or $(q^1 = 16, q^2 = 0)$ or $(q^1 = 16, q^2 = 16)$. In other words total output could have the value 0, 16, or 32, so of course average output has the value 0, 8, or 16. Notice that the average supply in the market is almost like that for each firm, but there is an additional 'blob' at $q = 8$.

We can extend this idea to a market with more firms. We do this by considering more replications. This is illustrated in Figure 3.5. Notice that in the top left-hand panel where there are four firms, there are three intermediate blobs. The top right-hand panel and the bottom left-hand panel display the result of two more replications of the firms in the market—to 8 firms and 16 firms respectively.[2] So we can see that in the limit this large number of small firms looks indistinguishable from a market incorporating firms each of which has a continuous supply curve, as illustrated in the bottom right-hand panel of Figure 3.5.

So, if we can appeal to a regularity condition—in our example a large number of small, similar firms in the market—the elementary diagram incorporating a continuous supply curve is a valid approach for the analysis of market equilibrium. Fortunately this regularity condition can be generalised, but the principle of 'large numbers, small firms' remains.

? Mini Problems

2 If there are n_f identical firms, how many blobs will there be? Use this argument to show why in the limit the average supply curve of the industry looks as though it is continuous.

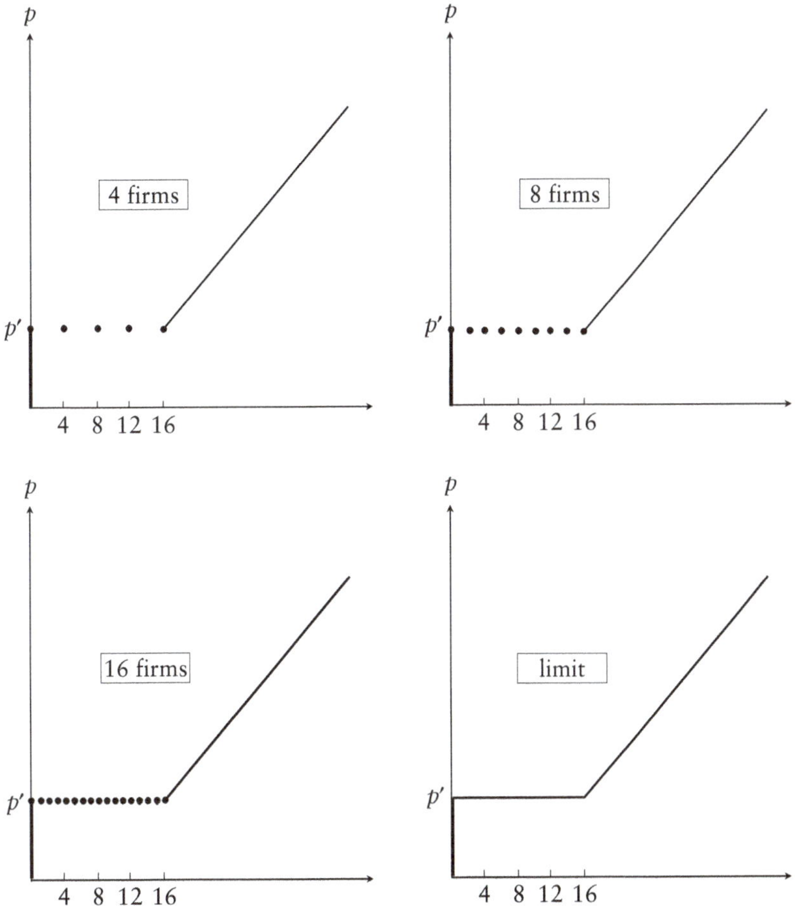

Figure 3.5 Average supply of lots of firms

3.4 Interaction amongst firms

All of the preceding analysis has been predicated on the basis that each firm's production possibilities are independent of every other firm's production decisions. However, we also need to take into account the possibility of technological interactions between firms—interactions that do not occur through conventional market mechanisms. One firm's choice of outputs and inputs affects the others' technological possibilities. This interaction could be in either of two directions: *negative externalities* whereby the increase in the output by one firm—a polluter perhaps—raises the marginal costs of other firms, and *positive externalities* whereby the increase in output by one firm—perhaps a firm that undertakes the general training of workers in an area—lowers the marginal costs of other firms.

Consider a negative externality in the case of two identical firms. If one firm increases its output, the other firm's marginal costs are pushed up. So the position of either firm's

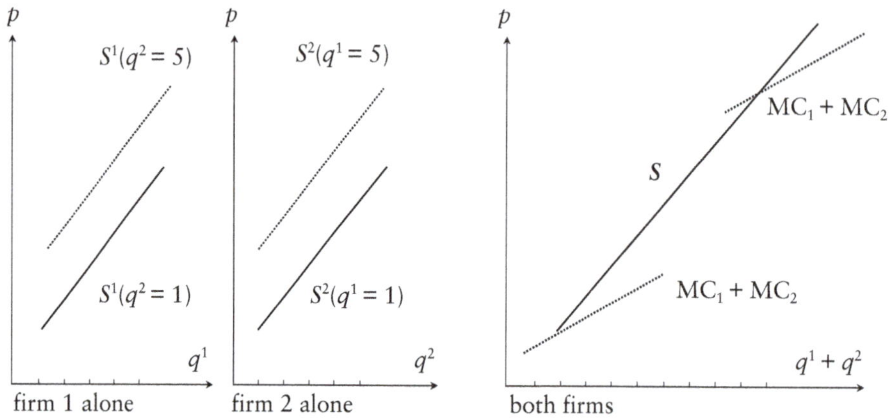

Figure 3.6 Industry supply with negative externality

supply curve depends on the other's output decision. This is illustrated in Figure 3.6. Suppose that market price is such that each firm wants to supply one unit of output: the firm's supply curve is as shown by the solid line in each of the first two panels. Then market demand rises: the price goes up and each firm expands output, let us say to five units. Because of the negative externality each firm's expansion pushes up marginal costs of the other firm—see the firm supply curves drawn as broken lines. When we draw in the supply curve for the market notice that the slope is steeper than would have been the case had there been no externality (in the third panel compare the supply curve *S* with the two broken lines).

We can also consider the effect of a positive externality simply by interchanging the labels in each part of the above figure. In this case, as each firm expands output, the other firm's marginal costs fall. Again we can run through the same story of what happens as market demand rises, but now the firm's supply curves shift the other way. If you do this notice that, for this particular case, the aggregate supply curve is less steeply upward sloping than that for either firm—see Figure 3.7. However, the resulting market supply curve could be horizontal or even be forward falling.[3]

3.5 The size of the industry

In the elementary examples of constructing market supply curves from the behavioural response of individual firms (sections 3.2 and 3.3) we made the unwarranted assumption that there was a known, fixed, number of firms n_f. Rather than just *assuming* that there are 2, 4, 8, 16, ... firms we need to examine the economic principle that will determine the size of the industry.

? Mini Problems

3 Suppose each firm's individual supply curve is upward sloping but that the market curve is forward falling. Explain what happens as market demand increases.

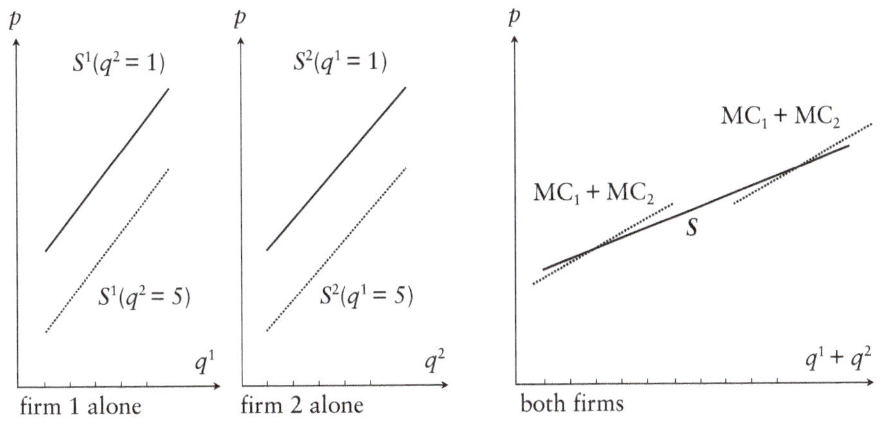

Figure 3.7 Industry supply with positive externality

Again we work within the context of price-taking firms. If all firms are earning positive profits, as depicted by the shaded area in Figure 3.8, then it is clear why this fixed-n_f approach to constructing the analysis of the supply and demand equilibrium in the market will not do. The reason is that other new firms may be able to set up and make a profit. If so, then presumably they will try to do this. How many firms will do so? How will the number of firms n_f be determined?

We can answer this by extending the elementary argument of the last paragraph. Let the firms be numbered in the order in which they would enter the industry, $1, 2, \ldots, N, \ldots$ and suppose the number of firms currently in the industry is n_f. Let q^N be the profit-maximising output for firm N in a price-taking equilibrium (in other words the optimal output and inputs given market prices as we considered for the single competitive firm on page 26). Allow n_f gradually to increase: 1,2,3. . . : output price p will fall

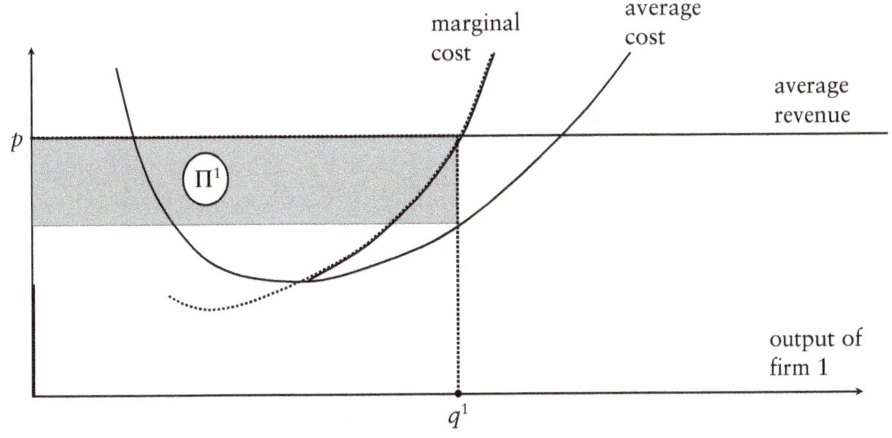

Figure 3.8 Temporary equilibrium of one firm

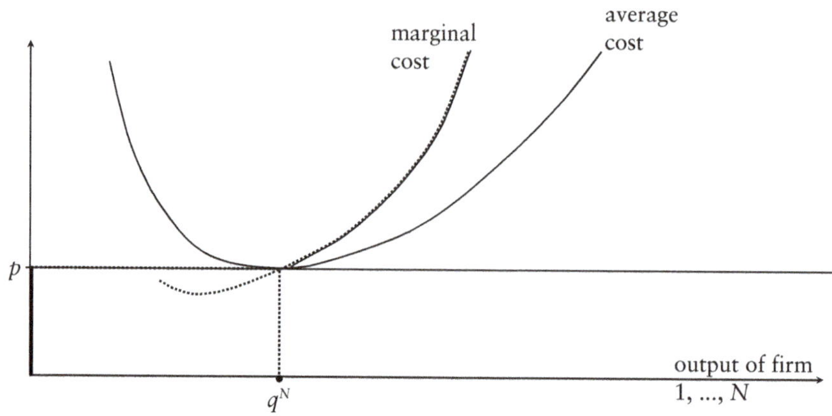

Figure 3.9 Equilibrium of the marginal competitive firm

if the market demand curve is downward sloping.[4] If there is a value N such that

$$\Pi^N(q^N) \geq 0 \tag{3.4}$$

and

$$\Pi^{N+1}(q^{N+1}) < 0 \tag{3.5}$$

then $n_f = N$ must represent an equilibrium number of firms.[5] In this full equilibrium we will find that the 'marginal firm' is in the situation as depicted in Figure 3.9: profit is zero since the firm is producing where

$$p = MC = AC. \tag{3.6}$$

Thus in the full market equilibrium the behaviour of each firm is determined by the standard 'price = marginal cost' rule, and the number of firms is solved by a zero-profit condition.

3.6 Price setting

So far we have assumed that the firm just accepts all prices as parametrically given. This seems reasonable if the firm has no market power, but it would be interesting to see how the optimisation problem would change were the firm in a position to make a price. We

? Mini Problems

4 Explain what will happen to input prices if factors are not in perfectly elastic supply.

5 Provide a one-line argument to explain why this is so.

will look at three straightforward developments of the basic model of the firm to examine the effect on the firm's behaviour of having market power.

3.6.1 Simple monopoly

We begin with a case that is easy and unrealistic, but that forms a very useful starting point. We shall assume that the markets for all inputs are competitive as before: so we can be sure that the derivation of the cost function will go through in just the same manner as we did it originally. The only effective change to our model is that we shall assume that the product price is a determinate function of output.[6] In other words there is an *inverse demand curve* for output given by:

$$p = p(q). \tag{3.7}$$

This gives the 'price that the market will bear'. It is useful to introduce the *product demand elasticity* η (a negative number):

$$\eta(q) := \frac{d\log q}{d\log p} = \frac{p(q)}{qp_q(q)}. \tag{3.8}$$

This encapsulates important information for the monopolist. If the monopolist considers what percentage change in price the market will bear given a 1 per cent change in the volume of output unloaded on to the market, then this is exactly $1/\eta(q)$.

Profits may now be written as the expression

$$p(q)q - C(\mathbf{w}, q). \tag{3.9}$$

The first-order condition for a maximum is:

$$p(q) + p_q(q)q = C_q(\mathbf{w}, q). \tag{3.10}$$

It is worth pausing for a moment to consider the implication of this in comparison with the analysis of competitive firms. By definition competitive firms active in the market have no individual power: so the best that they can do is accept the going price p in the market as the marginal revenue they get from selling each item and arrange production so that this equals the marginal cost of producing the item—equations (2.36) for the single firm and (3.6) for the industry. In assuming just one firm facing a given demand curve, we have endowed that firm with market power. The monopolist exercises this power rationally and takes full advantage of its knowledge of the given, downward-sloping demand curve. The firm therefore uses a rule that takes into account the erosion of price $p(q)$ every time an additional unit of output is unloaded on the market—the

? Mini Problems

6 Under what circumstances in the industry would this specification be insufficient? What other information about the market or about the 'rules of the game' might be required in order for the firm to determine the price of p at which it can sell its output?

second term on the left of (3.10). In plain language (3.10) says that the optimal rule for exercising the monopolist's market power is:

marginal revenue	=	marginal cost

where 'marginal revenue' explicitly takes account of the price-erosion effect.

Solving equation (3.10) for q determines the monopolist's optimal output—see the point q^* in Figure 3.10 where the AR (average revenue curve) is the demand curve and MR is marginal revenue.[7] But what of the price?

Condition (3.10) can be expressed in another way that illuminates the rational behaviour of the monopolist. A rearrangement of (3.10) gives:[8]

$$p = \frac{C_q(\mathbf{w}, q)}{1 + 1/\eta(q)}. \tag{3.11}$$

The denominator in (3.11) is smaller than 1. So this means that the price maker uses his market power to force price above marginal cost.

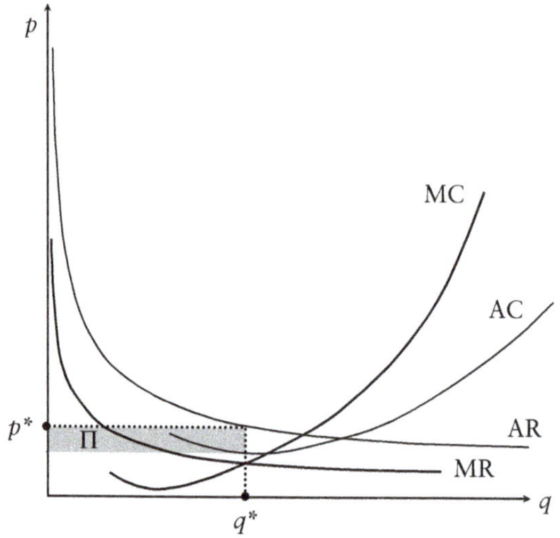

Figure 3.10 Equilibrium of the monopolist

? Mini Problems

7 (a) The average revenue and marginal curves have been drawn for the case where η is a constant. Write down explicit formulae for these curves in this special case. (b) Now suppose that market price is given by the relationship $p = a - bq$. Draw the AR and MR curves.

8 For this condition to be meaningful we must have $\eta < -1$. Explain what happens if this condition is violated. [Hint: plot (3.9) on a graph and think about what happens as $q \to 0$.]

A simple interpretation of (3.11) is that the monopolist uses information about the *shape* of the market demand curve (captured in the parameter η) and not just the price to determine how much of the product to supply to the market. So, in the sense of Definition 2.7 there is no determinate supply curve for the monopolistic firm. Nevertheless, there is a determinate solution to the monopolist's problem.

3.6.2 Discriminating monopolist

However, this is just one narrow interpretation of market power. What if the monopolist had yet more power? Suppose for example that the firm could effectively divide the market and sells in two separated markets with prices p^1, p^2 determined as follows

$$p^1 = p^1\left(q^1\right)$$

$$p^2 = p^2\left(q^2\right)$$

where q^1 and q^2 are the amounts delivered to each market and total output is $q = q^1 + q^2$. Profits are now:

$$p^1\left(q^1\right)q^1 + p^2\left(q^2\right)q^2 - C(\mathbf{w}, q). \tag{3.12}$$

To find a maximum we need the following pair of expressions

$$p^i_q\left(q^i\right)q^i + p^i\left(q^i\right) = C_q(\mathbf{w}, q),\ i = 1, 2. \tag{3.13}$$

The outcome of the profit-maximisation problem is one of two types: a solution where the monopolist sells in one market only[9] and, more interestingly, the case where the monopolist sells in both markets and (3.13) yields

$$p^1_q\left(q^1\right)q^1 + p^1\left(q^1\right) = p^2_q\left(q^2\right)q^2 + p^2\left(q^2\right) = C_q(\mathbf{w}, q)$$

or, if η^1 and η^2 are the demand elasticities in the two markets:

$$p^1\left[1 + \frac{1}{\eta^1}\right] = p^2\left[1 + \frac{1}{\eta^2}\right] = C_q(\mathbf{w}, q). \tag{3.14}$$

It is clear that profits are higher[10] than in the case of the simple monopolist and—from (3.14)—that if $\eta^1 < \eta^2 < -1$ then $p^2 > p^1$. We have the intuitively reasonable result that if the monopolistic firm can split the market then it will charge the higher price in the submarket that has the less elastic demand.

3.6.3 Entry fee

Could the monopolist do more—perhaps exercise market power by setting an entry fee for the market? Here is a quick and easy approach to the problem.

? Mini Problems

9 Write down the condition that must be satisfied in this case, derived from (3.13).

10 Provide an intuitive argument to show that this is true.

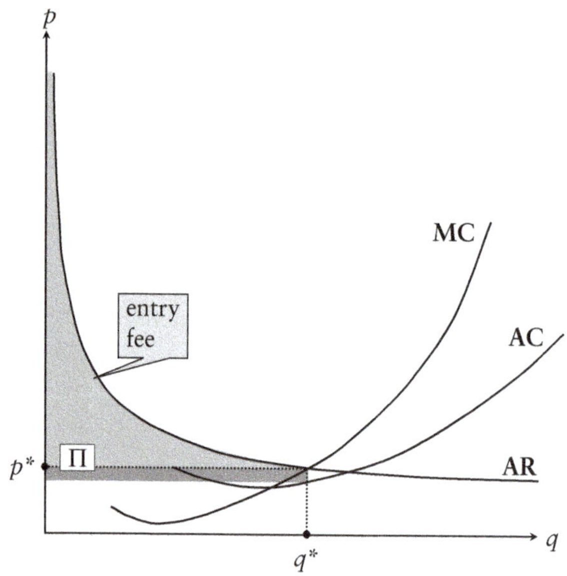

Figure 3.11 Monopolistic market with an entry fee

One way of interpreting the demand curve (AR) in Figure 3.10 is that the height of the curve $p(x)$ at any output level x gives the consumer's willingness to pay for an extra unit of output given that x units have already been supplied; if this is above the current market price then the consumer is enjoying a 'surplus'—the willingness to pay minus the price. Given that an amount q is actually being supplied to the market and that the price is $p(q)$, the total amount of this surplus is given by the expression

$$\int_0^q p(x)\,dx - p(q)\,q, \tag{3.15}$$

the large shaded area in Figure 3.11.

The concept of consumer's surplus is discussed further in chapter 4 (page 91); we use it here to give some extra leverage to the monopolist. Suppose the firm were able to charge an entry fee F_0 to the market in order to capture the consumer's surplus. Then in addition to the conventional profits term $p(q)\,q - C(\mathbf{w}, q)$ (the shaded rectangle in Figure 3.11) the firm also has the fee revenue F_0 equal to (3.15) so that in this case total profits are

$$\begin{aligned} & p(q)\,q - C(\mathbf{w}, q) + F_0 \\ &= p(q)\,q - C(\mathbf{w}, q) + \left[\int_0^q p(x)\,dx - p(q)\,q\right] \\ &= \int_0^q p(x)\,dx - C(\mathbf{w}, q). \end{aligned}$$

Differentiating this with respect to q the FOC for this problem is just

$$p(q) - C_q(\mathbf{w}, q) = 0 \tag{3.16}$$

so that we have the nice result that in this case the monopolist sets price equal to marginal cost—see Figure 3.11. Here the firm uses a *two-part tariff* (p, F_0) to charge for its provision of the good.[11]

Example 3.1

The monopoly-with-entry-fee model has been applied to Disneyland (Oi 1971). Here the marginal cost of some individual entertainments is effectively zero so that the entry fee is set in such a way as to capture the consumer surplus and the rides are then free of charge.

This model raises further, deeper issues that will be discussed in chapter 11 (page 333).

3.7 Product variety

Consider again the issue of many firms and industry equilibrium but, in contrast to section 3.5, pose the question: What if the firms are not all making an identical product? If there is effective product differentiation, then individual firms act as *quasi-monopolists*, with downward-sloping demand curves as in section 3.6 instead of facing a given market price. The form of the equilibrium, however, is fairly similar to the homogeneous product case. We need to set out the analogue to perfectly competitive equilibrium in which we discussed the determination of the number of firms: in effect an equilibrium under product differentiation.

Because each firm may have a local monopoly, its behaviour will be different from that discussed in section 3.5. In order to analyse this let us first of all take the situation where the market contains a fixed number of firms. Each firm will make quasi-monopolistic profits (as shown in Figure 3.12), the size of which will depend on the degree of market power that it enjoys through the effective product differentiation which 'ties' a section of the market to it.

But, as we saw in section 3.5 which dealt with homogeneous goods, the fixed-number assumption will not do. If all firms are making positive profits then other firms making products that are differentiated (perhaps only slightly differentiated) will enter the market in the hope of capturing some of these profits. Now, if any new firm enters the market, this will affect the AR and MR curves of other firms: the extent to which this happens will depend on the extent to which the new firm's product is perceived to be a close substitute for the outputs of other firms. The equilibrium is a form of 'monopolistic competition'; for the marginal firm, the situation is as in Figure 3.13. It makes zero profits but faces a downward-sloping demand curve.

? Mini Problems

11 What type of goods could be charged for in this way?

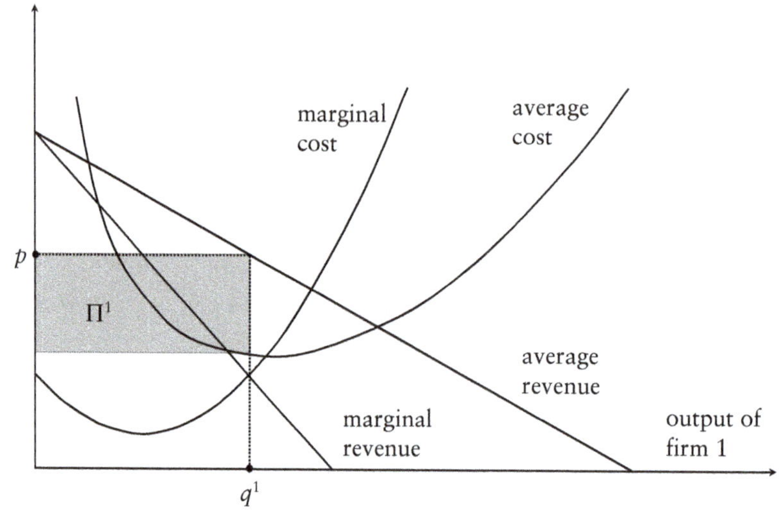

Figure 3.12 Short run equilibrium for the local monopolist

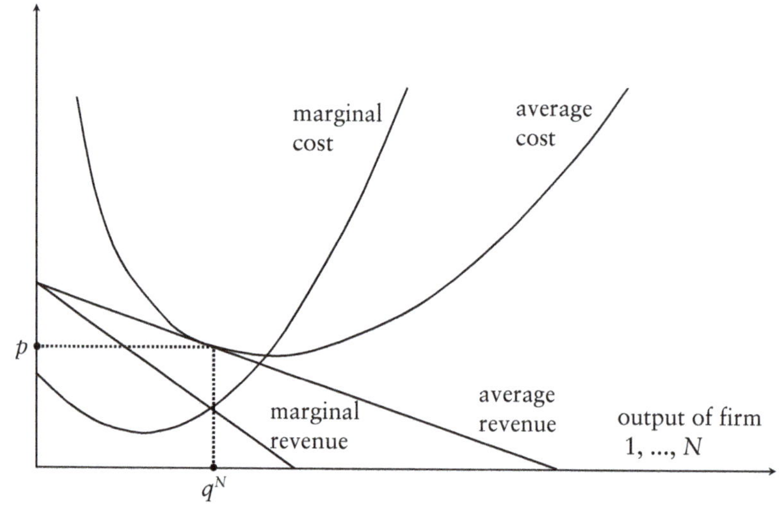

Figure 3.13 Long run equilibrium for the local monopolist

Example 3.2

What makes one type of good 'close' to another in monopolistic competition? One might expect competition amongst firms to be localised in that people are loyal to brands and do not regard products from other firms as perfect substitutes. But how could you identify this localised competition empirically? Schmalensee (1985) shows how to do this in the case of the breakfast cereal industry.

Summary

Extending the analysis of a firm in isolation to the mass of firms in the market is fairly straightforward as long as we make a key assumption about the economic environment in which they operate. Each firm faces a determinate demand curve for its product or, in the case where there is product variety, a determinate pattern of demand curves for the various products. On this assumption we can then move on from the approach of chapter 2 and find straightforward, interpretable conditions for firms' equilibrium behaviour. A marginal condition determines the equilibrium output for each firm and a condition on market demand and average costs determines how many firms will be present in the market.

The question of what happens when there is no determinate demand curve is a deep one and will be addressed after we have thought anew about firms' interaction and equilibrium.

Reading notes

The classic reference on monopolistic competition is Chamberlin (1933); see also Dixit and Stiglitz (1977) that is used as a basis for Exercise 3.2. Various types of discriminating monopoly are treated by Pigou (1952), chapter 17.

Exercises

3.1 (The phenomenon of 'natural monopoly') Consider an industry in which all the potential member firms have the same cost function C. Suppose it is true that for some level of output $\overline{q}$ and for any non-negative outputs q, q' of two such firms such that $q + q' \leq \overline{q}$ the cost function satisfies the 'subadditivity' property

$$C(\mathbf{w}, q + q') < C(\mathbf{w}, q) + C(\mathbf{w}, q').$$

1. Show that this implies that for all integers $N > 1$

$$C(\mathbf{w}, q) < NC\left(\mathbf{w}, \frac{q}{N}\right), \text{ for } 0 \leq q \leq \overline{q}.$$

2. What are the implications for the shape of average and marginal cost curves?
3. May one conclude that a monopoly must be more efficient in producing this good?

3.2 In a particular industry there are n profit-maximising firms each producing a single good. The costs for firm i are

$$C_0 + cq_i$$

where C_0 and c are parameters and q_i is the output of firm i. The goods are not regarded as being exactly identical by the consumers and the inverse demand function for firm i is given by

$$p_i = \frac{Aq_i^{a-1}}{\sum_{j=1}^{n} q_j^a}$$

where a measures the degree of substitutability of the firms' products, $0 < a \leq 1$.

1. Assuming that each firm takes the output of all the other firms as given, write down the first-order conditions yielding firm 1's output conditional on the outputs $q_2, \ldots, q_n$. Hence, using the symmetry of the equilibrium, show that in equilibrium the optimal output for any firm is

$$q_i^* = \frac{Aa\,[n-1]}{n^2 c}$$

and that the elasticity of demand for firm i is

$$\frac{n}{n - na + a}.$$

2. Consider the case $a = 1$. What phenomenon does this represent? Show that the equilibrium number of firms in the industry is less than or equal to $\sqrt{\frac{A}{C_0}}$.

3.3 A firm has the cost function

$$F_0 + \frac{1}{2}aq_i^2$$

where q_i is the output of a single homogeneous good and F_0 and a are positive numbers.

1. Find the firm's supply relationship between output and price p; explain carefully what happens at the minimum-average-cost point $\underline{p} := \sqrt{2aF_0}$.
2. In a market of a thousand consumers the demand curve for the commodity is given by

$$p = A - bq$$

where q is total quantity demanded and A and b are positive parameters. If the market is served by a single price-taking firm with the cost structure in part 1 explain why there is a unique equilibrium if $b \leq a\left[A/\underline{p} - 1\right]$ and no equilibrium otherwise.

3. Now assume that there is a large number N of firms, each with the above cost function: find the relationship between average supply by the N firms and price and compare the answer with that of part 1. What happens as $N \to \infty$?
4. Assume that the size of the market is also increased by a factor N but that the demand per thousand consumers remains as in part 2 above. Show that as N gets large there will be a determinate market equilibrium price and output level.

3.4 A firm has a fixed cost F_0 and marginal costs

$$c = a + bq$$

where q is output.

1. If the firm were a price-taker, what is the lowest price at which it would be prepared to produce a positive amount of output? If the competitive price were above this level, find the amount of output q^* that the firm would produce.
2. If the firm is actually a monopolist and the inverse demand function is

$$p = A - \frac{1}{2}Bq$$

(where $A > a$ and $B > 0$) find the expression for the firm's marginal revenue in terms of output. Illustrate the optimum in a diagram and show that the firm will produce

$$q^{**} := \frac{A - a}{b + B}.$$

What is the price charged p^{**} and the marginal cost c^{**} at this output level? Compare q^{**} and q^*.

3. The government decides to regulate the monopoly. The regulator has the power to control the price by setting a ceiling $p_{\max}$. Plot the average and marginal revenue curves that would then face the monopolist. Use these to show:
   (a) If $p_{\max} > p^{**}$ the firm's output and price remain unchanged at q^{**} and p^{**}.
   (b) If $p_{\max} < c^{**}$ the firm's output will fall below q^{**}.
   (c) Otherwise output will rise above q^{**}.

3.5 A monopolist has the cost function

$$C(q) = 100 + 6q + \frac{1}{2}[q]^2.$$

1. If the demand function is given by

$$q = 24 - \frac{1}{4}p$$

calculate the output-price combination which maximises profits.

2. Assume that it becomes possible to sell in a separate second market with demand determined by

$$q = 84 - \frac{3}{4}p.$$

Calculate the prices which will be set in the two markets and the change in total output and profits from case 1.

3. Now suppose that the firm still has access to both markets, but is prevented from discriminating between them. What will be the result?

4 The Consumer

Consumer: A person who is capable of choosing a president but incapable of choosing a bicycle without help from a government agency.
Herbert Stein, *Washington Bedtime Stories* (1979)

4.1 Introduction

It is now time to introduce the second of the principal economic actors in the economic system—the consumer. In a sense this is the heart of microeconomics. Why else speak about 'consumer sovereignty'? For what else, ultimately, is the economy's productive activity organised?

We will tackle the economic principles that apply to the analysis of the consumer in the following broad areas:

- Analysis of preferences.
- Consumer optimisation in perfect markets.
- Consumer's welfare.

This, of course, is just an introduction to the economics of individual consumers and households; in this chapter we concentrate on just the consumer in isolation. Issues such as the way consumers behave *en masse* in the market, the issues concerning the supply by households of factors such as labour and savings to the market, and whether consumers 'substitute' for the market by producing at home are deferred until chapter 5. The big topic of consumer behaviour under uncertainty forms a large part of chapter 8.

In developing the analysis we will see several points of analogy where we can compare the theory of the consumer with the theory of the firm. This can make life much easier analytically and can give us several useful insights into economic problems in both fields of study.

4.2 The consumer's environment

As with the firm we begin by setting out the basic ingredients of the problem. First, a preliminary word about who is doing the consuming. I shall sometimes refer to 'the individual', sometimes to 'the household' and sometimes—more vaguely—to 'the consumer', as appropriate. The distinction does not matter as long as (a) if the consumer is a multiperson household, that household's membership is taken as given and (b) any multiperson household acts as though it were a single unit. However, in later work the distinction will indeed matter—see chapter 9.

Having set aside the issue of the consumer we need to characterise and discuss three ingredients of the basic optimisation problem:

- the commodity space;
- the market;
- motivation.

The commodity space

We assume that there is a known list of n commodities where n is a finite, but perhaps huge, number. A consumption bundle is just a list of commodities $\mathbf{x} := (x_1, x_2, \ldots, x_n)$. We shall refer to the set of all *feasible* consumption bundles as X. In most cases we shall assume that X is identical to $\mathbb{R}^n_+$, the set of all non-negative n-vectors—see Figure 4.1; the implications of this are that a negative amount of any commodity makes no sense,

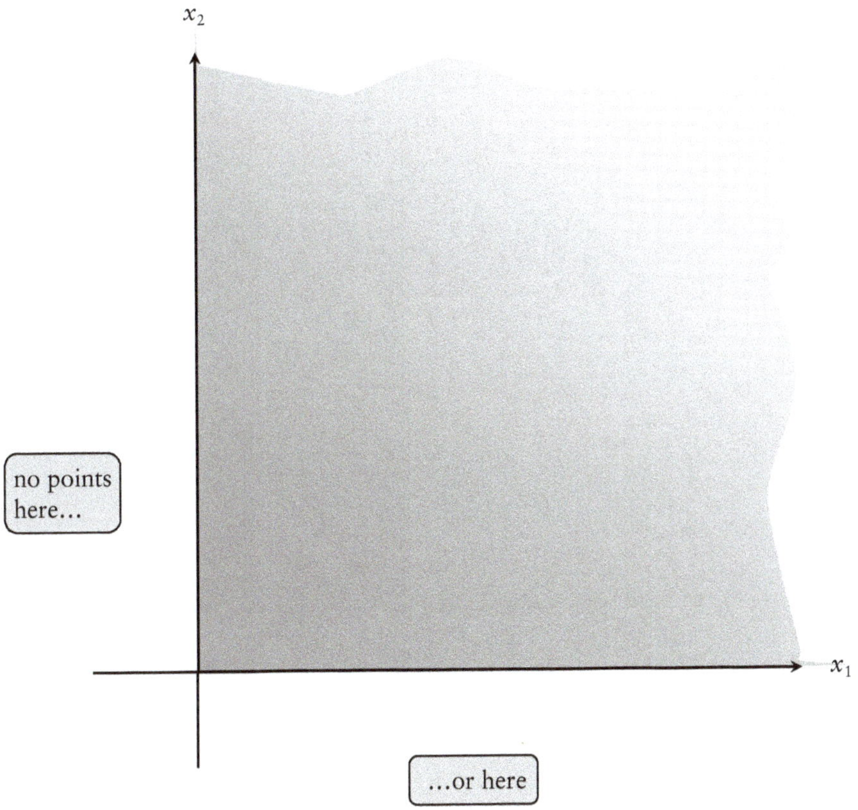

Figure 4.1 The consumption set: standard assumptions

that all commodities are divisible, and there is no physical upper bound to the amount of any one commodity that an individual could consume (that bound is going to be set by the budget, which we will come to in a moment).[1]

How do you draw the boundaries of goods classifications? This depends on the type of model you want to analyse. Very often you can get by with cases where you only have two or three commodities—and this is discussed further in chapter 5. Commodities could, in principle, be differentiated by space, time, or the state-of-the-world.

The market

As in the case of the competitive firm, we assume that the consumer has access to a market in which the prices of all n goods are known: $\mathbf{p} := (p_1, p_2, \ldots, p_n)$. These prices will, in part, determine the individual's budget constraint.

However, to complete the description, there are two versions (at least) of this constraint which we may wish to consider using in our model of the consumer. These two versions are presented in Figure 4.2.

- In the left-hand version a fixed amount of money y is available to the consumer, who therefore finds himself constrained to purchase a bundle of goods $\mathbf{x}$ such that

$$p_1x_1 + p_2x_2 \leq y \tag{4.1}$$

If all income y were spent on good 1 the person would be able to buy a quantity $x_1 = y/p_1$.

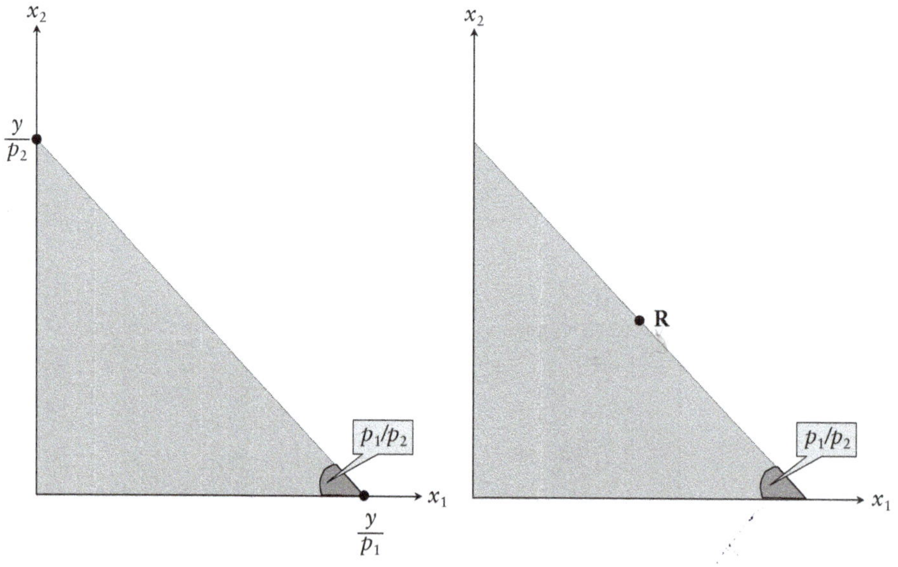

Figure 4.2 Two versions of the budget constraint

? Mini Problems

1 How might one model indivisibilities in consumption? Describe the shape of the set X if good 1 is food, and good 2 is (indivisible) refrigerators.

- In the right-hand version the person has an endowment of resources $\mathbf{R} := (R_1, R_2)$, and so his chosen bundle of goods must satisfy

$$p_1x_1 + p_2x_2 \leq p_1R + p_2R_2. \tag{4.2}$$

The two versions of the budget constraint look similar, but will induce different responses when prices change.[2]

Motivation

This is not so easy to specify as in the case of the firm, because there is no overwhelmingly strong case for asserting that individuals or households maximise a particular type of objective function if, indeed anything at all. Households could conceivably behave in a frivolous fashion in the market (if *firms* behave in a frivolous fashion in the market then presumably they will go bust). But if they are maximising something, what is it that they are maximising? We will examine two approaches that have been attempted to this question, each of which has important economic applications. In the first we suppose that people make their choices in a way that reveals their own preferences. Secondly we consider a method of introspection.

The Consumer: basic notation

x_i	amount consumed of good i
$\mathbf{x}$	$(x_1, \ldots, x_n)$
X	the set of all $\mathbf{x}$
p_i	price of good i
$\mathbf{p}$	$(p_1, \ldots, p_n)$
y	income
$\succcurlyeq$	weak preference relation
$\triangleright$	revealed preference relation
U	utility function
υ	utility level

4.3 Revealed preference

We shall tackle first the difficult problem of the consumer's motivation. To some extent it is possible to deduce a lot about a firm's objectives, technology, and other constraints from external observation of how it acts. For example, from data on prices and on firms'

? Mini Problems

2 (i) For each type of budget constraint sketch what will happen if the price of good 1 falls. (ii) Repeat this exercise for a rise in the price of good 2. (iii) Redraw the right-hand case for the situation in which the price at which one can buy a commodity is greater than the price at which one can sell the same commodity.

costs and revenue we could investigate whether firms' input and output decisions appear to be consistent with profit maximisation. Can the same sort of thing be done with regard to consumers?

The general approach presupposes that individuals' or households' actions in the market reflect the objectives that they were actually pursuing, which might be summarised as 'what-you-see-is-what-they-wanted'.

Definition 4.1

A bundle $\mathbf{x}$ is *revealed preferred* to a bundle $\mathbf{x}'$ (written in symbols $\mathbf{x} \rhd \mathbf{x}'$) if $\mathbf{x}$ is actually selected when $\mathbf{x}'$ was also available to the consumer.

The idea is almost self-explanatory and is given operational content by the following axiom.

Axiom 4.1 (Axiom of rational choice)

The consumer always makes a choice, and selects the most preferred bundle that is available.

This means that we can draw inferences about a person's preferences by observing the person's choices; it suggests that we might adopt the following simple—but very powerful—assumption.

Axiom 4.2 (Weak Axiom of Revealed Preference)

If $\mathbf{x} \rhd \mathbf{x}'$ then $\mathbf{x}' \not\rhd \mathbf{x}$.

In the case where purchases are made in a free market this has a very simple interpretation. Suppose that at prices $\mathbf{p}$ the household could afford to buy either of two commodity bundles, $\mathbf{x}$ or $\mathbf{x}'$; assume that $\mathbf{x}$ is actually bought. Now imagine that prices change from $\mathbf{p}$ to $\mathbf{p}'$ (while income remains unchanged); if the household now selects $\mathbf{x}'$ then the weak axiom of revealed preference states that $\mathbf{x}$ cannot be affordable at the new prices $\mathbf{p}'$. Thus the axiom means that if

$$\sum_{i=1}^{n} p_i x_i \geq \sum_{i=1}^{n} p_i x_i' \tag{4.3}$$

then

$$\sum_{i=1}^{n} p_i' x_i > \sum_{i=1}^{n} p_i' x_i'. \tag{4.4}$$

If you do not choose today something that you chose yesterday (when today's bundle was also available and affordable) it must be because now you cannot afford yesterday's bundle: see Figure 4.3.

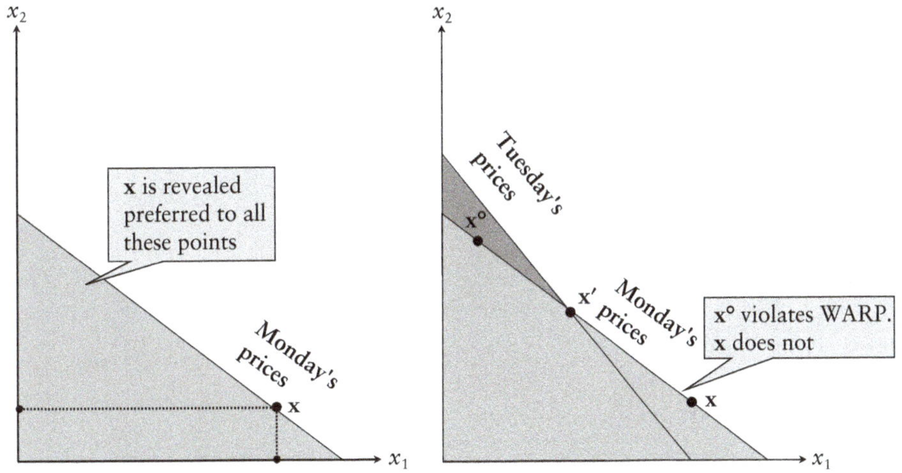

Figure 4.3 **x** is chosen Monday; **x**′ is chosen Tuesday

You can get a long way in consumption theory with just this. Indeed with a little experimentation it seems as though we are almost sketching out the result of the kind of cost-minimisation experiment that we performed for the firm, in which we traced out a portion of a contour of the production function. Perhaps we might even suspect that we are on the threshold of discovering a counterpart to isoquants by the back door (we come to a discussion of 'indifference curves' on page 76 below). For example, examine Figure 4.4: let $\mathbf{x} \rhd \mathbf{x}'$, and $\mathbf{x}' \rhd \mathbf{x}''$, and let $N(\mathbf{x})$ denote the set of points to which **x** is not revealed-preferred. Now consider the set of consumptions represented by the unshaded area: this is $N(\mathbf{x}) \cap N(\mathbf{x}') \cap N(\mathbf{x}'')$ and since **x** is revealed preferred to $\mathbf{x}'$ (which in turn is revealed preferred to $\mathbf{x}''$ we might think of this unshaded area as the set of points which are—directly or indirectly—revealed to be at least as good as $\mathbf{x}''$: the set is convex and the boundary does look a bit like the kind of contour we discussed in production theory. However, there are quite narrow limits to the extent that we can push the analysis. For example, it would be possible to have the following kind of behaviour: $\mathbf{x} \rhd \mathbf{x}'$, $\mathbf{x}' \rhd \mathbf{x}''$, $\mathbf{x}'' \rhd \mathbf{x}'''$ and yet also $\mathbf{x}''' \rhd \mathbf{x}$. To avoid this problem actually you need an additional axiom—the Strong Axiom of Revealed Preference—which explicitly rules out cyclical preferences.

4.4 Preferences: axiomatic approach

In contrast to section 4.3 let us use the method of introspection. Instead of just drawing inferences from people's purchases, we approach the problem of specifying their preferences directly. We proceed by setting out a number of axioms which it might be reasonable to suppose that a consumer's preferences should satisfy. There is no special magic in any one axiom or set of axioms: they are just a way of trying to capture a structure

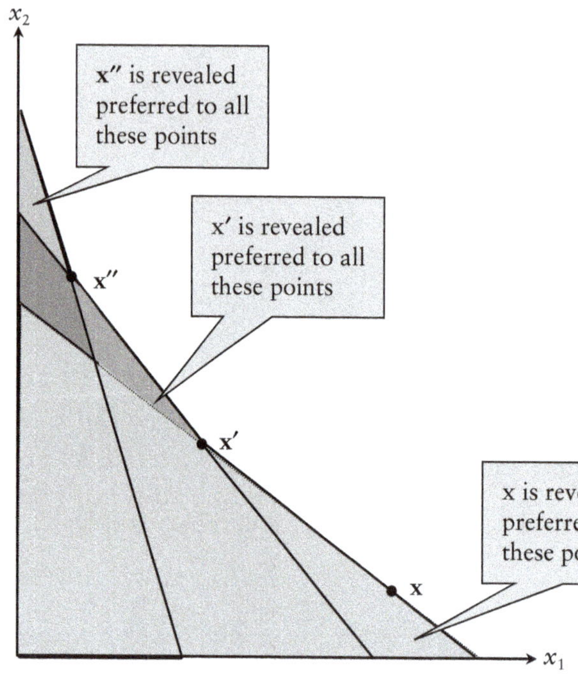

Figure 4.4 Extension of the revealed preference concept

that seems appropriate in the light of everyday experience. There is a variety of ways in which we might coherently axiomatise a model of consumer choice. Our fundamental concept is:

Definition 4.2

The *weak preference relation* $\succeq$ is a binary relation on X. If $\mathbf{x}, \mathbf{x}' \in X$ then the statement '$\mathbf{x} \succeq \mathbf{x}'$' is to be read '$\mathbf{x}$ is at least as good as $\mathbf{x}'$'.

From this we can define two related concepts. The expression '$\mathbf{x} \succ \mathbf{x}'$' is to be read '$\mathbf{x}$ is strictly better than $\mathbf{x}'$' and is equivalent to saying that '$\mathbf{x} \succeq \mathbf{x}'$' is true and '$\mathbf{x}' \succeq \mathbf{x}$' is not true. The expression '$\mathbf{x} \sim \mathbf{x}'$' is to be read '$\mathbf{x}$ is just as good as $\mathbf{x}'$' and is equivalent to saying that both '$\mathbf{x} \succeq \mathbf{x}'$' and '$\mathbf{x}' \succeq \mathbf{x}$' are true.

To make the weak-preference relation useful we shall consider three basic axioms on preference.

Axiom 4.3 (Completeness)

For every $\mathbf{x}, \mathbf{x}' \in X$, either $\mathbf{x} \succeq \mathbf{x}'$ is true, or $\mathbf{x}' \succeq \mathbf{x}$ is true, or both statements are true.

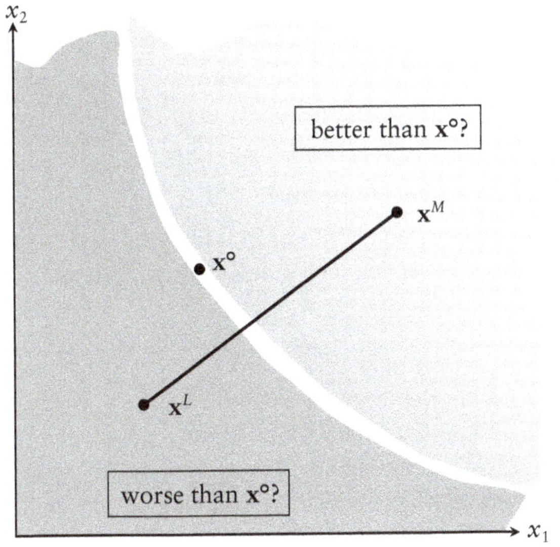

Figure 4.5 The continuity axiom

Axiom 4.4 (Transitivity)
For any $\mathbf{x}, \mathbf{x}', \mathbf{x}'' \in X$, if both $\mathbf{x} \succcurlyeq \mathbf{x}'$ and $\mathbf{x}' \succcurlyeq \mathbf{x}''$, then $\mathbf{x} \succcurlyeq \mathbf{x}''$.

Axiom 4.5 (Continuity)[3]
For any $\mathbf{x} \in X$, the not-better-than-$\mathbf{x}$ set and the not-worse-than-$\mathbf{x}$ set are closed in X.

Completeness means that people do not shrug their shoulders helplessly when confronted with a choice; transitivity implies that (in a sense) they are consistent;[4] if these two properties hold then the person may be said to have *rational* preferences.

To see what the continuity axiom implies do the experiment illustrated in Figure 4.5. In a two-commodity diagram put some point $\mathbf{x}^\circ$ that represents positive amounts of both goods; plot any other point $\mathbf{x}^M$ that represents *m*ore of both goods, and some other point $\mathbf{x}^L$ that represents *l*ess of both goods (relative to $\mathbf{x}^\circ$); suppose the individual strictly prefers $\mathbf{x}^M$ to $\mathbf{x}^\circ$ and $\mathbf{x}^\circ$ to $\mathbf{x}^L$. Now consider points in the line $(\mathbf{x}^L, \mathbf{x}^M)$: clearly points 'close' to $\mathbf{x}^M$ may reasonably be considered to be better than $\mathbf{x}^\circ$ and points 'close' to $\mathbf{x}^L$

? Mini Problems

3 What are the implications of dropping the continuity assumption?

4 Each day I buy one piece of fruit for my lunch. On Monday apples and bananas are available, but no oranges: I buy an apple. On Tuesday bananas and oranges are available, but no apples: I buy a banana. On Wednesday apples and oranges are available (sorry we have no bananas): I buy an orange. Am I inconsistent?

worse than $\mathbf{x}^\circ$. But will there be a point in $(\mathbf{x}^L, \mathbf{x}^M)$ which is just indifferent to $\mathbf{x}^\circ$? If the continuity axiom holds then indeed this is always so. We can then draw an *indifference curve* through any point such as $\mathbf{x}^\circ$ (the set of points $\{\mathbf{x} : \mathbf{x} \in X;\ \mathbf{x} \sim \mathbf{x}^\circ\}$) and we have the following useful result (see Appendix C):

Theorem 4.1 (Preference representation)

Given completeness, transitivity and continuity (axioms 4.3–4.5) there exists a continuous function U from X to the real line such that $U(\mathbf{x}) \geq U(\mathbf{x}')$ if and only if $\mathbf{x} \succcurlyeq \mathbf{x}'$, for all $\mathbf{x}, \mathbf{x}' \in X$.[5]

The utility function makes life much easier in the analysis which follows. So, almost without exception, we shall assume that axioms 4.3 to 4.5 hold, and so we can then work with the notation U rather than the slightly clumsy-looking $\succcurlyeq$.

Notice that this function is just a way of ordering all the points in X in a very simple fashion; as such any strictly increasing transformation—any *cardinalisation*—of U would perform just as well. So, if you plotted the utility values for some particular function U as $\mathbf{x}$ ranged over X, you would get the same pattern of values—the same ordering—if you plotted instead a function such such as U^2, U^3, or $\exp(U)$.[6] The utility function will tell you whether you are going uphill or downhill in terms of preference, which is important; but what it might suggest about how fast you are going uphill, or how high off the ground you are is completely irrelevant. Figure 4.6 shows two utility functions depicting exactly the same set of preferences: the (vertical) graphs of utility against (x_1, x_2) may look different, but the functions project the same pattern of contours—the indifference curves—on to the commodity space. The preference contour map has the same shape even if the labels on the contours differ.

? Mini Problems

5 Old George is a dipsomaniac. Friends speak in hushed tones about his lexicographic indifference map (this has nothing to do with his appointment in the University Library): he always strictly prefers the consumption bundle that has the greater amount of booze in it, regardless of the amount of other goods in the bundle; if two bundles contain the same amount of booze then he strictly prefers the bundle containing the greater amount of other goods. Sketch old George's preferences in a diagram. Which of the axioms used in Theorem 4.1 is violated by such an ordering? Are old George's preferences rational?

6 A consumer has a preference map represented by the utility function

$$U(\mathbf{x}) = x_1^{a_1} x_2^{a_2} \ldots x_n^{a_n}$$

Can this also be represented by the following utility function?

$$\hat{U}(\mathbf{x}) = \sum_{i=1}^{n} a_i \log(x_i)$$

Can it also be represented by this utility function?

$$\tilde{U}(\mathbf{x}) = \sum_{i=1}^{n} a_i \log(x_i + 1)$$

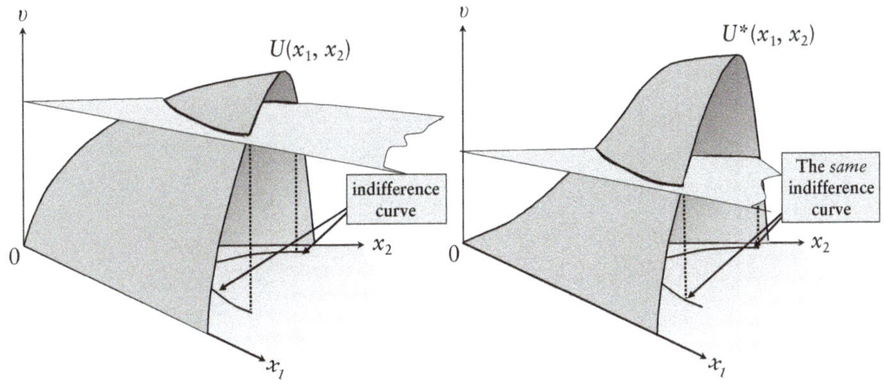

Figure 4.6 Two utility functions representing the same preferences

---

Axiom 4.6 (Greed)

If $\mathbf{x} > \mathbf{x}'$(i.e. $x_i \geq x_i'$ for all i with strict inequality for at least one i) then $U(\mathbf{x}) > U(\mathbf{x}')$.

This assumption implies that indifference curves can never be horizontal or vertical; furthermore they cannot bend round the wrong way as shown in Figure 4.7.[7] In particular, as far as we are concerned, there is no such thing as economic bliss (the peak of the 'mountain' in Figure 4.7). The final two assumptions concern the shape of the *indifference curves*, the contours of the function U.

Axiom 4.7 (Strict quasiconcavity)

[8]Let $\mathbf{x}', \mathbf{x}'' \in X$ be such that $U(\mathbf{x}') = U(\mathbf{x}'')$; then for any number t such that $0 < t < 1$ it is true that $U(t\mathbf{x}' + [1-t]\mathbf{x}'') > U(\mathbf{x}')$.

The immediate implication of this is that there can be no bumps or flat segments in the indifference curves—see Figure 4.8. Points $\mathbf{x}'$ and $\mathbf{x}''$ represent consumption vectors that yield the same level of utility. A point $\mathbf{x}^t$ on the line joining them, ($\mathbf{x}^t := t\mathbf{x}' + [1-t]\mathbf{x}''$) represents a 'mix' of these two vectors. Clearly $\mathbf{x}^t$ must lie on a higher indifference curve.

? Mini Problems

7 If the budget constraint actually passed 'north-west' of the bliss point (so that the bliss point lay in the interior of the budget set) explain what the person would do.

8 Notice that for a lot of results you can manage with the weaker requirements of *concave contours (quasiconcavity)*:

$$U(t\mathbf{x}' + [1-t]\mathbf{x}'') \geq U(\mathbf{x}'),$$

where $0 \leq t \leq 1$ and $U(\mathbf{x}') = U(\mathbf{x}'')$. For the results which follow, identify those that go through with this weaker assumption rather than strictly concave contours.

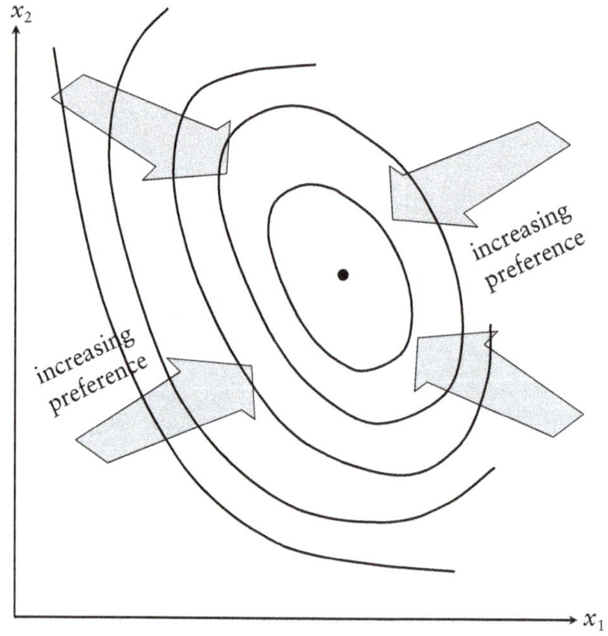

Figure 4.7 A bliss point

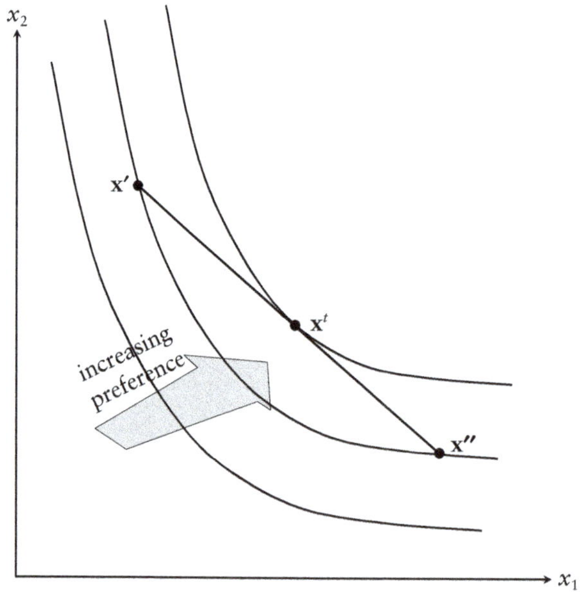

Figure 4.8 Strictly quasiconcave (concave-contoured) preferences

The deeper significance of this is that it presupposes that the consumer has a preference for mixtures of goods over extremes.[9]

Axiom 4.8 (Smoothness)

U is everywhere twice differentiable and its second partial derivatives commute—for any pair of goods i and j we have $U_{ij}(\mathbf{x}) = U_{ji}(\mathbf{x})$.

This means that there can be no kinks in the indifference curves. Given that a person's preferences satisfy the smoothness requirement, an important tool then becomes available to us:

Definition 4.3

The *marginal rate of substitution* of good i for good j (written MRS_{ij}) is $U_j(\mathbf{x})/U_i(\mathbf{x})$.

Here, as before, $U_i(\mathbf{x})$ means $\partial U(\mathbf{x})/\partial \mathbf{x}_i$. A quick check confirms that MRS_{ij} is independent of the cardinal representation of U.[10] The marginal rate of substitution has an attractive intuition: MRS_{ij} is the person's marginal willingness to pay for commodity j, measured in terms of commodity i—a 'subjective price ratio'. This leaves us with a fairly general specification of the utility function. We will see later two cases where we might want to impose further restrictions on the class of admissible functions for use in representing a person's preferences

- aggregation over consumers—see chapter 5, page 114.
- analysis of uncertainty—see chapter 8, page 178.

4.5 Consumer optimisation: fixed income

There is more than one way of representing the optimisation problem that the consumer faces; perhaps the intuitively obvious way in which to do this involves finding a point on the highest utility contour within the appropriate constraint set—for example the kind of sets illustrated in Figure 4.2. In the case of a perfect market with exogenously fixed income y we have the standard problem of choosing a basket of goods $\mathbf{x}$ from the feasible

? Mini Problems

9 Every Friday I go out for a drink with the lads. I regard one pint of cider and one pint of beer as of equal utility; and one pint of either is strictly preferable to $\frac{1}{2}$ pint of both. Draw my indifference curves.

10 Suppose that the utility function $\tilde{U}$ can be obtained from U by a differentiable monotonic transformation φ: i.e. $\tilde{U}(\mathbf{x}) = \varphi(U(\mathbf{x}))$ for all $\mathbf{x} \in X$. Prove this assertion about the MRS_{ij}.

set X so as to maximise utility subject to a budget constraint that is a simple generalisation of (4.1)

$$\sum_{i=1}^{n} p_i x_i \leq y. \tag{4.5}$$

This is illustrated in the left-hand part of Figure 4.9: note the direction of increasing preference and the particular vector $\mathbf{x}^*$ which represents the optimum.

However, we could also look at the optimisation problem in another way. Use the utility scale to fix a target utility level or standard of living (the units in which this is to be measured are arbitrary—dollars, tons, utils, quarks—since the cardinalisation of U is unimportant) and find the smallest budget that will enable the consumer to attain it. This yields an equivalent optimisation problem which may be regarded as the economic 'dual' of the one we have just described. This involves minimising the budget $\sum_i p_i x_i$ subject to the non-negativity condition and a *utility constraint*

$$U(\mathbf{x}) \geq \upsilon \tag{4.6}$$

where υ is the exogenously specified utility level—see the right-hand part of Figure 4.9.

A glance at the two halves of Figure 4.9 reveals that the utility-maximisation and the cost-minimisation problems are effectively equivalent, if the values of y and υ are appropriately specified. Obviously, in connecting these two problems, we would take υ as being the maximum utility obtainable under the first problem and y as minimum cost in the second problem. So in the left-hand diagram we are saying 'maximise the utility obtainable under a given budget': we are maximising a quasiconcave function over a convex set—the budget set. In the right-hand diagram we are saying 'minimise the cost of getting to any given utility level': we are minimising a linear function over a convex set—the

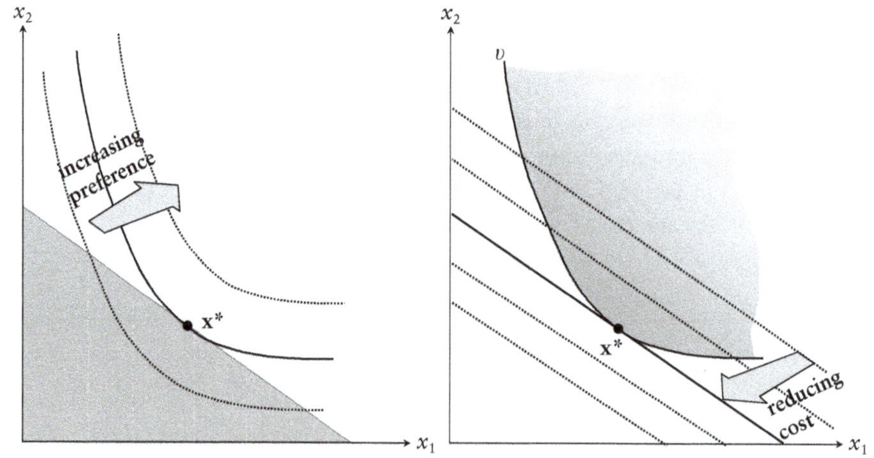

Figure 4.9 Two views of the consumer's optimisation problem

'better-than' set given by satisfying (4.6). We shall return to the 'primal' problem of utility maximisation, but for the moment let us look at the solution to the problem depicted in the right-hand panel of Figure 4.9.

4.5.1 Cost minimisation

Formally, the budget-minimising problem is one of minimising the Lagrangean

$$\mathcal{L}(\mathbf{x}, \lambda; \mathbf{p}, \upsilon) := \sum_{i=1}^{n} p_i x_i + \lambda[\upsilon - U(\mathbf{x})] \tag{4.7}$$

for some specified utility level υ, subject to the restrictions that $x_i \geq 0$ for every commodity i. Now inspection of (4.7) and comparison with the cost-minimisation problem for the firm reveals that the problem of cost minimisation subject to a target utility level is formally equivalent to the firm's cost-minimisation problem subject to a target output level, where all input prices are given. So we may exploit all the results on the economic analysis of the firm that dealt with this problem. For this aspect of the problem we can literally rub out and replace notation from our analysis of the firm. For example, we introduce the following counterpart:

Definition 4.4

The consumer's *cost function* or *expenditure function* is a real valued function C of the price vector and the utility index such that:

$$C(\mathbf{p}, \upsilon) := \min_{\{x_i \geq 0, U(\mathbf{x}) \geq \upsilon\}} \sum_{i=1}^{n} p_i x_i. \tag{4.8}$$

The cost function (expenditure function) plays a key rôle in analysing the microeconomic behaviour of individuals and households, just as it did in the case of the firm. All of the properties of the function carry straight over from chapter 2, so we do not need to prove them again here. Just use Theorem 2.2 and replace the symbol **w** by **p**, the symbol q by υ and z_i^* by x_i^*:[11]

? Mini Problems

11 Suppose an individual has the utility function

$$x_1 x_2^3.$$

(a) Explain why this utility function could be written equivalently as

$$\frac{1}{4}\log x_1 + \frac{3}{4}\log x_2.$$

(b) Write down the Lagrangean for the consumer's cost-minimisation problem for a given utility level υ and explain why we can be sure that it will not have a corner solution. (c) Find the FOCs for a minimum. (d) What are the cost-minimising values of goods x_1 and x_2? (e) What is the cost (expenditure) function? [Hint. Check Mini Problem 15 in Chapter 2.]

Theorem 4.2 (Properties of consumer's cost function)

The consumer's cost function $C(\mathbf{p}, \upsilon)$ is non-decreasing and continuous in $\mathbf{p}$, homogeneous of degree one in $\mathbf{p}$ and concave in $\mathbf{p}$. It is strictly increasing in υ and in at least one p_i. At every point where the differential is defined

$$\frac{\partial C(\mathbf{p}, \upsilon)}{\partial p_i} = x_i^*, \tag{4.9}$$

the optimal demand for good i.

Analogously to the firm we can also introduce a demand function conditioned on the given utility level υ. Incidentally, the terminology explains the rationale behind the usage of the letter H to denote this kind of demand function, for the firm and for the consumer—it is in honour of Sir John Hicks:

Definition 4.5

The *compensated demand functions* or *Hicksian demand functions* for goods $i = 1, 2, \ldots, n$ constitute a set of real-valued functions H^i of prices and a utility level such that

$$x_i^* = H^i(\mathbf{p}, \upsilon) \tag{4.10}$$

where $(x_1^*, x_2^*, \ldots, x_n^*)$ are the cost-minimising purchases for $\mathbf{p}$ and υ.

Of course, if the 'constraint set' in the cost-minimisation problem, defined by (4.6), is appropriately shaped then we can borrow another result from the theory of the firm, and then introduce the household's counterpart to the firm's conditional demand functions. The basic result on demand functions carries over from the firm, with just some rebadging:

Theorem 4.3 (Existence of compensated demand functions)

If the utility function is strictly concave contoured then compensated demand functions are always well defined and continuous for all positive prices.

We can also follow through the comparative statics arguments on the sign of the partial derivatives of the demand functions; again we only need to change the notation.

Theorem 4.4 (Properties of compensated demand functions)

(a) H_j^i, the effect of an increase in the price of good j on the compensated demand for good i, is equal to H_i^j the effect of an increase in the price of good i on the compensated demand for good j. (b) H_i^i, the effect of an increase in the price of good i on the compensated demand for good i must be non-positive. If the smoothness axiom holds, then H_i^i is strictly negative.

The analogy between the two applications of cost-minimisation could be extended further.[12] However, the particular point of special interest in the case of the household is the close relationship between this problem and the 'primal' problem of utility maximisation subject to a budget constraint. Some very useful results follow from this relationship, as we shall see.

4.5.2 Utility maximisation

So let us now tackle problem 1 which we can set up, once again, as a standard Lagrangean:

$$\mathcal{L}(\mathbf{x}, \mu; \mathbf{p}, y) := U(\mathbf{x}) + \mu \left[y - \sum_{i=1}^{n} p_i x_i \right] \tag{4.11}$$

where μ is the Lagrange multiplier. The FOC for the maximum yield[13]

$$U_i(\mathbf{x}^*) \leq \mu^* p_i \tag{4.12}$$

and also the boundary of the budget constraint:

$$\sum_{i=1}^{n} p_i x_i^* = y. \tag{4.13}$$

Notice that not all goods may be demanded at the optimum; this observation enables us to distinguish between the two cases of equation (4.12):

1. If '<' holds in (4.12) for commodity i then we must have $x_i^* = 0$.[14]
2. Otherwise (case '=') we could have $x_i^* = 0$ or $x_i^* > 0$.

Again we find a very neat immediate consequence of the first-order condition (4.12): if utility maximisation requires a positive amount of good i then for any other good j:[15]

$$\frac{U_j(\mathbf{x}^*)}{U_i(\mathbf{x}^*)} \leq \frac{p_j}{p_i} \tag{4.14}$$

? Mini Problems

12 What is the equivalent of the 'short run' in the case of the consumer?

13 [Exercise for the mathematically inclined.] Use the Kuhn—Tucker conditions (A.50)–(A.53) for an optimum to set out the solution to the problem in detail and to verify the statements made in the text.

14 Draw a figure for the case where '<' holds in (4.14).

15 Interpret this condition using the idea of the MRS as 'marginal willingess to pay" mentioned on page 79 (i) where one has '<' in (4.14) and (ii) where one has '=' in (4.14).

with equality in (4.14) if commodity j is also purchased in positive amounts. So in the case where the cost-minimising amounts of both commodities are positive we have:

$$\boxed{\text{MRS}} = \boxed{\text{price ratio}}$$

This characterises the tangency solution clearly seen in the left-hand panel of Figure 4.9.[16]

Let us examine more closely the properties of the solution to the utility-maximisation problem. We have already established (by analogy with the case of the cost-minimising firm) the circumstances under which the household's compensated (or conditional) demands can be represented by a well-defined function of prices and utility. Now let us introduce the following result,[17] proved in Appendix C, and a new concept:

Theorem 4.5 (Existence of ordinary demand functions)

If the utility function is strictly concave contoured then the *ordinary demand functions* for good i constitute a set of real-valued functions D^i of prices and income

$$x_i^* = D^i(\mathbf{p}, y), \tag{4.15}$$

are well defined and continuous for all positive prices, where $(x_1^*, x_2^*, \ldots, x_n^*)$ are the utility-maximising commodity demands for $\mathbf{p}$ and y.

? Mini Problems

16 Suppose an individual has preferences represented by the utility function in Mini Problem 11. The budget constraint is

$$p_1x_1 + p_2x_2 \leq y.$$

Verify that the following three methods of solution are equivalent.

(a) Using the MRS=price ratio 'tangency rule', find the optimal ratio of input demands x_1^*/x_2^* as a function of the ratio of prices p_1/p_2; assuming the budget constraint is binding then find x_1^* and x_2^* in terms of p_1, p_2 and y.

(b) Assuming that the budget constraint is binding, substitute for x_2 in terms of x_1, p_1, p_2 and y; find the utility-maximising value x_1^* in terms of p_1, p_2, and y; hence find the utility-maximising value x_2^*.

(c) Set up a Lagrangean for the utility-maximisation problem; assuming that there is no corner solution [why?] find the first-order conditions; solve the FOCs to obtain x_1^* and x_2^*.

17 Suppose that instead of the regular budget constraint (4.13) the consumer is faced with a quantity discount on good 1 ('buy 5 items and get the 6th one free'). Draw the budget set and draw in an indifference curve to show that optimal commodity demand may be non-unique. What can be said about commodity demand as a function of price in this case?

However, as the implicit definition of the set of demand functions suggests, we cannot just write out some likely-looking equation involving prices and income on the right-hand side and commodity quantities on the left-hand side and expect it to be a valid demand function. To see why, note two things:

1. Because of the budget constraint, binding at the optimum (equation 4.13), it must be true that the set of n functions (4.15) satisfy
$$\sum_{i=1}^{n} p_i D^i(\mathbf{p}, y) = y. \tag{4.16}$$
2. Again focus on the binding budget constraint (4.13). If all prices $\mathbf{p}$ and income y were simultaneously rescaled by some positive factor t (so the new prices and income are $t\mathbf{p}$ and ty) it is clear that the FOC remain unchanged and so the optimal values $(x_1^*, x_2^*, \ldots, x_n^*)$ remain unchanged. In other words
$$D^i(t\mathbf{p}, ty) = D^i(\mathbf{p}, y). \tag{4.17}$$

This enables us to establish:[18]

Theorem 4.6 (Properties of ordinary demand functions)

(a) The set of ordinary demand functions is subject to a linear restriction in that the sum of the demand for each good multiplied by its price must equal total income; (b) the ordinary demand functions are homogeneous of degree zero in all prices and income.

Now let us look at the way in which the optimal commodity demands $\mathbf{x}^*$ respond to changes in the consumer's market environment. To do this use the fact that the utility-maximisation and cost-minimisation problems that we have described are two ways of approaching the same optimisation problem: since problems 1 and 2 are essentially the same, the solution quantities are the same. So:
$$H^i(\mathbf{p}, \upsilon) = D^i(\mathbf{p}, y). \tag{4.18}$$

The two sides of this equation are just two ways of getting to the same answer (the optimised x_i^*) from different bits of information. Substituting the cost function into (4.18) we get:
$$H^i(\mathbf{p}, \upsilon) = D^i\left(\mathbf{p}, C(\mathbf{p}, \upsilon)\right). \tag{4.19}$$

Take equation (4.19) a stage further. If we differentiate it with respect to any price p_j we find:
$$H_j^i(\mathbf{p}, \upsilon) = D_j^i(\mathbf{p}, y) + D_y^i(\mathbf{p}, y) C_j(\mathbf{p}, \upsilon). \tag{4.20}$$

Then use (4.9) to give the *Slutsky equation*:
$$D_j^i(\mathbf{p}, y) = H_j^i(\mathbf{p}, \upsilon) - x_j^* D_y^i(\mathbf{p}, y). \tag{4.21}$$

? Mini Problems

18 Prove this using the properties of the cost function established earlier.

The formula (4.21) may be written equivalently as

$$\frac{\partial x_i^*}{\partial p_j} = \left.\frac{dx_i^*}{dp_j}\right|_{\upsilon=\text{const}} - x_j^* \frac{\partial x_i^*}{\partial y} \tag{4.22}$$

and we may think of this decomposition formula (4.21 or 4.22) of the effect of a price change as follows:

total effect	=	substitution effect	+	income effect

This can be illustrated by Figure 4.10 where $\mathbf{x}^*$ denotes the original equilibrium: the equilibrium after good 1 has become cheaper is denoted by $\mathbf{x}^{**}$ on the higher indifference curve. Note the point on this indifference curve marked '∘': this is constructed by increasing the budget at unchanged relative prices until the person can just reach the new indifference curve. Then the *income effect*—the change in consumption of each good that would occur if the person's real spending power alone increased—is given by the notional shift from $\mathbf{x}^*$ to '∘'. This effect could in principle be positive or negative: we will use the term *inferior good* to apply to any i for which the income effect is negative,

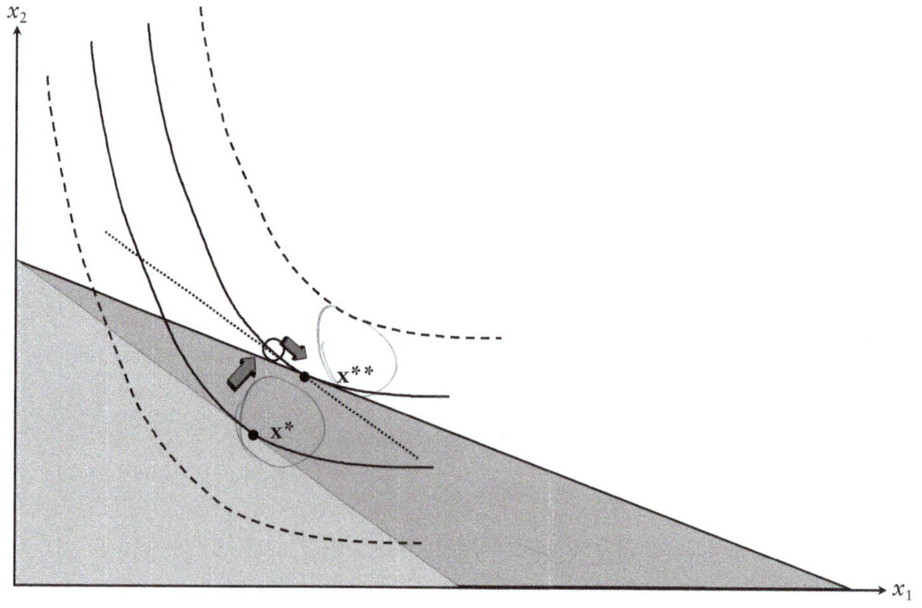

Figure 4.10 The effects of a price fall

and *normal good* for the other case.[19] The notional shift from $\mathbf{x}^*$ to the new equilibrium $\mathbf{x}^{**}$ represents the effect on commodity demands that would arise if the relative price of good 1 were to fall while the budget was adjusted to keep the person on the same indifference curve. This is the *substitution effect*. (Since we are actually talking about infinitesimal changes in prices we could have equally well done this diagrammatic representation the other way round—i.e. first consider the substitution effect along the original indifference curve and then consider the notional income change involved in moving from one indifference curve to the other).

The substitution effect could be of either sign if $n > 2$ and j and i in (4.21) represent different goods (jelly and ice-cream let us say). We say that commodities i and j are *net substitutes* if $H^i_j > 0$ and *net complements* if the reverse inequality is true. Now, we know that $H^i_j = H^j_i$. So if jelly is a net substitute for ice-cream then ice-cream is a net substitute for jelly.[20]

Now let us take the 'own-price' case; for example, let us look at the effect of the price of ice-cream on the demand for ice-cream. We get this by putting $j = i$ in (4.21). This gives us:

$$D^i_i(\mathbf{p},y) = H^i_i(\mathbf{p},\upsilon) - x^*_i D^i_y(\mathbf{p},y). \tag{4.23}$$

Once again we know from the analysis of the firm that $H^i_i < 0$ for any smooth-contoured function (see page 33 in chapter 2). So the compensated demand curve (which just picks up the substitution effect) must be everywhere downward sloping. But what of the income effect? As we have seen, this could be of either sign (unlike the 'output effect' in the own-price decomposition for a firm's input demand). So it is, strictly speaking, possible for the ordinary demand curve to slope upwards for some price and income combinations—the unusual case of the *Giffen good*.[21] But if the income effect is positive or zero (a normal good) we may state the following fundamental result:

Theorem 4.7 (Own-price effect)

If a consumer's demand for a good never decreases when his income (alone) increases, then his demand for that good must definitely decrease when its price (alone) increases.[22]

Notice throughout this discussion the difficulties caused by the presence of income effects. If all we ever had to consider were pure substitution effects—sliding around indifference curves—life would have been so much easier. However, as we shall see in other topics later in this book, income effects are nearly always a nuisance.

? Mini Problems

19 How might commodity grouping influence the income effect?

20 (a) Why can we not say the same about gross substitutes and complements? (b) Explain why—in a two-good model—the goods must be net substitutes.

21 Draw the income and substitution effects for a Giffen good.

22 Prove this using the own-price version of the Slutsky equation (4.23).

Example 4.1

Giffen goods are an interesting theoretical curiosity, but are they more than that? Do instances of such things arise in practice? For rational household consumption behaviour to conform to this pattern it is clear from (4.23) that not only must the good in question be inferior, but the income effect must be—in absolute terms—very large, so that it dominates the substitution effect. It has been suggested that in some special cases this could apply to necessities where the expenditure on the good forms a very large proportion of the budget—i.e. $p_i x_i^* / y$ is very large

- Giffen's original case applied to staple food in nineteenth-century Britain. '...as Sir R. Giffen has pointed out, a rise in the price of bread makes so large a drain on the resources of the poorer labouring families and raises so much the marginal utility of money to them, that they are forced to curtail their consumption of meat and the more expensive farinaceous foods: and, bread being still the cheapest food which they can get and will take, they consume more, and not less of it. But such cases are rare; when they are met with, each must be treated on its own merits.' (Marshall (1890), Bk. III, Ch.VI, paragraph 17)
- In modern times it has been claimed that this could apply to cheap heating/cooking fuel (Bopp 1983).
- It has also been suggested that consumer behaviour in the great Irish famine (1845–9) was consistent with potatoes being a Giffen good. But there is little economic evidence to support this claim, in contrast to more conventional explanations of behaviour during the crisis (Dwyer and Lindsey 1984, Rosen 1999). Robert Giffen never made the suggestion and the linking of his name with the famine has been characterised as a misunderstanding or even a hoax (McDonough and Eisenhauer 1995).

4.6 Welfare

Now look again at the solution to the consumer's optimisation problem, this time in terms of the market environment in which the consumer finds himself. We will do this for the case where y is fixed although we could easily extend it to the endogenous-income case. To do this work out optimised utility in terms of $\mathbf{p}, y$:

Definition 4.6

The *indirect utility function* is a real-valued function V of prices and income such that:

$$V(\mathbf{p}, y) := \max_{\left\{\begin{array}{c} x_i \geq 0, \\ \sum_{i=1}^{n} p_i x_i \leq y \end{array}\right\}} U(\mathbf{x}). \tag{4.24}$$

I should stress that this is not really new. As Figure 4.9 emphasises there are two fundamental, equivalent ways of viewing the consumer's optimisation problem and, just as (4.8) represents the solution to the problem as illustrated in the right-hand panel of the figure, so (4.24) represents the solution from the point of view of the left-hand panel. Because these are two aspects of the same problem we may write

$$y = C(\mathbf{p}, \upsilon) \tag{4.25}$$

and

$$\upsilon = V(\mathbf{p}, y) \tag{4.26}$$

where y is both the minimised cost in (4.8) and the constraint income in (4.24), while υ is both the constraint utility in (4.8) and the maximal utility in (4.24).

In view of this close relationship the function V must have properties that are similar to C. Specifically we find:[23]

- V's derivatives with respect to prices satisfy $V_i(\mathbf{p}, y) \leq 0$.[24]
- $V_y(\mathbf{p}, y) = \mu^*$, the optimal value of the Lagrange multiplier which appears in (4.12).[25]
- A further derivative property can be found by substituting the cost function from (4.25) into (4.26) we have

  $$V(\mathbf{p}, C(\mathbf{p}, \upsilon)) = \upsilon\,; \tag{4.27}$$

  then, differentiating (4.27) with respect to p_i and rearranging, we get:

  $$x_i^* = -\frac{V_i(\mathbf{p}, y)}{V_y(\mathbf{p}, y)}, \tag{4.28}$$

  a result known as *Roy's Identity*.[26]
- V is homogeneous of degree zero in all prices and income[27] and quasiconvex in prices (see Appendix C).

We can use (4.24) in a straightforward fashion to measure the welfare change induced by, say, an exogenous change in prices. To fix ideas let us suppose that the price of commodity 1 falls while other prices and income y remain unchanged—the story that we saw briefly in Figure 4.10. Denote the price vector before the fall as $\mathbf{p}$, and that after the fall

? Mini Problems

23 Suppose an individual has preferences represented by the utility function in Mini Problem 11. Verify that the bullet-point properties hold for V. [Hint: make use of the results from Mini Problem 16.]

24 Explain why V_i may be zero for some, but not all goods i.

25 Use your answer to Chapter 2's Mini Problem 21 (pages 25 and 523) to explain why this is so.

26 Use (4.27) to derive (4.28).

27 Show this using the properties of the cost function.

as $\mathbf{p}'$. Define the utility level υ as in (4.26) and υ' thus:

$$\upsilon' := V(\mathbf{p}', y). \tag{4.29}$$

This price fall is good news if the consumer was actually buying the commodity whose price has fallen. So we know that υ' is greater than υ: but how much greater?

One approach to this question is to take prices at their new values $\mathbf{p}'$, and then to compute that change in income which would bring the consumer back from υ' to υ. This is what we mean by the *compensating variation* of the price change $\mathbf{p} \to \mathbf{p}'$. More formally it is an amount of income CV such that

$$\upsilon = V(\mathbf{p}', y - \mathrm{CV}) \tag{4.30}$$

—compare this with (4.26) and (4.29). Now equation (4.27) suggests that we could write this same concept using the cost function C instead of the indirect utility function V. Doing so, we get:[28]

$$\mathrm{CV}(\mathbf{p} \to \mathbf{p}') := C(\mathbf{p}, \upsilon) - C(\mathbf{p}', \upsilon). \tag{4.31}$$

This suggests yet another way in which we could represent the CV. Consider Figure 4.11 which depicts the compensated demand curve for good 1 at the original utility level υ: the amount demanded at prices $\mathbf{p}$ and utility level υ is x_1^*. Now remember that

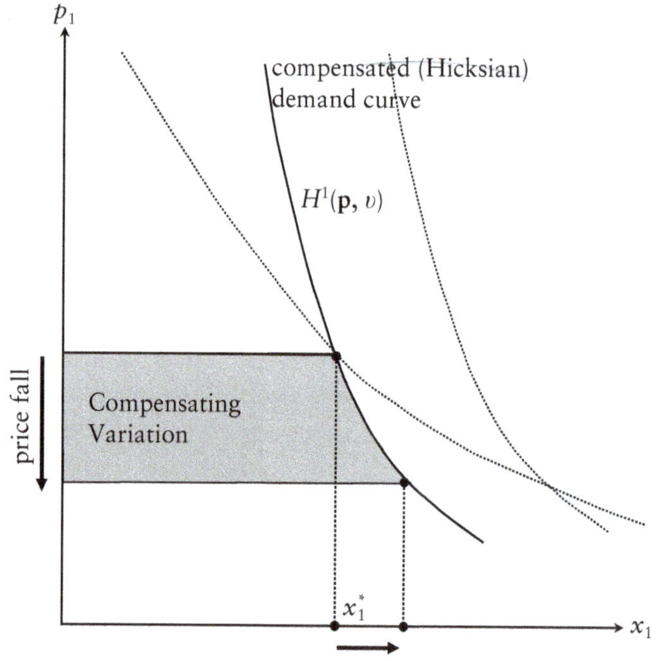

Figure 4.11 Compensated demand and the value of a price fall

? Mini Problems

28 Use (4.27) to fill in the one line that enables you to get (4.31) from equation (4.30).

Shephard's Lemma tells us that the derivative of the cost function C with respect to the price p_1 is $x_1^* = H^1(\mathbf{p}, v)$: this means that we can write the CV of a price fall of commodity 1 to the new value p_1' as the following integral:

$$\text{CV}(\mathbf{p} \to \mathbf{p}') := \int_{p_1'}^{p_1} H^1(\rho, p_2, \ldots, p_n, v) \, d\rho. \qquad (4.32)$$

So the CV of the price fall that we have been discussing is just the shaded area trapped between the compensated demand curve and the axis.

It is worth repeating that equations (4.30)–(4.32) all contain the same concept, just dressed up in different guises. However, there are alternative ways in which we can attempt to calibrate the effect of a price fall in monetary terms. For example, take the prices at their original values $\mathbf{p}$, and then compute that change in income which would have brought the consumer from v to v'; this is known as the *equivalent variation* of the price change $\mathbf{p} \to \mathbf{p}'$. Formally we define this as an amount of income EV such that

$$v' = V(\mathbf{p}, y + \text{EV}) \qquad \text{cost old/new utility} \qquad (4.33)$$

or, in terms of the cost function:

$$\text{EV}(\mathbf{p} \to \mathbf{p}') := C(\mathbf{p}, v') - C(\mathbf{p}', v') \qquad \leftarrow \text{cost new/new utility} \qquad (4.34)$$

—see Figure 4.12.

We can see that CV and EV will be positive if and only if the change $\mathbf{p} \to \mathbf{p}'$ increases welfare—the two numbers always have the same sign as the welfare change.[29] We also see that, by definition:

$$\text{CV}(\mathbf{p} \to \mathbf{p}') = -\text{EV}(\mathbf{p}' \to \mathbf{p}). \qquad (4.35)$$

The CV and the EV represent two different ways of assessing the value of the fall: the former takes as a reference point the original utility level; the latter takes as a reference the terminal utility level. Clearly either has a claim to our attention, as may other utility levels, for that matter.[30]

At this point we ought to mention another method of trying to evaluate a price change that is often found convenient for empirical work. This is the concept of *consumer's surplus* (CS):

$$\text{CS}(\mathbf{p} \to \mathbf{p}') := \int_{p_1'}^{p_1} D^1(\rho, p_2, \ldots, p_n, y) \, d\rho \qquad (4.36)$$

which is just the area under the ordinary demand curve—compare (4.36) with (4.32).

The relationship amongst these three concepts is illustrated in Figure 4.13. Here we have modified Figure 4.11 by putting in the compensated demand curve for the situation after the price fall (when the amount consumed is x_1^{**}) and the ordinary demand curve:

? Mini Problems

29 Use (4.26)–(4.34) to explain in words why this is so.

30 Using Figure 4.10 show how a fall in the price of good 1 can be evaluated using (a) the CV measured in units of good 2 and (b) the EV measured in units of good 2.

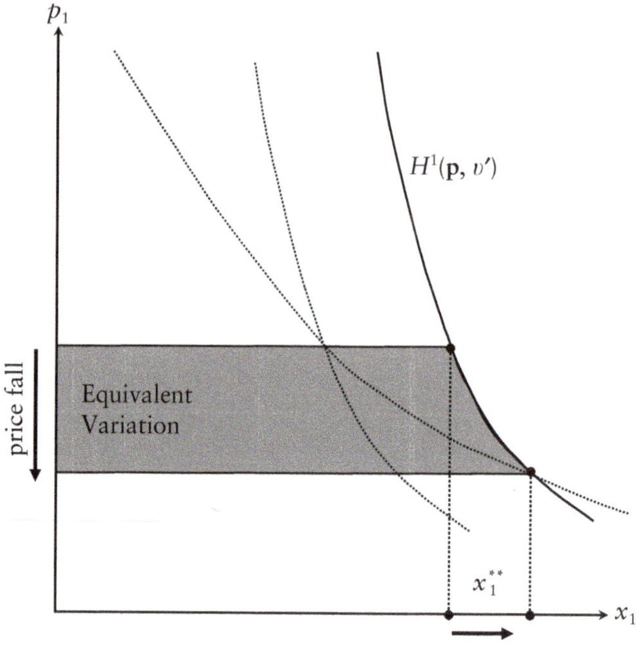

Figure 4.12 Compensated demand and the value of a price fall (2)

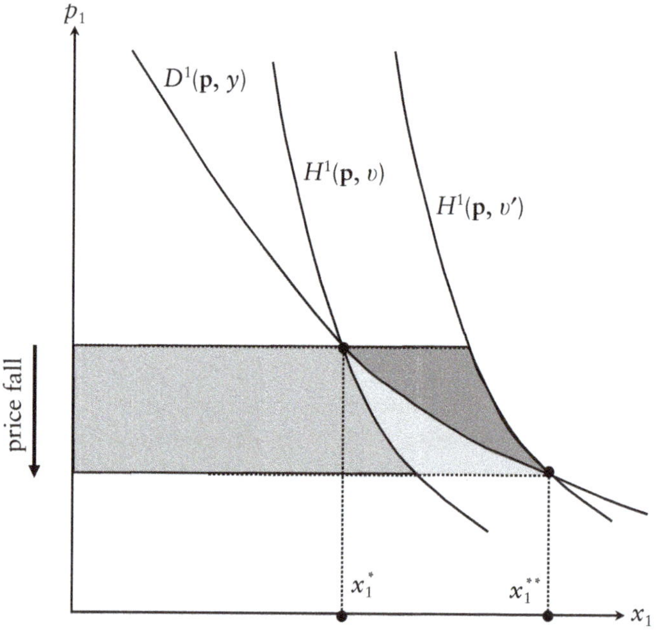

Figure 4.13 Three ways of measuring the benefits of a price fall

this has been drawn for the case of a normal good (where the curve marked D^1 is not steeper than the curve marked H^1 in Figure 4.13).[31] From Figure 4.13 we can see that the CV for the price fall is the smallest shaded area; by the same argument, using equation (4.34), the EV is the largest shaded area (made up of the three shaded components); and using (4.36) the CS is the intermediate area consisting of the area CV plus the triangular shape next to it.

So we can see that for normal goods the following must hold:

$$\text{CV} \leq \text{CS} \leq \text{EV}$$

and for the case of inferior goods we just replace '$\leq$' by '$>$'. Of course all three concepts coincide if the income effect for the good in question is zero.

4.6.1 An application: price indices

We can use the analysis that we have just developed as a basis for specifying a number of practical tools. Suppose we wanted a general index of changes in the cost of living. This could be done by measuring the proportionate change in the cost that a 'representative consumer' would face in achieving a particular reference level of utility as a result of the change in price from $\mathbf{p}$ to $\mathbf{p}'$. The analysis suggests we could do this using either the 'base-year' utility level υ (utility before the price change—the CV concept) or the 'current-year' utility level υ' (utility after the price change—the EV concept) which would give us two cost-of-living indices:

$$I_{\text{CV}} = \frac{C(\mathbf{p}', \upsilon)}{C(\mathbf{p}, \upsilon)}, \tag{4.37}$$

$$I_{\text{EV}} = \frac{C(\mathbf{p}', \upsilon')}{C(\mathbf{p}, \upsilon')}. \tag{4.38}$$

These are exact price indices in that no empirical approximations have to be used. However, in general each term in (4.37) and (4.38) requires a complete evaluation of the cost function, which can be cumbersome, and unless preferences happen to be such that the cost function can be rewritten neatly like this:

$$C(\mathbf{p}, \upsilon) = a(\mathbf{p})b(\upsilon) \tag{4.39}$$

then the indices in (4.37) and (4.38) will depend on the particular reference level utility, which is very inconvenient (more on this in Exercise 4.10).

? Mini Problems

31 Use the Slutsky decomposition to explain why this property of the slopes of the two curves must be true.

What is often done in practice is to adopt an expedient by using either of two corresponding approximation indices—the *Laspeyres* and the *Paasche* indices—which are given by:

$$I_L = \frac{\sum_{i=1}^{n} p'_i x_i}{\sum_{i=1}^{n} p_i x_i}, \tag{4.40}$$

$$I_P = \frac{\sum_{i=1}^{n} p'_i x'_i}{\sum_{i=1}^{n} p_i x'_i}. \tag{4.41}$$

These indices are easier to compute, since you just work out two 'weighted averages', in the case of I_L using the base-year quantities as weights, and in the case of I_P using the final-year quantities. But unfortunately they are biased since examination of (4.37)–(4.41) reveals that $I_L \geq I_{CV}$ and $I_P \leq I_{EV}$: the potential bias arises because the indices I_L and I_P ignore the possibility that consumers substitute between goods when relative prices change.[32] So the Laspeyres index—commonly used in practice—will overestimate the rise in the cost of living if the appropriate basis for evaluating welfare changes is the CV concept.

Furthermore, it is important to note that the model in this section is based on the welfare and behaviour of a single consumer and we have not addressed the difficult question of aggregation over individuals. Some of the issues of aggregation of welfare are addressed in chapter 9.

Example 4.2

National statistical offices usually publish some form of cost-of-living index, typically based on some version of the Laspeyres approach. But *whose* cost of living? 'Average' consumers? Should the rich or the elderly be excluded as atypical, as in the UK's Retail Price Index? Or should all households be covered, as in the UK's Consumer Price Index? Would a price index that focused on the poor differ dramatically from a more generally based index? The answer for the US Consumer Price Index, according to Garner et al. (1996) is, No.

Summary

The optimisation problem has many features that are similar to the optimisation problem of the firm, and many of the properties of demand functions follow immediately from results that we obtained for the firm. A central difficulty with this subfield of microeconomics is that an important part of the problem—the consumer's motivation—lies outside the realm of direct observation and must in effect be 'invented' by the model

? Mini Problems

32 Use the definition of the cost function and to prove these assertions. Explain the conditions under which there will be exact equality rather than a weak inequality.

builder. The consumer's objectives can be modelled either on the basis of indirect observation—market behaviour—or on an a priori basis.

If we introduce a set of assumptions about the structure of preferences that enable representation by a well-behaved utility function, considerable progress can be made. We can then formulate the economic problem of the consumer in a way that is very similar to that of the firm that we analysed in chapter 2; the cost function finds a natural reinterpretation for the consumer and makes it easy to derive some basic comparative-static results. Extending the logic of the cost-function approach also provides a coherent normative basis for assessing the impact of price and income changes upon the welfare of consumers. This core model of the consumer also provides the basis for dealing with some of the more difficult questions concerning the relationship between the consumer and the market as we will see in chapter 5.

Reading notes

On the fundamentals of consumer theory see Deaton and Muellbauer (1980), chapters 2 and 7.

The pioneering work on revealed-preference analysis is due to Samuelson (1938, 1948) and Houthakker (1950); for a thorough overview see Suzumura (1983), chapter 2. The representation theorem 4.1 is due to Debreu (1954); for a comprehensive treatment of axiomatic models of preference see Fishburn (1970). On indifference curve analysis the classic reference is Hicks (1946). There are several neat treatments of the Slutsky equation—see for example Cook (1972). For the original contributions see Slutsky (1915), Allen (1936). The indirect utility function was developed in Roy (1947), the concept of consumer's surplus is attributable to Dupuit (1844) and the relationship of this concept to compensating and equivalent variation is in Hicks (1956). For a discussion of the use of consumer's surplus as an appropriate welfare concept see Willig (1976).

For a general treatment of price indices see Pollack (1989). An excellent overview of the CPI in the United States is provided in Fixler (1993). The United Kingdom's Retail Price Index is documented in Central Statistical Office (1991); the UK's more recent CPI is based on the European Union's Harmonised Index of Consumer Prices (O'Donoghue and Wilkie 1998).

Exercises

4.1 You observe a consumer in two situations: with an income of \$100 he buys 5 units of good 1 at a price of \$10 per unit and 10 units of good 2 at a price of \$5 per unit. With an income of \$175 he buys 3 units of good 1 at a price of \$15 per unit and 13 units of good 2 at a price of \$10 per unit. Do the actions of this consumer conform to the basic axioms of consumer behaviour?

4.2 Draw the indifference curves for the following four types of preferences:

$$\text{Type A} : a \log x_1 + [1 - a] \log x_2$$

$$\text{Type B} : \beta x_1 + x_2$$

$$\text{Type C} : \gamma [x_1]^2 + [x_2]^2$$

$$\text{Type D} : \min \{\delta x_1, x_2\}$$

where x_1, x_2 denote respectively consumption of goods 1 and 2 and a, β, γ, δ are strictly positive parameters with $a < 1$. What is the consumer's cost function in each case? [Hint: check the solution to Exercises 2.4 and 2.5.]

4.3 Suppose a person has the Cobb–Douglas utility function

$$\sum_{i=1}^{n} a_i \log(x_i)$$

where x_i is the quantity consumed of good i, and $a_1, \ldots, a_n$ are non-negative parameters such that $\sum_{j=1}^{n} a_j = 1$. If he has a given income y, and faces prices $p_1, \ldots, p_n$, find the ordinary demand functions. What is special about the expenditure on each commodity under this set of preferences?

4.4 The elasticity of demand for domestic heating oil is -0.5, and for gasoline is -1.5. The price of both sorts of fuel is 60¢ per litre: included in this price is an excise tax of 48¢ per litre. The government wants to reduce energy consumption in the economy and to increase its tax revenue. Can it do this (a) by taxing domestic heating oil? (b) by taxing gasoline?

4.5 Define the uncompensated and compensated price elasticities as

$$\varepsilon_{ij} := \frac{p_j}{x_i^*} \frac{\partial D^i(\mathbf{p}, y)}{\partial p_j}, \varepsilon_{ij}^* := \frac{p_j}{x_i^*} \frac{\partial H^i(\mathbf{p}, \upsilon)}{\partial p_j}$$

and the income elasticity

$$\varepsilon_{iy} := \frac{y}{x_i^*} \frac{\partial D^i(\mathbf{p}, y)}{\partial y}.$$

Show how equations (4.20) and (4.21) can be expressed in terms of these elasticities and the expenditure share of each commodity in the total budget.

4.6 You are planning a study of consumer demand. You have a data set which gives the expenditure of individual consumers on each of n goods. It is suggested to you that an appropriate model for consumer expenditure is the *Linear Expenditure System* (Stone 1954):

$$e_i = \xi_i p_i + a_i \left[y - \sum_{j=1}^{n} p_j \xi_j \right]$$

where p_i is the price of good i, e_i is the consumer's expenditure on good i, y is the consumer's income, and $a_1, \ldots, a_n$, $\xi_1, \ldots, \xi_n$ are non-negative parameters such that $\sum_{j=1}^{n} a_j = 1$.

1. Find the effect on x_i, the demand for good i, of a change in the consumer's income and of an (uncompensated) change in any price p_j.
2. Find the substitution effect of a change in price p_j on the demand for good i.
3. Explain how you could check that this demand system is consistent with utility maximisation and suggest the type of utility function which would yield the demand functions implied by the above formula for consumer expenditure. [Hint: compare this with Exercise 4.3.]

4.7 Suppose a consumer has a two-period utility function of the form labelled type A in Exercise 4.2. where x_i is the amount of consumption in period i. The consumer's resources consist just of inherited assets A in period 1, which is partly spent on consumption in period 1 and the remainder invested in an asset paying a rate of interest r.

1. Interpret the parameter a in this case.
2. Obtain the optimal allocation of (x_1, x_2).
3. Explain how consumption varies with A, r, and a.
4. Comment on your results and examine the 'income' and 'substitution' effects of the interest rate on consumption.

4.8 Suppose a consumer is rationed in his consumption of commodity 1, so that his consumption is constrained thus $x_1 \leq a$. Discuss the properties of the demand functions for commodities $2, \ldots, n$ of a consumer for whom the rationing constraint is binding. [Hint: use the analogous set of results from section 2.4.]

4.9 A person has preferences represented by the utility function

$$U(\mathbf{x}) = \sum_{i=1}^{n} \log x_i$$

where x_i is the quantity consumed of good i and $n > 3$.

1. Assuming that the person has a fixed money income y and can buy commodity i at price p_i find the ordinary and compensated demand elasticities for good 1 with respect to p_j, $j = 1, \ldots, n$.
2. Suppose the consumer is legally precommitted to buying an amount A_n of commodity n where $p_n A_n < y$. Assuming that there are no additional constraints on the choices of the other goods find the ordinary and compensated elasticities for good 1 with respect to p_j, $j = 1, \ldots n$. Compare your answer to part 1.
3. Suppose the consumer is now legally precommitted to buying an amount A_k of commodity k, $k = n - r, \ldots, n$ where $0 < r < n - 2$ and $\sum_{k=n-r}^{n} p_k A_k < y$. Use the above argument to explain what will happen to the elasticity of good 1 with respect to p_j as r increases. Comment on the result.

4.10 Show that if the utility function is homothetic, then $I_{\text{CV}} = I_{\text{EV}}$ [Hint: use the result established in Exercise 2.8.]

4.11 Suppose an individual has Cobb–Douglas preferences given by those in Exercise 4.2.

1. Write down the consumer's cost function and demand functions.
2. The republic of San Serrife is about to join the European Union. As a consequence the price of milk will rise to eight times its pre-entry value, but the price of wine will fall by 50 per cent. Use the compensating variation to evaluate the impact on consumers' welfare of these price changes.
3. San Serrife economists have estimated consumer demand in the republic and have concluded that it is closely approximated by the demand system derived in part 1. They further estimate that the people of San Serrife spend more than three times as much on wine as on milk. They conclude that entry to the European Union is in the interests of San Serrife. Are they right?

4.12 In a two-commodity world a consumer's preferences are represented by the utility function

$$U(x_1, x_2) = a x_1^{\frac{1}{2}} + x_2$$

where (x_1, x_2) represent the quantities consumed of the two goods and a is a non-negative parameter.

1. If the consumer's income y is fixed in money terms find the demand functions for both goods, the cost (expenditure) function, and the indirect utility function.
2. Show that, if both commodities are consumed in positive amounts, the compensating variation for a change in the price of good 1 $p_1 \to p_1'$ is given by

$$\frac{a^2 p_2^2}{4}\left[\frac{1}{p_1'} - \frac{1}{p_1}\right].$$

3. In this case, why is the compensating variation equal to the equivalent variation and consumer's surplus?

4.13 Take the model of Exercise 4.12. Commodity 1 is produced by a monopolist with fixed cost C_0 and constant marginal cost of production c. Assume that the price of commodity 2 is fixed at 1 and that $c > a^2/4y$.

1. Is the firm a 'natural monopoly' (page 65)?
2. If there are N identical consumers in the market find the monopolist's demand curve and hence the monopolist's equilibrium output and price p_1^*.
3. Use the solution to Exercise 4.12 to show the aggregate loss of welfare $L(p_1)$ of all consumers' having to accept a price $p_1 > c$ rather than being able to buy good 1 at marginal cost c. Evaluate this loss at the monopolist's equilibrium price.
4. The government decides to regulate the monopoly. Suppose the government pays the monopolist a performance bonus B conditional on the price it charges where

$$B = K - L(p_1)$$

and K is a constant. Express this bonus in terms of output. Find the monopolist's new optimum output and price p_1^{**}. Briefly comment on the solution.

5 The Consumer and the Market

The consumer, so it is said, is the king ... each is a voter who uses his money as votes to get the things done that he wants done

Paul Samuelson, *Economics* (1948)

5.1 Introduction

There is a small collection of big issues that remain in connection with the consumer. These focus on the consumer's interaction with the surrounding economic environment and cover the following:

- *Determination of incomes.* Just as the market determines the prices of the goods that consumers buy, so too it may determine a large part, if not all, of their incomes. Instead of receiving a lump sum, members of a household generate their income by trading in the market. The price system therefore has a fuller rôle in influencing consumer behaviour than we accorded it in the simple model of chapter 4 (section 5.2).
- *Supply by households.* Implicit in the issue of income determination is the idea that the household will be selling goods and services to the market, as well as buying. We need to see how the basic analysis of the consumer can be adapted to include this phenomenon (section 5.3).
- *Household production.* Not all the objects in the utility function are on sale in the market. Instead the household may perform activities similar to that of a firm by buying market goods not for their own sake but in order to use them as inputs in the production of the things that it really wants (section 5.4).
- *Aggregation over goods and households.* Analysing the choices of a single agent over bundles of n commodities is a useful base on which to build a theory of consumers' behaviour. However, the extension of our analysis to more general economic models suggests—and data limitations usually require—(i) that we consider broadly defined *groups* of commodities and (ii) that we analyse demands by *groups* of consumers (sections 5.5 and 5.6)

We begin with a re-examination of the consumer's budget constraint.

5.2 The market and incomes

So far we have taken the consumer's budget constraint to be of the form (4.5) where y is an exogenously given number of dollars, euros, or pounds. We have assumed that the consumer's income is like a state pension for the elderly or pocket money for the young. This is clearly somewhat restrictive. In order to make progress we need to use something like that depicted in the right-hand panel of Figure 4.2.

To do this we introduce an elementary system of property rights. An individual owns $R_1, R_2, \ldots, R_n$ of commodities $1, 2, \ldots, n$; some of the R_i could be zero (if the consumer possesses none of that commodity) but no R_i can be negative. The person's income comes from selling in the market some of the resources that he owns. Given market prices $p_1, p_2, \ldots, p_n$ we have

$$y = \sum_{i=1}^{n} p_i R_i. \tag{5.1}$$

A small point that we need for the future is that if incomes are determined by (5.1) and the price of good j changes then the person's money income changes as follows:

$$\frac{dy}{dp_j} = R_j. \tag{5.2}$$

Obviously, other specifications of income are possible. For example, we could also have a hybrid case where the consumer had some income from the sale of resources, some shares in the profits of firms (we will be dealing with that in chapter 7) and some income fixed in money terms; but (5.1) is rich enough for present purposes. Obviously, too, we could translate all this from the case where the consumer is an individual to that where the consumer is a household.

5.3 Supply by households

Now the consumer's problem can be expressed: 'maximise utility subject to the constraint that expenditure is less than or equal to the value of resources'. To solve this we form the Lagrangean:

$$\mathcal{L}(\mathbf{x}, \mu; \mathbf{p}, \mathbf{R}) := U(\mathbf{x}) + \mu \left[\sum_{i=1}^{n} p_i R_i - \sum_{i=1}^{n} p_i x_i \right]. \tag{5.3}$$

This is essentially of the same form as (4.11) in chapter 4, and so has essentially the same solution. Accordingly, the demand for good i, $D^i(\mathbf{p}, y)$, can in this case be written

$$x_i^* = D^i \left(\mathbf{p}, \sum_{i=1}^{n} p_i R_i \right). \tag{5.4}$$

Obviously a change in prices will in general induce a change in resource incomes as well as changes in consumption demand. Consider the implications of the demand function (5.4). Obviously if, for some i, the optimum value of x_i^* is greater than R_i we have a fairly conventional case of consumption demand for this good; but if $x_i^* < R_i$ (and $p_i > 0$) then an amount $R_i - x_i^*$ is being *supplied* to the market. Factor supply by households can thus be treated symmetrically with consumption demand by households within this simple model.

Now let us examine the comparative statics of these demand functions (since each R_i is fixed, to get the effect on the supply in each case below, simply put a minus sign in front). First consider the effect on consumer demand of an increase in the endowment R_j: this simply augments the person's income by an amount proportional to p_j. So the net result is a simple modification of the income effect that we introduced above:

$$\frac{dx_i^*}{dR_j} = D_y^i(\mathbf{p}, y)p_j. \tag{5.5}$$

Next consider a change in p_j, the price of good j: this now has a direct effect through the first argument of D^i; and if y were somehow to be held constant then we know that the Slutsky decomposition formula (4.21) would apply; but of course y is not held constant: equation (5.1) makes clear that if the consumer has a positive stock of good j then as p_j increases, so too does y, as given by equation (5.2). Taking into account this indirect effect of p_j as well, we have to modify the exogenous-income formula (4.21) to read[1]

$$\frac{dx_i^*}{dp_j} = H_j^i(\mathbf{p}, \upsilon) - \left[x_j^* - R_j\right] D_y^i(\mathbf{p}, y). \tag{5.6}$$

Notice the importance of the sign of the term $[x_j^* - R_j]$ in (5.6). Let us suppose that good i (oil) is a normal good (so that the term D_y^i is positive). If the price of oil goes up and you are a net oil *demander* (so $x_j^* > R_j$) this event is bad news and it is clear from (5.4) that the impact on demand is similar to the exogenous income case; but if you are a net oil *supplier* (for whom $x_j^* < R_j$) this is good news and the income effect goes in the other direction.

The offer curve

In cases where $R_j - x_j^* > 0$—where the individual is a net supplier—you may get responses to price changes that might appear to be strange. To see this, look at Figure 5.1, which introduces a useful concept for cases where consumers' incomes are determined endogenously, the *offer curve*. This is the set of consumption bundles demanded (trades offered) at different prices. The initial resource endowment is denoted $\mathbf{R}$ and the original budget constraint is indicated by the shaded triangle: clearly the optimal consumption bundle is at $\mathbf{x}^*$ where the person supplies an amount $R_1 - x_1^*$ in order to buy extra units of commodity 2. If the price of good 1 rises (equivalently, the price of good 2 falls) then the optimum shifts to $\mathbf{x}^{**}$ and then to $\mathbf{x}^{***}$. Notice that, while the consumption of good 2 increases steadily, the supply of good 1 at first rises and then falls. The locus of equilibrium points (on which $\mathbf{x}^*$, $\mathbf{x}^{**}$, and $\mathbf{x}^{***}$ lie) is the offer curve and its shape clearly depends on the position of $\mathbf{R}$.

? Mini Problems

1 Fill in the one missing step in going from (4.21) to (5.6).

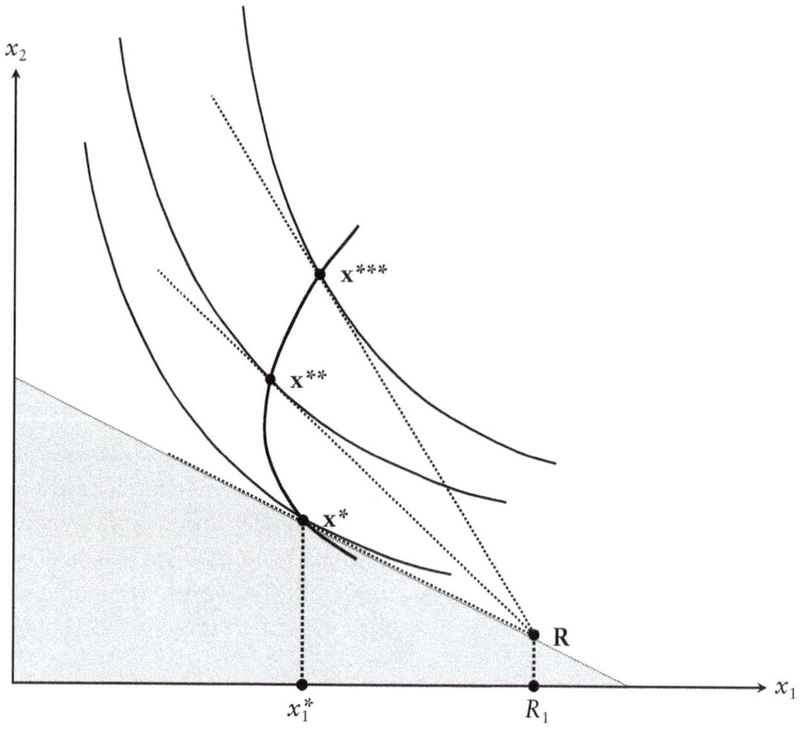

Figure 5.1 The offer curve

Household supply function

From the analysis that yields the offer curve we can get another useful tool. Plot the slope of the budget line in Figure 5.1 against $R_1 - x_1$. Then we have the *household supply curve*—see Figure 5.2.[2] Notice how the way the offer curve bends around in Figure 5.1 (due, of course to the rôle of the income effect) is reflected in the shape of the curve in Figure 5.1: in this case the supply curve eventually 'bends backwards'.

5.3.1 Labour supply

To get a usable model of labour supply we just need to reinterpret the elements of the above model. Suppose commodity 1 represents 'time' that is desired as a consumption good in its own right. Time can either be spent in paid work earning money income (so as to buy the other consumption goods) or is spent at home in the form of leisure. So x_1, the consumption of good 1, represents hours of leisure. R_1 is the total number of hours available (168 per week?) to the worker, so that the expression $\ell := R_1 - x_1$ is obviously

? Mini Problems

2 To get from Figure 5.1 to Figure 5.2 it is convenient to use an intermediate figure showing quantity of good 2 demanded against quantity of good 1 supplied. Describe how to generate this figure.

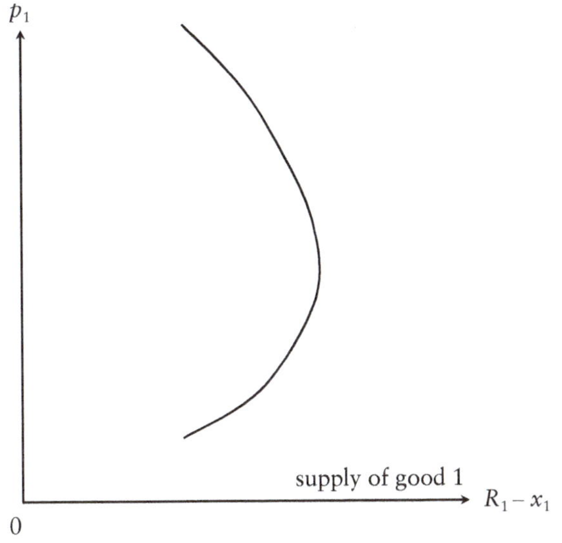

Figure 5.2 The household's supply of good 1

hours spent at work. p_1, the price of commodity 1, is the hourly wage rate: for convenience let us relabel this as w. In principle we have total income determined thus:[3]

$$y = w\ell + y_0 \tag{5.7}$$

where y_0 is any non-labour income of the household.

Now, remembering that $d\ell = -dx_1$, we can modify (5.6) to get the effect of a small change in the wage rate on an individual's labour supply:

$$\frac{\partial \ell}{\partial w} = \left.\frac{d\ell}{dw}\right|_{\upsilon=\text{const}} + \ell\frac{\partial \ell}{\partial y}. \tag{5.8}$$

Define ordinary and compensated wage elasticities and income elasticity for the supply of labour (cf. Exercise 4.5) as follows:

$$\varepsilon := \frac{w}{\ell}\frac{\partial \ell}{\partial w}, \; \varepsilon^* := \frac{w}{\ell}\left.\frac{d\ell}{dw}\right|_{\upsilon=\text{const}}, \; \varepsilon_y := \frac{y}{\ell}\frac{\partial \ell}{\partial y}.$$

Then, if non-labour income, y_0, is zero, (5.8) gives us:

$$\varepsilon = \varepsilon^* + \varepsilon_y. \tag{5.9}$$

? Mini Problems

3 Suppose that instead of (5.7) the individual were offered a premium rate for working overtime.

(a) Write down the budget constraint and draw a sketch of the budget set in (x_1, x_2)-space.
(b) Do the same in (ℓ, y)-space.
(c) What will be the implications of the shape of this set for the labour supply function? Hint: check out the answer to Mini Problem 17 in Chapter 4—see page 84.]

Example 5.1

The relationship (5.9) can be used to analyse the estimates of the labour-supply response of workers from sample survey data. Table 5.1 gives a typical picture for the UK.

		ε	ε^*	ε_y
Men		−0.23	+0.13	−0.36
Women				
	No children	+0.43	+0.65	−0.22
	One child	+0.10	+0.32	−0.22
	Two children	−0.19	+0.03	−0.22

Source: Blundell and Walker (1982).

Table 5.1 Own-wage labour-supply responses for different types of UK workers

Notice that the second column (the substitution effect) *has* to be positive, but the last column (the effect of an extra £1 of 'other income' on a person's market work) could be of either sign and of any magnitude. Men have a labour-supply curve which slopes the 'wrong' way (a negative elasticity overall because of the big negative income effect), but women (without too many children) have a conventional, upward-sloping labour-supply curve; also the more children she has, the less responsive is a woman's labour supply to the market wage rate (look at the substitution effect).

5.3.2 Savings

Again we just need to reinterpret the basic model components. First, the commodities: a lot of progress can be made just by taking a two-period model ('the present', 'the future') where x_i is consumption in period i, $i = 1, 2$. The consumer may have an endowment of resource in each of the two periods (R_1, R_2) and savings are simply the supply by household of commodity 1 to the market $R_1 - x_1$ (a negative value, of course, is interpreted as borrowing).

What about prices? Suppose that there is a rate of interest r in this two-period world—one unit of consumption saved in the present yields an additional r units in the future. So one unit of good 1 is worth $1 + r$ units of good 2; in other words

$$\frac{p_1}{p_2} = 1 + r \tag{5.10}$$

is the relative price of good 1 using good 2 as the unit of value, or *numéraire*.

There is a terminological difficulty with 'income' in this interpretation of the model. Common parlance refers to the monetary flow to the household per period as its 'income' for that period. But of course this is not the same as the concept of income that we have used throughout this chapter and chapter 4. Suppose the savings and loans market is such that there is everywhere a uniform interest rate r—the same whether you are a lender or a borrower. Of course such a 'perfect' market is a strong assumption (Exercises 5.3 and 5.4 invite you to think through the consequences of dropping it) but it permits a natural extension and interpretation of the approach epitomised in equation (5.1). The income concept that we want is the total value of the household's resources over the two periods (R_1, R_2). Using (5.10) this can be expressed in units of good 2 as $[1+r]\,R_1 + R_2$; however, it is slightly more convenient to express it in units of good 1, in which case the value of household resources is

$$\bar{y} := R_1 + \frac{R_2}{1+r}. \tag{5.11}$$

Obviously (5.11) is just a simple present-value expression, commonly referred to as 'lifetime income'. Under the perfect market assumption the budget constraint can then be written

$$x_1 + \frac{x_2}{1+r} \leq \bar{y} \tag{5.12}$$

where $\bar{y}$ is given by (5.11).

Consider preferences in this model. It is convenient to impose a more specific form on the structure of utility function

$$U(x_1, x_2) = u(x_1) + \delta u(x_2) \tag{5.13}$$

where u is an increasing, concave function.[4] It is not necessary to do this for the main results which follow, and it may not be an appropriate representation of some people's intertemporal preferences.[5] However, the special structure permits a natural and appealing intuition: consider a consumption vector that gives the person equal amounts in each of the two periods then, using Definition 4.3 (page 79),we have $\text{MRS}_{12} = \delta$; we can think of the parameter as the rate of pure time preference.

? Mini Problems

4 (a) Extend the formulation in (5.13) to the case where the consumer makes a choice over n periods. If n tends to infinity, why would it make sense to impose the restriction $\delta < 1$? (b) Suppose an individual consumes both bread (good 1) and jam (good 2) today (period 1) and tomorrow (period 2) so that (5.13) is generalised to

$$U(\mathbf{x}_1, \mathbf{x}_2) = u(\mathbf{x}_1) + \delta u(\mathbf{x}_2)$$

where $\mathbf{x}_1 = (x_{11}, x_{12})$, $\mathbf{x}_2 = (x_{21}, x_{22})$ and, for example x_{22} represents the quantity of jam tomorrow. How is the marginal rate of substitution between bread and jam in period 1 related to the marginal rate of substitution between bread and jam in period 2? Interpret the parameter δ in this case.

5 A consumer lives for three periods: BREAKFAST, LUNCH, and TEA. If he gets higher consumption at LUNCH this increases the amount of consumption at BREAKFAST that he is prepared to sacrifice in order to increase his consumption at TEA. Explain why these preferences are inconsistent with the type of model given in (5.13) and generalised in Mini Problem 4.

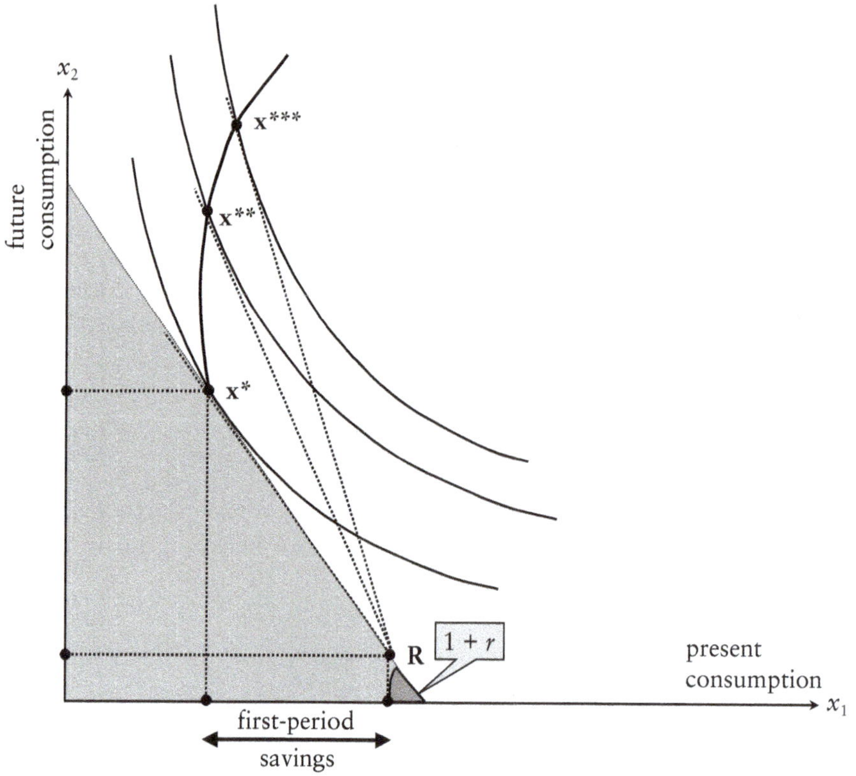

Figure 5.3 The savings problem

Now examine the equilibrium. If we work with the perfect-market assumption then the model and its solution are illustrated in Figure 5.3. The case drawn shows someone with a lot of resources in period 1 but very little in period 2.[6] Furthermore, it illustrates the point (actually just a rehash of the same point made in the case of labour supply in 5.3.1 above) that savings may eventually decrease with the interest rate. If the interest rate goes up just a little you may be persuaded to cancel your next visit to the pub in order to save more for a rainy day; but if the rate trebles, then the overall effect on your resources may be so huge that you invite others to the pub to celebrate.

Will the consumer bias his consumption towards the present or the future? Intuition suggests that if the pure rate of time preference is high then the person is likely to spend more of lifetime resources on future rather than present consumption. In fact we have[7]

$$x_2^* \gtrless x_1^* \text{ according as } \delta \gtrless \frac{1}{1+r}.$$

Mini Problems

6 Identify on the diagram the interest income that the household receives in period 2.

7 Show this. [Hint: set up the Lagrangean for the case where utility is given by (5.13) and the budget constraint is given by (5.12).]

Example 5.2

How do consumption and savings respond to interest rates? A generalisation of the model in (5.13) can be used to provide an answer. Attanasio and Weber (1993) do this for the case of an *isoelastic utility function*—see Exercise 5.6 for the specification. Using seventeen years of the UK's Family Expenditure Survey (FES) they estimate equations of the form

$$\Delta \log (x_t^*) = k + \sigma r_t + \varepsilon_t$$

where σ is the elasticity of intertemporal substitution and ε_t is a disturbance term. The intertemporal substitution elasticity is defined as

$$\sigma (x) = -\frac{u'(x)}{xu''(x)} \geq 0$$

and is constant for the isoelastic form.

Cohorts			All FES
Young	Middle	Old	
0.559	0.747	0.317	0.379

Source: Attanasio and Weber (1993), Table 1.

Table 5.2 Elasticity of substitution of consumption between periods

Table 5.2 provides a brief glimpse of the results (the impact of demographic factors has been omitted for the sake of simplicity). It is clear that the sensitivity of consumption growth to the interest rate depends on the person's position in the life cycle It also appears that the estimates of the intertemporal substitution elasticity is lower for aggregate data than for average cohort data.

5.4 Household production

Some items of household consumption cannot be bought and sold on the market—or at least there are no obvious close substitutes. Instead they must be produced within the household using other purchased goods as inputs. Family home videos, child care, vacation trips are possible examples, as are many other leisure activities where time and other commodities are expended within the household to produce 'goods' that are enjoyed directly, but which cannot be bought or sold.

Suppose the household faces a perfect market in some commodities but that certain consumption goods are not purchasable. Although in practice there may be goods that are used both as inputs and which yield utility directly, to fix ideas let us suppose that there are just two categories of commodities:

1. m 'household inputs' which do not yield utility directly, but which may be purchased (or sold) at prices $w_1, \ldots, w_m$.

2. n 'household outputs' $x_1, \ldots, x_n$, which yield utility directly, but cannot be bought or sold in the market.

The household has a technology for transforming the purchased inputs into outputs. The household needs both to select the right bundle of outputs and to find the appropriate technique (i.e. combination of market inputs) for producing that bundle.

Fixed-proportions technology

Take first a fixed proportions technology of the sort introduced in Exercise 2.11 in chapter 2. The production function here for outputs $x_1, \ldots, x_n$ from inputs $z_1, \ldots, z_m$ is given by

$$x_i = \min \left\{ \frac{z_1}{a_{i1}}, \ldots, \frac{z_m}{a_{im}} \right\} \quad i = 1, \ldots, n \tag{5.14}$$

where a_{ij} is the minimum amount of input j needed to produce one unit of output i. As long as at least one good i has positive marginal utility, the household would wish to transform inputs into outputs efficiently. If the person wants to consume an amount x_i of that good this will require $a_{ij}x_i$ units of input j. Hence the minimum cost of producing a bundle $\mathbf{x}$ is

$$C(\mathbf{w}, \mathbf{x}) = \sum_{i=1}^{n} \sum_{j=1}^{m} w_j a_{ij} x_i$$

$$= \sum_{i=1}^{n} \rho_i x_i \tag{5.15}$$

where

$$\rho_i := \sum_{j=1}^{m} a_{ij} w_j \tag{5.16}$$

is the notional 'price' of output i to the consumer given the household's production technology.

The household's income is given by a minor adaptation of (5.1) as

$$y = \sum_{j=i}^{m} R_j w_j. \tag{5.17}$$

So, using (5.15)–(5.17) in the case of a fixed-proportions technology, the attainable set of vectors $\mathbf{x}$ that can be reached by a consumer with resources $\mathbf{R}$ and facing input prices $\mathbf{w}$ is

$$\left\{ \mathbf{x} : \mathbf{x} \in X, \ \sum_{i=1}^{n} \rho_i x_i \leq y \right\}. \tag{5.18}$$

In general the idea of the attainable set can be thought of as a generalisation of the consumer's budget set, although in this case the attainable set (5.18) is equivalent to a simple linear budget constraint—see Figure 4.2.

Example 5.3

How is poverty to be appropriately characterised? Two standard approaches to determining whether a household of given needs is in poverty are:

- An income criterion: a critical income level $\bar{y}$ (1$ a day? 2$ a day?) is set by, for example, an international organisation—see for instance World Bank (2005). If income $y < \bar{y}$ then the household is considered to be poor.
- An expenditure criterion: similar to the above but relying observed household expenditures rather than their recorded incomes.

But neither approach takes account of the way people manage their resources in order to function in the society in which they live. Sen has pointed out that the technology available to households may be crucial to their access to basic services. For example a child in North America or Europe might need a television in the home in order to follow a basic educational programme, but a child in some African countries might not; the way the technology changes through time is going to have important implications for the appropriate measurement of poverty through time (see for example Sen 1983). Atkinson develops this using the fixed-proportions technology (5.14)–(5.15)—see Atkinson (1998: 92–105)

Substitution in household production

The analysis of the household-production problem becomes even more interesting if it is possible to substitute amongst inputs in the production process. Assume that the domestic 'firm' will be operated as an efficient economic unit, so that inputs $z_1, \ldots, z_m$ are adjusted to minimise cost. This yields a cost function $C(\mathbf{w}, \mathbf{x})$, the minimum value of $\sum_{j=1}^{m} w_j z_j$ required to obtain the specified n-vector of output $\mathbf{x}$. Obviously this cost must not exceed y, the value of the household's resources, so the attainable set of outputs A is given by

$$A(\mathbf{R}, \mathbf{w}) := \left\{ \mathbf{x} : C(\mathbf{w}, \mathbf{x}) \leq \sum_{j=1}^{m} R_j w_j \right\}. \tag{5.19}$$

Clearly the effective budget constraint need no longer be a straight line. But the attainable set must be convex if the household's production technology is convex—see Figure 5.4.[8]

The remainder of the household's optimisation problem can be illustrated in Figure 5.4. Given the attainable set the consumer selects the optimum combination

? Mini Problems

8 Use Definition A.19 to show why this must be true.

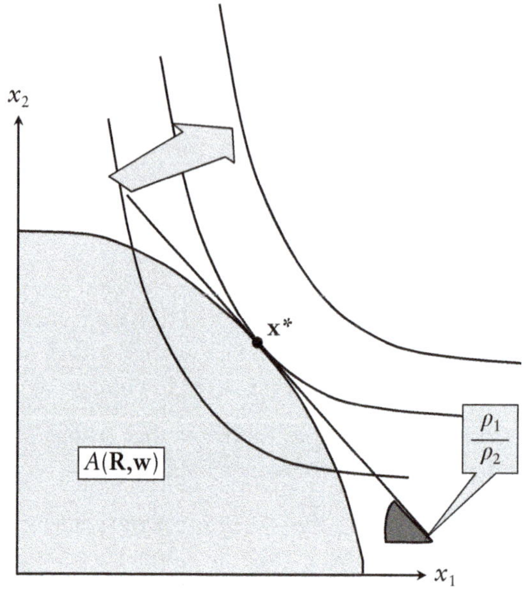

Figure 5.4 General household production model

of non-market goods in the usual fashion by a constrained maximisation of $U(\mathbf{x})$. This determines a point such as $\mathbf{x}^*$, which in turn determines the optimal combination of purchased inputs through the appropriate technique in the household production set.

Once again let us see what effects certain exogenous changes have upon the household's consumption plan. In the fixed proportions case (5.14) a change in any of the input prices $w_1, \ldots, w_m$ or a change in any of the production coefficients a_{ij} will shift the budget constraint.[9] However, if some substitution is possible, a more interesting picture emerges. To see this, consider another special case: the general linear technology. Let input j have a constant marginal productivity b_{ij} in the production of output i. Then, if the input vector $z_1, \ldots, z_m$ is selected, the amounts of consumption goods $i = 1, 2, \ldots, n$ produced are given by[10]

$$\left.\begin{array}{lllll} x_1 = & b_{11}z_1 + b_{12}z_2 + & \ldots + b_{1j}z_j + & \ldots + b_{1m}z_m \\ x_2 = & b_{21}z_1 + b_{22}z_2 + & \ldots + b_{2j}z_j + & \ldots + b_{2m}z_m \\ \vdots & \vdots & \vdots & \vdots \\ x_i = & b_{i1}z_1 + b_{i2}z_2 + & \ldots + b_{ij}z_j + & \ldots + b_{im}z_m \\ \vdots & \vdots & \vdots & \vdots \\ x_n = & b_{n1}z_1 + b_{n2}z_2 + & \ldots + b_{nj}z_j + & \ldots + b_{nm}z_m \end{array}\right\} \tag{5.20}$$

? Mini Problems

9 Provide a one-line explanation of why this happens.

10 Show how the model of Exercise 2.13 can be interpreted in terms of the system (5.20).

Contrast this with the fixed proportions technology (5.14). If $m > n$, not all inputs will be purchased—in fact at least $m - n$ will be redundant, in that optimal purchases of them will be zero. Which ones are redundant depends on the input prices $\mathbf{w}$ and the objective function U. The situation is illustrated in Figure 5.5 for the case $n = 2$, $m = 7$. The household's attainable set is a polyhedron, so that the boundary is piecewise linear. The coordinates of any vertex are

$$\left(\frac{b_{1j}}{w_j}y, \frac{b_{2j}}{w_j}y\right). \tag{5.21}$$

This shows the amount of x_1 and x_2 that could be produced if the entire budget were spent on input z_j. The slope of the frontier between vertex j and vertex $j + 1$ is

$$\frac{w_j b_{2j+1} - w_{j+1} b_{2j}}{w_j b_{1j+1} - w_{j+1} b_{1j}}. \tag{5.22}$$

We can think of this as the ratio of notional prices ρ_1/ρ_2. So it is clear that a simple increase in the budget y (from a larger resource endowment) just 'inflates' the attainable set—look at the way each vertex (5.21) changes with y—without altering the relative slopes of different parts of the frontier (5.22). However, changes in input prices or productivities will change the shape of the frontier.[11]

As illustrated the household would consume at $\mathbf{x}^*$ using a combination of input (market good) 4 and input 5 to provide itself with output goods 1 and 2. The household does not bother buying market good 3 because its market price is too high. Now suppose something happens to reduce the price of market good 3—w_3 falls in (5.21) and (5.22). Clearly the frontier is deformed by this—vertex 3 is shifted out along the ray through 0. Assume that $R_3 = 0$: then, if the price of market good 3 falls only a little, nothing happens to the household's equilibrium;[12] the new frontier shifts slightly outwards at vertex 3 and the household carries on consuming at $\mathbf{x}^*$. But suppose the price w_3 falls a lot, so that the vertex moves out as shown in Figure 5.6. Note that techniques 4 and 5 have now both dropped out of consideration altogether and lie inside the new frontier. Market good 3 has become so cheap as to render them inefficient: the consumer uses a combination of the now inexpensive market good 3 and market good 6 in order to produce the

? Mini Problems

11 In the case where $n = 2$ suppose the consumer wants to provide a specific amount of the two consumption goods (x_1, x_2).

(a) If there is just one market input available at price w_1 what is the minimum cost of providing this bundle?

(b) If there is a second market input available at price w_2 how large would w_2 have to be to ensure that a cost-minimising consumer would never purchase any of it if input 1 were still available at price w_1?

(c) So what condition would have to hold to ensure that both available inputs are actually used?

(d) If the condition in (c) is satisfied what amounts of the two inputs should be used? Under these circumstances what is the cost of the bundle (x_1, x_2)?

12 How would this behaviour change if $R_3 > 0$?

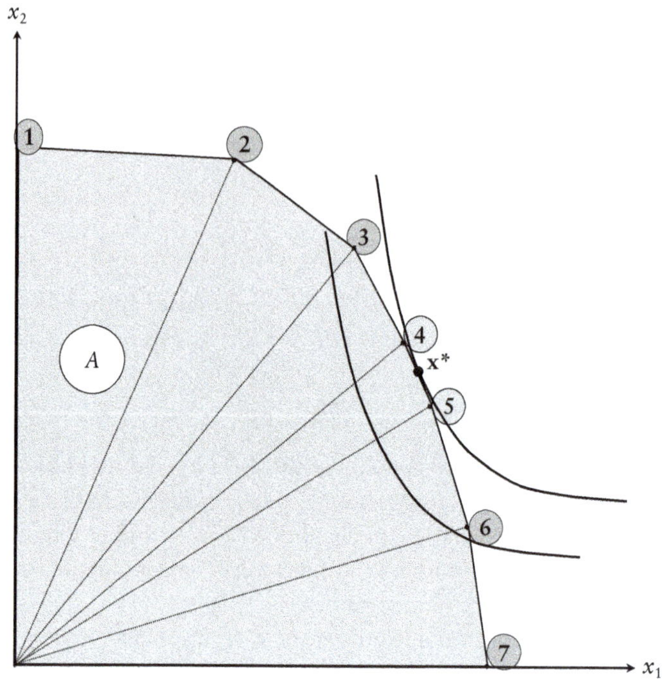

Figure 5.5 Consumption in the household-production model

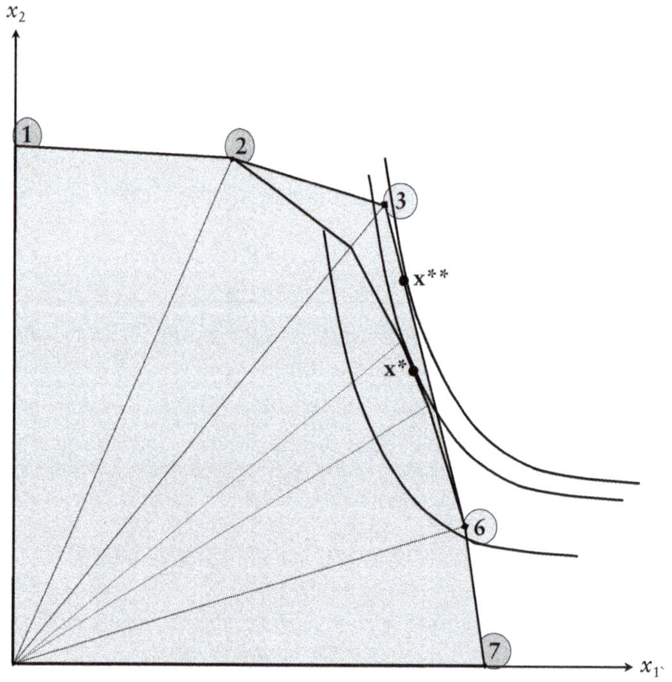

Figure 5.6 Market price change causes a switch

desired consumption goods that yield utility directly. The household's new consumption point is at $\mathbf{x}^{**}$.

The fact that some commodities are purchased by households not for direct consumption but as inputs to produce other goods within the household enables us to understand a number of phenomena that are difficult to reconcile in the simple consumer-choice model of section 4.5 (Chapter 4):

- If $m > n$, some market goods may not be purchased. By contrast, in the model of chapter 4, if all indifference curves are strictly convex to the origin, all goods must be consumed in positive amounts.
- If the market price of a good falls, or indeed if there is a technical improvement in some input this may lead to no change in the consumer's equilibrium.
- Even though each x_i may be a 'normal' good, certain purchased market goods may appear 'inferior' if preferences are non-homothetic.[13]
- The demand for inputs purchased in the market may exhibit jumps: as the price of an input drops to a critical level we may get a sudden switch from one facet to another in the optimal consumption plan.

5.5 Aggregation over goods

If we were to try to use any of the consumer models in an empirical study we would encounter a number of practical difficulties. If we want to capture the fine detail of consumer choice, distinguishing not just broad categories of consumer expenditure (food, clothing, housing ...) but individual product types within those categories (olive oil, peanut oil) almost certainly this would require that a lot of components in the commodity vector will be zero. Zero quantities are awkward for some versions of the consumer model, although they fit naturally into the household production paradigm of section 5.4; they may raise problems in the specification of an econometric model. Furthermore, attempting to implement the model on the kind of data that are likely to be available from budget surveys may mean that one has to deal with broad commodity categories anyway.

This raises a number of deeper questions: How is n, the number of commodities, determined? Should it be taken as a fixed number? What determines the commodity boundaries?

These problems could be swept aside if we could be assured of some degree of consistency between the model of consumer behaviour where a very fine distinction is made between commodity types and one that involves coarser groupings. Fortunately we can appeal to a standard commonsense result (proof is in Appendix C):

? Mini Problems

13 Provide an intuitive argument why this may occur.

Theorem 5.1 (Composite commodity)

Suppose that the relative price of good 3 in terms of good 2 always remains the same. Then maximising $U(x_1, x_2, x_3)$ subject to $p_1x_1 + p_2x_2 + p_3x_3 \leq y$ is equivalent to maximising a function $\overline{U}(x_1, \overline{x})$ subject to $p_1x_1 + \overline{p}\overline{x} \leq y$ where $\overline{p} := p_2 + p_3$, $\overline{x} := ax_2 + [1 - a]x_3$, $a := p_2/\overline{p}$.

An extension of this result can be made from three to an arbitrary number of commodities,[14] so effectively resolving the problem of aggregation over groups of goods. The implication of Theorem 5.1 is that if the relative prices of a group of commodities remain unchanged we can treat this group as though it were a single commodity.

The result is powerful, because in many cases it makes sense to simplify an economic model from n commodities to two: Theorem 5.1 shows that this simplification is legitimate, providing we are prepared to make the assumption about relative prices.

5.6 Aggregation of consumers

Translating the elementary models of consumption to a real-world application will almost certainly involve a second type of aggregation—over consumers. We are not talking here about subsuming individuals into larger groups—such as families, households, tribes—that might be considered to have their own coherent objectives.[15] We need to do something that is much more basic—essentially we want to do the same kind of operation for consumers as we did for firms in section 3.2 of chapter 3. We will find that this can be largely interpreted as treating the problem of analysing the behaviour of the mass of consumers as though it were that of a 'representative' consumer—representative of the mass of consumers present in the market.

To address the problem of aggregating individual or household demands we need to extend our notation a little. Write an h superscript for things that pertain specifically to household h so:

- y^h is the income of household h,
- x_i^h means the consumption by h of commodity i,
- D^{hi} is the corresponding demand function.

We also write n_h for the number of households.

The issues that we need to address are: (a) How is aggregate (market) demand for commodity i related to the demand for i by each individual household h? (b) What additional conditions, if any, need to be imposed on preferences in order to get sensible results from the aggregation? Let us do this in three steps.

? Mini Problems

14 Provide a one-line argument of why this can be done.

15 Is there any sensible meaning to be given to aggregate preference orderings?

Adding up the goods

Suppose we know exactly the amount that is being consumed by each household of a particular good:

$$x_i^h, \quad h = 1, \ldots, n_h. \tag{5.23}$$

To get the total amount of i that is being consumed in the economy, it might seem that we should just stick a summation sign in front of (5.23) so as to get

$$\sum_{h=1}^{n_h} x_i^h. \tag{5.24}$$

But this step would involve introducing an important, and perhaps unwarranted, assumption—that all goods are 'rival' goods. By this we mean that my consumption of one more unit of good i means that there is one less unit of good i for everyone else. We shall, for now, make this assumption; in fact we shall go a stage further and assume that we are only dealing with *pure private goods*—goods that are both rival and 'excludable' in that it is possible to charge a price for them in the market.[16] We shall have a lot more to say about rivalness and excludability in chapters 9 onwards.

The representative consumer

If all goods are 'private goods' then we get *aggregate demand* x_i as a function of $\mathbf{p}$ (the same price vector for everyone) simply by adding up individual demand functions:

$$x_i(\mathbf{p}) := \sum_{h=1}^{n_h} D^{hi}\left(\mathbf{p}, y^h\right). \tag{5.25}$$

The idea of equation (5.25) is depicted in the two-person case in Figure 5.7 and it seems that the elementary process is similar to that of aggregating the supply of output by firms, depicted in Figures 3.1 and 3.2. There are similar caveats on aggregation and market

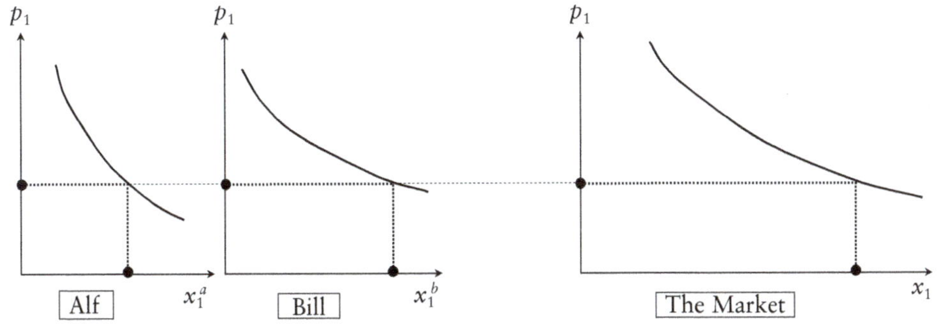

Figure 5.7 Aggregation of consumer demand

? Mini Problems

16 Can you think of a good or service that is not rival? One that is not excludable?

equilibrium as for the firm[17]—see pages 52 to 54 for a reminder—but in the case of aggregating over consumers there is a more subtle problem.

Will the entity in (5.25) behave like a 'proper' demand function? The problem is that a demand function typically is defined on prices and some simple measure of income—but clearly the right-hand side of (5.25) could be sensitive to the *distribution* of income amongst households, not just its total. One way of addressing this issue is to consider the problem as that of characterising the behaviour of a representative consumer. This could be done by focusing on the person with average income[18]

$$\bar{y} := \frac{1}{n_h}\sum_{h=1}^{n_h} y^h$$

and the average consumption of commodity i

$$\bar{x}_i := \frac{1}{n_h}\sum_{h=1}^{n_h} x_i^h.$$

Then the key question to consider is whether it is possible to write the commodity demands for the person on average income as:

$$\bar{x}_i = \bar{D}^i(\mathbf{p}, \bar{y}) \tag{5.26}$$

where each $\bar{D}^i$ behaves like a conventional demand curve. If such a relationship exists, then we may write (5.26) as:

$$\bar{D}^i(\mathbf{p}, \bar{y}) = \frac{1}{n_h}\sum_{h=1}^{n_h} D^{hi}\left(\mathbf{p}, y^h\right). \tag{5.27}$$

If you were to pick some set of functions D^{hi} out of the air—even though they were valid demand functions for each individual household—they might well not be capable of satisfying the aggregation criterion in (5.26) and (5.27) above. In fact we can prove (see Appendix C)

Theorem 5.2 (Representative consumer)

Average demand in the market can be written in the form (5.26) if and only if, for all prices and incomes, individual demand functions have the form

$$D^{hi}\left(\mathbf{p}, y^h\right) = a_i^h(\mathbf{p}) + y^h b_i(\mathbf{p}). \tag{5.28}$$

? Mini Problems

17 Take the beer-and-cider example of chapter 4's Mini Problem 9 (page 79). Show that my demand for cider on a Friday night has a discontinuity. Suppose my tastes and income are typical for everyone in London. Explain why London's demand for cider on a Friday night is effectively continuous.

18 This is a very narrow definition of the 'representative consumer' that makes the calculation easy: suggest some alternative implementable definitions.

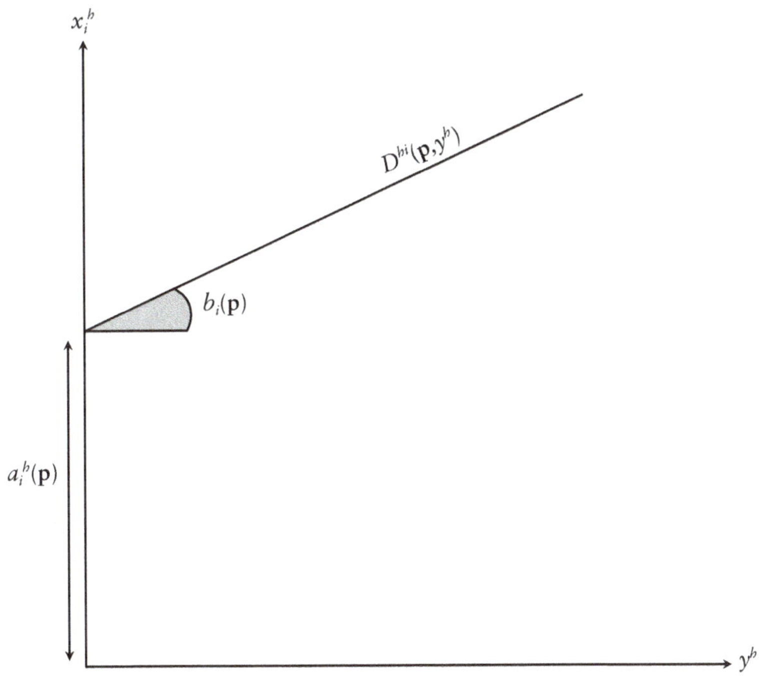

Figure 5.8 Aggregable demand functions

In other words aggregability across consumers imposes a stringent requirement on the ordinary demand curves for any one good i—for every household h the so-called Engel curve for i (demand for i plotted against income) must have the same slope (the number $b_i(\mathbf{p})$). This is illustrated in Figure 5.8. Of course imposing this requirement on the demand function also imposes a corresponding condition on the class of utility functions that allow one to characterise the behaviour of the market as though it were that of a representative consumer.

Market demand and WARP

What happens if this regularity condition is *not* satisfied? Aggregate demand may behave very oddly indeed. There is an even deeper problem than just the possibility that market demand may depend on income distribution. This is illustrated in Figure 5.9 which allows for the possibility that incomes are endogenously determined by prices as in (5.1). Alf and Bill each have conventionally shaped utility functions: although clearly they differ markedly in terms of their income effects: in neither case is there a 'Giffen good' . The original prices are shown by the budget sets in the first two panels: Alf's demands are at point $\mathbf{x}^a$ and Bill's at $\mathbf{x}^b$. Prices then change so that good 1 is cheaper (the budget constraint is now the flatter line): Alf's and Bill's demands are now at points $\mathbf{x}^{a\prime}$ and $\mathbf{x}^{b\prime}$ respectively; clearly their individual demands satisfy the Weak Axiom of Revealed Preference. However, look now at the combined result of their behaviour (third panel): the average demand shifts from $\mathbf{x}$ to $\mathbf{x}'$. It is clear that this change in average demand

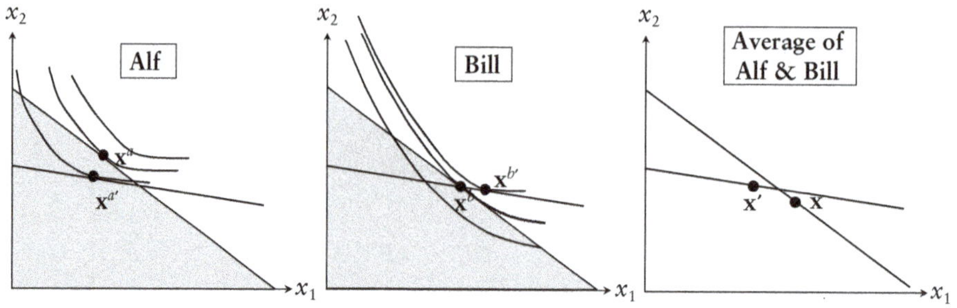

Figure 5.9 Odd things happen when Alf and Bill's demands are combined

could not be made consistent with the behaviour of some imaginary 'representative consumer'—it does not even satisfy WARP!

Summary

The demand analysis that follows from the structure of chapter 4 is powerful: the issue of the supply to the market by households can be modelled using a minor tweak of standard demand functions, by making incomes endogenous. This in turn opens the door to a number of important applications in the economics of the household—to the analysis of labour supply and of the demand for loans and the supply of savings, for example.

Introducing the production model of chapter 2 alongside conventional preference analysis permits a useful separation between 'goods' that enter the utility function directly and 'commodities' that are bought in the market, not for their own sake, but to produce the goods. It enables us to understand market phenomena that are not easily reconciled with the workings of the models described in chapter 4 such as jumps in commodity demand and the fact that large numbers of individual commodities are not purchased at all by some consumers. We will also find—in chapter 8—that it can form a useful basis for the economic analysis of financial assets.

There are a number of cases where it makes good sense to consider a restricted class of utility functions. To be able to aggregate consistently it is helpful if utility functions belong to the class that yield demand functions that are linear in income.

These developments of the basic consumer model to take into account the realities of the market place facilitate the econometric modelling of the household and they will provide some of the building blocks for the analysis of chapters 6 and 7.

Reading notes

The consumer model with endogenous income is covered in Deaton and Muellbauer (1980), chapters 11 and 12. The additive separability property used in the discussion of savings follows from the parallel result in the theory of production (see page 45 in chapter 2 for references). However, this relies on a differentiability assumption. For a more general approach see Debreu (1960).

The basis of the household production model is given in Lancaster (1966)'s seminal work on goods and characteristics; this type of model had already been used in an early unpublished version of Gorman (1980). Becker (1965) pioneered a version of the household production model focusing on the allocation of time.

Exercises

5.1 A peasant consumer has the utility function

$$a \log (x_1) + [1 - a] \log (x_2 - k)$$

where good 1 is rice and good 2 is a 'basket' of all other commodities, and $0 < a < 1, k \geq 0$.

1. Briefly interpret the parameters a and k.
2. Assume that the peasant is endowed with fixed amounts (R_1, R_2) of the two goods and that market prices for the two goods are known. Under what circumstances will the peasant wish to supply rice to the market? Will the supply of rice increase with the price of rice?
3. What would be the effect of imposing a quota ration on the consumption of good 2?

5.2 Take the model of Exercise 5.1. Suppose that it is possible for the peasant to invest in rice production. Sacrificing an amount z of commodity 2 would yield additional rice output of

$$b\left[1 - e^{-z}\right]$$

where $b > 0$ is a productivity parameter.

1. What is the investment that will maximise the peasant's income?
2. Assuming that investment is chosen so as to maximise income find the peasant's supply of rice to the market.
3. Explain how investment in rice production and the supply of rice to the market is affected by b and the price of rice. What happens if the price of rice falls below $1/b$?

5.3 Consider a household with a two-period utility function of the form specified in Exercise 4.7 (page 97). Suppose that the individual receives an exogenously given income stream (y_1, y_2) over the two periods, assuming that the individual faces a perfect market for borrowing and lending at a uniform rate r.

1. Examine the effects of varying y_1,y_2 and r on the optimal consumption pattern.
2. Will first-period savings rise or fall with the rate of interest?
3. How would your answer be affected by a total ban on borrowing?

5.4 A consumer lives for two periods and has the utility function

$$a \log (x_1 - k) + [1 - a] \log (x_2 - k)$$

where x_t is consumption in period t, and a, k are parameters such that $0 < a < 1$ and $k \geq 0$. The consumer is endowed with an exogenous income stream (y_1, y_2) and he can lend on the capital market at a fixed interest rate r, but is not allowed to borrow.

1. Interpret the parameters of the utility function.
2. Assume that $y_1 \geq \bar{y}$ where

$$\bar{y} := k - \frac{a}{1-a}\left[\frac{y_2 - k}{1+r}\right].$$

Find the individual's optimal consumption in each period.

3. If $y_1 \geq \bar{y}$ what is the impact on period 1 consumption of
   (a) an increase in the interest rate?
   (b) an increase in y_1?
   (c) an increase in y_2?
4. How would the answer to parts (b) and (c) change if $y_1 < \bar{y}$?

5.5 In an n-commodity economy a consumer lives for T periods and has preferences that are represented by a differentiable utility function.

1. Show that Theorem C.1 in Appendix C implies that if the marginal rate of substitution between commodity i and commodity j in period t is independent of consumption in any other period then the person's preferences can always be represented by the additive form

$$\sum_{t=1}^{T} v(\mathbf{x}_t; t) \tag{5.29}$$

where $\mathbf{x}_t$ is the vector of consumption goods at time t and the within-period utility function $v(\cdot; t)$ may be different in each period.

2. Show that if the MRS_{ij} in period t equals the MRS_{ij} in period t' whenever $\mathbf{x}_t = \mathbf{x}_{t'}$ then within-period utility in (5.29) can be written as

$$v(\mathbf{x}; t) = u(\mathbf{x})\,\varphi(t) \tag{5.30}$$

3. Suppose that v in (5.30) has the property that, whenever the consumption vector is the same in all periods, the MRS of good i in period t for good i in period $t+1$ is independent of t. Show that within-period utility can then be written

$$v(\mathbf{x}; t) = \delta^t u(\mathbf{x}) \tag{5.31}$$

5.6 Suppose an individual lives for T periods and has a utility function of the form (5.29) where within-period utility is given by (5.31), consumption in period t is given by the scalar x_t and the function u has the isoelastic form

$$u(x) = \frac{1}{1-\beta}x^{1-\beta} \tag{5.32}$$

where β is a non-negative parameter.

1. Suggest an appropriate limiting form for u as $\beta \to 1$.
2. The individual has a known exogenous income stream $(y_1, y_2, \ldots, y_T)$ and the interest rate in period t is r_t. Find the first-order condition for maximising utility.

3. Using the approximation $\log(1+z) \simeq z$ show that the optimum consumption path is approximated by

$$\Delta \log\left(x_t^*\right) = k + \sigma r_t.$$

where k and are σ constants.

4. How is σ related to the parameter β?

5.7 Suppose a person is endowed with a given amount of non-wage income $\bar{y}$ and an ability to earn labour income which is reflected in his or her market wage w. He or she chooses ℓ, the proportion of available time worked, in order to maximise the utility function $x^a [1-\ell]^{1-a}$ where x is total money income—the sum of non-wage income and income from work. Find the optimal labour supply as a function of $\bar{y}$, w, and a. Under what circumstances will the person choose not to work?

5.8 A household consists of two individuals who are both potential workers and who pool their budgets. The preferences are represented by a single utility function $U(x_0, x_1, x_2)$ where x_1 is the amount of leisure enjoyed by person 1, x_2 is the amount of leisure enjoyed by person 2, and x_0 is the amount of the single, composite consumption good enjoyed by the household. The two members of the household have, respectively (T_1, T_2) hours which can either be enjoyed as leisure or spent in paid work. The hourly wage rates for the two individuals are w_1, w_2 respectively, they jointly have non-wage income of $\bar{y}$, and the price of the composite consumption good is unity.

1. Write down the budget constraint for the household.
2. If the utility function U takes the form

$$U(x_0, x_1, x_2) = \sum_{i=0}^{2} \beta_i \log(x_i - a_i)\,. \tag{5.33}$$

where a_i and β_i are parameters such that $a_i \geq 0$ and $\beta_i > 0$, $\beta_0 + \beta_1 + \beta_2 = 1$, interpret these parameters. Solve the household's optimisation problem and show that the demand for the consumption good is:

$$x_0^* = a_0 + \beta_0 \left[\left[\bar{y} + w_1 T_1 + w_2 T_2\right] - \left[a_0 + w_1 a_1 + w_2 a_2\right]\right].$$

3. Write down the labour supply function for the two individuals.
4. What is the response of an individual's labour supply to an increase in
   (a) his/her own wage,
   (b) the other person's wage, and
   (c) the non-wage income?

5.9 Let the demand by household 1 for good 1 be given by

$$x_1^1 = \left\{ \begin{array}{ll} \dfrac{y}{4p_1} & \text{if } p_1 > a \\ \dfrac{y}{2p_1} & \text{if } p_1 < a \\ \dfrac{y}{4a} \text{ or } \dfrac{y}{2a} & \text{if } p_i = a \end{array} \right\},$$

where $a > 0$.

1. Draw this demand curve and sketch an indifference map that would yield it.

2. Let household 2 have identical income y: write down the average demand of households 1 and 2 for good 1 and show that at $p_1 = a$ there are now three possible values of $\frac{1}{2}[x_1^1 + x_1^2]$.
3. Extend the argument to n_h identical consumers. Show that $n_h \to \infty$ the possible values of the consumption of good 1 per household becomes the entire segment $\left[\frac{y}{4a}, \frac{y}{2a}\right]$.

6 A Simple Economy

> I had nothing to covet; for I had all that I was now capable of enjoying. I was lord of the whole manor; or, if I pleased, I might call myself king, or emperor over the whole country which I had possession of. There were no rivals. I had no competitor, none to dispute sovereignty or command with me. . . . But all I could make use of was all that was valuable. . . . The nature and experience of things dictated to me upon just reflection that all the good things of this world are no farther good to us than they are for our use.
>
> Daniel Defoe, *Robinson Crusoe*, pp. 128, 129.

6.1 Introduction

Now that we have seen how each of the principal actors in microeconomic models behaves and how their responses to price signals can be modelled, we could just go ahead and build a fully formed, multi-featured general model of price-taking equilibrium. This will indeed be done in chapter 7. But first we need to focus on just one point: the issues that arise from 'closing' the economic system, without yet introducing the complication of large numbers of economic agents. To do this we will build a self-contained model of a very simple economy.

The initial step of building a self-contained model of an economic system will yield an important insight. In the discussion so far we have treated the analysis of the firm and of the household as logically separate problems and have assumed there is access to a 'perfect' market which permits buying and selling at known prices. Now we will be able to see some economic reasons why this logical separation of consumption and production decisions may make sense.

6.2 Another look at production

In chapter 2 (section 2.5) we focused on the case of a single firm that produced many outputs using many inputs. We need to look at this again because the multiproduct-firm model is an ideal tool for switching the focus of our analysis from an isolated enterprise to an entire economy. It is useful to be able to think about a collection of production processes that deal with different parts of the economy and their relationship to one another. Fortunately there is a comparatively easy way of doing this.

6.2.1 Processes and net outputs

In order to describe the technological possibilities it is useful to use the concept briefly introduced in chapter 2:

Definition 6.1

The *net output vector* $\mathbf{q}$ is a list of all potential inputs to and outputs from a production process, using the convention that outputs are measured positively and inputs negatively.

We can apply this concept at the level of a particular production process or to the economy as a whole. At each level of operation if more of commodity i is being produced than is being used as input, then q_i is positive, whereas if more of i is used up than is produced as output, then q_i is negative. To illustrate this usage and its application to multiple production processes, consider Figure 6.1 which illustrates three processes in which labour, land, pigs, and potatoes are used as inputs, and pigs, potatoes, and sausages are obtained as outputs.

We could represent process 1 in vector form as

$$\mathbf{q}^1 = \begin{bmatrix} 0 & [\text{sausages}] \\ 990 & [\text{potatoes}] \\ 0 & [\text{pigs}] \\ -10 & [\text{labour}] \\ -1 & [\text{land}] \end{bmatrix} \tag{6.1}$$

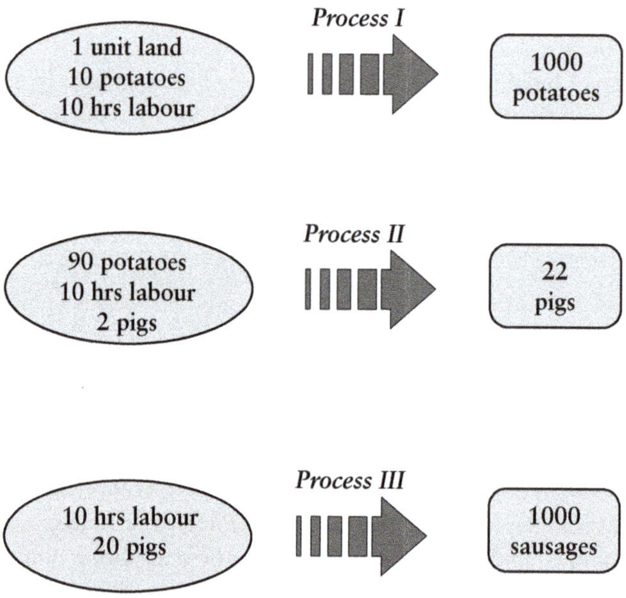

Figure 6.1 Three basic production processes

and processes 2 and 3, respectively as:

$$\mathbf{q}^2 = \begin{bmatrix} 0 & \text{[sausages]} \\ -90 & \text{[potatoes]} \\ +20 & \text{[pigs]} \\ -10 & \text{[labour]} \\ 0 & \text{[land]} \end{bmatrix} \tag{6.2}$$

$$\mathbf{q}^3 = \begin{bmatrix} +1000 & \text{[sausages]} \\ 0 & \text{[potatoes]} \\ -20 & \text{[pigs]} \\ -10 & \text{[labour]} \\ 0 & \text{[land]} \end{bmatrix} \tag{6.3}$$

Expressions (6.1) to (6.3) give a succinct description of each of the processes. But we could also imagine a simplified economy in which these five commodities were the only economic goods and $\mathbf{q}^1$ to $\mathbf{q}^3$ were the only production processes. If we wanted to view the situation in the economy as a whole we can do so by just adding up the vectors in (6.1) to (6.3): $\mathbf{q} = \mathbf{q}^1 + \mathbf{q}^2 + \mathbf{q}^3$: netting out intermediate goods and combining the three separate production stages we find the overall result described by the net output vector

$$\mathbf{q} = \begin{bmatrix} +1000 \\ +900 \\ 0 \\ -30 \\ -1 \end{bmatrix} \tag{6.4}$$

So, viewed from the point of view of the economy as a whole, our three processes produce sausages and potatoes as outputs, using labour and land as inputs; pigs are a pure intermediate good.

In sum, we have a simple method of deriving the production process in the economy as a whole, $\mathbf{q}$, from its constituent parts. But this leaves open a number of issues: How do we handle multiple techniques in each process? What is the relationship of this approach to the production function introduced in section 2.5? Is the simple adding-up procedure always valid?

6.2.2 The technology

The vectors in (6.1) to (6.3) or their combination (6.4) describe one possible list of production activities. It is useful to be able to describe the 'state of the art', the set of all available processes for transforming inputs into outputs—i.e. the technology. We shall accordingly refer to Q, a subset of Euclidean n-space, $\mathbb{R}^n$, as the *technology set* (also known as the production set). If we write $\mathbf{q} \in Q$ we mean simply that the list of inputs and outputs given by the vector is technically feasible. We assume the set Q is exogenously given—a preordained collection of blueprints of the production process. Our immediate task is to consider the possible structure of the set Q: the characteristics of the set that incorporate the properties of the technology.

We approach this task by imposing on Q a set of axioms which seem to provide a plausible description of the technology available to the community. These axioms will then form a basis of almost all our subsequent discussion of the production side of the economy, although sometimes one or other of them may be relaxed. We shall proceed by first providing a formal statement of the axioms, and then considering what each means in intuitive terms.

The first four axioms incorporate some very basic ideas about what we mean by the concept of production: it is always feasible to do nothing; zero inputs mean zero outputs; production cannot be 'turned around' so that outputs become inputs and vice versa; it is technologically feasible to 'waste' outputs or inputs. Formally:

Axiom 6.1 Possibility of inaction

$$0 \in Q.$$

① it is feasible to do nothing

Axiom 6.2 No free lunch

$$Q \cap \mathbb{R}^n_+ = \{0\}.$$

② φ inputs → φ outputs

Axiom 6.3 Irreversibility

$$Q \cap (-Q) = \{0\}.$$

③

Axiom 6.4 Free disposal

If $q^\circ \in Q$ and $q \leq q^\circ$ then $q \in Q$. ④

The next two axioms introduce rather more sophisticated ideas and, as we shall see, are more open to question. They relate, respectively, to the possibility of combining and dividing production processes.

Axiom 6.5 Additivity

If q' and $q'' \in Q$ then $q' + q'' \in Q$.

Axiom 6.6 Divisibility

If $0 < t < 1$ and $q^\circ \in Q$ then $tq^\circ \in Q$.

Let us see the implications of all six axioms by using a diagram. Accordingly, take Process III in Figure 6.1 and consider the technology of turning pigs (good 3) and labour (good 4) into sausages (good 1). In Figure 6.2 the vector q°

$$q^\circ = (1800, 0, -18, -20, 0) \tag{6.5}$$

S P pigs L labour

represents one specific technique in terms of the list of the two inputs and the output they produce;

$$q' = (500, 0, -10, -5, 0) \tag{6.6}$$

represents another, less labour-intensive technique producing less output. The three unlabelled vectors represent other techniques for combining the two inputs to produce

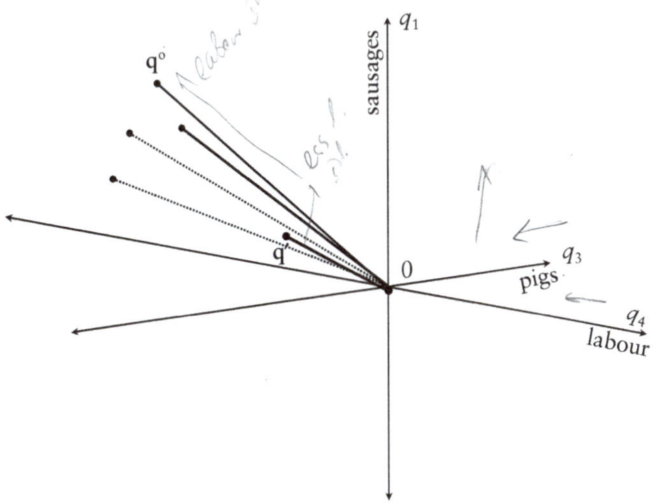

Figure 6.2 Labour and pigs produce sausages

sausages: note that all five points lie in the $(+,\cdot,-,-,\cdot)$ orthant indicating that sausages are the output $(+)$, pigs and labour the inputs $(-)$—the two '·' symbols are there just to remind us that goods 2 (potatoes) and 5 (land) are irrelevant in this production process.

These axioms can be used to build up a picture of the technology set in Figure 6.3. Axiom 6.1 simply states that the origin 0 must belong to the technology set—no pigs, no labour: no sausages. Axiom 6.2 rules out there being any points in the $(\cdot,+,\cdot,+,+,\cdot)$ orthant—you cannot have a technique that produces sausages *and* pigs *and* labour time to be enjoyed as leisure. Axiom 6.3 fixes the 'direction' of production in that the sausage machine does not have a reverse gear—if $\mathbf{q}$ is technically possible, then there is no feasible vector $-\mathbf{q}$ lying in the $(\cdot,-,\cdot,+,+,\cdot)$ direction whereby labour time and pigs are produced from sausages. Axiom 6.4 just says that outputs may be thrown away and inputs wasted, so that the entire negative orthant belongs to Q.

The implications of the additivity axiom are seen if we introduce $\mathbf{q}'' = (0,0,-12,0,0)$ in Figure 6.3: this is another feasible (but not very exciting) technique, whereby if one has pigs but not labour one gets zero sausages. Now consider again $\mathbf{q}'$ in (6.6); then additivity implies that $(500,0,-22,-5,0)$ must also be a technically feasible net output vector: it is formed from the sum of the vectors $\mathbf{q}'$ and $\mathbf{q}''$. Clearly a further implication of additivity is, for example, that $(1000,0,-20,-10,0)$ is a technically feasible vector: it is formed just by doubling $\mathbf{q}'$. The divisibility axiom says that if we have a point representing a feasible input/output combination then any point on the ray joining it to the origin must represent a feasible technique too. Hence, because $\mathbf{q}^\circ$ in (6.5) is feasible, the technique $\frac{1}{2}\mathbf{q}^\circ = (900,0,-9,-10,0)$ is also technologically feasible; hence also the entire cone shape in Figure 6.3 must belong to Q.

Axioms 6.1—6.3 are fairly unexceptionable, and it is not easy to imagine circumstances under which one would want to relax them. The free disposal Axiom 6.4 is

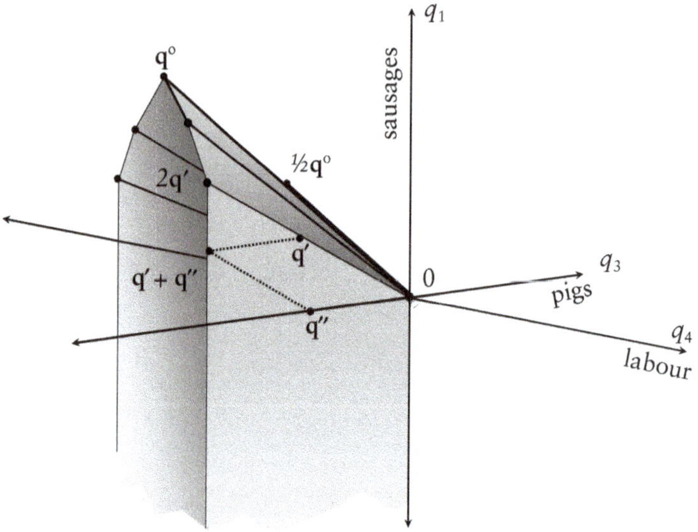

Figure 6.3 The technology set Q

almost innocuous: perhaps only the case of noxious wastes and the like need to be excluded. However, we should think some more about Axioms 6.5 and 6.6 before moving on.

The additivity axiom rules out the possibility of decreasing returns to scale—defined analogously to the way we did it for the case of a single output on page 17. As long as every single output is correctly identified and accounted for this axiom seems reasonable: if, say, land were also required for sausage making then it might well be the case that multiplying the vector **q**′ by 2000 would produce less than a million sausages, because the sausage makers might get in each other's way—but this is clearly a problem of incomplete specification of the model, not the inappropriateness of the axiom. However, at the level of the individual firm (rather than across the whole economy) apparent violations of additivity may be relevant. If certain essential features of the firm are non-expandable, then decreasing returns may apply within the firm; in the whole economy additivity might still apply if 'clones' of individual firms could be set up.

The divisibility axiom rules out increasing returns (since this implies that any net output vector can be 'scaled down' to any arbitrary extent) and is perhaps the most suspect. Clearly some processes do involve indivisibilities, and whilst it is reasonable to speak of single pigs or quarter pigs in process III, there is an obvious irreducible minimum of two pigs required for process II![1] However, as we shall see later, in large economies it may be possible to dismiss these indivisibilities as irrelevant: so for most of the time we shall assume that the divisibility axiom is valid. Evidently, if both additivity and divisibility hold, then decreasing and increasing returns to scale are ruled out: we again have

? Mini Problems

1 Sketch in two dimensions a technology set Q that violates Axiom 6.6.

constant returns to scale: in the multi-output case this means that if $\mathbf{q}$ is technologically feasible, then so is $t\mathbf{q}$ where t is any non-negative scalar.[2]

6.2.3 The production function again

The extended example in section 6.2.2 dealt with one production process; but all the principles discussed there apply to the combined processes for the whole economy. Naturally there is the difficulty of trying to visualise things in five dimensions—so, to get a feel for the nature of the technology set Q it is useful to look at particular sections of the set. One particularly useful instance of this is illustrated in Figure 6.4 that illustrates the technological possibilities for producing the two outputs in the five-good economy (sausages and potatoes), for given values of the three other goods. The kinks in the boundary of the set correspond to the specific techniques of production that were discussed earlier.[3] In the case where there are lots of basic processes, this view of the technology set, giving the production possibilities for the two outputs, will look like Figure 6.5. Clearly we

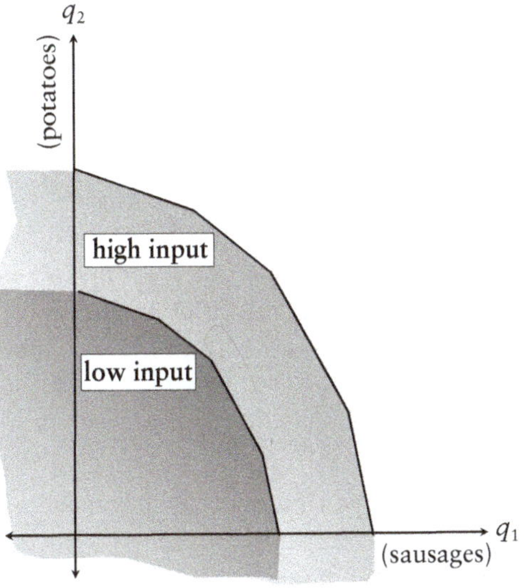

Figure 6.4 The potato-sausage tradeoff

? Mini Problems

2 Consider a two-good economy (good 1 an input good 2 an output) in which there are potentially two technologies as follows

$$Q^\circ := \{\mathbf{q} : q_2 = 0 \text{ if } q_1 > -1;\, q_2 \leq 1 \text{ otherwise}\}$$

$$Q' := \{\mathbf{q} : q_2 \leq -q_1 \text{ for all } q_1 \leq 0\}.$$

If both technologies were available at the same time, what would be the combined technology set?

3 Draw similar figures to illustrate (a) the relationship between one input and one output (given the levels of other outputs); (b) the isoquants corresponding to the pig-labour-sausage figure.

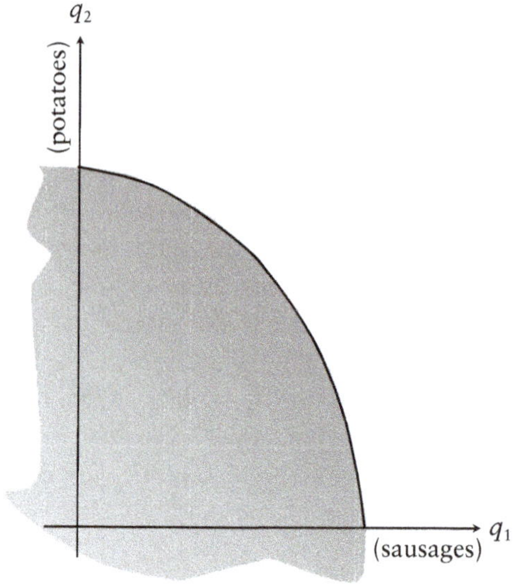

Figure 6.5 Smooth potato-sausage tradeoff

have recreated Figure 2.17, which we introduced rather abruptly in chapter 2's discussion of the single multiproduct firm.

This connection of ideas suggests a further step. Using the idea of the technology set Q we can then write the production function for the economy as a whole. This specifies the set of net output vectors (in other words the set of input-output combinations) that are feasible given the technology available to the economy. Put differently, this is a function Φ such that[4]

$$\Phi(\mathbf{q}) \leq 0 \tag{6.7}$$

if and only if $\mathbf{q} \in Q$. The particular feature of the production function highlighted in Figures 6.4 and 6.5 is of course the transformation curve—the implicit tradeoff between outputs given any particular level of inputs.

6.2.4 Externalities and aggregation

The simple exercise in section 6.2.1 implicitly assumed that there were no technological interactions amongst the three processes. We have already met—in chapter 3, page 55—the problem that one firm's production possibilities depend on another firm's activities. This concept can be translated into the net-output language of processes as follows: if Q^1 and Q^2 are the technology sets for processes 1 and 2 respectively then, if

? Mini Problems

4 Take a firm that produces a single output q from quantities of inputs z_1, z_2 subject to the explicit production function $q \leq \phi(z_1, z_2)$; rewrite this production function in implicit form using Φ notation. Sketch the set of technologically feasible net output vectors.

there are no externalities, the technology set for the combined process is just $Q^1 + Q^2$ [check (A.24) in Appendix A for the definition of the sum of sets]. So, if there are no externalities, we have a convenient result:[5]

Theorem 6.1 (Convexity in aggregation)

If each technology set or firm is convex and if there are no production externalities, then the technology set for the economy is also convex.

If, to the contrary, there were externalities, then it is possible that the aggregate technology set is non-convex. Clearly the independence implied by the absence of externalities considerably simplifies the step of moving from the analysis of the individual firm or process to the analysis of the whole economy.

6.3 The Robinson Crusoe economy

Now that we have a formal description of the production side of our simple economy we need to build this into a complete model. The model will incorporate both production and consumption sectors and will take into account the natural resource constraints of the economy. To take this step we turn to a well-known story that contains an appropriately simple account of economic organisation—the tale of Robinson Crusoe.

To set the scene we are on the sunny shores of a desert island which is cut off from the rest of the world so that:

- there is no trade with world markets,
- we have a single economic agent (Robinson Crusoe),
- all commodities on the island have to be produced or found from existing stocks.

Some of these restrictions will be dropped in the course of our discussion; but even in this highly simplified model, there is an interesting economic problem to be addressed.

The problem consists in trying to reach Crusoe's preferred economic state by choosing an appropriate consumption and production plan. To make this problem specific, assume that he has the same kind of preference structure as we discussed previously; this is represented by a function U defined on the set X of all feasible consumption vectors; each vector $\mathbf{x}$ is just a list of quantities of the n commodities that are potentially available on the island. Requiring that the consumption vector be feasible imposes the restriction

$$\mathbf{x} \in X. \tag{6.8}$$

But what determines the other constraints under which the optimisation problem is to be solved? The two main factors are the technological possibilities of transforming some

? Mini Problems

5 Use Theorem A.6 (page 497) to provide a 1-line proof of this.

commodities into others, and the stocks of resources that are already available on the island.

The desert island economy

$\mathbf{x}$	consumption goods
$\mathbf{q}$	net outputs
U	utility function
Φ	production function
$\mathbf{R}$	resource stocks

Clearly we need to introduce the technology set or the production function. Take, for example, the technology set from section 6.2 depicted in Figure 6.5. This merely illustrates what is technologically feasible: the application of the technology will be constrained by the available resources; furthermore the amount of any commodity that is available for consumption will obviously be reduced if that commodity is also used in the production process. To incorporate this point we introduce the assumption that there are known resource stocks $R_1, R_2, \ldots, R_n$, of each of the n commodities, where each R_i must be positive or zero. Then we can write down the *materials balance* condition for commodity i:

$$x_i \leq q_i + R_i \tag{6.9}$$

which simply states that the amount consumed of commodity i must not exceed the total production of commodity i plus pre-existing stocks of i. Technology and resources enable us to specify the attainable set for consumption in this model, sometimes known as the *production-possibility set*.[6] This follows from the conditions (6.7) and (6.9):

$$A(\mathbf{R}; \Phi) := \left\{\mathbf{x} : \mathbf{x} \in X, \mathbf{x} \leq \mathbf{q} + \mathbf{R}; \; \Phi\left(\mathbf{q}\right) \leq 0\right\}. \tag{6.10}$$

Two examples of the attainable set A are illustrated in Figure 6.6: the left-hand side assumes that there are given quantities of resources $R_3, \ldots, R_n$ and zero stocks of goods 1 and 2 ($R_1 = R_2 = 0$); the case on the right-hand side of Figure 6.6 assumes that there are the same given quantities of resources $R_3, \ldots, R_n$, a positive stock of R_1 and $R_2 = 0$.

So the 'Crusoe problem' is to choose net outputs $\mathbf{q}$ and consumption quantities $\mathbf{x}$ so as to maximise $U(\mathbf{x})$ subject to the constraints (6.7)–(6.9). This is represented in Figure 6.7 where the attainable set has been copied across from Figure 6.6 (for the case where $R_1 = R_2 = 0$) and a standard set of indifference curves has been introduced to represent Crusoe's preferences. Clearly the maximum will be at the point where[7]

$$\frac{\Phi_i(\mathbf{q})}{\Phi_j(\mathbf{q})} = \frac{U_i(\mathbf{x})}{U_j(\mathbf{x})} \tag{6.11}$$

? Mini Problems

6 Use the production model of Exercise 2.11. If Crusoe has stocks of three resources R_3, R_4, R_5 sketch the attainable set for commodities 1 and 2.

7 Show this, using standard Lagrangean methods.

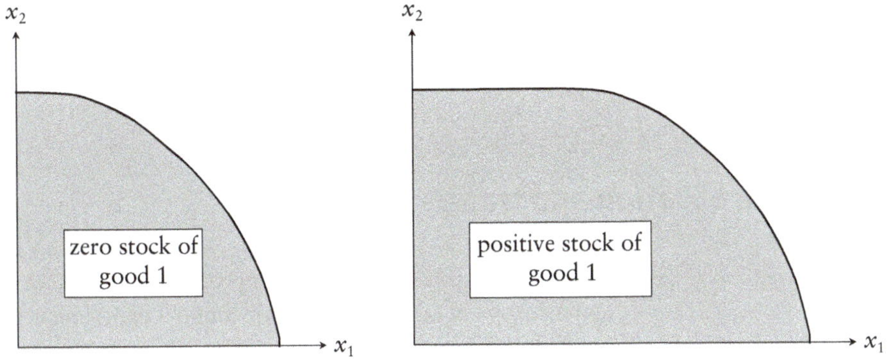

Figure 6.6 Crusoe's attainable set

for any pair of goods that are produced in non-zero quantities, and consumed in positive quantities at the optimum. This condition is illustrated in Figure 6.7 where the highlighted solution point (representing both optimal consumption $\mathbf{x}^*$ and optimal net outputs $\mathbf{q}^* = \mathbf{x}^* - \mathbf{R}$) is at the common tangency of the surface of the attainable set and a contour of the utility function. You would probably think that this is essentially the same shape as 5.4 (the model with household production) and you would be right: the linkage between the two is evident once one considers that in the household-production model the consumer buys commodities to use as inputs in the production of utility-yielding goods that cannot, by their nature, be bought; Crusoe uses resources on the island to produce consumer goods that cannot be bought because he is on a desert island.

The comparative statics of this problem are straightforward. Clearly, a technical change or a resource change will usually involve a simultaneous change in both net

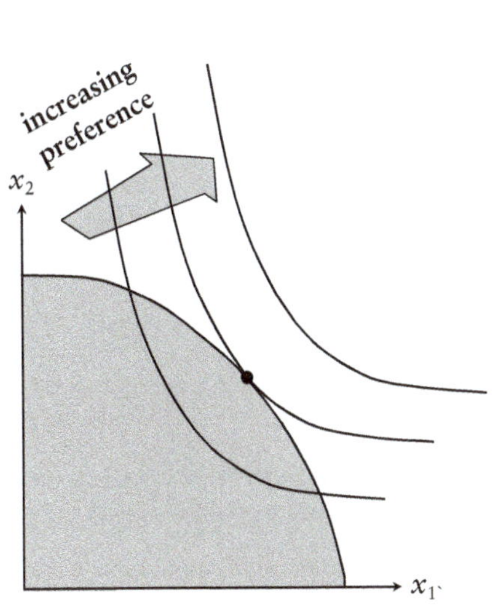

Figure 6.7 Robinson Crusoe problem: summary

outputs **q** and consumption **x**.[8] Moreover, a change in Crusoe's tastes will also usually involve a change in production techniques as well as consumption: again this is to be expected from chapter 5's household-production model.[9]

6.4 Decentralisation and trade

In the tidy self-contained world of Robinson Crusoe there appears to be no room for prices. However, this is not quite true: we will carry out a little thought experiment that will prove to be quite instructive.

6.4.1 Reorganisation on the island?

Re-examine the left-hand panel of Figure 6.6 and consider the expression

$$\Pi := \rho_1 q_1 + \rho_2 q_2 + \ldots + \rho_n q_n \tag{6.12}$$

where $\rho_1, \rho_2, \ldots, \rho_n$ are some notional prices. (I have used a different symbol for prices here because at the moment there is no market, and therefore there are no 'prices' in the usual meaning of the word (if we want to invent a story for this, let us suppose that Robinson Crusoe does some accounting as a spare-time activity). If we were to draw the projection of (6.12) on the diagram for different values of the sum Π, we would generate a family of isoprofit lines similar to those on page 42 but with these notional prices used instead of real ones.[10] If we draw the same family of lines in the right-hand panel of Figure 6.6, then clearly we have a set of notional valuations of resources $R_1, R_2, \ldots, R_n$ plus profits, and if we do the same in Figure 6.7, then we have a family of budget constraints corresponding to various levels of income at a given set of notional prices $\rho_1, \cdots, \rho_n$.

Now suppose that there is an extra person on the island. Although the preferences of this person (called 'ManFriday', after the original *Robinson Crusoe* book) play no rôle in the objective function and although he owns none of the resources, he plays a vital rôle in the economic model: he acts as a kind of intelligent slave to whom production can be delegated by Robinson Crusoe. We can then imagine the following kind of story.

Crusoe writes down his marginal rates of substitution—his personal 'prices' for all the various goods in the economy—and passes the information on to Man Friday with the instruction to organise production on the island so as to maximise profits. If the

? Mini Problems

8 Use your answer to the exercise in Mini Problem 6 to illustrate the effect of an increase in the stock R_4.

9 Use the diagram in the text to show the effect of a technological improvement that enables Crusoe to produce more of commodity i for every input combination.

10 Use the definition of net outputs to explain how to rewrite the expression for profits in (6.12) the more conventional format of 'Revenue—Cost'.

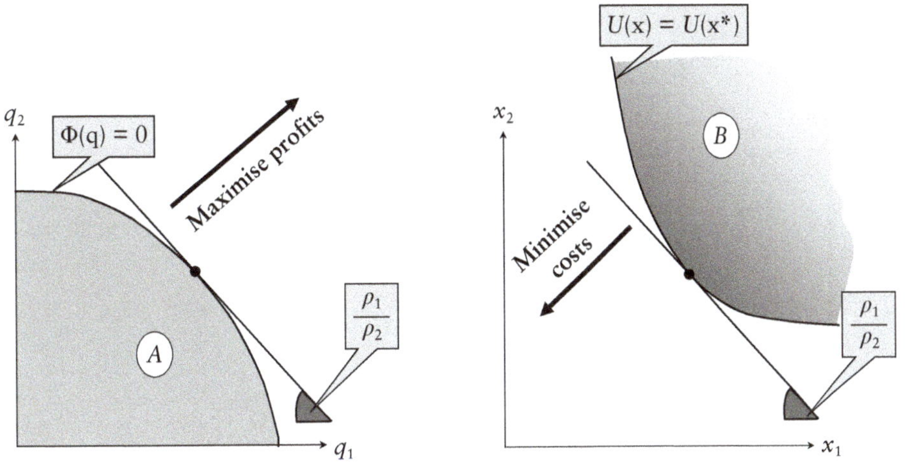

Figure 6.8 The separating role of prices

notional prices $p_1, \cdots, p_n$ are set equal to these announced MRS values then a simple geometrical experiment confirms that the profit-maximising net outputs $\mathbf{q}$ chosen by Friday (left-hand panel of Figure 6.6) lead to a vector of commodities available for consumption $\mathbf{q} + \mathbf{R}$ (right-hand panel of Figure 6.6) that exactly corresponds to the optimal $\mathbf{x}$ vector (Figure 6.7).

In the light of this story we can interpret the numbers $p_1, \cdots, p_n$ as *shadow prices*—the imputed values of commodities given Crusoe's tastes. The notional 'shadow profits' made by the desert island at any net output vector $\mathbf{q}$ will be given by (6.12). So the notional valuation of the whole island at these shadow prices is just

$$\Pi := p_1 [q_1 + R_1] + p_2 [q_2 + R_2] + \ldots + p_n [q_n + R_n]. \tag{6.13}$$

To summarise, see Figure 6.8. Crusoe has found a neat way to manage production on the desert island—he gets Friday to maximise profits (6.12) at shadow prices (left-hand panel); this requires

$$\frac{\Phi_i(\mathbf{q})}{\Phi_j(\mathbf{q})} = \frac{p_i}{p_j}. \tag{6.14}$$

Crusoe then maximises utility given the income consisting of the value of his resource endowment plus the profits (6.12) generated by Friday (right-hand panel);[11] this requires

$$\frac{U_i(\mathbf{x})}{U_j(\mathbf{x})} = \frac{p_i}{p_j}. \tag{6.15}$$

We have a simple decentralisation parable: the problem with FOC (6.11) is broken down into the two separate problems with FOCs (6.14) and (6.15) respectively.

? Mini Problems

11 How would this sort of problem change if Crusoe could not thoroughly monitor Friday's actions?

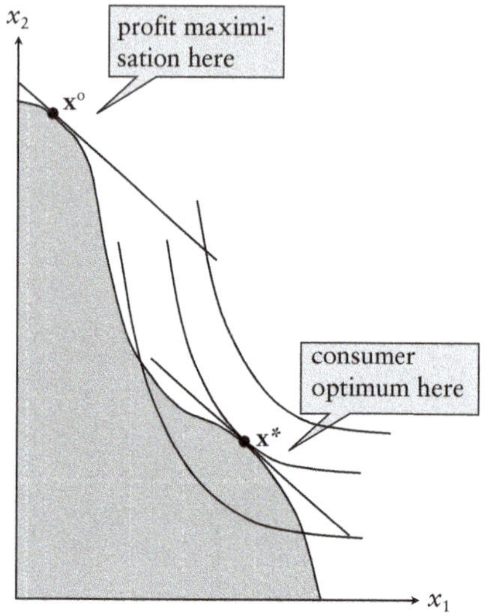

Figure 6.9 Optimum cannot be decentralised

But will decentralisation always work? Not if there are indivisibilities in the technology set that render the attainable set non-convex. To see that this is the case recall that such non-convexities will be present if there are indivisibilities in the production process. In such a case profit maximisation could lead to selection of an inappropriate input-output combination as illustrated in Figure 6.9. Notice that if Crusoe announces the prices that correspond to point $\mathbf{x}^*$, profit maximisation will actually result in production, not at point $\mathbf{x}^*$, but at point $\mathbf{x}^{\circ}$.

Comparing the diagrams we have used so far should give the clue to the following general result, proved in Appendix C:

Theorem 6.2 (Decentralisation)

If the attainable set is convex and the utility function is concave contoured and satisfies the greed axiom, then there exists a set of imputed shadow prices $\rho_1, \cdots, \rho_n$ such that the problem

$$\max_{\{\mathbf{x},\mathbf{q}\}} U(\mathbf{x}) \text{subject to} \left\{ \begin{array}{l} \mathbf{x} \in X \\ \Phi(\mathbf{q}) \leq 0 \\ \mathbf{x} \leq \mathbf{q} + \mathbf{R} \end{array} \right\} \tag{6.16}$$

is equivalent to the two-stage problem

$$\max_{\mathbf{q}} \sum_{i=1}^{n} \rho_i \left[q_i + R_i\right] \text{ subject to } \Phi(\mathbf{q}) \leq 0 \tag{6.17}$$

$$\max_{\mathbf{x}} U(\mathbf{x}) \text{subject to} \quad \begin{array}{l} \sum_{i=1}^{n} \rho_i x_i \leq y \\ \mathbf{x} \in X \end{array} \tag{6.18}$$

where y is the maximal value of (6.17).

Theorem 6.2 relies on the powerful results given in Appendix A as Theorems A.8 and A.9. To oversimplify what these results state, if you have two convex sets A and B with no points in common, then you can 'separate' them with a hyperplane, an n-dimensional generalisation of a line in (in two dimensions) or a plane (in three dimensions); if A and B have only boundary points in common, then you can pass a hyperplane through their common boundary points so that it 'supports' A and B. The two sets here are:

- A: the attainable set (from 6.10)

$$A(\mathbf{R}; \Phi) := \{\mathbf{x} : \mathbf{x} \in X, \mathbf{x} \le \mathbf{q} + \mathbf{R}; \ \Phi(\mathbf{q}) \le 0\}. \tag{6.19}$$

- B: the *better-than-x** set,

$$B(\mathbf{x}^*) := \{\mathbf{x} : U(\mathbf{x}) \ge U(\mathbf{x}^*)\}. \tag{6.20}$$

(Purists will note that I should have called B the 'at-least-as-good-as-$\mathbf{x}^*$' set or the 'not-worse-than-$\mathbf{x}^*$'; but purists will have to put up with this nomenclature for the sake of linguistic euphony). The hyperplane here is determined by the notional prices $\rho_1, \cdots, \rho_n$ and is represented by the straight line in each panel of Figure 6.8—for a formal definition see page 499.[12] The problem in (6.17) is equivalent to maximising profits $\sum_{i=1}^n \rho_i q_i$; maximising profits gives the solution in the left-hand panel of Figure 6.8. The right-hand panel of Figure 6.8 reinterprets Crusoe's utility-maximisation problem as one of cost-minimisation (as we did in the discussion of the consumer in chapter 4); consumer costs in this case are given by $\sum_{i=1}^n \rho_i x_i$. The decentralisation result is further illustrated in Figure 6.10, which puts together the two parts of Figure 6.8. Figure 6.10 represents the basic utility-maximisation problem, as in Figure 6.7, but also illustrates the two convex sets A and B corresponding to the two component optimisation problems—profit maximisation subject to a technological feasibility constraint, and cost minimisation subject to a utility constraint. Notice that the same price line applies to these two problems, and

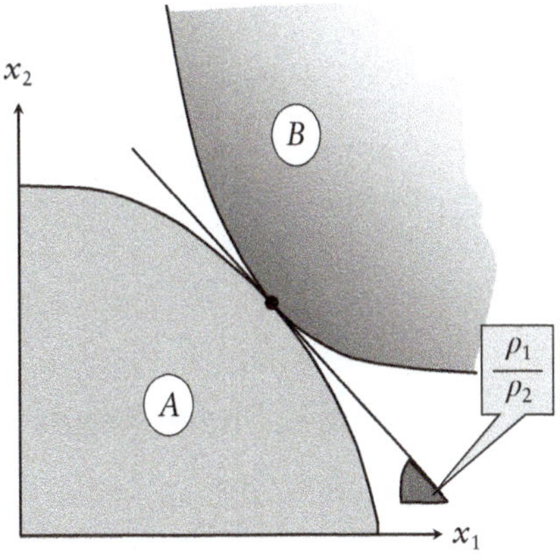

Figure 6.10 Crusoe problem: another view

 Mini Problems

12 Discuss the way Theorem 6.2 can be applied to the household production model in section 5.4.

is the line that just 'separates' the two sets in Figure 6.10. This is the first example of economic decentralisation which will play an important rôle later in the book.

Example 6.1

Decentralisation can even be seen as a revolutionary concept. After the trauma of the civil war in Russia that followed the 1917 revolution and the events leading to the Kronstadt rebellion a rethink in communist economic organisation was mooted in what came to be known as the New Economic Policy:

> The most urgent thing at the present time is to take measures that will immediately increase the productive forces of peasant farming. Only in this way will it be possible to improve the conditions of the workers and strengthen the alliance between the workers and peasants, to strengthen the dictatorship of the proletariat ... This cannot be done without a serious modification of our food policy. Such a modification [effected by NEP] was the substitution of the surplus-appropriation system [i.e. forcible acquisition of grain production above what is needed for subsistence] by the tax in kind [i.e., handing over of grain in amounts to satisfy tax due], which implies free trade...
>
> The tax in kind is one of the forms of transition from that peculiar 'War Communism,' which we were forced to resort to by extreme want, ruin and war, to the proper socialist exchange of products. The latter, in its turn, is one of the forms of transition from Socialism, with the peculiar features created by the predominance of the small peasantry among the population, to Communism. The essence of the peculiar 'War Communism' was that we actually took from the peasant, all the surplus grain—and sometimes even not only surplus grain, but part of the grain the peasant required for food—to meet the requirements of the army and sustain the workers ... It was a temporary measure. The correct policy of the proletariat which is exercising its dictatorship in a small-peasant country is to obtain grain in exchange for the manufactured goods the peasant requires... only such a policy can strengthen the foundations of Socialism and lead to its complete victory...
>
> The effect will be the revival of the petty bourgeoisie and of capitalism on the basis of a certain amount of free trade ... This is beyond doubt. It would be ridiculous to shut our eyes to it. (Lenin 1921: 329–65)

So Lenin saw the benefits of decentralisation, irrespective of the system of ownership in society. But it could not last: the NEP was finally abandoned under Stalin in 1928 (Bandera 1970).

6.4.2 Opening up the economy

Now let us suppose that Crusoe has access to a world market with prices $\mathbf{p}$: all goods are tradeable at those prices and there are no transactions costs to trade.[13] An immediate

? Mini Problems

13 Rework the analysis of this section for the case where there are fixed costs to trade.

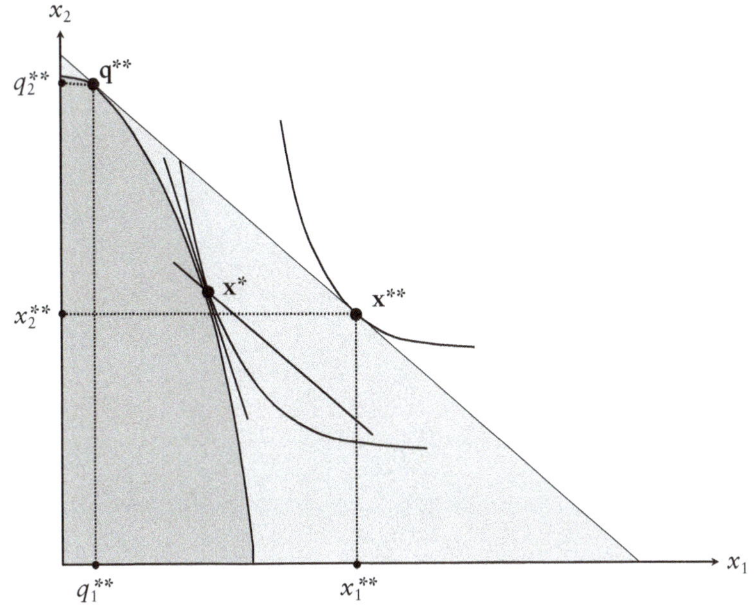

Figure 6.11 Crusoe's island trades

consequence of this is that the attainable set may be enlarged. To see this let us reuse the graphical tools we have already developed.

Let us depict production possibilities as in the heavily shaded area in Figure 6.11: this is the original (no-trade) attainable set. Note that the best that can be done on the desert island without trade is given by point $\mathbf{x}^*$ (compare this with our previous diagram, Figure 6.7). At point $\mathbf{x}^*$ an indifference curve is tangential to the original attainable set and the slope of the common tangent (the steep line through $\mathbf{x}^*$) can be interpreted as relative prices in the economy before trade is opened up.

Now we allow contact with the outside world. There, good 1 is much cheaper relative to good 2, as depicted by the slope of the shallow line through $\mathbf{x}^*$. If we introduce the possibility of buying and selling as much as Crusoe likes at these new prices then, of course, any point on this line becomes feasible—all such points lie in Crusoe's 'budget set' given by the world prices $\mathbf{p}$. So clearly the attainable set has now been enlarged. However, Crusoe can do better than points on this budget line through $\mathbf{x}^*$. This is one of a whole family of lines with the equation

$$\sum_{i=1}^{n} p_i \left[q_i + R_i\right] = \textbf{constant} \tag{6.21}$$

each one of which puts a particular valuation on net output plus resources—so why not pick the budget line that maximises this valuation? This is shown by the parallel line through $\mathbf{q}^{**}$ and $\mathbf{x}^{**}$: Crusoe's island produces at $\mathbf{q}^{**}$, but trade with the market permits consumption at $\mathbf{x}^{**}$. There is a substantial gain to Crusoe from

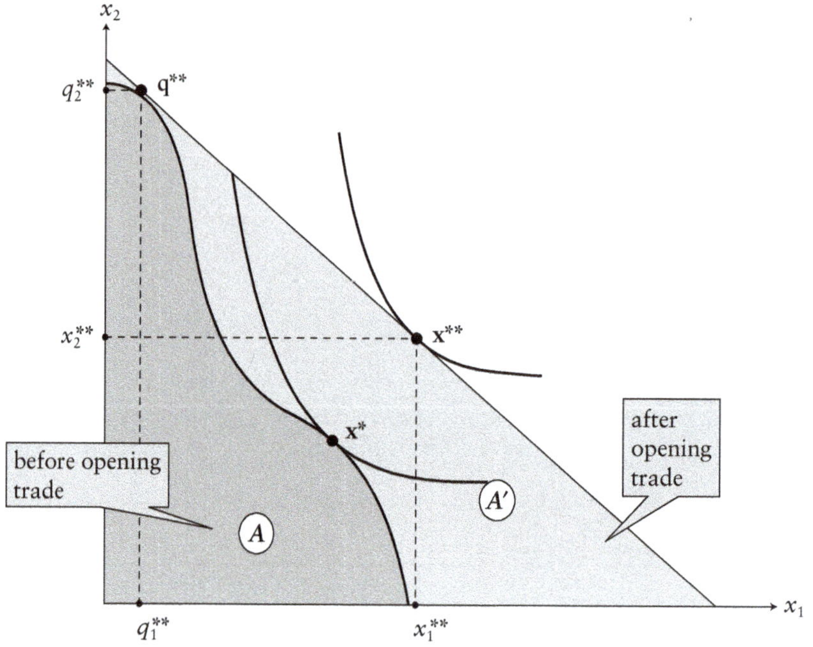

Figure 6.12 Convexification of the attainable set

this depicted by the fact that $\mathbf{x}^{**}$ lies on a higher indifference curve than does $\mathbf{x}^{*}$.[14]

A second result immediately follows. Trade will 'convexify' the attainable set, so that we do not have to worry about the decentralisation problem. This result is illustrated in Figure 6.12: the pre-trade attainable set for Crusoe is given by A and has deliberately drawn as non-convex; the after-trade attainable set for Crusoe is given by the convex set A'. So the exact shape of the pre-trade attainable set is largely irrelevant to the utility outcome for the consumer; as drawn Crusoe gets the same utility whether the pre-trade attainable set is convex (Figure 6.11) or non-convex (Figure 6.12).[15]

Trade thus permits the transformation of the optimisation problem into the following two stages:

- You choose $\mathbf{q}$ so as to maximise the value of 'South Seas' Inc.
- You then choose $\mathbf{x}$ from the budget set determined by this maximised value.

An important lesson from this exercise is that the market accomplishes decentralisation in a beautifully simple fashion—it takes over the 'Man Friday' rôle by ensuring that

? Mini Problems

14 Use a diagram similar to the ones shown here to show the amount that Crusoe exports to the market and the amount that he imports from the market.

15 Explain in words why this happens.

the correct signals are given the consumption and production sectors ensuring that their optimisation problems can be separated out from each other. We shall make extensive use of this property in the next few chapters.

Example 6.2

In the mid-nineteenth century a remarkable change occurred in Japan. After the arrival of Commodore Matthew Perry in 1854 a peace treaty was established between Japan and the United States. There followed a transformation from almost complete economic isolation from the rest of the world (rather like our story of Crusoe's island, but a self-imposed situation rather than the result of a shipwreck) to a situation of active involvement in world trade. What happened? The sketch in Figure 6.11 should give us a good idea. Before opening up trade relative prices of key commodities in Japan were way out of line with world markets: in Japan a pound of tea had cost 1.3 times a pound of iron, but on the London market a pound of tea had cost 11 times a pound of iron.

The impact on the Japanese economy was abrupt. Within a little over a decade foreign trade increased 70-fold. The change in terms of trade led to a rise in national income of, perhaps, 65 per cent. (Huber 1971).

Summary

We have seen some of the basic elements of a complete economic system. The characterisation of the system is facilitated by using the compact net-output language for production and an explicit axiomatisation of the technology. Although the economic model at the heart of this chapter is very simple, it is capable of illustrating some of the deep points of standard economic analysis of decentralisation and the market. It lays the basis for a richer model that we will analyse in chapter 7.

Reading notes

For a good introduction to the Robinson Crusoe economy see Koopmans (1957).

Exercises

6.1 In an economy the activity of digging holes in the ground is carried out by self-employed labourers (single–person firms). The production of one standard-sized hole requires a minimum input of one unit of labour. No self-employed labourer can produce more than one hole.

1. Draw the technology set Q for a single firm.
2. Draw the technology set Q for two firms.
3. Which of Axioms 6.1 to 6.6 are satisfied by this simple technology?

6.2 Consider the following four examples of technology sets Q:

$$A: \left\{\mathbf{q} : q_1^2 + q_2^2 + q_3 + q_4 \leq 0;\ \ q_1, q_2 \geq 0; q_3, q_4 \leq 0\right\}$$

$$B: \left\{\mathbf{q} : q_1^\alpha - [-q_2]^\beta - [-q_3]^\gamma \leq 0;\ \ q_1 \geq 0; q_2, q_3 \leq 0\right\}$$

$$C: \left\{\mathbf{q} : \log q_1 - \frac{1}{2}\log\left(q_2 q_3\right) \leq 0;\ \ q_1 \geq 0; q_2, q_3 \leq 0\right\}$$

$$D: \left\{\mathbf{q} : q_1 + q_2 + \max\left(q_3, \frac{q_4}{a}\right) \leq 0;\ \ q_1, q_2 \geq 0; q_3, q_4 \leq 0\right\}$$

1. Check whether Axioms 6.1 to 6.6 are satisfied in each case.
2. Sketch their isoquants and write down the production functions.
3. In cases B and C express the production function in terms of the notation used in chapter 2.
4. In cases A and D draw the transformation curve.

6.3 Suppose two identical firms each produce two outputs from a single input. Each firm has exactly 1 unit of input. Suppose that for firm 1 the amounts q_1^1, q_2^1 it produces of the two outputs are given by

$$q_1^1 = \alpha\theta^1$$

$$q_2^1 = \beta[1 - \theta^1]$$

where θ^1 is the proportion of the input that firm 1 devotes to the production of good 1 and α and β depend on the activity of firm 2 thus

$$\alpha = 1 + 2\theta^2$$

$$\beta = 1 + 2[1 - \theta^2].$$

where θ^2 is the proportion of the input that firm 2 devotes to good 1. Likewise for firm 2:

$$q_1^2 = \alpha'\theta^2$$

$$q_2^2 = \beta'[1 - \theta^2]$$

$$\alpha' = 1 + 2\theta^1$$

$$\beta' = 1 + 2[1 - \theta^1].$$

1. Draw the production possibly set for firm 1 if firm 2 sets $\theta^2 = \frac{1}{2}$ and firm 2's production possibly set if firm 1 sets $\theta^1 = \frac{1}{2}$.
2. Draw the combined production-possibility set.

6.4 Take the model of Exercise 2.14. Assuming that production is organised to maximise profits at given prices show that profit-maximising net outputs of goods 1 and 2 are:

$$q_1 = \frac{A}{2}p_1$$

$$q_2 = \frac{A}{2}p_2$$

where p_i is the price of good i expressed in terms of commodity 3, and that maximised profits are

$$\Pi = A\frac{[p_1]^2 + [p_2]^2}{4}.$$

6.5 Take the model of Exercise 5.3 but suppose that income is exogenously given at y_1 for the first period only. Income in the second period can be obtained by investing an amount z in the first period. Suppose $y_2 = \phi(z)$, where ϕ is a twice-differentiable function with positive first derivative and negative second derivative and $\phi(0) = 0$, and assume that there is a perfect market for lending and borrowing.

1. Write down the budget constraint.
2. Explain the rôle of Theorem 6.2 in this model.
3. Find the household's optimum and compare it with that of Exercise 5.3.
4. Suppose $\phi(z)$ were to be replaced by $\tau\phi(z)$ where $\tau > 1$; how would this affect the solution?

6.6 Apply the model of Exercise 6.5 to an individual's decision to invest in education.

1. Assume the parameter τ represents talent. Will more talented people purchase more education?
2. How is the demand for schooling related to exogenous first-period income y_1?

6.7 Take the savings model of Exercise 5.4 (page 119). Suppose now that by investing in education in the first period the consumer can augment his future income. Sacrificing an amount z in period 1 would yield additional income in period 2 of

$$\tau\left[1 - e^{-z}\right]$$

where $\tau > 0$ is a productivity parameter.

1. Explain how investment in education is affected by the interest rate. What would happen if the interest rate were higher than $\tau - 1$?
2. How is the demand for borrowing affected by (i) an increase in the interest rate r and (ii) an increase in the person's productivity parameter τ?

7 General Equilibrium

Every individual . . . intends only his own gain, and he is in this as in many other cases led by an invisible hand to promote an end which was no part of his intention. By pursuing his own interest he frequently promotes that of society more effectually than when he really intends to promote it.

Adam Smith, *Wealth of Nations* (1776).

7.1 Introduction

We are now able to examine the problem of general competitive equilibrium: in other words the conditions under which you can get some sort of harmony in a market economy full of selfish individuals, and the ways in which this harmony is achieved. General equilibrium analysis can be 'general' in a number of ways; some or all of the following features may be present in a general-equilibrium model:

- The number of economic actors—households and firms—can be general. We could have n_h households and n_f firms.
- Behavioural assumptions can be general—there is no need to assume that everyone acts as price takers.
- The system can be general: instead of a single market, or collection of markets, we deal with a complete, closed economic unit incorporating consumption, exchange, and (perhaps) production.

The last of these features was present in the Robinson Crusoe model of chapter 6: in the Crusoe economy production and consumption took place within the same closed universe and (at least at first) there was no market, no world outside with which to trade. But we can now extend the model of the economic system to one that incorporates the first two features, multiple agents and the possibility of non-price-taking behaviour.

7.2 A more interesting economy

We begin by building on the simple closed model of the Robinson Crusoe economy: we need to make it richer and capable of handling large numbers of economic agents. To do this we need first to reconsider the basic economic ingredients of the economic problem.

There are three fundamental elements to the kind of economy that we shall be talking about:

- *Households* who have given preferences represented by utility functions

$$U^h,\ h = 1, 2, \ldots, n_h; \tag{7.1}$$

- *Firms* that have specific technologies described in production functions

$$\Phi^f,\ f = 1, 2, \ldots, n_f; \tag{7.2}$$

- *Resource stocks* R_i of the commodities $i = 1, 2, \ldots, n$.

Assume that there are markets in all commodities, and that all agents are perfectly informed about what is going on in the economy. We shall also usually assume that they act as price takers in each of the markets. Finally let us mention the rôle of time within the model: essentially it does not exist, but we shall examine a rudimentary model involving time in section 7.4.4 below.

Quite a bit more is needed to complete the description of the economy—how the households' budget constraints are determined, who runs the firms, and so on—but for now this gives us enough to start a meaningful discussion of an equilibrium system. Some of the issues which suggest themselves within this framework are:

- Why do people act as price takers?
- Where do the prices come from?

Elements of the economy

HOUSEHOLDS

x_i^h	consumption by h of good i
$\mathbf{x}^h$	$\left(x_1^h, x_2^h, \ldots, x_n^h\right)$
$[\mathbf{x}]$	$\left[\mathbf{x}^1, \mathbf{x}^2, \mathbf{x}^3, \ldots\right]$
U^h	h's preferences

FIRMS

q_i^f	net output by f of good i > 0 if i is an output < 0 if i is an input
$\mathbf{q}^f$	$\left(q_1^f, q_2^f, \ldots, q_n^f\right)$
$[\mathbf{q}]$	$\left[\mathbf{q}^1, \mathbf{q}^2, \mathbf{q}^3, \ldots\right]$
Φ^f	f's technology

R_i	resource stock of i

- Will an economic system have an equilibrium? More than one equilibrium?
- Is there a mechanism driving the economy towards the equilibrium?

7.2.1 Allocations

To make further headway we need to describe a state of the economy. We shall assume that a state is completely described by a snapshot of what is going on in every household and in every firm at some particular moment: we are, for the moment, unconcerned about the processes which have led to the snapshot that we observe.

Definition 7.1

A *state of the economy* or an *allocation* in an economy consists of an allocation of consumption vectors to each household $[\mathbf{x}]$, and an allocation of net output vectors to each firm $[\mathbf{q}]$.

As a reminder of the meaning of this notation, check the details in the notation box.

Suppose there is a market in operation: prices are denoted by $p_1, \ldots, p_n$ and household h's income is written as y^h, for $h = 1, \ldots, n_h$. The profits of firm f are given by[1]

$$\Pi^f = \sum_{i=1}^{n} p_i q_i^f \tag{7.3}$$

for $f = 1, \ldots, n_f$. Clearly we would be interested in *market allocations* that take into account the prices as well as the collection of consumption bundles $[\mathbf{x}]$ and the collection of net-output vectors $[\mathbf{q}]$. However, to make progress it is more useful to introduce the following more carefully defined concept:

Definition 7.2

A *competitive allocation* is a market allocation:

$$\mathbf{a} = ([\mathbf{x}], [\mathbf{q}], \mathbf{p})$$

where $\mathbf{x}^h$ is utility-maximising for household $h = 1, 2, \ldots, n_h$, and $\mathbf{q}^f$ is profit maximising for firm $f = 1, 2, \ldots, n_f$ at prices $\mathbf{p}$.

What this means is that, given the prices $\mathbf{p}$, each $\mathbf{x}^h$ in the allocation must be the solution to

$$\max_{(\mathbf{x}^h)} U^h(\mathbf{x}^h) \text{ subject to } \left\{ \begin{array}{c} \mathbf{x}^h \in X \\ \\ \sum_{i=1}^{n} p_i x_i^h \leq y^h \end{array} \right\} \tag{7.4}$$

and each $\mathbf{q}^f$ in the allocation must be the solution to

$$\max_{(\mathbf{q}^f)} \sum_{i=1}^{n} p_i q_i^f \text{ subject to } \Phi^f(\mathbf{q}^f) \leq 0. \tag{7.5}$$

? Mini Problems

1 Using this notation explain what happens to profits if two firms, which previously traded with each other, now merge.

This implies that, in a competitive allocation, each consumer's bundle must be on his offer curve. To 'close' the system we again use the materials balance condition—(6.9) generalised to allow for the multiplicity of households and firms. This raises a tricky point that is too easily glossed over. Can we just add up the household consumption demands to get the overall demand for input i and add up the firms' net outputs? This simple aggregation property would be satisfied if:

- All goods are purely private goods (like bread) and do not permit joint consumption (like bridges and broadcast TV). We have used this assumption before when considering the relationship between market and household demand (page 114). Technically it requires the property of 'rivalness' discussed on page 234.
- There are no externalities in production. Then, if $\mathbf{q}^1$ is technologically feasible for firm 1 and $\mathbf{q}^2$ is technologically feasible for firm 2, the combined net output vector $\mathbf{q}^1 + \mathbf{q}^2$ is also feasible—see the discussion on pages 55 and 131.

If we assume the simple aggregation property then the generalised materials balance condition for any commodity i is:

$$\sum_{h=1}^{n_h} x_i^h \leq \sum_{f=1}^{n_f} q_i^f + \sum_{h=1}^{n_h} R_i^h; \tag{7.6}$$

or, writing $x_i = \sum_{h=1}^{n_h} x_i^h$, $q_i = \sum_{f=1}^{n_f} q_i^f$ and $R_i = \sum_{h=1}^{n_h} R_i^h$, for the aggregates over households and firms, we can express (7.6) equivalently in vector form as

$$\mathbf{x} \leq \mathbf{q} + \mathbf{R}. \tag{7.7}$$

What this means is that, if an allocation is to be feasible, demand cannot exceed supply, where 'supply' of any commodity covers the aggregate of all the net outputs of the firms plus the aggregate of all pre-existing stocks. Then we can introduce our main concept:

Definition 7.3

A *competitive equilibrium* is a competitive allocation $\mathbf{a}^* := ([\mathbf{x}^*], [\mathbf{q}^*], \mathbf{p})$ in which the materials balance condition holds.

So there are two principal components to the definition of a competitive equilibrium: the price-taking maximising behaviour by each of the agents—households, firms—and the feasibility condition incorporated in the fundamental constraint (7.6). However, it is important to note that we still have no explanation of why people and firms should take the prices $\mathbf{p}^*$ parametrically nor of where these prices come from.

7.2.2 Incomes

But what about the incomes? Where are they derived from? Although there are many possibilities we shall consider one of the simplest—a private ownership economy in which income comes from two sources, thus:

household income	=	value of resources	+	share in the firms' profits

To make this work we need to specify R_i^h, the ownership by household h of resource stock i, and also ς_f^h, the proportionate share in firm f's profits to which h is entitled. Then we may express household income formally as:

$$y^h = \sum_{i=1}^{n} p_i R_i^h + \sum_{f=1}^{n_f} \varsigma_f^h \Pi^f \tag{7.8}$$

Compare this with Robinson Crusoe and his income: Crusoe's notional 'income' consisted of a valuation of all the resources on the island plus all of the surplus (profit) from the production activity. We may rewrite (7.8) as:[2]

$$y^h = \sum_{i=1}^{n} p_i \left[R_i^h + \sum\nolimits_{f=1}^{n_f} \varsigma_f^h q_i^f \right]. \tag{7.9}$$

So y^h is homogeneous of degree 1 in prices.

The distribution of property—in other words the distribution of the income-yielding assets—is given as:

$$\mathbf{d} := ([\mathbf{R}], [\varsigma]). \tag{7.10}$$

Example 7.1

The approach to 'incomes' here is rather like a modern system of national accounts. There is also an interesting precedent for this from medieval England: the Domesday Book. The Norman king William I ordered a comprehensive survey to take place in 1085–86, manor by manor. In each manor the reeve (farm manager) and six peasants were questioned; the answers were carefully checked and there were heavy punishments for false information. The survey questions included:

- How many ploughs are there in the manor?
- How many mills and fishponds?
- How many freemen, villagers, and slaves are there in the manor?
- How much woodland, pasture, meadow?
- What does each freeman owe in the manor?
- How much is the manor worth?

? Mini Problems

2 Show this using the definition of profits given in equation (7.3).

7.2.3 An illustration: the exchange economy

The essence of a competitive equilibrium can be conveniently illustrated in a model of an economy without production—an *exchange economy*. The elements of this simple economy are illustrated in Figures 7.1 and 7.2. The left-hand side of Figure 7.1 shows the solution to a conventional utility-maximisation problem for Alf:[3] Alf is endowed with a bundle of resources $\mathbf{R}^a$; given his preference map and the price line shown in the figure he chooses to trade so as to be able to consume at point $\mathbf{x}^a$. The right-hand side of Figure 7.1 shows a similar solution for Bill, rotated through 180°.[4]

Given that Alf and Bill face the same prices we can simply stick these two diagrams together to get the diagram in Figure 7.2—conventionally known as an *Edgeworth box*. The box shape in this figure is of length R_1 and height R_2.[5] The point in the box marked [**R**] is the *endowment point* representing the property distribution—the resource-vectors (R_1^a, R_2^a) and $\left(R_1^b, R_2^b\right)$ with which Alf and Bill are endowed before trading takes place. From our earlier argument concerning Figure 7.1 it is clear that the competitive equilibrium allocation is given by point [$\mathbf{x}^*$], and the equilibrium price ratio p_1/p_2 is given by the slope of the line joining the points [**R**] and [$\mathbf{x}^*$]; it is also clear that the competitive equilibrium depends crucially on the property distribution, captured in this case, by the endowment point [**R**].

Example 7.2

Some types of prisoner-of-war camp are appropriately modelled as a simple exchange economy. Radford (1945) discusses (from personal experience) the key elements of such an economy including the determination of equilibrium prices and allocations and the impact of changes in endowments.

To summarise, the economic system can be summarised schematically as

$$\mathbf{d} \to (\mathbf{a}^*, \mathbf{p}^*). \tag{7.11}$$

The 'rules of the game' which apply to this simple economic model are as follows:

- acceptance of **d**;
- price-taking behaviour by each of the participants.

Why is this set of rules appropriate?

? Mini Problems

3 Write down the budget constraint and first-order conditions for a maximum.

4 In the example as shown what trade takes place between Alf and Bill?

5 Explain why. What happens to the diagram if Alf suddenly receives a present of 10 more units of good 1? What happens if both Alf and Bill get 10 more units of good 1?

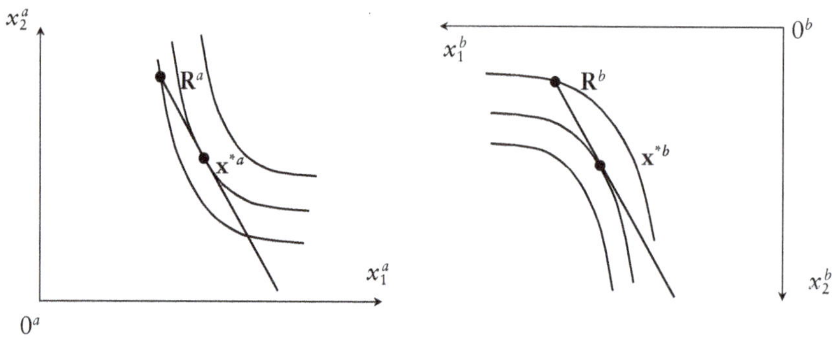

Figure 7.1 Utility-maximising choices for Alf and Bill

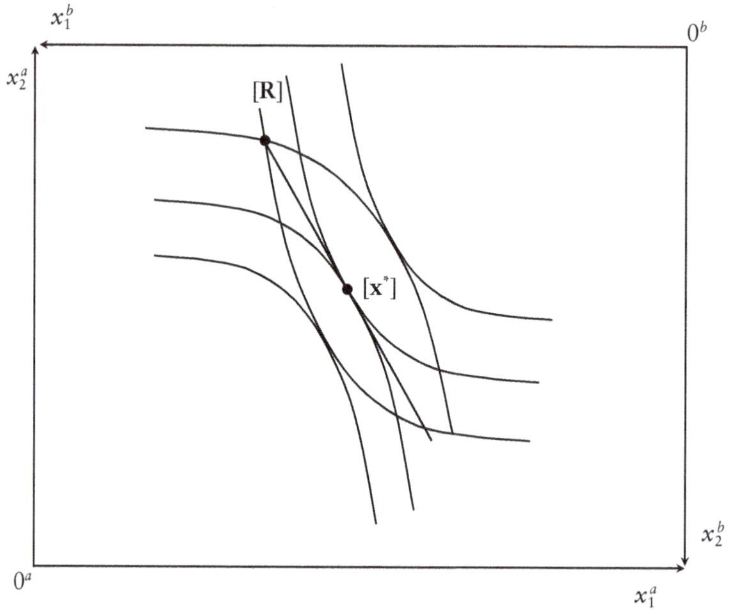

Figure 7.2 Competitive equilibrium: exchange economy

7.3 The logic of price taking

I do not think we can contribute much to the discussion of the first of these rules in the present context. However, we can say something about the second. What we will do is use a simplified model of the economy in order to characterise a very general concept of equilibrium trades.

Suppose we are in an *exchange economy* where there is no production and all income is derived from the endowment of resources. You can think of an exchange economy as

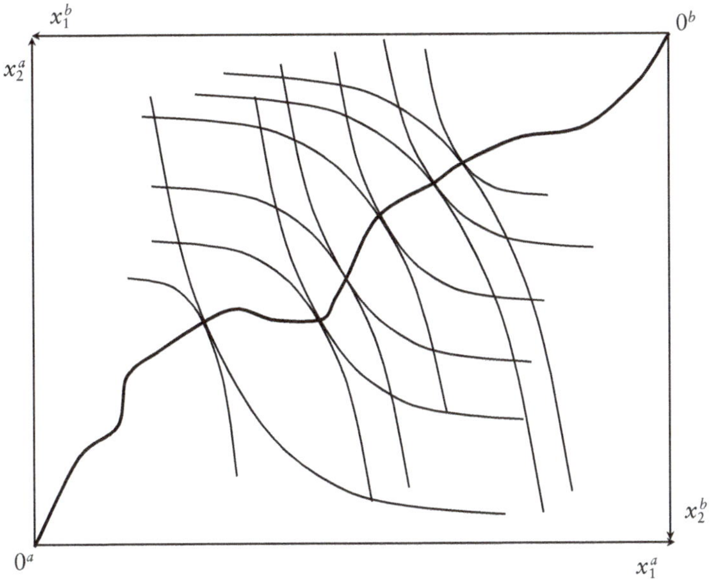

Figure 7.3 The contract curve

the prisoner-of-war camp in the example above where the inmates get a regular endowment of food parcels and may wish to trade the contents of the parcels with each other. In this case $\mathbf{d} = [\mathbf{R}]$: the property distribution is just the initial distribution of parcels in the camp. This is illustrated in Figure 7.3, which is derived from Figure 7.2. The path joining the two origins 0^a and 0^b is the locus of points where an a-indifference curve is tangential to a b-indifference curve. This path—usually known as the so-called *contract curve*—has considerable attraction because it is the key to the general solution concept that we seek.

To see this let us consider the set of allocations that could emerge as a potential solution in such an economy assuming that the agents (households or individuals) have perfect information and tell the truth.[6] We allow all sorts of negotiation amongst them that respects their personal property rights—nobody is compelled to trade and nobody is able to steal other people's resources. Given that all agents are well informed and self-interested we can assume that they will not be prepared to agree to allocations that they know they could improve on, either by themselves or in cooperation with others in the economy. This idea is made formal using the following two definitions:

Definition 7.4

A *coalition* is a non-empty subset K of the set of households $\{1, 2, \ldots, n_h\}$.

? Mini Problems

6 What might happen to all this if people had imperfect information, or if they were to lie?

Definition 7.5

A coalition K *blocks* an allocation $[\hat{\mathbf{x}}]$ if there exists a set of consumption vectors $\{\mathbf{x}^h : h \in K\}$ such that, for every h in K:

$$U^h(\mathbf{x}^h) \geq U^h(\hat{\mathbf{x}}^h) \tag{7.12}$$

with strict inequality for at least one h, and

$$\sum_{h \in K} \mathbf{x}^h \leq \sum_{h \in K} \mathbf{R}^h. \tag{7.13}$$

The idea of blocking yields the solution concept to the problem of exchange in an economy of truthful agents. It is simply this:

Definition 7.6

The *core* is the set of unblocked feasible allocations given the preferences $(U^1, U^2, \ldots)$ for the n_h households and the property distribution $\mathbf{d}$.

7.3.1 The core of the exchange economy

Let us have a look at the core in Figure 7.4 in which again we have just the two agents called Alf and Bill. There are three coalitions that could be formed {Alf}, {Bill}, and

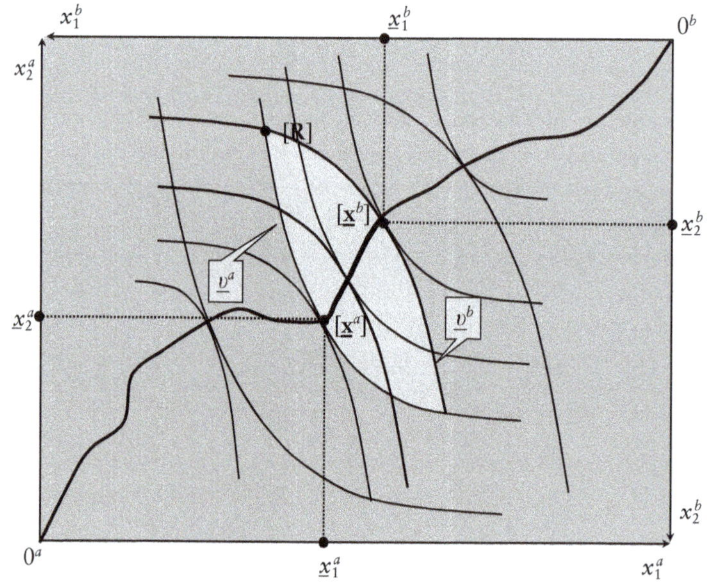

Figure 7.4 The core in the two-person case

{Alf, Bill}. The way the diagram works in the analysis is largely determined by the location of the endowment point [**R**].

Let the utility level for Alf at point [**R**] be $\underline{\upsilon}^a$: this is his *reservation utility*, since he can always guarantee it for himself by just refusing to trade; the same thing can be said about the Bill indifference curve labelled $\underline{\upsilon}^b$ that passes through [**R**]. So it is clear that one or other of the two agents would form a 1-person coalition to block any proposed allocation that fell outside the lens-shaped area in Figure 7.4 bounded by $\underline{\upsilon}^a$ and $\underline{\upsilon}^b$. Moreover, we can see that, working together, they would block any point that does not lie on the contract curve,[7] the locus of common tangencies. The core is therefore the little segment of the curve along joining $[\underline{\mathbf{x}}^a]$ and $\left[\underline{\mathbf{x}}^b\right]$—including the endpoints—that consists entirely of points of common tangencies.

As with the discussion of the competitive equilibrium in section 7.2.3 we should note the dependence of the core on the property distribution, again given by the endowment point [**R**].

7.3.2 Competitive equilibrium and the core: small economy

The core is a basic solution concept and of considerable interest in its own right. However, it is particularly interesting to see how this concept relates to other approaches to the general equilibrium problem. The following result (proof in Appendix C) in particular is very useful:[8]

Theorem 7.1 (Competitive equilibrium and the core)

If no consumer has a bliss point, any competitive equilibrium allocation must always be in the core.

Theorem 7.1 is quite powerful. For example, it is not restricted to cases where there is just one competitive equilibrium in the economy. It could indeed happen that in a certain economy there are multiple competitive equilibria: the theorem establishes that all of them must lie in the core. Figure 7.5 illustrates this: both [**x***] and [**x****] are competitive equilibrium allocations each with its own set of equilibrium prices. To see this check first the allocation [**x***]: the straight line that passes through [**R**] and [**x***] plays the rôle of a budget constraint for both Alf and Bill; given this budget constraint both parties maximise utility at point [**x***]. But all of this is also true of the allocation [**x****]: it involves a different budget constraint corresponding to different relative prices, of course, but at those prices [**x****] is also a utility-maximising allocation.[9]

? Mini Problems

7 Show this by considering a point that is off the contract curve and showing graphically how they could find an allocation that would make at least one of them better off, without reducing the utility of the other.

8 In a two-person economy describe the competitive equilibrium in terms of the offer curve for each trader. Use this to provide an intuitive argument for Theorem 7.1.

9 Draw in the offer curves in the case of multiple equilibria (Cf. Mini Problem 8).

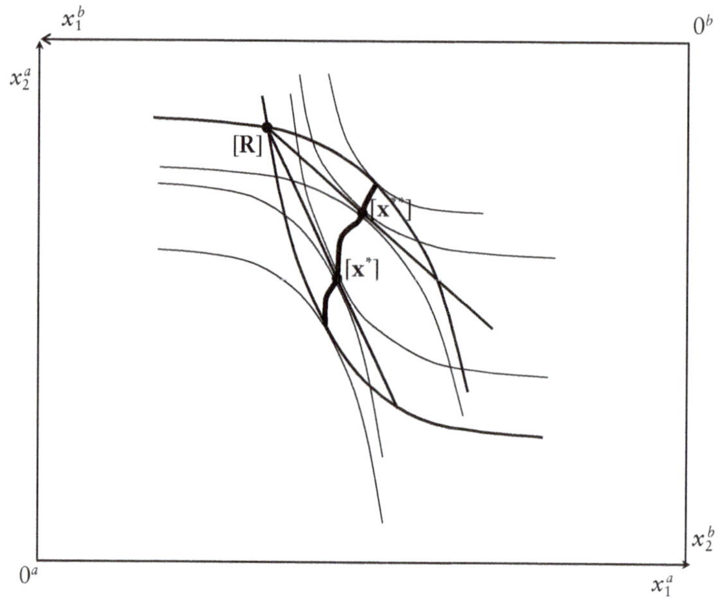

Figure 7.5 Any CE must lie in the core

Even in the multiple-equilibrium case depicted in Figure 7.5 it is clear that the set of equilibrium allocations is rather sparse: there are lots of allocations in the core other than the competitive equilibria. But are these other allocations relevant as solutions to the trading problem?

7.3.3 Competitive equilibrium and the core: large economy

The answer to this question depends on whether we take the Alf and Bill story as literally a two-person economy or as a parable for an economy with many agents. If it is a parable then many of the core allocations in the two-person story may turn out to be irrelevant in a large economy.

To see why let us suppose that the economy is *replicated*. We mean by this that we take one or more identical copies of the agents and their endowments: note that this is a rather narrowly defined way of proceeding from the two-person paradigm to a large economy. So, in the replication economy Alf is now joined by his twin brother Arthur; Bill is accompanied by his brother Ben. The Alf-and-Arthur twins have the same utility functions and the same resources. The same goes for Bill and Ben. The immediate consequence of this is that there are likely to be more possibilities of forming coalitions: all the old coalitions in the two-person model are still available, plus some new ones. This suggests that the core may not contain as many allocations as before because the new coalitions may now be able to block some of them.

This is in fact just what happens. Consider whether a point such as $[\underline{\mathbf{x}}^a]$ in Figure 7.4 is still a valid solution for the Alf-Arthur-Bill-Ben economy; could it still be in the core?

Some elementary reasoning shows that an allocation that places both sets of twins at this point must surely be blocked.

To show this note first that the consumption bundle of one of the b-twins at point $[\underline{\mathbf{x}}^a]$ would be given by

$$\overline{\mathbf{x}}^b := \mathbf{R}^b + \mathbf{R}^a - \underline{\mathbf{x}}^a \tag{7.14}$$

where, of course, $\underline{\mathbf{x}}^a$ is the consumption bundle of one of the a-twins at point $[\underline{\mathbf{x}}^a]$. Next let us write down what the consumption bundle of one of the a-twins would be if he were located at a point exactly halfway between $[\mathbf{R}]$ and $[\underline{\mathbf{x}}^a]$; it is

$$\hat{\mathbf{x}}^a := \frac{1}{2}\left[\mathbf{R}^a + \underline{\mathbf{x}}^a\right]. \tag{7.15}$$

So, imagine a coalition of Alf, Arthur, and Bill with associated consumption bundles as set out in the top half of Table 7.1 (poor old Ben gets left out of the coalition and so just has to consume his original endowment).

Examining this proposed allocation we find that the resources required to satisfy the consumption vectors of members of the coalition amount exactly to the combined endowments of Alf, Arthur, and Bill.[10] Furthermore, if we look at the situation diagrammatically in Figure 7.6, it is clear that by ensuring that the a-twins can consume at $\hat{\mathbf{x}}^a$ given by (7.15) they are placed on a strictly higher indifference curve than if they had been forced to consume $\underline{\mathbf{x}}^a$ (look at the point marked '$\circ$'). So the allocation proposed by the coalition is feasible *and* Alf and Arthur prefer it. Therefore it is clear that the allocation given by the bundles in Table 7.1 blocks $[\underline{\mathbf{x}}^a]$.[11]

The significance of this exercise is that an allocation that had been in the core of the original two-person economy is blocked in the four-person economy: the core must have shrunk in the replication process.[12]

It is important to note that it is not just the 'extreme' allocations that are knocked out of the core by the replication process taking us from the Alf-Bill economy to the

THE COALITION		
Alf	$\hat{\mathbf{x}}^a$	(7.15)
Arthur	$\hat{\mathbf{x}}^a$	(7.15)
Bill	$\overline{\mathbf{x}}^b$	(7.14)
(OUT OF COALITION)		
Ben	$\mathbf{R}^b$	

Table 7.1 Alf, Arthur, and Bill cut Ben out of the coalition

? Mini Problems

10 Use the information in Table 7.1 to check this.

11 The allocation in Table 7.1 is not in the core of the four-person economy either—can you see why?

12 What might happen in this process if the replication were carried out in an unbalanced way?

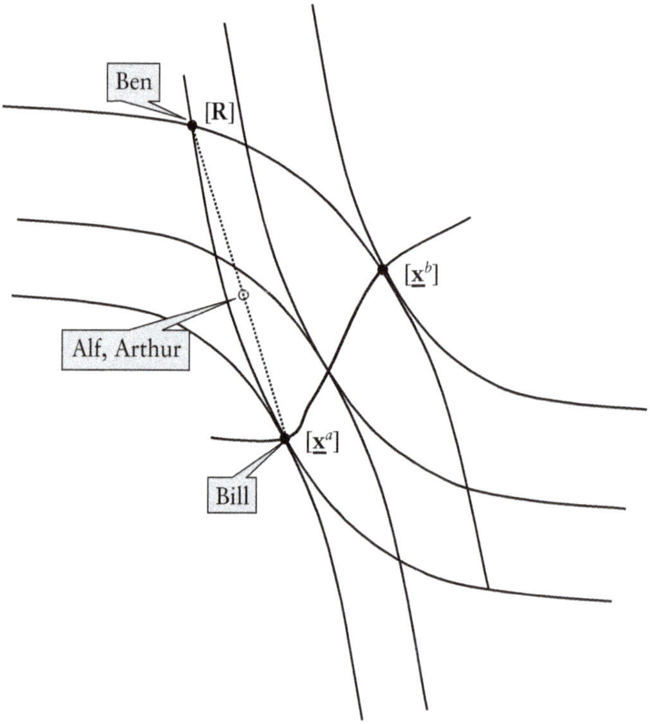

Figure 7.6 An allocation that blocks $[\underline{\mathbf{x}}^a]$

Alf-Arthur-Bill-Ben economy. Let $[\tilde{\mathbf{x}}]$ represent any point on the little bit of the contract curve joining $[\underline{\mathbf{x}}^a]$ and $[\underline{\mathbf{x}}^b]$ in Figure 7.6 that is *not* a competitive equilibrium; this assumption means that the tangent to the two indifference curves at $[\tilde{\mathbf{x}}]$ does not pass through $[\underline{\mathbf{R}}]$. Look again at the way in which we constructed the example to show that point $[\underline{\mathbf{x}}^a]$ was no longer in the core; the presence of two representatives of each type of agent enabled us to consider a consumption vector that split in half the line from $[\underline{\mathbf{R}}]$ to $[\underline{\mathbf{x}}^a]$. It is clear that we could have done the same kind of thing with many of these other points $[\tilde{\mathbf{x}}]$ that would have belonged to the two-person core—i.e. we could have split the line from $[\underline{\mathbf{R}}]$ to $[\tilde{\mathbf{x}}]$ and found a point that makes the *a*-twins better off than they would have been at $[\tilde{\mathbf{x}}]$. But we can be more specific than this vague assertion.

Suppose now that we replicate the economy *N*-fold: there are *N* persons in the Alf tribe and *N* persons in the Bill tribe, and all the members of the same tribe have identical preferences and identical endowments. If *N* were 4, let us say, then coalitions could be formed that will not just split the line from $[\underline{\mathbf{R}}]$ to $[\tilde{\mathbf{x}}]$ in the proportion $\frac{1}{2} : \frac{1}{2}$ (as in Figure 7.6) but also in the proportions $\frac{1}{4} : \frac{3}{4}$, for example; and if *N* were to be very large, coalitions could be formed that could secure for members of the Alf tribe any arbitrary point on this line. By this method we can show that in a sufficiently large economy any point $[\tilde{\mathbf{x}}]$ as defined in the previous paragraph must be blocked by some coalition.[13]

The implication of this is that as $N \to \infty$ with balanced replication all allocations that are not competitive equilibria are eliminated from the set of possible solutions: in the limit the core is reduced to the set of competitive equilibria. In other words, under carefully specified conditions, large numbers suggest that only price-taking behaviour survives in equilibrium.[14]

7.4 The excess-demand approach

Let us recall the two major elements of our discussion of general equilibrium so far :

- The combination of a market allocation and the materials balance condition yields what we have called a *competitive equilibrium* (section 7.2.1).
- Price taking is the limiting behaviour of rational economic agents in the context of a 'core' equilibrium (section 7.3.3).

Using these two elements we can represent the issues concerning general equilibrium in terms of a very convenient economic device. We introduce the *excess demand function*, for each commodity *i*. The excess demand function encodes the information about aggregate demand and aggregate supply for a particular good at some given set of market prices; it is defined as a function $E_i(\cdot)$ such that:[15]

$$E_i(\mathbf{p}) := x_i(\mathbf{p}) - q_i(\mathbf{p}) - R_i. \tag{7.16}$$

The derivation of the excess demand function can be illustrated as follows.

First, we need to derive the aggregate demand for each commodity as a function of prices $\mathbf{p}$: Figure 5.7 in chapter 5 shows the idea of how it is done in a two-person economy for $x_1(\cdot)$, the demand for commodity 1. We then do a similar exercise for the net output of each commodity by aggregating firms' supply curves to get $q_1(\cdot)$ (illustrated for the two-firm case in Figures 3.1 or 3.2 in chapter 3). Finally we subtract the net output and resource stocks of each commodity from the demand, as shown in Figure 7.7, which summarises the relationship between market demand from consumers, net output from firms, resource stocks and excess demand in the case of commodity 1.

? Mini Problems

13 Assuming that N is very large use a geometrical argument—similar to that in Figure 7.6 to show the composition of a coalition that could be formed to block such an allocation $[\tilde{\mathbf{x}}]$.

14 It is sometimes argued that in practice in economies with large numbers of individuals this blocking process does not appear to work automatically, so that some can deviate from price-taking behaviour. Why might this be so?

15 Briefly explain the relationship between the excess demand function in an exchange economy and households' offer curves.

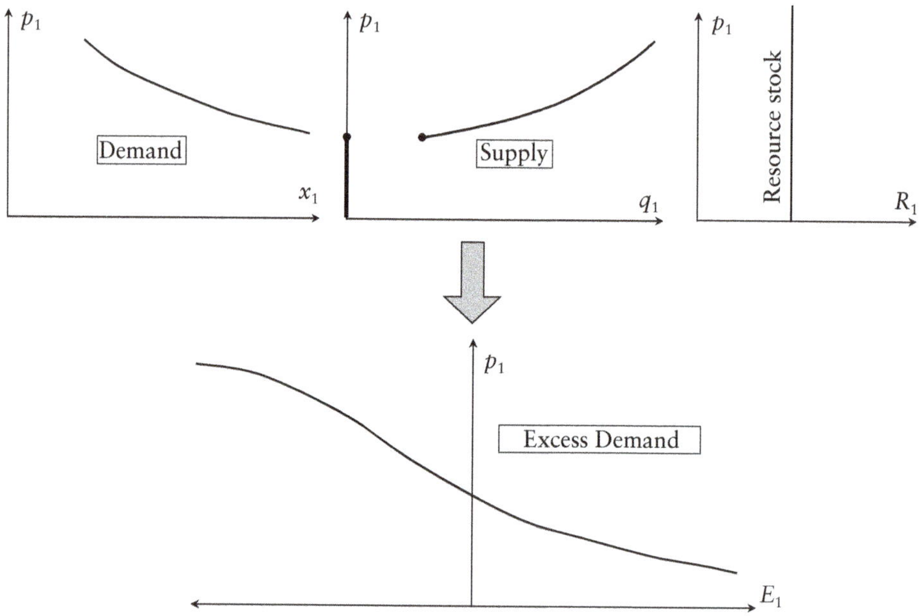

Figure 7.7 Construction of excess demand curve

We may then write the conditions for equilibrium in terms of the excess demand functions. An equilibrium price vector $\mathbf{p}^*$ must satisfy the following conditions:

$$\left.\begin{array}{r} E_i(\mathbf{p}^*) \leq 0, \\ p_i^* \geq 0, \\ p_i^* E_i(\mathbf{p}^*) = 0 \end{array}\right\} \tag{7.17}$$

for each commodity $i = 1, \ldots, n$. The three statements in (7.17) mean that, in equilibrium, there cannot be excess demand—that would violate materials balance—and any good for which there is excess supply must be a free good.[16]

The excess demand function will prove to be an effective tool for understanding some of the basic issues in determining and characterising a competitive equilibrium. This is pursued below; before doing that we need to examine the properties of the system of excess demand functions.

7.4.1 Properties of the excess demand function

Inherent in any system of excess demand functions, $\mathbf{E} = (E_1, \ldots, E_n)$, are a couple of features that are fundamental to the way a competitive market system works and that make computation of the equilibrium much easier. They are summarised in the following two

? Mini Problems

16 Explain in words the circumstances under which you could have excess supply of some commodity in equilibrium.

results that follow directly from the properties of firms' and consumers' response functions (chapters 2 and 4) and that are really only a reinterpretation of results that we have already established.

Theorem 7.2 (Homogeneity of excess-demand functions)

Each excess-demand function must be homogeneous of degree zero.[17]

Theorem 7.3 (Walras's law)

For any price vector $\mathbf{p}$ and fully informed, rational, non-satiated agents in a private-ownership economy, the set of n excess demand functions must satisfy[18]

$$\sum_{i=1}^{n} p_i E_i(\mathbf{p}) = 0 \tag{7.18}$$

It is, perhaps, worth labouring the point that these two properties are generally true in a world of price-taking optimisers: they hold for all configurations of preferences and production functions, not just well-behaved ones; they hold for all price vectors, not just at equilibrium. Let us look more closely at their implications.

Homogeneity of degree zero

This property means that we can normalise the prices arbitrarily. There are lots of ways in which this normalisation could be done, but let us briefly consider two alternative methods that one often finds in actual applications.

We could measure everything in terms of a *numéraire* good, let us say good n. Then, if the non-normalised prices were given by the vector $\widehat{\mathbf{p}}$, we would find that normalised prices under this normalisation method were given by

$$\left.\begin{array}{lcl} p_i & = & \dfrac{\hat{p}_1}{\hat{p}_n} \\ p_2 & = & \dfrac{\hat{p}_2}{\hat{p}_n}, \\ \dots & & \dots \\ p_{n-1} & = & \dfrac{\hat{p}_{n-1}}{\hat{p}_n} \\ p_n & = & 1. \end{array}\right\} \tag{7.19}$$

Alternatively we could write the prices in such a way that they sum to 1. Again writing non-normalised prices as the vector $\widehat{\mathbf{p}}$, we find that this second method would yield the

? Mini Problems

17 Explain why. Prove it using the results on the firm's demand and supply functions and the consumer's demand functions.

18 Prove this law, using the facts that (a) for each household income equals expenditure, and that (b) each household's income is derived from the resources it owns and its shares in the firms' profits. [Hint: Check equations (2.69) and (4.13).]

following set of normalised prices:

$$\left.\begin{array}{lcl} p_1 & = & \dfrac{\hat{p}_1}{\hat{p}_1+\hat{p}_2+\cdots+\hat{p}_n}, \\ p_2 & = & \dfrac{\hat{p}_2}{\hat{p}_1+\hat{p}_2+\cdots+\hat{p}_n}, \\ \ldots & & \ldots \\ p_n & = & \dfrac{\hat{p}_n}{\hat{p}_1+\hat{p}_2+\cdots+\hat{p}_n}. \end{array}\right\} \quad (7.20)$$

This procedure might seem a bit odd, but in fact it sometimes proves to be a very convenient device. The reason that it is so convenient is that it ensures that every normalised price must lie between zero and one inclusive. Furthermore, if we consider the set J of all possible normalised prices

$$J := \left\{\mathbf{p} : \mathbf{p} \geq 0; \sum_{i=1}^{n} p_i = 1\right\} \quad (7.21)$$

it can be shown that is convex and compact (see page A.6 in Appendix A)—properties that are handy for some results that we will come to in a moment.

Example 7.3

Take a two-good economy with non-normalised prices $\widehat{p}_1, \widehat{p}_2$. Using the normalisation scheme in (7.20) yields normalised prices $p_1 = \widehat{p}_1/[\widehat{p}_1 + \widehat{p}_2]$, $p_2 = 1 - p_1$. Figure 7.8 depicts the set J and illustrates the normalised price vector $\mathbf{p} = (0.75, 0.25)$.[19]

Walras's Law

This property of excess demand functions means that there is a linear restriction on the system of n demand functions. In particular, if you know $E_1, \ldots, E_{n-1}$ you can find E_n from the following formula:

$$E_n(\mathbf{p}) = -\frac{1}{p_n} \sum_{i=1}^{n-1} p_i E_i(\mathbf{p}). \quad (7.22)$$

Hence, although there are n commodities—and thus n prices and n excess demands—the two restrictions that we have discussed imply that when we solve the system (7.17) we have, in effect, only $n-1$ equations in $n-1$ unknowns. In simple models this can be a great advantage. If, say, we had an economy where $n = 3$, then this means that to find the equilibrium price vector we effectively have a system of two simultaneous equations in two unknowns, that can probably be solved explicitly by hand, instead of a cumbersome 3×3 system.

? Mini Problems

19 Draw the set J for the case $n = 3$ and depict the normalised prices $\mathbf{p} = (0.5, 0.25, 0.25)$.

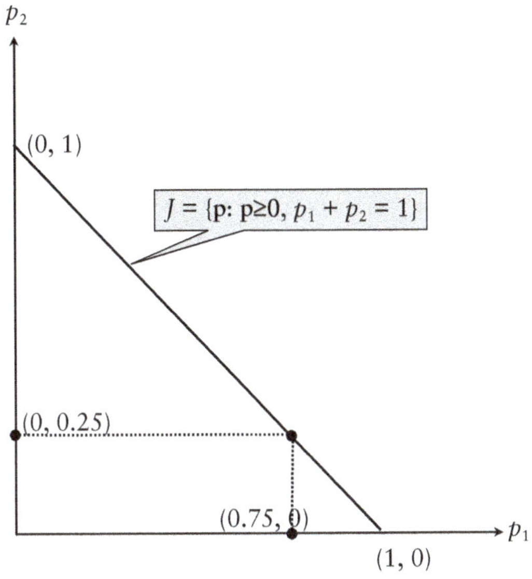

Figure 7.8 Normalised prices, $n = 2$

Now that we have a clearer idea of how the system of excess demand functions E makes the representation of the competitive system easier by encapsulating information about the responses of the mass of individual economic agents, we can investigate a number of fundamental issues about equilibrium. We shall address three principal questions:

- the conditions for the *existence* of a solution (7.17)—in section 7.4.2;
- the *uniqueness* or otherwise of the solution (7.17)—in section 7.4.3;
- the *stability* of equilibrium—in section 7.4.4.

7.4.2 **Existence**

An idealised 'well-behaved' case is illustrated in Figure 7.9: there is a specific value p_1^* of the price of commodity 1 such that the excess demand for commodity 1 is exactly zero and, by (7.22) we know that the excess demand for commodity 2 must be zero at this point as well. However, this neat solution begs a number of questions that we will examine over the next few pages.

The most basic question that we need to address is whether, in general, the general-equilibrium system has a solution at all: in other words, can we be sure that for some specific set of excess demand functions **E** there is going to be any vector **p*** such that (7.17) holds? To convince ourselves that this question is not vacuous, let us look at a couple of examples in a two-commodity model.

The properties of boundedness and continuity are evidently important. If there are discontinuities in the excess demand function, then we might find that excess demand jumps from negative to positive without ever being 0: look at the gap that straddles the p_1 axis in Figure 7.10. If excess demand for some good is unbounded below then you might be

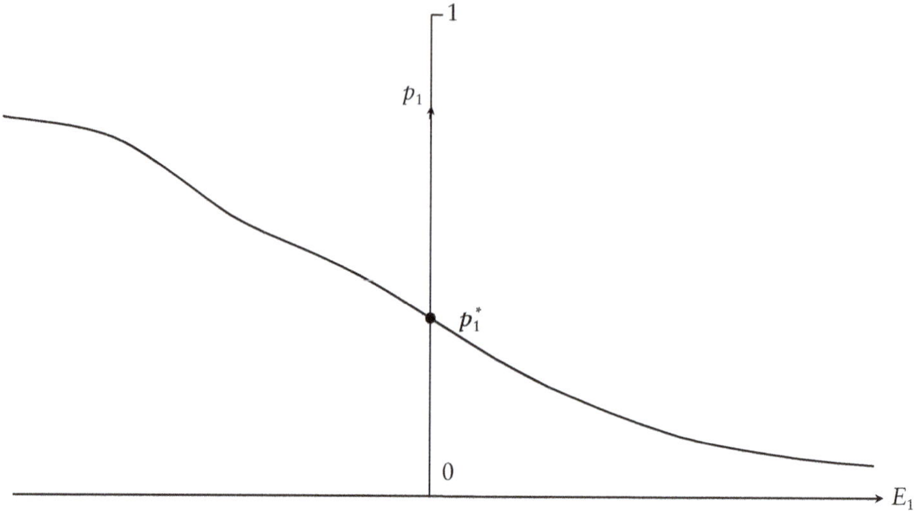

Figure 7.9 Existence of a unique equilibrium price

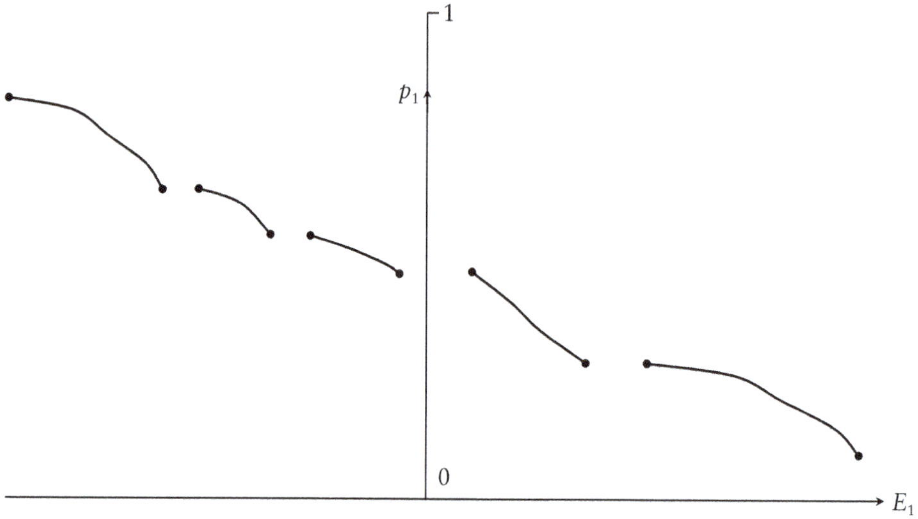

Figure 7.10 Discontinuous excess demand

able to go on increasing the price of the other good indefinitely without reaching an equilibrium—see Figure 7.11.[20]

Boundedness is not terribly worrying: all that you need is a requirement that there could not be infinite aggregate supply of any one commodity. However, continuity may

? Mini Problems

20 Show that in Figure 7.11 excess supplies of some of the other goods must be infinite.

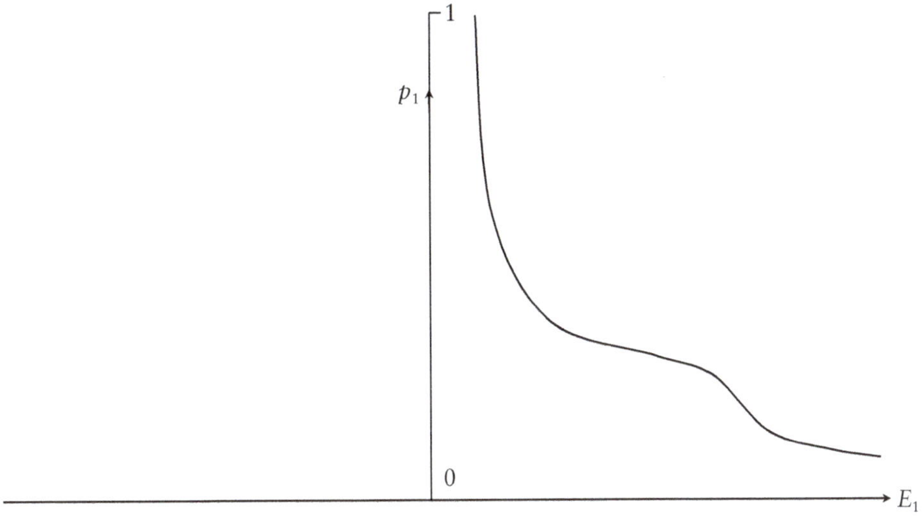

Figure 7.11 Excess demand for good 2 unbounded below

present greater difficulties—we have already seen instances where apparently standard assumptions about the structure of firms' costs can lead to discontinuous supply functions.

The following result (proved in Appendix C) formalises our discussion of Figures 7.9 to 7.11.

Theorem 7.4 (Existence of competitive equilibrium)

If each $E_i(\cdot)$ is a continuous function from J to the real line and is bounded below, then there exists $\mathbf{p}^* \in J$ which is an equilibrium price vector.

A sufficient condition to ensure continuity of each E_i is that each production function Φ^f be strictly concave (strict convexity of the technology set), and each utility function U^h be strictly quasiconcave. In fact these requirements are considerably stronger than necessary. One can establish the existence of equilibrium using only concavity of each production function and quasiconcavity (rather than the 'strict' concavity). But a general proof of an existence result is technically quite demanding.

7.4.3 **Uniqueness**

We have already seen that even in a pure exchange economy there could be more than one equilibrium: this was illustrated in the Edgeworth box diagram of Figure 7.5. The pattern of indifference curves and endowments that permits this multiplicity of equilibria produces some rather 'twisty' offer curves (if you have not done so yet, checking the answer to Mini Problem 9 could be helpful here) and a set of excess demand curves that have several turning points: see Figure 7.12.

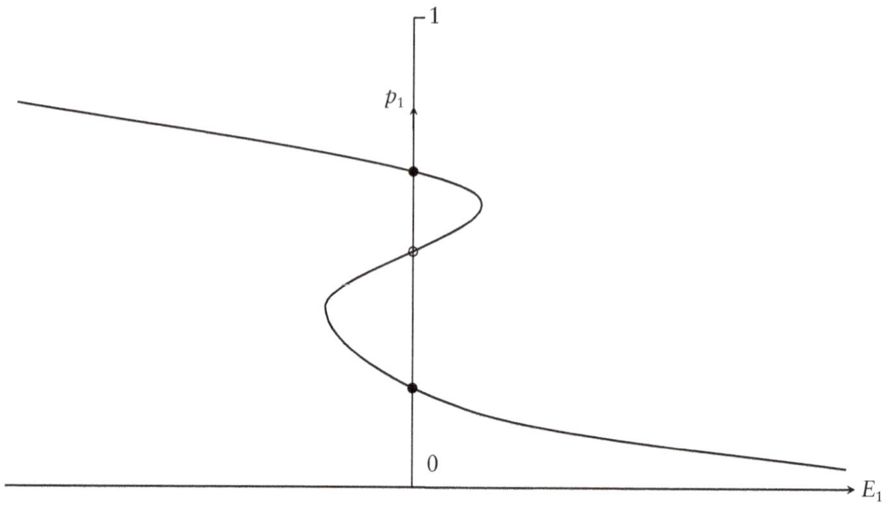

Figure 7.12 Multiple equilibria

We might wonder what condition on the functions E could avoid this. Basically we need well-behaved demand and supply curves that do not slope the 'wrong way', so that we do not find multiple intersections in Figure 7.12, for example. But why might demand curves (in the aggregate) slope the 'wrong way'? The main problem is the presence of income effects, as we have already seen in the discussion of the aggregation of the market behaviour of consumers in chapter 5. If Alf and Bill have very different income effects, then as different price vectors are tried out the changes in incomes could lead to perverse switches in demand in the aggregate.

What conditions in the economic system could ensure that situations do not arise? The clue lies in our earlier discussion of Figure 5.9 (page 118): we noted there that the apparent oddity that arose when Alf's and Bill's demands were aggregated was that, although their individual behaviour was rational and consistent, jointly it did not satisfy the minimal requirement of the Weak Axiom of Revealed Preference; so, could this violation of WARP be key to understanding the odd things that seem to be going on in the case of multiple competitive equilibria? This insight is summarised in the following theorem (proved in Appendix C):

Theorem 7.5 (Uniqueness of competitive equilibrium)

If $\mathbf{p}^*$ is a normalised equilibrium price vector in a private ownership economy and if aggregate consumer demands satisfy the Weak Axiom of Revealed Preference with reference to $\mathbf{p}^*$, then $\mathbf{p}^*$ must be unique.

It is interesting to note that WARP, a principle that might have appeared as blindingly obvious for an individual, plays a subtle and important rôle in characterising the regularity conditions needed for the mass of consumers to act in a way that makes competitive equilibrium 'well behaved'.[21]

7.4.4 Stability

In order to make precise the problem of specifying what stability of the system means and the conditions under which it might be achieved, we need some explicit story of dynamics—a process through time—something that we have in general shied away from.

Our first step is to introduce an artificial device. Suppose there is an 'auctioneer' who adjusts prices. This is not one of the ordinary economic agents of our model, but a disembodied institution that manipulates the vector $\mathbf{p}$ in response to market conditions. A reasonable sort of rule might be that, if there is currently excess demand for commodity i, then the auctioneer ought to put p_i up a bit; if there is excess supply ($E_i < 0$) then, if the price is not already zero, it ought to come down a bit—see Figures 7.13 and 7.14. We could formalise this general idea in the following specific process:

Definition 7.7

the economy follows a *linear tâtonnement process* if

$$\frac{dp_i(t)}{dt} = \left\{ \begin{array}{l} a_i E_i\left(\mathbf{p}(t)\right) \text{ if } p_i(t) \geq 0 \\ \\ 0 \text{ otherwise} \end{array} \right\} \tag{7.23}$$

$i = 1, \ldots, n$, where a_i is some positive scalar.

Tâtonnement processes—linear or non-linear—are very convenient analytical simplifications, but are rather strange in terms of their economic interpretation. The process described in (7.23) implies that if there is positive excess demand for a good then that good's price rises, and vice versa. But the functions E_i are defined relative to a given distribution $\mathbf{d}$, so that the price-adjustment rule above implicitly assumes that $\mathbf{d}$ does not change during the process. Obviously once people do trade, these resource endowments for the 'next period' will change; so the *tâtonnement* process effectively assumes that no trading occurs before equilibrium is reached. In many cases this is a manifestly absurd assumption. However, let us see how the system adjusts under this simple-minded process where, for convenience we shall take $a_i = 1$ for all i.

To do this let us introduce a notion of 'distance' of prices at any time t from equilibrium prices; this may be defined as

$$\Delta(t) := \sqrt{\sum_{i=1}^{n} \left[p_i(t) - p_i^*\right]^2} \tag{7.24}$$

? Mini Problems

21 You might think that the phenomenon of multiple equilibria is just a technicality; but it could have important policy implications. What might happen in a situation such as Figure 7.12 if one were to try to influence the equilibrium incomes of poor agricultural producers by changing resource endowments?

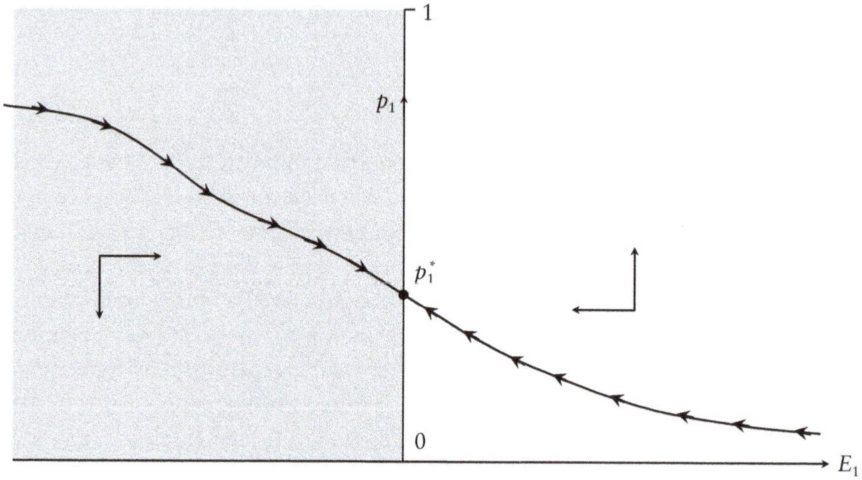

Figure 7.13 Global stability

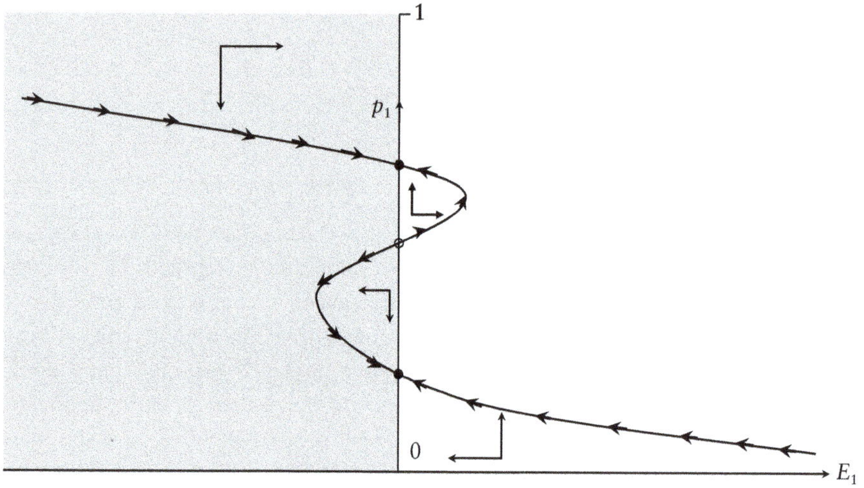

Figure 7.14 Local instability

To examine the issue of stability, we need to examine how this distance changes as time goes by. Differentiate (7.24) with respect to time; then using the definition of the *tâtonnement* process we get[22]

$$\frac{d\Delta(t)}{dt} = -\frac{1}{\Delta(t)} \sum_{i=1}^{n} p_i^* E_i\left(\mathbf{p}(t)\right). \tag{7.25}$$

? Mini Problems

22 Establish this result by squaring (7.24), differentiating and then using Walras's Law.

However, if aggregate consumption demands $\mathbf{x}(\mathbf{p})$ obey the Weak Axiom of Revealed Preference with reference to $\mathbf{p}^*$, so also do the excess demand functions $\mathbf{E}(\mathbf{p})$.[23] The Weak Axiom of Revealed Preference implies

$$\sum_{i=1}^{n} p_i^* E_i(\mathbf{p}^*) < \sum_{i=1}^{n} p_i^* E_i(\mathbf{p}(t)). \tag{7.26}$$

But the left-hand side of (7.26) is zero, because of Walras's Law. From this result we can see that the right-hand side of equation (7.25) must be negative. This means that the distance to equilibrium always decreases over time. So we may conclude that the system is stable.[24]

These three topics in the excess-demand approach have enabled us to focus on the key issues in the determination of an equilibrium price vector. We now need to use the information derived from this analysis to complete the characterisation of general equilibrium.

Example 7.4

General-equilibrium analysis is a valuable theoretical tool. But it also has fruitful practical applications.

- Most modern macroeconomic models are general-equilibrium models.
- A further important offshoot is that of *Computable General Equilibrium* modelling. This enables the policy analyst to construct large-scale quantitative models, typically on large-scale questions. For example they can be used to investigate the implications of economic reform for an economy in transition. An example of this for the case of China is provided by Zhang (1998) who explicitly allows for the divergence between plan prices and market prices that characterise the transition process.

7.5 The rôle of prices

In section 7.2 we summarised the underlying story of the competitive equilibrium system as a mapping from the distribution of resources and share ownership to a special allocation of goods and production activities in the economy (7.11). We have now seen two key steps in the explanation of that mapping:

? Mini Problems

23 Show this using the definition of WARP (Axiom 4.2 on page 72) and the definition of profit maximisation.

24 What might happen if people were to sell things along the way?

- *A rationale for the price-taking paradigm.* The results on the core in section 7.3 clarify why it makes sense to assume that self-interested consumers act as price takers in a large economy. If everyone does act as a price taker then an important component of the fundamental mapping is that the property distribution and the price system determine desired consumptions and outputs through the demand and supply functions

$$(\mathbf{d},\mathbf{p}) \rightarrow \left[\mathbf{x}^1(\mathbf{p}),\mathbf{x}^2(\mathbf{p}),\ldots\right] \tag{7.27}$$

$$\mathbf{p} \rightarrow \left[\mathbf{q}^1(\mathbf{p}),\mathbf{q}^2(\mathbf{p}),\ldots\right]. \tag{7.28}$$

- *A tool for analysing the properties of equilibrium price vectors.* The system of excess demands discussed in section 7.4 encapsulates all the information about the price-taking responses by aggregating the two relationships (7.27, 7.28) over all the agents. This simplifies (7.27) and (7.28) to

$$(\mathbf{d},\mathbf{p}) \rightarrow \mathbf{E}(\mathbf{p}) \tag{7.29}$$

  We now know that under (perhaps?) reasonable conditions the excess-demand system (7.17) will yield a unique equilibrium price-vector $\mathbf{p}^*$.

It is clear that the rôle of prices is central to each of these steps in the argument. There remain for us two important tasks that exploit this central rôle. First, we need to use these two steps to complete the characterisation of a general competitive equilibrium. Second, we need to re-examine the decentralisation function of prices that we discussed in chapter 6, taking into account that, by contrast to the chapter 6 model, we are now in a large-numbers economy.

7.5.1 The equilibrium allocation

The solution to the excess-demand system discussed in section 7.4 gives us a specific set of normalised prices; we can notionally represent this as

$$(7.17) \rightarrow \mathbf{p}^*. \tag{7.30}$$

Given (7.30) we can then take the final step in the mapping from the property distribution to the equilibrium allocation. This is simply to plug the $\mathbf{p}^*$ that emerges from (7.30) into the response functions (7.27) and (7.28). What is going on here is that each household or firm in the economy freely chooses the appropriate consumption bundle or collection of net outputs at the equilibrium prices: it is the result of their acting as optimising economic agents. We can summarise this as 'equilibrium prices determine the allocation':

$$\mathbf{p}^* \rightarrow \mathbf{a}^*. \tag{7.31}$$

Putting together the three bits of the story (7.29)–(7.31) we then have a complete account of the fundamental mapping $\mathbf{d} \rightarrow \mathbf{a}^*$.

As a final remark here, let us not overlook the fact that associated with the distribution of bundles of goods in the allocation $\mathbf{a}^*$ there is also a distribution of utilities. The general equilibrium determines how well off each person is. This is something that ought to be of interest to anyone concerned with how economies work. The issue will be pursued in chapter 9.

7.5.2 Decentralisation again

There is another important interpretation of the rôle of prices that we can see just by borrowing material from the Crusoe model (chapter 6). This is the decentralisation result, the essence of which is depicted in Figure 7.15: this figure is obviously very similar to Figure 6.10 used for the decentralisation result in the Robinson Crusoe economy, but there are two small differences.

The first difference is that we are now talking about real market prices, not shadow prices as in the discussion of Figure 6.10. The hyperplane defined by the equilibrium price vector $\mathbf{p}^*$ is depicted as the straight line in Figure 7.15. In the figure this line is seen to pass between two sets marked A and B: again these are the *attainable set* of consumptions, A, given by

$$\{\mathbf{x} : \mathbf{x} \leq \mathbf{q} + \mathbf{R}, \Phi(\mathbf{q}) \leq 0\} \tag{7.32}$$

and the *better-than-x* set*, B, given by

$$\left\{ \sum_{h=1}^{n_h} \mathbf{x}^h : U^h(\mathbf{x}^h) \geq U^h(\mathbf{x}^{*h}) \right\}, \tag{7.33}$$

where $\mathbf{x}$, $\mathbf{q}$, and $\mathbf{R}$ represent vectors of consumption, net output, and resources aggregated over the whole economy as in (7.7). The attainable set A is much as we discussed on page 132 in chapter 6. The set B is the second of the slight differences from the previous discussion: it represents the set of aggregate consumption vectors that would permit

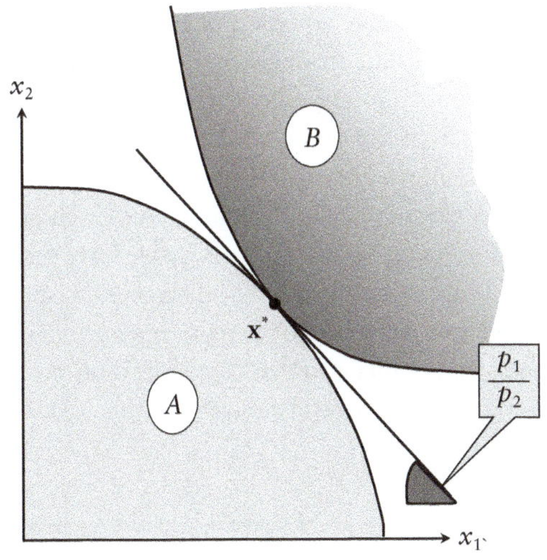

Figure 7.15 Decentralisation in general equilibrium

each household to achieve the same or higher utility level that it achieves in equilibrium. This set must also be convex if all households have conventional concave-contoured utility functions.[25]

To interpret the decentralisation function of prices in this case define aggregate expenditure (income) in equilibrium as

$$y := \sum_{i=1}^{n} p_i^* x_i^*.$$

Then the hyperplane illustrated in Figure 7.15 is the set of points

$$\left\{ \mathbf{x} : \sum_{i=1}^{n} p_i^* x_i = y \right\}. \tag{7.34}$$

This hyperplane 'supports' the sets A and B as in the following result (see Appendix C):

Theorem 7.6 Valuation in general equilibrium

If A given by (7.32) and B given by (7.33) are both convex sets, then there are prices $\mathbf{p}^*$ and a consumption vector $\mathbf{x}^*$ such that, for all $\mathbf{x} \in A$:

$$\sum_{i=1}^{n} p_i^* x_i \leq y \tag{7.35}$$

and for all $\mathbf{x} \in B$

$$\sum_{i=1}^{n} p_i^* x_i \geq y. \tag{7.36}$$

where $y := \sum_{i=1}^{n} p_i^* x_i^*$.

This means that $\mathbf{x}^*$ simultaneously maximises the valuation of aggregate income over the attainable set A and minimises the valuation of aggregate expenditure over the set B.

Now, while we can borrow results from chapter 6 we must also admit that there is a problem that carries over from chapter 6. One of the lessons drawn from the Robinson Crusoe analogy was that it might not be possible to decentralise in the presence of non-convexities. This appears to affect Theorem 6.2 which relies on the sets A and B being convex.[26] We might have suspected this in the light of the discussion of the possibility of non-existence of equilibrium (page 162)—after all, as we have seen, non-convexity of an agent's constraint set can lead to discontinuity of the agent's response function.

However, given that we are using a model that represents arbitrarily many agents, we may be able to get around this problem by appealing to a result that we have already glimpsed a couple of times previously (see section 3.3). Consider a very simple

? Mini Problems

25 Explain why (7.33) must be convex using Theorem A.6 in Appendix A.

26 Use the Robinson Crusoe analogy and a diagram like Figure 7.15 to show why decentralisation may not be possible (a) if A is non-convex, and (b) if B is non-convex.

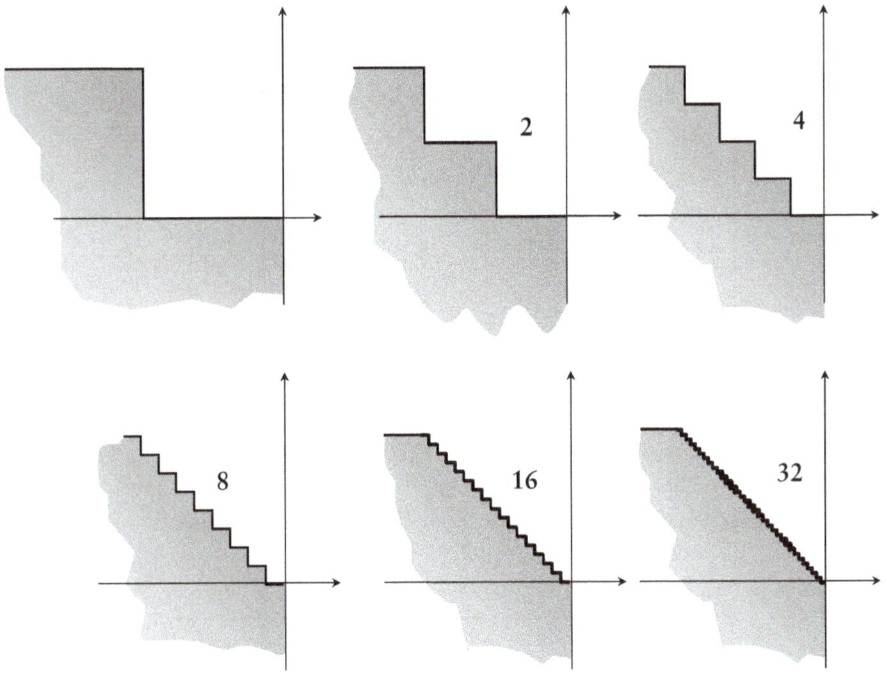

Figure 7.16 Convexification of production through aggregation

production function, where good 1 is an input, and good 2 an output (this is based on Exercise 6.1 in chapter 6):

$$\left\{ \begin{array}{ll} q_2 = 0 & q_1 > -1 \\ q_2 = 1 & q_1 \leq -1 \end{array} \right\} \tag{7.37}$$

This technology is illustrated in the first panel of Figure 7.16. Clearly there is a simple indivisibility in the production process and, as a consequence, the technology set is non-convex. If we were to replicate a firm with this technology set and plot the feasible combinations of inputs and outputs on a half-scale diagram, we would get the second panel in the figure; successive replications yield the subsequent panels, scaled down by $\frac{1}{4}, \frac{1}{8}$, and so on. As we can see this process of replication enables one to consider the aggregate technology set being 'almost' convex if the replication factor were to be large enough. The same kind of result can be obtained in the case of non-convex preferences. Examine Figure 7.17 in which the shaded area represents the B-set for a single person, Bill. Consider the line that bridges the 'dent' in B. If the economy consists of Bill, and his identical twin brother Ben, then not only the end points of the line but also the midpoint will belong to the B-set. If there are indefinitely many of the Bill tribe, then *all* of this line belongs to the B-line: in fact you just shaded in the dent that you had in the one person B-set.

The allocation in each of these two cases involves placing similar agents in dissimilar situations: some firms will produce ($q_2 = 1$), others will not ($q_2 = 0$); some consumers

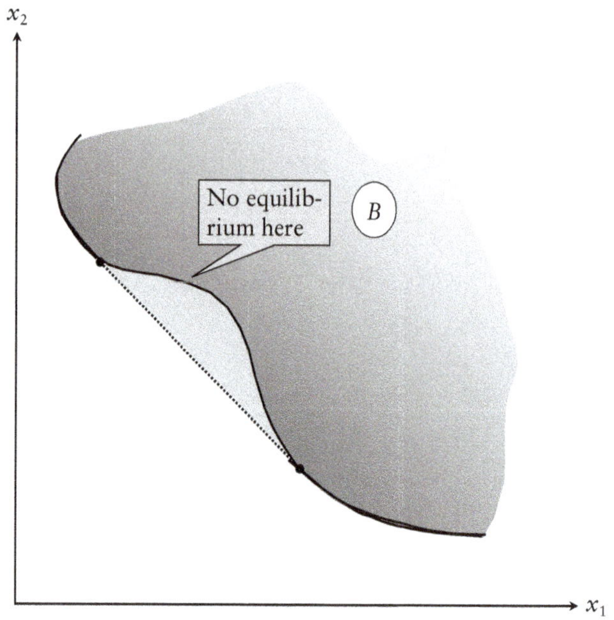

Figure 7.17 Non-convex preferences

will be at the left-hand end of the dent in Figure 7.17, others at the right-hand end. But in each case the firms and the consumers are acting as maximisers. What this means is that we can still decentralise if individual sets are non-convex, but agents are 'small'.

Summary

Without too much additional effort and complication the Robinson Crusoe economy of chapter 6 can be generalised to an economy with many agents—consumers and firms—in a way that preserves the main Crusoe insights. Furthermore, it is clear that the general-equilibrium model has much that is familiar from earlier chapters: along with bits of the Crusoe story it incorporates bits from the equilibrium analysis of the firm and of the consumer. Some components of microeconomic models have popped up again in a new guise: for example WARP that originally appeared as a basic axiom of consumer behaviour re-emerges as a condition on excess-demand functions that enables us to characterise whether the system is well behaved.

However, there are three areas where the general-equilibrium analysis presented here does more than just pull together results from previous analysis, but rather contributes important new insights.

Ownership

The anchor point of the type of model that we have analysed is the system of property rights—who owns the resources and the rights to the profits from the firms. From this follows the endogenous determination of household incomes; from this also follows the fundamental mapping $\mathbf{d} \rightarrow \mathbf{a}$ from the property distribution to the allocation of consumption bundles amongst the households and net-output vectors amongst the firms. Taking the property distribution as a given enables us to focus clearly on the principles governing the operation of the competitive market system, but it may seem to be as an abdication of responsibility on the part of the economist.

Numbers

The presence of many economic agents might at first have seemed just an unfortunate but necessary complication in the basic economic model. However, there are two points where a 'large-numbers argument' is a particular advantage in establishing key economic insights.

The first large-numbers argument concerns the analysis of the core and competitive equilibrium (section 7.3.3). The limit theorem enables us to see why and under what circumstances the competitive parable provides a coherent account of how self-interested economic agents behave.

The second large-numbers argument concerns the decentralisation story (section 7.5.2). This works in basically the same way as in Robinson Crusoe, but there is a new twist. In the Crusoe story decentralisation might break down if there were some substantial indivisibility in production that led to the attainable set being non-convex. That could happen in the general-equilibrium model too, but the large-numbers argument provides some reassurance: building on a lesson from chapter 3 the presence of large numbers of small agents approximately convexifies the model, ensures that the excess-demand function is effectively continuous and so ensures the existence of equilibrium prices that do the job of decentralisation.

Prices

As an oversimplification, the central problem of characterising a general competitive equilibrium can be resolved into a two-stage process:

1. Find the equilibrium price vector $\mathbf{p}^*$ from the aggregate market-clearing conditions.
2. Use $\mathbf{p}^*$ to get the equilibrium allocation $\mathbf{a}^*$ through the price responses of individual agents.

It is evident that the price system is the engine that drives this model; how it does this is an issue that we shall have cause to re-examine in later chapters.

Reading notes

The origin of general equilibrium is largely attributable to Walras (1954). The connection between the core and competitive equilibrium was anticipated in Edgeworth (1881); the key result is in Debreu and Scarf (1963); an easier treatment of this is in Schweizer (1982). The classic reference on the existence of equilibrium is Arrow and Debreu (1954); comprehensive treatment of general equilibrium models is to be found in Arrow and Hahn (1971). Stability analysis is considered further in Hahn (1982). For the application of convexity arguments in competitive models see Farrell (1959).

Exercises

7.1 Suppose there are 200 traders in a market, all of whom behave as price takers. Suppose there are three goods and the traders own initially the following quantities:

- 100 of the traders own 10 units of good 1 each;
- 50 of the traders own 5 units of good 2 each;
- 50 of the traders own 20 units of good 3 each.

All the traders have the utility function

$$U = x_1^{\frac{1}{2}} x_2^{\frac{1}{4}} x_3^{\frac{1}{4}}.$$

What are the equilibrium relative prices of the three goods? Which group of traders has members who are best off?

7.2 Consider an exchange economy with two goods and three persons. Alf always demands equal quantities of the two goods. Bill's expenditure on group 1 is always twice his expenditure on good 2. Charlie never uses good 2.

1. Describe the indifference maps of the three individuals and suggest utility functions consistent with their behaviour.
2. If the original endowments are respectively (5, 0), (3, 6), and (0, 4), compute the equilibrium price ratio. What would be the effect on equilibrium prices and utility levels if
   (a) 4 extra units of good 1 were given to Alf;
   (b) 4 units of good 1 were given to Charlie?

7.3 In a two-commodity economy assume a person has the endowment $(0, 20)$.

1. Find the person's demand function for the two goods if his preferences are represented by each of the types A to D in Exercise 4.2. In each case explain what the offer curve must look like.
2. Assume that there are in fact two equal sized groups of people, each with preferences of type A, where everyone in group 1 has the endowment (10,0) with $a = \frac{1}{2}$ and everyone in group 2 an endowment (0,20) with $a = \frac{3}{4}$. Use the offer curves to find the competitive equilibrium price and allocation.

7.4 The agents in a two-commodity exchange economy have utility functions

$$U^a(\mathbf{x}^a) = \log(x_1^a) + 2\log(x_2^a) U^b(\mathbf{x}^b) = 2\log(x_1^b) + \log(x_2^b)$$

where x_i^h is the consumption by agent h of good i, $h = a, b$; $i = 1, 2$. The property distribution is given by the endowments $\mathbf{R}^a = (9, 3)$ and $\mathbf{R}^b = (12, 6)$.

1. Obtain the excess demand function for each good and verify that Walras's Law is true.
2. Find the equilibrium price ratio.

3. What is the equilibrium allocation?
4. Given that total resources available remain fixed at $\mathbf{R} := \mathbf{R}^a + \mathbf{R}^b = (21, 9)$, derive the contract curve.

7.5 Which of the following sets of functions are legitimate excess demand functions?

$$\left.\begin{array}{l} E_1(\mathbf{p}) = -p_2 + \dfrac{10}{p_1} \\ E_2(\mathbf{p}) = p_1 \\ E_3(\mathbf{p}) = -\dfrac{10}{p_3} \end{array}\right\} \quad (7.38)$$

$$\left.\begin{array}{l} E_1(\mathbf{p}) = \dfrac{p_2 + p_3}{p_1} \\ E_2(\mathbf{p}) = \dfrac{p_1 + p_3}{p_2} \\ E_3(\mathbf{p}) = \dfrac{p_1 + p_2}{p_3} \end{array}\right\} \quad (7.39)$$

$$\left.\begin{array}{l} E_1(\mathbf{p}) = \dfrac{p_3}{p_1} \\ E_2(\mathbf{p}) = \dfrac{p_3}{p_2} \\ E_3(\mathbf{p}) = -2 \end{array}\right\} \quad (7.40)$$

7.6 In a two-commodity economy let ρ be the price of commodity 1 in terms of commodity 2. Suppose the excess demand function for commodity 1 is given by

$$1 - 4\rho + 5\rho^2 - 2\rho^3.$$

How many equilibria are there? Are they stable or unstable? How might your answer be affected if there were an increase in the stock of commodity 1 in the economy?

7.7 Consider the following four types of preferences:

$$\text{Type A} : \alpha \log x_1 + [1 - \alpha] \log x_2$$

$$\text{Type B} : \beta x_1 + x_2$$

$$\text{Type C} : \gamma [x_1]^2 + [x_2]^2$$

$$\text{Type D} : \min\{\delta x_1, x_2\}$$

where x_1, x_2 denote respectively consumption of goods 1 and 2 and $\alpha, \beta, \gamma, \delta$ are strictly positive parameters with $\alpha < 1$.

1. Draw the indifference curves for each type.
2. Assume that a person has an endowment of 10 units of commodity 1 and zero of commodity 2. Show that, if his preferences are of type A, then his demand for the two commodities can be represented as

$$\mathbf{x} := \begin{bmatrix} x_1 \\ x_2 \end{bmatrix} = \begin{bmatrix} 10\alpha \\ 10\rho[1 - \alpha] \end{bmatrix}$$

where ρ is the price of good 1 in terms of good 2. What is the person's offer curve in this case?

3. Assume now that a person has an endowment of 20 units of commodity 2 (and zero units of commodity 1). Find the person's demand for the two goods if his preferences are represented by each of the types A to D. In each case explain what the offer curve must look like.
4. In a two-commodity economy there are two equal-sized groups of people. People in group 1 own all of commodity 1 (10 units per person) and people in group 2 own all of commodity 2 (20 units per person). If Group 1 has preferences of type A with $a = \frac{1}{2}$ find the competitive equilibrium prices and allocations in each of the following cases:
   (a) Group 2 have preferences of type A with $a = \frac{3}{4}$
   (b) Group 2 have preferences of type B with $\beta = 3$.
   (c) Group 2 have preferences of type D with $\delta = 1$.
5. What problem might arise if group 2 had preferences of type C? Compare this case with case 4(b).

7.8 In a two-commodity exchange economy there are two equal-sized groups of people. Those of type a have the utility function

$$U^a\left(\mathbf{x}^a\right) = -\frac{1}{2}\left[x_1^a\right]^{-2} - \frac{1}{2}\left[x_2^a\right]^{-2}$$

and a resource endowment of $(R_1, 0)$; those of type b have the utility function

$$U^b\left(\mathbf{x}^b\right) = x_1^b x_2^b$$

and a resource endowment of $(0, R_2)$.

1. How many equilibria does this system have?
2. Find the equilibrium price ratio if $R_1 = 5$, $R_2 = 16$.

7.9 In a two-person, private-ownership economy persons a and b each have utility functions of the form

$$V^h\left(\mathbf{p}, y^h\right) = \log\left(y^h - p_1\beta_1^h - p_2\beta_2^h\right) - \frac{1}{2}\log\left(p_1 p_2\right)$$

where $h = a, b$ and β_1^h, β_2^h are parameters. Find the equilibrium price ratio as a function of the property distribution $[\mathbf{R}]$.

7.10 In an economy there are large equal-sized groups of capitalists and workers. Production is organised as in the model of Exercises 2.14 and 6.4. Capitalists' income consists solely of the profits from the production process; workers' income comes solely from the sale of labour. Capitalists and workers have the utility functions $x_1^c x_2^c$ and $x_1^w - \left[R_3 - x_3^w\right]^2$ respectively, where x_i^h denotes the consumption of good i by a person of type h and R_3 is the stock of commodity 3.

1. If capitalists and workers act as price takers find the optimal demands for the consumption goods by each group, and the optimal supply of labour $R_3 - x_3^w$.

2. Show that the excess demand functions for goods 1,2 can be written as

$$\frac{\Pi}{2p_1} + \frac{1}{2\,[p_1]^2} - \frac{A}{2}p_1$$

$$\frac{\Pi}{2p_2} - \frac{A}{2}p_2$$

where Π is the expression for profits found in Exercise 6.4. Show that in equilibrium $p_1/p_2 = \sqrt{3}$ and hence show that the equilibrium price of good 1 (in terms of good 3) is given by

$$p_1 = \left[\frac{3}{2A}\right]^{1/3}$$

3. What is the ratio of the money incomes of workers and capitalists in equilibrium?

8 Uncertainty and Risk

The lottery is the one ray of hope in my otherwise unbearable life.
Homer Simpson.

8.1 Introduction

All of the economic analysis so far has been based on the assumption of a certain world. Where we have touched on the issue of time it can effectively be collapsed into the present through discounting. Now we explicitly change that by incorporating uncertainty into the microeconomic model. This also gives us an opportunity to think more about the issue of time. We deal with a specific, perhaps rather narrow, concept of uncertainty that is, in a sense, exogenous. It is some external ingredient that has an impact upon individual agents' economic circumstances (it affects their income, their needs...) and also upon the agents' decisions (it affects their consumption plans, the pattern of their asset holding...)

Although there are some radically new concepts to be introduced, the analysis can be firmly based on the principles that we have already established, particularly those used to give meaning to consumer choice. However, the approach will take us on to more general issues: by modelling uncertainty we can provide an insight into the definition of risk, attitudes to risk, and a precise concept of risk aversion.

8.2 Consumption and uncertainty

We begin by looking at the way in which elementary consumer theory can be extended to allow for the fact that the future is only imperfectly known. To fix ideas, let us consider two examples of a simple consumer choice problem under uncertainty.

1. *Budget day.* You have a licence for your car which must be renewed annually and which still has some weeks before expiry. The government is announcing tax changes this afternoon which may affect the fee for your licence: if you renew the licence now, you pay the old fee, but you forfeit the unexpired portion of the licence; if you wait, you may have to renew the licence at a higher fee.
2. *Election day.* Two parties are contesting an election, and the result will be known at noon. In the morning you hold an asset whose value will be affected by the outcome of the election. If you do not sell the asset immediately your wealth will rise if the Red party wins, and drop if the Blue party wins.

	'Budget day'	'Election day'
States of the world	fee does/does not increase	Blue/Red wins
Payoffs (outcomes)	−£20 or £0, depending on ω	capital gain/capital loss, depending on ω
Prospects	states and outcomes seen from the morning	states and outcomes seen from the morning
Ex ante/ex post	before/after 3pm	before/after the Election results

Table 8.1 Two simple decision problems under uncertainty

The essential features in these two examples can be summarised in Table 8.1, and the following points are worth noting:

- The *states of the world* indexed by ω act like labels on physically different goods.
- The set of all states of the world Ω in each of the two examples is very simple—it contains only two elements. But in some interesting economic models may be (countably or uncountably) infinite.
- The *payoffs* in the two examples are scalars (monetary amounts); but in more general models it might be useful to represent the payoff as a consumption bundle—a vector of goods $\mathbf{x}$.
- Timing is crucial. Use the time-line Figure 8.1 as a simple parable; the left-hand side represents the 'morning' during which decisions are made; the outcome of a decision is determined in the afternoon and will be influenced by the state of the world ω. The dotted boundary represents the point at which exactly one ω is realised out of a whole rainbow of possibilities. You must make your choice *ex ante*. It is too late to do it *ex post*—after the realisation of the event.
- The *prospects* could be treated like consumption vectors.

8.2.1 The nature of choice

It is evident from these examples that the way we look at choice has changed somewhat from that analysed in chapter 4. In our earlier exposition of consumer theory actions by consumers were synonymous with consequences. You choose the action 'buy x_1 units of commodity 1' and you get to consume x_1 units of commodity 1: it was effectively a model of instant gratification. We now have a more complex model of the satisfaction of wants. The consumer may choose to take some action (buy this or that, vote for him or her) but the consequence that follows is no longer instantaneous and predictable. The payoff—the consequence that directly affects the consumer—depends both on the action and on the outcome of some event.

To put these ideas on an analytical footing we will discuss the economic issues in stages: later we will examine a specific model of utility that appears to be well suited for

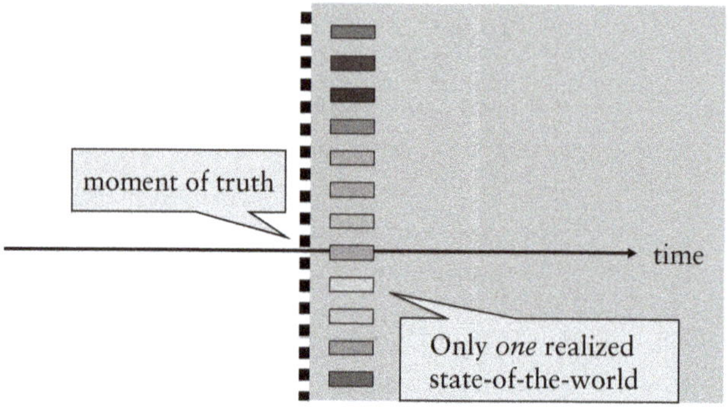

Figure 8.1 The *ex-ante*/*ex-post* distinction

representing choice under uncertainty and then consider how this model can be used to characterise attitudes to risk and the problem of choice under uncertainty. However, first we will see how far it is possible to get just by adapting the model of consumer choice that was used in chapter 4.

8.2.2 State-space diagram

As a simplified introduction, take the case where there are just two possible states of the world, denoted by the labels RED and BLUE, and scalar payoffs; this means that the payoff in each state of the world ω can be represented as the amount of a composite consumption good x_ω. Then consumption in each of the two states of the world x_{RED} and x_{BLUE} can be measured along each of the two axes in Figure 8.2. These are *contingent goods*: that is x_{RED} and x_{BLUE} are quantities of consumption that are contingent on which state of the world is eventually realised. An individual prospect is represented as a vector of contingent goods such as that marked by the point P_0 and the set of all prospects is represented by the shaded area in Figure 8.2. If instead there were three states in Ω with scalar payoffs, then a typical prospect would be such as P_0 in Figure 8.3. So the description of the environment in which individual choice is to be exercised is rather like that of ordinary consumption vectors—see page 70. However, the 45° ray in Figure 8.2 has a special significance: prospects along this line represent payoffs under complete certainty. It is arguable that such prospects are qualitatively different from anywhere else in the diagram and may accordingly be treated differently by consumers; there is no counterpart to this in conventional choice under certainty.

Now consider the representation of consumers' preferences—as viewed from the morning—in this uncertain world. To represent an individual's ranking of prospects we can use a weak preference relation of the form introduced in Definition 4.2. If we copy across the concepts used in the world of certainty from chapter 4, we might postulate indifference curves defined in the space of contingent goods—as in Figure 8.4. This of course will require the standard axioms of completeness, transitivity, and continuity introduced in chapter 4 (see page 75). Other standard consumer axioms might also seem to be intuitively reasonable in the case of ranking prospects. An example of this is 'greed' (Axiom 4.6 on page 77): prospect P_1 will, presumably, be preferred to P_0 in Figure 8.4.

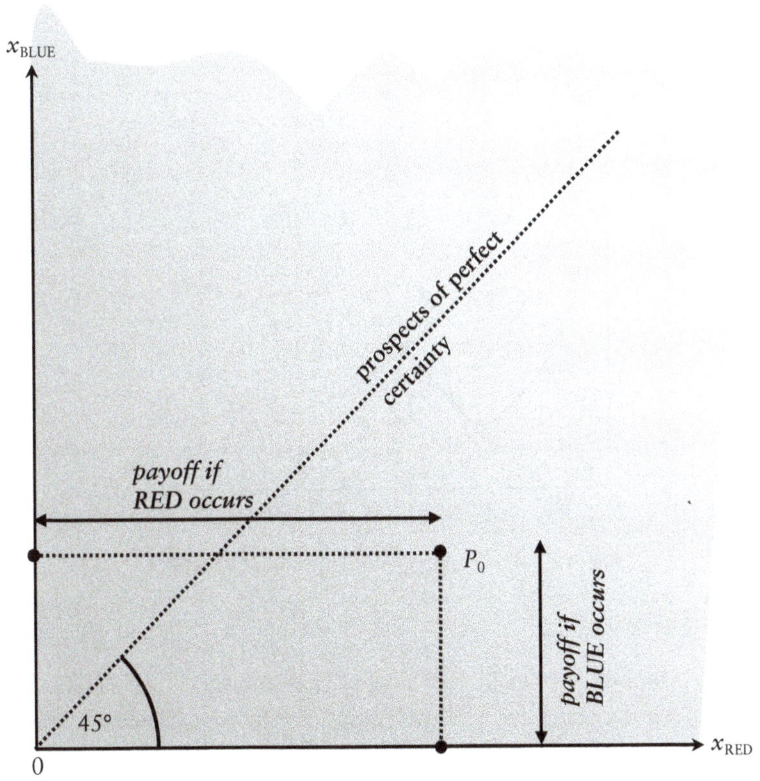

Figure 8.2 The state-space diagram: $\#\Omega = 2$

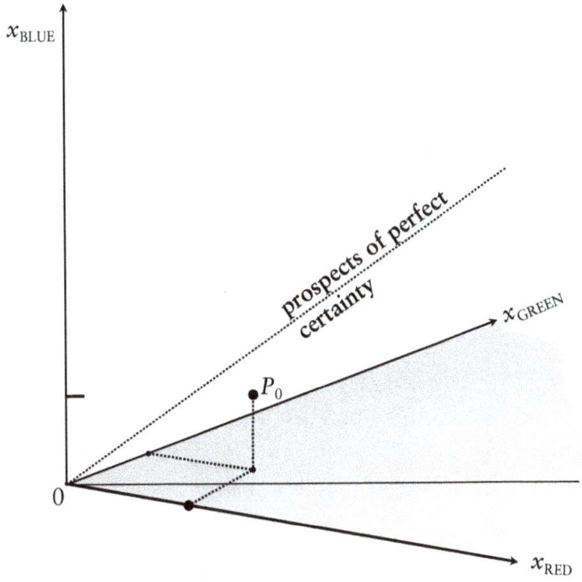

Figure 8.3 The state-space diagram: $\#\Omega = 3$

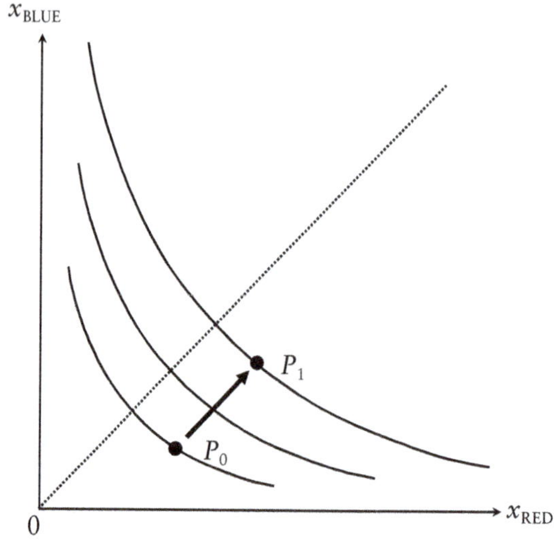

Figure 8.4 Preference contours in state-space

But this may be moving ahead too quickly. Axioms 4.3 to 4.5 might seem fairly unexceptionable in the context where they were introduced—choice under perfect certainty—but some people might wish to question whether the continuity axiom is everywhere appropriate in the case of uncertain prospects. It may be that people who have a pathological concern for certainty have preferences that are discontinuous in the neighbourhood of the 45° ray: for such persons a complete map of indifference curves cannot be drawn.[1]

However, if the individual's preferences are such that you can draw indifference curves, then you can get a very useful concept indeed: the *certainty equivalent* of any prospect P_0. This is point E with coordinates (ξ, ξ) in Figure 8.5; the amount ξ is simply the quantity of the consumption good, guaranteed with complete certainty, that the individual would accept as a straight swap for the prospect P_0. It is clear that the existence of this quantity depends crucially on the continuity assumption.

Let us consider the concept of the certainty equivalent further. To do this, connect prospect P_0 and its certainty equivalent by a straight line, as shown in Figure 8.6. Observe that all points on this line are weakly preferred to P_0 if and only if the preference map is quasiconcave (you might find it useful to check the definition of quasiconcavity on page 503 in Appendix A). This suggests an intuitively appealing interpretation: if the individual always prefers a mixture of prospect P with its certainty equivalent to prospect P alone, then one might claim that in some sense he or she has 'risk-averse' preferences. On this interpretation 'risk aversion' implies, and is implied by, convex-to-the-origin

? Mini Problems

1 If the continuity axiom is violated in this way describe the shape of the individual's preference map.

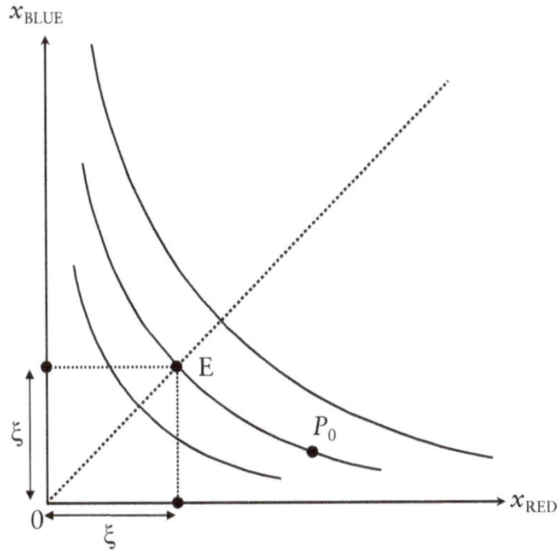

Figure 8.5 The certainty equivalent

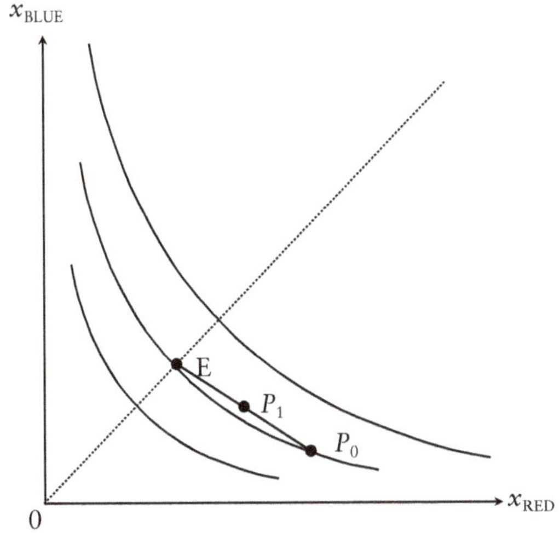

Figure 8.6 Quasiconcavity reinterpreted

indifference curves (I have used the quote marks around risk aversion because we have not defined what risk *is* yet).[2]

Now for another point of interpretation. Suppose RED becomes less likely to win (as perceived by the individual in the morning)—what would happen to the indifference

? Mini Problems

2 What would the curves look like for a risk-neutral person? For a risk-lover?

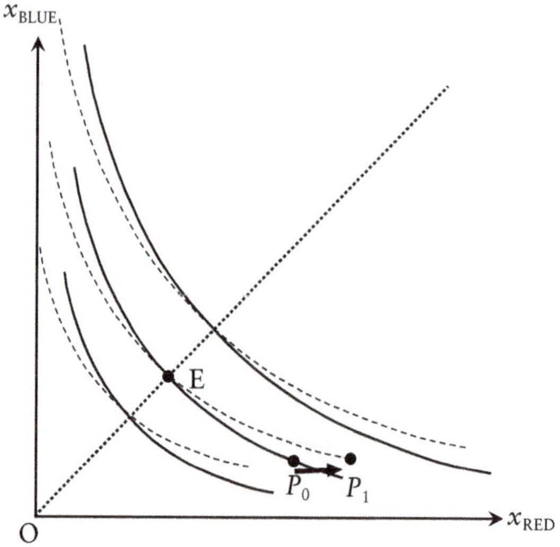

Figure 8.7 A change in perception

curves? We would expect them to shift in the way illustrated in Figure 8.7. By replacing the existing light indifference curves with the heavy indifference curves. The reasoning behind this is as follows. Take E as a given reference point on the 45° line—remember that it represents a payoff that is independent of the state of the world that will occur. Before the change the prospects represented by points E and P_0 are regarded as indifferent; however, after the change it is P_1—that implies a higher payoff under RED—that is regarded as being of 'equal value' to point E.[3]

? Mini Problems

3 Consider a choice between the following two prospects:

$$P: \begin{cases} \$1\,000 & \text{with probability } 0.7 \\ \$100\,000 & \text{with probability } 0.3 \end{cases}$$

$$P': \begin{cases} \$1\,000 & \text{with probability } 0.2 \\ \$30\,000 & \text{with probability } 0.8 \end{cases}$$

Starting with Lichtenstein and Slovic (1983) a large number of experimental studies have shown the following behaviour

1. When a simple choice between P and P' is offered, many experimental subjects would choose P'.
2. When asked to make a dollar bid for the right to either prospect many of those who had chosen then put a higher bid on P than on P'.

This phenomenon is known as *preference reversal*. Which of the fundamental axioms appears to be violated?

8.3 A model of preferences

So far we have extended the formal model of the consumer by reinterpreting the commodity space and reinterpreting preferences in this space. This reinterpretation of preference has included the first tentative steps toward a characterisation of risk including the way in which the preference map 'should' change if the person's perception about the unknown future should change. It appears that we could—perhaps with some qualification—represent preferences over the space of contingent goods using a utility function as in Theorem 4.1 and the associated discussion on page 76.

However, some might complain all this is a little vague: we have not specified exactly what risk is, nor have we attempted to move beyond an elementary two-state example. To make further progress, it is useful to impose more structure on preferences. By doing this we shall develop the basis for a standard model of preference in the face of uncertainty and show the way that this model depends on the use of a few powerful assumptions.

8.3.1 Key axioms

Let us suppose that all outcomes can be represented as vectors $\mathbf{x}$ which belong to $X \subset \mathbb{R}^n$. We shall introduce three more axioms.

Axiom 8.1 (State-irrelevance)

The state that is realised has no intrinsic value to the person.

In other words, the colour of the state itself does not matter. The intuitive justification for this is that the objects of desire are just the vectors $\mathbf{x}$ and people do not care whether these materialise on a 'red' day or a 'blue' day; of course it means that one has to be careful about the way goods and their attributes are described: the desirability of an umbrella may well depend on whether it is a rainy or a sunny day.

Axiom 8.2 (Independence)

Let $P_{\mathbf{z}}$ and $\widehat{P}_{\mathbf{z}}$ be any two distinct prospects specified in such a way that the payoff in one particular state of the world is the same for both prospects: $\mathbf{x}_\omega = \widehat{\mathbf{x}}_\omega = \mathbf{z}$. Then, if prospect $P_{\mathbf{z}}$ is preferred to prospect $\widehat{P}_{\mathbf{z}}$ for *one* value of $\mathbf{z}$, $P_{\mathbf{z}}$ is preferred to $\widehat{P}_{\mathbf{z}}$ for *all* values of $\mathbf{z}$.

To see what is involved, consider Table 8.2, in which the payoffs are scalar quantities. Suppose P_{10} is preferred to $\hat{P}_{10}$: would this still hold even if the payoff 10 (which always comes up under state GREEN) were to be replaced by the value 20? Look at the preference map depicted in Figure 8.8: each of the 'slices' that have been drawn in shows a glimpse of the $(x_{\text{RED}}, x_{\text{BLUE}})$-contours for one given value of x_{GREEN}. The independence

	RED	BLUE	GREEN
P_{10}	1	6	10
$\hat{P}_{10}$	2	3	10

Table 8.2 Example for independence axiom

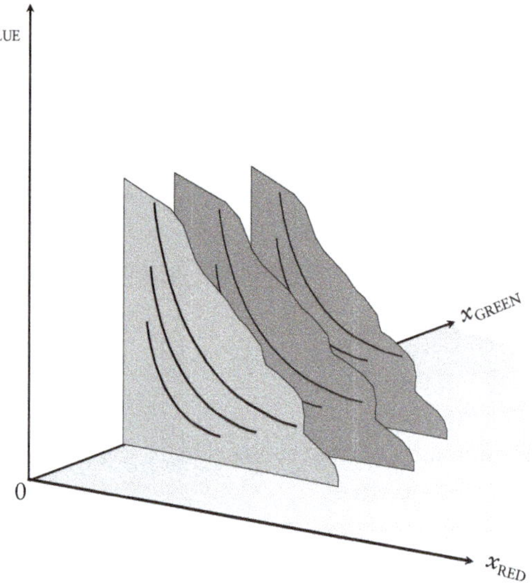

Figure 8.8 Independence axiom: illustration

property also implies that the individual does not experience disappointment or regret—see Exercises 8.5 and 8.6.[4]

Axiom 8.3 (Revealed likelihood)

Let $\mathbf{x}^*$ and $\mathbf{x}$ be two payoffs such that under certainty $\mathbf{x}^*$ would be weakly preferred to $\mathbf{x}$. Let Ω_0 and Ω_1 be any two given subsets of the set of all states of the world Ω and suppose the individual weakly prefers the prospect

$$P_0 = [\mathbf{x}^* \text{ if } \omega \in \Omega_0; \mathbf{x} \text{ if } \omega \notin \Omega_0]$$

to the prospect

$$P_1 = [\mathbf{x}^* \text{ if } \omega \in \Omega_1; \mathbf{x} \text{ if } \omega \notin \Omega_1]$$

for *some* such $\mathbf{x}^*, \mathbf{x}$. Then he prefers P_0 to P_1 for *every* such $\mathbf{x}^*$, $\mathbf{x}$.

Mini Problems

4 Compare Exercises 8.5 and 8.6. What is the essential difference between regret and disappointment?

	RED	ORANGE	YELLOW	GREEN	BLUE	INDIGO	VIOLET
P_0	apple	apple	apple	apple	apple	banana	banana
P_1	banana	banana	banana	apple	apple	apple	apple

Table 8.3 Prospects with fruit

	RED	ORANGE	YELLOW	GREEN	BLUE	INDIGO	VIOLET
P'_0	cherry	cherry	cherry	cherry	cherry	date	date
P'_1	date	date	date	cherry	cherry	cherry	cherry

Table 8.4 Prospects with different fruit

Consider an example illustrating this property. Let the set of all states-of-the-world be given by

$$\Omega = \{\text{RED,ORANGE,YELLOW,GREEN,BLUE,INDIGO,VIOLET}\}.$$

Now, suppose we have a person who prefers one apple to one banana, and also prefers one cherry to one date. Consider two prospects P_0, P_1 which each have as payoffs an apple or a banana in the manner defined in Table 8.3.

Furthermore, let us define two subsets of Ω, namely

$$\Omega_0 := \{\text{RED,ORANGE,YELLOW,GREEN,BLUE}\}$$

$$\Omega_1 := \{\text{GREEN,BLUE,INDIGO,VIOLET}\};$$

we see that P_0 and P_1 then have the property described in the axiom. Suppose the individual prefers P_0 to P_1. Then the revealed-likelihood axiom requires that he also prefer P'_0 to P'_1, defined as in Table 8.4; it further implies that the above hold for any other arbitrary subsets Ω_0, Ω_1 of the set of all states of the world.

The intuition is that the pairs (P_0, P_1) and (P'_0, P'_1) have in common the same pattern of subsets of the state-space where the 'winner' comes up. By consistently choosing P_0 over P_1, P'_0 over P'_1, and so on, the person is revealing that he thinks that the subset of events Ω_0 is 'more likely' than Ω_1. This assumption rules out so-called 'ambiguity aversion'—see Exercise 8.7.

The three new assumptions then yield this important result, proved in Appendix C:

Theorem 8.1 (Expected utility)

Assume that preferences over the space of state-contingent goods can be represented by a utility function as in Theorem 4.1. If preferences also satisfy state irrelevance, independence, and revealed likelihood (Axioms 8.1–8.3), then they can be represented in the form

$$\sum_{\omega\in\Omega} \pi_\omega u(\mathbf{x}_\omega) \tag{8.1}$$

where the π_ω are real numbers and u is a real-valued function on X that is defined up to an increasing, affine transformation.

In honour of its origin the special form (8.1) is often known as a *von Neumann–Morgenstern utility function*. One way of thinking about this follows naturally from our discussion of the savings problem in chapter 5—see equation (5.13) and Mini Problem 4 on page 105. Instead of discrete time periods indexed by t we now have discrete states of the world indexed by ω; the principal difference between the two versions—that there is a natural sequence in the case of time periods that is absent from the uncertainty problem—is not relevant here. So, given that the problems have the same shape, they can be tackled in the same way. The proof of Theorem 8.1 is essentially that of Exercise 5.5, but with a change of notation.

As with the problem of aggregation discussed in chapter 5 (see page 114), once again the additional requirements imposed on the representation of preferences induce a set of restrictions on the class of admissible utility functions. It is difficult to overstate the importance of this result (and its alternate version in Theorem 8.4 below) for much of modern microeconomic analysis. Nevertheless, before we press on to its interpretation and some of its many applications, it is worth reminding ourselves that the additional structural axioms on which it rests may be subject to challenge as reasonable representations of people's preferences in the face of uncertainty. Specifically, experimental evidence has repeatedly rejected the independence axiom as a representation of people's preferences in the face of choice under uncertainty.

8.3.2 Von Neumann–Morgenstern utility

What does this special utility function look like? To scrutinise the properties of (8.1) and how they work we can extract a lot of information from the simple case of scalar payoffs—e.g. payoffs in money—as in section 8.2.2 above.

First the function u. Here we encounter a terminologically awkward corner. We should not really call u 'the utility function' because the whole expression (8.1) is the person's utility; so u is sometimes known as the individual's *cardinal utility function* or *felicity function*; arguably neither term is a particularly happy choice of words. The last part of Theorem 8.1 means that the function u could be validly replaced by $\hat{u}$ defined by

$$\hat{u} := a + bu \tag{8.2}$$

where a is an arbitrary constant and $b > 0$: the scale and origin of u are unimportant. However, although these features of the function u are irrelevant, other features, such as its curvature, are important because they can be used to characterise the individual's attitude to risk: this is dealt with in section 8.4.

Now consider the set of weights $\{\pi_\omega : \omega \in \Omega\}$ in (8.1). If they are normalised so as to sum to 1,[5] then they are usually known as the *subjective probabilities* of the individual. Notice that the concept of probability has emerged naturally from the structural

? Mini Problems

5 Show that, given the definition of u, this normalisation can always be done.

assumptions that we have introduced on personal preferences, rather than as an explicit construct. Furthermore, being 'subjective', they could differ from one individual to another—one person might quite reasonably put a higher weight on the outcome 'The red party will win the election' than another. We shall have much more to say about this and other aspects of probability later in this chapter.

In view of the subjective-probability interpretation of the πs the von Neumann–Morgenstern utility function (8.1) can be interpreted as *expected utility*, and may more compactly be written $\mathcal{E}u(\mathbf{x})$. In the two-state, scalar payoff case that we used as an example earlier this would be written:

$$\pi_{\text{RED}} u(x_{\text{RED}}) + \pi_{\text{BLUE}} u(x_{\text{BLUE}}) \tag{8.3}$$

Using Figure 8.9 for the two-state case we can see the structure that (8.3) introduces to the problem:[6]

- The slope of the indifference curve where it crosses the 45°-line is (−) the ratio of the probabilities $\pi_{\text{RED}}/\pi_{\text{BLUE}}$.
- A corollary of this is that all the contours of the expected utility function must have the same slope at the point where they intersect the 45°-line.
- For any prospect such as point P_0 in Figure 8.9, if we draw a line with this slope through P_0, the point at which it cuts the 45°-line represents the *expected value* of the prospect P; the value of this is represented (on either axis) as $\mathcal{E}x$, where $\mathcal{E}$ is the usual expectations operator (see Definition A.30 on page 513).

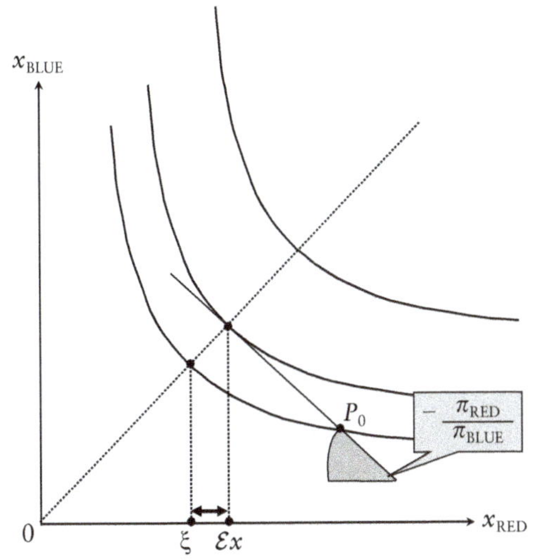

Figure 8.9 Contours of the Expected-Utility function

? Mini Problems

6 Explain why these results are true, using (8.3).

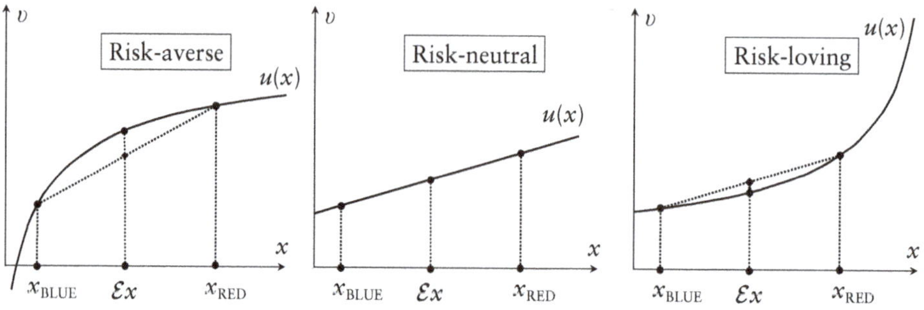

Figure 8.10 Attitudes to risk

8.3.3 The 'felicity' function

Let us now interpret the function u in terms of individual attitudes. To fix ideas let us take the two-state case and suppose that payoffs are scalars; further assume that the individual assigns equal probability weight to the two states (this is not essential, but it makes the diagram more tractable). Figure 8.10 illustrates three main possibilities for the shape of u.

- In the left-hand panel look at the diagonal line joining the points $(x_{\text{BLUE}}, u(x_{\text{BLUE}}))$ and $(x_{\text{RED}}, u(x_{\text{RED}}))$; halfway along this line we can read off the individual's expected utility (8.3); clearly this is strictly less than $u(\mathcal{E}x)$. So if u had this shape an individual would strictly prefer the expected value of the prospect (in this case $\pi_{\text{RED}}x_{\text{RED}} + \pi_{\text{BLUE}}x_{\text{BLUE}}$) to the prospect itself. It follows from this that the person would reject some 'better-than-fair' gambles i.e. gambles where the expected payoff is higher than the stake money for the gamble.
- In the right-hand panel we see the opposite case; here the individual's expected utility is higher than $u(\mathcal{E}x)$ and so the person would accept some unfair gambles (where the expected payoff is strictly less than the stake money).[7]
- Finally the middle panel. Here the expected utility of the gamble just equals $u(\mathcal{E}x)$.

Clearly each of these cases is saying something important about the person's attitude to risk; let us investigate this further.

8.4 Risk aversion

We have already developed an intuitive approach to the concept of risk aversion. If the utility function U over contingent goods is quasiconcave (so that the indifference curves in the state-space diagram are convex to the origin) then we have argued that the

? Mini Problems

7 Would a rational person buy lottery tickets?

person is risk averse—see page 183 above. However, we can now say more: if, in addition to quasiconcavity the utility function takes the von Neumann–Morgenstern form (8.1), then the felicity function u must be concave.[8] This is precisely the case in the left-hand panel of Figure 8.10 and accords with the accompanying story explaining that the individual might reject some fair gambles, which is why the panel has been labelled 'risk averse'. By the same argument the second and third panels depict risk-neutral and risk-loving attitudes, respectively.[9] However, we can extract more information from the graph of the felicity function.

8.4.1 Risk premium

We have already introduced the concept of the certainty equivalent in 8.2.2: as shown in Figure 8.5 this is the amount of perfectly certain income that you would be prepared to exchange for the random prospect lying on the same indifference curve. Now, using the von Neumann–Morgenstern utility function, the certainty equivalent can be expressed using a very simple formula: it is implicitly determined as the number ξ that satisfies

$$u(\xi) = \mathcal{E}u(x). \tag{8.4}$$

Furthermore, we can use the certainty equivalent to define the *risk premium* as

$$\mathcal{E}x - \xi. \tag{8.5}$$

This is the amount of income that the risk-averse person would sacrifice in order to eliminate the risk associated with a particular prospect: it is illustrated on the horizontal axis of Figure 8.9.

Now we can also use the graph of the felicity function to illustrate both the certainty equivalent and the risk premium—see Figure 8.11. In this figure $\pi_{\text{RED}} > \pi_{\text{BLUE}}$ and on the horizontal axis $\mathcal{E}x$ denotes the point $\pi_{\text{RED}}x_{\text{RED}} + \pi_{\text{BLUE}}x_{\text{BLUE}}$; on the vertical axis $\mathcal{E}u(x)$ denotes the point $\pi_{\text{RED}}u\,(x_{\text{RED}}) + \pi_{\text{BLUE}}u\,(x_{\text{BLUE}})$. Use the curve to read off on the horizontal axis the income ξ that corresponds to $\mathcal{E}u(x)$ on the vertical axis. The distance between the two points ξ and $\mathcal{E}x$ on the horizontal axis is the risk premium.

But we can say more about the shape of the function u by characterising risk aversion as a numerical index.

8.4.2 Indices of risk aversion

Why quantify risk aversion? It is useful to be able to describe individuals' preferences in the face of uncertainty in a way that has intuitive appeal: a complex issue is made manageable through a readily interpretable index. However, it should not come as a surprise to know that there is more than one way of defining an index of risk aversion, although the good news is that the number of alternative approaches is small.

? Mini Problems

8 Prove this. [Hint: use Figure 8.9 and extend the line through P_0 with slope $-\pi_{\text{RED}}/\pi_{\text{BLUE}}$ to cut the indifference curve again at a point P_1; then use the definition of quasiconcavity.]

9 Draw an example of a u-function similar to those in Figure 8.9 but where the individual is risk loving for small risks and risk averse for large risks.

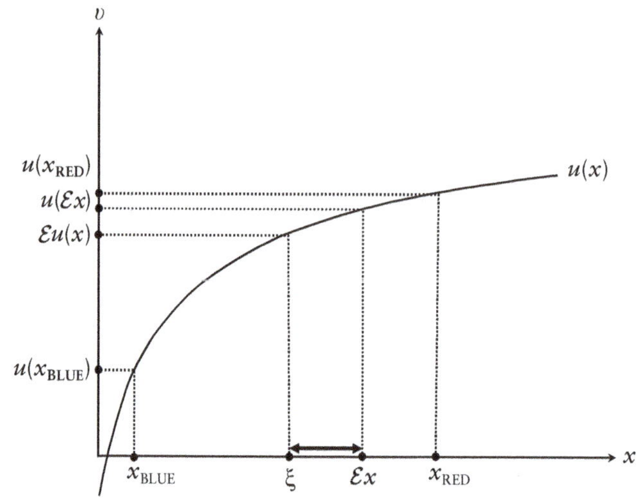

Figure 8.11 The 'felicity' or 'cardinal utility' function u

Assume that preferences conform to the standard von Neumann–Morgenstern configuration. In the case where the payoff is a *scalar* (as in our diagrammatic examples above), we can define an index of risk aversion in a way that encapsulates information about the function u depicted in Figure 8.11. Use the subscript notation u_x and u_{xx} to denote the first and second derivatives of the felicity function u. Then we can introduce two useful definitions of risk aversion.

Absolute risk aversion

The first of the two risk-aversion concepts is just the normalised rate of decrease of marginal felicity:

Definition 8.1

The index of *absolute risk aversion* is a function a given by

$$a(x) := -\frac{u_{xx}(x)}{u_x(x)}.$$

We can also think of $a(\cdot)$ as a sort of index of 'curvature' of the function u; in general the value of $a(x)$ may vary with the level of payoff x, although we will examine below the important special case where a is constant. The index a is positive for risk-averse preferences and zero for risk-neutral preferences (reason: follows immediately from the sign of $u_{xx}(\cdot)$). Furthermore, a is independent of the scale and origin of the function u.[10]

? **Mini Problems**

10 Show why this property is true.

This convenient representation enables us to express the risk premium in terms of the index of absolute risk aversion and the variance of the distribution of x:[11]

Theorem 8.2 (Risk premium and variance)

For small risks the risk premium is approximately $\frac{1}{2}a(x)\text{var}(x)$.

Relative risk aversion

The second standard approach to the definition of risk aversion is this:

Definition 8.2

The index of *relative risk aversion* is a function ϱ given by

$$\varrho(x) := -x\frac{u_{xx}(x)}{u_x(x)}.$$

Clearly this is just the 'elasticity of marginal felicity'. Again it is clear that $\varrho(x)$ must remain unchanged under changes in the scale and origin of the function u. Also, for risk-averse or risk-neutral preferences, increasing absolute risk aversion implies increasing relative risk aversion (but not vice versa).[12]

Comparisons of risk attitudes

We have already seen above (page 190) that a concave u-function can be interpreted as risk aversion everywhere, a convex u-function as risk preference everywhere. We can now be more precise about the association between concavity of u and risk aversion: if we apply a strictly concave transformation to u, then either index of risk aversion must increase, as in the following theorem.[13]

Theorem 8.3 (Concavity and risk aversion)

Let u and $\widehat{u}$ be two felicity (cardinal utility) functions such that $\widehat{u}$ is a concave transformation of u. Then $\widehat{a}(x) \geq a(x)$ and $\widehat{\varrho}(x) \geq \varrho(x)$.

So, the more 'sharply curved' is the cardinal-utility or felicity function u, the higher is risk aversion (see Figure 8.12) on either interpretation. An immediate consequence of

? Mini Problems

11 Prove this. Hint, use a Taylor expansion around $\mathcal{E}x$ on the definition of the risk premium (see page 492).

12 Show this by differentiating the expression in Definition 8.2.

13 Prove this by using the result that the second derivative of a strictly concave function is negative.

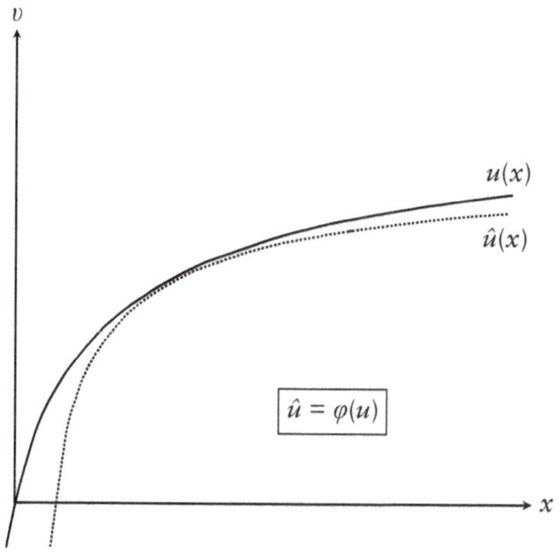

Figure 8.12 Concavity of u and risk aversion

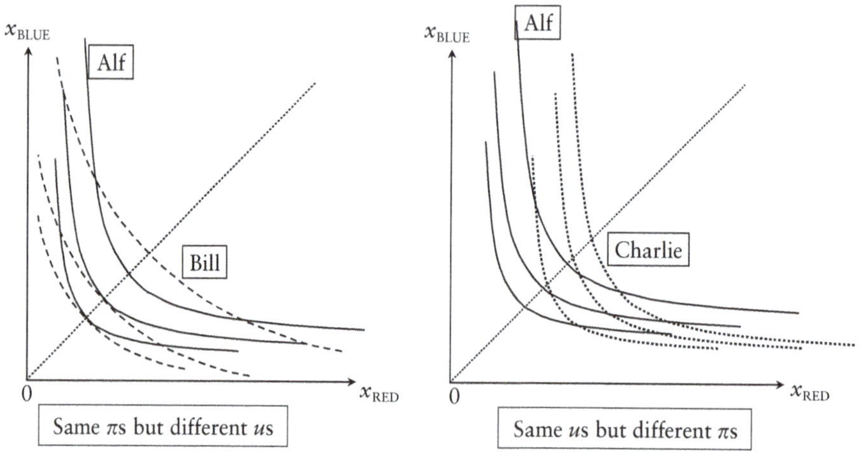

Figure 8.13 Differences in risk attitudes

this is that the more concave is u, the higher is the risk premium (8.5) on any given prospect.[14]

This gives us a convenient way of describing not only how an individual's attitude to risk might change, but also how one can compare the risk attitudes of different people in terms of their risk aversion. Coupled with the notion of differences in subjective probabilities (page 188) we have quite a powerful method of comparing individuals' preferences. Examine Figure 8.13. On the left-hand side we find that Alf and Bill attach the

? Mini Problems

14 Show this using Jensen's inequality (see page 514 in Appendix A).

same subjective probabilities to the two states RED and BLUE: for each of the two sets of indifference curves in the state-space diagram the slope where they intersect the 45° line is the same. But they have differing degrees of risk aversion—Alf's indifference curves are more sharply convex to the origin (his felicity function u will be more concave) than is the case for Bill. By contrast, on the right-hand side, Alf and Charlie exhibit the same degree of risk aversion (their indifference curves have the same 'curvature' and their associated u-functions will be the same), but Charlie puts a higher probability weight on state RED than does Alf (look at the slopes where the indifference curves cross the 45° line).

8.4.3 Special cases

The risk-aversion indices $\alpha(\cdot)$ and $\varrho(\cdot)$ along with the felicity function $u(\cdot)$ are quite general. However, for a lot of practical modelling it is useful to focus on a particular form of u. Among the many possibly fascinating special functional forms that might be considered it is clearly of interest to consider preferences where either $\alpha(x)$ or $\varrho(x)$ is constant for all x. In each case we get a particularly convenient formula for the felicity function u.

Constant absolute risk aversion

In the case of constant *absolute* risk aversion the felicity function must take the form:[15]

$$u(x) = -\frac{1}{\alpha}e^{-\alpha x} \tag{8.6}$$

or some increasing affine transformation of this—see (8.2) above. Figure 8.14 illustrates the indifference curves in state-space for the utility function (8.1) given a constant α: note that along any 45° line the MRS between consumption in the two states of the world is constant.[16]

Constant relative risk aversion

In the case of constant *relative* risk aversion the felicity function must take the form:[17]

$$u(x) = \frac{1}{1-\varrho}x^{1-\varrho} \tag{8.7}$$

illustrated in Figure 8.15[18] or some transformation of (8.7) of the form (8.2). Figure 8.14 illustrates the indifference curves in state-space for the utility function (8.1) given a constant ϱ: in this case we see that the MRS is constant along any ray through the origin.

Other special cases are sometimes useful, in particular the case where u is a quadratic function—see Exercise 8.8.

? Mini Problems

15 Use Definition 8.1 to establish (8.6) if $\alpha(x)$ is everywhere a constant α.

16 Suppose individual preferences satisfy (8.1) with u given by (8.6). Show how Figure 8.14 alters if (a) π_ω is changed, (b) α is changed.

17 Use Definition 8.2 to establish (8.7) if $\varrho(x)$ is everywhere a constant ϱ.

18 Suppose individual preferences satisfy (8.1) with u given by (8.7). Show how Figure 8.15 alters if (a) π_ω is changed, (b) ϱ is changed.

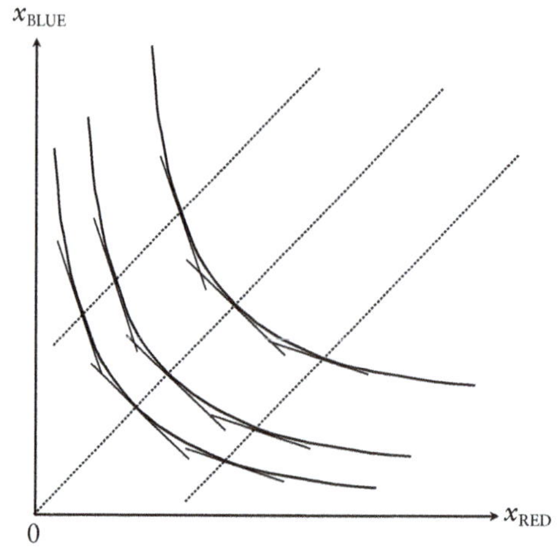

Figure 8.14 Indifference curves with constant absolute risk aversion

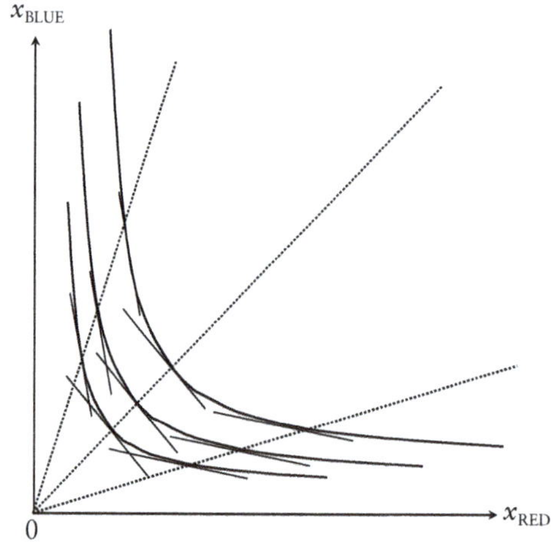

Figure 8.15 Indifference curves with constant relative risk aversion

Example 8.1

How risk averse are people? Barsky et al. (1997) used survey questions from the Health and Retirement Survey—a panel survey of a nationally representative sample of the US population aged 51 to 61 in 1992—to elicit information on risk aversion, subjective rate of time preference, and willingness to substitute intertemporally. The

continued...

...continued

questions involved choice in hypothetical situations about willingness to gamble on lifetime income. Their principal evidence concerns the degree of 'relative risk tolerance'—the inverse of $\varrho(x)$—by individuals at different points in the income distribution. The implications of these estimates for relative risk aversion by income and wealth groups group is shown in Figure 8.16.

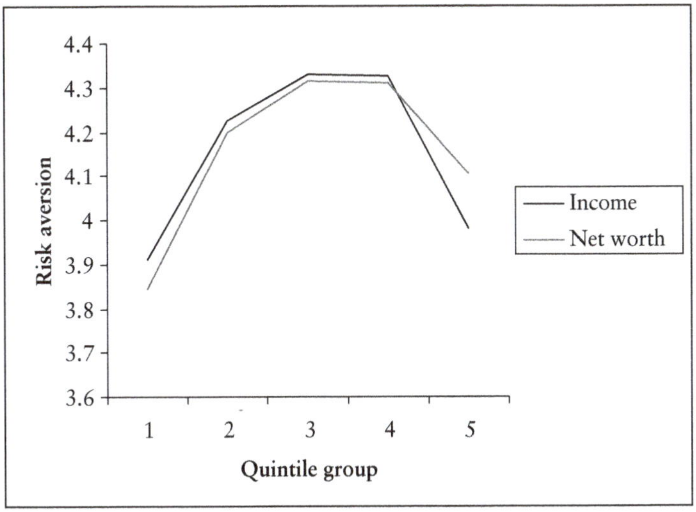

Figure 8.16 Estimates of ϱ by quintiles from Barsky et al. (1997)

8.5 Lotteries and preferences

Sections 8.2 to 8.4 managed quite well without reference to probability, except as a concept derived from the structure of preferences in the face of the unknown future. This is quite a nice idea where there is no particular case for introducing an explicit probability model, but now we are going to change that. By an explicit probability model I mean that there is a well-defined concept of probability conforming to the usual axioms, and that the probability distribution is objectively knowable (section A.8 on page 512 reviews information on probability distributions). Where the probabilities come from—a coin tossing, a spin of the roulette wheel—we do not enquire, but we just take them to be known entities.

We are going to consider the possibility that *probability distributions* are themselves the objects of choice. The motivation for this is easy to appreciate if we think of the individual making a choice amongst lotteries with a given set of prizes associated with the various possible states of the world: the prizes are fixed but there are different probability vectors associated with different lotteries.

8.5.1 The probability space

To formalise this assume a finite set of states of the world ϖ as in (A.64): this is not essential, but it makes the exposition much easier. There is a payoff $\mathbf{x}_\omega$ and a probability π_ω associated with each state. We can imagine preferences being defined over the space of probability distributions, a typical member of which can be written as a ϖ-dimensional vector π given by

$$\pi := (\pi_{\text{RED}}, \pi_{\text{BLUE}}, \pi_{\text{GREEN}}, \ldots) \tag{8.8}$$

such that

$$\sum_{\omega \in \Omega} \pi_\omega = 1. \tag{8.9}$$

Figure 8.17 depicts the case $\varpi = 2$ where the set of points representing the lottery distributions is the 45° line from $(0, 1)$ to $(1, 0)$: the specific distribution $(0.75, 0.25)$ is depicted as a point on this line. Alternatively, for the case $\varpi = 3$, we can use Figure 8.18 where the set of points representing valid probability distributions is the shaded triangle with vertices $(1, 0, 0)$, $(0, 1, 0)$, $(0, 0, 1)$; the specific distribution $(0.5, 0.25, 0.25)$ is illustrated in the figure. (Figures 8.17 and 8.18 are essentially exactly the same as the normalised price diagrams, Figures 7.8 and B.25) The $\varpi = 3$ case can be seen more clearly in Figure 8.19 where the probability triangle has been laid out flat.

8.5.2 Axiomatic approach

Now, suppose we consider an individual's preferences over the space of lotteries. Again we could try to introduce a 'reasonable' axiomatisation for lotteries and then use this

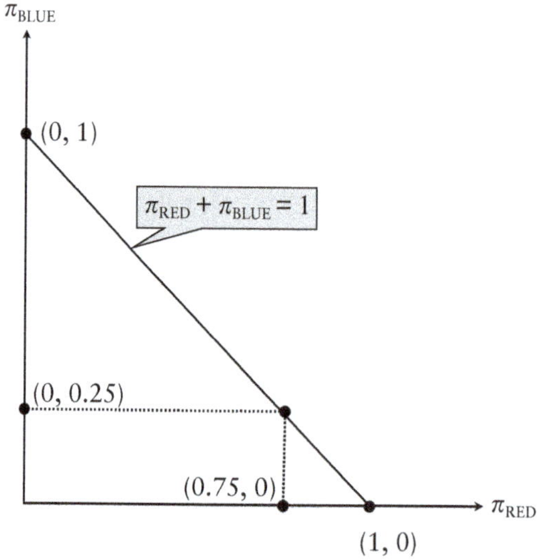

Figure 8.17 The probability diagram: $\#\Omega = 2$

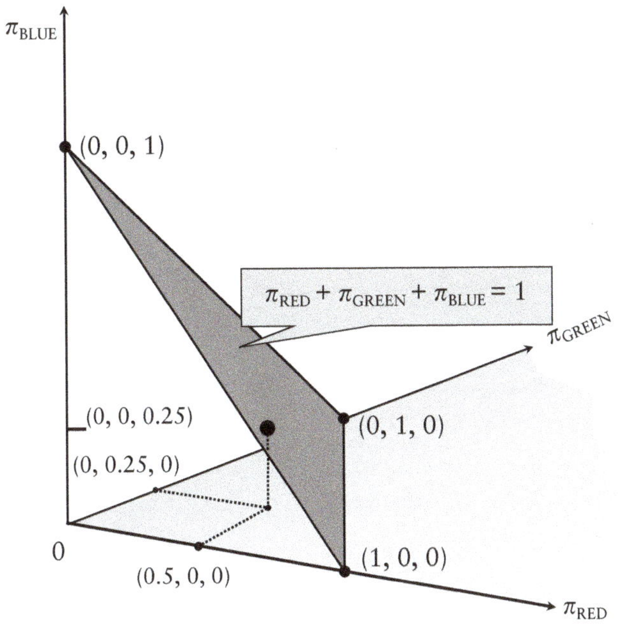

Figure 8.18 The probability diagram: $\#\Omega = 3$

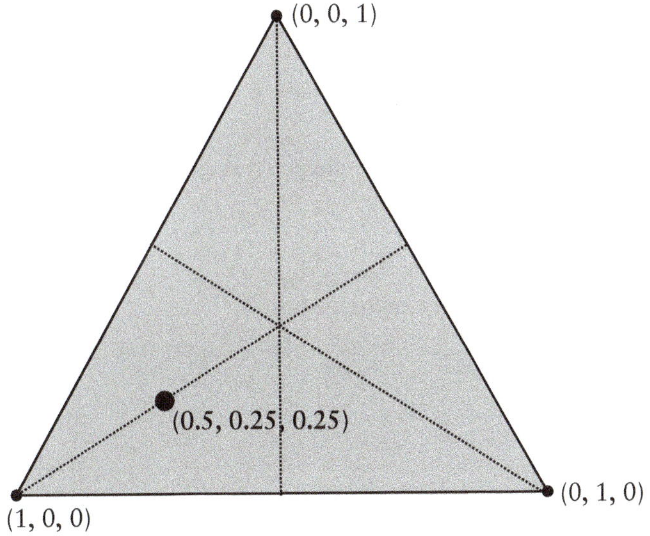

Figure 8.19 The probability diagram: $\#\Omega = 3$ (close-up)

to characterise the structure of preference maps—a particular class of utility functions—that are to be regarded as suitable for problems of choice under uncertainty.

The three axioms that follow form the standard way of doing this axiomatisation. Here π°, π', and π'' are lotteries with the same payoffs, each being ϖ-vectors of the form (8.8). The payoffs associated with the given set of prizes for each of the ϖ states-of-the-world is the ordered list of consumption vectors $[\mathbf{x}_{\text{RED}}, \mathbf{x}_{\text{BLUE}}, \mathbf{x}_{\text{GREEN}}, \ldots]$ and $(0, 1)$ is the set of numbers greater than zero but less than 1.

It is convenient to reintroduce the inelegant 'weak preference' notation that was first used in chapter 4. Remember that the symbol '$\succcurlyeq$' should be read as 'is at least as good as'. Here are the basic axioms:

Axiom 8.4 (Transitivity over lotteries)

If $\pi^\circ \succcurlyeq \pi'$ and $\pi' \succcurlyeq \pi''$ then $\pi^\circ \succcurlyeq \pi''$.

Axiom 8.5 (Independence of lotteries)

If $\pi^\circ \succcurlyeq \pi'$ and $\lambda \in (0, 1)$, then

$$\lambda\pi^\circ + [1 - \lambda]\,\pi'' \succcurlyeq \lambda\pi' + [1 - \lambda]\,\pi''.$$

Axiom 8.6 (Continuity over lotteries)

If $\pi^\circ \succ \pi' \succ \pi''$ then there are numbers $\lambda, \mu \in (0, 1)$ such that

$$\lambda\pi^\circ + [1 - \lambda]\,\pi'' \succ \pi'$$

and

$$\pi' \succ \mu\pi^\circ + [1 - \mu]\,\pi''$$

Now for a very appealing result that obviously echoes Theorem 8.1 (for proof see Appendix C):

Theorem 8.4 (Lottery preference representation)

If Axioms 8.4–8.6 hold then preferences can be represented as a *Von Neumann–Morgenstern utility function*:

$$\sum_{\omega\in\Omega} \pi_\omega u\left(\mathbf{x}_\omega\right) \tag{8.10}$$

where u is a real-valued function on X that is defined up to an increasing, affine transformation.

So with the set of three axioms over lotteries the individual's preference structure once again takes the expected utility form

$$\mathcal{E}u\left(\mathbf{x}\right).$$

Furthermore, it is clear that the utility function (8.10) can be rewritten as a simple 'bilinear' form

$$\sum_{\omega \in \Omega} \pi_\omega \upsilon_\omega \tag{8.11}$$

where $\upsilon_\omega := u(\mathbf{x}_\omega)$ is the payoff in state of the world ω, expressed in utility terms. We can see the objective function (8.11) in two equivalent ways:

1. As a weighted sum of payoffs (the payoffs are the utilities derived from consumption; the weights are the probabilities).
2. As a weighted sum of probabilities (the weights are the scalar utility payoffs).

Version 1 is exactly what we already found from our first pass through the axiomatisation of preferences under uncertainty in section 8.3. Version 2 is perhaps the more natural when it is the probability distributions themselves that are the objects of choice.

The linearity of the expression (8.11) implies that indifference curves must take the form illustrated[19] in Figure 8.20 and will exhibit the following properties:[20]

- The indifference curves must be parallel straight lines.

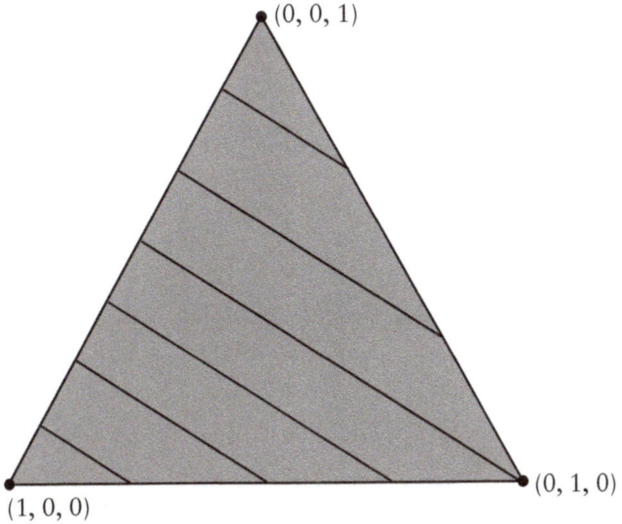

Figure 8.20 π-indifference curves

? Mini Problems

19 Another convenient way of representating the set of all probability distributions when $\varpi = 3$ can be constructed by plotting π_{RED} on the horizontal axis and π_{GREEN} on the vertical axis of a conventional two-dimensional diagram. (a) What shape will the set of all possible lotteries have in this diagrammatic representation? (b) How is π_{BLUE} to be determined in this diagram? (c) What shape will an expected-utility maximiser's indifference curves have in this diagram?

20 In the case where $\varpi = 3$ show that these are true by using the fundamental property (8.9) and the bilinear form of utility (8.11).

- If $\upsilon_{\text{RED}} > \upsilon_{\text{GREEN}} > \upsilon_{\text{BLUE}}$, the slope $\frac{d\pi_{\text{BLUE}}}{d\pi_{\text{RED}}}$ is positive.
- If υ_{BLUE} increases, then the slope also increases.

So we now have a second approach to the expected-utility representation of individual's preferences under uncertainty. This alternative way of looking at the problem of uncertainty and choice is particularly useful when probabilities are well defined and apparently knowable. It might seem that this is almost a niche study of rational choice in situations involving gaming machines, lotteries, horse-race betting, and the like. But there is much more to it. We will find in chapter 10 that explicit randomisation is often appropriate as a device for the analysis and solution of certain types of economic problem: the range of potential application there is enormous.

Uncertainty and risk: notation

π_ω	probability that state of the world ω occurs
π_ω^h	subjective probability of ω according to h
u	felicity or cardinal utility function
β_j	holding of bonds of type j.
$r_{j\omega}$	rate of return on bonds of type j in state ω
$p_{i\omega}$	price of good i contingent on state ω
$\bar{y}$	initial wealth
y_ω	wealth in state ω

8.6 Trade

We now have a fairly extensive view of how individuals' preferences under uncertainty can be mapped; so we should try to put the analysis to work. To do this, let us start by considering the logical extension of the exchange-economy analysis of chapter 7 to a world of uncertainty. We again make use of the timing convention introduced in Figure 8.1.

8.6.1 Contingent goods: competitive equilibrium

If there are n physical commodities (anchovies, beef, champagne,...) and ϖ possible states of the world (RED, BLUE,...) then, viewed from the morning, there are $n\varpi$ possible 'contingent goods' (anchovies-under-RED, anchovies-under-BLUE, beef-under-RED,... It is possible that there are markets, open in the morning, in which titles to these contingent goods can be bought and sold. Then, using the principles established in chapter 7, one can immediately establish the following:

Theorem 8.5 (Equilibrium in contingent goods)

If all individuals are risk averse or risk neutral then there are market-clearing contingent-goods prices

$$[p_{i\omega}], i = 1, \ldots, n, \omega \in \Omega \tag{8.12}$$

that will support an exchange equilibrium.[21]

If there is just one physical commodity ($n = 1$) and two states of the world the situation can be depicted as in Figure 8.21. Here, Alf has the endowment $(0, y_{\text{BLUE}})$ and Bill has the endowment $(y_{\text{RED}}, 0)$ where the size of the box is $y_{\text{RED}} \times y_{\text{BLUE}}$. Note that Alf's indifference curves all have the same slope where they intersect the 45° line through the origin 0^a; Bill's indifference curves all have the same slope where they intersect the 45° line through the origin 0^b; as drawn Alf and Bill have different subjective probabilities about the two events:

$$\frac{\pi^a_{\text{RED}}}{\pi^a_{\text{BLUE}}} > \frac{\pi^b_{\text{RED}}}{\pi^b_{\text{BLUE}}}$$

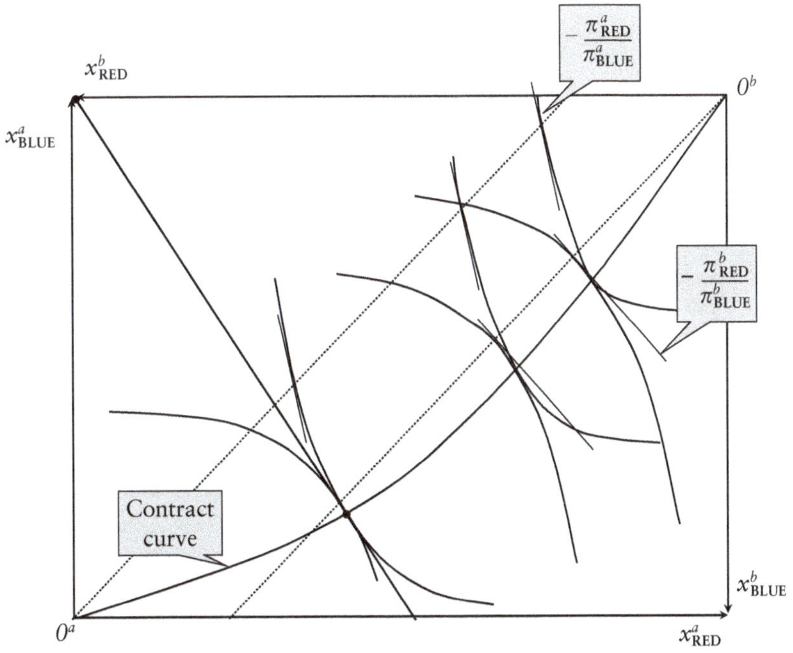

Figure 8.21 Contingent goods: equilibrium trade

? Mini Problems

21 Under what circumstances might it be possible to drop the assumption about risk aversion in this theorem?

Equilibrium contingent-goods prices are shown as the line from the endowment point (top left-hand corner) to the equilibrium point on the contract curve.[22]

But the number of contingent goods $n\varpi$ may be huge, which suggests that it might be rather optimistic to expect all these markets to exist in practice. Could the scale of the problem be reduced somewhat?

8.6.2 Financial assets

Let us introduce 'securities'—in other words financial assets. These securities are simply pieces of paper which say 'the bearer is entitled to \$1 if state ω occurs'. If person h has an endowment y^h of wealth in the morning, and if the price on the securities market (open in the morning) of an ω-security is σ_ω, then the following constraint holds:

$$\sum_{\omega \in \Omega} \sigma_\omega z_\omega^h \leq y^h$$

where z_ω^h is the amount h buys of a ω-security. If the (morning) price of a claim on commodity i contingent on state ω is $p_{i\omega}$, and if $p_i|\omega$ is the (afternoon) price of commodity i given that state ω has actually occurred at lunchtime, then equilibrium in the securities market, with all firms breaking even, requires:

$$\sigma_\omega p_i|\omega = p_{i\omega}$$

which, set out in plain language, says:

price of an ω security	×	price of champagne when ω has occured	=	contingent price of champagne given ω

There is in effect a two-stage budgeting process:

1. Choose the securities z_ω^h: this, along with the realisation of ω, determines income in the afternoon.
2. Given that state ω has occurred, choose the purchases $\mathbf{x}_\omega^h$ in the afternoon so as to maximise $u^h(\mathbf{x}_\omega^h)$.

This seems to reduce the scale of the problem by an order of magnitude, and to introduce a sensible separation of the optimisation problem.

But there is a catch. People have to do their financial shopping in the morning (lunchtime is too late). Now, when they are doing this, will they know what the $p_i|\omega$ would

? Mini Problems

22 Redraw Figure 8.21 for two special cases: (a) where overall wealth in the economy is constant, independent of the state of the world; (b) where Alf and Bill have the same subjective probabilities.

be for each commodity i in each possible state ω? This seems rather a demanding requirement, but they need to have this information in order to make sensible purchases of the securities z^h_ω in stage 1. Despite this logically awkward corner the two-stage simplification provides us a way of making the individual decision maker's problem more tractable.

8.7 Individual optimisation

In the light of the two-stage problem discussed in section 8.6.2 we can now extend the elementary modelling of the household's preferences and constraints to build in the essential characteristics of uncertainty. We will draw both upon standard consumer behaviour as presented in chapter 4, and the model of household production that was introduced in chapter 5. We shall develop further the idea of financial assets introduced in section 8.6.2 in order to focus upon the comparative statics of behaviour under risk.

To set the scene, consider a general version of the consumer's optimisation problem in an uncertain world. You have to go shopping for food, clothing, and so on in the afternoon. The amount that you will have available to spend then may be stochastic (viewed from the morning), but that you can influence the probability distribution affecting your income by some choices that you make in the morning. These choices concern the disposition of your financial assets including the purchase of bonds and of insurance contracts.

Before we get down to the detail of the model, let us again use Figure 8.1 to anchor the concepts that we need in developing the analysis. The timing of matters is in the following order:

- The initial endowment is given. The person makes decisions on financial assets.
- The state of the world ω is revealed: this and the financial decisions already made determine final wealth in state ω.
- Given final wealth the person determines consumptions using *ex-post* utility function and prices then ruling.

An explicit model of this is set out in section 8.7.2 below: first we will examine in more detail what the shape of the individual's attainable set is going to be in a typical problem of choice under uncertainty.

8.7.1 The attainable set

We need to consider the opportunities that may be open to the decision maker under uncertainty—the market environment and budget constraint. We have already introduced one aspect of this in that we have considered whether an individual would swap a given random prospect x for a certain payoff ξ: there may be some possibility of trading away undesirable risk. Is there, however, an analogue to the type of budget set we considered in chapters 4 and 5?

There are many ways that we might approach this question. However, we will proceed by focusing on two key cases—where the individual's endowment is perfectly certain, and where it is stochastic—and then reasoning on a leading example of each case.

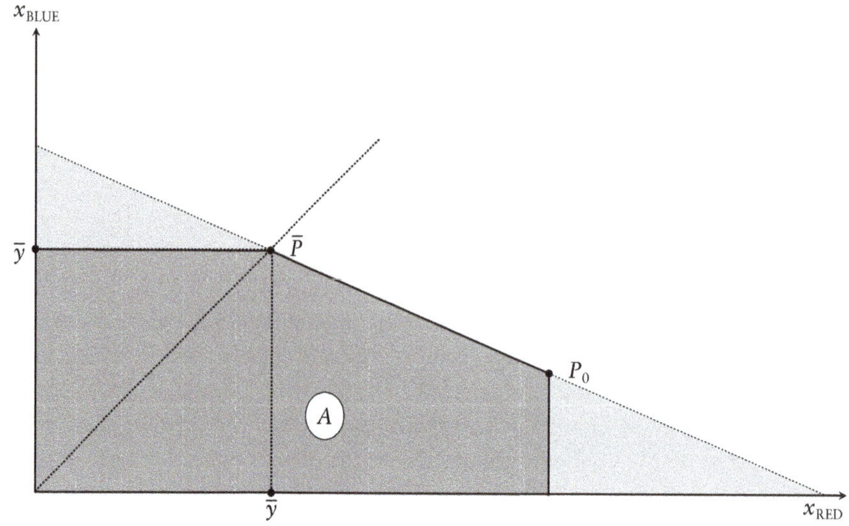

Figure 8.22 Attainable set: safe and risky assets

Determinate endowment: portfolio choice

Return to the two-state 'RED/BLUE' examples above and examine Figure 8.22 which represents the attainable set for a simple portfolio composition problem. Imagine that an individual is endowed with an entitlement to a sum $\bar{y}$ (denominated in dollars) whichever state-of-the-world is realised. We may think of this as money. He may use one or more of these dollars to purchase bonds in dollar units. For the moment, to keep things simple, there is only one type of bond: each bond has a yield of r° if state BLUE is realised, and r' if state RED is realised where we assume that

$$r' > 0 > r^\circ > -1.$$

So if the individual purchases an amount β of bonds and holds the balance $\bar{y} - \beta$ in the form of money then the payoff in terms of *ex-post* wealth is either

$$y_{\text{RED}} = [\bar{y} - \beta] + \beta[1 + r']$$

or

$$y_{\text{BLUE}} = [\bar{y} - \beta] + \beta[1 + r^\circ].$$

In other words

$$(y_{\text{RED}}, y_{\text{BLUE}}) = (\bar{y} + \beta r', \bar{y} + \beta r^\circ). \quad (8.13)$$

By construction of the example, for all positive β we have $y_{\text{RED}} > \bar{y} > y_{\text{BLUE}}$. In Figure 8.22 the points $\bar{P}$ and P_0 represent, respectively, the two cases where $\beta = 0$ and $\beta = \bar{y}$. Clearly the slope of the line joining $\bar{P}$ and P_0 is r'/r°, a negative number, and the coordinates of P_0 are

$$([1 + r']\bar{y},\ [1 + r^\circ]\bar{y}).$$

Given that he has access to such a bond market, any point on this line must lie in the feasible set; and assuming that free disposal of his monetary payoff is available in either case, the attainable set A must include all the points in the heavily shaded area shown in Figure 8.22. Are there any more such points? Perhaps.

First of all, consider points in the lightly shaded area above the set A. If one could 'buy' a negative amount of bonds, then obviously the line from P_0 to $\bar{P}$ could be extended until it met the vertical axis. What this would mean is that the individual is now selling bonds to the market. Whether this is a practical proposition or not depends on other people's evaluation of him as to his 'financial soundness': will he pay up if RED materialises? With certain small transactions—betting on horse races among one's friends, for example—this may be quite reasonable. Otherwise one may have to offer an extremely large r' relative to r° to get anybody to buy one's bonds.

Secondly, consider points in the area to the right of A. Why can't we just extend the line joining $\bar{P}$ and P_0 downwards until it meets the horizontal axis? In order to do this one would have to find someone ready to sell bonds 'on credit' since one would then be buying an amount $\beta > \bar{y}$. Whoever extends this credit then has to bear the risk of the individual going bankrupt if BLUE is realised. So lenders might be found who would be prepared to advance him cash up to the point where he could purchase an amount $-\bar{y}/r^\circ$ of bonds. Again, we can probably imagine situations in which this is a plausible assumption, but it may seem reasonable to suppose that one may have to pay a very high premium for such a facility. Accordingly, the feasible set might look like Figure 8.23, although for many purposes Figure 8.22 is the relevant shape.

There might be a rôle for many such financial assets—particularly if there were many possible states of the world—in which case the attainable set A would have many vertices, a point to which we return in section 8.7.2.

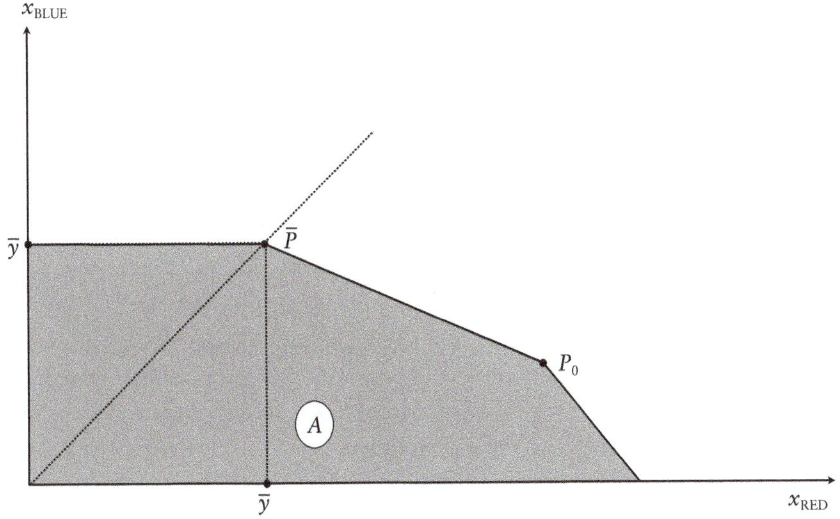

Figure 8.23 Attainable set: safe and risky assets (2)

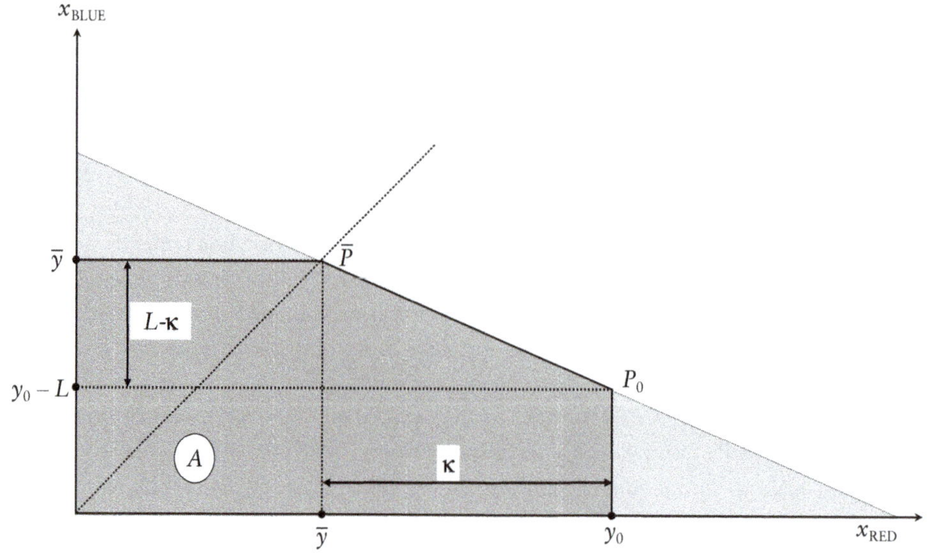

Figure 8.24 Attainable set: insurance

Stochastic endowment: the insurance problem

Now consider a different problem using the same diagrammatic approach—see Figure 8.24. Suppose that the individual's endowment is itself stochastic—it equals y_0 if RED is realised and $y_0 - L$ if BLUE is realised, where $0 < L < y_0$. As a simple example, state BLUE might be having one's house destroyed by fire and state RED is its not being destroyed, y_0 is the total value of your assets in the absence of a disaster, and L is the monetary value of the loss. Let us suppose that fire insurance is available and interpret Figure 8.24. If full insurance coverage is available at a premium represented by

$$\kappa = y_0 - \bar{y} \tag{8.14}$$

then the outcome for such full insurance will be at point $\bar{P}$. If the individual may also purchase partial insurance at the same rates, then once again the whole of the line segment from $\bar{P}$ to P_0—and hence the whole shaded pentagonal area—must lie in the attainable set A.

In this case too we can see that it may be that there are no further points available to the individual. Again consider the implications of enlarging the set A in the region above the horizontal line through point $\bar{P}$. At any point in this area the individual would in fact be better off if his house burned down than if it did not. The person has over-insured himself, a practice which is usually frowned upon. The reason that it is frowned upon is to be found in the concept of *moral hazard*. Moral hazard refers to the influence that the actions of the insured may have on the probability of certain events' occurrence. Up until now we have taken the probabilities—'objective' or 'subjective'—attached to different events as exogenously given. But in practice the probability of a person's house burning down depends in part on his carelessness or otherwise. He may be more inclined to be careless if he knows that he has an insurance company to back him up if one day the house does burn down; furthermore the person may be inclined to be criminally negligent if he knows that he stands to *gain* by event BLUE being realised. So insurance companies usually prevent over-insurance and may indeed include an 'excess clause' (otherwise known as 'coinsurance') so that not even all of the shaded area is attainable.

Furthermore, for reasons similar to those of the portfolio selection example, it is unlikely that the points in the shaded area to the right of A could be included in the attainable set.

8.7.2 Components of the optimum

To set out the individual's optimisation problem let us assume that the person's opportunities are based on the model of section 8.7.1 with a determinate endowment. However, we will introduce one further consideration—the possibility of there being multiple financial assets in the form of 'bonds'. The person has a given amount of wealth $\bar{y}$ initially which he or she could invest in bonds of types $1, \ldots, m$. Denote by β_j the amount held of a type-j bond; then, under any particular state of the world ω we can define income yielded by bond j as:

return on j in state ω	$\times$	holding of bond j	$=$	$r_{jw}\beta_j$

Then the value of one's wealth after the financial decision becomes

$$y_\omega = \bar{y} + \sum_{j=1}^{m} r_{j\omega}\beta_j \tag{8.15}$$

—see equation (8.13). We could then further specify a standard consumer optimisation model conditional upon the realisation of a particular state of the world ω

$$\max_{\mathbf{x}} U(\mathbf{x}) \text{ subject to } \sum_{i=1}^{n} p_i x_i \leq y_\omega$$

where I have written p_i as shorthand for $p_i|\omega$, the actual goods prices once state of the world ω has been realised, and obtain a set of demand functions conditional upon ω:

$$x_i^* = D^i(\mathbf{p}, y_\omega).$$

If we assume that goods' prices are known to be fixed then we may write the maximised utility in state ω as $u(y_\omega) := V(\mathbf{p}, y_\omega)$ where V is the conventional indirect utility function (Definition 4.6, page 88).

Suppose that there is a finite number of all possible states of the world. Then clearly one also has to solve the problem:

$$\max_{\beta_1,\ldots,\beta_m} \sum_{\omega\in\Omega} \pi_\omega u(y_\omega)$$

subject to

$$y_\omega = \bar{y} + \sum_{j=1}^{m} r_{j\omega}\beta_j.$$

But we have analysed this type of economic problem before. There is a close analogy with the general 'household production' or 'goods and characteristics' model discussed in chapter 5 (page 107). We just need some translation of terminology; in the present case:

- $y_{\text{RED}}, y_{\text{BLUE}}, \ldots$ are the 'consumption goods' from which one derives utility directly.
- $\beta_1, \ldots, \beta_m$ correspond to the 'market goods' or 'inputs' which are purchased by the household.
- Given uniform interest rates, one has a linear technology which transforms purchased assets into spendable income in each state of the world using (8.15).

This is illustrated in Figure 8.25 where the vertices of the attainable set A correspond to the various types of bond.[23] The slope of each facet is given by

$$\frac{r_{j+1,\text{BLUE}} - r_{j,\text{BLUE}}}{r_{j+1,\text{RED}} - r_{j,\text{RED}}}. \tag{8.16}$$

Drawing on the analysis of section 5.4 what can one say about the person's decisions regarding the purchase of financial assets in this set-up? Dominated financial assets will obviously be irrelevant to the optimal choice. There may be many zeros amongst the m

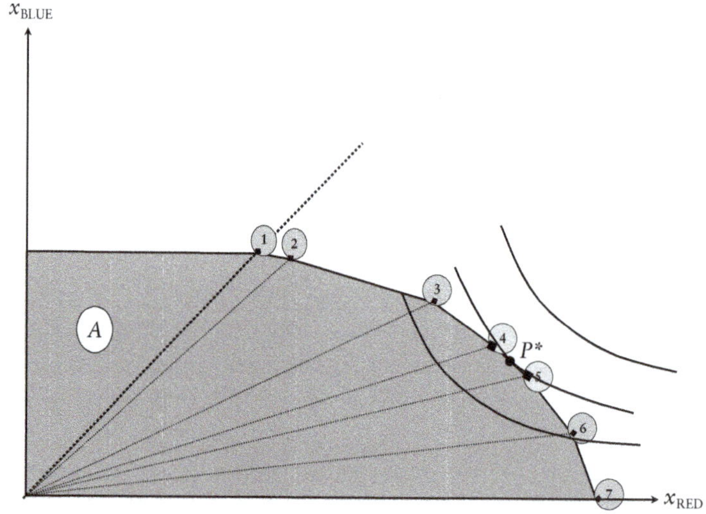

Figure 8.25 Consumer choice with a variety of financial assets

? Mini Problems

23 As depicted bonds 1 and 7 are likely to be uninteresting—briefly explain what they are.

assets—as illustrated in Figure 8.25 just two types of asset are purchased. As a result of this, when rates of return change one may get jumps in demand for financial assets as particular assets are brought into or dropped from the solution. One could also expect jumps in demand as initial wealth grows if the individual's indifference curves are not homothetic.[24] But can we say more about the way that this demand for financial assets will respond to changes in the distribution of rates of return?

8.7.3 The portfolio problem

We can say much more if we restrict attention to what happens on just one facet—i.e. if we rule out switching between facets of A as we change the parameters of the model. Then, in the case where there are two states of the world, the problem is effectively equivalent to that discussed earlier in section 8.7.1. However, although we will illustrate it for the two-state case using diagrams based on Figure 8.22, our approach will be more general in that we will allow for arbitrarily many possible states of the world.

So we take a model in which there are just two assets: money and bonds. The person is endowed with a determinate amount of initial wealth $\bar{y}$. The rate of return on bonds is given by r, a random variable with a known distribution having positive, finite mean; the density function of r is illustrated in Figure 8.26.

If the person chooses to hold an amount β in the form of bonds, then wealth after the financial decision has been made is

$$y = \bar{y} + \beta r, \tag{8.17}$$

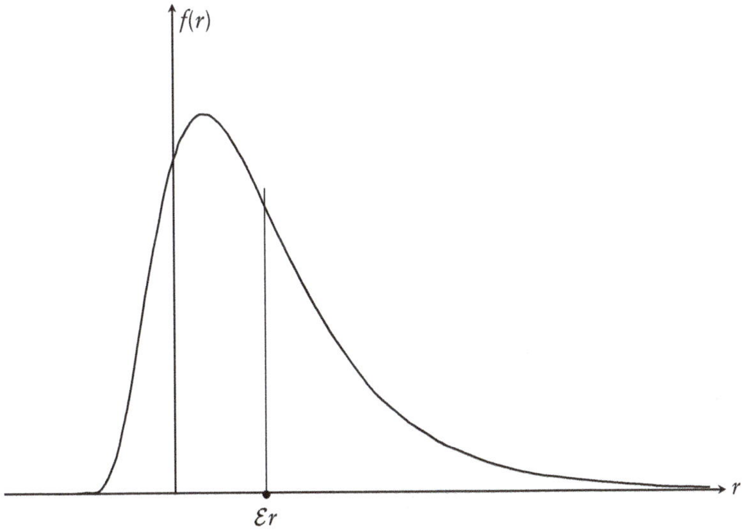

Figure 8.26 Distribution of returns

? **Mini Problems**

24 Explain why you get jumps in the demand for bonds in this case.

also a random variable—compare this with equations (8.13) and (8.15). Assume that the person's preferences are represented by a utility function of the form $\mathcal{E}u(y)$ where y is given by (8.17).

We can now set out the simplified optimisation problem:

$$\max_{\beta} \mathcal{E}u\left(\bar{y} + \beta r\right) \tag{8.18}$$

$$\text{subject to } 0 \leq \beta \leq \bar{y}.$$

Letting u_y denote the first derivative of u with respect to y, the first-order condition for this maximisation problem is

$$\mathcal{E}\left(ru_y\left(\bar{y} + \beta r\right)\right) = 0 \tag{8.19}$$

for an interior solution—see Figure 8.27.[25]

Assuming the interior solution we can, in principle, solve equation (8.19) in order to derive the optimal purchases of bonds β^* which will be a function of the endowment of assets $\bar{y}$ and of the probability distribution of the rate of return r.

One clear-cut conclusion can easily be drawn from this approach. Consider what happens in the neighbourhood of point $\bar{P}$ in Figure 8.27; specifically consider the effect on

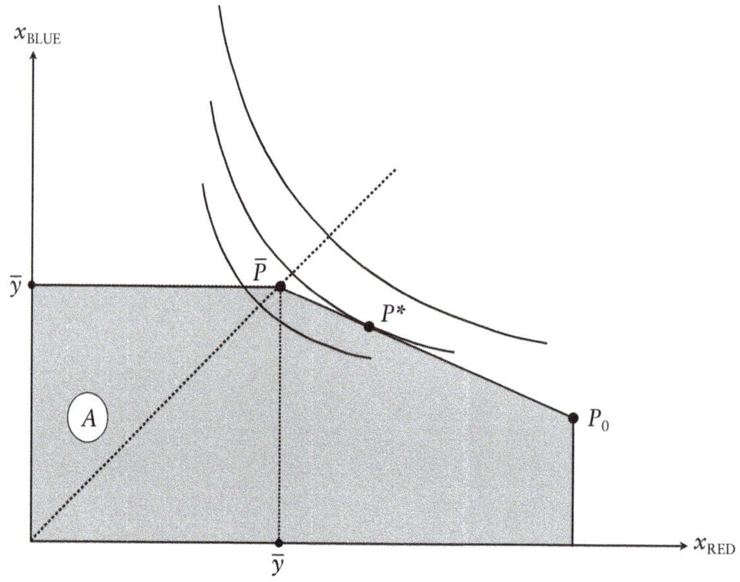

Figure 8.27 Consumer choice: safe and risky assets

? Mini Problems

25 What would be the FOC corresponding to (8.19) for the two possible corner solutions (a) where the individual chooses to leave all resources in the riskless asset, (b) where the individual puts all resources into bonds?

the person's utility of a small increase in β away from 0:

$$\left.\frac{\partial\mathcal{E}\left(u\left(\bar{y}+\beta r\right)\right)}{\partial\beta}\right|_{\beta=0} = u_y\left(\bar{y}\right)\mathcal{E}r. \tag{8.20}$$

So, given that $u_y\left(\bar{y}\right) > 0$, the impact of β on utility is positive if $\mathcal{E}r$ is positive. In other words:

Theorem 8.6 (Risk taking)

If the individual is non-satiated and has a von Neumann–Morgenstern utility function and if the expected return to risk taking is positive, then the individual will hold a positive amount of the risky asset.

It would be interesting to know how this optimal demand for risky assets β^* changes in response to changes in the market environment by modelling the appropriate changes in the person's budget constraint. We can use the first-order condition (8.19) to look at a number of issues in comparative statics.

An increase in endowment

Let us analyse the effect of a change in the person's assets by differentiating (8.19) with respect to $\bar{y}$:

$$\mathcal{E}\left(ru_{yy}\left(\bar{y}+\beta^* r\right)\left[1+r\frac{\partial\beta^*}{\partial\bar{y}}\right]\right) = 0 \tag{8.21}$$

which implies

$$\frac{\partial\beta^*}{\partial\bar{y}} = \frac{-\mathcal{E}\left(ru_{yy}\left(\bar{y}+\beta^* r\right)\right)}{\mathcal{E}\left(r^2 u_{yy}\left(\bar{y}+\beta^* r\right)\right)}. \tag{8.22}$$

The denominator of (8.22) is unambiguously negative, since u_{yy} is everywhere negative (the assumption of risk aversion) and r^2 is non-negative. However, the numerator could be positive or negative, since the risky asset could turn out to make a profit ($r > 0$) or a loss ($r < 0$). So it appears that the effect of wealth upon risk taking is ambiguous.

In order to resolve this ambiguity, it is common to find the following additional assumption about preferences:

Axiom 8.7 (Decreasing absolute risk aversion)

$a(x)$ decreases with x.

This introduces a further restriction on the felicity function u.[26] But if we introduce decreasing absolute risk aversion along with the other standard assumptions, then we can show (see Appendix C):

? Mini Problems

26 This further restriction can be expressed as a condition on the third derivative of u: what is the condition?

Theorem 8.7 (Risk-taking and wealth)

If an individual has a von Neumann–Morgenstern utility function with decreasing absolute risk aversion and holds a positive amount of the risky asset, then the amount invested in the risky asset will increase as initial wealth increases.

People whose risk aversion decreases with their endowment will buy more risky assets if their wealth increases. Notice that the result for any distribution of returns for which $\beta^* > 0$. This can be illustrated in Figure 8.28. The original equilibrium is at P^* and the lightly shaded area shows the increase in the attainable set when $\bar{y}$ increases to $\bar{y} + \Delta$. From (8.13) it is clear that if bond holdings were kept constant at β^* as $\bar{y}$ increased then point P^* would move out along a 45° line. However, the indifference curves as drawn show decreasing absolute risk aversion (constant relative risk aversion) and the new equilibrium is at P^{**}, to the right of the 45° line through P^*: the holding of bonds must have increased.

A rightward shift of the distribution

What happens to risk-taking if the returns on the risky asset change in an unambiguously favourable fashion? We can analyse this by supposing that the probability distribution of r is 'translated' by adding the same determinate amount τ to every possible value of r (see Figure 8.29); then we look at how β^* changes in response to small changes in τ, in the neighbourhood of $\tau = 0$.

Adding the amount τ to r as mentioned the FOC (8.19) becomes:

$$\mathcal{E}\left([r+\tau]\, u_y\left(\bar{y} + \beta^*[r+\tau]\right)\right) = 0 \tag{8.23}$$

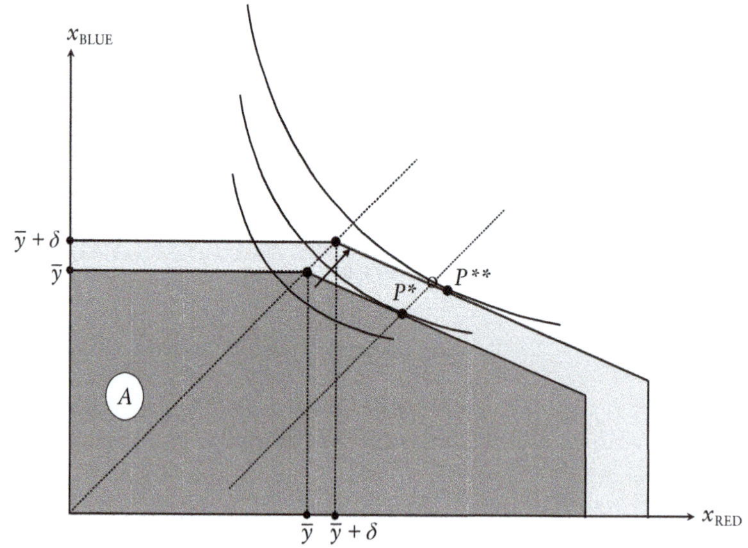

Figure 8.28 Effect of an increase in endowment

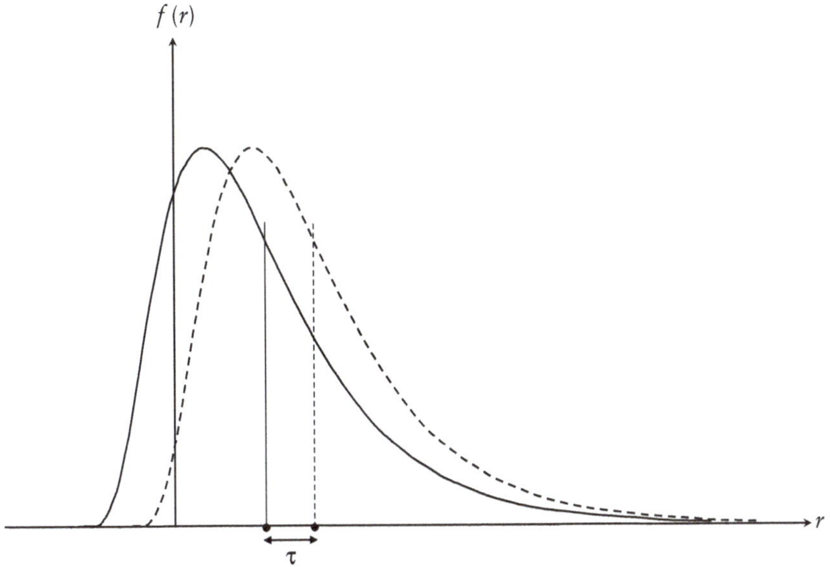

Figure 8.29 A rightward shift

Differentiate (8.23) with respect to τ:

$$\mathcal{E}\left(u_y\left(\bar{y}+\beta^*[r+\tau]\right)\right)+\beta^*\mathcal{E}\left([r+\tau]\,u_{yy}\left(\bar{y}+\beta^*[r+\tau]\right)\right)$$
$$+\frac{\partial\beta^*}{\partial\tau}\mathcal{E}\left([r+\tau]^2\,u_{yy}\left(\bar{y}+\beta^*[r+\tau]\right)\right)=0 \tag{8.24}$$

Setting $\tau = 0$ we find

$$\mathcal{E}\left(u_y(y)\right)+\beta^*\mathcal{E}\left(ru_{yy}(y)\right)+\frac{\partial\beta^*}{\partial\tau}\mathcal{E}\left(r^2u_{yy}(y)\right)=0$$

where y is given by (8.17). So, in the neighbourhood of $\tau = 0$, we have

$$\frac{\partial\beta^*}{\partial\tau}=-\frac{\mathcal{E}\left(u_y(y)\right)}{\mathcal{E}\left(r^2u_{yy}(y)\right)}-\beta^*\frac{\mathcal{E}\left(ru_{yy}(y)\right)}{\mathcal{E}\left(r^2u_{yy}(y)\right)} \tag{8.25}$$

and, given (8.22), equation (8.25) becomes

$$\frac{\partial\beta^*}{\partial\tau}=-\frac{\mathcal{E}\left(u_y(y)\right)}{\mathcal{E}\left(r^2u_{yy}(y)\right)}+\beta^*\frac{\partial\beta^*}{\partial\bar{y}} \tag{8.26}$$

From the way that (8.26) is written it is clear that if β^* increases with personal wealth $\bar{y}$, then it must also increase with this favourable shift in the distribution. Decreasing absolute risk aversion is a sufficient condition (although not a necessary condition) for this.

This is illustrated in Figure 8.30. The attainable set A expands in an unbalanced way: the point P_0 moves out along a 45° line, so that the boundary of A rotates through $\bar{P}$ as shown. Once again the dotted line through P^* is the locus that would be followed if the absolute amount of bonds bought β stayed constant: clearly the new equilibrium P^{**} must lie to the right of where this line intersects the new boundary of A (marked by '∘').

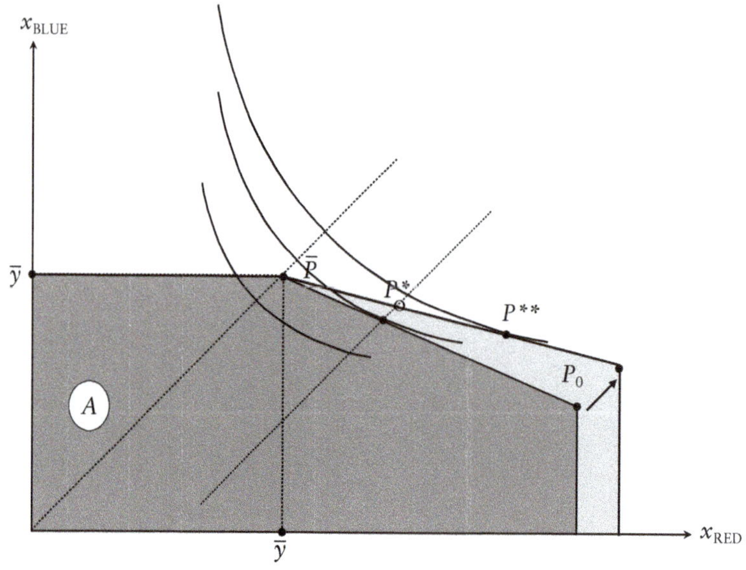

Figure 8.30 Effect of a rightward shift in the distribution

An increased spread of the distribution

We can handle this by supposing that the probability distribution of r is 'scaled' by multiplying every possible value of r by a determinate constant t; then we look at how changes in t affect β^* in the neighbourhood of $t = 1$. The FOC becomes:

$$\mathcal{E}\left(tru_y\left(\bar{y} + \beta^* tr\right)\right) = 0. \tag{8.27}$$

Differentiating this with respect to t we now find:[27]

$$\frac{t}{\beta^*}\frac{\partial \beta^*}{\partial t} = -1. \tag{8.28}$$

Equation (8.28) implies that the optimal purchase of bonds, β^*, is bound to decrease; the elasticity of bond purchases with respect to the scale factor t is -1. We do not need a special assumption about risk aversion in order to get this result.

8.7.4 Insurance

From section 8.7.1 it appears that the economic problem of insurance can be treated in essentially the same way as the portfolio problem just discussed—i.e. as a tradeoff between safe and risky assets that is determined by the person's own subjective probability of events, the nature of risk aversion, and the returns to the risky asset. Some results can indeed just be copied across. In particular, Theorem 8.6 shows that if the expected

? Mini Problems

27 Fill in the missing lines from the differentiation and illustrate the outcome using a figure similar to Figure 8.30.

return to risk is positive, then the individual will choose to hold a positive amount of the risky asset: let us see how this translates.

From Figure 8.24 and the accompanying discussion we can deduce the following. If the risk of loss is π_{BLUE} and the size of the loss is L, then the expected payout equals the expected receipts for an insurance company if

$$\pi_{\text{BLUE}} L = \kappa \tag{8.29}$$

where κ, the premium, is given by (8.14). A quick check reveals that this is equivalent to

$$\frac{L - \kappa}{\kappa} = \frac{\pi_{\text{RED}}}{\pi_{\text{BLUE}}} \tag{8.30}$$

where the left-hand side is clearly the slope of the boundary of the attainable set A and the right-hand side is the slope of the indifference curve where it crosses the 45° line. So if the insurance premium is set such that the insurance company expects to break even (8.29) then the indifference curve is tangential to the opportunity set at point $\bar{P}$: the person fully insures at the optimum. This means that if the terms of the insurance are unfair (replace the '=' by '<' in expressions 8.14 and 8.29), then the individual will take out less than full insurance or no insurance at all—i.e. equilibrium will be in either the interior of or at the right-hand end of the line joining $\bar{P}$ and P_0. This is the exact translation of the result concerning the positive expected return to risk.

Other results will work in the same way. For example, if an individual with decreasing risk aversion chooses to be partially insured then, if his wealth grows, the amount of his insurance coverage cannot increase (see Exercise 8.12).[28] However, this type of analysis assumes that an insurance market exists for this type of risk—but under what circumstances would such a market exist?

First, there is a necessary condition of large numbers in the market to permit the pooling of risks. Take a simple example of an economy consisting of clones. Each clone faces an identical independent risk on his wealth, and evaluates the risk with identical subjective probability: \$2,000 with probability 0.4 and \$4,000 with probability 0.6. Let us suppose the clones assemble themselves and agree to pool their wealth and share equally the combined realised payoff. Clearly the mathematical expectation is \$3,200. Now consider Figure 8.31. As the economy is replicated to 2, 4, 8, 16, . . . persons, we can see that the distribution of payoffs to the individual soon becomes symmetric and concentrated about the expected value. In the limit, of course, the probability of any payoff different from the expected value becomes infinitesimal. If the insurance company is owned by a large number of 'small' individuals—that is if the shares in the profits and losses from insurance are reasonably diffuse—then the risks are not only pooled but also *spread*. Under such circumstances there may be the basis for effective competition in both the demand side and the supply side of a market for insurance.

? Mini Problems

28 Suppose that the individual is partially insured and that the insurance company cuts the premium. Assuming decreasing absolute risk aversion use a diagram similar to Figure 8.30 to show what happens to the amount of insurance coverage chosen.

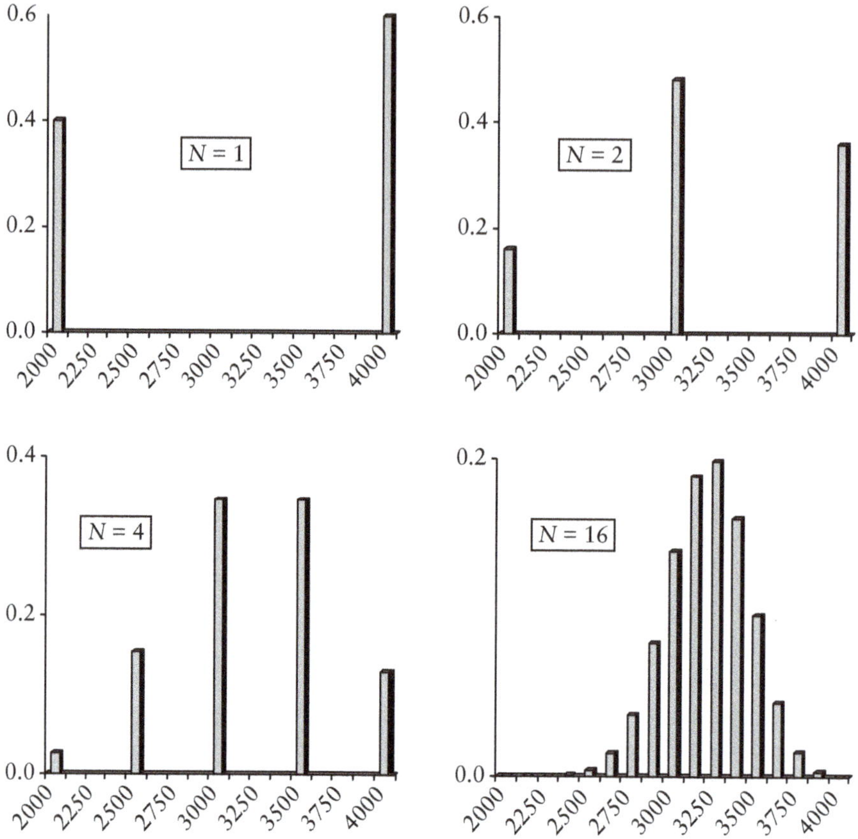

Figure 8.31 Effect of numbers

So it appears that with a very large number of agents each one ought to be able to 'buy insurance' against the risk on his income at an actuarially fair price corresponding to the probabilities given above. But the example also reveals some obvious pitfalls:

- There is the 'moral hazard' problem as described above. We must assume that no person can have direct influence on the probability of any particular payoff being realised.
- Each agent must be 'small' in the limit.
- The *risks must be independent*—the results will not work if all the agents' risks are closely correlated.
- The payoffs must be *tradeable* amongst the individuals in the form of some transferable commodity. Obviously there are some risks which people confront where the payoffs cannot be thus transferred, and where losses cannot be compensated for in money.

For any of these reasons a market may simply not exist; more on this and related problems in chapter 11.

Summary

The basic approach to decision making under uncertainty can be analysed as a straightforward extension of consumer theory, by considering a class of utility functions that are additively separable over the states of the world. Furthermore, the analysis of market equilibrium and of individual portfolio behaviour in the face of risk follows on immediately from the core analysis of previous chapters once we have appropriately modelled preferences and opportunities.

It is evident that at the core of the approach is the concept of expected utility—see the two Theorems 8.1 and 8.4. But why do the job twice over? Our first approach to the subject showed that the special structure of utility function follows naturally from a coherent representation of preferences over a space of 'contingent goods' without a specific construct of probability; the second approach shows what happens when one treats probability distributions—lotteries—as the focus of the choice problem. The first approach provides an essential link to the standard analysis of decision making treated in chapters 2 to 7; we shall find this second approach is essential in providing the basis for the analysis of games in chapter 10.

Reading notes

On the foundations of expected-utility analysis in terms of choices over lotteries refer to von Neumann and Morgenstern (1944) and Friedman and Savage (1948) and for early, penetrating critiques see Allais (1953) and Ellsberg (1961). The von Neumann–Morgenstern approach in some ways builds on the classic contribution by Bernouilli (1954) originally published in 1738; for this reason some refer to a von Neumann–Morgenstern utility function as a *Bernoulli utility function.* A useful survey is to be found in Machina (1987). The consumer-theoretic approach to uncertainty is developed in Deaton and Muellbauer (1980).

The concept of risk aversion developed in Arrow (1970) and Pratt (1964). On the discussion of conditions such as increasing risk aversion see Menezes et al. (1980).

Exercises

8.1 Suppose you have to pay \$2 for a ticket to enter a competition. The prize is \$19 and the probability that you win is $\frac{1}{3}$. You have an expected utility function with $u(x) = \log x$ and your current wealth is \$10.

1. What is the certainty equivalent of this competition?
2. What is the risk premium?
3. Should you enter the competition?

8.2 You are sending a package worth 10 000€. You estimate that there is a 0.1 per cent chance that the package will be lost or destroyed in transit. An insurance company offers you insurance against this eventuality for a premium of 15€. If you are risk-neutral, should you buy insurance?

8.3 Consider the following definition of risk aversion. Let $P := \{(x_\omega, \pi_\omega) : \omega \in \Omega\}$ be a random prospect, where x_ω is the payoff in state ω and π_ω is the (subjective) probability of state ω, and let $\mathcal{E}x := \sum_{\omega \in \Omega} \pi_\omega x_\omega$, the mean of the prospect, and let $P_\lambda := \{(\lambda x_\omega + [1 - \lambda]\mathcal{E}x, \pi_\omega) : \omega \in \Omega\}$ be a 'mixture' of the original prospect with the mean. Define an individual as risk averse if he always prefers P_λ to P for $0 < \lambda < 1$.

1. Illustrate this concept on a diagram similar to Figure 8.6 and contrast it with the concept of risk aversion mentioned on page 183.
2. Show that this definition of risk aversion need not imply convex-to-the-origin indifference curves (Rothschild and Stiglitz 1970).

8.4 This is an example of the *Allais paradox* (Allais 1953). Suppose you are asked to choose between two lotteries. In one case the choice is between P_1 and P_2, and in the other case the choice offered is between P_3 and P_4, as specified below:

$$P_1 : \quad \$1\,000\,000 \quad \text{with probability } 1$$

$$P_2 : \begin{cases} \$5\,000\,000 & \text{with probability } 0.1 \\ \$1\,000\,000 & \text{with probability } 0.89 \\ \$0 & \text{with probability } 0.01 \end{cases}$$

$$P_3 : \begin{cases} \$5\,000\,000 & \text{with probability } 0.1 \\ \$0 & \text{with probability } 0.9 \end{cases}$$

$$P_4 : \begin{cases} \$1\,000\,000 & \text{with probability } 0.11 \\ \$0 & \text{with probability } 0.89 \end{cases}$$

It is often the case that people prefer P_1 to P_2 and then also prefer P_3 to P_4. Show that these preferences violate the independence axiom.

8.5 This is an example to illustrate disappointment (Bell 1988, Machina 1989). Suppose the payoffs are as follows

x''	weekend for two in your favourite holiday location
x'	book of photographs of the same location
x°	fish-and-chip supper.

Your preferences under certainty are $x'' \succ x' \succ x^\circ$. Now consider the following two prospects

$$P_1 : \begin{cases} x'' & \text{with probability } 0.99 \\ x' & \text{with probability } 0 \\ x^\circ & \text{with probability } 0.01 \end{cases}$$

$$P_2 : \begin{cases} x'' & \text{with probability } 0.99 \\ x' & \text{with probability } 0.01 \\ x^{\circ} & \text{with probability } 0 \end{cases}$$

Suppose a person expresses a preference for P_1 over P_2. Briefly explain why this might be the case in practice. Which axiom in section 8.3 is violated by such preferences?

8.6 An example to illustrate regret. Let

$$P := \{(x_\omega, \pi_\omega) : \omega \in \Omega\}$$

$$P' := \{(x'_\omega, \pi_\omega) : \omega \in \Omega\}$$

be two prospects available to an individual. Define the expected regret if the person chooses P rather than P' as

$$\sum_{\omega \in \Omega} \pi_\omega \max\left\{x'_\omega - x_\omega, 0\right\} \tag{8.31}$$

Now consider the choices amongst prospects presented in Exercise 8.4. Show that if a person is concerned to minimise expected regret as measured by (8.31), then it is reasonable that the person select P_1 when P_2 is also available and then also select P_3 when P_4 is available (Bell 1982, Loomes and Sugden 1982).

8.7 An example of the Ellsberg paradox (Ellsberg 1961). There are two urns marked *Left* and *Right*, each of which contains 100 balls. You know that in Urn L there are exactly 49 white balls and the rest are black and that in Urn R there are black and white balls, but in unknown proportions. Consider the following two experiments:

1. One ball is to be drawn from each of L and R. The person must choose between L and R before the draw is made. If the ball drawn from the chosen urn is black there is a prize of \$1000, otherwise nothing.
2. Again one ball is to be drawn from each of L and R; again the person must choose between L and R before the draw. Now if the ball drawn from the chosen urn is white there is a prize of \$1000, otherwise nothing. You observe a person choose Urn L in both experiments. Show that this violates Axiom 8.3.

8.8 An individual faces a prospect with a monetary payoff represented by a random variable x that is distributed over the bounded interval of the real line $[\underline{a}, \overline{a}]$. He has a utility function $\mathcal{E}v(x)$ where

$$u(x) = a_0 + a_1 x - \frac{1}{2} a_2 x^2$$

and a_0, a_1, a_2 are all positive numbers.

1. Show that the individual's utility function can also be written as $\varphi(\mathcal{E}x, var(x))$. Sketch the indifference curves in a diagram with $\mathcal{E}x$ and $var(x)$ on the axes, and discuss the effect on the indifference map altering (i) the parameter a_1, (ii) the parameter a_2.

2. For the model to make sense, what value must $\bar{a}$ have? [Hint: examine the first derivative of u.]
3. Show that both absolute and relative risk aversion increase with x.

8.9 A person lives for 1 or 2 periods. If he lives for both periods he has a utility function given by (5.13) where the parameter δ is the pure rate of time preference. The probability of survival to period 2 is γ, and the person's utility in period 2 if he does not survive is 0.

1. Show that if the person's preferences in the face of uncertainty are represented by the functional form in (8.1) then the person's utility can be written as
$$u(x_1) + \delta' u(x_2). \tag{8.32}$$
What is the value of the parameter δ'?
2. What is the appropriate form of the utility function if the person could live for an indefinite number of periods, the rate of time preference is the same for any adjacent pair of periods, and the probability of survival to the next period given survival to the current period remains constant?

8.10 A person has an objective function $\mathcal{E}u(y)$ where u is an increasing, strictly concave, twice-differentiable function, and y is the monetary value of his final wealth after tax. He has an initial stock of assets K which he may keep either in the form of bonds, where they earn a return at a stochastic rate r, or in the form of cash where they earn a return of zero. Assume that $\mathcal{E}r > 0$ and that $\Pr\{r < 0\} > 0$.

1. If he invests an amount β in bonds $(0 < \beta < K)$ and is taxed at rate t on his *income*, write down the expression for his disposable final wealth y, assuming full loss offset of the tax.
2. Find the first-order condition which determines his optimal bond portfolio β^*.
3. Examine the way in which a small increase in t will affect β^*.
4. What would be the effect of basing the tax on the person's *wealth* rather than income?

8.11 An individual taxpayer has an income y that he should report to the tax authority. Tax is payable at a constant proportionate rate t. The taxpayer reports x where $0 \leq x \leq y$ and is aware that the tax authority audits some tax returns. Assume that the probability that the taxpayer's report is audited is π, that when an audit is carried out the true taxable income becomes public knowledge and that, if $x < y$, the taxpayer must pay both the underpaid tax and a surcharge of s times the underpaid tax.

1. If the taxpayer chooses $x < y$, show that disposable income c in the two possible states of the world is given by
$$c_{\text{NOAUDIT}} = y - tx,$$
$$c_{\text{AUDIT}} = [1 - t - st]\, y + stx.$$
2. Assume that the individual chooses x so as to maximise the utility function
$$[1 - \pi]\, u(c_{\text{NOAUDIT}}) + \pi u(c_{\text{AUDIT}})$$

where u is increasing and strictly concave.

(a) Write down the FOC for an interior maximum.

(b) Show that if $1 - \pi - \pi s > 0$ then the individual will definitely under-report income.

3. If the optimal income report x^* satisfies $0 < x^* < y$:

(a) Show that if the surcharge is raised then under-reported income will decrease.

(b) If true income increases will under-reported income increase or decrease?

8.12 A risk-averse person has wealth y_0 and faces a risk of loss $L < y_0$ with probability π. An insurance company offers cover of the loss at a premium $\kappa > \pi L$. It is possible to take out partial cover on a pro-rata basis, so that an amount tL of the loss can be covered at cost $t\kappa$ where $0 < t < 1$.

1. Explain why the person will not choose full insurance.
2. Find the conditions that will determine t^*, the optimal value of t.
3. Show how t will change as y_0 increases if all other parameters remain unchanged.

8.13 Consider a competitive, price-taking firm that confronts one of the following two situations:

- 'uncertainty': price p is a random variable with expectation $\overline{p}$.
- 'certainty': price is fixed at $\overline{p}$.

It has a cost function $C(q)$ where q is output and it seeks to maximise the expected utility of profit.

1. Suppose that the firm must choose the level of output before the particular realisation of p is announced. Set up the firm's optimisation problem and derive the first- and second-order conditions for a maximum. Show that, if the firm is risk averse, then increasing marginal cost is not a necessary condition for a maximum, and that it strictly prefers 'certainty' to 'uncertainty'. Show that if the firm is risk neutral then the firm is indifferent as between 'certainty' and 'uncertainty'.
2. Now suppose that the firm can select q *after* the realisation of p is announced, and that marginal cost is strictly increasing. Using the firm's competitive supply function write down profit as a function of p and show that this profit function is convex. Hence show that a risk-neutral firm would strictly prefer 'uncertainty' to 'certainty'.

8.14 Every year Alf sells apples from his orchard. Although the market price of apples remains constant (and equal to 1), the output of Alf's orchard is variable yielding an amount R_1, R_2 in good and poor years respectively; the probability of good and poor years is known to be $1 - \pi$ and π respectively. A buyer, Bill offers Alf a contract for his apple crop which stipulates a down payment (irrespective of whether the year is good or poor) and a bonus if the year turns out to be good.

1. Assuming Alf is risk averse, use a diagram similar to Figure 8.21 to sketch the set of such contracts which he would be prepared to accept. Assuming that Bill is also risk averse, sketch his indifference curves in the same diagram.

2. Assuming that Bill knows the shape of Alf's acceptance set, illustrate the optimum contract on the diagram. Write down the first-order conditions for this in terms of Alf's and Bill's utility functions.

8.15 In exercise 8.14, what would be the effect on the contract if (i) Bill were risk neutral; (ii) Alf risk neutral?

9 Welfare

Society is a kind of parent to its members. If it, and they, are to thrive, its values must be clear, coherent and generally acceptable

Milton R. Sapirstein, *Paradoxes of Everyday Life* (1955), 8.

9.1 Introduction

What is social welfare? In this chapter we shall look at a number of interpretations of this concept. Perhaps it is not too contentious to say that 'social welfare' has to do with the welfare of individuals. Accordingly, the following questions appear to be particularly relevant:

- What do we mean by an individual's 'welfare'?
- What do we mean by 'social welfare'?
- How are the two related?

For the most part we shall continue to make a very simple assumption about the first issue—that an individual's (or household's) welfare is determined by the consumption of goods and services that he enjoys. However, larger issues may well be involved. For example, one person's utility may be affected by another person's consumption levels if he is afflicted with altruism or envy. So it is also useful to consider the wider aspects of individuals' preferences about social states, especially when we come to consider the second and third questions above. The issues raised are so many and varied that it is difficult to combine them all into a single unified theme. Accordingly, to bring out some of the main points, we shall adopt a piecemeal method of attack. We shall consider three approaches:

1. We investigate whether 'social preferences', taken as an ordering over all possible social states, can logically be derived from individual citizens' orderings of all possible social states.
2. We examine whether certain apparently reasonable principles provide a satisfactory basis for evaluating social states.
3. We consider the implications of imposing a specific structure of social preferences that to some extent respect individual preferences.

Of course these approaches are not necessarily incompatible, but they represent alternative, fruitful, lines of enquiry as to what can usefully be done in the name of welfare economics.

9.2 The constitution

How should we carry forward the idea of choice from the individual to the social setting? We might think it reasonable to start by reusing of some of the tools from Chapter 4—perhaps something related to utility and indifference curves. However, rather than attempting to define and specify in detail 'social indifference curves' as such, we shall investigate a more basic concept: that of the existence of a 'social ordering'—in other words a ranking by 'society' of all possible social states. This approach allows us to examine at a fundamental level the problem of how to organise an economy or a society.

9.2.1 A model of social choice

Let us begin with some terminology and notation.

The setting

When we come to consider issues that affect the entire community it seems reasonable to allow social states to be described in very broad terms. A social state θ may be taken to include, for example, the allocation $\mathbf{a}$ of all the private goods, the supply of public goods, and other non-economic entities; the set of all conceivable social states is Θ.

Each household or individual h has a well-defined ordering $\succeq^h$ over the social states in Θ; this means that each agent's ranking of social states satisfies the axioms of completeness and transitivity, and is also reflexive (so that θ is ranked at least as good as itself). We read the statement '$\theta \succeq^h \theta'$' as: 'h thinks social state θ is no worse than social state θ'.' Denote by $\succeq$ (note the absence of h-superscript) the ordering over social states that is to be taken as the *social ordering*, and use the symbols $\succ^h$ and $\succ$ to denote *strict* preference by household h and by society respectively. This is just a slight adaptation of the notation first introduced for individual choice on page 74.

It may be that there is some systematic way of deriving this $\succeq$ from all individual $\succeq^h$. In other words it may be that we have some function Σ such that:

$$\succeq = \Sigma(\succeq^1, \succeq^2, \ldots, \succeq^h, \ldots,) \tag{9.1}$$

The rule Σ will be termed a *constitution* (it is also referred to as a social welfare function in some of the literature.). The constitution Σ has as its argument a 'profile' of preferences—in other words, a collection of individual orderings or utility *functions*—not utility levels—one for each household;[1] it yields an ordering as its result.

? Mini Problems

1 Suppose we use a utility function U^h to represent preferences $\succeq^h$. If we were then to replace U^h by $a + bU^h$ in (9.1) what would happen to $\succeq$? If we were to replace U^h by $\varphi(U^h)$ in (9.1) what would happen to $\succeq$?

The problem

The constitution Σ is thus a notional device for aggregating preferences. A central issue of welfare economics is whether such a preference-aggregating constitution can be found that meets certain 'reasonable' preconditions. This is of primary interest in giving substance to the idea of 'social preferences' or a 'social ordering'. After all, one might argue, of what does society consist but its citizens? So, if the concept is to have any meaning, either social preferences are imposed from the outside, or they are somehow related to individual preferences about social states. The question that needs to be addressed immediately is this: what characteristics might the constitution Σ possess for it to be seen as a 'reasonable' way of relating $\succeq$ to the individual $\succeq^h$? Consider the following four requirements which we shall state as axioms.

Axiom 9.1 (Universality)

The constitution is defined over all logically possible profiles of individual orderings.

Axiom 9.2 (Pareto unanimity)

For any $\theta, \theta' \in \Theta$ if $\theta \succ^h \theta'$ for all h then $\theta \succ \theta'$.

Axiom 9.3 (Independence of irrelevant alternatives)

Let two different profiles be identical over some subset ($\hat{\Theta} \subset \Theta$). Then the social orderings corresponding to each of these profiles are identical over $\hat{\Theta}$.

Axiom 9.4 (Non-dictatorship)

There is no individual h such that for all $\theta, \theta' \in \Theta : \theta \succ^h \theta' \Rightarrow \theta \succ \theta'$.

The first of these requirements is self-explanatory. Axiom 9.2 requires that the constitution is such that if there is unanimous agreement that one social state is strictly preferred to another, then 'society' strictly prefers the said social state. Axiom 9.3 is analogous to the requirement of 'independence' (Axiom 8.2) in the theory of choice under uncertainty and choice amongst lotteries (Axiom 8.5). Axiom 9.4 requires that there be no individual who is always decisive as to whether society shall rank one particular state above another.

A key result

We have run through this list of axioms quite rapidly, because the principal result that one has in this area is extremely simple and, unfortunately, rather negative in tone.

Theorem 9.1 (Arrow's impossibility theorem)

If there are more than two social states then there is no Σ satisfying axioms 9.1 to 9.4.

Should this negative result be regarded as overwhelmingly disturbing? Not if one is careful about interpreting what it is actually saying. In fact, on reflection, it may not be all that surprising—given the potential conflicts of interest in a community one might be rather amazed if the Impossibility Theorem did not hold.

Point of the result

Note that the result does *not* say that reasonable constitutions can never exist, which is a relief because societies seem to arrange for themselves constitutions that are not wholly bizarre. But it does suggest that it is too ambitious to expect a rule like Σ for deriving the 'social will' or 'social preferences' that simultaneously satisfy the requirements to be:

- a bona fide ordering;
- as general and as appealing as implied in Axioms 9.1 to 9.4;
- a function only of citizens' orderings over social states.

This remark suggests three possible ways forward from the apparent impasse posed by the Impossibility Theorem.

9.2.2 A response to the Impossibility Theorem?

One possible response to Theorem 9.1 is to resign oneself to the unpalatable conclusion that if Axioms 9.1 to 9.4 are to be accepted, then 'social preferences' just will not work like individual preferences in that they may not exhibit either the property of completeness or of transitivity which characterise an 'ordering' as conventionally understood. Furthermore, this result concerns not only the possibility of deriving rational *social* preferences, but also preferences in other smaller groups. Collective choice, whether it is by a nation, a club, a corporation—or even a household—may therefore not be 'rational' in the sense that we usually assume individuals to be rational. Some progress can be made by relaxing one or other of these two properties to some extent,[2] but even then some version of the above 'Impossibility Theorem' will still apply.

The second way forward is to examine whether one or more of Axioms 9.1 to 9.4 could, under certain circumstances, be done away with or modified to some extent. There are several ways in which this might be done, but let us take as given Axioms 9.2 and 9.4 (there does not seem to be much future in a specification of a social choice rule that perversely flies in the face of the Pareto unanimity criterion or that abdicates choice to a Führer). How may one usefully relax Axioms 9.1 and 9.3?

The problem with Axiom 9.1 is that one may be demanding far more of one's constitution Σ than one is ever likely to need, since Axiom 9.1 requires that Σ shall work for *every conceivable* pattern of individual preferences. In practice it may be reasonable to limit the range of 'relevant' preferences in some fashion, either by some empirical generalisation ('your average American wants less government interference') or by restricting the jurisdiction over which individual preferences are to count. One aspect of this latter approach is pursued below.

Consider the possibility that only certain *types* of preferences may be empirically relevant. It might be true that, even though there is substantial disagreement in the relative

? Mini Problems

2 Some authors have suggested relaxing the requirement of transitivity to *quasi-transitivity* which could allow for the possibility that while (i) $\theta \succ \theta'$ and (ii) θ and θ'' are regarded as different, yet (iii) θ and θ'' are *also* regarded as indifferent. Consider the usefulness of this concept in making judgements about social states.

desirability of social states, nevertheless all citizens' orderings have a similar structure. Consider, for example, a situation in which all the social states could be represented by a single variable—let us say the proportion of (homogeneous) national resources devoted to national defence; every other possible variable is fixed. Now sketch the preferences of army veteran Alf, ban-the-bomb Bill, and common-sense Charlie: the horizontal axis measures the proportion of national resources devoted to defence and the vertical axis indicates intensity of preference of each person for each person over the range of θ—see Figure 9.1. The scale of the vertical axis is arbitrary: if you like, you can imagine that this axis measures utility where utility scales need not be in any way comparable between people. Observe that Alf always prefers more resources to be devoted to defence; Bill has the opposite type of preference structure; Charlie dislikes extremes of either sort. All three are examples of *single-peaked* preferences—where there is at most one peak along the line representing social states. Let us assume that *all* persons' preferences have this single-peaked structure, and consider a simple majority voting scheme as a possible candidate for Σ in equation (9.1) (so that, given a choice between θ and θ', then θ is ranked over θ' if and only if the number of people who prefer θ to θ' is greater than the number of people who prefer θ' to θ). Then simple experimentation will reveal that (in Figure 9.1) this condition produces a well-behaved ordering of the states $[\theta', \theta, \theta'']$—majority voting ranks the states in exactly that order, in fact.

By contrast, if preferences looked like those in Figure 9.2 then majority voting will *not* produce a well-defined ordering of the three states: in this case one will find apparent intransitivities in the social choice rule.[3] This property on preferences generalises.

Theorem 9.2 (Black's Theorem)

If the number of voters is odd and all individuals have single-peaked preferences, then the majority voting procedure produces a complete, transitive social ordering.

Unfortunately one should not get too excited about this result. In the first place single-peakedness may be quite a strong assumption in some cases. Secondly, the 'single-peakedness' idea is quite difficult to apply to cases where the set of social states Θ is multidimensional.[4] It appears that simply restricting the pattern of admissible preferences is not in itself of much help in dealing with the result of the 'Impossibility' Theorem.

? Mini Problems

3 Write out Alf's, Bill's, and Charlie's preferences over $\{\theta, \theta', \theta''\}$ in terms of rankings. Show that for the preferences in Figure 9.1 majority voting over pairs of states produces a well-defined winner (known as a *Condorcet winner*) and that for the preferences in Figure 9.2 majority voting does not produce a well-defined winner.

4 Consider a situation where social states have two dimensions—expenditure on defence and expenditure on welfare. Suppose Alf, Bill, and Charlie have a similar structure of preferences over the set $\{\theta, \theta', \theta''\}$ as in Mini Problem 3; Alf always prefers more on defence and less on welfare; Bill prefers the opposite; Charlie prefers a middling amount of both. What restriction on the set of alternatives $\{\theta, \theta', \theta''\}$ would be required for the 'single-peakedness' property to obtain?

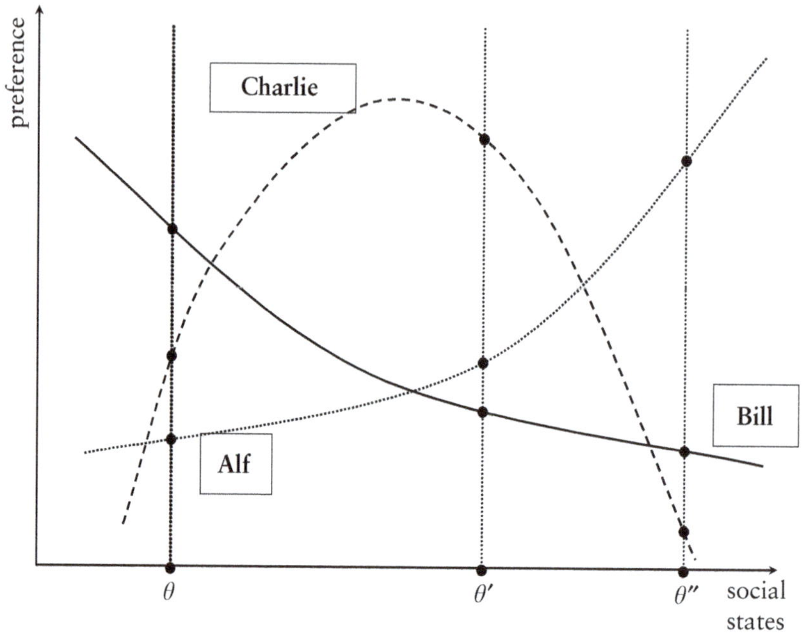

Figure 9.1 Alf, Bill, Charlie and the Bomb

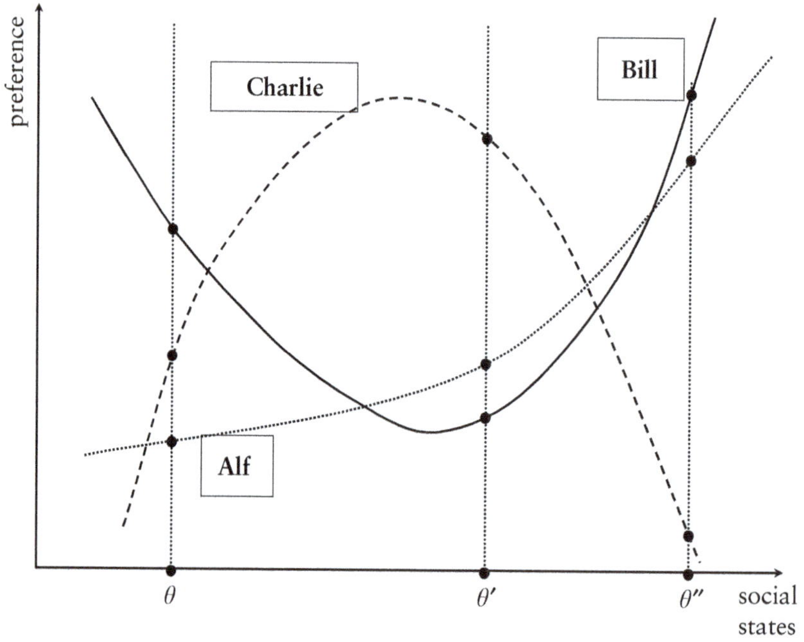

Figure 9.2 Alf, Bill, Charlie and the Bomb (2)

If one relaxes Axiom 9.3, the independence of irrelevant alternatives, then one can certainly obtain a well-defined social ordering. But again it is not clear whether this is necessarily a major step forward. Consider two simple examples of voting systems that relax IIA:

1. *Plurality voting (First-past-the-post)*. Put all the social states simultaneously to the vote. Choose that which attains the largest number of votes. The problem with this system is that it focuses only on the 'top candidate' states and takes no account of voter preference in the rest of the distribution. Votes for middle- and low-order candidate states might be considered 'wasted'.
2. *Rank-order point voting (or de Borda voting)*. Let every voter assign the number 1 to the worst alternative, the number 2 to the next worst, 3 to the next worst, ... and so on. Let $\#(\theta)$ be the total number of points voted for state θ; then the constitution ranks θ above θ' if and only if $\#(\theta) > \#(\theta')$. Manifestly the use of $\#(\theta)$ provides a complete, transitive ordering; but the ordering will depend crucially on the particular point system attached to the votes. For example, if instead of the points $[1, 2, 3, 4, \ldots]$ one assigned the point system $[1, 2, 4, 8, \ldots]$ then a different social ordering might emerge. However, there is a more disturbing feature of this constitution, which illustrates directly why the independence of irrelevant alternatives assumption may be attractive. Consider the subset of social states that beat all others under this constitution; now reduce the size of the set of social states by discarding *only* some of the inferior states—one may find that even though the original subset of 'best states' is still available, they may not still be considered 'best' when the choice is made from the more restricted set of states.[5]

The third approach to coping with the Impossibility Theorem is to change the domain of Σ. Recall that Σ is defined on a space of *orderings*; so, if one imputed a utility function U^h to household h, one might apply an arbitrary increasing transformation to U^h without affecting the social ordering generated by Σ. If one abandons this and imputes a cardinal significance to the utility functions U^h, one is in effect allowing the constitution to take account of individuals' intensity of preference. This obviously demands much more information about households' preferences; we examine this later when we consider an explicit social-welfare function (section 9.5). There are many examples of the oddities of voting systems in social decision rules.

? Mini Problems

5 Consider an economy with this voting scheme, where there are four social states and three individuals with preferences thus:

Alf	Bill	Charlie
θ	θ'''	θ'
θ''	θ	θ'''
θ'	θ''	θ''
θ'''	θ'	θ

Calculate the aggregate number of votes for each state, (a) on the assumption that $\Theta = \{\theta, \theta', \theta'', \theta'''\}$:(b) assuming that $\Theta = \{\theta, \theta'''\}$. Show that under (a) θ is ranked equal to θ''' and that they are regarded as superior to all other states. Show that under (b) θ is ranked inferior to θ'''.

Example 9.1

The selection by the International Olympic Committee of the location of the games in the year 2000 is given in Table 9.1. Each column shows a round of voting with an elimination at each round. Consider the ranking revealed by the collection of columns. Clearly whether Sydney is ranked over Peking depends on whether or not Manchester is forced to have a zero weight (compare columns 3 and 4). The implied constitution violates the independence of irrelevant alternatives.

Round	1	2	3	4
Sydney	30	30	37	45
Peking	32	37	40	43
Manchester	11	13	11	—
Berlin	9	9	—	—
Istanbul	7	—	—	—

Table 9.1 How the IOC voted 1993

9.2.3 The importance of the constitution approach

The rather downbeat feel of the results examined here might lead us to suppose that we have just been chasing down a blind alley. This is not really so. Rather the results on the constitution perform two very important services. First, the analysis makes very clear not just that social-choice problems are fundamentally difficult, but *why* they are difficult; we need this before moving on to look at other approaches to social welfare. Second, it lays the groundwork for some important developments in the field of economic design. This is dealt with in detail in Chapter 12.

9.3 Principles for social judgements: efficiency

Now let us turn to the second of three routes outlined in the introduction: the search for 'reasonable' principles on which to assess social states. The most obvious of these principles is, perhaps, efficiency. Because this issue is so important we will consider not only the principle itself but also, in some detail, its application to the type of economic model considered in chapter 7.

We often take the notion of efficiency for granted. This is, perhaps, attributable in part to the way in which we usually represent these problems graphically. You see a production-possibility set—and the eye immediately focuses on the boundary. You see a budget constraint and again the eye focuses on the boundary, where none of the budget is 'wasted'. Moreover efficiency appears to be something which we might consider as a desirable attribute of economic systems. How can it be expressed more generally?

First let us introduce some notation. Let v^h be the utility level of household h. For any state $\theta \in \Theta$ write

$$v^h = v^h(\theta) \tag{9.2}$$

where $v^h(\cdot)$ is a kind of 'reduced-form' function giving the utility of person or household h in state θ: the function encapsulates all the detailed information of how the person's utility level is determined through the market allocation. We introduce the following two concepts:

Definition 9.1

For any two states θ, θ', the state θ is *Pareto superior* to the state θ' if and only if (a) for all households $h : v^h(\theta) \geq v^h(\theta')$ and (b) for at least one household h: $v^h(\theta) > v^h(\theta')$.

As a synonym to the phrase 'is Pareto superior to' we will sometimes use the term 'Pareto-dominates'. If social states are adequately described there is a presumption to reject as 'inefficient' any state θ' when a Pareto-superior alternative exists. This leads to a definition of efficiency.

Definition 9.2

A state θ is Pareto efficient if and only if (a) θ is feasible ($\theta \in \Theta$), and (b) there is no other feasible θ' that is Pareto superior to θ.

The set of all Pareto-efficient outcomes is illustrated in Figure 9.3. The shaded area represents $\mathbb{U}$, the *utility-possibility set*—the attainable set of utility levels of Alf and Bill, given the technology of the economy total resources, and possibly other constraints. The parts of the boundary marked with a heavy curve are the Pareto-efficient points.[6] Once we have grasped these fundamental ideas, a number of questions spring to mind:

- What type of allocations yield a Pareto-efficient outcome?
- In what way does the specification of a Pareto-efficient state depend on the characteristics of goods?
- What is the relation of efficiency to the concept of equilibrium?
- How should departures from efficiency be quantified?

We will defer the last item on this list until chapter 13. In order to come to grips with the other three issues we need to consider the relationship between goods and services at the level of the individual household and commodities in the economy as a whole.

? Mini Problems

6 (a) How would this diagram alter if Alf's and Bill's utility functions U^h were replaced by the transformed utility functions $\alpha + \beta U^h$? (b) How would the diagram alter if the utility functions were replaced with the transformed functions $\varphi^h(U^h)$, where φ^h is a monotonic increasing function? (c) Plot an arbitrary point in the utility-possibility set, and show the set of points which are Pareto superior to it.

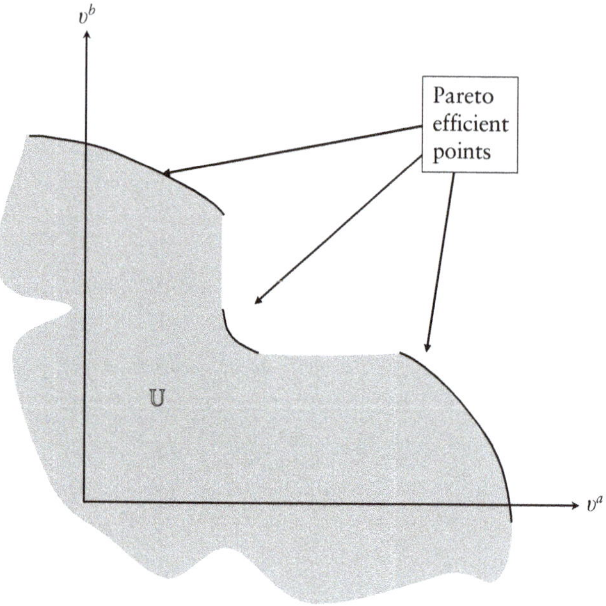

Figure 9.3 The utility possibility set

	Rival	Non-Rival
Excludable	Pure private goods	?
Non-excludable	?	Pure public goods

Table 9.2 Classification of goods

We introduce a simple classification of goods by their innate physical characteristics or the characteristics of the means by which they are delivered; these are summarised in Table 9.2.

One cell of Table 9.2 is already familiar: we have encountered the idea of 'private goods' when considering the issue of aggregating commodity demands over households in demand analysis (page 115) and in general equilibrium (pages 147 and 157). It is often the standard unspoken assumption in microeconomics that all goods are purely private. But in fact this assumption requires that associated with each good are two properties that, in some cases, may just be inappropriate for the commodity in question. The two properties are as follows.

1. *Rivalness.* Suppose there are n_h consumers, each consuming at least one unit of good i and that the marginal cost production of good i in terms of other goods is c. Now imagine that one additional person (person $n_h + 1$) arrives and demands good i. If the nature of good i is such that the provision of one unit to the new person requires

a sacrifice of c units of other goods, we will say that good i is *rival*. If the provision of one unit to the new consumer requires a sacrifice of 0 units of other goods, we will say that good i is *non-rival*.

2. *Excludability*. Suppose there are n_h consumers, each consuming at least one unit of good i. If it is possible costlessly to prevent an extra person from consuming one unit of good i, then good i is said to be *excludable*. If it is impossible to prevent the extra individual from consuming one unit of good i, then good i is said to be *non-excludable*.

A simple example of (pure) excludability is where one can charge a price for the good without having to incur any compliance costs to ensure that the consumer has actually paid. Clearly both rivalness and excludability properties may change as technology changes. Clearly also excludability depends on the institutions assumed to be present in the economy—for example whether it is legal to deny individuals consumption of a particular commodity. Using these two concepts we have:

Definition 9.3

Good i is a *pure private* good if it is rival and excludable.

Definition 9.4

Good i is a *pure public* good if it is non-rival and non-excludable.

Other types of good—for example the cases marked '?' in Table 9.2—are also economically interesting. For example, consumption externalities—see section 13.4—are examples of rival but non-excludable goods and page 448 gives an example of non-rival excludable goods.

Elements of the efficiency problem

x_i^h	consumption by h of good i
q_i^f	net output by f of good i
R_i	resource stock of i
U^h	h's preferences
Φ^f	f's technology
LAGRANGE MULTIPLIERS	
λ_h	utility constraint
μ_f	technical feasibility
κ_i	materials balance

9.3.1 Private goods and the market

Let us outline a simple methodology for deriving the economic conditions which characterise a Pareto-efficient allocation. We do this within the type of economic environment that we used for the standard competitive equilibrium approach. In this environment there are n goods, n_h households, and n_f firms; household h consumes x_i^h of good i, and firm f produces a net output q_i^f of good i; the n-vector $\mathbf{x}^h$ (whose ith component is x_i^h) represents the consumption basket of household h; and n-vector $\mathbf{q}^f$ (whose ith component is q_i^f) represents firm f's activity. The social state θ in such a world is completely determined by the allocation which we denote by $\mathbf{a} := ([\mathbf{x}], [\mathbf{q}])$, where $[\mathbf{x}]$ is shorthand for $[\mathbf{x}^1, \mathbf{x}^2, \ldots, \mathbf{x}^h, \ldots]$, the list of consumption vectors for households $h = 1, 2, \ldots, n_h$, and $[\mathbf{q}]$ is shorthand for $[\mathbf{q}^1, \mathbf{q}^2, \ldots, \mathbf{q}^f, \ldots]$, the list of net output vectors for firms $f = 1, 2, \ldots, n_f$.

Now let us see how to characterise economic efficiency in this environment. The method is as follows:

- We specify an economy in terms of its three basic components: preferences, technology and total resources—see the notation box.
- For each household except household 1 we pick an arbitrary (feasible) utility level $\bar{\upsilon}^h$. There is no special significance in choosing household 1 as the exception: any other household could have been chosen.
- Then we maximise the utility of household 1 subject to three constraints. Every other household must achieve at least its target utility level specified above:

$$U^h(\mathbf{x}^h) \geq \bar{\upsilon}^h \tag{9.3}$$

for $h = 2, \ldots, n_h$; every firm's production must be technologically feasible:

$$\Phi^f(\mathbf{q}^f) \leq 0, \tag{9.4}$$

and the materials balance condition must hold for each commodity:

$$x_i \leq q_i + R_i. \tag{9.5}$$

If we consider this problem in the case of *pure private goods* with no production externalities, then the following aggregation properties hold:

$$x_i = \sum_{h=1}^{n_h} x_i^h \tag{9.6}$$

$$q_i = \sum_{f=1}^{n_f} q_i^f. \tag{9.7}$$

We may then set out the efficiency problem as one of maximising the following Lagrangean:

$$\left.\begin{array}{rcl} \mathcal{L}([\mathbf{x}], [\mathbf{q}], \lambda, \mu, \kappa; \bar{\upsilon}, R) & := & U^1(\mathbf{x}^1) + \sum_{h=2}^{n_h} \lambda_h [U^h(\mathbf{x}^h) - \bar{\upsilon}^h] \\ & & - \sum_{f=1}^{n_f} \mu_f \Phi^f(\mathbf{q}^f) \\ & & + \sum_{i=1}^{n} \kappa_i [R_i + q_i - x_i] \end{array}\right\} \tag{9.8}$$

where we have introduced the three sets of Lagrange multipliers λ_h, μ_f, and κ_i for the three constraints (9.3) to (9.5). The standard FOCs for a maximum are:[7]

$$\frac{\partial \mathcal{L}}{\partial x_i^h} = \lambda_h U_i^h(\mathbf{x}^h) - \kappa_i \leq 0 \tag{9.9}$$

$$\frac{\partial \mathcal{L}}{\partial q_i^f} = -\mu_f \Phi_i^f(\mathbf{q}^f) + \kappa_i \leq 0 \tag{9.10}$$

for all h, f, and i, where the inequalities in (9.9) and (9.10) would be replaced by the corresponding equalities if the relevant consumption or net output (x_i^h or q_i^f respectively) is not zero at the maximum of $\mathcal{L}$. To complete the FOCs we also need to differentiate $\mathcal{L}$ with respect to the three sets of Lagrange multipliers: doing this we then get conditions (9.3) to (9.5) again, with each inequality replaced by an equality if the corresponding Lagrange multiplier is not zero at the maximum.

From these FOCs and the standard Kuhn-Tucker complementary slackness conditions (page 510) we can deduce the following features of an efficient state:

- If a household h is not satiated, then $\lambda_h > 0$ (condition 9.3).
- If there is at least one household that is not satiated with good i and that is consuming a positive amount of good i then $\kappa_i > 0$ (condition 9.9): the 'scarcity price' of good i is positive in an efficient allocation.
- If so, then there can be no idle stocks of good i (condition 9.5).
- If $\kappa_i > 0$, and if the net output of good i by firm f is not zero, then $\mu_f > 0$ (condition 9.10).
- If $\mu_f > 0$ then $\Phi^f(\mathbf{q}^f) = 0$ (condition 9.4): this implies that any active firm must operate in a technically efficient manner.

There are furthermore a couple of very strong points that we can infer from the FOCs. Consider any household that consumes both goods i and j in positive amounts:[8]

$$\lambda_h U_i^h(\mathbf{x}^h) = \kappa_i \tag{9.11}$$

$$\lambda_h U_j^h(\mathbf{x}^h) = \kappa_j \tag{9.12}$$

the right-hand sides of which are independent of h. Likewise for any firm f using or producing goods i, j in non-zero amounts:

$$\mu_f \Phi_i^f(\mathbf{q}^f) = \kappa_i \tag{9.13}$$

$$\mu_f \Phi_j^f(\mathbf{q}^f) = \kappa_j. \tag{9.14}$$

? Mini Problems

7 In fact condition (9.9) is very slightly different for household 1. Write down the modified condition that applies in this case.

8 Rework conditions (9.11) to (9.14) for the cases where (a) good i is not consumed by one or more households, (b) good i is neither produced nor used by one or more firms.

Using the standard definitions of the marginal rate of substitution of good i for good j and of the marginal rate of transformation of good i into good j then, on dividing (9.12) by (9.11) and (9.14) by (9.13) we find the following result:

Theorem 9.3 (Efficiency with purely private goods)

In a Pareto-efficient state without externalities for any pair of pure private goods i and j that are consumed by each household and produced by each firm:

$$\begin{aligned} \mathrm{MRS}_{ij}^{1} &= \mathrm{MRS}_{ij}^{2} = \cdots = \mathrm{MRS}_{ij}^{n_h} = \frac{\kappa_j}{\kappa_i}, \\ \mathrm{MRT}_{ij}^{1} &= \mathrm{MRT}_{ij}^{2} = \cdots = \mathrm{MRT}_{ij}^{n_f} = \frac{\kappa_j}{\kappa_i} \end{aligned} \tag{9.15}$$

Every household equates its marginal rate of substitution to the 'shadow price ratio' κ_j/κ_i which represents the relative scarcity of goods j and i in the economy. Likewise for firms' marginal rate of substitution.

Efficiency and equilibrium

Clearly the conditions for a Pareto-efficient allocation would be satisfied if there happened to be a competitive equilibrium in the economy under consideration. The reason is simple. If $(\mathbf{a}^*, \mathbf{p}^*)$ is a competitive equilibrium then, by definition, all households are maximising utility and all firms are maximising profits. But they do so by fulfilling FOCs that are very similar to those that we have just discussed. Any household that consumes both good 1 and good 2 ensures that its marginal rate of substitution from good 2 into good 1 exactly equals the cost of good 1 (in terms of good 2) in the market: p_1/p_2. Likewise every profit-maximising firm will equate its marginal rate of transformation of good 2 into good 1 to p_1/p_2. This is clearly just a special case of the result we have just considered, with the p_is replacing the ρ_is. So we have established:

Theorem 9.4 (Efficiency of competitive equilibrium)

If consumers are non-satiated, in a private ownership economy, without externalities and consisting entirely of pure private goods, any competitive equilibrium allocation is Pareto efficient.

So, in the very special circumstances of a pure private economy, competitive equilibrium must be Pareto efficient. This is illustrated in the case of an exchange economy. For, consider what the set of Pareto-efficient allocations must be in this model: fix Alf's utility at an arbitrary level $\bar{\upsilon}^a$; now keeping Alf on the given indifference curve $\bar{\upsilon}^a$, maximise Bill's utility; one obviously ends up on the contract curve. Hence in the exchange economy it is the contract curve itself which forms the set of Pareto-efficient allocations. We know that the core is a subset of the contract curve and that the competitive equilibrium allocation, if it exists, must lie in the core.

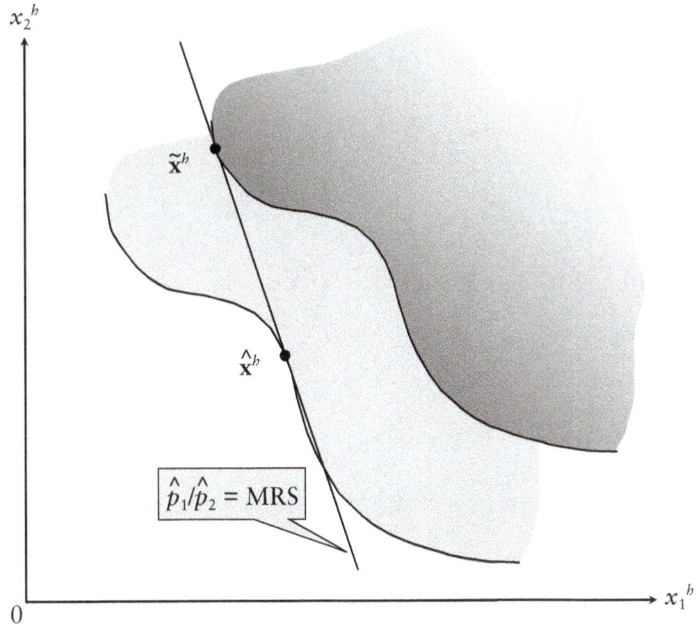

Figure 9.4 Household h will choose $\tilde{\mathbf{x}}^h$ not $\hat{\mathbf{x}}^h$.

What about the reverse? Suppose the preferences, technology, and resource totals are given. Consider a Pareto-efficient allocation $\hat{\mathbf{a}}$. Will there be some $\hat{\mathbf{d}}$ such that $\hat{\mathbf{a}}$ is a competitive equilibrium? In other words, can we find a property distribution $\hat{\mathbf{d}}$ and a price system $\hat{\mathbf{p}}$ such that people choose $\hat{\mathbf{a}}$? This is not always the case if there are non-convexities. This applies, in principle, to both households' preferences and to firms' production possibilities, and Figures 9.4 and 9.5 reveal what can happen:[9]

However, in the absence of such pathological structures we can state:

Theorem 9.5 (Support)

If the conditions for Theorem 9.4 hold, if the technology set of each firm is convex, and if consumers are greedy and have concave-contoured utility functions, then any Pareto-efficient allocation $\hat{\mathbf{a}}$ in which $\hat{x}_i^h > 0$ for all h and i can be supported by a competitive equilibrium.

For proof of this, see Appendix C. So it appears that under certain circumstances we can pick the Pareto-efficient allocation that we would like to see, and then arrange that the economy is automatically moved to this allocation by the process of

? Mini Problems

9 Use the contours in Figures 9.4 and 9.5 to sketch in the points that could not be supported by a competitive equilibrium.

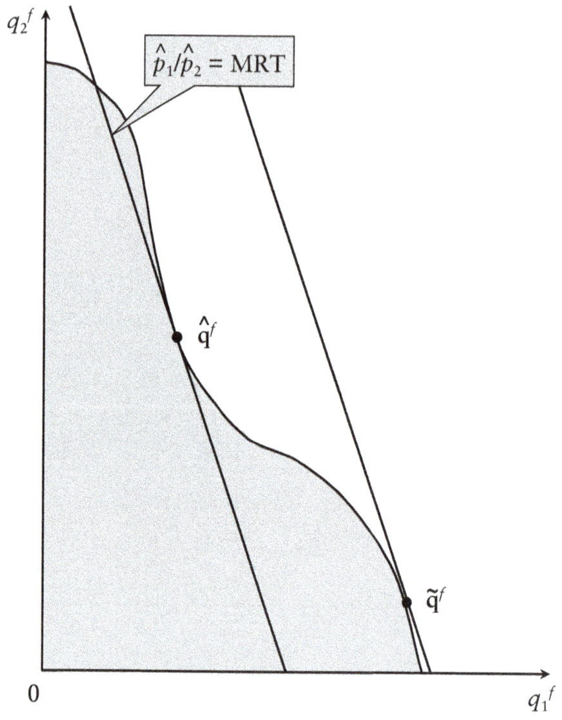

Figure 9.5 Firm f will choose $\tilde{\mathbf{q}}^f$ not $\hat{\mathbf{q}}^f$

competition—the competitive equilibrium 'supports' the allocation. But a few words of caution are appropriate here.

- First, in order to manipulate the economy in this way we need to have the right property distribution $\hat{\mathbf{d}}$ as a starting point. But how do we arrange for this distribution in the first place? If history has thrown up some other property distribution $\mathbf{d}$ then perhaps it is possible to arrange transfers of entitlements of property from one group of households to another before production and trade takes place. These transfers are not based on the activities or choices of any of the agents in the economy—in the jargon they are *lump-sum* transfers—and the political and administrative difficulties associated with them should not be taken lightly (more of this in chapter 13, page 463). A principal difficulty is that of identifying who is entitled to receive a transfer and who should be required to provide the resources. Some resource endowments are intrinsically non-observable;[10] some are intrinsically non-transferable.[11]

? Mini Problems

10 (a) Give an example of why this is so. (b) Because of the problems of non-observability policy makers often condition transfers on individuals' actions, as with the income tax. Why will this give rise to efficiency problems?

11 Again provide an example.

- Second, the conditions in Theorem 9.5 are fairly stringent. Reasonably we could ask what guidance is available on efficiency grounds once we try to accommodate real-world problems and difficulties. These difficulties will involve either departures from the ideals of perfect competition or relaxation of some of the assumptions that underpin the theorem. These issues are addressed in section 9.3.2.
- Third, the discussion of efficiency has been conducted in a world of perfect certainty. There are important issues raised by the model of uncertainty that we developed in chapter 8. These are handled in section 9.3.5.

9.3.2 Departures from efficiency

The pair of theorems, 9.4 and 9.5, are undeniably attractive but, to be applicable they clearly impose somewhat idealistic requirements. So, two things deserve further consideration: (1) In situations where we have a private goods economy with technology and preferences that satisfy the conditions of Theorems 9.4 and 9.5, how does one quantify departures from the ideal? It may be useful to have some guidance on this to have an idea of whether one imperfect state is 'better' or 'worse' than another in efficiency terms. (2) What if the underlying assumptions about the private-goods economy were relaxed? What could we then say about the conditions for an efficient allocation? We deal with each of these in turn.

Waste

Consider the problem of quantifying inefficiency. Suppose that we are in a purely private-good economy. All the conditions for a competitive equilibrium are present—which would involve prices $\mathbf{p}^*$ and incomes $y^{*1}, y^{*2}, \ldots$—but we find that in fact one good (good 1) has its price fixed up above p_1^*. This price wedge might be caused by a sales tax, for example, and it will in general distort all other prices. Can we measure the loss that is induced by the price wedge?

Let us suppose that we actually observe the consumer prices $(p_1, p_2, \ldots, p_n)$ and producer prices $(\tilde{p}_1, \tilde{p}_2, \ldots, \tilde{p}_n)$ such that

$$\left.\begin{array}{lcl} p_1 & = & \tilde{p}_1[1+\delta], \\ p_2 & = & \tilde{p}_2, \\ p_3 & = & \tilde{p}_3 \\ \ldots & \ldots & \ldots \\ p_n & = & \tilde{p}_n \end{array}\right\} \tag{9.16}$$

where δ is the price wedge imposed exogenously upon good 1. To make the argument easier assume that all prices are positive and that all markets clear. To measure waste we need a reference point. Since we have argued that under the idealised conditions of a competitive equilibrium, it seems natural to use as the reference point the prices $\mathbf{p}^*$ that would have prevailed in equilibrium. Furthermore, let

$$\Delta p_i := p_i - p_i^* \tag{9.17}$$

denote the deviations from the reference prices for each good $i = 1, 2, \ldots, n$. Given that all consumers are maximising utility we must have that

$$\mathrm{MRS}_{ij}^{h} = \frac{p_j}{p_i} \tag{9.18}$$

for all goods i and j, and all households h,[12] and

$$\left.\begin{array}{lcl} \mathrm{MRT}_{1j} & = & \frac{p_j}{p_1}[1+\delta] \\ \mathrm{MRT}_{2j} & = & \frac{p_j}{p_2} \\ \ldots & \ldots & \ldots \\ \mathrm{MRT}_{nj} & = & \frac{p_j}{p_n} \end{array}\right\} \tag{9.19}$$

Now consider the net gain that person h would experience were one to go from the reference allocation $\mathbf{a}^*$ to the actual allocation $\mathbf{a}$:

$$\mathrm{EV}^h = C^h(\mathbf{p}^*, \upsilon^h) - C^h(\mathbf{p}, \upsilon^h) - [y^{*h} - y^h] \tag{9.20}$$

where C^h is h's cost function. Summing (9.20) over all h expresses the total loss measured in the same units as income. Assume that all producer prices remain constant—an implicit assumption of infinite supply elasticities. Then (minus) the aggregation over the consumers of the loss in equation (9.20) gives the total measure of waste involved in the price distortion $\Delta\mathbf{p}$ thus:[13]

$$\Lambda(\Delta\mathbf{p}) := \sum_{h=1}^{n_h}\left[C^h(\mathbf{p}, \upsilon^h) - C^h(\mathbf{p} - \Delta\mathbf{p}, \upsilon^h)\right] - \sum_{i=1}^{n} R_i \Delta p_i - \sum_{i=1}^{n} q_i \Delta p_i. \tag{9.21}$$

We have $\Lambda(0) = 0$ and Shephard's Lemma implies:

$$x_i^h = C_i^h(\mathbf{p}, \upsilon^h). \tag{9.22}$$

Using the materials' balance condition and taking an approximation we then get[14]

$$\Lambda(\Delta\mathbf{p}) \approx -\frac{1}{2}\sum_{i=1}^{n}\sum_{j=1}^{n}\sum_{h=1}^{n_h} \frac{\partial H^{hi}(\mathbf{p}, \upsilon^h)}{\partial p_j} \Delta p_i \Delta p_j \tag{9.23}$$

where $\frac{\partial H^{hi}(\mathbf{p}, \upsilon^h)}{\partial p_j}$ is the substitution effect of a rise in the price of commodity j on the demand for commodity i by household h—in other words the slope of the compensated or Hicksian demand curve.[15]

? Mini Problems

12 Sketch a diagram similar to Figure 9.5, but with a convex production possibility set, and superimpose a set of indifference curves; use this to illustrate the conditions (9.18) and (9.19).

13 Use equations (7.8), (7.9), and theorem 2.7 to show how (9.21) follows from (9.20).

14 Show how to derive (9.23) using a Taylor approximation (see page 492).

15 Show how the expression for waste must be modified if supply elasticities are less than infinite.

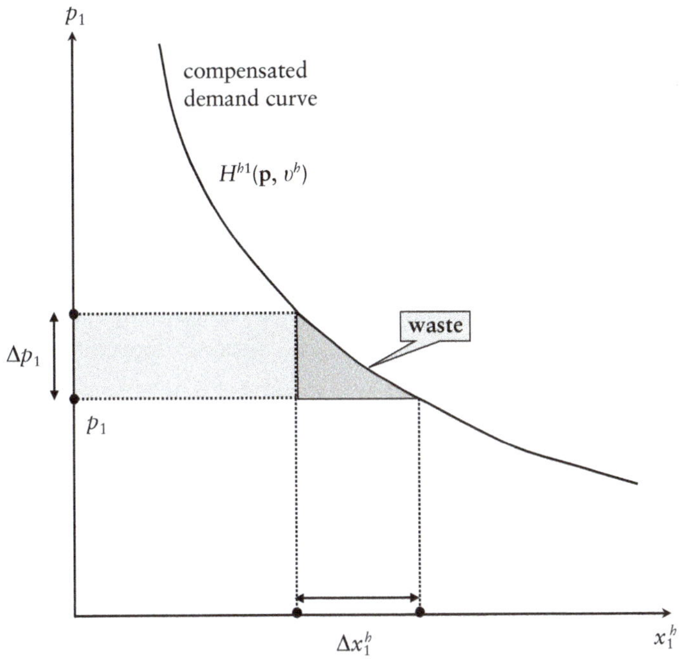

Figure 9.6 Component of efficiency loss

The interpretation of this can be based on the analysis of cost changes that we developed for the firm (page 34) and the consumer (page 92). The price increase leads to an income increase for someone (because of the effect on sales revenue) and the contribution to this from agent h's consumption this is given by the lightly shaded rectangle with dimension $p_1 x_1^h$ in Figure 9.6. However, the component of cost increase to agent h represented by the change in price Δp_1 is represented by the whole shaded area in Figure 9.6. The difference between the two represents the component of the waste generated by the price distortion faced by person h directly from Δp_1. It is illustrated in Figure 9.6 as (−) the area of the heavily shaded 'triangle' shape, approximated by

$$-\frac{1}{2}\Delta p_1 \Delta x_1^h$$

where

$$\Delta x_1^h = \frac{\partial H^{h1}(\mathbf{p}, \upsilon^h)}{\partial p_1}\Delta p_1.$$

Of course, one needs to take into account the other components of waste that are generated from the induced price changes: the sum of the little triangles such as that in Figure 9.6 gives the expression for loss (9.23).[16]

? Mini Problems

16 (a) Suppose there is only a single firm producing good 1 that uses the market power it enjoys to force up the price of good 1. If we neglect cross-price effects and use consumer's

This idea of quantifying waste gives us the basis for developing a coherent analysis of economic policy that may be aimed at yielding welfare improvements rather than shooting just at a welfare optimum. More of this in chapter 13.

Efficiency and market 'failures'

Now let us turn to the other main thing that needs consideration. This introduces us to a class of economic problems that are sometimes—perhaps somewhat unfairly—characterised as instances of 'market failure'. It is perhaps better to say that these are instances where unqualified reliance on the market mechanism cannot be relied upon to produce an efficient outcome. This is hardly astonishing: the requirements for the 'support' result in Theorem 9.5 may appear to be unacceptably strong. Relaxing these requirements raises two key issues.

1. *The characterisation problem.* Where the conditions for Theorem 9.4 are violated the FOCs (9.12)–(9.13) are no longer valid. Furthermore, in the presence of non-convexities the FOCs are no longer sufficient to pin down a unique allocation—see the two parts of the figure where points on different parts of a contour have the same MRS or MRT. So in all these cases the FOCs for the Pareto-efficient allocation need to be replaced or supplemented in order to characterise an efficient allocation.
2. *The implementation problem.* If the market mechanism cannot do the job of supporting a particular allocation in this case, then what else might work?

We shall discuss non-convexities and the difficult implementation issue further in chapters 12 and 13. The characterisation issue where the conditions for Theorem 9.4 are violated can be handled by a series of tweaks as follows in sections 9.3.3 and 9.3.4.

9.3.3 Externalities

We have already seen the mechanics of externalities in a simple example of interactions amongst firms, discussed in chapter 3 (pages 56ff). Here we also need to take into account a similar phenomenon of interactions amongst consumers. We will handle each in turn under the labels production and consumption externalities.

Production externalities

Unfortunately there are all too many practical examples of 'negative' production externalities—emissions into rivers, acid rain, traffic congestion—where the unregulated actions by one firm significantly affect the cost function of other firms. So we shall focus on such detrimental interactions, although virtually all of the results can be easily reworked to deal with positive externalities too. We can see the essential nature of the problem by considering a two-firm example. Suppose that q_1^1 the output of good-1 by firm 1 affects the technological possibilities of other firms: firm 1 produces glue. Consider the position of firm 2, a restaurant. In the no-externality case we would normally

? Mini Problems

surplus as an approximation to EV interpret the model as one of the waste that is attributable to monopoly. [Hint: use the equilibrium condition given in (3.11).]

(b) How is the waste related to the elasticity of demand for good 1?

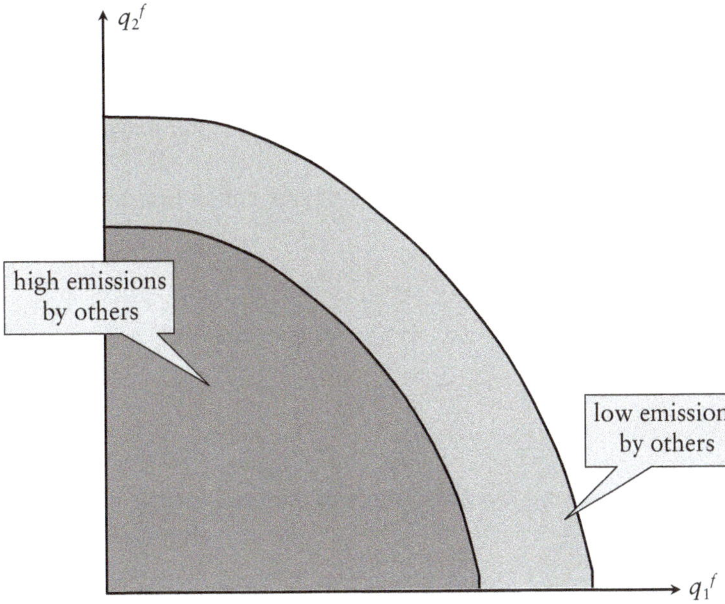

Figure 9.7 The effect of pollution on a victim's production set

write $\Phi^2(\mathbf{q}^2) \leq 0$ to characterise the net-output vectors $\mathbf{q}^2$ that are technologically feasible. However, in view of the externality, firm 1's output (q_1^1) will shift firm 2's production function. If the externality is detrimental (the smell of glue does not enhance enjoyment of the restaurant's meals), then we have:

$$\frac{\partial \Phi^2}{\partial q_1^1} > 0. \tag{9.24}$$

Why? Consider a net output vector $\hat{\mathbf{q}}^2$ that was just feasible for firm 2, before firm 1 increased its output; this means that—in terms of the figure—the relevant point lies on the boundary, so that $\Phi^2(\mathbf{q}^2) = 0$. Now suppose that firm 1 increases its output q_1^1: if the externality is strictly detrimental,[17] then this must mean that $\hat{\mathbf{q}}^2$—which had hitherto been just in the feasible set—must now be infeasible (you have to use more electricity to run air conditioning). This in turn means that we now find $\Phi^2(\hat{\mathbf{q}}^2) > 0$ and that q_1^1 has shifted Φ^2 inwards: in other words condition (9.24) holds—see Figure 9.7.[18]

We could then appropriately define the value, at the margin, of the damage inflicted upon firm 2 by the externality generated by firm 2. We could measure this in terms of

? Mini Problems

17 Suppose firms 1 and 2 experience diminishing returns to scale and generate negative externalities: will production overall exhibit diminishing returns to scale?

18 Rework the analysis in equations (9.24) to (9.29) for a favourable externality.

firm 2's output:

$$-\frac{1}{\Phi_2^2}\frac{\partial \Phi^2}{\partial q_1^1} \tag{9.25}$$

where Φ_2^2 is the conventional differential of firm 2's production function with respect to its own output.

More generally, in the multifirm case, we can represent an externality by writing the production function for firm g as:

$$\Phi^g\left(\mathbf{q}^g; q_1^1, q_1^2, \ldots, q_1^{g-1}, q_1^{g+1}, \ldots\right) \tag{9.26}$$

and if the externality generated by any of these firms is potentially detrimental we would have:

$$\frac{\partial \Phi^g}{\partial q_1^f} > 0. \tag{9.27}$$

Once again this means that if the detrimental externality (noxious emissions) by other firms were to increase, then firm g's production possibilities are reduced—see Figure 9.7.

The general form of the marginal externality caused by firm f when it produces good 1 (again evaluated in terms of good 2) may thus be written:

$$e_{21}^f := \sum_{g=1}^{n_f} \frac{1}{\Phi_2^g}\frac{\partial \Phi^g}{\partial q_1^f}. \tag{9.28}$$

We can then plug the production function with externalities into the problem defining an efficient allocation. We then find:[19]

$$\frac{\Phi_1^f}{\Phi_2^f} - e_{21}^f = \frac{\kappa_1}{\kappa_2} \tag{9.29}$$

which can be expressed as:

MRT	−	externality	=	ratio of shadow prices

One implication of this is that market prices, that the firm would use, do not correspond to the 'scarcity prices' of commodities in an efficient allocation: there is a 'wedge' between them corresponding to the value of the marginal externality.[20] This is illustrated in Figure 9.8. If the MRT were to equal just the ratio of scarcity prices, then the firm

? Mini Problems

19 Substitute (9.26) into equation (9.8) and differentiate to get this result.

20 Discuss how equation (9.29) might be interpreted as a simple rule for setting a 'polluter pays' levy on output.

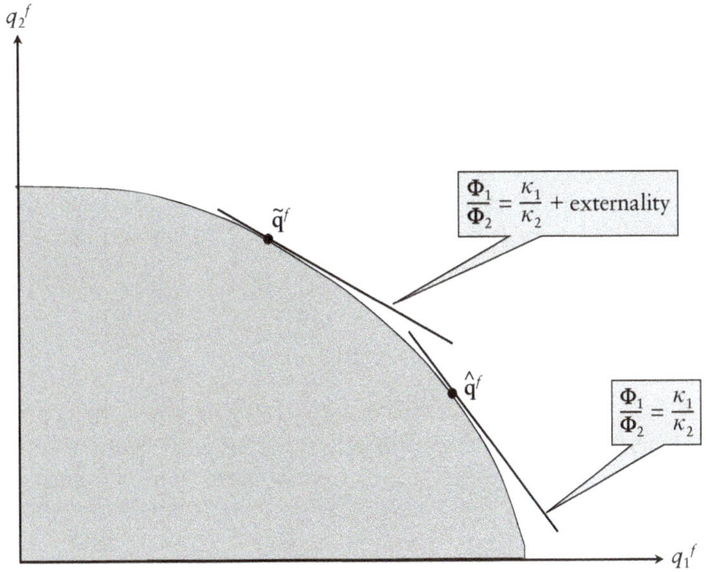

Figure 9.8 Production boundary and efficiency with externalities

would produce at point $\hat{\mathbf{q}}^f$. If the scarcity prices are adjusted by the marginal externality then we find the efficient allocation at point $\tilde{\mathbf{q}}^f$.

Consumption externalities

Consumption externalities can be handled in a similar manner, and the main idea conveyed by means of a simple example. Alf is an asthmatic non-smoker who is affected by the actions of Bill, a boorish smoker. To simplify the example we use the device of bundling together all goods in the economy except one. Let good 1 be tobacco, and good 2 the composite of everything else. Then, we can write the utility function for Bill as $U^b(x_1^b, x_2^b)$ and for Alf as $U^a(x_1^a, x_2^a; x_1^b)$. The signs of the partial derivatives of these functions are fairly obvious; in particular we may assume that $\partial U^a / \partial x_1^b < 0$, since Alf suffers when Bill consumes commodity 1. But how awful is it for asthmatic Alf to be in boorish Bill's company? One way of capturing this is to try to measure Alf's marginal willingness to pay to have the nuisance reduced—to get Bill to cut down on the tobacco. We can do this by computing the amount that Alf would be prepared to sacrifice in order to get Bill to have one less cigarette; this is:

$$e_{21}^b := \frac{1}{U_2^a} \frac{\partial U^a}{\partial x_1^b} \leq 0 \tag{9.30}$$

where U_2^a is Alf's marginal utility derived from other goods in the usual way. From Alf's point of view expression (9.30) is the marginal externality—or the marginal damage—inflicted through the consumption of good 1 by Bill the boor. Translating this into our more general model of efficiency with n goods and n_h households, let us suppose the consumption of good 1 by any household h potentially affects the utility of some other household ℓ, possibly as the result of some side effect. We would then write:

$$v^\ell = U^\ell(\mathbf{x}^\ell, x_1^1, x_1^2, \dots, x_1^{\ell-1}, x_1^{\ell+1}, \dots). \tag{9.31}$$

If the externality is detrimental by nature then we have

$$\frac{\partial U^\ell}{\partial x_1^h} \leq 0 \tag{9.32}$$

for any two distinct households h and ℓ. Analogous to (9.30) we may define the marginal externality imposed on others by household h as:

$$e_{21}^h := \sum_{\ell=1}^{n_h} \frac{1}{U_2^\ell} \frac{\partial U^\ell}{\partial x_1^h}. \tag{9.33}$$

Notice that the summation is required because we want to know the marginal damage inflicted on *all* parties, evaluated appropriately at the sufferers' marginal utility of other goods. When we take this relationship into account in the FOCs for efficiency, we find the following:[21]

$$\frac{U_1^h}{U_2^h} + e_{21}^h = \frac{\kappa_1}{\kappa_2}. \tag{9.34}$$

In other words we again have a simple relationship:

MRS	+	externality	=	ratio of shadow prices

Clearly, if there is a negative externality, then the marginal rate of substitution of good 2 into good 1 will be greater than the price ratio in an efficient allocation.[22]

The interaction between firms or between consumers leads to fairly straightforward extensions of the rules covering the characterisation of efficient allocations. However, although the characterisation problem is relatively simple in this case, the implementation problem may prove to be intractable—even for production externalities—in the absence of external intervention.

9.3.4 Public goods

The precise meaning of a public good is given in Definition 9.3. So, if good 1 is a pure public good it must be non-rival which requires that

$$x_1^h = x_1$$

? Mini Problems

21 Substitute (9.31) into equation (9.8) and differentiate to get this result.

22 In a two-good model, show how condition (9.34) might be used to suggest an appropriate tax on the good causing the externality, or an appropriate subsidy on the other good.

for all non-satiated households. It must also be non-excludable, which can be interpreted as an extreme case of consumption externality: once provided there is no means of charging for it.

Let us explore the efficiency implications of non-rivalness. In fact we only require a different form of aggregation in the efficiency condition. Notice that in this case if, for some household h we have $x_1^h < x_1$ and yet $U_1^h > 0$, then a Pareto-superior allocation can be attained by allowing household h's consumption of good 1 to increase (as long as x_1^h is strictly less than x_1 no additional resources have to be used up to increase h's consumption of this non-rival good, so we might as well let household h increase its own utility since it will not thereby reduce any one else's utility). Therefore at the Pareto-efficient allocation for each household h, either $x_1^h = x_1$ so that the household is consuming the non-rival good to its maximum capacity, or $x_1^h < x_1$ and $U_1^h = 0$ so that the household is consuming less than it could, but is satiated with the public good 1. Let us assume that everyone is non-satiated;[23] each person must consume exactly the same amount at a Pareto-efficient allocation. Thus we put $x_1^h = x_1, h = 1, \ldots, n_h$ in the Lagrangean (9.8) as our new aggregation condition. Differentiate the Lagrangean with respect to x_1 and set it equal to zero:

$$\sum_{h=1}^{n_h} \lambda_h U_1^h(\mathbf{x}^h) = \kappa_1. \tag{9.35}$$

Now pick any other pure private good i that is being consumed in positive amounts by everyone: from equation (9.35) we get

$$\sum_{h=1}^{n_h} \frac{U_1^h(\mathbf{x}^h)}{U_i^h(\mathbf{x}^h)} = \frac{\kappa_1}{\kappa_i}. \tag{9.36}$$

So we have established the result:

Theorem 9.6 (Efficiency with public goods)

In a Pareto-efficient state without externalities for any pure private good i consumed by everyone and a non-rival good 1 we have:

$$\left.\begin{aligned} MRS_{i1}^1 + MRS_{i1}^2 + \cdots + MRS_{i1}^{n_h} &= \frac{\kappa_1}{\kappa_i} \\ &= MRT_{i1}^f, f = 1, \ldots, n_f. \end{aligned}\right\} \tag{9.37}$$

Figure 9.9 illustrates the two-good, two-person case where production is carried out by a single firm. The top part of the diagram plots Alf's marginal rate of substitution of the private good (good 2) for the public good (good 1) as a function of the total supply of good 1. It is a graph of his willingness to pay for additional units of the public good and it is downward sloping on the assumption that Alf's utility function is quasiconcave. The second part of the diagram does the same job for Bill. At any level of provision

? Mini Problems

23 Derive the same condition assuming that the first h^* households are non-satiated, and the remaining $n_h - h^*$ households are satiated.

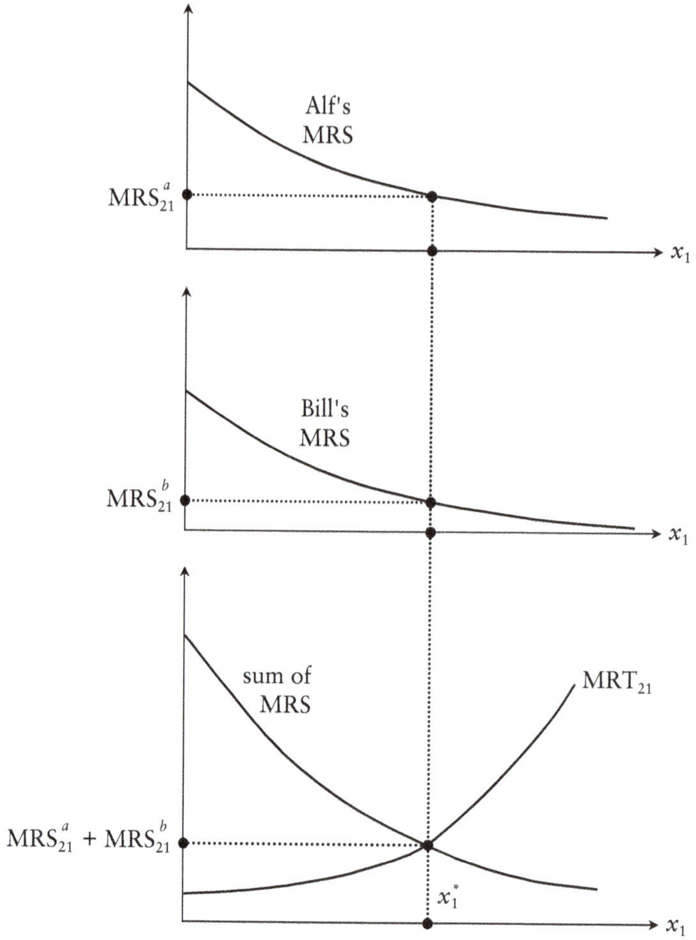

Figure 9.9 Conditions for efficient provision of public goods

of the public good x_1 we can imagine asking ourselves 'what is the total willingness to pay for an extra unit of the public good' (remember: because it is non-rival both parties will benefit from the extra unit). The graph of this total willingness to pay is the downward-sloping line in the bottom part of the figure (MRS_{21}^a+MRS_{21}^b); the marginal cost of providing the public good is given by the graph of MRT_{21} against x_1; the intersection of these two curves gives the efficient supply of public goods x_1^*.

9.3.5 Uncertainty

It is reasonably straightforward to apply the efficiency concept in definition 9.2 to the case where an economy is characterised by uncertainty, following on the analysis of section 8.6. The key issue is whether efficiency is to be viewed before or after the uncertain state of the world is revealed (be careful not to confuse the concept of a state of the world $\omega \in \Omega$ with that of a social state $\theta \in \Theta$). A standard approach is as follows.

Consider a situation in which social states are completely described by allocations. Take an allocation $\hat{\mathbf{a}}$ in which the consumption of household h under state of the world ω is $\hat{\mathbf{x}}^h_\omega$ and the resulting utility for household h is $\hat{\upsilon}^h$, $h = 1, 2, \ldots, n_h$.

Definition 9.5

An allocation $\hat{\mathbf{a}}$ is *ex-ante Pareto efficient* if it is feasible and there is no other feasible allocation $\mathbf{a}$ with associated utility levels $\upsilon^h, h = 1, 2, \ldots, n_h$ such that, for all h,

$$\upsilon^h \geq \hat{\upsilon}^h \tag{9.38}$$

with strict inequality for at least one h.

This is a general approach. If we wish to impose the restriction that each person or household's utility conform to axioms 8.1 to 8.3 (page 185) that underpin the von Neumann–Morgenstern functional form of utility (Theorem 8.1) then we may write

$$\upsilon^h = \mathcal{E}^h u^h\left(\mathbf{x}^h\right) = \sum_{\omega\in\Omega} \pi^h_\omega u^h\left(\mathbf{x}^h_\omega\right) \tag{9.39}$$

where π^h_ω denotes the system of (subjective) probability weights used by household h, and $\mathcal{E}^h$ denotes expectation with respect to this set of subjective probabilities. Using (9.39) the condition (9.38) becomes

$$\sum_{\omega\in\Omega} \pi^h_\omega \left[u^h\left(\mathbf{x}^h_\omega\right) - u^h\left(\hat{\mathbf{x}}^h_\omega\right)\right] \geq 0. \tag{9.40}$$

So *ex-ante* efficiency has the interpretation that there is no other allocation which dominates it in terms of expected utility. However, it is also reasonable to consider efficiency only from the *ex-post* standpoint, after the state of the world has been realised.

Definition 9.6

The allocation $\hat{\mathbf{a}}$ is *ex-post Pareto efficient* if there is no other feasible allocation $\mathbf{a}$ with associated utility levels $\upsilon^h = u^h\left(\mathbf{x}^h_\omega\right), h = 1, 2, \ldots, n_h$ such that, for all h, and all $\omega \in \Omega$

$$u^h\left(\mathbf{x}^h_\omega\right) - u^h\left(\hat{\mathbf{x}}^h_\omega\right) \geq 0 \tag{9.41}$$

with strict inequality for at least one h.

Comparing (9.40) and (9.41) we can see that the following must be true:

Theorem 9.7 (*Ex-ante* efficiency)

If there is no state of the world which is regarded by any household as impossible, then any *ex-ante* Pareto-efficient allocation must also be *ex-post* Pareto efficient.

However, the reverse is not true; one can easily find social states that are efficient *ex post*, but not *ex ante*. Figure 9.10 illustrates this point. The axes of the diagram viewed

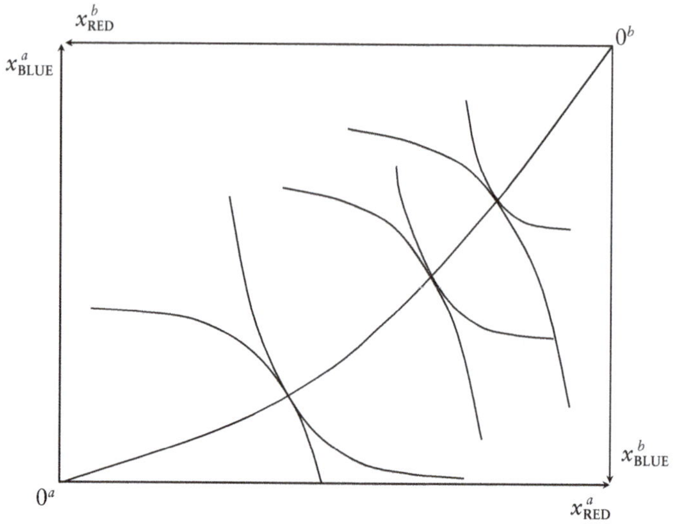

Figure 9.10 Ex-ante and ex-post efficiency

from origin 0^a are the same as in Figure 8.2 and give consumption of a single commodity by person a in the two states of the world; the axes of the diagram viewed from origin 0^b do the same job for person b. The points along the contract curve from 0^a to 0^b represent *ex-ante*-efficient allocations; points off the curve are not efficient *ex ante*: you can then increase the expected utility of one person without reducing the expected utility of the other. However, *any* point in Figure 9.10 is *ex-post* efficient: once the state of the world ω is known you can only increase the *ex-post* utility of one person by reducing the consumption (and hence the utility) of the other.

Theorem 9.8 (*Ex-ante* efficiency)

If a competitive equilibrium exists in the market for contingent goods, then it is *ex-ante* Pareto efficient.

The proof of this result is straightforward, since the existence of all the contingent markets permits one to extend the standard results on competitive equilibrium and Pareto efficiency just by redefining the particular markets involved. Likewise we have:

Theorem 9.9 (*Ex-ante* support)

If consumers are greedy and have concave-contoured utility functions, then any *ex-ante* Pareto-efficient allocation with positive incomes for all consumers can be supported by a competitive equilibrium.

Again this follows by a simple extension of the results that we obtained in the elementary model of efficiency and equilibrium in the absence of uncertainty in section 9.3 above. For the result to go through we require, in principle, lump-sum transfers to be available in all states of the world ω, and the existence of a full set of $n\varpi$ markets in contingent goods.

9.3.6 Extending the efficiency idea

Let us reconsider the Pareto superiority criterion. Whilst it appears to have an attractive interpretation in some welfare terms—'approve a switch from state θ' to state θ if no one is worse off in θ than he would have been in θ' and at least one person is strictly better off'—it is very limited as a general policy rule. A principal reason for this is that it is so wretchedly indecisive. There are a lot of pairs of possible social states which just cannot be compared using this criterion; and, as it is quite difficult to think up lots of real-life examples where there have been demonstrable Pareto improvements, the Pareto-superiority criterion does not strike one as overwhelmingly useful in practice.

Let us consider what might be done to make the Pareto-superiority criterion more discriminating and, perhaps, more useful as a criterion for making welfare judgements. To do this, we convert the problem into a two-stage decision process.

To fix ideas, consider the example of a government which has to decide whether or not to build an airport, and assume that the airport is a 'one-off' project—either one has an airport of given size and quality or one does not. There is in fact a huge range of possible social states associated with this decision, even though there is only one type of airport which could be built: the reason for this is that there are all sorts of ways in which the gains and losses arising from the project may be distributed amongst the community. So it may make sense to consider (a) all the social states that could be obtained through a pure redistribution (for example, by taxes and transfers) given that resources have been committed to the airport; and (b) all the states of the world that could be obtained (by similar methods) given that the airport is *not* built. In either case we describe these other states (obtainable through redistribution) as being *accessible* from the reference state. So the decision process is something like this:

1. look first at the resource commitment that is involved in building the airport;
2. then consider the states you can generate from the outcome of step 1 by a further rearrangement of incomes.

On a more general note—with many possible projects of different types and sizes—the idea in step 1 is that the alternatives are mutually exclusive and irreversible, and that in step 2 all the states can be reached from one another by steps that are in principle reversible. Clearly the distinction between the two may be somewhat arbitrary and is reminiscent of the distinction between the 'short' and 'long run'. Nevertheless, one can perhaps think of many practical decisions where such a distinction could reasonably be drawn.

To see how we may use this to extend the Pareto-superiority criterion, let θ and θ' be the two states under consideration ('airport' and 'no airport') and let $\hat{\Theta}(\theta)$ be the subset of Θ that is accessible from θ. Then consider the following:

Definition 9.7

The state θ is *potentially superior* to θ' if there exists $\theta^* \in \hat{\Theta}(\theta)$ such that θ^* is Pareto superior to θ'.

The idea is this: θ is potentially superior to θ' if there is some other state, accessible from θ, which is actually Pareto superior to θ'. In the airport example, the rule says: 'building the airport (state θ) is potentially superior to not building the airport (state θ'), even if some people actually lose out thereby, if it can be shown that, once the airport is built, there is some *hypothetical* income redistribution which (were it to be actually implemented) would mean that everyone was at least as well off as before and no one was worse off (state θ^*)'.

Again there are some obvious drawbacks to this criterion. One is on moral grounds. The state θ is counted as being superior to θ' on the above conditions *even though the switch by income redistribution to θ^* never takes place.* To some people this will seem manifestly objectionable.

There is a second, powerful objection, this time on the grounds of logic. In Figure 9.11 $\mathbf{v}(\theta^\circ)$ represents $\left(v^a(\theta^\circ), v^b(\theta^\circ)\right)$, the vector of utility payoffs corresponding to θ°, and $\mathbf{v}(\theta')$ is the utility vector corresponding to θ'. The set of utility vectors corresponding to states accessible from θ°, and the set of points corresponding to states accessible from θ' have been sketched in. Clearly, there are points in the set accessible from θ° that lie to the north-east of θ', and so $\theta' \in \hat{\Theta}(\theta)$ and thus, θ° is potentially superior to θ'. However,

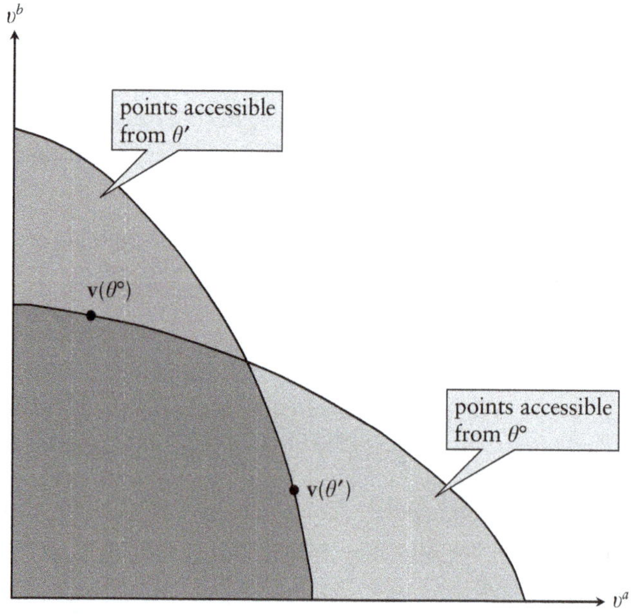

Figure 9.11 θ° is accessible from θ' and θ' is accessible from θ°

we could just as easily turn the argument round, examine the points lying to the north and east of θ°, and find that $\theta^{\circ} \in \hat{\Theta}(\theta')$. We have the extraordinary conclusion that θ° is potentially superior to θ' and θ' is potentially superior to θ°! The solution to this problem that seems to suggest itself is to strengthen the definition so that such apparent contradictions cannot occur. Consider the following:

Definition 9.8

The state θ° is *unambiguously potentially superior* to θ' if θ° is potentially superior to θ' but θ' is not potentially superior to θ°.

Unfortunately this apparently more attractive criterion may be vacuous since it could just restore the indecisiveness of the original Pareto-superiority principle, and it may also lead to intransitive rankings of social states. However, despite the problem of 'reversals' associated with the simple 'potential superiority criterion' there is a useful interpretation of this concept in terms of the aggregate 'willingness to pay' expressed as $\sum_{h=1}^{n_h} \mathrm{CV}^h$, the sum of all households' compensating variations. Here $\mathrm{CV}^h\left(\theta' \to \theta\right)$ means just the cost of restoring household h to state θ' from state θ and is positive if the move from θ' to θ is a welfare gain for h. In the case where 'accessibility' is defined as above in terms of monetary transfers at given prices $\mathbf{p}$, we have:

Theorem 9.10 (Potential superiority)

A necessary and sufficient condition for θ to be potentially superior to θ' is that $\sum_{h=1}^{n_h} \mathrm{CV}^h(\theta' \to \theta) > 0$.

Note that this uses a strong definition of accessibility. For weaker versions of accessibility it is usually the case that the condition $\sum_{h=1}^{n_h} \mathrm{CV}^h > 0$ is necessary, but not sufficient for potential superiority.

The practical importance of Theorem 9.10 is considerable. Potential Pareto superiority is used as the intellectual basis for a broad range of applied welfare economics. It provides a powerful tool for policy makers and advisers.

Example 9.2

This approach is the basis for the technique of cost-benefit analysis. Who gains, who loses from a new bridge, a rerouted highway, a lengthened airport runway? There is room for debate over the valuation of individual benefits CV^h (which may involve valuing things such as travel-time savings and improvements in safety) and on the simple method of aggregation (the straight sum from 1 to n_h which ignores how the benefits and costs are distributed amongst rich and poor). A particularly powerful example of the application of these techniques is the argument for the construction of the Victoria Line on London's Underground System—see Beesley and Foster (1965).

9.4 Principles for social judgements: equity

We turn to another broad general principle that might be considered as a 'reasonable' basis for welfare economics. However, rather than an extension of Pareto efficiency—as in the case of potential efficiency—in this case it is a separate criterion that complements principles of efficiency, namely equity. We will have two attempts at this.

9.4.1 Fairness

In our first attempt equity is interpreted as 'fairness'. Furthermore, 'fairness' is to be given a very specific interpretation that enables us to carry through the analysis with information about households that is no more specific than in our treatment of efficiency.

To assist in the exposition of this version of the equity principle it is convenient to suppose that each social state θ is adequately described by the allocation $\mathbf{a}$ of goods embedded in it. In particular, let a particular household's evaluation of a social state depend *only* on $\mathbf{x}^h$, the consumption vector that household enjoys: households are selfish. Under this restricted interpretation it is convenient to use the conventional utility function $U^h(\mathbf{x}^h)$ as an index of household h's preferences.

Definition 9.9

A consumption allocation $[\mathbf{x}]$ is *fair* if, for every pair of households $h, \ell = 1, 2, \ldots, n_h$, it is true that $U^h(\mathbf{x}^h) \geq U^h(\mathbf{x}^\ell)$.

In other words an allocation is fair if it is such that no one in the community wishes he had somebody else's bundle instead of his own: fairness is the absence of envy. This then yields:[24]

Theorem 9.11 (Fairness of competitive equilibrium)

If all households have equal incomes then a competitive equilibrium is a fair allocation.

Of course not only would such an equal-income equilibrium be fair, it would also be Pareto efficient—which appears to be a powerful endorsement.

However, just because it meets both the requirements of efficiency and 'no-envy' fairness, one should *not* assume that such an equilibrium is ideal. Indeed one has only to imagine two households, one of which consists of several physically disabled people and

? Mini Problems

24 Prove this. Hint: Note that the definition of competitive equilibrium implies that, for every household $h : U^h(\mathbf{x}^{*h}) \geq U^h(\mathbf{x}^h)$ for all $\mathbf{x}^h$ such that $\sum_i p_i x_i^h \leq y^h$. Now consider the utility h would enjoy were it to receive the consumption bundle of household h' under this equilibrium, and note that all households face the same budget constraints.

the other is composed of a single, able-bodied person, to see that such an allocation of equal incomes, regardless of differences between households, is not very attractive. The 'fairness' concept is, therefore, not of itself overwhelmingly powerful or compelling.

9.4.2 Concern for inequality

It is reasonable to say that the fairness interpretation of the equity principles is somewhat special, possibly even a touch artificial. Perhaps one might have in mind that equity should involve the opposite of inequality—interpreted in terms of the distribution of income, somehow defined, or the distribution of utility. But here we reach a temporary check to our analytical progress. If one is to interpret equity in this way, one cannot avoid detailed utility comparison between households, something that we have not yet introduced to the discussion of this chapter. To make further progress we would first need to impose a lot more structure on the welfare analysis.

9.5 The social-welfare function

Therefore let us look at what can be done using a third, more restrictive, approach to social welfare, one that underpins a lot of work in applied economics. This will involve four main elements:

- a restriction on the range of issues on which each household's preferences is to count;
- an assumption that one either knows, or one may impute, the preferences of households;
- a basis for comparing the levels and scales of utility of one household with another;
- a function for aggregating the utilities enjoyed by (or imputed to) each household.

To incorporate all these features we shall take a specific *social welfare function*. This is individualistic in nature in that it explicitly respects individual agents' preferences. The particular form that we shall use is:

$$W(U^1(\mathbf{x}^1), U^2(\mathbf{x}^2), \ldots, U^h(\mathbf{x}^h), \ldots) \tag{9.42}$$

Notice that W is defined on the space of individual utilities—not on orderings, as was the 'constitution' function Σ. This enables us to impose much more structure on the problem of describing what is meant by social welfare. We have further assumed that individual utilities are determined by their own consumptions thus:

$$\upsilon^h = U^h(\mathbf{x}^h), h = 1, 2, \ldots, n_h. \tag{9.43}$$

So in this specification welfare is not only individualistic but also self-interested. Clearly we have a rule which assigns a welfare level (some number W) to any consumption allocation $[\mathbf{x}]$ by a two-stage process

$$[\mathbf{x}] \overset{(1)}{\rightarrow} (\upsilon^1, \upsilon^2, \upsilon^3, \ldots) \overset{(2)}{\rightarrow} W. \tag{9.44}$$

Where does W come from? Of the various answers that have been attempted in the social science literature over the last few decades I shall draw attention to two in particular:

- *Equal ignorance.* Even though individuals may be perfectly informed about what society actually looks like, society is supposed to form judgements about alternative social states behind a 'veil of ignorance'. It is as though a representative individual were to make choices amongst alternative social states without knowing the identity that he or she would have within the social state. If society chooses among distributions in the same way that an individual makes choices amongst uncertain prospects then it is appropriate to let W have the same basic structure as an individual utility function under uncertainty (see Exercise 9.3).
- *The PLUM principle: People Like Us Matter.* Someone in the community makes the decisions, and he/she/they impute their values to everybody else. In practice this may mean that W is determined by the preferences of a particular political interest group.

9.5.1 Welfare, national income, and expenditure

To see the implications of assuming a well-defined social-welfare function W as a representation of social preferences, let us consider how the welfare level changes when there is a small change in the allocation. Let each person's consumption of each commodity change by an amount dx_i^h. We find

$$dW = \sum_{i=1}^{n} \sum_{h=1}^{n_h} W_h U_i^h dx_i^h \tag{9.45}$$

Notice the following features which can be inferred from this simple relationship:

- the issues on which W ranks states are limited: each $\mathbf{x}^h$ is assessed only on the basis of h's preferences for it.
- the cardinalisation of U^h is important here, since we need to aggregate—add up—the changes in utilities.[25]
- as a result a person's 'weight' depends on both W_h and U_i^h—the importance of his utility to social welfare, and the marginal utility to him of good i.

Suppose the government can choose the allocation $[\mathbf{x}^h]$, subject to some overall constraint

$$\left.\begin{array}{c} \Phi(x_1, \ldots, x_n) \leq 0, \\ \text{where } x_i := \sum_{h=1}^{n_h} x_i^h,\ i = 1, 2, \ldots, n \end{array}\right\}$$

Clearly we will find that for any pair of goods that are being consumed by any two households:

$$\frac{U_i^h}{U_j^h} = \frac{U_i^\ell}{U_j^\ell}. \tag{9.46}$$

? Mini Problems

25 How will social welfare change if each U^h is subjected to an arbitrary affine transformation?

(This we knew anyway from our consideration of efficiency problems.) However, we will also find the condition

$$W_h U_i^h = W_\ell U_i^\ell. \tag{9.47}$$

Why? Because if the cost of producing good i is the same whoever consumes it, then we shall only be at a welfare maximum if W cannot be increased by some small transfer of bread, butter, or toothpaste from h to ℓ.

Now let us examine the properties of the social welfare function (9.42) in the case of a market economy. Each household h maximises its utility $U^h(\mathbf{x}^h)$ subject to a budget constraint $\sum p_i x_i^h \le y^h$ where y^h is the household's income: the argument can easily be extended to the case where y^h is endogenously determined. We may substitute from the demand functions for each household back into its utility function to obtain the indirect utility function for each household $V^h(\mathbf{p}, y^h)$. This then yields the social welfare function in terms of prices and households' incomes:

$$W(V^1(\mathbf{p}, y^1), V^2(\mathbf{p}, y^2), \ldots, V^h(\mathbf{p}, y^h), \ldots). \tag{9.48}$$

Recall that for a consumer's optimum purchases in a free market we have $U_i^h = \mu^{*h} p_i$ if good i is purchased in positive amounts where the term μ^{*h} is the marginal utility of money income for household h and equals $\partial V^h / \partial y^h$—see (4.12) and page 89. So the social optimality condition (9.47) can be rewritten, in the case of a market economy, as

$$W_h V_y^h = W_\ell V_y^\ell \tag{9.49}$$

for any pair of households h and ℓ. This is the effect on social welfare of giving one dollar to any household at the optimum; let us call it M. Hence it is immediate that if there is some economic change affecting individual incomes (for example a change in natural resource endowments or in the technology), the change in social welfare is

$$dW = \sum_{h=1}^{n_h} W_h dU^h = \sum_{h=1}^{n_h} W_h V_y^h dy^h = M \sum_{h=1}^{n_h} dy^h. \tag{9.50}$$

The right-hand side of (9.50) is proportional to the change in national income $y^1 + y^2 + \cdots + y^{n_h}$.

Now consider a change in the prices $\mathbf{p}$ leaving incomes y^h unchanged. Differentiating (9.48) we find that the effect on social welfare is

$$\sum_{h=1}^{n_h} W_h \left[\sum_{i=1}^{n} V_i^h dp_i \right]. \tag{9.51}$$

But, since each household is assumed to be maximising utility, (9.51) becomes[26]

$$-\sum_{h=1}^{n_h} W_h V_y^h \sum_{i=1}^{n} x_i^{*h} dp_i = -M \sum_{i=1}^{n} x_i^* dp_i. \tag{9.52}$$

This is simply $-M$ times the change in the cost of aggregate expenditure (by all households on all goods) as a result of the price changes. In a market economy, aggregate

? Mini Problems

26 Prove this. [Hint: try using Roy's identity.]

expenditure equals national income; so we have established that, whatever the reason for the change in the social state, the following result holds:

Theorem 9.12 (National income)

In the neighbourhood of a welfare optimum, welfare changes are measured by changes in national income.

Unless we believe that somehow the distribution of resources just happens to be ideal in every case we wish to examine this result is of limited appeal. What of other cases?

9.5.2 Inequality and welfare loss

In our earlier discussion of equity as a general welfare principle (section 9.4) we recognised that a method of comparing individual utilities would be necessary in order to introduce a meaningful criterion based on the commonsense notion of inequality. The social-welfare function approach enables us to take the necessary steps.

Clearly there is some form of loss that would result if households' money incomes were not 'correctly' adjusted—according to the social-welfare function W—so as to be able to invoke Theorem 9.12. We can examine the nature of this loss using an approach that is somewhat reminiscent of quantifying departures from efficiency—'waste'—discussed in section 9.3.2 above. To do this let us make two further simplifying assumptions:[27]

- all the V^h are identical, and
- W is a symmetric and concave function.

Given that all the households are assumed identical, the assumption of symmetry is a natural one: it implies that there is no significance in the labelling of individual households $1, \ldots, n_h$. The assumption that W is concave implies that 'society'—as represented by the social-welfare function—is weakly averse to an unequal distribution of income. Now national income is equal to the value of all the resources in the community plus all the profits made by firms which, in a market economy, can be written:

$$\left.\begin{array}{l} \sum_{h=1}^{n_h} y^h = \sum_{i=1}^{n} p_i R_i + \sum_{f=1}^{n_f} \Pi^{*f}(\mathbf{p}), \\ \text{where} \\ \Pi^{*f}(\mathbf{p}) = \sum_{i=1}^{n} p_i q_i^f(\mathbf{p}). \end{array}\right\} \quad (9.53)$$

So obviously national income will be fixed for a given price vector $\mathbf{p}$ and for given resources and technology. So, in view of the concavity and symmetry of W, we can see that, for a given $\mathbf{p}$, W would be maximised in a situation where every household receives an equal share of national income; in other words where everybody gets *mean income* $\mathcal{E}y := \sum_h y^h / n_h$.

? Mini Problems

27 Suppose the economy is composed of two types of households single individuals, and couples (who share their income). Show how the results in this section can be established if households are weighted by size and incomes adjusted to 'per-person equivalents'.

Consider now situations in which every household is not receiving an equal share. A natural way of measuring the apparent loss attributable to the less-than-ideal property distribution suggests itself in the light of chapter 8's discussion of using the risk premium concept in the context of the expected-utility model (see page 191). Consider the income that, were it to be given identically to every household, would yield the same level of social welfare as the actual incomes $y^1, y^2, \ldots, y^{n_h}$. This income is clearly less than or equal to $\mathcal{E}y$, and the difference between the two can be regarded as a money measure of the shortfall in social welfare attributable to the inequality of incomes.

Definition 9.10

(a) The *equally distributed equivalent income* ξ is a real number such that

$$W(V(\xi, \mathbf{p}), V(\xi, \mathbf{p}), \ldots) = W(V(y^1, \mathbf{p}), V(y^2, \mathbf{p}), \ldots). \tag{9.54}$$

(b) The *inequality index* is $1 - \xi / \mathcal{E}y$.

This is illustrated, for a two-household example, in Figure 9.12. The ray through the origin is at 45° to the axes: any point on this represents a situation of exact equality of income distribution. So, given an actual distribution of income (y^a, y^b) represented by the point $\hat{\mathbf{y}}$ we find the mean by drawing a perpendicular from $\hat{\mathbf{y}}$ to the 45° ray: this perpendicular meets the ray at the point $\mathcal{E}\mathbf{y}$. The contour of the social-welfare function $W(V(\mathbf{p}, y^a), V(\mathbf{p}, y^b))$ that passes through $\hat{\mathbf{y}}$ is symmetric about the ray, and cuts the ray

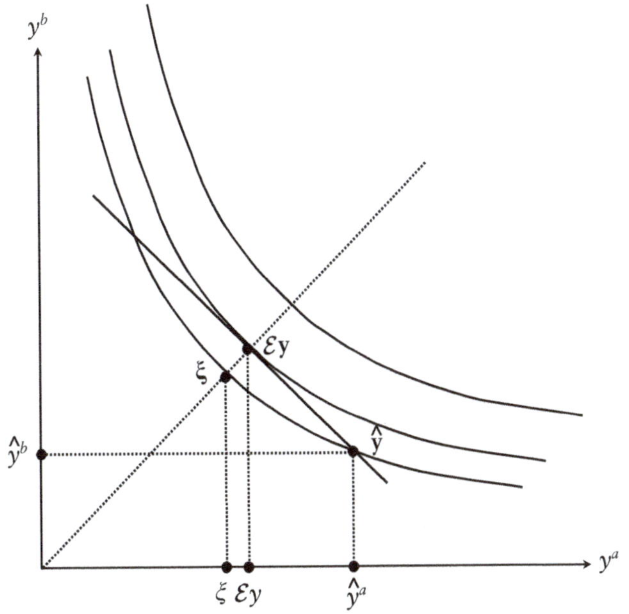

Figure 9.12 The social-welfare function

at point ξ, with coordinates (ξ, ξ). The more sharply curved is this contour, the greater the inequality $1-\xi/\bar{y}$.

You may have already spotted the similarity of these concepts to the concepts of certainty equivalence and risk premium. This becomes even more evident if we impose a further restriction on the social-welfare function W. If we assume that it is additively separable (analogous to the von Neumann–Morgenstern utility function[28]) then, suppressing the price vector $\mathbf{p}$ (assumed to be held invariant) we may rewrite (9.48) as

$$\sum_{h=1}^{n_h} \zeta(y^h) \tag{9.55}$$

where ζ is an increasing, concave function of one variable. Then the equation defining the equally distributed equivalent income can be rewritten

$$\xi = \zeta^{-1}\left(\frac{1}{n_h}\sum_{h=1}^{n_h} \zeta(y^h)\right) \tag{9.56}$$

Recall that in the case of choice under uncertainty the curvature of the function reflected the degree of risk aversion, and hence the risk premium to be imputed to any particular prospect. Likewise the curvature of ζ determines the degree of 'inequality aversion' that is implicit in the social-welfare function: in fact, assuming differentiability of ζ, we conventionally define the following:

Definition 9.11

The *(relative) inequality aversion* of a social-welfare function is given by

$$\iota(y) := -y\frac{\zeta_{yy}(y)}{\zeta_y(y)}. \tag{9.57}$$

Then, borrowing results from the theory of choice under uncertainty we may immediately state:[29]

Theorem 9.13 (Concavity and inequality aversion)

Let ζ and $\hat{\zeta}$ be increasing, concave functions of one variable, such that $\hat{\zeta}$ is a concave transformation of ζ. Then (a) $\hat{\iota} \geq \iota$; (b) $\hat{\xi} \leq \xi$.

So the greater is the inequality aversion implicit in the social-welfare function, the greater is the apparent loss attributable to any given unequal distribution of income. It is important to emphasise that this is an *apparent* loss since there is no reason to suppose that in practice it is legitimate to take total income as given.

? Mini Problems

28 In this application what is the counterpart to the probabilities used in the von Neumann–Morgenstern case?

29 Prove this using the results from Chapter 8.

Example 9.3

In Chapter 8 we saw one study that attempted to determine how risk averse individuals are (page 197). What about the welfare-economics counterpart? Can we find evidence of an appropriate value range for the inequality-aversion parameter ι? Amiel et al. (1999) suggest a method based on a 'leaky bucket' thought experiment. The compelling leaky-bucket parable is due to Okun (1975): we might think it socially desirable that some income be redistributed from rich person R to poor person P, but would we still think the transfer worthwhile if a proportion of the income taken from R 'leaks out of the bucket' because of administrative costs? The larger the value of ι the more willing would one be to consider the transfer as appropriate, despite the leak. Amiel et al. find a rather low value of ι from their experiment, compared to the private values of risk aversion ρ mentioned on page 197.

9.5.3 The social-welfare function approach: assessment

The narrowly focused type of social-welfare function used here provides a way of interpreting intuitive criteria such as national income comparisons as well as a tool for analysing questions of distributional equity.

Social-welfare functions that are not individualistic and self-interested may well be worth considering. For example, if households had other people's incomes or utilities as arguments of their own utility functions then it is clear that a modified form of the above analysis will still go through. It may also provide a basis for assuming W to be strictly concave in incomes: if households 'feel bad' about income inequality (in a manner that is similar to the way they are adversely affected by other externalities) and if the social orderings respect individual tastes then the social-welfare function will exhibit inequality aversion. However, this may not, in itself, be an entirely satisfactory reason for supposing the social-welfare function to be inequality averse.

Summary

Moving from individual preferences and decision making—as in chapter 4—to preferences and decision making for society is a challenge. Our three approaches to social welfare show why this is so:

- The Arrow impossibility result (Theorem 9.1) is of fundamental importance in understanding why it is intrinsically so difficult to express social preferences as a general function of individual preferences.
- Of the principles for social judgement it is clear that Pareto efficiency is overwhelmingly important. It has a natural definition in models of perfect certainty and can be extended without much difficulty to uncertainty. In a pure private-goods economy the conditions for efficiency are very straightforward and can be fulfilled by a competitive

equilibrium. But it is difficult to extend the notion of Pareto superiority (on which efficiency is based) to criteria that permit general application.

- The social-welfare function seems like a useful way of cutting through the difficulties where general principles appear indecisive. But where is it supposed to come from? On what basis can we compare the utility levels or utility scales of one person with another?

We will find the issues raised in this chapter essential when dealing with the important questions that form the basis of Chapters 12 and 13. But before getting to that material we need to broaden considerably the analysis of economic decision making by introducing the idea of strategic behaviour.

Reading notes

A good overview of the main issues in welfare economics is provided by Boadway and Bruce (1984). On the 'constitution' approach see Arrow (1951), Black (1958), and the excellent paper by Vickrey (1960); for the basis of Theorem 9.2 see Black (1948).

The standard references on efficiency with public goods are Samuelson (1954, 1955).

Keenan and Snow (1999) summarise a variety of criteria for potential superiority and the relationship between them; the literature on the 'reversals' problems associated with potential superiority was initiated by Kaldor (1939), Hicks (1946), and Scitovsky (1941). The fairness discussion is based on an important contribution by Varian (1974).

Using the individual's attitude to risk as the basis for a social-welfare function is attributable to Vickrey (1945) and Harsanyi (1955). On the social-welfare interpretation of inequality and income distribution and its relationship to risk aversion see Atkinson (1970). The developments of social-welfare criteria for use in applied economics are reviewed in Harberger (1971) and Slesnick (1998).

Exercises

9.1 In a two-commodity exchange economy there are two large equal-sized groups of traders. Each trader in group a has an endowment of 300 units of commodity 1; each person in group b has an endowment of 200 units of commodity 2. Each a-type person has preferences given by the utility function

$$U^a(\mathbf{x}^a) = x_1^a x_2^a$$

and each b-type person's utility can be written as

$$U^b(\mathbf{x}^b) = \frac{x_1^b x_2^b}{x_1^a}$$

where x_i^h means the consumption of good i by an h-type person.

1. Find the competitive equilibrium allocation

2. Explain why the competitive equilibrium is inefficient.
3. Suggest a means whereby a benevolent government could achieved an efficient allocation.

9.2 Consider a constitution Σ based on a system of rank-order voting whereby the worst alternative gets 1 point, the next worst, 2, ... and so on, and the state that is awarded the most points by the citizens is the one selected. Alf's ranking of social states changes during the week. Bill's stays the same:

Monday:		*Tuesday:*	
Alf	**Bill**	**Alf**	**Bill**
θ	θ'	θ	θ'
θ'	θ	θ''	θ
θ''	θ''	θ'	θ''

What is the social ordering on Monday? What is it on Tuesday? How does this constitution violate Axiom 9.3?

9.3 Consider an economy that consists of just three individuals, $\{a, b, c\}$ and four possible social states of the world. Each state of the world is characterised by a monetary payoff y^h thus:

	a	b	c
θ	3	3	3
θ'	1	4	4
θ''	5	1	3
θ'''	2	6	1

Suppose that person h has a utility function $U^h = \log(y^h)$.

1. Show that if individuals know the payoffs that will accrue to them under each state of the world, then majority voting will produce a cyclic decision rule.
2. Show that the above conditions can rank unequal states over perfect equality.
3. Show that if people did not know which one of the identities $\{a, b, c\}$ they were to have before they vote, if they regard any one of these three identities as equally likely and if they are concerned to maximise expected utility, then majority voting will rank the states strictly in the order of the distribution of the payoffs.
4. A group of identical schoolchildren are to be endowed at lunchtime with an allocation of pie. When they look through the dining hall window in the morning they can see the slices of pie lying on the plates: the only problem is that no child knows which plate he or she will receive. Taking the space of all possible pie distributions as a complete description of all the possible social states for these schoolchildren, and assuming that *ex-ante* there are equal chances of any one child receiving any one of the plates discuss how a von Neumann–Morgenstern utility function may be used as a simple social-welfare function.
5. What determines the degree of inequality aversion of this social-welfare function?
6. Consider the possible problems in using this approach as a general method of specifying a social-welfare function.

	Left-handers				Right-handers	
#	10	6	6	12	18	17
	θ	θ'	θ'	θ''	θ	θ''
	θ'	θ	θ''	θ	θ''	θ
	θ''	θ''	θ	θ'	θ'	θ'

Table 9.3 Left-handed and right-handed voters

9.4 Table 9.3 shows the preferences over three social states for two groups of voters; the row marked '#' gives the number of voters with each set of preferences; preferences are listed in row order, most preferred at the top.

1. Find the Condorcet winner (see Mini Problem 3) among right-handed voters only.
2. Show that there is a cycle among left-handed voters only.
3. Suppose that the cycle among the left-handed voters is broken by ignoring the vote that has the smallest winner. Show that the winner is then the same as that among the right-handed voters.
4. Show that if the two groups are merged there is a Condorcet winner but is different from the winners found for the left-handers and the right-handers separately!
5. Would the above paradox occur if one used de Borda voting? (Moulin 2003)

9.5 Suppose social welfare is related to individual incomes y^h thus:

$$W = \sum_{h=1}^{n_h} \zeta(y^h)$$

where $\zeta(\cdot)$ has the form

$$\zeta(x) = \frac{x^{1-\varepsilon} - 1}{1 - \varepsilon}$$

and ε is a non-negative parameter.

1. What form does ζ take for $\varepsilon = 1$? [Hint, use l'Hôpital's rule.]
2. What is relative inequality aversion for this W?
3. Draw the contours of the social welfare function for the cases $\varepsilon = 1$, $\varepsilon \to 0$, $\varepsilon \to \infty$. What is equally-distributed-equivalent income in each case?
4. If, instead of a finite population $\{1, \ldots, n_h\}$, there is a continuum of individuals distributed on $\mathbb{R}$ with density at income y given by $f(y)$ write down the equivalent form of the social-welfare function W in general and in the particular cases cited in part 3 (Atkinson 1970).

9.6 In a two-commodity exchange economy there are two groups of people: type a have the utility function $2\log(x_1^a) + \log(x_2^a)$ and an endowment of 30 units of commodity 1 and k units of commodity 2; type b have the utility function $\log(x_1^b) + 2\log(x_2^b)$ and an endowment of 60 units of commodity 1 and $210 - k$ units of commodity 2.

1. Show that the equilibrium price, ρ, of good 1 in terms of good 2 is $\frac{210+k}{150}$. [Hint: use the answer to Exercise 7.4 (page 174).]
2. What are the individuals' incomes (y^a, y^b) in equilibrium as a function of k? As a function of ρ?
3. Suppose it is possible for the government to carry out lump-sum transfers of commodity 2, but impossible to transfer commodity 1. Use the previous answer to show the set of income distributions that can be achieved through such transfers. Draw this in a diagram.
4. If the government has the social-welfare function

$$W(y^a, y^b) = \log(y^a) + \log(y^b)$$

find the optimal distribution of income using the transfers mentioned in part 3. [Hint: use the diagram constructed earlier.]
5. If instead the government has the social-welfare function

$$W(y^a, y^b) = y^a + y^b$$

find the optimal distribution of income using transfers. Comment on the result.

9.7 This is an example of *rent seeking*. In a certain industry it is known that monopoly profits $\overline{\Pi}$ are available. There are N firms that are lobbying to get the right to run this monopoly. Firm f spends an amount c^f on lobbying; the probability that firm f is successful in its lobbying activity is given by

$$\pi^f := \frac{c^f}{\sum_{j=1}^{N} c^j}.$$

1. Suppose firm f makes the same assumptions about other firms activities as in Exercise 3.2 (page 65). It chooses c^f so as to maximise expected returns to lobbying assuming the other firms' lobbying expenditures are given. What is the first-order condition for a maximum?
2. If the firms are identical show that the total lobbying costs chosen by the firms must be given by

$$Nc^* = \overline{\Pi}\left[1 - \frac{1}{N}\right].$$

3. If lobbying costs are considered to contribute nothing to society what is the implication for the measurement of 'waste' attributable to monopoly, as discussed in Mini Problem 16 (Tullock 1967)?

9.8 In an economy there are n commodities and n_h individuals, and there is uncertainty: each individual may have good or poor health. The state of health is an independently distributed random variable for each individual and occurs after the allocation of goods has taken place. Individual h gets the following utility in state of the world ω:

$$u^h\left(\mathbf{x}^h, \omega\right) := a^h\left(x_1^h, \omega\right) + \sum_{i=2}^{n} b^h\left(x_i^h\right)$$

where $\mathbf{x}^h := \left(x_1^h, x_2^h, \ldots, x_n^h\right)$, x_i^h is the amount of commodity i consumed by h, the functions a^h,b^h are increasing and concave in consumption, and ω takes one of the two values 'poor health' or 'good health' for each individual; good 1 is health-care services.

1. The government estimates that for each individual the probability of state of the world ω is π_ω. If aggregate production possibilities are described by the production constraint $\Phi(\mathbf{x}) = 0$ (where $\mathbf{x} := (x_1, x_2, \ldots, x_n)$ and x_i is the aggregate consumption of commodity i) and the government has a social-welfare function

$$\sum_{h=1}^{n_h} \sum_{\omega} \pi_\omega u^h\left(\mathbf{x}^h, \omega\right)$$

find the first-order conditions for a social optimum.

2. The government also has the ability to tax or subsidise commodities at different rates for different individuals: so individual h faces a price p_i^h for commodity i. If the person has an income y^h and estimates that the probability of state of the world ω is π_ω^h, and if he maximises expected utility, write down the first-order conditions for a maximum.

3. Show that the solutions in parts 1 and 2 can only coincide if

$$\frac{p_i^h}{p_j^h} = \frac{\Phi_i(\mathbf{x})}{\Phi_j(\mathbf{x})}, \quad i, j = 2, \ldots, n$$

$$\frac{p_1^h}{p_j^h} = \frac{\Phi_1(\mathbf{x})}{\Phi_j(\mathbf{x})} \times \left[\frac{\sum_\omega \pi_\omega^h a_1^h\left(x_1^h, \omega\right)}{\sum_\omega \pi_\omega a_1^h\left(x_1^h, \omega\right)}\right], \; j = 2, \ldots, n$$

Is there a case for subsidising health care? Is there a case for subsidising any other commodity (Sandmo 1983)?

9.9 Revisit the economy of San Serrife (Exercise 4.11 on page 97). Heterogeneity amongst the inhabitants of San Serrife was ignored in Exercise 4.11. However, it is now known that although all San Serrife residents have preferences of the form Exercise 4.2 they differ in their tastes: Northern San Serrifeans spend 34 per cent of their budget on milk and only 2 per cent on wine, while Southern San Serrifeans spend just 4 per cent of their budget on milk and 32 per cent on wine. The question of entry to the EU is to be reviewed; the consequences for the prices of milk and wine of entry to the EU are as in Exercise 4.11.

1. Assume that there are eight times as many Southerners as Northerners in the San Serrife population, but that the average income of a Northerner is four times that of a Southerner. On the basis of the potential-superiority criterion, should San Serrife enter the EU?
2. Suppose Northerners and Southerners had equal incomes. Should San Serrife enter the EU?
3. What would be the outcome of a straight vote on entry to the EU?

10 Strategic Behaviour

You know my methods [Watson]. Apply them.
Sherlock Holmes (Sir Arthur Conan Doyle, *The Sign of Four*)

10.1 Introduction

In this chapter we focus on the conflict and cooperation that are fundamental to microeconomic problems. The principles of economic analysis that we will develop will provide a basis for the discussion of chapters 11 and 12 and provide essential tools for the wider study of microeconomics. Why a change in the direction of analysis?

Our analysis of strategic behaviour in economics focuses on the theory of games. Game theory is an important subject in its own right and it is impossible to do it justice within a chapter or so. Here we use it as a further powerful analytical tool. The methodology that we will introduce in this chapter offers new insights on concepts and techniques we have discussed earlier including the specification of the optimisation process and the nature of equilibrium. The logical processes may require some mental adjustment in order to grasp the methods involved. But, having mastered the methods, one can apply them—Sherlock Holmes style—to a wide variety of models and problems.

The chapter covers the topics in strategic behaviour by grouping them into three broad areas as follows:

- *The essential building blocks.* In sections 10.2 and 10.3 we review some of the ideas that were taken for granted in the case of perfect markets (chapters 2–7) and rethink the notion of equilibrium. Section 10.4 applies these concepts to 'industrial organisation'—the interaction of firms in a market.
- *Time.* In section 10.5 we examine how the sequencing of decisions in strategic interactions will affect notions of rationality and equilibrium. Section 10.6 examines these principles in the context of market structure.
- *Uncertainty.* In section 10.7 we introduce some of the issues raised in chapter 8 to the context of strategic interaction. The resulting models are quite rich and the analysis here is continued into chapter 11.

10.2 Games: basic concepts

Many of the concepts and methods of game theory are quite intuitive but, in order to avoid ambiguity, let us run through a preliminary list of its constituent parts and note those that will require fuller treatment.

10.2.1 Players, rules, and payoffs

The literature offers several alternative thumbnail sketches of the elementary ingredients of a game. The following four-part summary has a claim to be a consensus approach.

Players

The 'players' are the individual entities that are involved in the economic problem represented by the game. We will take these to be economic agents such as firms, households, or the government. But occasionally one needs to extend the set of players in games that involve an element of exogenous uncertainty. It can be convenient to treat the random elements of the game as the actions of an extra player known as 'Nature', a kind of invisible bogeyman rolling the dice behind the scenes.

Rules of play

The rules of the game focus on *moves* or *actions* of the players. The concept of 'action' is a wide-ranging idea covering, for example, the consumption choices made by households, the output decisions of firms, level of taxes . . .

In a parlour game it is clearly specified what moves each player can legally make at each stage of the game. For a well-specified game in microeconomics this must obviously be done too. But more is involved: in both parlour games and economic problems: the *information* that is available at the point of each move can be crucial to the specification of the game. To illustrate, there is a variant of chess known as Kriegsspiel, in which the players can see their own pieces, but not those of their opponent; kings, queens, pawns, and so on all work in the same way, but the rules of the game obviously become fundamentally different from ordinary chess in the light of this difference in information.

Determination of the outcome

For each set of actions or moves (including moves by 'Nature' to cover the rôle of uncertainty) there is a specific outcome that is then determined almost mechanistically. The outcome could be defined in terms of lists of outputs, baskets of goods, or other economic quantities. It could be something as simple as the answer to the question 'who wins?' It is given economic meaning by an evaluation in terms of the *payoffs* that accrue to the players given a particular outcome of the game.

Payoffs

The players' objectives (maximisation of utility, profits, . . .) are just as we have introduced them in earlier chapters. The nature of the payoffs that are associated with the outcomes could be quite different for different types of game. As in the analysis of previous chapters we have to be careful to distinguish cases where the payoffs can be treated as purely ordinal concepts (utility in chapter 4) from those where they have cardinal significance (profits in chapter 2 or 'felicity' in chapter 8).

These basic ingredients collectively permit a description of what the game is about, but not how it is to be played. To see what more is involved we have to examine some of the game's ingredients more closely: we particularly need to consider the rôle of information.

10.2.2 Information and beliefs

Uncertainty and progressively changing information can greatly influence the possible outcomes of a game: simply turning over cards in an elementary two-person card game or in solitaire is enough to convince one of that. However, more is involved. Take the Kriegsspiel versus ordinary chess example again: without being a chess expert oneself, one can see that it would be useful for player A to try to discover ways of moving his own pieces that will force player B to reveal information about the disposition of B's concealed pieces. What players think that they know is going to affect the way that they play the game and will, in turn, influence the way that information develops through time.

Because information plays such a central rôle in the way a game can unfold it is important to incorporate a precise representation of this within the microeconomic model. The key concept in characterising the situation for an individual agent at any point in the game is the agent's *information set*: this is a full description of the exact state of what is known to the agent at a particular point in the game and will usually (although not necessarily) embody complete recall about everything that has happened previously in the game. Obviously the same individual will usually have a different information set at different stages of the game. We will be able to make the definition of the information set precise once we have considered how to represent the game precisely—in 10.2.4 below.

A central idea in the discussion of 'who knows what?' is the concept of 'common knowledge'. An appeal to common knowledge is frequently a feature of the reasoning required to analyse strategic problems and clearly has much intuitive appeal. However, the term has a precise interpretation in the context of games and microeconomics: a piece of information is common knowledge if it is known by all agents and all agents know that the other agents know it... and so on, recursively. The idea is quite powerful. Suppose we assume that it is common knowledge that all players in the game are rational: this greatly simplifies the analysis but, although this assumption is standard in economic modelling of strategic interaction, you can probably recall playing parlour games where it was wildly inappropriate.

For cases not covered by the comforting quasi-certainty of 'common knowledge', we need to introduce some concept of individual *beliefs* about the way the game works. Of course in some very special cases beliefs are almost irrelevant to the modelling of a game. But usually the use of available information in the modelling of beliefs is an important extension to the concept of rationality that we have employed in earlier chapters. If the individual agent were not making a maximising choice subject to the reasonable beliefs that he has we could say that the individual is irrational. Of course this begs the question of what constitutes 'reasonable' beliefs. It also leaves open the issue of how the beliefs could or should be updated in the light of hard information that becomes available during the playing of the game, a point to which we return in section 10.7.

The explicit treatment of uncertainty in models of strategic behaviour and the unfolding of information with the passage of time are important features of microeconomic models and are considered in further detail below.

10.2.3 Strategy

The essence of the game-theoretic approach—and the reason for the title of this chapter—is the focus on *strategy*. A player's strategy needs to be clearly distinguished from the idea of an action. Think of the kind of chess puzzle you sometimes see in newspapers or magazines: a few pieces are on the board and the challenge 'White to play and mate in four moves.' You, acting out the rôle of White then work through the various sequences of moves and counter-moves from Black to see if, indeed, you can find a way of winning the game in four moves. The detailed plan that you form in your mind 'if I move here, Black would respond by moving here or here, in which case...' is your strategy; the individual moves are your actions. Of course we can imagine some very simple games where the whole strategy consists of just one single action, but these are rather special.

Simply stated, player h's strategy is a complete contingent plan of action for all possible situations that could conceivably arise in the course of a game. It can be expressed formally as follows. Take the collection of all the information sets for agent h corresponding to reachable points within the game: a strategy s^h for agent h is a mapping from this collection to the set of actions feasible for h.

The individual's strategy is the fundamental tool that we will use to analyse the working and outcomes of games.

10.2.4 Representing a game

A game is usually a complex form of strategic interaction. To make sense of it a clear method of representation is required. There are two main forms

- The game in *extensive form* is a kind of tree diagram. The root of the tree is where the game starts and the beginning of each new branch—each *node*—characterises the situation reached at a given moment from a given sequence of actions by the players. At each terminal node (i.e. where the game ends) there is a vector of payoffs, one for each agent. For now these payoffs could be considered to be purely ordinal and need not be comparable between different agents—we will see below situations when these assumptions are no longer satisfactory.

- The game in *strategic form* (also known as *normal form*) is a kind of multidimensional spreadsheet. Each dimension (row, column, etc.) of the spreadsheet corresponds to the set of strategies for each separate player; each cell in the spreadsheet gives a list of numbers corresponding to the payoffs of the outcome associated with that particular combination of strategies.

A simple example of the two forms of representation can help here. Figure 10.1 depicts the extensive form of a game where the two players each make a move simultaneously and then the game ends. In this case the strategies for both agents are very simple—each strategy consists of exactly one action. The top of the diagram depicts Alf's choice between the two strategies s_1^a (play [LEFT]) and s_2^a (play [RIGHT]): his choice then determines whether the left- or the right-hand node in the middle of the diagram is the relevant one. In the bottom part of the diagram Bill makes his choice (between the actions [left] and [right]); but in view of the simultaneous move he does not, of course, know whether the left-hand or the right-hand node is the relevant one; this lack of clarity is depicted by the shaded box around the two nodes depicting the fact that both nodes are in Bill's information set.[1] At the bottom of the figure is the list of (Alf, Bill)-payoffs resulting from each $\left(s_i^a, s_j^b\right)$-combination. Table 10.1 shows the same game in strategic form. The rows correspond to Alf's choice of strategy; the columns to Bill's choice; the contents of each cell correspond exactly to the bottom line of Figure 10.1.

Note the way the concept of the information set is implicitly defined in Figure 10.1. If the agent knows for certain which node the game has reached when he has to make a move then he has very precise information to use in making his choice—all the basket of detail associated with the knowledge of being exactly at that node. In such a case the information set contains just one point. If there is the possibility of more than one node being relevant—if the information set contains multiple points—then information is less precise. More formally we have:

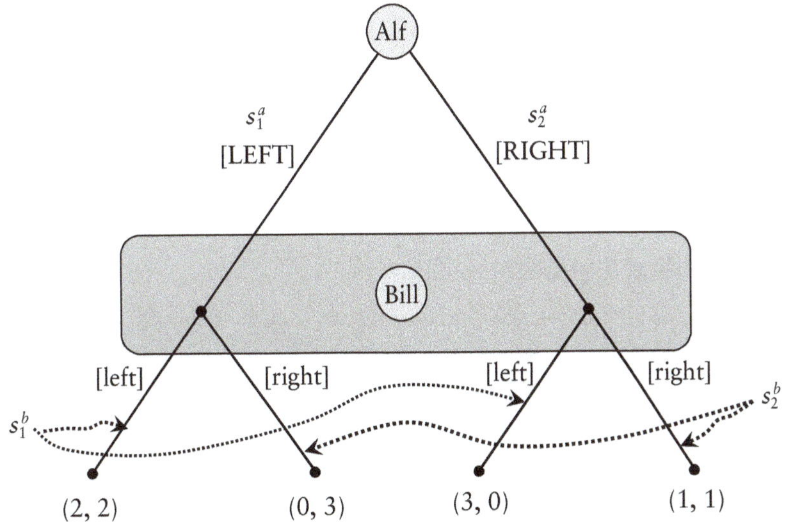

Figure 10.1 Simultaneous move, extensive form

? Mini Problems

1 The game could also be one where Alf moves first but conceals the move that he has made: briefly explain why.

		s_1^b [left]	s_2^b [right]
s_1^a	[LEFT]	2, 2	0, 3
s_2^a	[RIGHT]	3, 0	1, 1

Table 10.1 Simultaneous move, strategic form

Definition 10.1

Agent h's *information set* is the set of nodes that h knows might be the actual node, but that cannot be distinguished by direct observation.

Does it matter whether extensive form or strategic form is used? In most cases that are relevant to microeconomic modelling the choice between the two forms is largely a matter of expositional convenience, as long as the representation in each of the two forms has been properly done.[2] However, it is worth noting that one particular strategic-form representation may correspond to more than one extensive-form representation—it is just that the alternative extensive-form representations turn out to be economically equivalent in terms of the way the game is actually played.[3]

10.3 Equilibrium

The players—economic agents—come to the game with their strategies: what would constitute an equilibrium of the economic problem being represented by the game? To address this we can draw on the understanding of equilibrium set out in several contexts in chapters 2 to 7. However, we will find that several new issues are raised and that even the concept of equilibrium itself requires some care. We begin our discussion with a deceptively simple version of equilibrium.

10.3.1 A simplified approach

The simplified approach consists of introducing an idea that should appear rather persuasive and that leads naturally on to a description of equilibrium in some kinds of games; it also makes the method of finding the equilibrium obvious. However, as we shall see, it has some limitations.

? Mini Problems

2 A couple want to decide on an evening's entertainment. He prefers to go to the West End (there's a new play); she wants to go to the East End (dog races). If they go as a couple each person gets utility level 2 if it is his/her preferred activity and 1 otherwise. However, for each person the evening would be ruined if the partner were not there to share it (utility level 0). Depict this as a game in (a) strategic form (b) extensive form.

3 Draw another extensive-form game tree that corresponds to the strategic form given in Table 10.1.

Dominance

The dominance concept and its relationship to equilibrium can be introduced by a simple example in a two-person game of the sort already introduced. Suppose that Alf finds that, whatever his opponent does, he would do better for himself if he played the strategy [RIGHT]. Then the strategy [RIGHT] can be said to dominate any other strategy as far as Alf is concerned. Admittedly this is not saying very much in a game such as that of Table 10.1 since there is only one other strategy that Alf could consider. But the idea of a dominant strategy and of a dominated strategy (in this case the strategy [LEFT]) easily generalises to cases where there are many strategies available.

Suppose further that Bill finds that the situation facing him is essentially the same—it is true that he always does better by playing [right] whatever his opponent (Alf) does. Again we have a dominant strategy. Furthermore, if there is a dominant strategy for a rational player h then it is reasonable to assume that h would definitely use that strategy in playing the game. It is a very short step from that thought to a simple solution.

Applying dominance

The associated solution is a no-brainer. If each player h has a dominant strategy then the situation where each h plays the dominant strategy can be characterised as an equilibrium: everyone is taking an action that, apparently, cannot be improved upon and so no one wants to deviate from this dominant-strategy outcome.

We can apply this immediately to the game in Table 10.1 as follows. If Bill plays [left] Alf does better for himself by playing [RIGHT] (he gets a payoff of 3 rather than 2); if Bill plays [right] Alf again does better for himself by playing [RIGHT] (he gets a payoff of 1 rather than 0); so Alf would seem justified in eliminating the strategy [LEFT] from further consideration. The set-up is symmetric so we can immediately see that Bill would seem justified in eliminating the strategy [left] from further consideration. What remains is the pair of strategies [RIGHT], [right] yielding the payoff (1,1). So, finding an equilibrium in the kind of uncomplicated games that we have used thus far appears to be quite easy. It can of course be extended to cases where there are more than two strategies available for each player and where there are many players.[4]

We could even extend this elimination argument in the following way. Consider the case where there are two players but more than two strategies available for each of them. Suppose there is no strategy that immediately emerges as dominant for either player. But maybe, on checking the situation for Bill, say, it is clear that there are some strategies that are *dominated* in the sense just explained (i.e. Bill has available some other strategy that would always give him a higher payoff whatever Alf chooses to do). We could consider that choosing such a strategy would be irrational for Bill. We might therefore eliminate dominated strategies from the table and then look again to see if there is, in the reduced

? Mini Problems

4 Consider the game in the following table. Assuming that both agents are rational, what is the game's solution? In what way does it differ fundamentally from the game in Table 10.1?

	s_1^b	s_2^b
s_1^a	3, 3	1, 2
s_2^a	2, 1	0, 0

table, a dominant strategy for each player.[5] If necessary the process could be repeated, eliminating yet more dominated strategies until (we hope) a pair of dominant strategies emerges. The method essentially follows Sherlock Holmes's dictum 'when you have eliminated the impossible, whatever remains, however improbable, must be the truth'. In the kind of case we have been thinking about, when you have eliminated the inappropriate (i.e. the dominated strategies), whatever remains must be the equilibrium.

Overall the dominance approach seems to be attractively simple. However, there are two big difficulties

1. It is often the case that there is no dominant strategy, even if one were to use the iterative method outlined above. In richer models the solution method can be much less straightforward. This is why we need to introduce a more general approach right away.
2. The apparently reasonable solution that we have just outlined can, in some cases, lead to a rather odd outcome. Maybe you can already see what the problem is just by eyeballing Table 10.1. We will come back to study this in 10.3.4 below.

10.3.2 A general approach

In order to make further progress in discussing equilibrium we need to put the discussion on to a more formal footing.

Some more notation

First, we introduce a concept that facilitates the definition of further concepts by reusing a term from chapter 9. A *profile* of strategies is a particular collection of strategies, one for each player in the game. Write this as

$$[s] := \left[s^1, s^2, \ldots\right].$$

Note that we use the same [ ] notation as for allocations in chapter 7. We also need a notation to describe the strategy being played by all those other than agent h; this is of course just the profile $[s]$ with the hth component deleted, so we express this as

$$[s]^{-h} := \left[s^1, s^2, \ldots, s^{h-1}, s^{h+1}, s^{h+2}, \ldots\right]. \tag{10.1}$$

In order to evaluate the outcome of the game we will write payoffs as utilities. It makes sense to write utility as a function of strategies—in a kind of reduced form. So, for a given profile of strategies $[s]$, we write h's utility as

$$v^h\left(s^h, [s]^{-h}\right); \tag{10.2}$$

person h's utility is dependent on his own choice of strategy s^h and on those of everyone else in the game $[s]^{-h}$.

? Mini Problems

5 In extending the method in this way we are making an important assumption about the information available to each player. Can you see what it is?

Let us denote the set of all feasible strategies for agent h as S^h: this gives a comprehensive description of what h can do and when he can do it. Then for a given set of agents (players) we can completely describe a game by just two objects, a profile of payoff functions and the corresponding list of strategy sets, as follows:

$$\left[v^1, v^2, \ldots\right]; \left[S^1, S^2, \ldots\right]. \tag{10.3}$$

'Best response'

These elementary building blocks allow us to introduce the essential concept to grasp in any consideration of economic strategy. This is the idea of an agent's 'best response' to other agents' strategies and is defined as follows:

Definition 10.2

The strategy $\hat{s}^h$ is h's *best response* to $[s]^{-h}$ if

$$v^h\left(\hat{s}^h, [s]^{-h}\right) \geq v^h\left(s^h, [s]^{-h}\right) \tag{10.4}$$

for all $s^h \in S^h$ or, equivalently, if

$$\hat{s}^h \in \arg\max_{s^h} v^h\left(s^h, [s]^{-h}\right). \tag{10.5}$$

The form (10.5) uses the 'argmax' notation to denote the set of values of s^h that do the required maximisation job—see Appendix section A.7.5 for a formal definition. We could, of course, alter the definition to 'strongly best' by replacing the '$\geq$' with '$>$' in (10.4) in which case the set on the right-hand side of (10.5) has just one element.

The best-response idea is indeed a logical extension of what we have assumed about agents in earlier chapters that focused on perfect markets. There we can see each profit-maximising firm making a 'best response' in terms of inputs and outputs to a ruling set of market prices; the utility-maximising consumer makes the 'best response' to the market in the light of the household budget and his or her own preferences. But now, instead of the sharp information about market conditions, the individual agent has to form a view as to what the consequences will be of his own actions as they are observed and interpreted by other agents.

Contained within the concept of Definition 10.2, there is the very special case that we introduced in 10.3.1 above. A *dominant strategy* is one that remains a best-response strategy whatever the actions of the other players in the game: there is a dominant strategy for agent h if $\hat{s}^h$ in (10.5) is actually independent of $[s]^{-h}$. Of course in many interesting cases dominant strategies just do not exist—but they are of particular interest in certain important applications as we will see in chapter 12.

Nash equilibrium

The idea of the best response leads us on to the fundamental concept of equilibrium of a game.

Definition 10.3

A *Nash equilibrium* is a profile of strategies $[s^*]$ such that, for each agent $h, 1, \ldots, n_h$:

$$s^{*h} \in \arg\max_{s^h} v^h\left(s^h, [s^*]^{-h}\right). \tag{10.6}$$

The plain language interpretation of this is as follows. The Nash equilibrium is a situation where everyone is making the best response to everyone else. We can imagine each agent thinking 'I want to select the strategy that will give the best outcome for me, given what I believe are the strategy choices of all the other agents.' Under these circumstances no agent has a unilateral incentive to deviate from his strategy given that all the other agents do not deviate from their policy.

An illustration

To see how the equilibrium concept works in a simple case consider the game illustrated in Table 10.2. Let us enumerate the best responses:

- If Bill plays [left] Alf's best response is to play [LEFT].
- If Bill plays [right] Alf's best response is to play [RIGHT].
- If Alf plays [LEFT] Bill's best response is to play [left].
- If Alf plays [RIGHT] Bill's best response is to play [left].

So the unique Nash equilibrium is given by the strategy profile [LEFT],[left]. It is clear that there is no dominant strategy for Alf, although there is a dominant strategy for Bill. Exercise 10.2 provides a richer example with more strategies.

A word of caution

Although the Nash equilibrium is the main plank on which our approach to strategic behaviour is based we ought to take immediate note of three serious difficulties that are frequently encountered in applying the Nash concept to microeconomic and other problems. These difficulties are handled in 10.3.3 to 10.3.4.

10.3.3 Multiple equilibria

In many interesting economic cases there is more than one Nash equilibrium. For example, in Table 10.3 both $\left[s_1^a, s_1^b\right]$ and $\left[s_2^a, s_2^b\right]$ are equilibria. Clearly the former

		s_1^b [left]	s_2^b [right]
s_1^a	[LEFT]	2, 3	0, 2
s_2^a	[RIGHT]	0, 1	1, 0

Table 10.2 A game with a unique Nash equilibrium

	s_1^b	s_2^b
s_1^a	3, 3	1, 0
s_2^a	0, 1	2, 2

Table 10.3 Multiple equilibria 1

	s_1^b	s_2^b
s_1^a	2, 2	1, 3
s_2^a	3, 1	0, 0

Table 10.4 Multiple equilibria 2

generates outcomes that Pareto-dominate the latter but, as far as the Nash concept is concerned, each is equally valid as an equilibrium outcome of the game.[6] The second example—a version of the so-called Chicken game—appears more problematic. In Table 10.4 the strategy profiles $\left[s_1^a, s_2^b\right]$ and $\left[s_1^a, s_2^b\right]$ (yielding payoffs (3, 1) and (1, 3) respectively) are both Nash equilibria: in contrast to the previous example they are the (only) unequal outcomes of the game—either Alf is exalted and Bill ends in near despair, or vice versa.[7]

So, in each game there are two equilibria: how to choose between them? In some cases the economic context will provide an answer (more on this below); but the Nash concept by itself is of no help.

10.3.4 Efficiency

The terminology 'best response' that was used to underpin the Nash equilibrium concept should be treated with caution—'best' in what sense? If we are tempted to reply 'best in the sense that a rational agent makes the choice that maximises his own payoff, given the environment that he is in,' then we should be aware that rationality needs

? Mini Problems

6 Suppose we were to change the model a little and allow the participants to communicate their intentions before they play the game—would this help to resolve the choice between the equilibria?

7 Recreate the Chicken game from the following information. Two lads want to impress each other by appearing to be very brave. They stand on the highway when a truck is coming. The first to jump out of the way of the truck is 'chicken' and suffers ignominy, the other lad is then free to follow him and is considered a local hero. If both jump out of the way simultaneously they equally suffer embarrassment. If neither jumps out of the way they are both dead.

(a) What is the utility ordering of 'death', 'embarrassment', 'hero', 'ignominy' required in order to yield the same structure as Table 10.4?

(b) Would preplay communication assist in resolving the problem of multiple equilibria in this case?

(c) What would happen to the structure of this game if, instead, 'ignominy' were considered worse than 'death'?

careful interpretation here. This can be illustrated by the example just considered in Table 10.3—only one of the two equilibria is efficient, but both equilibria are characterised by 'best responses'.

The point comes out even more forcefully in the next example. To set the scene let us pose an important question about games in general—what is the worst that can happen to a rational economic agent? Formally we could write this as the *minimax* payoff for agent h:

$$\underline{\upsilon}^h := \min_{[s]^{-h}} \left[\max_{s^h} \upsilon^h \left(s^h, [s]^{-h} \right) \right]; \tag{10.7}$$

Checking back to Definition 10.2 we see that expression enclosed in [ ] of (10.7) means that h is making the best response to everyone else's strategy; the 'min' operator in (10.7) means that everyone else is trying to punish him within the rules of the game. This minimax value plays the rôle of reservation utility and provides a useful reference point in judging the outcomes of games in terms of their payoffs.

Now for the example: this is the game introduced in Figure 10.1 and briefly discussed in 10.3.1—a game form known as the *Prisoner's Dilemma*.[8] Note first from the associated Table 10.1 that there is a single Nash equilibrium at $\left[s_2^a, s_2^b\right]$; note second that it is inefficient: the strategy profile $\left[s_1^a, s_1^b\right]$ would yield higher payoffs for both agents! This is illustrated in Figure 10.2 where the utility possibilities representing the payoffs from the game consist of just the four dots.[9] The Nash equilibrium yields in fact the minimax outcome shown in the figure as the utility pair $\left(\underline{\upsilon}^a, \underline{\upsilon}^b\right)$.[10] The equilibrium is myopically and individualistically rational, by definition. However, it is arguable that the Pareto-efficient outcome of $(3, 3)$ is where some sense of group rationality ought to lead us.[11]

? Mini Problems

8 Recreate the Prisoner's Dilemma from the following. Two bad guys have been arrested and are held in separate locations. The problem for the authorities is to prove that they are bad guys: evidence is only likely to come from the individuals themselves. So the authorities announce to each bad guy that if he confesses and implicates the other he will get off with a token sentence of 1 year while the other will go down for 20 years; if they both confess then they each get 10 years. Both of them know, however, that if they both stay shtumm the authorities can only get them for bad driving during the police chase: this will incur a sentence of 2 years each.

Write the game in strategic form and show that there is a dominant strategy for each of the two bad guys. Find the Nash equilibrium payoffs and explain why it appears inefficient from the bad guys' point of view.

Suppose that the bad guys get the opportunity to communicate and are then put back into their separate cells: will this make a difference to the outcome of the game?

9 Draw the same kind of diagram for the games depicted in Mini Problem 2 ('Battle of the Sexes') and in Table 10.4 ('Chicken').

10 Suppose all of Alf's payoffs are subjected to a given monotonically increasing transformation; and that Bill's payoffs are subjected to another monotonically increasing transformation. Show that the outcome of the game is unaffected.

11 Practical common sense might suggest that the way to resolve this is for the agents (the prisoners) to sign some sort of binding contract. Why is this apparently neat 'solution' somewhat misleading?

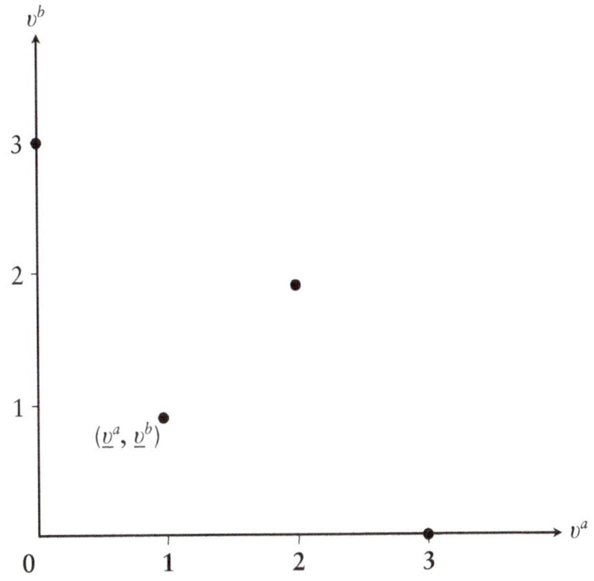

Figure 10.2 Utility possibilities: Prisoner's Dilemma

This is not just a bizarre example carefully selected in order to make a recondite theoretical point. The Prisoner's Dilemma issue lies at the heart of many economic questions where group interests and narrowly defined individual interests do not coincide: we will discuss one important example from the field of industrial organisation in 10.4 below; another important area is introduced in chapter 12 and its consequences are further examined in chapter 13.

10.3.5 **Existence**

There may be no Nash equilibrium at all. To see this consider the problem depicted in strategic form in Table 10.5 (more on this in exercise 10.3). Again it is set up so that strategies coincide with actions. In this case if Alf (agent a) were to select strategy s_1^a then Bill's best response is to select strategy s_2^b; but if Bill selects strategy s_2^b then Alf's best response is to go for strategy s_2^a;... and so on round the cycle. There is no strategy profile where each agent is simultaneously making the best response to the other. What is at the bottom of the problem and can one find a way round it?[12]

? Mini Problems

12 'Matching pennies' is a simple game that you can play at home. Each player chooses to hold a concealed penny either heads up or tails up; the players simultaneously reveal the pennies; if the pennies are both the same way up, player b pays player a \$1; if one is head and one is tails then a pays b \$1. Use a table similar to Table 10.1 to depict the strategic form of the game. Show the best responses on the table. Is there a Nash equilibrium?

	s_1^b	s_2^b
s_1^a	2, 2	0, 3
s_2^a	0, 1	1, 0

Table 10.5 No equilibrium in pure strategies

A suggested solution

Consider the best response for agent a as a function of agent b's strategy, and vice versa: it is clear that they are discontinuous, because in this simple model the choices are discrete. We may recall from our previous discussion of agents in perfect markets that where the response function was discontinuous it might be that there was, strictly speaking, no market equilibrium (see, for example, pages 53ff. in chapter 3); we may also recall that there is a commonsense argument to 'rescue' the equilibrium concept in conventional cases. The query might come to mind whether a similar issue arises with strategic models like those depicted in Table 10.5: is lack of equilibrium in some way attributable to the discontinuity of response in this case? And is there a similar 'rescue' argument? In the case of the firm and the market it made sense to appeal to a large numbers argument—on average the supply function is continuous and then we know that there is a price-taking equilibrium. But the large numbers device may not be appropriate here—perhaps there really are only two players. However, there is an approach that has a similar flavour. This involves introducing an explicit probabilistic device that allows an agent to enlarge the set of available strategies. We will see how this works in the particular case of the game in Table 10.5 and then examine the issues that are involved in the extra step that apparently offers us the solution.

Suppose that Alf announces that he will adopt strategy s_1^a with probability π^a and strategy s_2^a with probability $1 - \pi^a$. Likewise Bill announces that he will adopt strategies $\left(s_1^b, s_2^b\right)$ with probabilities $\left(\pi^b, 1 - \pi^b\right)$ respectively. Furthermore, let us take the criterion for each of the agents as being their expected payoff (in utility terms). Then, from Table 10.5, if Alf takes π^b as given and chooses probability π^a his expected utility is[13]

$$\left[3\pi^b - 1\right]\pi^a + 1 - \pi^b, \tag{10.8}$$

and if Bill takes π^a as given and chooses probability π^b, then his expected utility is

$$\left[1 - 2\pi^a\right]\pi^b + 3\pi^a. \tag{10.9}$$

We can use (10.8) to derive Alf's choice of π^a as a best response to Bill's choice of π^b. Clearly if $\pi^b = \frac{1}{3}$ the value of π^a has no impact on Alf's expected payoff; but if $\pi^b > \frac{1}{3}$ then (10.8) is increasing in π^a and it would pay Alf to push π^a as high as it will go ($\pi^a = 1$)—i.e. he would then adopt strategy s_1^a with certainty; if $\pi^b < \frac{1}{3}$ the converse happens—(10.8) is then decreasing in π^a and Alf would adopt strategy s_2^a with certainty. Alf's best-response behaviour is summarised by the correspondence $\chi^a(\cdot)$ in Figure 10.3

? Mini Problems

13 Use Table 10.5 to derive (10.8) and (10.9).

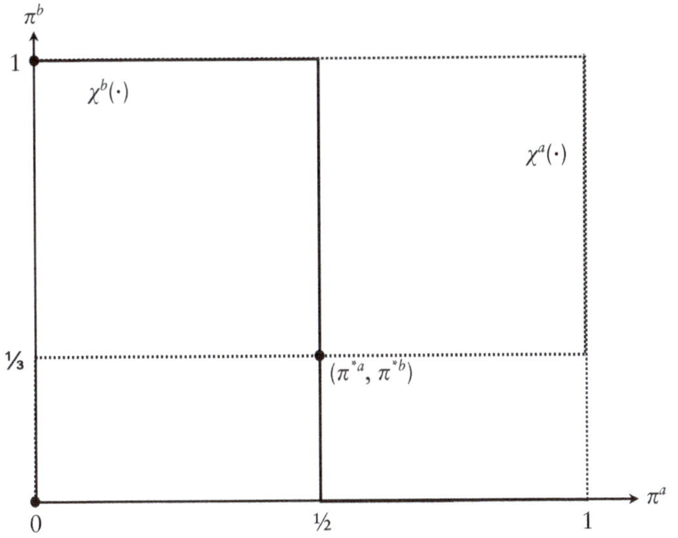

Figure 10.3 Equilibrium in mixed strategy

(we are being picky here: χ^a is a correspondence rather than a function because it is multi-valued at the point $\pi^b = \frac{1}{3}$). The expression $\chi^a\left(\pi^b\right)$ will give the set of values of π^a that constitute Alf's best response to an announced π^b.

Now think about Bill's best response to Alf's chosen probability. From (10.9) we see that his expected payoff is increasing or decreasing in π^b as $\pi^a < \frac{1}{2}$ or $\pi^a > \frac{1}{2}$, respectively. So, by similar reasoning to the Alf case, Bill's best-response correspondence $\chi^b(\cdot)$ is as depicted in Figure 10.3: for low values of π^a Bill uses strategy s_1^b with certainty and for high values of π^a he adopts s_2^b with certainty.

But now we can see an apparent solution staring at us from Figure 10.3. Put the question, 'is there a probability pair such that $\pi^a \in \chi^a\left(\pi^b\right)$ and $\pi^b \in \chi^b(\pi^a)$ simultaneously?' and it is clear that the pair $\left(\pi^{*a}, \pi^{*b}\right) = \left(\frac{1}{2}, \frac{1}{3}\right)$ does the job exactly. If Alf and Bill respectively select exactly these probabilities when randomising between their two strategies then each is making a best response to the other. Again we seem to have an equilibrium in the Nash sense.

To summarise the suggested resolution of the problem, we see that each agent

- invents his own lottery that affects the other agent's payoffs;
- knows and believes the probability with which the other agent will adopt any particular strategy;
- formulates a best-response policy by maximising expected utility in the light of that belief.

However, to make clear what is happening with this methodological development we need to re-examine the basic concepts and their meaning.

'Mixed' strategies

First let us refine the description of strategies. We ought to refer to those that have been discussed so far as *pure strategies*. If S^a, the set of pure strategies for agent a, is finite we can imagine each pure strategy as a separate radio button that agent a can press.[14] If in a particular game there were just three pure strategies (three buttons) then we could depict the situation as on the left-hand side of Figure 10.4: each of the agent's three 'buttons' is labelled both with the strategy name (s_i^a) and with what looks like the binary code for the button—(0, 0, 1) and so on.[15]

By introducing randomisation we can change the whole idea of strategies at a stroke. The picture on the right-hand side of Figure 10.4 is borrowed directly from Figure 8.18 in chapter 8. It depicts the set of lotteries amongst the three pure strategies—the shaded triangle with vertices at $(0,0,1)$, $(0,1,0)$, and $(1,0,0)$. Conventionally each such lottery is known as a *mixed strategy* and the dot in the centre of the picture denotes a mixed strategy where agent a adopts s_1^a, s_2^a, s_3^a with probabilities $0.5, 0.25, 0.25$ respectively. Obviously the idea extends readily to any situation where the number of pure strategies is finite:

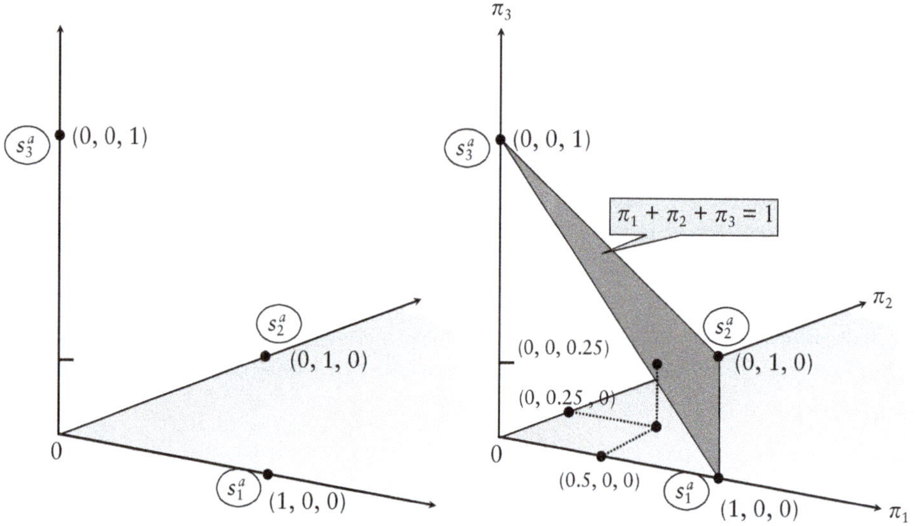

Figure 10.4 Alf's pure and mixed strategies

? Mini Problems

14 In the example of Table 10.5 just discussed think of Alf and Bill pressing radio buttons corresponding to their pure strategies (actions). If Bill is randomising amongst his actions, what distribution over actions will make Alf indifferent as to which radio button to press? If Alf is randomising amongst his actions, what distribution over actions will make Bill indifferent as to which radio button to press?

15 Take the 'matching pennies' game of Mini Problem 12. What is the equilibrium in mixed strategies?

Definition 10.4

Given a finite set S^h of pure strategies for agent h, a *mixed strategy* is a probability distribution over the elements of S^h.

We can represent the mixed strategy by writing out the elements of S^h in vector form $\left(s_1^h, s_2^h, \ldots\right)$ and representing the probability distribution by $\pi^h := \left(\pi_1^h, \pi_2^h, \ldots\right)$ such that π_i^h is the probability that s_i^h is the strategy that is actually adopted by h.[16]

Expected utility

The extension to a mixed-strategy equilibrium also requires a new view of payoffs. In previous examples of games and strategic behaviour we were able to assume that payoffs were purely ordinal. However, by assuming that expected utility is an appropriate criterion, we now have to impose much more structure on individual agents' evaluation of outcomes. In the light of the discussion of chapter 8 (see, for example, page 188) this is not something that we should automatically assume is appropriate.

Two results

The advantage of the extended example based on Table 10.5 is that it conveniently introduces a powerful result lying at the heart of the game-theoretic approach to strategic behaviour:

Theorem 10.1 (Nash equilibrium in mixed strategies)

Every game with a finite number of pure strategies has an equilibrium in mixed strategies.

The equilibrium in mixed strategies can include degenerate cases where $\pi^h = (0, 0, \ldots, 1, \ldots)$ (by a linguistic paradox, of course, these 'degenerate' cases involve *pure* strategies only!). It is not hard to see where the result in Theorem 10.1 comes from in view of the result on competitive equilibrium in chapter 7. There a mapping from a convex compact set into itself was used to establish the existence of a general competitive equilibrium using a 'fixed point' result (see the discussion in Appendix section C.5.2); the mapping was induced by price adjustments using the excess demand function; and the set in question was the set of all normalised prices. Here we have a very similar story: the mapping is the best-response correspondence; the set is the set of mixed strategies, which has exactly the same form as in the general-equilibrium problem—compare Figure 10.4 with Figure B.25 (page 547).

However, in reviewing why this result works the thought might occur whether there is some other way of obtaining an existence result without using the mixed-strategy device—perhaps by appealing to the same fixed-point argument but in a transformed

? Mini Problems

16 Introducing the possibility of mixed strategies will not change the outcome in the case of the prisoner's dilemma game form. Show this from Table 10.1 using the same reasoning as for equations (10.8) and (10.9) in the case of the game in Table 10.5.

problem. Indeed there is, and for a class of problems that is especially relevant to microeconomic applications. Suppose, in contrast to Theorem 10.1 and the examples used so far, the set of pure strategies is infinite: for example a firm might select an output level anywhere between 0 and $\overline{q}$, or a worker might put in any effort level between 0 and $\overline{z}$. Then, in many cases we can use the following:

Theorem 10.2 (Nash equilibrium with infinite strategy sets)

If the game is such that, for all agents h, the strategy sets S^h are convex, compact subsets of $\mathbb{R}^n$ and the payoff functions v^h in (10.2) are continuous and quasiconcave, then the game has a Nash equilibrium in pure strategies.

Mixed strategies: assessment

A mixed strategy can be seen as a theoretical artifice that closes up an otherwise awkward hole in the Nash-equilibrium approach to strategic behaviour. Whether it is an appropriate device depends on the specific context of the microeconomic model in which it is employed and the degree to which one finds it plausible that economic actors observe and understand the use of randomisation devices as strategic tools.

This is not the last occasion on which we will find it necessary to refine the concept of equilibrium as new features and subtleties are introduced into the model of strategic behaviour. We will need to keep picking away at the concept of equilibrium as the concept of the game becomes more sophisticated and more interesting.

Example 10.1

Does it make sense for firms to randomise prices? The question may sound odd, but Varian (1980) provides an argument that, for large retail chains in the United States, this policy makes sense. The heart of the argument is that the situation where two large firms each try to capture customers and profits by running 'sales' (promotions, special offers at low prices) is appropriately seen as a mixed-strategy equilibrium. They can do this because they know their customers are a mixture of the well informed (who always know where the best bargains are to be had) and the uninformed who just shop as usual. A simplified version of the story with just two retailers a and b is presented in Table 10.6, in which each retailer can choose one of two pricing strategies with the associated profits denoted by the Π values, where $\Pi_2 > \Pi_1 > \Pi_0$. From analysing the best response of each agent it is clear that there are two

		s_1^b [normal]	s_2^b [sale]
s_1^a	[NORMAL]	Π_1, Π_1	Π_1, Π_2
s_2^a	[SALE]	Π_2, Π_1	Π_0, Π_0

Table 10.6 Profits under 'normal' or 'sales' pricing

continued...

...continued

equilibria in pure strategies, where one of them sets 'normal' prices and the other 'sales' prices. But there is also a symmetric mixed-strategy equilibrium where each retailer sets 'normal' prices with probability π and 'sales' prices with probability $1 - \pi$ where

$$\pi := \frac{\Pi_1 - \Pi_0}{\Pi_2 - \Pi_0}.$$

Strategic behaviour: notation

s^h	strategy for agent h
S^h	strategy set for agent h
$[s]^{-h}$	strategies for all agents other than h
v^h	payoff function for agent h
χ	best-response correspondence
π^h	randomisation vector for agent h
τ^h	type of agent h

10.4 Application: duopoly

It is time to put the analysis to work. One of the most obvious gaps in the discussion of chapter 3 was the idea that each firm in a market might have to operate without having a given, determinate demand function—see section 3.1. The classic instance of this is oligopoly—competition amongst the few. Each firm has to condition its behaviour not on the parameters of a determinate market environment but on the conjectured behaviour of the competition.

We are going to treat this by taking a very simple version of the strategic problem. The rules of the game limit the players to exactly two—*duopoly* as a special case of oligopoly. How the game is to be played will depend on whether decisions about prices or decisions about quantities are to be treated as actions by the firms; it will also depend on whether the firms have to make their move simultaneously (more on this below).

10.4.1 Competition in quantities

We will first examine the classic version of the *Cournot model* and then interpret it in terms of the principles of strategic behaviour that we have set out earlier in this chapter. The Cournot model assumes that firms make decisions over output quantities—the market price will be determined mechanically by market demand—and they make their decisions simultaneously. As a reminder, in this simple world we can treat these quantity decisions, the actions, as strategies.

Model specification

There are two firms simultaneously making decisions on the production of the same homogeneous good. So total market output of the good is given by

$$q = q^1 + q^2 \tag{10.10}$$

where q^f is the output of firm $f = 1, 2$. There is a known market-demand curve for this single good that can be characterised by $p(\cdot)$, the *inverse demand function* for the market: this is just a way of saying that there is a known market price for any given total market output q, thus:

$$p = p(q).$$

Each firm f has a known cost function C^f that is a function just of its own output. So the profits for firm f are:

$$p(q)\,q^f - C^f\left(q^f\right). \tag{10.11}$$

Optimisation

Firm 1 assumes that q^2, the output of firm 2, is a number that is exogenously given. So, using the case $f = 1$ in (10.11), we can see that it is attempting to maximise

$$\Pi^1\left(q^1; q^2\right) := p\left(q^1 + q^2\right)q^1 - C^1\left(q^1\right) \tag{10.12}$$

on the assumption that q^2 is a constant. This is illustrated in Figure 10.5 where firm 1's objectives are represented by a family of isoprofit contours: each contour is in the form of an inverted U and profits for firm 1 are increasing in the direction of the arrow.[17] To find firm 1's optimum given the particular assumption that firm 2's output is constant at q_0^2 just draw a horizontal line at the level q_0^2; this can be repeated for any other given value of firm 1's output conditioned on a particular value of q^2. The graph of these points is conventionally known as firm 1's *reaction function*, which is a slight misnomer. The reaction function might be thought of as what a firm would do if it were to know of a change in the other firm's action—in simultaneous move games of course this changing about cannot actually happen.

Formally, differentiating (10.12), we have the FOC:

$$\frac{\partial \Pi^1(q^1; q^2)}{\partial q^1} = p_q\left(q^1 + q^2\right)q^1 + p\left(q^1 + q^2\right) - C_q^1\left(q^1\right) \le 0$$
$$= 0 \text{ if } q^1 > 0. \tag{10.13}$$

We find q^1 as a function of q^2:

$$q^1 = \chi^1\left(q^2\right) \tag{10.14}$$

where $\chi^1(\cdot)$ is a function satisfying (10.13): this is also illustrated in Figure 10.5.[18]

? Mini Problems

17 Give a one-line verbal explanation for each of these two assertions.

18 Give a brief interpretation of the straight segment of the reaction function for $q^2 > \overline{q}^2$.

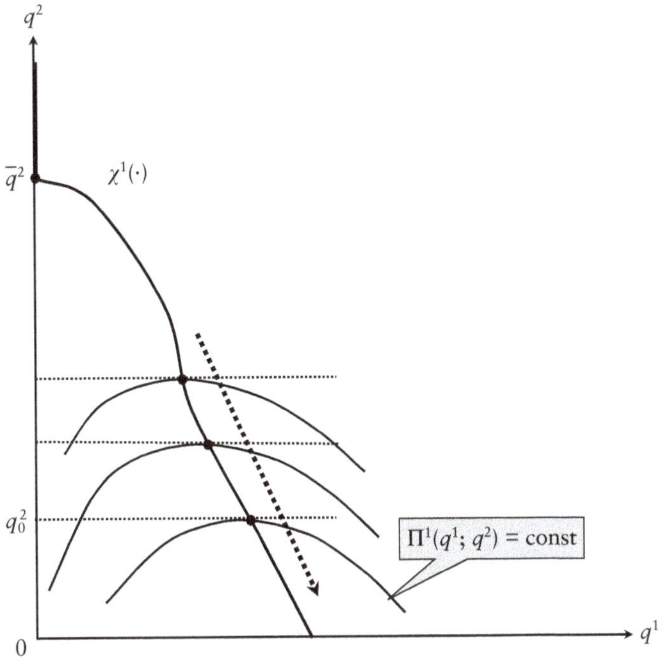

Figure 10.5 Cournot—the reaction function

Likewise for firm 2 we get a relationship χ^2 giving q^2 as a function of some arbitrary value q^1 of the output of firm 1:

$$q^2 = \chi^2\left(q^1\right). \tag{10.15}$$

Equilibrium and efficiency

Treating χ^1 and χ^2 as characterising the firms' best responses and combining them, the *Cournot–Nash* solution is then evident—see the point labelled (q_C^1, q_C^2) in Figure 10.6.[19]

Closer inspection of Figure 10.6 reveals a problem, however. Check the two sets of isoprofit contours for the two firms (firm 2's contours are those that run across the diagram in the form of a reverse C-shape): we know that any point lying below firm 1's contour that passes through the Cournot–Nash equilibrium would yield higher profits for firm 1; by the same reasoning, any point to the left of firm 2's contour through the Cournot–Nash outputs means higher profits for firm 2; so any point in the shaded area would mean higher profits for *both* firms. Both firms would benefit if they were able to restrict output and move away from the Cournot–Nash point into this zone. Clearly the Cournot–Nash equilibrium is dominated.

? Mini Problems

19 Using Theorem 10.2 explain under what conditions we can be sure that the Cournot–Nash equilibrium will exist.

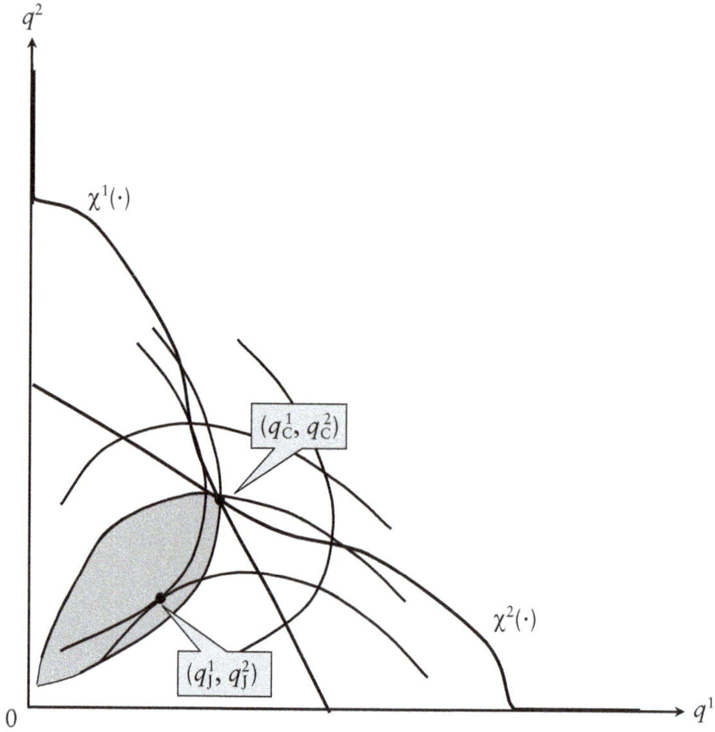

Figure 10.6 Cournot-Nash equilibrium

Collusion

Let us tackle the problem from a different direction. Suppose the two firms were able to join forces and pursue their common interest in profit: they form a *cartel*. In the context of the simple model just developed we consider the possibility that the two firms maximise joint profits and split the result between them in some agreed fashion—in effect we are treating the two firms as though they were a single monopoly with two separate plants.

In general the profits for this two-plant monopoly would be

$$p(q)\,q - C^1\left(q^1\right) - C^2\left(q^2\right) \tag{10.16}$$

where q is given by (10.10). Differentiating (10.16) with respect to q^f we get:

$$p_q(q)\,q + p(q) - C^f_q\left(q^f\right) = 0 \tag{10.17}$$

$f = 1, 2$. So joint profit maximisation occurs where

$$C^1_q\left(q^1\right) = p_q(q)\,q + p(q) \tag{10.18}$$

$$C^2_q\left(q^2\right) = p_q(q)\,q + p(q) \tag{10.19}$$

—marginal cost for each 'plant' (each firm) equals overall marginal revenue. From this pair of equations we get the joint-profit maximising outputs $\left(q_J^1, q_J^2\right)$ illustrated in Figure 10.6.[20]

It is clear that the overall profits associated with $\left(q_J^1, q_J^2\right)$ are going to be higher than they would have been at (q_C^1, q_C^2).

Defection

However, if the joint-profit maximising solution is to survive the two firms would each need an iron resolution and a sharp eye. Each would be tempted by a possibility that is easily demonstrated in Figure 10.6. Draw a line horizontally from $\left(q_J^1, q_J^2\right)$ to the right: it is clear that along this line profits for firm 1 will increase for a while as one moves rightwards. What this means is that, if firm 1 believes that firm 2 is too slow-witted to observe what is happening, then firm 1 might try to 'chisel': increase its own output and profits while 2's output stays fixed.[21] Of course firm 2 may have the same temptation, with the rôles reversed (look what happens to its profits on a straight line upwards from the joint-profit-maximising solution).

By now we can see the familiar form of the Prisoner's Dilemma emerging. Take a stylised version of the problem we have been discussing: the two firms have identical cost structures and, instead of being able to choose output freely, must select just one of two output levels—either low output or high. We can then reconstruct Table 10.1 as Table 10.7. If both firms choose strategy 1 [low], then each gets the joint-profit maximising payoff Π_J, but if they both choose strategy 2 [high] then they get only the Cournot–Nash payoffs $\Pi_C < \Pi_J$; if they play different strategies then the one choosing [high] gets $\overline{\Pi} > \Pi_J$ while the one playing [low], gets 0 (this is just for simplicity it could be some positive value less than Π_C). Likewise we can reinterpret Figure 10.1 as the extensive form of the Cournot game in Figure 10.7.[22]

10.4.2 Competition in prices

Suppose we change the rules of the game for the duopoly: firms play by setting prices rather than quantities: total market output is determined by the market demand curve once the price is known. This is the classic *Bertrand model*, adapted slightly here to facilitate comparison with other models.

? Mini Problems

20 The point $\left(q_J^1, q_J^2\right)$ lies on the tangency of the two isoprofit curves such that the tangent passes through the origin. Show why this is so.

21 What will be happening to firm 2's profits? Why?

22 There is a possibility here that was not present when we discussed the Prisoner's Dilemma before. The payoffs can be transferred between players—contrast this with Figure 10.2 where the payoffs were in utility (that may or may not be transferable) or Mini Problem 8 where the payoffs were in length of prison sentence (not transferable). So firms in a cartel could agree on arbitrary divisions of total profits or on side-payments. Draw the set of possible payoffs in the Cournot game. Show that the transferability of the payoff makes no difference to the strategic outcome.

		s_1^2 [low]	s_2^2 [high]
s_1^1	[low]	Π_J, Π_J	$0, \overline{\Pi}$
s_2^1	[high]	$\overline{\Pi}, 0$	Π_C, Π_C

Table 10.7 Cournot model as Prisoner's Dilemma

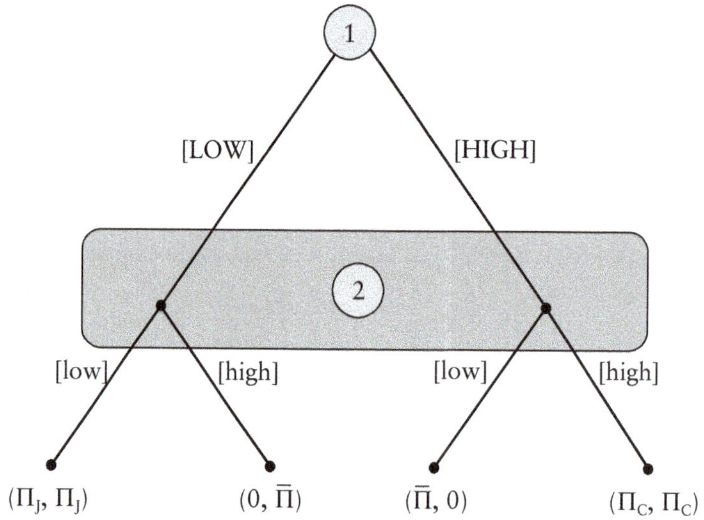

Figure 10.7 Simplified one-shot Cournot game

Model specification

There is a market for a single good with a known market-demand curve. We will assume a straight-line form of this curve so that the quantity sold in this market at price p is given by:

$$q = \frac{\beta_0 - p}{\beta} \tag{10.20}$$

where β_0 and β are positive parameters. If there were a single firm with constant marginal cost c operating in this market then it would announce the following monopoly price[23]

$$p_M = \frac{\beta_0 + c}{2}.$$

However, suppose two firms supply the market: each has zero fixed cost and constant marginal cost c. They compete on price as follows. Firm 1 announces price p^1 and firm 2 announces p^2; in the light of this announcement there are three possibilities:

1. If $p^1 < p^2$ firm 1 sells $\frac{\beta_0 - p^1}{\beta}$; firm 2 sells nothing.

? Mini Problems

23 Derive the monopolist's optimum price in this model.

2. If $p^1 > p^2$ the reverse happens—firm 2 sells $\frac{\beta_0 - p^2}{\beta}$; firm 1 sells nothing.

3. If $p^1 = p^2 = p$ the firms split the market equally and each sells $\frac{\beta_0 - p}{2\beta}$.

Equilibrium

How will the firms set the price? Consider the following steps of an argument:

- Clearly if one firm charges a price above the monopoly price p_M, the other can capture the whole market by charging exactly p_M.
- If one firm charges a price p above c and at or below p_M then the other could charge a price $p - \varepsilon$ (where ε is a small number) and again capture the whole market.
- If one firm charges a price c then the other firm would not charge a price below this (it would make a loss were it to do that); but it could exactly match the price c, in which case we assume that the market is equally split between the firms.

This gives a complete characterisation of a function $\chi^f(\cdot)$ for each firm that would enable us to conclude how it would set its own price given the price that it anticipates would be set by the rival. In the case of firm 1 we have

$$\chi^1\left(p^2\right) = \begin{cases} p_M & \text{if } p^2 > p_M \\ p^2 - \varepsilon & \text{if } p_M \geq p^2 > c \\ c & \text{if } p^2 \leq c \end{cases} \tag{10.21}$$

It is clear from (10.21) that there is a Nash equilibrium at (c, c)—see Figure 10.8.[24]

Taken at face value the result seems really remarkable. It appears that there is, effectively, a competitive outcome with just two firms. Contrast this with the case of monopoly (analysed in chapter 3) where the firm sets a price strictly greater than marginal cost with a consequent loss of efficiency. However, it is important to recognise that the rules of the game here are rather restrictive: there are constant marginal costs and no capacity constraints; the product of the two firms is perceived as identical by the customers; the game is played out simultaneously and once only—there is no idea of a true price war. Relaxing any of these assumptions would generate a much richer model; but we can think of the Bertrand model and its solution as an instructive limiting case.

? Mini Problems

24 In this case, strictly speaking, χ^f is not a 'best-response' function: why? Take a modified version of this model where for administrative reasons it is only possible to set prices as integer values (payment is by coins in a slot machine). Marginal cost is c, an integer, and $p_M = 4c$. Illustrate the game in strategic form; explain why, in this modified model, there *is* a well-defined best-response function for each firm and confirm that the Nash equilibrium outcome is as above.

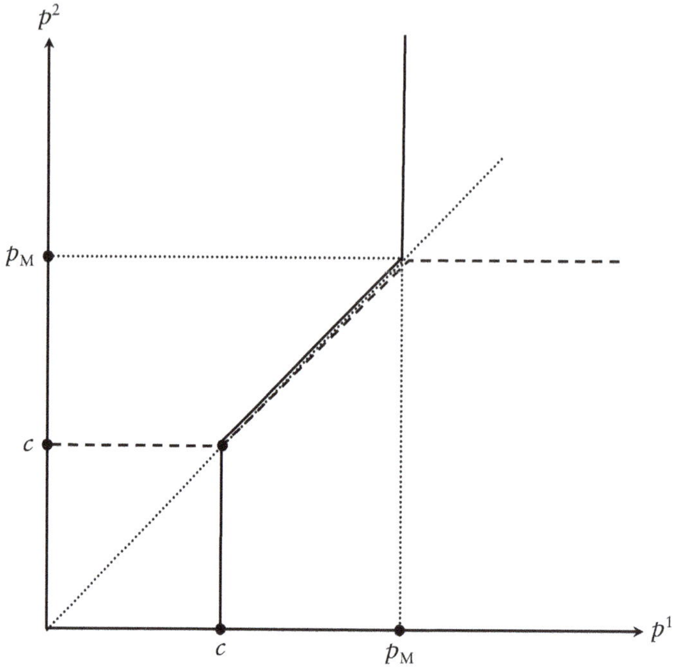

Figure 10.8 Bertrand model

Example 10.2

Bresnahan (1987) uses a version of the Bertrand price-competition model to analyse the United States automobile industry in 1955. The 'good' in question here is the quality of cars: consumers derive utility from such things as horsepower, weight, length, and so on. The year is a particularly interesting one because it was a year when prices fell during macroeconomic expansion and there was a dramatic 'blip' in sales—output was 45 per cent higher than a year before or a year after. The explanation for this phenomenon can be sought in the collapse of a tacit collusive arrangement among the producers leading to a price war. Bresnahan develops an ingenious econometric method to establish that this was the case.

10.5 Time

Until now, there has been a significant omission in the analysis of strategic behaviour: the lack of an explicit treatment of time. However, 'time' here has a significance different from that where it has popped up in earlier chapters. We have seen time in its rôle as the scope for economic flexibility (see the discussion of the short run in section 2.4) and time as a characteristic of an economic good (see the discussion of savings in section 5.3.2). Now we focus on time in its rôle of sequencing—the *ordering* of decision making. In many economic models this feature is crucial.[25]

Taking this step means that much more becomes possible within a strategic microeconomic model. Several intuitive concepts in analysing games just make no sense without the introduction of time into the model. One cannot speak about reactions, an equilibrium path, or even threats without modelling the sequence of decision making and careful consideration of the rôle of information in that sequence. It also means that we have to be particularly careful about the distinction between strategies and actions that we highlighted on page 272.[26]

With this temporal dimension of the strategic problem we will find it important to extend the use and application of the tools introduced in sections 10.2 and 10.3. The distinction between strategies and actions will emerge with greater clarity and we will also need to refine the equilibrium concept. This can be illustrated by re-examining the standard game introduced in Figure 10.1. Suppose the two players now move in sequence—Alf, then Bill. The new situation is represented in extensive form in Figure 10.9. Representing the game in strategic form is a bit more complex and less

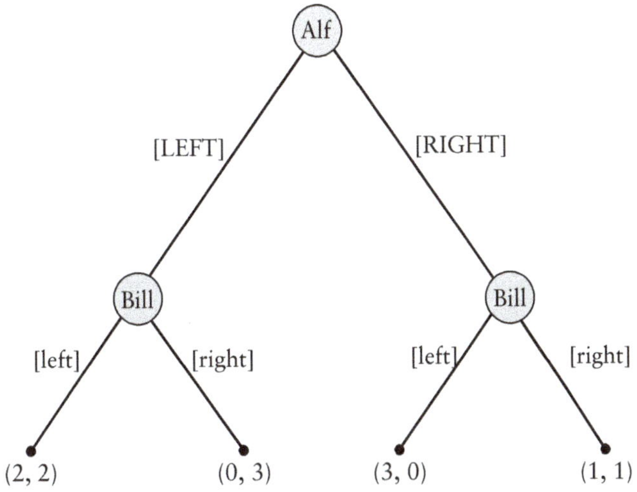

Figure 10.9 Sequential move, extensive form

? Mini Problems

25 Consider a variant of the 'matching pennies' game (see Mini Problem 12): player *a* first chooses one side of the coin, and then shows which side of the coin he chose; then player *b* chooses to show his side; if the sides match, player *a* gets a dollar from *b* (as before) otherwise player *b* gets a dollar from *a* (as before). If you were invited to play and could choose whether to be player *a* or player *b*, which would you choose?

26 It is important to distinguish between 'real' time (when the moves are made) from 'playing' time (the order of decisions). Use the case of Cournot competition (section 10.4.1) to explain how a game which is 'sequential' in real time could be 'simultaneous' in playing time.

		s_1^b [left-left]	s_2^b [left-right]	s_3^b [right-left]	s_4^b [right-right]
s_1^a	[LEFT]	2, 2	2, 2	0, 3	0, 3
s_2^a	[RIGHT]	3, 0	1, 1	3, 0	1, 1

Table 10.8 Sequential move, strategic form

transparent; but it is done in Table 10.8. There is one small development in notation here; since Bill moves second he has to condition his strategy on what Alf does when making the first move; so we will write, for example, [left-right] for the strategy which states 'move left if Alf has chosen [LEFT] and move right if Alf has chosen [RIGHT].' Although at each stage of the game there are exactly two possible actions that a player can take (move left or move right) as far as Bill is concerned there are now *four* strategies $s_1^b, \ldots, s_4^b$ as shown in the columns of the table.[27]

Will sequencing the play in this way alter the likely outcome of the game? In the case of this particular game the outcome is much the same[28] but in others there can be a drastic change.[29] However, before we treat the solution to this properly we need to consider how the explicit introduction of time allows for more elaborate and illuminating game structures. In doing so we will assume that there is *perfect information* in that everyone knows exactly what happened at earlier stages of the game (this assumption about information will be dropped in section 10.7).

10.5.1 Games and subgames

Let us begin by extending the kind of extensive-form diagram depicted in Figures 10.1 and 10.9. In Figure 10.10 there is a further stage of the game, in other words a further level of decision-making with additional nodes; the payoffs after the final stage of the game are given by the payoff profiles $[\upsilon_1], \ldots, [\upsilon_8]$ where $[\upsilon_i] := \left(\upsilon_i^a, \upsilon_i^b\right)$ gives the payoffs to Alf and Bill in terminal node i.

There is an obvious and useful way of referring to the position of nodes in the structure. Take, for example, the nodes highlighted at the bottom of the diagram, which are those that can be reached from node labelled *: we can think of these as *successor nodes* to *. This enables us to make precise an important new concept. A glance at the figure suggests that by deleting part of the tree we can again end up with another viable game tree starting from *. Indeed it is often true that some subsets of the extensive form game can themselves be considered as games and it is these that are of special economic interest:

? Mini Problems

27 Using a table similar to Table 10.8 construct the strategic-form version of the modified matching-pannies game in Mini Problem 25.

28 Explain why. [Hint: put yourself in Bill's position and ask 'what would I do if Alf had played [LEFT]? What would I do if he had played [RIGHT]?' Then put yourself in the role of Alf and think about what is going to happen after you have made your move.]

29 Take the model of Mini Problem 2. What happens if the players move sequentially? What if they have to move simultaneously?

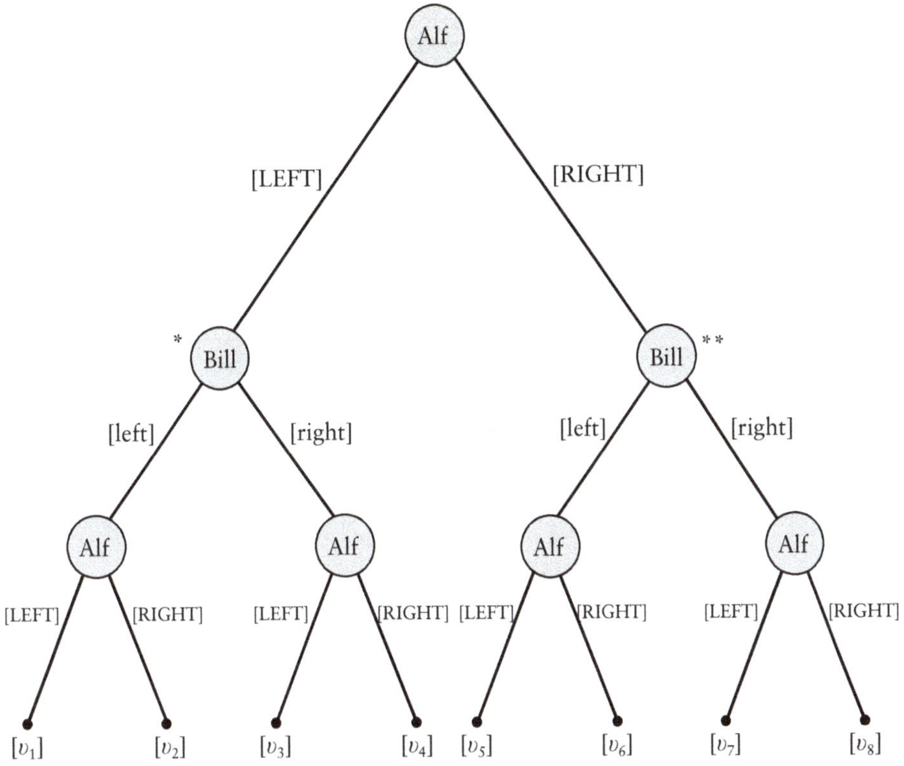

Figure 10.10 Game and subgame (1)

Definition 10.5

A *subgame* of a game in extensive form is a subset of the game such that

1. It begins at a single node;
2. It contains all the successor nodes;
3. If the game contains an information set with multiple nodes then either all of these nodes are in the subset or none of them is.

With reference to Figure 10.10 it is clear that the successor nodes to the node marked * form a subgame as do the successor nodes to the node marked **. But suppose we consider a modified structure as in Figure 10.11: here Alf's choice of actions at the start of the game has been expanded (there is a [MID] option); furthermore there is an information set with multiple nodes (indicated by the shaded area). Again * marks the beginning of a subgame; but the successor nodes to the node marked # do not form a subgame.[30]

? Mini Problems

30 Explain why.

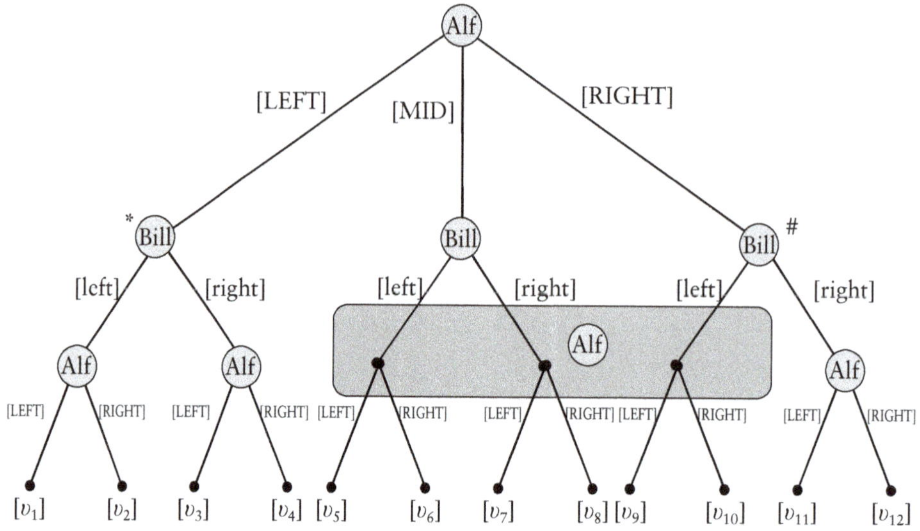

Figure 10.11 Game and subgame (2)

The advantage of this new concept is that it permits a naturally intuitive description of the way a game unfolds through time. Think again about the chess analogy used earlier. Even if you are not a chess player you may have seen the kind of chess puzzles that appear in newspapers: typically you are given the position that a game has reached after many moves; then you are asked to finish off the game. Given that the position shown in the puzzle can be reached by a sequence of legal chess moves the puzzle is a subgame of the original game.

In the same way it is interesting to examine the 'endgame' of situations of strategic economic interaction. By analysing the endgame one gets a better understanding of the whole of the game: this leads us naturally on to a further discussion of solution concepts.

10.5.2 Equilibrium: more on concept and method

In the light of the multi-period nature of games we need not only to re-examine the way in which a solution is derived but also what is meant by a satisfactory solution. The reason for this is that, as we will see, some Nash equilibria can appear as unattractive when examined from the point of view of each subgame.

So, how to solve for an equilibrium in this case? We will start with some useful intuition and then move on to a more formal concept. Again we can use another good principle from Sherlock Holmes (from *A Study in Scarlet*): 'In solving a problem of this sort, the grand thing is to be able to reason backwards. That is a very useful accomplishment, and a very easy one, but people do not practise it much.' This intuition is exactly what is required: start at the end of the game and work back through the stages of the game—a process usually known as backwards induction. The principle is easily grasped, but the possible complexity in practice should not be underestimated. Take the imaginary chess problem mentioned in section 10.2.3—'White to play and mate in four moves.' You do not need to be a chess expert to see that the number of final (check-mate) positions is itself likely to be large; and the number of possible paths to each of those positions could be huge.

To see how the backwards-induction method works—albeit in a very simple case—let us apply the method to solve the game in the case of Figure 10.10. Suppose it is true that $\upsilon_1^a > \upsilon_2^a$ and $\upsilon_3^a > \upsilon_4^a$ and so on (we could easily retell the story if the inequalities were different). Then, if the game had reached the lower left-hand node where it is Alf's turn to play, obviously Alf would choose 1; so the value of reaching this node is effectively $[\upsilon_1] = \left(\upsilon_1^a, \upsilon_1^b\right)$; reasoning in this way we can see that the value associated with reaching each of the other nodes on the same level of this diagram is $[\upsilon_3]$, $[\upsilon_5]$, $[\upsilon_7]$ respectively. We have effectively reduced a three-stage game to a two-stage game with payoffs $[\upsilon_1]$, $[\upsilon_3]$, $[\upsilon_5]$, $[\upsilon_7]$. We can then solve the two-stage game using the same method—see Mini Problem 28 above.

Associated with the backward-induction method we can now introduce a refined concept of equilibrium in a multi-stage game:

Definition 10.6

A profile of strategies is a *subgame-perfect equilibrium* for a game if

1. It is a Nash equilibrium
2. It induces actions that are consistent with a Nash equilibrium in every subgame.

Three key points about this concept and the associated backwards-induction algorithm should be noted right away:

- All subgame-perfect equilibria are Nash equilibria, but the reverse is not true. Some Nash equilibria that are not subgame perfect involve agents making threats that are just not credible. There is an important practical example of this in the discussion of market entry in Section 10.6.2 below.
- Definition 10.6 is quite demanding because it says something about *all* the subgames, even if one might have thought that some individual subgames are not particularly interesting and are unlikely to be actually reached in practice.
- The straightforward backward-induction method is not going to be suitable for all games with richer information sets. We will come back to this point in section 10.7.4 below.

Now for the reason why the concept of equilibrium needs to be refined in this way when we take into account the temporal sequence of a game: some Nash equilibria involve strategies that lack credibility. What we mean by this is as follows. Imagine reaching the final stage of a game at a position where a specific move by player h may well damage the opponent(s) but would cause serious damage to player h himself. Taking the subgame starting from this position as a game in its own right it is clear that h would not rationally make the move; so, in the context of the overall game, threatening to make this move should the position be reached is unlikely to be impressive. Yet there may well be Nash equilibria of the whole game that imply the use of such empty threats: clearly there is a good case for discarding such strategy combinations as candidates for equilibria and focusing just on those that satisfy subgame perfection (Definition 10.6).

This point is illustrated in Figure 10.12. Alf gets to play first; Bill knows that if Alf plays [RIGHT] then Bill gets a payoff of 2; but if they play the sequence [LEFT],[right] then the situation would be disastrous for Bill—he would get a payoff of no more than 1. Can Bill dissuade Alf from playing [LEFT] by threatening to play [left] as well, so reducing Alf's payoff to 0?

On checking the strategic form in Table 10.9 we can see that there are four Nash equilibria $\left[s_2^a, s_1^b\right]$, $\left[s_2^a, s_2^b\right]$, $\left[s_1^a, s_3^b\right]$, and $\left[s_1^a, s_4^b\right]$: the first two of these are equivalent in their outcomes; likewise the third and fourth equilibria are equivalent. So it appears that the case where Alf's strategy is to play [RIGHT] and Bill's strategy is to play [left] whatever Alf does $\left[s_2^a, s_1^b\right]$ is a valid equilibrium outcome of the game. But it is a bit odd. Put the case that on Monday Alf plays [LEFT] anyway and then says to Bill (who plays on Tuesday) 'what are you going to do about that?' Presented with this *fait accompli* one could imagine Bill thinking on Monday night that maybe he ought to make the best of a bad job and play [right]: the reasoning is that on Monday night we are at the node marked * and, viewed from this standpoint, Bill would do better to play [right] on Tuesday in order to secure a payoff of 1 rather than 0. Knowing that this is how a rational opponent would reason on Monday night, Alf is unlikely to be impressed by a threat from Bill on Sunday of 'I'll play [left] whatever happens.' So, although $\left[s_2^a, s_1^b\right]$ is a Nash equilibrium, it is not subgame perfect.[31]

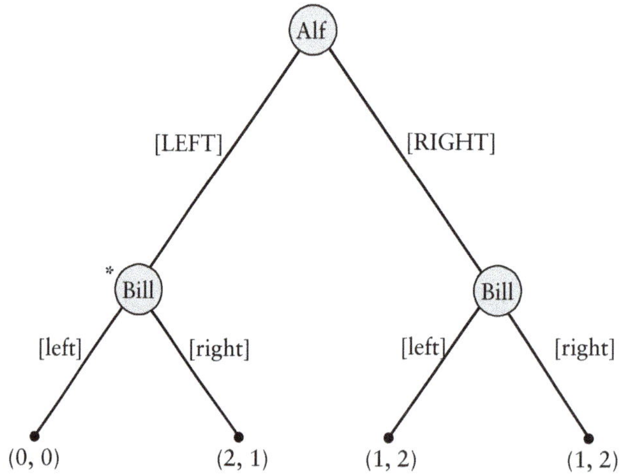

Figure 10.12 An incredible threat

? Mini Problems

31 Back in the 1960s nuclear strategists (seriously?) discussed the idea of a 'Doomsday machine'. This was to be a gizmo that would automatically launch a world-devastating nuclear strike if (a) any nuclear missile landed on its home territory or (b) any attempt was made to disarm it. Could a similar device assist Bill?

		s_1^b [left-left]	s_2^b [left-right]	s_3^b [right-left]	s_4^b [right-right]
s_1^a	[LEFT]	0,0	0,0	**2,1**	**2,1**
s_2^a	[RIGHT]	**1,2**	**1,2**	1,2	1,2

Table 10.9 Incredible threat: strategic view

By restricting attention to equilibria that satisfy subgame perfection we are insisting on an important aspect of consistency in economic behaviour. In doing this we have to consider what a player would do in positions that are not actually played out.

10.5.3 Repeated interactions

For some purposes it is useful to jump from the case of comparatively few stages to the case of arbitrarily many. The principles that can be learned from this apparently arbitrary exercise have some profound implications. They can illuminate the possibilities for long-term cooperative outcomes that may appear absent from a myopic analysis of a simple model of strategic interaction. The refinements of equilibrium that we have introduced enable us to simplify the analysis of the many-stage game: by focusing on subgame perfection we can rule out empty threats and incredible promises that could have arisen on paths of the game that are not actually played in equilibrium.

The basic idea of a *repeated game* is simple. One joins together multiple instances of an atemporal game: the analysis models a repeated encounter between the players in apparently the same simple situation of economic conflict. Figure 10.13 shows an outline of the setup for the Prisoner's Dilemma game: the same players face the same outcomes from their actions that they may choose in periods $1, 2, \ldots, t, \ldots$ The example of the Prisoner's Dilemma is particularly instructive given its importance in microeconomics and, as noted earlier (page 280), the somewhat pessimistic outcome of an isolated implementation of the game.

What makes the repeated game different from a collection of unrelated games of identical structure with identical players? The key point is history. One typically assumes that everyone can know all the information about actual play that has accumulated at any particular stage of the game—the perfect-information assumption again. Individual strategies can then be conditioned on this information and may be used to support equilibrium outcomes that could not have arisen from play by rational economic agents of an isolated single encounter.

The stage game

The basic building block of repeated-interactions analysis is the *stage game*. This is just an instance of one of the simultaneous-play atemporal games that were considered in section 10.3: in particular we can see that each stage in Figure 10.13 is just a copy of Figure 10.1. It is important to distinguish between what goes on in a single play of the stage game and strategy in the game as a whole. If an instance of the stage game were to be played in isolation, of course, we can take strategies as being equivalent to actions; but if the stage game is taken as a component of the repeated game then the individual

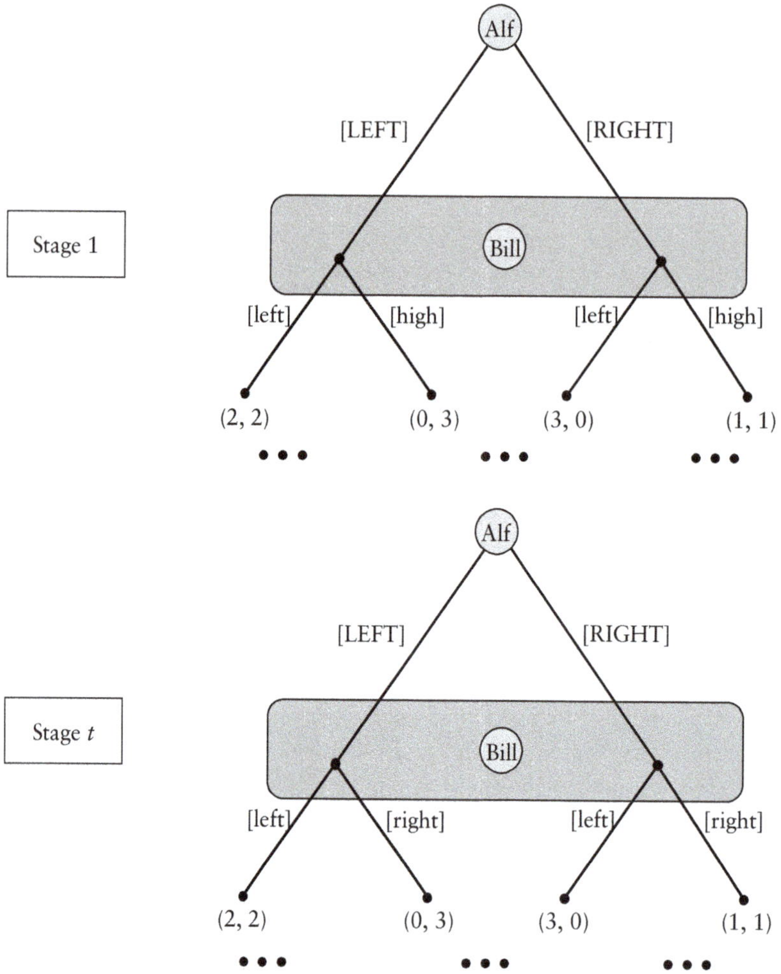

Figure 10.13 Repeated Prisoner's Dilemma

strategies refer to planned choices over the entire sequence of play: the actions at stage $t+1$ will have been conditioned by the sequence of behaviour up to t.

It is also important to understand the relationship between the payoffs that emerge from an isolated instance of the stage game and those that might be obtainable from a repeated version of the game in which strategies can be conditioned on history. In Figure 10.14, based on Figure 10.2, we have introduced the set of all payoffs that could be reached by mixing the payoffs from the pure strategy combinations in the basic Prisoner's Dilemma game: these are represented by the heavily shaded lozenge shape. The mixes could be achieved by agreeing on a coordinated randomisation plan or by taking it in turns to use different strategy combinations, for example. Note the following features of this figure:

- The 'south-west' corner of the shaded set represents the minimax outcomes for the two players—the worst that can happen to player h in a particular instance of the stage game; as we know it is also the Nash-equilibrium outcome of the stage game.

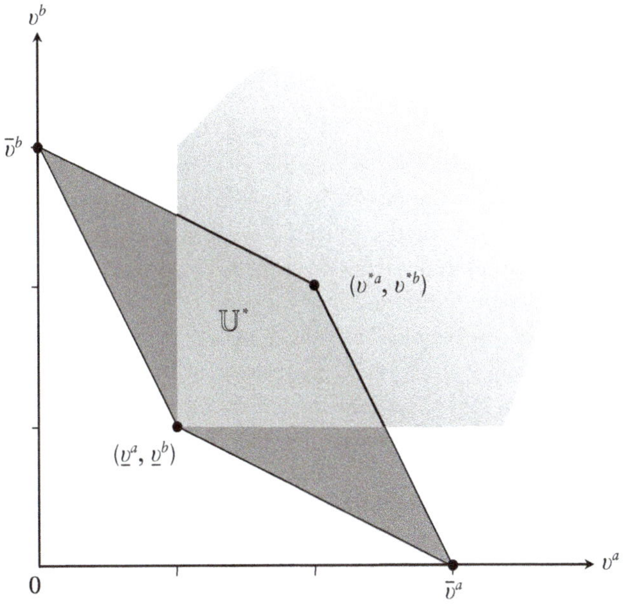

Figure 10.14 Utility possibilities: Prisoner's Dilemma with 'mixing'

- The set represented by lightly shaded area north-east of this point consists of all the payoffs that would be Pareto improvements over the Nash-equilibrium outcome.
- The set $\mathbb{U}^*$, as the intersection of these two sets, consists of payoffs that are an improvement on the Nash outcome and that can be represented as mixtures of payoffs in a one-shot stage game.
- The points on the north-east boundary of $\mathbb{U}^*$ correspond to the Pareto-efficient outcomes.

The issue is, can one achieve a Pareto-efficient outcome in $\mathbb{U}^*$ or, indeed, anything other than the minimax value at $\left(\underline{\upsilon}^a, \underline{\upsilon}^b\right)$? As we know (check Mini Problem 16) the use of mixed strategies in an isolated play of Prisoner's Dilemma does nothing to alter the single Nash-equilibrium outcome at $\left(\underline{\upsilon}^a, \underline{\upsilon}^b\right)$; however, it may be that through the structure of repetitive play other points in $\mathbb{U}^*$ are implementable as equilibrium outcomes.

The repeated game

To investigate this possibility we need a model of payoffs in an infinite-horizon world. Obviously this is based on the model of payoffs in a typical stage game: but we also need a method of aggregating payoffs across the stages. The aggregation method is a generalisation of the intertemporal utility function in equation (5.13). Specifically, let $\upsilon^h(t)$ denote the payoff for agent h in period t and introduce the possibility of pure time preference in the form of a discount factor δ that is greater than or equal to zero and less than one. Then the value of payoff stream $\left(\upsilon^h(1), \upsilon^h(2), \ldots, \upsilon^h(t)\ldots\right)$ is given by

$$[1-\delta]\sum_{t=1}^{\infty}\delta^{t-1}\,\upsilon^h(t)\,. \qquad (10.22)$$

Note two technical points about the specification of (10.22). First, the term $[1-\delta]$ performs a normalisation rôle: if the payoff in the stage game were constant throughout all time, so that $\upsilon^h(t) = \upsilon_0$, then the overall payoff is itself υ_0. Second, if we allow $\delta \to 1$ then the overall payoff approaches a simple average with current utility components being given equal weight with those in the indefinite future.

Why an infinite number of periods? The short answer is that this ensures that there is always a tomorrow. In many situations if there were to be a known Last Day then the game would 'unravel': you just have to imagine yourself at the Last Day and then apply the Sherlock Holmes working-backwards method that we outlined in section 10.5.2 above.[32]

How could rational players use the information from a history of play in a repeated game? We can illustrate a method in an argument by example on Figure 10.14. Suppose Alf and Bill collectively recognise that it would be in their interests if they could maintain actions in each period that would guarantee them the Pareto-efficient payoffs $\left(\upsilon^{*a}, \upsilon^{*b}\right)$ in each period; to do this they need to play [LEFT],[left] every period. The problem is they cannot trust each other, nor indeed themselves: Alf has the temptation to jump at the possibility of getting the payoff $\overline{\upsilon}^a$ by being antisocial and playing [RIGHT]; Bill has a similar temptation. To forestall this suppose that they each adopt a strategy that (1) rewards the other party's cooperative behaviour by responding with the action [left] and (2) punishes antisocial behaviour with the action [right], thus generating the minimax payoffs $\left(\underline{\upsilon}^a, \underline{\upsilon}^b\right)$. What gives the strategy bite is that the punishment action applies to *every* period after the one where the antisocial action occurred: should the punishment be invoked the offender is cast into outer darkness and minimaxed for ever. This is known as a *trigger strategy*.

Consider the trigger strategy for Bill, s_{T}^b, set out in detail in Table 10.10: would it persuade Alf to behave cooperatively? The gain to Alf from behaving antisocially in period t is $\overline{\upsilon}^a - \upsilon^{*a}$. The consequence for Alf in every period from $t+1$ onwards is a difference in

? Mini Problems

32 (a) It is Thursday morning. The world is going to end on Friday afternoon. The stage game in Table 10.1 is to be played at lunchtime on both days. The discount rate is 0.01 per day. What is the subgame-perfect equilibrium? (b) It is Sunday morning. The information in part (a) remains unchanged but in this case the stage game is to be played at lunchtime every day of the week from now until the end of the world. Again, what is the subgame-perfect equilibrium? (c) Take the repeated game of part (b) . Consider a strategy profile that involves Alf playing [LEFT] on Tuesday and Wednesday and [RIGHT] on every other day and Bill playing [left] on Thursday and Friday (with Bill's actions on Sunday,...,Wednesday left unspecified. Show that this cannot be a Nash equilibrium for the repeated game. What may we therefore conclude about Nash equilibria in this finitely repeated game? (d) How would the situation change if the interest rate were twice that in parts (a)–(c) ?

Alf's action in $0,\ldots,t$	Bill's action at $t+1$
[LEFT][LEFT]... [LEFT]	[left]
Anything else	[right]

Table 10.10 Bill's trigger strategy s_{T}^{b}

utility given by $\upsilon^{*a} - \underline{\upsilon}^{a}$ per period; so Alf would not find it worthwhile to behave antisocially if[33]

$$\overline{\upsilon}^{a} - \upsilon^{*a} \leq \frac{\delta}{1-\delta}\left[\upsilon^{*a} - \underline{\upsilon}^{a}\right]. \tag{10.23}$$

The trigger strategy for Alf follows the same reasoning—just interchange the a and b labels.

Now let us examine whether the strategy pair $\left[s_{\mathrm{T}}^{a}, s_{\mathrm{T}}^{b}\right]$ constitutes an equilibrium that would support the Pareto-efficient payoffs. Note first that if there were antisocial behaviour at t then the sequence of actions prescribed by Table 10.10 and its counterpart for s_{T}^{a} together constitute a Nash equilibrium for the subgame that would then start at $t+1$: Alf could not increase his payoff by switching from [RIGHT] to [LEFT] given that Bill is playing [left]; likewise for Bill. The same conclusion follows for any subgame starting after $t+1$. Note second that if δ is large enough[34] and [LEFT],[left] has been played in every period up till t then it is clear from (10.23) that Alf would not wish to switch to [RIGHT]; again a similar statement follows for Bill. So $\left[s_{\mathrm{T}}^{a}, s_{\mathrm{T}}^{b}\right]$ is a subgame-perfect equilibrium that will implement $\left(\upsilon^{*a}, \upsilon^{*b}\right)$.[35]

It is important to recognise that this reasoning is not specific to an isolated example, as the following key result shows:

Theorem 10.3 (The Folk Theorem)

In a two-person infinitely repeated game any combination of actions observed in any finite number of stages is the outcome of a subgame-perfect equilibrium if the discount factor is sufficiently close to 1.

Theorem 10.3—known as the Folk Theorem because informal versions of it were around well before it was formally stated and proved—tells us that *any* point in $\mathbb{U}^*$ can be supported as a subgame-perfect equilibrium, given a condition on the utility function

? Mini Problems

33 Explain why.

34 We need to have $\underline{\delta} \leq \delta \leq 1$. What is the value of $\underline{\delta}$?

35 In the answer to Mini Problem 10 it is shown that a monotonic transformation of utilities does not change the outcome of the Prisoner's Dilemma one-shot game. Could such a transformation affect the repeated game?

in (10.22). However, this does not mean that the result turns just on a quirk of individuals' intertemporal preferences. We can consider the discount factor to be a product of a factor derived from a person's impatience—a pure preference parameter—and the probability that the person will be around to enjoy utility in the next period. (Check out the reasoning in Exercise 8.9 to convince yourself of this). So, in this case we can imagine that although in principle the game could go on forever, there is a probability that it will end in finite time. Then Theorem 10.3 requires both that this probability be 'sufficiently low' and that the individual agents be 'sufficiently patient'.

Although Theorem 10.3 has been tagged as *The* Folk Theorem there is actually a family of results that deal with this type of issue in the field of repeated games: the version stated here is somewhat conservative. Some results focus only on Nash equilibria (which, perhaps, rather misses the point since credibility is important), some deal with more than two agents (but ensuring subgame perfection then gets a bit tricky) and some discuss repeated games of finite length. However, in assessing the contribution of the Folk Theorem(s) it is important to be clear about the main message of the result.

The implication of Theorem 10.3 is that there is a wide range of possible equilibria in infinitely repeated games: it does not predict that rational behaviour will generate one specific outcome. Should it seem troubling that there are so many equilibrium outcomes for the repeated game? Perhaps not: we can think of Theorem 10.3 as a kind of possibility result demonstrating that strategic problems that do not have 'sensible' solutions in the short run may yet be susceptible of sensible solution in the long run through induced cooperation.

Example 10.3

How do collusive arrangements between firms—cartels—survive? At first sight we might think of lax or non-existent regulation by government agencies. But more is required: as noted earlier (page 291) a collusive arrangement between firms may contain the seeds of its own destruction in that each firm typically has an incentive to defect from the agreement. In the case of international cartels, beyond the reach of national governments, it is the cooperation/defection issue that is central. The experience of the Organisation of Petroleum Exporting Countries (OPEC) provides an interesting example and an opportunity for examining in practice the degree to which it is possible to deter cheating. Table 10.11 shows who stood to gain from the possibility of cheating, according to a simulation model developed by Griffin and Xiong (1997) for the oil market projected forward from 1994.

Some points to note:

- Not all countries gain from cooperation over the Cournot outcome.
- There is a marked difference in potential returns to cheating between larger and smaller members.
- Saudi Arabia is modelled as a potential enforcer of the cooperative outcome.

continued...

...continued

To see the dynamics of cheating and enforcement and the role of the interest rate in determining whether cheating is worthwhile in the long run check Griffin and Xiong (1997).

	Cournot revenue*	Cooperative revenue*	gain over Cournot (%)	cheating revenue*	gain over Cooperative (%)
Gabon	37.6	41.5	10.4	46.9	11.5
Qatar	36.6	47.8	30.6	49.8	4.0
Algeria	133.1	159.9	20.1	176.2	9.3
Indonesia	242.8	294.9	21.5	327.3	9.9
Nigeria	303.3	368.3	21.4	411.4	10.5
Libya	326.6	351.6	7.7	420.1	16.3
Kuwait	717.5	638.1	−11.1	863.6	26.1
UAE	732.2	645.3	−11.9	878.8	26.6
Venezuela	915.8	842.6	−8.0	1114.4	24.4
Iran	922.8	1061.6	15.0	1208.8	12.2
Iraq	1194.5	1252.6	4.9	1477.2	15.2
Saudi Arabia	1960.9	2382.6	21.5		
Total	7523.7	8086.8			

Source: Griffin and Xiong (1997), Tables 1,3
*Net present values in $bn at 6% discount rate

Table 10.11 Comparison of payoffs for OPEC members: quota system versus Cournot

10.6 Application: market structure

The temporal sequence on which we have focused plays an important rôle in the analysis of industrial organisation. We will illustrate its contribution by considering three applications.

10.6.1 Market leadership

First, let us revisit the simple competition-in-quantities version of the duopoly model. Explicit recognition of the time sequence within the game structure permits the strategic modelling of an important economic phenomenon, market leadership.

Assume that social customs or institutional rules (of what sort, or from where, we do not enquire) ensure that firm 1 gets the chance to move first in deciding output—it is the *leader*. The follower (firm 2) observes the leader's output choice q^1 and then announces its output q^2. What would we expect as a solution?

First let us note that the Nash concept does not give us much leverage. In fact, using the reaction function given in (10.15), any non-negative output pair (q^1, q^2) satisfying $q^2 = \chi^2(q^1)$ can be taken as the outcome of a Nash equilibrium to the sequentially played game described above; but given the sequence of decision making we know that many of these equilibria will involve incredible threats—they are not subgame perfect.[36] To find the subgame-perfect equilibrium consider first the subgame that follows firm 1's output decision; clearly this involves firm 2 choosing $\chi^2(q^1)$ as a best response to whatever q^1 has been selected; reasoning backwards firm 1 will therefore select its output so as to maximise its profits conditional on firm 2's best response.

The upshot of this argument is that the leader effectively manipulates the follower by choosing its own output appropriately. Given the reaction function (10.15), the leader's expression for profits becomes

$$p\left(q^1 + \chi^2\left(q^1\right)\right) q^1 - C^1\left(q^1\right). \tag{10.24}$$

The prerogative of being the leader is the opportunity to construct an opportunity set for oneself from the responses of one's opponents: this is illustrated in Figure 10.15 where

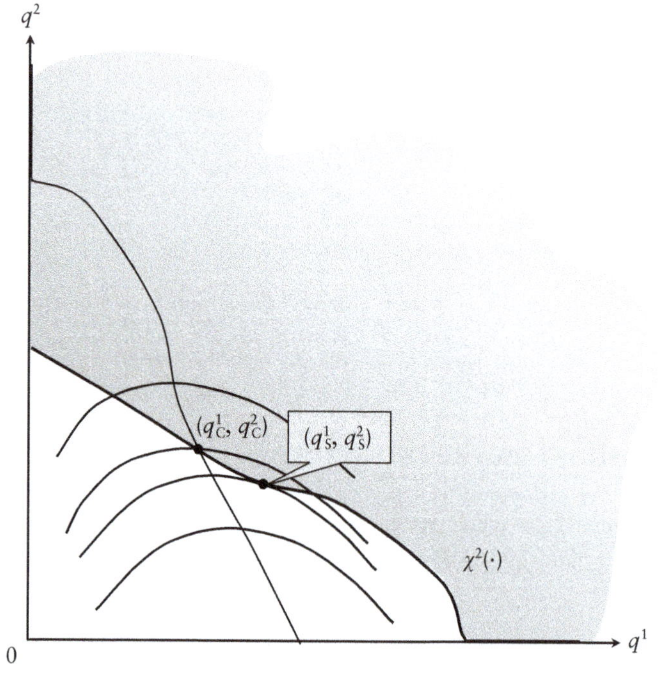

Figure 10.15 Leader-follower

? Mini Problems

36 Let q_M be the profit-maximising output for firm 2 if it were a monopolist and assume that $\chi^1(q_M) = 0$ in the case of simultaneous play—see (10.14). Show that in the sequential-play game a strategy pair yielding the output combination $(0, q_M)$ is a Nash equilibrium but is not a subgame-perfect solution.

firm 2's reaction function χ^2 marks out the boundary of firm 1's opportunity set. This is the essence of the *Stackelberg* model of duopoly.

The solution to the Stackelberg duopoly problem (10.24) is depicted by the point (q_S^1, q_S^2) in Figure 10.15: the leader's isoprofit contour is tangent to the follower's reaction function at this point. The leader has a *first-mover advantage* in that firm 1's profits will be higher than would be the case at the Cournot–Nash solution while firm 2 has profits correspondingly lower than at the Cournot–Nash solution.

However, the Stackelberg analysis leaves a fundamental and important question—what constitutes a credible leader? How is the leadership position maintained? There are two responses here. First, this special duopoly model establishes some important principles that are relevant for other economic applications (see chapter 12). Second, we can dig a little deeper into the issues of industrial organisation that are raised by this model; this we will handle in the topic of market entry.

10.6.2 Market entry

In chapter 3 we considered a simple economic process of introducing new firms to a market (page 56); but the process was almost mechanical and took no account of the strategic issues involved in the relationship between the incumbent firm(s) and the potential entrants that are challenging them. Here we will use the analysis of time in games as the basis for modelling a strategic model of entry.

The point of departure is the story depicted in Figure 10.12 and Table 10.9. Replace player Alf with a potential entrant firm (here [LEFT] means 'enter the industry', [RIGHT] means 'stay out') and Bill as the incumbent (so [left] means 'fight a potential entrant', [right] means 'accommodate a potential entrant'). The numbers in the example depict the case where the incumbent's position is relatively weak and so the subgame-perfect equilibrium is one where the incumbent immediately accommodates the potential entrant without a fight.[37]

However, the model is rather naive and inflexible: the relative strength of the positions of the incumbent and the challenger are just hardwired into the payoffs and do not offer much economic insight. What if the rules of the game were altered a little? Could an incumbent make credible threats? The principal way of allowing for this possibility within the model of market structure is to introduce a 'commitment device' (see Mini Problem 31). A simple and realistic example of this is where a firm incurs *sunk costs*: this means that the firm spends money on some investment that has no resale value.[38] A simple version of the idea is depicted in Figure 10.16.

Figure 10.16 is based on Figure 10.12, but there are now three stages of the game. Stages two and three correspond to the story that we have just described; the subgame

? Mini Problems

37 Suppose the first two payoff pairs in Figure 10.12 are changed from '(0, 0) (2, 1)' to '(0, 1) (2, 0)'. How will this alter the equilibrium of the game? What interpretation can be given in terms of the model of contested entry? What is the equilibrium?

38 You set up a window cleaning business. You buy a ladder, window cleaning fluid and 1000 leaflets to publicise your business in the neighbourhood. Identify (i) variable costs, (ii) fixed costs, (iii) sunk costs.

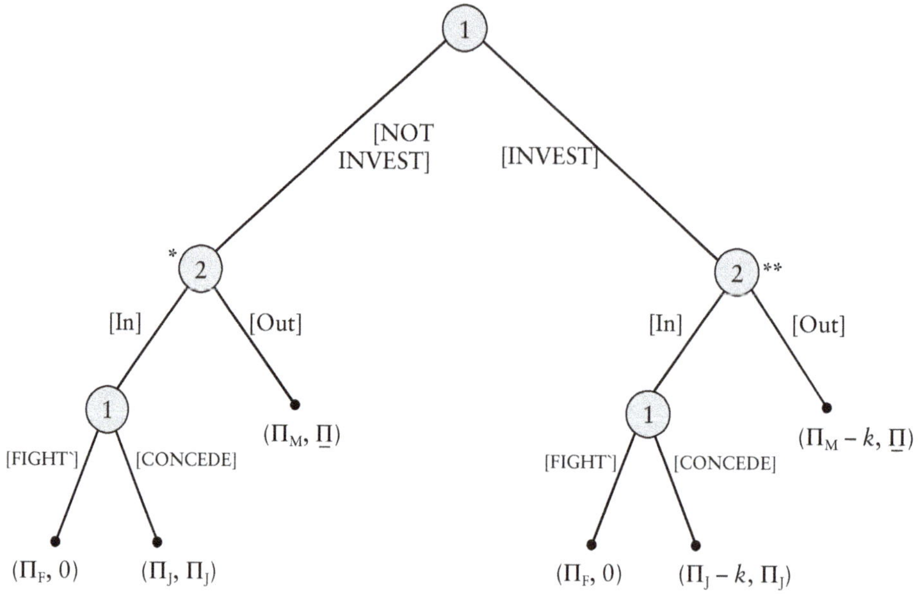

Figure 10.16 Entry deterrence

starting at the node marked * on the left is effectively the same game as we discussed before where the incumbent conceded immediately; in the corresponding subgame on the right-hand side (starting at the node marked **) the payoffs for the incumbent have been changed so that, in this case, it will no longer be profitable to concede entry to the challenger.[39] In the first stage the incumbent makes a decision whether or not to invest an amount that will cost a given amount k: this decision is publicly observable.

The decision on investment is crucial to the way the rest of the game works. The following is common knowledge.

- If the challenger stays out it makes a reservation profit level $\underline{\Pi}$ and the incumbent makes monopoly profits Π_M (less the cost of investment if it has been undertaken in stage 1).
- If the incumbent concedes to the challenger then they share the market and each gets Π_J.
- If the investment is not undertaken then the payoff if there is a fight is Π_F.
- If the investment is undertaken in stage 1 then it is recouped, dollar for dollar, should a fight occur. So, if the incumbent fights, it makes profits of exactly Π_F, net of the investment cost.

Now consider the equilibrium. Let us focus first on the subgame that follows on from a decision by the incumbent to invest (for the case where the incumbent does not invest

? Mini Problems

39 Show that the subgame starting at the left-hand node marked 2 in Figure 10.16 is essentially the same game, up to an ordinal transformation of payoffs, as the game in Figure 10.12.

see Exercise 10.13). If the challenger were to enter after this then the incumbent would find that it is more profitable to fight than concede as long as

$$\Pi_F > \Pi_J - k. \tag{10.25}$$

Now consider the first stage of the game: is it more profitable for the incumbent to commit the investment than just to allow the no-commitment subgame to occur? Yes if the net profit to be derived from successful entry deterrence exceeds the best that the incumbent could do without committing the investment:

$$\Pi_M - k > \Pi_J. \tag{10.26}$$

Combining the two pieces of information in (10.25) and (10.26) we get the result that deterrence works (in the sense of having a subgame-perfect equilibrium) as long as k has been chosen such that:

$$\Pi_J - \Pi_F < k < \Pi_M - \Pi_J. \tag{10.27}$$

In the light of condition (10.27) it is clear that, for some values of Π_F, Π_J, and Π_M, it may be impossible for the incumbent to deter entry by this method of precommitting to investment.

There is a natural connection with the Stackelberg duopoly model. Think of the investment as advance production costs: the firm is seen to build up a 'war chest' in the form of an inventory of output that can be released on to the market. If deterrence is successful, this stored output will have to be thrown away. However, should the challenger choose to enter, the incumbent can unload inventory from its warehouses without further cost. Furthermore, the newcomer's optimal output will be determined by the amount of output that the incumbent will have stashed away and then released. We can then see that the overall game becomes something very close to that discussed in the leader-follower model of section 10.6.1, but with the important difference that the rôle of the leader is now determined in a natural way through a commonsense interpretation of timing in the model.

10.6.3 Another look at duopoly

In the light of the discussion of repeated games (section 10.5.3) it is useful to reconsider the duopoly model of section 10.4.1. Applying the Folk Theorem enables us to examine the logic in the custom and practice of a tacit cartel. The story is the familiar one of collusion between the firms in restricting output so as to maintain high profits; if the collusion fails then the Cournot–Nash equilibrium will establish itself.

First we will oversimplify the problem by supposing that the two firms have effectively a binary choice in each stage game—they can choose one of the two output levels as in the discussion on page 292. Again, for ease of exposition, we take the special case of identical firms and we use the values given in Table 10.7 as payoffs in the stage game:

- If they both choose [low], this gives the joint-profit maximising payoff to each firm, Π_J.
- If they both choose [high], this gives the Cournot–Nash payoff to each firm, Π_C.
- If one firm defects from the collusive arrangement it can get a payoff $\overline{\Pi}$.

Using the argument for equation (10.23) (see also the answer to Mini Problem 34) the critical value of the discount factor is

$$\underline{\delta} := \frac{\overline{\Pi} - \Pi_J}{\overline{\Pi} - \Pi_C}.$$

So it appears that we could just carry across the argument of page 305 to the issue of cooperative behaviour in a duopoly setting. The joint-profit-maximising payoff to the cartel could be implemented as the outcome of a subgame-perfect equilibrium in which the strategy would involve punishing deviation from cooperative behaviour by switching to the Cournot–Nash output levels for ever after. But it is important to make two qualifying remarks.

First, suppose the market is expanding over time. Let $\tilde{\Pi}(t)$ be a variable that can take the value $\overline{\Pi}$, Π_J, or Π_C. Then it is clear that the payoff in the stage game for firm f at time t can be written

$$\Pi^f(t) = \tilde{\Pi}(t)\,[1+g]^{t-1}$$

where g is the expected growth rate and the particular value of $\tilde{\Pi}(t)$ will depend on the actions of each of the players in the stage game. The payoff to firm f of the whole repeated game is the following present value:

$$[1-\delta]\sum_{t=1}^{\infty}\delta^{t-1}\,\Pi^f(t)$$

$$= [1-\delta]\sum_{t=1}^{\infty}\tilde{\delta}^{t-1}\,\tilde{\Pi}(t) \qquad (10.28)$$

where $\tilde{\delta} := \delta\,[1+g]$. So it is clear that we can reinterpret the discount factor as a product of pure time preference, the probability that the game will continue, and the expected growth in the market. We can see that if the market is expected to be growing the effective discount factor will be higher and so in view of Theorem 10.3 the possibility of sustaining cooperation as a subgame-perfect equilibrium will be enhanced.

Second, it is essential to remember that the argument is based on the simple Prisoner's Dilemma where the action space for the stage game just has the two output levels. The standard Cournot model with a continuum of possible actions introduces further possibilities that we have not considered in the Prisoner's Dilemma. In particular, we can see that minimax level of profit for firm f in a Cournot oligopoly is *not* the Nash-equilibrium outcome, Π_C. The minimax profit level is zero—the other firm(s) could set output such that the f cannot make a profit (see, for example, point $\overline{q}_2$ in Figure 10.5). However, if one were to set output so as to ensure this outcome in every period from $t+1$ to ∞, this would clearly not be a best response by any other firm to an action by firm f (it is clear from the two-firm case in Figure 10.6 that $(0, \overline{q}_2)$ is not on the graph of firm 2's reaction function); so it cannot correspond to a Nash equilibrium to the subgame that would follow a deviation by firm f. Everlasting minimax punishment is not credible in this case.[40]

? Mini Problems

40 Draw a diagram similar to Figure B.38 to show the possible payoff combinations that are consistent with a Nash equilibrium in an infinitely repeated subgame. Would everlasting minimax

10.7 Uncertainty

As we have seen, having precise information about the detail of how a game is being played out is vital in shaping a rational player's strategy—the Kriegsspiel example on page 270 is enough to convince of that. It is also valuable to have clear ideas about the opponents' characteristics: a chess player might want to know whether the opponent is 'strong' or 'weak', the type of play that he favours, and so on.

These general remarks lead us on to the nature of the uncertainty to be considered here. In principle we could imagine that the information available to a player in the game is *imperfect* in that some details about the history of the game are unknown (who moved where at which stage?) or that it is *incomplete* in that the player does not fully know what the consequences and payoffs will be for others because he does not know what type of opponent he is facing (risk-averse or risk-loving individual? high-cost or low-cost firm?). Having created this careful distinction we can immediately destroy it by noting that the two versions of uncertainty can be made equivalent as far as the structure of the game is concerned. This is done by introducing one extra player to the game, called 'Nature'. Nature acts as an extra player by making a move that determines the characteristics of the players; if, as is usually the case, Nature moves first and the move that he/she/it makes is unknown and unobservable, then we can see that the problem of incomplete information (missing details about types of players) is, at a stroke, converted into one of imperfect information (missing details about history).

10.7.1 A basic model

We focus on the specific case where each economic agent h has a *type* τ^h. This type can be taken as a simple numerical parameter; for example it could be an index of risk aversion, an indicator of health status, a component of costs. The type indicator is the key to the model of uncertainty: τ^h is a random variable; each agent's type is determined at the beginning of the game but the realisation of τ^h is only observed by agent h.

Payoffs

The first thing to note is that an agent's type may affect his payoffs (if I become ill I may get a lower level of utility from a given consumption bundle than if I stay healthy) and so we need to modify the notation used in (10.2) to allow for this. Accordingly, write agent h's utility as

$$V^h\left(s^h, [s]^{-h};\ \tau^h\right) \tag{10.29}$$

where the first two arguments consist of the list of strategies (h's strategy and everybody else's strategy as in expression 10.2) and the last argument is the type associated with player h.

? Mini Problems

punishment be credible if the stage game involved Bertrand competition rather than Cournot competition?

Conditional strategies

Given that the selection of strategy involves some sort of maximisation of payoff (utility), the next point we should note is that each agent's strategy must be conditioned on his type. So a strategy is no longer a single 'button' as in the discussion on page 284 but is, rather, a 'button rule' that specifies a particular button to each possible value of the type τ^h. Write this rule for agent h as a function $\varsigma^h(\cdot)$ from the set of types to the set of pure strategies S^h. For example, if agent h can be of exactly one of two types {[HEALTHY],[ILL]} then agent h's button rule $\varsigma^h(\cdot)$ will generate exactly one of two pure strategies

$$s_0^h = \varsigma^h\left([\text{HEALTHY}]\right)$$

or

$$s_1^h = \varsigma^h\left([\text{ILL}]\right)$$

according to the value of τ^h realised at the beginning of the game.

Beliefs, probabilities, and expected payoffs

However, agent h does not know the types of the other agents who are players in the game. Instead he has to select a strategy based on some set of *beliefs* about the others' types. These beliefs are incorporated into a simple probabilistic model: F, the joint probability distribution of types over the agents, is assumed to be common knowledge. Although it is by no means essential, from now on we will simply assume that the type of each individual is just a number in $[0, 1]$.[41]

Figure 10.17 shows a stylised sketch of the idea. Here Alf, who has been revealed to be of type τ_0^a and who is about to choose [LEFT] or [RIGHT], does not know what Bill's type is at the moment of the decision. There are three possibilities, indicated by the three points in the information set. However, because Alf knows the distribution of types that Bill may possess he can at least rationally assign conditional probabilities $\Pr\left(\tau_1^b |\, \tau_0^a\right)$,

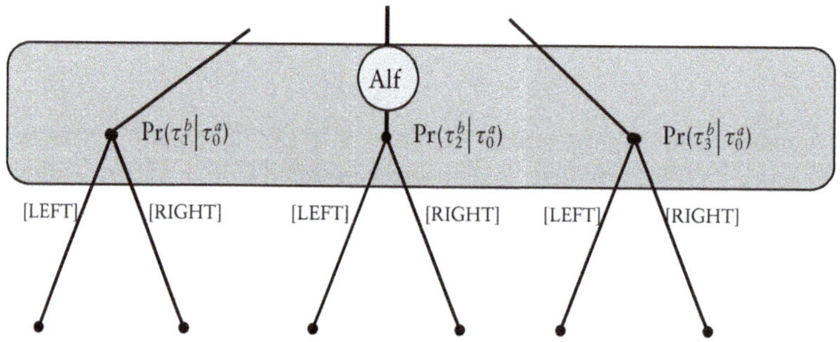

Figure 10.17 Alf's beliefs about Bill

? Mini Problems

41 This assumption about types is adaptable to a wide range of specific models of individual characteristics. Show how the two-case example used here, where the person is either of type [HEALTHY] or of type [ILL] can be expressed using the convention that agent h's type $\tau^h \in [0, 1]$ if the probability of agent h being healthy is π.

$\Pr\left(\tau_2^b | \tau_0^a\right)$, and $\Pr\left(\tau_3^b | \tau_0^a\right)$ to the three members of the information set, given the type that has been realised for Alf. These probabilities are derived from the joint distribution F, conditional on Alf's own type: these are Alf's beliefs (since the probability distribution of types is common knowledge then he would be crazy to believe anything else).

Consider the way that this uncertainty affects h's payoff. Each of the other agents' strategies will be conditioned on the type which 'Nature' endows them and so, in evaluating (10.29) agent h faces the situation that

$$s^h = \varsigma^h\left(\tau^h\right) \tag{10.30}$$

$$[s]^{-h} = \left[\varsigma^1\left(\tau^1\right), \ldots, \varsigma^{h-1}\left(\tau^{h-1}\right), \varsigma^{h+1}\left(\tau^{h+1}\right), \ldots\right]. \tag{10.31}$$

The arguments in the functions on the right-hand side of (10.30) and (10.31) are random variables and so the things on the left-hand side of (10.30) and (10.31) are also random. Evaluating (10.29) with these random variables one then gets

$$V^h\left(\varsigma^1\left(\tau^1\right), \varsigma^2\left(\tau^2\right), \ldots; \tau^h\right) \tag{10.32}$$

as the (random) payoff for agent h.

In order to incorporate the random variables in (10.30)–(10.32) into a coherent objective function for agent h we need one further step. We assume the standard model of utility under uncertainty that was first introduced in chapter 8 (page 187)—the von Neumann—Morgenstern function. This means that the appropriate way of writing the payoff is in expectational terms

$$\mathcal{E}V^h\left(s^h, [s]^{-h}; \tau^h\right) \tag{10.33}$$

where s^h is given by (10.30), $[s]^{-h}$ is given by (10.31), $\mathcal{E}$ is the expectations operator, and the expectation is taken over the joint distribution of types for all the agents.

Equilibrium

We need a further refinement in the definition of equilibrium that will allow for the type of uncertainty that we have just modelled. To do this note that the game can be completely described by three objects, a profile of utility functions, the corresponding list of strategy sets, and the joint probability distribution of types:

$$\left[V^1, V^2, \ldots\right]; \left[S^1, S^2, \ldots\right]; F. \tag{10.34}$$

However, we can recast the game in a way that is familiar from the discussion of section 10.3. We could think of each agent's 'button-rule' $\varsigma^h(\cdot)$ as a redefined strategy in its own right; agent h gets utility $v^h\left(\varsigma^h, [\varsigma]^{-h}\right)$ which exactly equals (10.33) and where v^h is just the same as in (10.2). If we use the symbol $\mathcal{S}^h$ for the set of these redefined strategies or 'button rules' for agent h then (10.34) is equivalent to the game

$$\left[v^1, v^2, \ldots\right]; \left[\mathcal{S}^1, \mathcal{S}^2, \ldots\right]. \tag{10.35}$$

Comparing this with (10.3) we can see that, on this interpretation, we have a standard game with redefined strategy sets for each player.

This alternative, equivalent representation of the Bayesian game enables us to introduce the definition of equilibrium:

Definition 10.7

A *pure strategy Bayesian Nash equilibrium* for (10.34) is a profile of rules $[\varsigma^*]$ that is a Nash equilibrium of the game (10.35).

This definition means that we can just adapt (10.6) by replacing the ordinary strategies ('buttons') in the Nash equilibrium with the 'button rules' $\varsigma^{*h}(\cdot)$ where

$$\varsigma^{*h}(\cdot) \in \underset{\varsigma^h(\cdot)}{\arg\max}\, v^h\left(\varsigma^h(\cdot), [\varsigma^*(\cdot)]^{-h}\right). \tag{10.36}$$

Identity

The description of this model of incomplete information may seem daunting at first reading, but there is a natural intuitive way of seeing the issues here. Recall that in chapter 8 we modelled uncertainty in competitive markets by, effectively, expanding the commodity space—n physical goods are replaced by $n\varpi$ contingent goods, where ϖ is the number of possible states of the world (page 202). A similar thought experiment works here. Think of the incomplete-information case as one involving players as superheroes where the same agent can take on a number of identities. We can then visualise a Bayesian equilibrium as a Nash equilibrium of a game involving a larger number of players: if there are two players and two types we can take this setup as equivalent to a game with four players (Batman, Superman, Bruce Wayne, and Clark Kent). Each agent in a particular identity plays so as to maximise his expected utility in that identity; expected utility is computed using the probabilities attached to each of the possible identities of the opponent(s); these probabilities are conditional on the agent's own identity. So Batman maximises Batman's expected utility having assigned particular probabilities that he is facing Superman or Clark Kent; Bruce Wayne does the same with Bruce Wayne's utility function although the probabilities that he assigns to the (Superman, Clark Kent) identities may be different.

This can be expressed in the following way. Use the notation $\mathcal{E}\left(\bullet \mid \tau_0^h\right)$ to denote conditional expectation—in this case the expectation taken over the distribution of all agents other than h, conditional on the specific type value τ_0^h for agent h—and write $[s^*]^{-h}$ for the profile of random variables in (10.31) at the optimum where $\varsigma^j = \varsigma^{*j}$, $j \neq h$. Then we have:

Theorem 10.4

A profile of decision rules $[\varsigma^*]$ is a Bayesian Nash equilibrium for (10.34) if and only if for all h and for any τ_0^h occurring with positive probability

$$\mathcal{E}\left(V^h\left(\varsigma^{*h}\left(\tau_0^h\right), [s^*]^{-h} \mid \tau_0^h\right)\right) \geq \mathcal{E}\left(V^h\left(s^h, [s^*]^{-h} \mid \tau_0^h\right)\right)$$

for all $s^h \in S^h$.

So the rules given in (10.36) will maximise the expected payoff of every agent, conditional on his beliefs about the other agents.

10.7.2 An application: entry again

We can illustrate the concept of a Bayesian equilibrium and outline a method of solution using an example that ties in with the earlier discussion of strategic issues in industrial organisation.

Figure 10.18 takes the story of section 10.6.2 a stage further. The new twist is that the monopolist's characteristics are not fully known by a firm trying to enter the industry. It is known that firm 1, the incumbent, has the possibility of committing to investment that might strategically deter entry: the investment would enhance the incumbent's market position. However, the firm may incur either high cost or low cost in making this investment: which of the two cost levels actually applies to firm 1 is something unknown to firm 2. So the game involves first a preliminary move by 'Nature' (player 0) that determines the cost type, then a simultaneous move by firm 1, choosing whether or not to invest, and firm 2, choosing whether or not to enter. Consider the following three cases concerning firm 1's circumstances and behaviour:

1. *Firm 1 does not invest.* If firm 2 enters then both firms make profits Π_J. But if firm 2 stays out then it just makes its reservation profit level $\underline{\Pi}$, where $0 < \underline{\Pi} < \Pi_J$, while firm 1 makes monopoly profits Π_M.
2. *Firm 1 invests and is low cost.* If firm 2 enters then firm 1 makes profits $\Pi_J^* < \Pi_J$ but firm 2's profits are forced right down to zero. If firm 2 stays out then it again gets just reservation profits $\underline{\Pi}$ but firm 1 gets enhanced monopoly profits $\Pi_M^* > \Pi_M$.

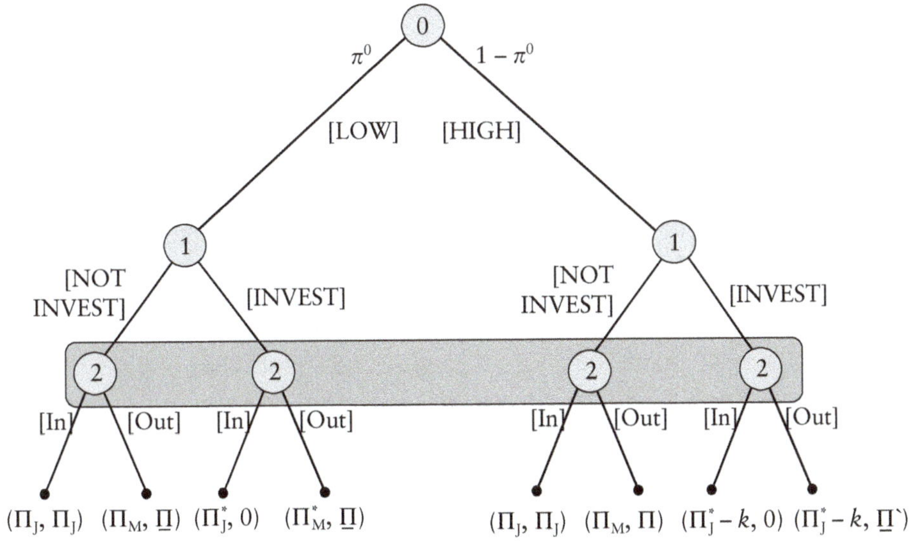

Figure 10.18 Entry with incomplete information

3. *Firm 1 invests and is high cost.* Story is as above, but firm 1's profits are reduced by an amount k, the cost difference.

To make the model interesting we will assume that k is fairly large, in the following sense:

$$k > \max\left\{\Pi_J^* - \Pi_J, \Pi_M^* - \Pi_M\right\}.$$

In this case it is never optimal for firm 1 to invest if it has high cost (check the bottom right-hand part of Figure 10.18 to see this).

To find the equilibrium in this model we will introduce a device that we used earlier, in section 10.3.5. Even though we are focusing on pure (i.e. non-randomised) strategies let us suppose that firm 1 and firm 2 each consider a randomisation between the two actions that they can take. To do this, define the following:[42]

- π^0 is the probability that 'Nature' endows firm 1 with low cost. This probability is common knowledge.
- π^1 is the probability that firm 1 chooses [INVEST] given that its cost is low.
- π^2 is the probability that firm 2 chooses [In].

Then, writing out the expected payoff to firm 1, $\mathcal{E}\Pi^1$ we find that:

$$\frac{\partial \mathcal{E}\Pi^1}{\partial \pi^1} > 0 \Longleftrightarrow \pi^2 < \frac{1}{1+\gamma} \tag{10.37}$$

where

$$\gamma := \frac{\Pi_J - \Pi_J^*}{\Pi_M^* - \Pi_M} > 0. \tag{10.38}$$

Furthermore, evaluating $\mathcal{E}\Pi^2$, the expected payoff to firm 2:

$$\frac{\partial \mathcal{E}\Pi^2}{\partial \pi^2} > 0 \Longleftrightarrow \pi^1 < \frac{\Pi_J - \underline{\Pi}}{\pi^0 \Pi_J}. \tag{10.39}$$

The restriction on the right hand of (10.39) only makes sense if the probability of being low-cost is large enough, that is, if

$$\pi^0 \geq 1 - \frac{\underline{\Pi}}{\Pi_J}. \tag{10.40}$$

To find the equilibrium in (conditional) pure strategies[43] check whether conditions (10.37)–(10.39) can be satisfied by probability pairs (π^1, π^2) equal to any of the values $(0, 0)$, $(0, 1)$, $(1, 0)$, or $(1, 1)$. Clearly condition (10.37) rules out $(0, 0)$ and $(1, 1)$. However, the pair $(0, 1)$ always satisfies the conditions, meaning that ([NOT INVEST],[In]) is always a pure-strategy Nash equilibrium. Likewise, if the probability of [LOW] is large enough that condition (10.40) holds, then ([INVEST],[Out]) will also be a pure-strategy Nash equilibrium.

? Mini Problems

42 Write out the expressions for expected payoff for firm 1 and for firm 2 and verify (10.37) and (10.39).

43 Will there also be a mixed-strategy equilibrium to this game?

The method is of interest here as much as is detail of the equilibrium solutions. It enables us to see a link with the solution concept that we introduced on page 284.

10.7.3 Mixed strategies again

One of the features that emerges from the description of Bayesian Nash equilibrium and the example in section 10.7.2 is the use of probabilities in evaluating payoffs. The way that uncertainty about the type of one's opponent is handled in the Bayesian game appears to be very similar to the resolution of the problem arising in elementary games where there is no equilibrium in pure strategies. The assumption that the distribution of types is common knowledge enables us to focus on a Nash equilibrium solution that is familiar from the discussion of mixed strategies in section 10.3.5.

In fact one can also establish that a mixed-strategy equilibrium with given players Alf, Bill, Charlie..., each of whom randomise their play, is equivalent to a Bayesian equilibrium in which there is a continuum of a-types all with Alf's preferences but slightly different types, a continuum of b-types all with Bill's preferences but with slightly different types, and so on, all of whom play pure strategies.

The consequence of this is that there may be a response to those who see strategic arguments relying on mixed strategies as artificial and unsatisfactory (see page 286). Large numbers and variability in types appear to 'rescue' the situation by showing that there is an equivalent, or closely approximating, Bayesian Nash equilibrium in pure strategies.

10.7.4 A 'dynamic' approach

The discussion of uncertainty thus far has been essentially static insofar as the sequencing of the game is concerned. But it is arguable that this misses out one of the most important aspects of incomplete information in most games and situations of economic conflict. With the passage of time each player gets to learn something about the other players' characteristics through observation of the other players' actions at previous stages; this information will be taken into account in the way the game is planned and played out from then on.

In view of this it is clear that the Bayesian Nash approach outlined above only captures part of the essential problem. There are two important omissions:

1. *Credibility.* We have already discussed the problem of credibility in connection with Nash equilibria of multi-stage games involving complete information (see pages 300 ff). The same issue would arise here if we considered multi-stage versions of games of incomplete information.

2. *Updating.* As information is generated by the actions of players this can be used to update the probabilities used by the players in evaluating expected utility. This is typically done by using Bayes's rule (see Appendix A, page 514).

So in order to put right the limitations of the uncertainty model one would expect to combine the 'perfection' involved in the analysis of subgames with the logic of the

Bayesian approach to handling uncertainty. This is exactly what is done in the following further refinement of equilibrium

---

Definition 10.8

A *perfect Bayesian equilibrium* in a multi-stage game is a collection of strategies and beliefs at each node of the game such that:

1. the strategies form a subgame-perfect equilibrium, given the beliefs;
2. the beliefs are updated from prior beliefs using Bayes's rule at every node of the game that is reached with positive probability using the equilibrium strategies.

The two parts of the definition show a nice symbiosis: the subgame-perfect strategies at every 'relevant' node make use of the set of beliefs that is the natural one to use at that point of the game; the beliefs are revised in the light of the information that is revealed by playing out the strategies.

However, note that the definition is limited in its scope. It remains silent about what is supposed to happen to beliefs out of equilibrium—but this issue raises complex questions and takes us beyond the scope of the present book. Note too that in some cases the updating may be simple and drastic so that the problem of incomplete information is resolved after one stage of the game. However, despite these qualifications, the issue of strategic interactions that incorporate learning is so important and so multifaceted that we shall be devoting all of chapter 11 to it.

Summary

Strategic behaviour is not just a new microeconomic topic but a new method and a fresh way of looking at economic analysis. Game theory permits the construction of an abstract framework that enables us to think through the way economic models work in some cases where the simplified structure of price taking is inapplicable or inappropriate.

But how much should one expect from game theory? It clearly provides a collection of important general principles for microeconomics. It also offers some truly striking results, for example the demonstration that cooperative outcomes can be induced from selfish agents by the design of credible strategies that involve future punishment for 'anti-social' behaviour (the Folk Theorem). On the other hand game theory perhaps warrants an enthusiasm that is tempered by considerations of practicality. Game-theoretic approaches do not always give clear-cut answers but may rather point to a multiplicity of solutions and, where they do give clear-cut answers in principle, these answers may be almost impossible to work out in practice. To illustrate: finding all the outcomes in chess is a computable problem, but where is the computer that could do the job?

To summarise the ways in which this chapter has illustrated the contribution of the game-theoretic approach to economic principles and to point forward to later chapters let us focus on three key aspects:

- *The nature of equilibrium.* In moving to an economic environment in which strategic issues are crucial we have had to introduce several new definitions of equilibrium; in the formal literature on this subject there are even more intellectual constructions that are candidates for equilibrium concepts. Do the subtle differences between the various definitions matter? Each can be defended as the correct way of modelling coherence of agents' behaviour in a carefully specified strategic setting. Each incorporates a notion of rationality consistent with this setting. However, as the model structure is made richer, the accompanying structure of beliefs and interlocking behaviour can appear to be impossibly sophisticated and complex. The difficulty for the economic modeller is, perhaps, to find an appropriate location on the spectrum from total naivety to hyper-rationality (more on this in chapter 12).
- *Time.* The sequencing of decisions and actions is a crucial feature of many situations of potential economic conflict because it will often affect the way the underlying game is played and even the viability of the solution concept. A modest extension of fairly simple games to more than one period enables one to develop models that incorporate the issues of power and of induced cooperation.
- *Uncertainty.* In chapter 8 uncertainty and risk appeared in economic decision making in the rôle of mechanistic chance. Here, the mechanistic chance can be a player in the game and clear-cut results carry over from the complete-information case, although they rest on quite strong assumptions about individual beliefs and understanding of the uncertain universe. However, we can go further. The Bayesian model opens the possibility of using the acquisition of information strategically and has implications for how we model the economics of information. This is developed in chapter 11.

Reading notes

A good introduction is provided by Dixit and Skeath (2004), Gardner (2003), Osborne (2004), or Rasmusen (2001); the older Gibbons (1992) still provides an excellent and thorough overview of the main issues; for a more advanced treatment Vega-Redondo (2003) is useful. The Nash equilibrium concept first appeared in Nash (1951); on the appropriateness of using it as a solution concept see Kreps (1990). The rationale of mixed-strategy equilibria is discussed in Harsanyi (1973) and the argument for treating 'nature' as a player in the game is developed in Harsanyi (1967). For the history and precursors of the concept of Nash equilibrium see Myerson (1999); on Nash equilibrium and behaviour see Mailath (1998) and Samuelson (2002). Subgame perfection as an equilibrium concept is attributable to Selten (1965, 1975).

The folk theorem and variants on repeated games form a substantial literature. For an early statement in the context of oligopoly see Friedman (1971). A key result establishing subgame perfection in repeated games is proved in Fudenberg and Maskin (1979).

How people actually conduct themselves in strategic situations has been the focus of a huge literature on experimental game theory. For a good introduction see Crawford (2002).

The standard reference on industrial organisation is the thorough treatment by Tirole (1988). For more recent treatment of oligopoly models and analytical tools see Vives (1999) and Shy (1995), section II. The original classic contributions whose logic underlies so much modern work are to be found in Bertrand (1883), Cournot (1838), and von Stackelberg (1934).

Exercises

10.1 Table 10.12 is the strategic form representation of a simultaneous move game in which strategies are actions.

1. Is there a dominant strategy for either of the two agents?
2. Which strategies can always be eliminated because they are dominated?
3. Which strategies can be eliminated if it is common knowledge that both players are rational?
4. What are the Nash equilibria in pure strategies?

	s_1^b	s_2^b	s_3^b
s_1^a	0, 2	3, 1	4, 3
s_2^a	2, 4	0, 3	3, 2
s_3^a	1, 1	2, 0	2, 1

Table 10.12 Elimination and equilibrium

10.2 Table 10.13 again represents a simultaneous move game in which strategies are actions.

1. Identify the best responses for each of the players a, b.
2. Is there a Nash equilibrium in pure strategies?

	s_1^b	s_2^b	s_3^b
s_1^a	0, 2	2, 0	3, 1
s_2^a	2, 0	0, 2	3, 1
s_3^a	1, 3	1, 3	4, 4

Table 10.13 Pure-strategy Nash equilibria

10.3 A taxpayer has income y that should be reported in full to the tax authority. There is a flat (proportional) tax rate γ on income. The reporting technology means that that taxpayer must report income in full or zero income. The tax authority can choose whether or not to audit the taxpayer. Each audit costs an amount φ and if the audit uncovers under-reporting then the taxpayer is required to pay the full amount of tax owed plus a fine F.

1. Set the problem out as a game in strategic form where each agent (taxpayer, tax-authority) has two pure strategies.

2. Explain why there is no simultaneous-move equilibrium in pure strategies.
3. Find the mixed-strategy equilibrium. How will the equilibrium respond to changes in the parameters γ, φ and F?

10.4 Take the 'battle-of-the-sexes' game of Mini Problem 2 (the strategic form is given in Table B.1 on page 560).

1. Show that, in addition to the pure-strategy, Nash equilibria there is also a mixed-strategy equilibrium.
2. Construct the payoff-possibility frontier (as in Figure B.38 on page 565). Why is the interpretation of this frontier in the battle-of-the-sexes context rather unusual in comparison with the Cournot-oligopoly case?
3. Show that the mixed-strategy equilibrium lies strictly inside the frontier.
4. Suppose the two players adopt *the same* randomisation device, observable by both of them: they know that the specified random variable takes the value 1 with probability π and 2 with probability $1 - \pi$; they agree to play $\left[s_1^a, s_1^b\right]$ with probability π and $\left[s_2^a, s_2^b\right]$ with probability $1 - \pi$; show that this *correlated mixed strategy* always produces a payoff on the frontier.

10.5 Rework Exercise 10.4 for the case of the Chicken game in Table 10.4.

10.6 Consider the three-person game depicted in Figure 10.19 where strategies are actions. For each strategy combination, the column of figures in parentheses denotes the payoffs to Alf, Bill, and Charlie, respectively (Fudenberg and Tirole 1991: 55).

1. For the simultaneous-move game shown in Figure 10.19 show that there is a unique pure-strategy Nash equilibrium.
2. Suppose the game is changed. Alf and Bill agree to coordinate their actions by tossing a coin and playing [LEFT],[left] if heads comes up and [RIGHT],[right] if tails comes up. Charlie is not told the outcome of the spin of the coin before making his move. What is Charlie's best response? Compare your answer to part 1.
3. Now take the version of part 2 but suppose that Charlie knows the outcome of the coin toss before making his choice. What is his best response? Compare your answer to parts 1 and 2. Does this mean that restricting information can be socially beneficial?

10.7 Consider a duopoly with identical firms. The cost function for firm f is

$$C_0 + cq^f, f = 1, 2.$$

The inverse demand function is

$$\beta_0 - \beta q$$

where C_0, c, β_0, and β are all positive numbers and total output is given by $q = q^1 + q^2$.

1. Find the isoprofit contour and the reaction function for firm 2.
2. Find the Cournot–Nash equilibrium for the industry and illustrate it in (q^1, q^2)-space.

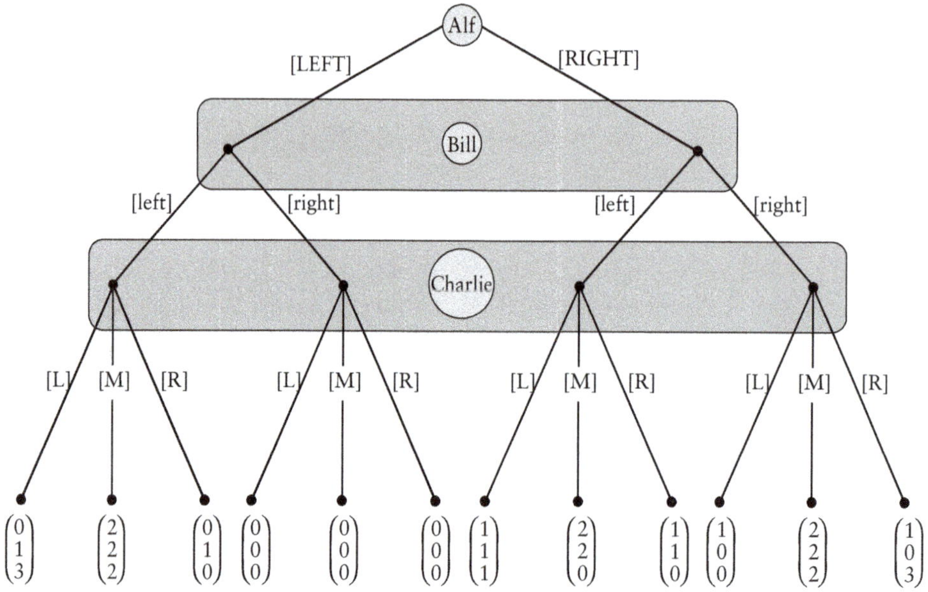

Figure 10.19 Benefits of restricting information

3. Find the joint-profit maximising solution for the industry and illustrate it on the same diagram.
4. If firm 1 acts as leader and firm 2 as a follower find the Stackelberg solution.
5. Draw the set of payoff possibilities and plot the payoffs for cases 2-4 and for the case where there is a monopoly.

10.8 An oligopoly contains N identical firms. The cost function is convex in output. Show that if the firms act as Cournot competitors then as N increases the market price will approach the competitive price.

10.9 Two identical firms consider entering a new market; setting up in the new market incurs a once-for-all cost $K > 0$; production involves constant marginal cost c. If both firms enter the market Bertrand competition then takes place afterwards. If the firms make their entry decision sequentially, what is the equilibrium?

10.10 Two firms have inherited capacity from the past so that production must take place subject to the constraint

$$q^f \leq \bar{q}^f, \; f = 1, 2$$

There are zero marginal costs. Let $\chi(\cdot)$ be the Cournot (quantity-competition) reaction function for each firm. If the firms compete on prices (as in section 10.4.2) show that the following must be true in a pure-strategy equilibrium:

1. Both firms will charge the same price p.
2. $p = p(\bar{q}^1 + \bar{q}^2)$.

3. $p \geq p(\chi(\bar{q}^2) + \bar{q}^2)$.
4. $\bar{q}^1 \leq \chi(\bar{q}^2)$.

10.11 In winter two identical ice-cream firms have to choose the capacity that they plan to use in the summer. To install capacity $\bar{q}$ costs an amount $k\bar{q}$ where k is a positive constant. Production in the summer takes place subject to

$$q^f \leq \bar{q}^f, \ f = 1, 2$$

where $\bar{q}^f$ is the capacity that was chosen in the previous winter. Once capacity is installed there is zero marginal cost. The market for ice-cream is characterised by the inverse demand function $p(q^1 + q^2)$. There are thus two views: the 'before' problem when the decision on capacity has not yet been taken; the 'after' problem (in the summer) once capacity has been installed.

1. Let $\chi(\cdot)$ be the reaction function for either firm in the 'after' problem (as in Exercise 10.10). In the context of a diagram such as Figure 10.5 explain why this must lie strictly above the Cournot reaction function for the 'before' problem.
2. Let q_C be the Cournot-equilibrium quantity for the 'before' problem. Write down the definition of this in terms of the present model.
3. Suppose that in the summer competition between the firms takes place in terms of prices (as in Exercise 10.10). Show that a pure-strategy Bertrand equilibrium for the overall problem is where both firms produce q_C (Kreps and Sheinkman 1983).

10.12 There is a cake of size 1 to be divided between Alf and Bill. In period $t = 1$ Alf offers player Bill a share: Bill may accept now (in which case the game ends), or reject. If Bill rejects then, in period $t = 2$ Alf again makes an offer, which Bill can accept (game ends) or reject. If Bill rejects, the game ends one period later with exogenously fixed payoffs of γ to Alf and $1 - \gamma$ to Bill. Assume that Alf and Bill's payoffs are linear in cake and that both persons have the same, time-invariant discount factor $\delta < 1$.

1. What is the backwards induction outcome in the two-period model?
2. How does the answer change if the time horizon increases but is finite?
3. What would happen if the horizon were infinite (Rubinstein 1982, Ståhl 1972, Sutton 1986)?

10.13 Take the game that begins at the node marked '*' in Figure 10.16 (page 310).

1. Show that if $\Pi_M > \Pi_J > \Pi_F$ then the incumbent firm will always concede to a challenger.
2. Now suppose that the incumbent operates a chain of N stores, each in a separate location. It faces a challenge to each of the N stores: in each location there is a firm that would like to enter the local market. The challenges take place sequentially, location by location; at each point the potential entrant knows the outcomes of all previous challenges. The payoffs in each location are as in part 1 and the incumbent's overall payoff is the undiscounted sum of the payoffs over all locations. Show that, however large N is, all the challengers will enter and the incumbent never fights (Selten 1978).

10.14 In a monopolistic industry firm 1, the incumbent, is considering whether to install extra capacity in order to deter the potential entry of firm 2. Marginal capacity installation costs, and marginal production costs (for production in excess of capacity) are equal and constant. Excess capacity cannot be sold. The potential entrant incurs a fixed cost k in the event of entry (Dixit 1980, Spence 1977).

1. Let $\underline{q}^1$ be the incumbent's output level for which the potential entrant's best response yields zero profits for the entrant. Suppose $\underline{q}^1 \neq q_M$, where q_M is firm 1's output if its monopolistic position is unassailable (i.e. if entry deterrence is inevitable). Show that this implies that market demand must be non-linear.
2. In the case where entry deterrence is possible but not inevitable, show that if $q_S^1 > \underline{q}^1$, then it is more profitable for firm 1 to deter entry than to accommodate the challenger, where q_S^1 is firm 1's output level at the Stackelberg solution.

10.15 Two firms in a duopolistic industry have constant and equal marginal costs c and face market demand schedule given by $p = k - q$ where $k > c$ and q is total output.

1. What would be the solution to the Bertrand price-setting game?
2. Compute the joint-profit-maximising solution for this industry.
3. Consider an infinitely repeated game based on the Bertrand stage game when both firms have the discount factor $\delta < 1$. What trigger strategy, based on punishment levels $p = c$, will generate the outcome in part 2? For what values of δ do these trigger strategies constitute a subgame-perfect Nash equilibrium?

10.16 Consider a market with a very large number of consumers in which a firm faces a fixed cost of entry F. In period 0, N firms enter and in period 1 each firm chooses the quality of its product to be HIGH, which costs $c > 0$, or LOW, which costs 0. Consumers choose which firms to buy from, choosing randomly if they are indifferent. Only after purchasing the commodity can consumers observe the quality. In subsequent time periods the stage game just described is repeated indefinitely. The market demand function is given by

$$q = \begin{cases} \varphi(p) & \text{if quality is believed to be HIGH} \\ 0 & \text{otherwise} \end{cases}$$

where $\varphi(\cdot)$ is a strictly decreasing function and p is the price of the commodity. The discount rate is zero.

1. Specify a trigger strategy for consumers which induces firms always to choose high quality. Hence determine the subgame-perfect equilibrium. What price will be charged in equilibrium?
2. What is the equilibrium number of firms, and each firm's output level in a long-run equilibrium with free entry and exit?
3. What would happen if $F = 0$?

10.17 In a duopoly both firms have constant marginal cost. It is common knowledge that this is 1 for firm 1 and that for firm 2 it is either $\frac{3}{4}$ or $1\frac{1}{4}$. It is common knowledge that firm 1 believes that firm 2 is low cost with probability $\frac{1}{2}$. The inverse demand function is

$$2 - q$$

where q is total output. The firms choose output simultaneously. What is the equilibrium in pure strategies?

11 Information

As we know,
There are known knowns.
There are things we know we know.
We also know
There are known unknowns.
That is to say
We know there are some things
We do not know.
But there are also unknown unknowns,
The ones we don't know
We don't know.

Donald Rumsfeld. 12 Feb. 2002, Department of Defense news briefing.

11.1 Introduction

We have already seen that economics can do a lot more than just talk about the 'known knowns'. The economics of information builds on elementary reasoning about 'known unknowns' and incorporates elements of both exogenous uncertainty—blind chance—and endogenous uncertainty—the actions and reactions of others; it has connections with previous discussions both of uncertainty and risk (chapter 8) and of the economics of strategic behaviour (chapter 10).

In principle uncertainty can be incorporated into models of strategic behaviour in a variety of interesting ways, some of which were treated in chapter 10. Here we focus on just one important class of problem that can be categorised in terms of Bayesian games and we focus on perfect Bayesian equilibrium: but it is a rich class and the equilibrium behaviour can be readily interpreted in terms of microeconomic intuition.

The structure of the problem is closely related to the issue of timing in models of strategic behaviour. We imagine an economic relationship between two economic actors or players, one of whom has some information that is key to the economic relationship that the other does not possess—in the jargon it is a case of *asymmetric information*. The central questions concern (i) the nature of the hidden information and (ii) which of the players—the well informed or the uninformed—gets to make the first move.

The three main paradigms are highlighted in Table 11.1—they are discussed separately in the three main sections of this chapter, 11.2 to 11.4. However, before moving on to these two comments should be made on the simple classification in this table. First, the bottom right cell remains blank because the situation where the uninformed player cannot observe an action of the player who draws up the contract is not intrinsically very

	type of hidden information	
first move by...	*characteristics*	*actions*
uninformed	adverse selection	moral hazard
informed	signalling	—

Table 11.1 Types of incentive problem

interesting. Second, the term 'uninformed' is a slight misnomer. Quite a lot of information about characteristics and actions is common knowledge in these models, indeed it has to be so for the economic problem to be well defined. In order to obtain and analyse clear-cut principles to apply to the behaviour of economic agents we need to be clear about the precise form of the distribution of the relevant random variables that are used to represent the lack of specific information that characterises many economic problems. We need to impose a rigid structure on the 'known unknowns' in the Rumsfeldian terminology.

11.2 Hidden characteristics: adverse selection

We begin with the problem that information about some crucial parameter in an economic transaction—personal tastes or individual ability, let us say—is known to one party in the transaction but not to the other. We will treat this first in the context of a monopolist confronted by heterogeneous consumers. The reason for starting like this is that it is fairly easy to see exactly how and why the economic mechanism works in this case and to deduce the principles underlying the solution. Although we work out the results in the context of a highly simplified model the lessons are fairly general and can be extended to quite complex situations. Later we move on from monopoly to cases where there are many partially informed firms competing for customers—see subsections 11.2.5 and 11.2.6.

11.2.1 Information and monopoly power

In a two-good model suppose a monopolistic firm produces good 1 from good 2 at constant marginal cost c. The monopolist is free to set whatever fees or charges for good 1 that it wishes; the nature of good 1 is such that it is possible to prevent resale of the good.

The analysis of the monopolist's problem requires specification of a fee schedule F that gives the total amount to be paid $F(x_1)$ by a customer who consumes a quantity x_1 of good 1. For example, Figure 11.1 depicts three alternative forms that the fee schedule could take:

1. The simplest case with a uniform price p:

$$F(x_1) = px_1.$$

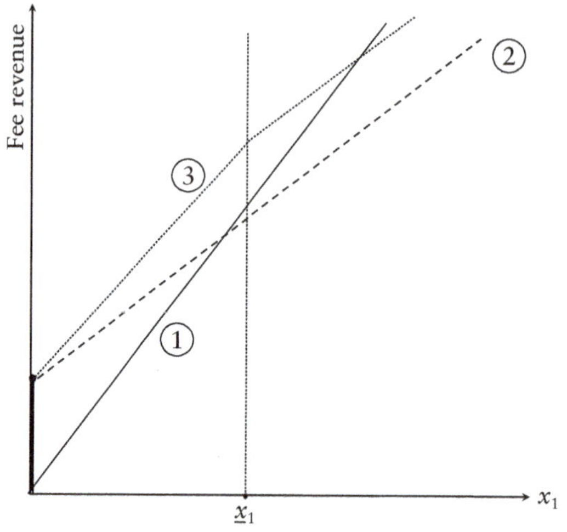

Figure 11.1 Alternative fee schedules

2. The two-part tariff comprising an entry fee F_0 (required to get access to the market) and a fixed price for the marginal unit of good 1:

$$F(x_1) = F_0 + px_1 \text{ if } x_1 > 0.$$

3. The multi-part tariff that can take a huge range of forms. One example is

$$\begin{aligned} F(x_1) &= F_0 + p'x_1 \text{ if } 0 < x_1 \leq \underline{x}_1 \\ &= F_0 + p'\underline{x}_1 + p''\left[x_1 - \underline{x}_1\right] \text{ if } x_1 > \underline{x}_1. \end{aligned}$$

The firm obviously needs to choose what sort of fee schedule is appropriate in order to maximise profits—not just what *values* parameters such as p and F_0 should take. But there is a further problem to be considered: in order to maximise profits would the firm want to distinguish between different groups of customers when setting its fee? If so, how should the firm take account of this potential difficulty in determining its fee structure?

We proceed by first setting out the problem in the special cases where informational problems do not arise (sections 11.2.2 and 11.2.3); then we look at the case where an informational problem arises and examine how to solve it (section 11.2.4). However, to make the discussion manageable we are going to limit the analysis in two important ways. First, we will only consider a simplified form of the informational problem; nevertheless, the principles that will be established are valid for a more general structure. Second, we are only going to examine a simplified version of the choice of fee schedule; more general issues of design proper are left until Chapter 12.

11.2.2 One customer type

To start with we shall in effect revisit the modelling of section 3.6 in chapter 3 but now with an explicit analysis of the welfare of the consumer; furthermore we do not assume in

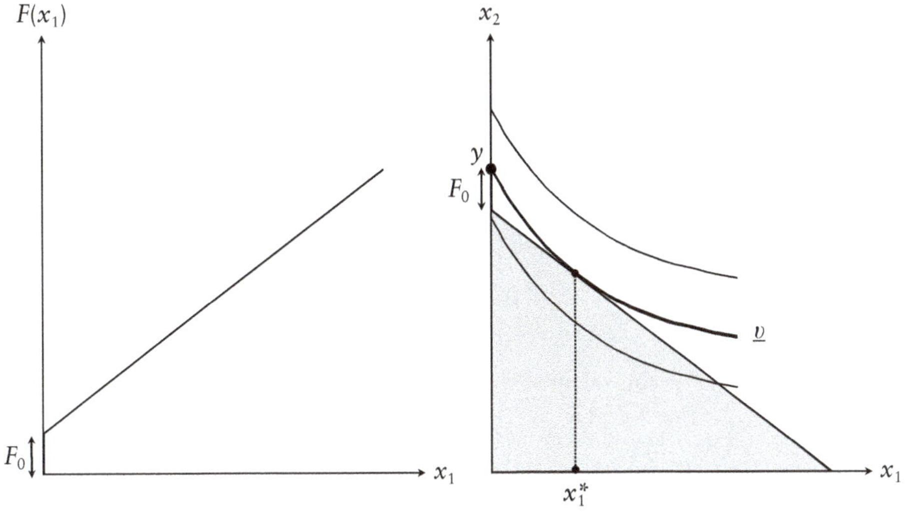

Figure 11.2 An exploitative contract: fee schedule and consumption possibilities

advance the type of charging scheme that will be adopted—that is going to emerge from the firm's optimisation problem. A typical customer has income y (denominated in units of good 2) and preferences represented by the utility function

$$U(x_1, x_2) = \psi(x_1) + x_2 \tag{11.1}$$

where $\psi(0) = 0$, $\psi_x(x) > 0$, $\psi_{xx}(x) < 0$ (subscripts on ψ denote first and second derivatives, following our usual convention); the indifference curves for this utility function are illustrated in Figure 11.2. Notice that the form (11.1) implies that the demand for good 1 has a zero income effect:[1] a convenient feature of such a utility function is that for changes in the fee schedule for good 1 there is a unique measure of consumer welfare: the consumer's surplus is equal to the compensating variation and to the equivalent variation—see page 93 in chapter 4.

The firm sets a fee schedule $F(\cdot)$ as discussed on page 329: from the consumer's point of view this fee schedule simply determines his budget constraint—just take a particular $F(\cdot)$ graph from Figure 11.1 and insert it, upside-down, into the standard diagram of the consumer's choices in commodity space (see for example Figure 11.2). So the individual's consumption of good 2 is

$$x_2 = \left\{ \begin{array}{ll} y - F(x_1) & \text{if } x_1 > 0 \\ y & \text{if } x_1 = 0 \end{array} \right\}$$

? Mini Problems

1 Explain why this is so.

and utility is given by

$$U(x_1, x_2) = \left\{ \begin{array}{cc} y + \psi(x_1) - F(x_1) & \text{if } x_1 > 0 \\ y & \text{if } x_1 = 0 \end{array} \right\}. \tag{11.2}$$

If a consumer has the opportunity of purchasing good 1 under a given fee schedule $F(\cdot)$ then the chosen amount x_1 is positive if and only if the top line in (11.2) is at least as great as the bottom line, in other words as long as the following *participation constraint* is satisfied:

$$U(x_1, x_2) \geq U(0, y). \tag{11.3}$$

This constraint (11.3) is equivalent to the condition

$$\psi(x_1) - F(x_1) \geq 0. \tag{11.4}$$

It is clear from (11.2) that—in the case where '>' holds in (11.4)—if the fee schedule $F(\cdot)$ were to be shifted upwards in Figure 11.1, then the consumer's utility would decrease. Increasing the fee transfers consumer's surplus to the monopolist's profits.

When the consumer can choose any amount x_1, the FOC for an internal solution to the consumer's maximisation problem is given by:

$$\psi_x(x_1) = p(x_1) \tag{11.5}$$

where $p(\cdot)$ is the first derivative of $F(\cdot)$—the unit price of a marginal amount of good 1. This has the interpretation 'marginal willingness to pay = price at the margin.' The solution, x_1^*. to (11.5) can be written implicitly as

$$x_1^*(F) = \left\{ \begin{array}{cc} \varphi(p(x_1^*)) & \text{if } F(x_1^*) \leq \psi(x_1^*) \\ 0 & \text{otherwise} \end{array} \right\}. \tag{11.6}$$

where $\varphi(\cdot)$ is the inverse of the function $\psi_x(\cdot)$.

The firm has freedom to choose whatever the fee schedule it wants subject to the consumer's response specified in (11.6). So its optimisation problem is to choose $F(\cdot)$ to maximise

$$F(x_1^*) - cx_1^* \tag{11.7}$$

where x_1^* is given by (11.6).

First note that if the case '>' were to hold in (11.4) then profits could be increased by shifting $F(\cdot)$ upwards in Figure 11.1. So at the firm's profit-maximising solution the case '=' in (11.4) must hold; in other words we have

$$F(x_1^*) = \psi(x_1^*). \tag{11.8}$$

Therefore the problem (11.7) can be written:

$$\max \psi(x_1) - cx_1 \tag{11.9}$$

subject to (11.6). Because the firm can arbitrarily manipulate the fee schedule it can effectively choose the amount x_1 that will be bought by the consumer, subject to the participation constraint. We will therefore treat (11.9) as a simple 'take-it-or-leave-it' problem: the firm offers a package consisting of

- a quantity x_1 of the good.
- a total sum to pay for this quantity.

The problem for the firm then is just to determine what the quantity x_1 should be.[2]

The FOC for the firm's problem is therefore

$$\psi_x(x_1) - c = 0 \qquad (11.10)$$

or equivalently

$$p(x_1) = c; \qquad (11.11)$$

the price of the marginal unit is everywhere equal to marginal cost, a constant in this special model.

It is clear that the profit-maximising allocation can be implemented by offering the individual a contract consisting of the simple fee schedule

$$F(x_1) = F_0 + px_1 \qquad (11.12)$$

where $p = c$ and F_0 is a fixed charge or 'entry fee' chosen such that (11.8) is satisfied. Given that (11.5) characterises the individual customer's reaction to the fee schedule offered by the firm, using (11.8), (11.6), and (11.12) we find

$$F_0 = \psi(\varphi(c)) - c\varphi(c). \qquad (11.13)$$

The resulting charging scheme is a two-part tariff summarised by the pair (p, F_0), first introduced in section 3.6.3 on page 61. We see now that it involves complete exploitation of the consumer (no consumer surplus is left): the individual consumer is forced to his reservation utility level $\underline{\upsilon} := U(0, y)$. This is illustrated in Figure 11.2: the left-hand side shows the fee schedule set by the firm, where the intercept is F_0 and the slope is simply marginal cost; the right-hand side shows the impact of the fee schedule on the consumer with income y; the reservation indifference curve has been emphasised a little and the attainable set—a triangle with a 'spike' on top—has been shaded in; the boundary of the attainable set is just the fee schedule from the left-hand panel, flipped vertically. However, although it is exploitative, the fee schedule is efficient: unlike a simple monopolistic pricing strategy (such as those outlined in sections 3.6.1 and 3.6.2 of chapter 3), the fee structure given in (11.12) and (11.13) does not force prices above marginal cost.

A final note: as we have seen the two-part-tariff (p, F_0) is not the only way of implementing the profit-maximising outcome. The firm could have actually offered a simple 'take-it-or-leave-it' contract. It is clear that this would have involved a package involving the quantity $\bar{x}_1 := \varphi(c)$ (the equilibrium outcome under the two-part tariff) and a payment of $\bar{F} := \psi(\bar{x}_1)$.

? Mini Problems

2 What about the payment? How is this to be determined by the firm?

Adverse selection: elements of the problem

a	high-valuation customer type
b	low-valuation customer type
τ	taste parameter
$\psi(\cdot)$	utility of good 1
y	individual income
c	marginal cost for good 1
π	proportion of high-valuation types
$F(\cdot)$	fee schedule

11.2.3 Multiple types: full information

It is more interesting to suppose that individuals differ in their tastes for good 1. Instead of the utility function (11.1) we have

$$U(x_1, x_2) = x_2 + \tau\psi(x_1) \tag{11.14}$$

where τ is a taste parameter. This special structure ensures that the indifference curves for different taste types satisfy a regularity requirement known as the *single-crossing condition*. This is illustrated in Figure 11.3 where each a-type indifference curve intersects a b-type indifference curve just once, from top left to bottom right; the a-type curves are unambiguously steeper in the sense that the value of τ is higher than for the b-type curves.[3]

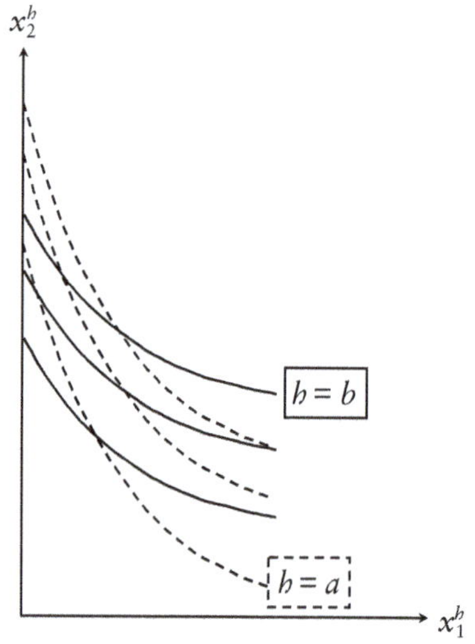

Figure 11.3 Two types: single-crossing condition

? Mini Problems

3 Explain why the single-crossing condition holds for utility functions of the form (11.14).

If the consumer of type τ is offered a fee schedule $F(\cdot;\tau)$ then the FOC for an internal solution to the maximisation problem is now:

$$p(x_1) = \tau\psi_x(x_1). \tag{11.15}$$

This characterises the consumer's solution as long as

$$\tau\psi(x_1) - F(x_1;\tau) \geq 0 \tag{11.16}$$

holds—the participation constraint again. Therefore consumption of good 1 is given by

$$x_1^*(F;\tau) = \left\{ \begin{array}{ll} \varphi\left(\frac{p(x_1^*)}{\tau}\right) & \text{if (11.16) holds} \\ 0 & \text{otherwise} \end{array} \right\}. \tag{11.17}$$

and utility is

$$U(\mathbf{x}^*) = \left\{ \begin{array}{ll} y + \tau\psi\left(x_1^*\right) - F\left(x_1^*;\tau\right) & \text{if (11.16) holds} \\ y & \text{otherwise} \end{array} \right\}. \tag{11.18}$$

Note that utility increases with the taste type.[4]

If the firm could correctly identify each person's taste type then it could set a separate fee schedule conditioned on the type $F(\cdot;\tau)$. Suppose there are many types, indexed by h; the proportion of consumers with taste type τ^h is known to be π^h. The firm's optimisation problem would then be to choose the fee schedule so as to maximise

$$\sum_h \pi^h \left[F\left(x_1^h;\tau^h\right) - cx_1^h\right] \tag{11.19}$$

where x_1^h satisfies (11.17). The firm knows the reaction of each of its customer types and recognises that the fee schedule has to be set in such a way that the participation constraint is satisfied for each type h.

It is clear that the firm could just separate out the problem and select $F\left(\cdot;\tau^h\right)$ so as to maximise each h-component enclosed in the [ ] in expression (11.19). The reason that this can be done is that the firm can isolate each specific group indexed by h as a separate submarket.

The solution is evidently that of section 11.2.2, slightly modified to allow for the distinct taste parameter in each group. Specifically we find that the optimal policy can be implemented by setting price equal to marginal cost

$$p\left(x_1^h\right) = c \tag{11.20}$$

(for all consumer types and all units of the good) and offering a consumer of type h the fee schedule

$$F\left(x_1;\tau^h\right) = F_0^h + px_1 \tag{11.21}$$

? Mini Problems

4 Show this by using (11.18).

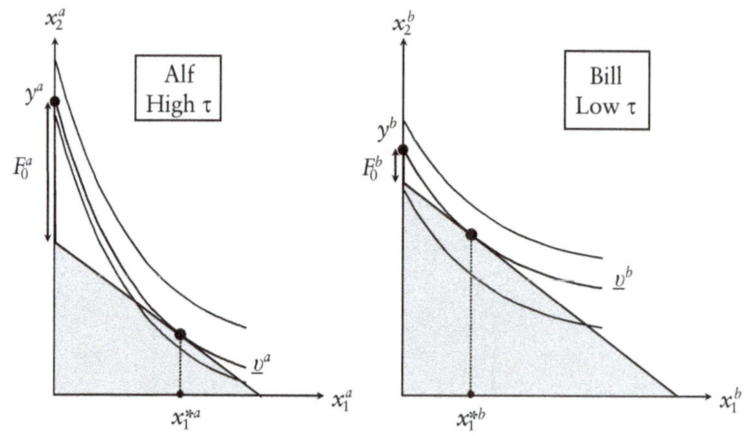

Figure 11.4 Full-information contracts: Consumption possibilities for each type

where $p = c$ and F_0^h is an entry fee that could be different for each group. It is given by

$$F_0^h = \tau^h \psi\left(\varphi\left(\frac{c}{\tau^h}\right)\right) - c\varphi\left(\frac{c}{\tau^h}\right). \tag{11.22}$$

This full-information solution—also known as the *First-Best solution*—is illustrated in Figure 11.4: Alf the a-type consumer has a higher taste parameter τ than Bill the b-type. On inspecting the solution in (11.20)–(11.22) and Figure 11.4 the following points stand out:

- Each person is forced down on to his reservation utility level $\underline{\upsilon}^h$.
- Each person faces the same unit price for the commodity (equal to marginal cost)—the slope of the budget constraint in each half of Figure 11.4.[5]
- Customer types with a higher value of the taste parameter τ pay a higher entry fee and consume more of good 1.[6]
- The firm maximises revenue by use of discriminatory fixed charges F_0^h.
- The outcome is efficient.

In other words the outcome of profit-maximising behaviour under these circumstances is achieved by setting of a fee schedule summarised by the pair $\left(p, F_0^h\right)$ that is extortionary, but not distortionary.[7] As a final comment let us note that once again the firm could

? Mini Problems

5 Draw a diagram similar to the left-hand side of Figure 11.2 to show the fee schedule for the firm in this case.

6 Use (11.17) and (11.22) to show this.

7 The optimal contract takes no account of the customer's income—why?

implement this allocation by offering each of the h-types a tailor-made 'take-it-or-leave-it' contract of the sort described on page 333 specifying an amount $\bar{x}_1^h := \varphi\left(c/\tau^h\right)$ in exchange for a given payment of $\bar{F}^h := \tau^h \psi\left(\bar{x}_1^h\right)$.[8]

11.2.4 Imperfect information

The outcome of the problem addressed in section 11.2.3 is clear-cut and the principles easy to grasp. But it might be argued that the main features of the model and its clear conclusions are likely to be hopelessly unrealistic. In many cases the precise information by taste type is just not going to be available, or at least not at low cost; even in situations where the information is theoretically available it is easy to imagine that firms may be prohibited by law from exercising the kind of discriminatory power that the model implies. One way or another it makes sense to consider the possibility that the firm cannot get access to, or is not allowed to use, the personal information that has been presupposed in section 11.2.3. So we now move from a model of explicit interpersonal discrimination by the firm to one of self-selection by the customers in the face of the apparently neutral fee schedule that the firm chooses to specify.

Although we are now going to focus on the problems of a lack of information it is important to recognise that in order to make the model precise and well structured we will assume that rather a lot of things are well known. In particular, we assume that the form of the utility function (11.14) and the distribution of types τ is common knowledge.

For the purposes of exposition we are going to take a simplified version of the distribution of tastes. Suppose that there are just two types of consumer a and b with taste parameters τ^a, τ^b such that

$$\tau^a > \tau^b \tag{11.23}$$

as before and that there are proportions π, $1 - \pi$ of a-types and b-types, respectively. The values of τ^a, τ^b, and π are all known by the firm and by all its potential customers. We will further assume that a person of type h has income y^h which, in view of (11.18), is the utility attained if he chooses not to consume good 1.

? Mini Problems

8 A question involving little more than flipping the diagram, changing notation, and modifying the budget constraint. In answering it check the answer to Mini Problem 3 in Chapter 5 (page 537).

Suppose leisure is commodity 1 and all other consumption is commodity 2. Alf and Bill are endowed with the same fixed amount of time and amounts y_0^a, y_0^b respectively of money income (measured in units of commodity 2). Alf and Bill each have the utility function (11.14) with $\tau^a > \tau^b$ (Alf values leisure more highly). Alf and Bill consider selling their labour to a monopsonistic firm; they have the same marginal productivity w. Because the firm is a monopsony it can demand an up-front payment of F^h from worker h as a condition of agreeing to employ h and can offer each worker h a different wage w^h.

(a) Write down the budget constraint for worker h giving total money income y^h (in terms of commodity 2) as a function of ℓ^h, labour supplied by h.

(b) Draw a diagram analogous to Figure 11.4 in (ℓ, y)-space to illustrate the full-information contracts that the firm will offer. Briefly describe the solution.

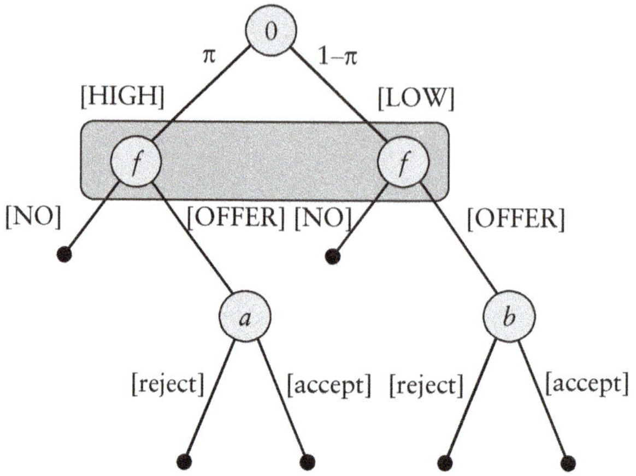

Figure 11.5 Screening: extensive-form game

As noted in the introduction we can see the core of the argument as the equilibrium of a Bayesian game. Here the situation is that the firm is involved in a *screening* process that can be outlined using Figure 11.5. The stages of the game are as follows:

0. 'Nature' makes the move that determines whether a particular customer is of [HIGH] or [LOW] type as far as the demand for the product is concerned. The probability of being a high-demand type is π.
1. The firm decides whether to offer a fee schedule.
2. The customer, knowing his type (a or b) decides whether or not to accept the contract implicit in the fee schedule.

This is just a sketch to clarify the timing of the various players' moves: the payoffs will be specified in detail below. As a final preliminary point we ought to note a further subtlety that may be relevant to some situations of asymmetric information. The customer's behaviour, having accepted the contract, may reveal something about the otherwise private information on tastes or other personal characteristics. Is this revelation important? Clearly this depends on the kind of contractual situation that is relevant for the particular economic problem that is being analysed. Roughly speaking we can imagine two versions of this situation

Version 1 There is a continuing relationship between client and provider—as between an insurance company and the insured person. Under these circumstances it may be that the contract could be invalidated by material information that subsequently comes to light: this might apply if what we have labelled 'taste' is in fact an unverifiable characteristic (health status?) that is of special relevance to the firm.

Version 2 Alternatively the economic problem may be no more than a one-off meeting of customer and supplier at the supermarket checkout. In this case information revealed in the transaction is of no further use.

We will see that most of the analysis goes through in the same way, albeit with slightly different interpretation, whichever of the two versions we take to be relevant.

The problem

From the above it is clear that the monopolist would want to offer fee schedules (p, F_0^a) and $\left(p, F_0^b\right)$ with $F_0^a > F_0^b$. But if it is possible for a high-demand a-type consumer to masquerade as a b-type—i.e. to claim a b-type contract, though he 'should' have an a-type contract—then he would certainly do so, because utility is decreasing in the component F_0: it always pays to find a contract with a lower fixed charge. This is a standard example of the problem of 'adverse selection'. If so then, de facto, we have a situation known as *pooling* where different types get exactly the same contract. The monopolist's profits are lower under pooling relative to the full-information solution. But can it avoid this situation? Should it do so?

The answers to these questions are yes and yes. To see why examine Figure 11.6. Suppose that the situation regarding private information corresponds to Version 1 described above.[9] The slope p of each of the budget lines in each case is equal to marginal cost c. Under the full-information solution the firm can offer the a-type customer a contract characterised by the two-part tariff (p, F_0^a) that forces the customer on to the reservation utility level $\underline{\upsilon}^a$, but which will be (just) accepted: the a-type consumes at point $\mathbf{x}^{*a}$ on

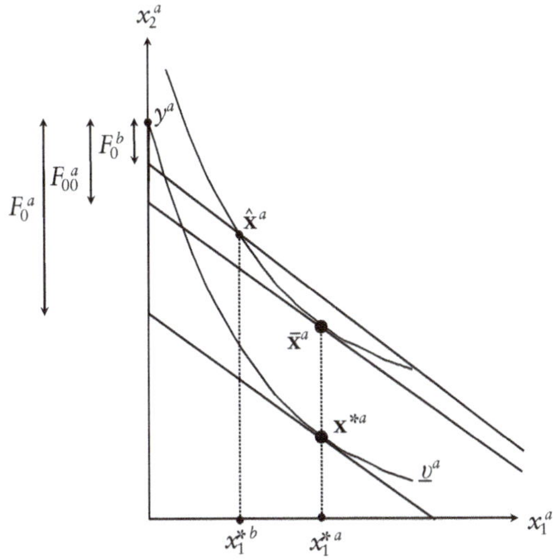

Figure 11.6 Possibility of masquerading

? Mini Problems

9 Show that the same conclusions can be reached in Version 2 if the firm offers its customers a choice of just two quantity-and-payment packages (x_1^{*a}, z^a) and $\left(x_1^{*b}, z^b\right)$ where the zs are the two specific (total) payment amounts. What are the appropriate values of z^a and z^b in this version of the story?

the bottom budget constraint. But if an a-customer can masquerade as a b-type he would clearly be better off consuming x_1^{*b} and paying just $F_0^b + px_1^{*b}$ in order to do so[10] (point $\hat{\mathbf{x}}^a$ on the topmost budget constraint). Now suppose that the firm changed the contract intended for the a-types to the two-part tariff (p, F_{00}^a) as illustrated by the middle budget constraint. Now an a-type would be (just) willing to accept this modified contract giving him consumption $\bar{\mathbf{x}}^a$ rather than pretend to be a b-type: note that the points $\hat{\mathbf{x}}^a$ and $\bar{\mathbf{x}}^a$ lie on the same indifference curve. This means that by persuading the a-type customers to move from $\hat{\mathbf{x}}^a$ to $\bar{\mathbf{x}}^a$ the firm can increase its profits relative to the masquerading outcome (the a-types are paying a fixed charge of F_{00}^a rather than F_0^b) without, of course, making any of its customers worse off.[11]

There is an alternative argument that is also illuminating. Again start with the pooling situation where the a-types find it worthwhile masquerading as b-types. But now suppose that the firm alters the fee structure by changing the b-type contract from $\left(p, F_0^b\right)$ to $\left(p + dp, F_0^b - dF_0^b\right)$ where dp is a small positive number and dF_0^b is calculated to keep a low-valuation b-type exactly on the reservation utility level $\underline{\upsilon}^b$ at the new, higher unit price; we have in fact[12]

$$\frac{dF_0^b}{dp} = x_1^b. \tag{11.24}$$

Furthermore, because this change isolates a pure substitution effect it is clear that

$$\left.\frac{dx_1^b}{dp}\right|_{U^b\left(\mathbf{x}^b\right)=\underline{\upsilon}^b} < 0. \tag{11.25}$$

Consider the effect of this change in contract on the utility of each of the two types: by construction the change in the b-type's utility is zero and, if an a-type attempts to continue the masquerade by reducing consumption just like the b-types, then the change in a-type utility is given by[13]

$$\frac{dU^a\left(\hat{\mathbf{x}}^a\right)}{dp} = \left[\tau^a - \tau^b\right]\psi_x\left(x_1^b\right)\left.\frac{dx_1^b}{dp}\right|_{U^b\left(\mathbf{x}^b\right)=\underline{\upsilon}^b}$$

which, by (11.23) and (11.25), must be strictly negative. What this means is that the small change in the b-contract leaves a genuine b-type no worse off, but would make any a-type masquerading as a b-type strictly worse off. So, by choosing a sufficiently large, compensated increase in the unit price in the b-contract the firm could separate the two types by making it worthwhile for a-types to choose the a-contract. In so doing, of

? Mini Problems

10 Why would an a-type not just take the b contract and consume an amount x_1^{*a} of good 1 anyway?

11 Take the labour-monopsony example of Mini Problem 8. Who has an incentive to misrepresent himself?

12 Use (11.15) and (11.18) to show why this is so.

13 Use (11.15) and (11.24) to establish this.

course, the firm will increase profits from what would have happened in the pooling situation (although not back to the profit level attainable under full information).

With the use of either of these two lines of argument we have established a negative, but important, result.

Theorem 11.1 No pooling

It is not optimal for the firm to propose payment schedules that lead the consumers to pool.

An approach

However, all this is suggestive: we have not yet established what the optimal policy of the firm should be if it cannot observe the taste parameter that affects the utility and behaviour of each of its customers. Let us see how this can be tackled.

First let us recognise the limitations on the firm in its quest for profit-maximising fee schedule. We know that it cannot condition the fee schedule upon the taste parameter τ, but perhaps it could use the information from customer demands for each type to improve its planning. All a-types will consume the same amount x_1^a and all b-types will consume the same amount x_1^b; the amounts x_1^a and x_1^b can be forced to be different by appropriate choice of fee schedule.

So the firm's objective function can now be written

$$\pi\left[F\left(x_1^a\right) - cx_1^a\right] + [1-\pi]\left[F\left(x_1^b\right) - cx_1^b\right]. \tag{11.26}$$

Here we can also interpret this expression probabilistically: the firm makes contact with a customer, but does not know what the customer's taste parameter is: the customer has taste τ^a with probability π (taste τ^b otherwise) and (11.26) then represents expected profits. The firm's problem is to find a fee schedule $F(\cdot)$ to maximise (11.26) subject, of course, to the participation constraint of each consumer type (11.4) but also to a constraint that ensures that no one has an incentive to reveal false information. This problem differs from that of section 11.2.3 because of these extra *incentive-compatibility* constraints: we can refer to this version as the information-constrained or *second-best* contract problem.

For convenience write

$$F^a := F\left(x_1^a\right)$$

$$F^b := F\left(x_1^b\right)$$

the total fee charged to someone with an a-type or a b-type contract respectively. We have already seen that there is usually more than one way of implementing a particular contract—see for example the equivalent two-part tariff and the take-it-or-leave-it contract in the full-information case. To solve the monopolist's second-best optimisation problem it is convenient to use the amounts sold to each customer (x_1^h) and the total payments (F^h) as controls and treat the problem as though it were one of selecting a take-it-or-leave-it offer. Later we will return to the question of the shape of the fee schedule.

So the problem can now be written:

$$\max_{\{x_1^a, x_1^b, F^a, F^b\}} \pi\left[F^a - cx_1^a\right] + [1-\pi]\left[F^b - cx_1^b\right] \tag{11.27}$$

subject to

$$\tau^a \psi\left(x_1^a\right) - F^a \geq 0 \tag{11.28}$$

$$\tau^b \psi\left(x_1^b\right) - F^b \geq 0 \tag{11.29}$$

$$\tau^a \psi\left(x_1^a\right) - F^a \geq \tau^a \psi\left(x_1^b\right) - F^b \tag{11.30}$$

$$\tau^b \psi\left(x_1^b\right) - F^b \geq \tau^b \psi\left(x_1^a\right) - F^a. \tag{11.31}$$

Constraints (11.28) and (11.29) are the participation constraints—as before these are required to ensure that the a-types and the b-types respectively stay in the market for good 1 rather than just consuming their bundle of other goods. Constraints (11.30) and (11.31) are the incentive-compatibility constraints that are required to prevent individuals from misrepresenting information about themselves: (11.30) ensures that an a-type would prefer the contract intended for him rather than a b-type contract; (11.31) is the counterpart to ensure that b-types do not masquerade as a-types.

Before proceeding to derivation of a solution it is useful to see whether the problem specified in (11.26)–(11.31) can be simplified. This is done by analysing whether each of the constraints is relevant at the optimum:

- First, note that if '>' were to hold in (11.29), then also one would have $\tau^a \psi\left(x_1^a\right) - F^a > 0$;[14] if so it would be possible for the firm to increase profits by increasing both F^a and F^b. This obviously means that the firm is not already maximising profits and so it must be the case that at the optimum:

$$\tau^b \psi\left(x_1^b\right) - F^b = 0. \tag{11.32}$$

- Next, if '>' were to hold in (11.30) then this would imply that $\tau^a \psi\left(x_1^a\right) - F^a > 0$;[15] but in turn this would mean that profits could be increased by increasing F^a, without violating the incentive-compatibility constraints. This again must mean that the firm is not maximising profits, so that at the optimum

$$\tau^a \psi\left(x_1^a\right) - F^a = \tau^a \psi\left(x_1^b\right) - F^b. \tag{11.33}$$

- Third, given (11.33), we must have:[16]

$$\tau^a \psi\left(x_1^a\right) - F^a > 0.$$

? Mini Problems

14 Show this by using (11.23) and (11.30).

15 Show this by using (11.23) and (11.32).

16 Show this by using (11.33) and (11.32).

- Finally, if '=' were to hold in (11.31) then this would imply that $x_1^a = x_1^b$.[17] But this is ruled out by Theorem 11.1, so at the optimum we must have

$$\tau^b \psi\left(x_1^b\right) - F^b > \tau^b \psi\left(x_1^a\right) - F^a.$$

So inpractice two of the constraints—the participation constraint of the high-valuation customer a and the incentive-compatibility constraint of the low-valuation customer b—can be dropped because they are never binding at the optimum. This means that the problem (11.26)–(11.31) can indeed be simplified since we only need to worry about constraints (11.32) and (11.33).

The solution

In the light of this reasoning the firm's optimisation problem can now be written as a Lagrangean incorporating just two constraints:

$$\begin{aligned} \max_{\left\{x_1^a, x_1^b, F^a, F^b\right\}} \quad & \pi\left[F^a - cx_1^a\right] + [1-\pi]\left[F^b - cx_1^b\right] \\ & + \lambda\left[\tau^b \psi\left(x_1^b\right) - F^b\right] \\ & + \mu\left[\tau^a \psi\left(x_1^a\right) - F^a - \tau^a \psi\left(x_1^b\right) + F^b\right] \end{aligned} \tag{11.34}$$

where λ is the Lagrange multiplier for the participation constraint of the low-valuation b-types (11.32) and μ is the Lagrange multiplier for the incentive-compatibility constraint of the high-valuation a-types (11.33).

The FOCs for (11.34) are

$$-\pi c + \mu\tau^a \psi_x\left(\tilde{x}_1^a\right) = 0$$

$$-[1-\pi]\,c + \lambda\tau^b \psi_x\left(\tilde{x}_1^b\right) - \mu\tau^a \psi_x\left(\tilde{x}_1^b\right) = 0$$

$$\pi - \mu = 0$$

$$1 - \pi - \lambda + \mu = 0$$

where $\tilde{x}_1^a$ and $\tilde{x}_1^b$ denote the second-best values of the consumption of good 1 by a-types and b-types, respectively. From these we see immediately $\mu = \pi$ and $\lambda = 1$:[18] so, substituting for these, we get

$$\tau^a \psi_x\left(\tilde{x}_1^a\right) = c, \tag{11.35}$$

$$\tau^b \psi_x\left(\tilde{x}_1^b\right) = \frac{c}{1 - \frac{\pi}{1-\pi}\left[\frac{\tau^a}{\tau^b} - 1\right]}. \tag{11.36}$$

? Mini Problems

17 Use (11.33) to show this.

18 Give a brief verbal interpretation of these values of the Lagrange multipliers.

The left-hand side of these two expressions is just the marginal rate of substitution for the two types of customer. Therefore at the optimum we have

$$\mathrm{MRS}^a_{21} = \mathrm{MRT}_{21}$$

$$\mathrm{MRS}^b_{21} > \mathrm{MRT}_{21}.$$

This establishes an important principle:

Theorem 11.2 No distortion at the top

In the second-best fee-setting optimum for the firm the high-valuation types are offered a non-distortionary (efficient) contract.

The principle carries over to richer models where there are many taste levels: the model then typically involves an incentive-compatibility constraint to make sure that a person of each valuation type has no incentive to masquerade as someone from the valuation type below; and for the topmost valuation type the contract ensures that MRS = MRT.

The solution (11.35, 11.36) implies that:[19]

$$\tilde{x}^a_1 > \tilde{x}^b_1 \tag{11.37}$$

and that, when we compare the second-best contract with the full-information contract, we find

$$\tilde{x}^a_1 = x^{*a}_1 \tag{11.38}$$

$$\tilde{x}^b_1 < x^{*b}_1. \tag{11.39}$$

These facts are illustrated in Figure 11.7. Let us examine the structure of this figure.

The right-hand panel represents the income y^b and preferences of Bill, a typical b-type. The point $\mathbf{x}^{*b}$, lying on the reservation indifference curve $\underline{\upsilon}^b$, represents the consumption bundle that Bill would get under the full-information contract: here $\mathrm{MRS}^b_{21} = \mathrm{MRT}_{21}$, the slope of the pale line in this figure. The second-best contract would give Bill a consumption bundle $\tilde{\mathbf{x}}^b$, also on the reservation indifference curve, but at a point where $\mathrm{MRS}^b_{21} > \mathrm{MRT}_{21}$; the total fee in the second-best contract is given by the amount $\tilde{F}^b$. Note that in contrast to the treatment of the high-valuation a-types the second-best optimal policy requires that the firm introduce a 'distortion' into the price that effectively faces the b-types.

The left-hand panel shows the corresponding situation for Alf, a typical a-type. The point $\mathbf{x}^{*a}$, on the reservation indifference curve, represents the consumption bundle that Alf would get under the full-information contract. The point with coordinates

? Mini Problems

19 Show that (11.37) is always true if the proportion of low-valuation types is non-zero. Explain what features of the model yield the results in (11.38) and (11.39).

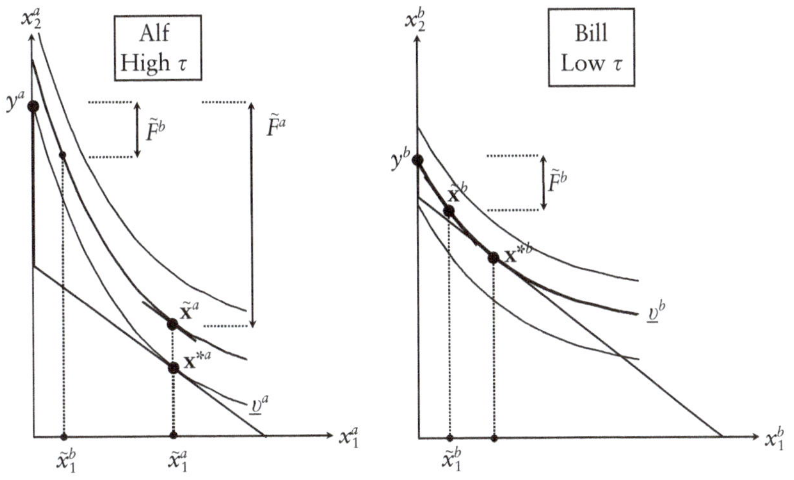

Figure 11.7 Second-best contracts: consumption for each of the two types

$\left(\tilde{x}_1^b, y^a - \tilde{F}^b\right)$ represents the consumption that Alf would get if he took a b-type contract and the indifference curve through this point represents the incentive-compatibility constraint for an a-type. The second-best contract would give Alf a consumption bundle $\tilde{\mathbf{x}}^a$ that lies on this indifference curve; this contract requires a total payment $\tilde{F}^a$; and for both the full-information and the second-best contract $\text{MRS}_{21}^a = \text{MRT}_{21}$.

Clearly this set of optimal contracts for the two types of customer could be implemented by 'take-it-or-leave-it' offers for each type. But what sort of shape would the fee schedule have? Clearly a simple two-part tariff will not work (the two types have to be at different marginal rates of substitution), but a multi-part tariff would. This is illustrated in Figure 11.8: panel (1) shows the fee schedule—note the kink at point $\underline{x}_1$—and panel (2) the implied attainable set with which a person of either type would be confronted, given this fee schedule;[20] as in Figure 11.2 flip the fee schedule in panel (1) to get the boundary of the attainable set in panel (2). However, a multi-part tariff is not the only way of specifying a suitable fee schedule—one could do the job with, for example, a 'quantity discount' system.[21]

The monopoly paradigm used here is a convenient vehicle for conveying some basic points about the model of hidden characteristics. But it is important to realise that the issues are by no means confined to the special case that has been discussed:

- First note the essentially same simple monopolistic framework can be adapted to a variety of economic issues. For example, the analysis is easily extended to monopsony

? Mini Problems

20 How would the firm rationally choose point $\underline{x}_1$?

21 Draw a diagram similar to those used above to show that this outcome could also be implemented by the firm using a system of quantity discounts. [Hint: check the answer to Mini Problem 17 in Chapter 4 on page 84.]

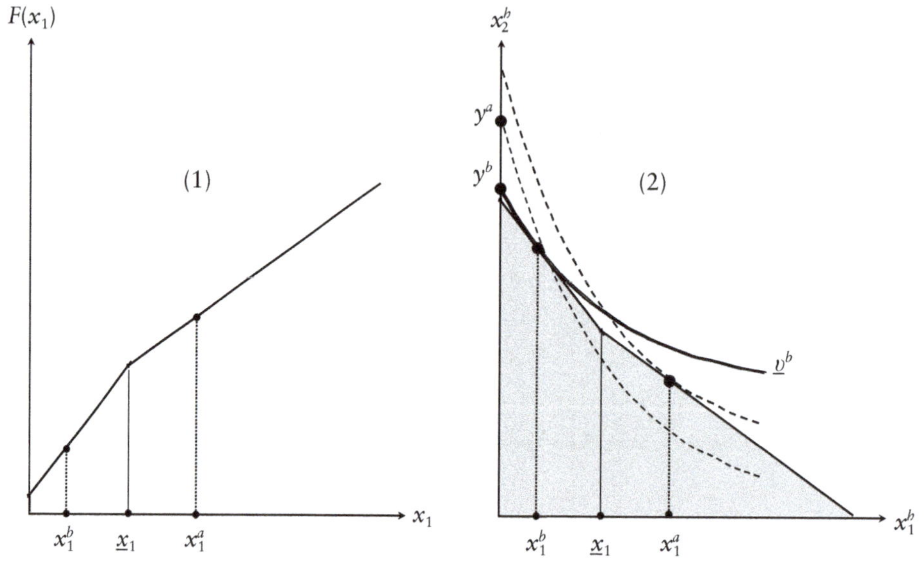

Figure 11.8 Second best contract: fee schedule and attainable set

in the labour market, as in Mini Problems 8 and 11;[22] Exercises 11.2 and 11.3 at the end of this chapter further illustrate the way the same paradigm can be applied. Chapter 12 builds on this structure when considering further the principles of economic design.

- Second, we can relax the monopoly assumption to examine the adverse selection model under competition.

Example 11.1

At several points we have noted that a suitable way of thinking about the type of contract offered by the firm to its customers is as a selection of simple 'packages'. It could be that we are talking about literal packages here. In response to a *Wall St Journal* headline 'Why Do Hot Dogs Come in Packs of 10 and Buns in 8s or 12s?' Gerstner and Hess (1987) suggest that the type of model presented in this section

continued...

? Mini Problems

22 Take the labour-monopsony example of Mini Problems 8 and 11.

(a) Show how the optimal labour contract is determined by using an analogy to Figure 11.7.
(b) What is the analogy to Figure 11.8 (2)? Show that this implies a kind of 'overtime' payment.

...continued

may satisfactorily explain the regularity of package sizes and price structure. This phenomenon is a way of segmenting the market in the face of consumer heterogeneity combined with asymmetric information.

11.2.5 Adverse selection: competition

The results on the full-information and second-best solutions for the monopolist are generally applicable and provide powerful insights; they also form the basis of an important branch of economic policy prescription (see chapter 12). But what would happen if the monopoly power of the firm in sections 11.2.1 to 11.2.4 were to be undermined? To address this question we can apply the same reasoning as in section 3.5 of chapter 3.

Given the fee schedule $F(\cdot)$, the profits that the firm makes out of the sales to a type-h customer are

$$\Pi^b = F\left(x_1^b\right) - cx_1^b. \tag{11.40}$$

This can be interpreted in Figure 11.9: the piecewise linear schedule $F(\cdot)$ is the fee schedule copied across from Figure 11.8 depicting the second-best contract. The straight line labelled $C(\cdot)$ is the cost function—again taken from the model in sections 11.2.1 to 11.2.4. So the vertical distance labelled Π^a in Figure 11.9 is therefore the amount of profit that the firm would make on each customer who accepts an a-type contract; a similar interpretation applies for Π^b. So, if this situation were the case for one particular firm, a potential entrant could seize the opportunity of making a profit by introducing a fee schedule that lies somewhere between $C(\cdot)$ and $F(\cdot)$. Such a revised fee schedule would obviously increase the utility of at least one of the customer types.

If there were no barriers to entry (by assumption fixed costs are zero) then it is clear that this would go on until Π^h in (11.40) is zero—i.e. until $p\left(x_1^h\right) = c$ for each customer type. The outcome would be an efficient allocation with $\mathrm{MRS}_{21}^h = \mathrm{MRT}_{21}$, for all types h.

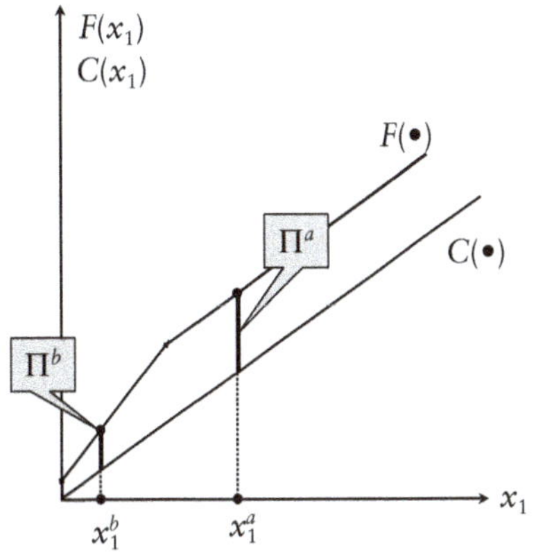

Figure 11.9 Profit on the contract

11.2.6 Application: insurance

The insurance market provides an important application of the insights from the hidden-characteristics model; in particular it highlights a particularly difficult aspect of the problem of adverse selection. We will assume that there is free entry to the insurance market so that the model of section 11.2.5 is the appropriate starting point.

Outline of the model

A heterogeneous group of people have effectively a stochastic endowment: all individuals have the same initial wealth y_0 and if state RED occurs all of their wealth remains available for their consumption; but if state BLUE occurs they suffer a loss worth L in monetary terms. The probability of this loss differs between subgroups: each member of subgroup h knows that he or she faces a probability of loss equal to π^h.

To see the situation facing the individuals let us use Figure 11.10, a variant on the diagram that we have already seen in Figure 8.24. The figure has been split into two halves to make it easier to see what is happening to each of two types of individuals. Point P_0 with coordinates $(y_0, y_0 - L)$ corresponds to the prospect that would face each individual in the absence of insurance. There is a high-risk group of a-types (left-hand side of diagram) for each of whom preferences are represented by the dashed indifference curves—the slope where each curve intersects the 45° line is $(-)\,\frac{1-\pi^a}{\pi^a}$; there is also a low-risk group of b-types (right-hand side of diagram) for each of whom preferences are represented by the solid indifference curves that intersect the 45° line at $(-)\,\frac{1-\pi^b}{\pi^b}$;[23] clearly

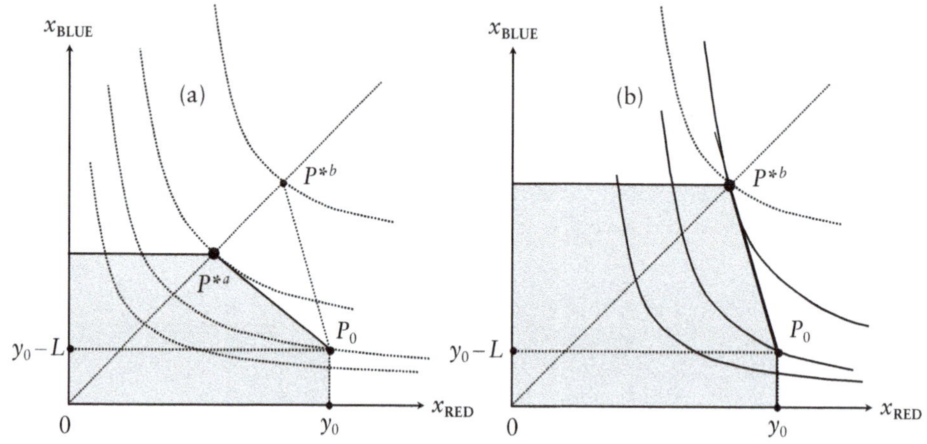

Figure 11.10 Insurance: efficient risk allocation

? Mini Problems

23 Why must the indifference curves have slope

$$-\frac{1-\pi^h}{\pi^h},\; h = a, b$$

where they cross the 45° line?

$\pi^a > \pi^b$—compare this with the right-hand panel of Figure 8.13. Both sets of indifference curves are of the form:

$$\pi^b u\left(x^b_{\text{BLUE}}\right) + \left[1 - \pi^b\right] u\left(x^b_{\text{RED}}\right) = \text{constant} \tag{11.41}$$

The form (11.41) ensures that the single-crossing condition is satisfied.[24]

Take a simple version of the individual's optimisation problem. Suppose an individual can buy insurance coverage z^b at a price p^b per unit of coverage where $0 \leq z^b \leq L$. This means that if state BLUE occurs (so that the individual suffers the loss L) he has the comfort of knowing that the insurance company will pay him z^b; the total premium required for this service is

$$\kappa^b = p^b z^b. \tag{11.42}$$

Then the expressions in (11.41)

$$x^b_{\text{BLUE}} = y_0 - L - \kappa^b + z^b$$

$$x^b_{\text{RED}} = y_0 - \kappa^b$$

give consumption in the two possible states of the world. Clearly $x^b_{\text{BLUE}} \gtreqless x^b_{\text{RED}}$ as $z^b \gtreqless L$. We can characterise an insurance contract as a pair (z^b, p^b); an b-type chooses the coverage in the light of the price p^b and the risk of loss, π^b. Given utility of the form (11.41) the FOC for the maximisation problem is

$$\left[1 - p^b\right] \pi^b u_x\left(x^b_{\text{BLUE}}\right) - p^b \left[1 - \pi^b\right] u_x\left(x^b_{\text{RED}}\right) = 0 \tag{11.43}$$

if $0 < z^b < L$, with '=' replaced by '$\geq$' in (11.43) if $z^b = L$ at the optimum. Condition (11.43) implies

$$\frac{u_x\left(x^b_{\text{BLUE}}\right)}{u_x\left(x^b_{\text{RED}}\right)} = \frac{p^b}{1 - p^b} \frac{1 - \pi^b}{\pi^b} \tag{11.44}$$

for an interior solution. Clearly the right-hand side is $\gtreqless 1$ as $p^b \gtreqless \pi^b$. So

- If $p^b = \pi^b$ the individual would buy full insurance ($z^b = L$).
- If $p^b < \pi^b$ the individual would want to over-insure.
- If $p^b > \pi^b$ the individual would under-insure.

In the first of these three cases—full insurance at fair rates—the attainable set for the a-types would be the shaded area bounded by the line P_0P^{*a} in part (a) of Figure 11.10; and for b-types it would be the shaded area bounded by P_0P^{*b} in part (b) of Figure 11.10—the reasoning underlying this shape for the attainable set was given on page 208.

Now consider the model from the point of view of a firm providing insurance. Using the expression (11.42) for the premium, the expected profit made by a firm on a contract

? Mini Problems

24 Use an argument similar to that of Mini Problem 3 to show that this is true. What would happen if individuals differed in terms of *risk aversion* as well as their risk characteristic?

sold to a type-h customer is:

$$\Pi^h = \kappa^h - z^h \pi^h$$
$$= \left[p^h - \pi^h\right] z^h. \tag{11.45}$$

From this we can immediately see that the firm avoids making a loss wherever it can set the price for insurance such that $p^h \geq \pi^h$. This also has a nice interpretation in Figure 11.10. We know that the slope of the line P_0P^{*a} is $\frac{1-\pi^a}{\pi^a}$ (left-hand side of the diagram); an insurance contract located along this line will have $p^a = \pi^a$ and so make zero profits; contracts to the left and below this line will have $p^a > \pi^a$ yielding positive profits; likewise contracts located above the line will have $p^a < \pi^a$ and would be loss-making. The same interpretation applies to the line P_0P^{*b} on the right-hand side of the diagram (the extra point P^{*b} marked on the left-hand side will be discussed in a moment).

However, we should note that in the expression for profits of a typical firm in (11.45) there is a subtle difference from the discussion of section 11.2.5. In the standard model of a firm or firms serving a market, although the customer's characteristics will affect their demand, they do not enter directly into the expression for profit—see equation (11.40); but here the characteristics of each customer do explicitly enter the expression for profit, because the probability π^h is going to determine the expected value of the firm's payout to a type-h person.

Full information

From these observations it is but a single step to see what would happen if there were full information in the insurance market. Figure 11.10 shows the situation where the characteristic that determines the individual's risk type is costlessly observable (sex? age?). Because individuals' characteristics are observable, insurance companies can condition the price of insurance on each person's probability of loss. The competitive price for insurance is obviously $p^h = \pi^h$ and so the high-risk a-types get complete insurance coverage at P^{*a} and low-risk b-types get complete coverage at P^{*b}.

Adverse selection: pooling

Now let us examine the difficult, but perhaps realistic, case where insurance companies cannot easily discern the differences between risk types. To make the point we shall make the extreme assumption that they know *nothing* about an individual customer's risk type, but they do know the distribution of risk types in the population. To make this specific let us work again with the case of two risk classes, the high-risk a-types and the low-risk b-types.

First let us note that the possibility of one type of customer trying to masquerade as another—the adverse selection problem—will inevitably arise, just as in section 11.2.4. To see this we need only glance back at Figure 11.10: it is clear that prospect P^{*b} lies on a higher a-type indifference curve than does P^{*a}, corresponding to the contract that a-types are 'supposed' to take. This is clear from part (a) of the diagram where the line P_0P^{*b} has been copied across from part (b). But if high-risk a-types successfully masquerade as low-risk and take b-type contracts (i.e. if they can attain point P^{*b}) this is a financial disaster for the insurance companies: since $p^b < \pi^a$ the companies will expect to lose money on every contract they sell to an a-type and, by assumption, at the point of sale the firms do not know which risk type the customer really is.

So, suppose instead that the insurance firms make no attempt to distinguish between customer types; they just try to sell insurance at a price that would be expected to make them break even in the population as a whole. If the proportion of a-types is γ then the probability of loss in the pooled group consisting of both types is

$$\bar{\pi} := \gamma\pi^a + [1-\gamma]\,\pi^b \tag{11.46}$$

and we can assume that the values of π^a, π^b, and γ are all common knowledge. Obviously $\pi^a > \bar{\pi} > \pi^b$. So, in the light of our argument on page 349, if an insurance company offers a single price for insurance at $p = \bar{\pi}$ then the low-risk people would want to under-insure and the high-risk people would want to over-insure.

Is such a 'pooling' approach viable? Let us assume that Version 1 of the private-information problem (page 338) applies so that evidence of false information may void the contract.[25] In Figure 11.11 the indifference curves for the two types and the initial endowment point P_0 is just the same as for Figure 11.10. The figure replicates the full-information contracts from Figure 11.10 as two pale lines; it also illustrates the offer of a pooled contract as the line segment $P_0\bar{P}$ with slope $\frac{1-\bar{\pi}}{\bar{\pi}}$. As we have just argued, because the price of insurance $p = \bar{\pi}$ is high for the a-types they would not

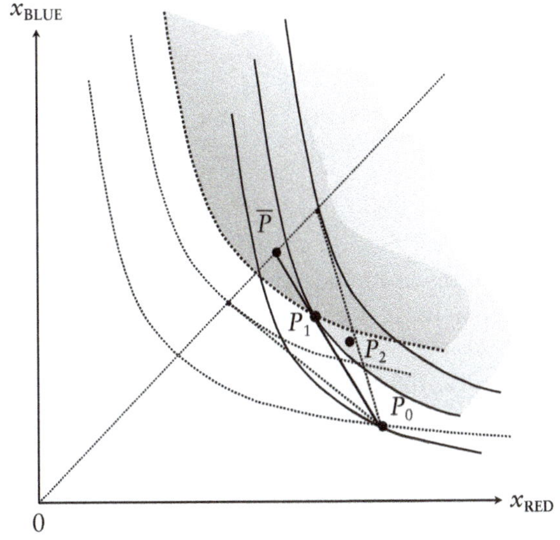

Figure 11.11 Insurance: pooling

? Mini Problems

25 Suppose, instead, that version 2 is the relevant one: how can the argument about pooling then be made?

want to insure fully and would therefore choose partial coverage that leaves them with a prospect represented by the point P_1, where the budget line is tangent to a b-type indifference curve. If a-types looked only at the terms of the contract and ignored what the other customers in the market might be doing then they would choose $\overline{P}$ (actually they would really like to move to a point further out along $P_0\overline{P}$ but we have supposed that over-insurance is ruled out). But, because information about the distribution of risk-types is common knowledge, the decision that b-types would rationally make is also common knowledge; so the a-types would use their common sense about this and realise that if they actually selected $\overline{P}$ then they would be revealing their true risk type to the insurance company, with obvious consequences. Better for them to behave just like b-types and also go to point P_1.

But the situation where everyone takes the partial-coverage contract represented by P_1 cannot be an equilibrium. The reason is the possibility of a contract such as P_2: if this were available the a-types would prefer it to P_1 and the b-types would not (check the 'better-than-P_1' sets that have been shaded in); furthermore if a firm offered P_2 it would expect to make money because the slope of P_0P_2 is less than $\frac{1-\pi^a}{\pi^a}$, so the price at which it offers the contract is greater than π^a. Contract P_2 thus clearly dominates P_1 and so we have established:

Theorem 11.3

There is no pooling equilibrium in the insurance market.

Of course this result is not entirely surprising in view of Theorem 11.1 that referred to monopoly provision.

Adverse selection: separation

So we have to return to the idea of the firms trying to offer separate contracts to the different risk types. We know that this has to be done in such a way that the high-risk a-types would not find it worthwhile masquerading. Figure 11.12 depicts the indifference curves and endowment point just as for figures 11.10 and 11.11; once again it shows the full-information budget line for each of the two risk types. Draw the a-type indifference curve that passes through the full-coverage point P^{*a}; the point $\tilde{P}^b$ is where this curve intersects the a-type's full-information budget line (the slope of $P_0\tilde{P}^b$ is $\frac{1-\pi^b}{\pi^b}$). Obviously if insurance companies allowed b-types complete freedom of choice on coverage they would choose full coverage ($z^b = L$); but then, as we have seen, the issue of a-types misrepresenting themselves as b-types would emerge. So, suppose the insurance companies restrict the choice of the low-risk b-types to just the coverage $\tilde{z} < L$ that allows them to reach the point $\tilde{P}^b$. Clearly at, or near to this point, the contracts offered will separate the two groups: a-types will voluntarily go to P^{*a} (the contract (L, π^a)) and b-types will select $\tilde{P}^b$ (the contract $(\tilde{z}^b, \pi^b)$). The a-indifference curve through P^{*a} and $\tilde{P}^b$ forms the incentive-compatibility constraint. Have we therefore found an equilibrium?

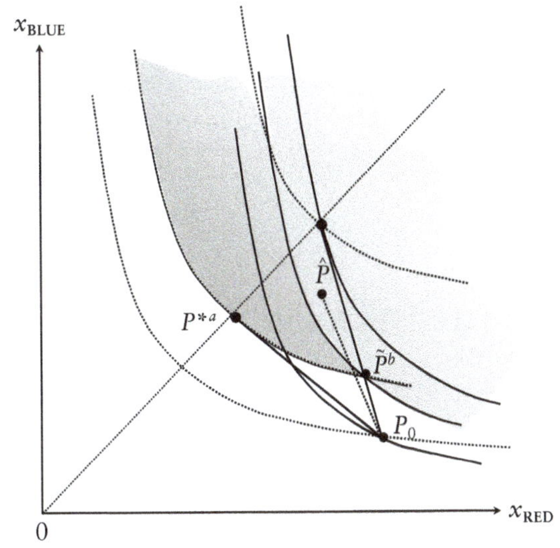

Figure 11.12 Insurance: Separating equilibrium?

Maybe, but maybe not. The answer depends on the exact distribution of types in the population.[26] Suppose there are a lot of low-risk types—γ is fairly small—such that the slope $\frac{1-\bar{\pi}}{\bar{\pi}}$ (where $\bar{\pi}$ is given by 11.46) is that depicted by the line $P_0\hat{P}$. Since $\hat{P}$ lies in the 'better-than' sets of both types (the shaded areas in Figure 11.12) it is clear that this pooling contract would dominate the pair of contracts that we have just suggested as a separating equilibrium.

So in addition to the strong negative conclusion that there is no pooling equilibrium we also have to accept the possibility that there may be no separating equilibrium either. Why does this difficulty arise in the insurance model when, after all, no hint of this arose in sections 11.2.4 and 11.2.5? The principal difficulty is one that we have already flagged up: the insurance problem is somewhat special in that the profits to be made on each customer depend directly on the customer's hidden characteristic, the risk type π^h.

Example 11.2

The market for individual health insurance is a classic example of the issues discussed here. Using the National Medical Care Expenditure Survey for the US Browne (1992) shows, amongst other things that high-risk consumers of insurance are subsidised by low-risk consumers—a classic feature of adverse selection. But are the apparent

continued...

? Mini Problems

26 Suppose the value of γ were the same as that used in the construction of Figure 11.11. Could a pooling contract somewhere on the line $P_0\overline{P}$ be used to dominate the separating contract depicted in Figure 11.12?

...continued

losses in consumer welfare that arise from adverse selection offset by beneficial cost reductions ? Cutler and Reber (1998) answer this question in the context of a case study of employees of Harvard University.

11.3 Hidden characteristics: signalling

Let us move on to a subtly different kind of 'hidden-characteristics' problem: one where the informed party makes the first move in the game. The move involves making a *signal* which, depending on the economic context of the model, could be a costly action such as physical investment, advertising, acquiring an educational certificate, or could be a costless message.

To motivate a simplified version of the model let us suppose that individuals differ in terms of some hidden talent τ. This talent is valuable in the market, but the difficulty is that the owner of the talent cannot convince the buyers in the market that he has it without providing a signal. If it is not possible to provide this signal a market equilibrium may not be possible.

11.3.1 Costly signals

We will begin with the case where the 'signal' costs something in terms of forgone income. Imagine that we are considering a labour market in which there are able ('above-average') people with type τ^a and 'below-average' people of type τ^b where $\tau^a > \tau^b$. There is a single type of job and potential employers know what the true product of a τ^a-person or a τ^b-person would be if only they could tell which was which at the time of making a job offer.

The story can be encapsulated in the oversimplified extensive-game form depicted in Figure 11.13, which is based on Figure 10.18. It is oversimplified because the figure assumes that workers can only make binary decisions on education (whether or not to invest) and firms can only make binary decisions on wages (high or low wage): of course in each case the decision would involve choice from a continuum of alternatives. The game has the following stages:

0. 'Nature' makes the move that determines whether each individual worker is of [LOW] or [HIGH] type. The probability of being a low type is π.
1. The individual workers decide on whether to spend time and money acquiring an educational certificate.
2. Firms make wage offers. The wage offers are simultaneous so that this stage of the game is effectively Bertrand competition (compare section 10.4.2).
3. Each worker decides whether or not to accept a particular offer.

Let us examine stages 1-3 in more detail.

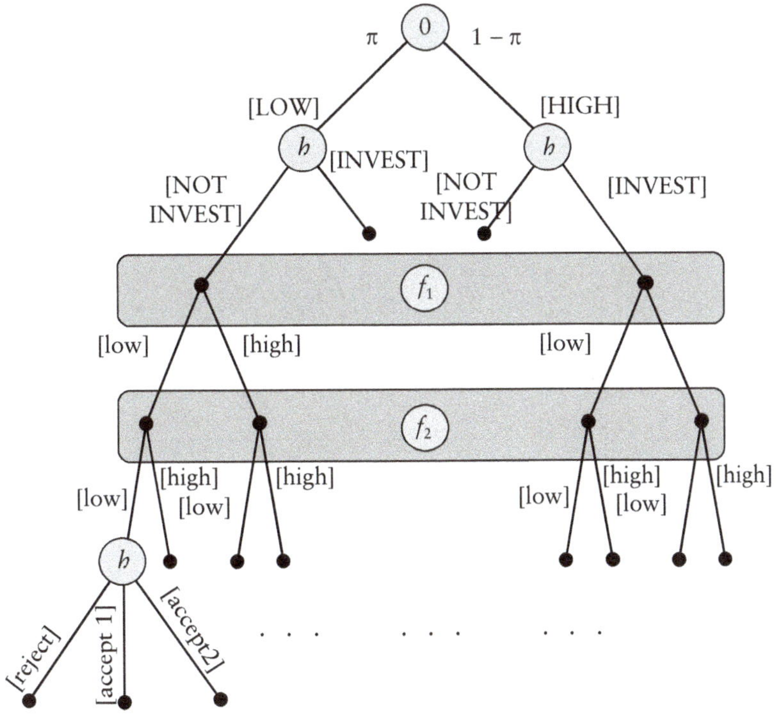

Figure 11.13 Signalling by workers

Educational 'investment'

Focus first on the decision by individuals about whether or not to acquire education. Suppose it is common knowledge that talent at doing the job is identical to talent at achieving educational credentials. Then it may be worth the person's while to 'invest' in the acquisition of such credentials. Note that the present discussion is in sharp contrast with the model discussed in Exercise 6.6 (page 143): in the simple model of Exercise 6.6 education worked like investment in human capital in that it actually enhanced a person's productivity. Here the person's education does *nothing* to enhance his or her productive ability: it is simply an informative message or credential that flags up innate talent; hence the quotation marks around the word investment. Of course one could construct more complicated combined models where education performs both the function of signalling inner qualities and the function of enhancing productivity.

The acquisition of education requires time and money on the part of the student. Let completed education be measured continuously by $z \geq 0$. The cost of acquiring education z for a person with talent τ is known to be $C(z, \tau) \geq 0$ where C is a differentiable function such that

$$C(0, \tau) = 0, \tag{11.47a}$$

$$C_z(z, \tau) > 0, \tag{11.47b}$$

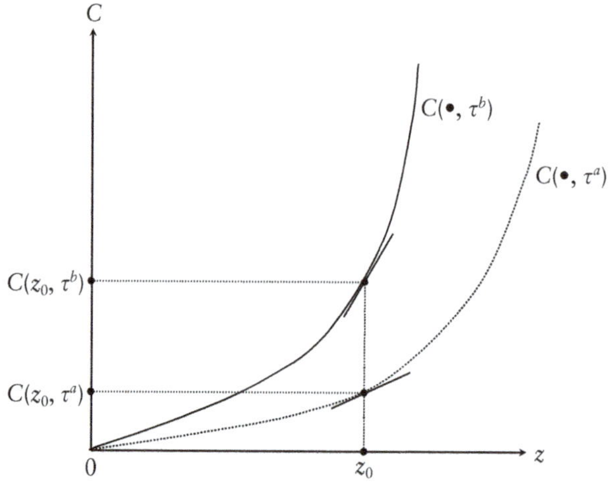

Figure 11.14 Costly signals

$$C_{zz}(z,\tau) > 0, \qquad (11.47c)$$

$$C_{z\tau}(z,\tau) < 0. \qquad (11.47d)$$

This cost structure is illustrated in Figure 11.14. Note that a person of any type faces a positive rising marginal cost of acquiring education and an able person incurs lower cost for a given amount of education (so that $C(z_0, \tau^a) < C\left(z_0, \tau^b\right)$ on the left-hand axis) and, for a given education level, has lower marginal cost (the slopes of the two schedules at z_0).

Assume that the talent indicator does not enter directly into the worker's utility function. The only thing that individuals care about is income so that we can measure utility directly in terms of income. However, if we were to write utility (net income) in terms of gross income y and education z we have:

$$v\left(y, z; \tau\right) := y - C(z, \tau); \qquad (11.48)$$

the dependency of v on τ, of course, arises from the fact that greater talent reduces the cost of net income.[27] Assume that a worker's gross income y is completely determined by his wage: if all know that the wage is conditioned on the 'signal' that they provide through the acquisition of educational credentials then a type-τ worker will choose z to maximise

$$w(z) - C(z, \tau) \qquad (11.49)$$

where $w(\cdot)$ is the wage schedule that the workers anticipate will be offered by firms.

? Mini Problems

27 Show that condition (11.47d) means that the indifference curves for the utility functions (11.48) satisfy the single-crossing condition. Illustrate this for the case where the cost of education is given by $C(z, \tau) = \frac{1}{\tau}z^2$.

Signalling: elements of the problem

a	'able' ('above-average') worker type
b	'below-average' worker type
$C(\cdot)$	cost of education
τ	ability parameter ('talent')
z	amount of education
$\phi(\cdot)$	productivity
$w(\cdot)$	wage schedule
π	proportion of low-talent types
$\tilde{\pi}(\cdot)$	firms' belief function

The firms' decisions

Firms make wage offers based on the information that is available to them about the supposed productivities of the workers. They know that an individual with talent τ would have a marginal productivity $\phi(\tau)$ and so, if there were full information about these talents firms would set a wage schedule based on talent—each person would get paid exactly $\phi(\tau)$. In the absence of full information the firms form beliefs about the talent of the individual workers presenting themselves for employment. At the beginning of the game all they know is that the probability of drawing a below-average person at random from the population is π. After the workers have made their education decisions the firms update their beliefs on the basis of this new information: they set a schedule of the form that has been assumed in (11.49). The beliefs form an integral part of the equilibrium model. It remains to characterise what that equilibrium is.

We need to distinguish between two types of equilibria, separating and pooling equilibria, corresponding to the cases that we have previously distinguished in models of adverse selection (see pages 341 and 350-352).

Separating equilibria

First we examine the case where the educational certificate seems to fulfil exactly the job that it is supposed to do. Higher ability is signalled by an appropriate education qualification and workers of each type are paid exactly their marginal products, $\phi(\tau^a)$ and $\phi(\tau^b)$. We can reason through the Bayesian equilibrium verbally.

If each type of agent is maximising then neither would have an incentive to switch to using the other's signal. So for the talented a-types we have

$$\phi(\tau^a) - C(z^a, \tau^a) \geq \phi\left(\tau^b\right) - C\left(z^b, \tau^a\right) \tag{11.50}$$

—i.e. the net benefit of being correctly identified as an a-type must be at least as great as the benefit from being misidentified as a b-type. Likewise for the b-types:

$$\phi(\tau^a) - C(z^a, \tau^b) \leq \phi\left(\tau^b\right) - C\left(z^b, \tau^b\right). \tag{11.51}$$

From this we can see that rationally the able individuals would acquire more education than the below-average individuals.[28] Furthermore, in the very simple model where there are just two types, at the optimum

$$z^b = 0. \tag{11.52}$$

The reason for this is that everyone knows that there are only two productivity types, education has no innate productivity-enhancing rôle and so there is no gain to b-types in buying any education at all. Conditions (11.50) and (11.51) then become[29]

$$C\left(z^a, \tau^a\right) \le \phi\left(\tau^a\right) - \phi\left(\tau^b\right) \tag{11.53}$$

$$C\left(z^a, \tau^b\right) \ge \phi\left(\tau^a\right) - \phi\left(\tau^b\right) \tag{11.54}$$

which implies a restriction on the value of z^a to be a credible signal of a type-a individual. Specifically z^a must lie in the interval $[z_0, z_1]$ where z_0 is the value that would ensure that condition (11.54) becomes an equality and z_1 is the value that would ensure that condition (11.53) becomes an equality.

Consider the position of the firms. If a firm is confronted with two groups of workers, one of which comes with a positive level of education and the other with zero education then, since it knows that there are only two levels of talent in the population, it can reasonably form the belief that the educated applicants are the high-talent ones. So if $\tilde{\pi}(z)$ denotes the firm's subjective probability that a person with education z has low ability, the belief system is very simple:

$$\left.\begin{array}{l} \tilde{\pi}(0) = 1 \\ \tilde{\pi}(z^a) = 0 \end{array}\right\}. \tag{11.55}$$

In the light of this the firm can confidently set a *wage schedule* $w(\cdot)$ conditioned on education such that

$$\left.\begin{array}{l} w(0) = \phi\left(\tau^b\right) \\ w(z^a) = \phi(\tau^a) \end{array}\right\}. \tag{11.56}$$

Thus there is, in fact, a family of separating equilibria in which both (11.55) and (11.56) hold, where low-talent optimal education is given by (11.52) and high-talent optimal education lies somewhere in the interval $[z_0, z_1]$.[30] This situation is illustrated in Figure 11.15.

Take panel (i) first. Firms offer a wage schedule indicated by the curve $w(\cdot)$: this fixes an attainable set for any worker shown by the solid shaded area. A typical indifference curve for a type-a person is labelled $\upsilon(\cdot, \tau^a)$ (utility is increasing in the 'north-west' direction) and it is clear that such a person maximises utility over the attainable set exactly at

? Mini Problems

28 Show that condition (11.51) implies $z^a > z^b$.

29 Show this.

30 Use a diagram like Figure 11.15 to show how z_0 and z_1 are determined.

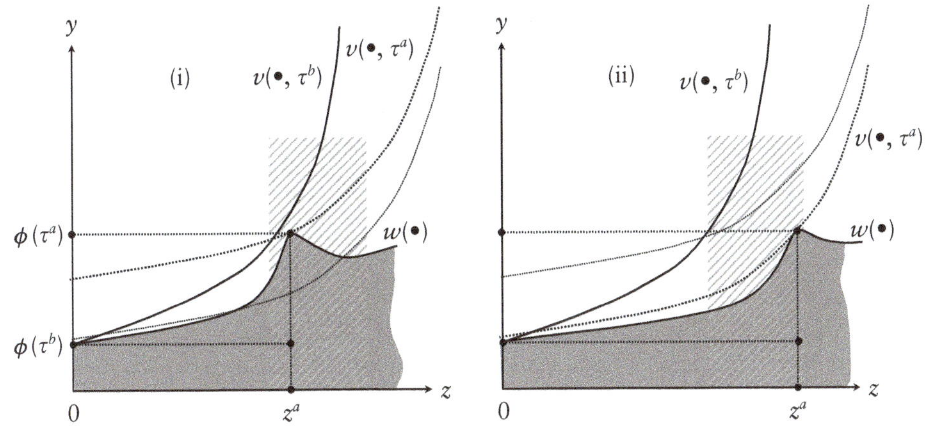

Figure 11.15 Separating equilibria

the point with coordinates $(z^a, \phi(\tau^a))$. Likewise a type-b (with indifference curve labelled $v(\cdot, \tau^b)$) evidently maximises utility at point $(0, \phi(\tau^b))$.

However, we could expect there to be other separating equilibria and one of these is illustrated in panel (ii) of Figure 11.15. The story set out in the preceding paragraph could be repeated for this case, but with a higher value for z^a and with the type-a people on a lower indifference curve. In both panels the cross-hatched area demarcates the interval $[z_0, z_1]$ and we could have constructed other separating equilibria with z^a somewhere else in this interval.

Notice that in either panel we could have redrawn the $w(\cdot)$-schedule, as long as the resulting attainable set for the workers still induced them to choose points $(z^a, \phi(\tau^a))$ and $(0, \phi(\tau^b))$ respectively. The shape of the $w(\cdot)$-schedule at other values of z is a reflection of the firms' beliefs about workers' types in situations that do not show up in equilibrium. So the characterisation of the perfect Bayesian equilibrium leaves open the form that these out-of-equilibrium beliefs may take.[31]

Finally, which of these equilibria 'should' emerge in practice? The requirements for the perfect Bayesian equilibrium do not help us to select among the separating equilibria, but common sense may do so. Since an a-type's payoff is strictly decreasing in z^a throughout the interval $[z_0, z_1]$ it is clear that any equilibrium that puts $z^a > z_0$ is Pareto dominated by the equilibrium at z_0: education level z_0 is the minimum-cost signal for the talented a-types. It would be nice if we could just assume away the Pareto-dominated equilibria as uninteresting, but from chapter 10 we know that there are important cases of strategic interaction that inevitably end up at Pareto-dominated outcomes. We need a proper argument, based on the reasonableness of such an equilibrium.

? Mini Problems

31 Let $z' \in [z_0, z_1]$. Sketch the $w(\cdot)$ schedule that corresponds to the beliefs that a worker with $z < z'$ must be of type b and all others are of type a. Show the separating equilibrium in this case.

So is an equilibrium at $z^a > z_0$ 'reasonable'? Note that, from Figure 11.15, such an equilibrium requires a wage schedule that sets $w(z') < \phi(\tau^a)$ for any z' greater than z_0 and less than z^a. This means that firms must be assigning the belief $\tilde{\pi}(z') > 0$. But imagine that someone were observed to deviate from the equilibrium and to choose z'. Who could this be? Even if a b-type were confident that he could pass himself off to firms as an a-type in this region it is clear that the b-type indifference curve passing through $(z', \phi(\tau^a))$ lies strictly below the b-type indifference curve through $(0, \phi(\tau^b))$ (z' lies in the interior of the interval marked by crosshatching). So, even if he were wildly optimistic, a b-type would know that he would be worse off than in the separating equilibrium and so would *never* go to $(z', \phi(\tau^a))$. Therefore, if there were someone at z' out of equilibrium, it would have to be an a-type. An *intuitive criterion* of assigning beliefs out of equilibrium therefore suggests that $\tilde{\pi}(z') = 0$, for any such z'. The implication of this intuitive criterion is that the only separating equilibrium worth considering is the one that places the a-types at $(z_0, \phi(\tau^a))$ and the b-types at $(0, \phi(\tau^b))$.

Pooling equilibria

On the other hand, it may be the case that there are equilibria where the educational signal does not work. It may be that the distribution of talents and the relationship between marginal productivity and talent is such that no one finds it profitable to 'invest' in education or, possibly, that all workers find themselves compelled to acquire the same specific amount of education z^*. Again let us reason through the equilibrium conditions.

Here the firms have no usable information on which to update their beliefs—by assumption all workers present themselves with the same credentials and are therefore indistinguishable. So firms' beliefs are just those derived from common knowledge about the distribution of talent in the population. The expected marginal productivity is[32]

$$\mathcal{E}\phi(\tau) := [1 - \pi]\,\phi(\tau^a) + \pi\phi(\tau^b)$$

and this is exactly the wage offered to any job applicant.

Figure 11.16 panel (i) represents a typical pooling equilibrium. As in Figure 11.15 the wage schedule forms the boundary of the attainable set for any worker (the heavily shaded area). However, in this case it is clear that a worker of either type will maximise utility at the point $(z^*, \mathcal{E}\phi(\tau))$. Given the wage schedule on offer type a people find that the cost of acquiring additional education to distinguish themselves from the common herd does not pay. On the other hand b-type people dare not enter the market with less than z^* for fear of being identified as below-average and therefore being paid less than the net income that they currently receive. If this is to be a serious worry to this group then it must be true that $z^* < z_2$ where z_2 is found from[33]

$$C\left(z_2, \tau^b\right) = [1 - \pi]\left[\phi(\tau^a) - \phi(\tau^b)\right] \qquad (11.57)$$

Mini Problems

32 Under what circumstances would it be in the interests of all workers if educational institutions were banned?

33 Show this. Use a diagram similar to Figure 11.16 to show how z_2 is determined.

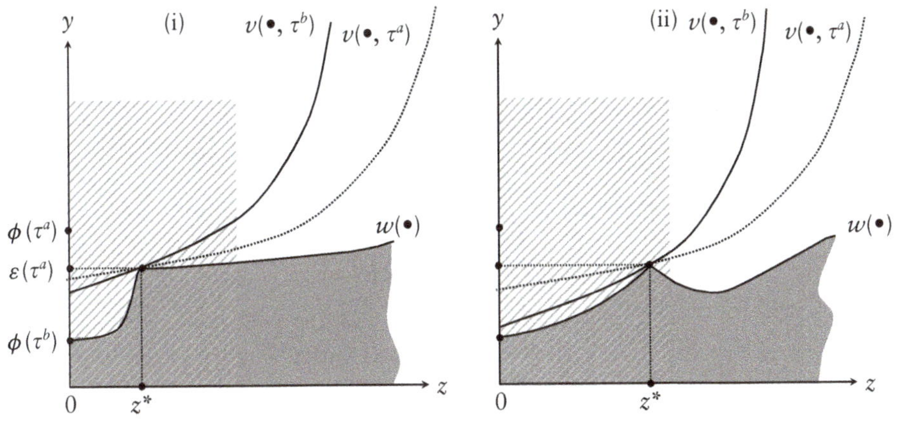

Figure 11.16 Pooling equilibria

However, once again the equilibrium is not unique. Panel (ii) shows another pooling equilibrium that fulfils the conditions described in the previous paragraph but with a higher equilibrium value of z^*. Other such equilibria can be found for values of z^* in the interval $[0, z_2]$ where z_2 is given by (11.57). This range of education values for which pooling equilibria are feasible is indicated by the cross-hatched area in Figure 11.16.[34]

11.3.2 Costless signals

Effectively costless signals are all around us—manufacturers' assurances of quality, promises by service deliverers, and so on. Whether they work is another matter. This is a difficult area so that we will highlight the issue with a simplified example.

There are N risk-neutral persons with a shared project. Each person chooses whether or not to participate, denoted by an effort indicator z^h that can take the values 1 or 0 respectively. Output is given by

$$q = a\left[z^1 \times z^2 \times z^3 \times \ldots\right]$$

where $0 < a < 1$. The output is a public good so that, for all h, consumption is $x^h = q$. Agent h incurs a cost of participation c^h that is known to himself, but unknown to others; it is common knowledge that these costs are rectangularly distributed on the interval $[0, 1]$ (so that $\Pr(c^h \leq c) = c$—see page 515). The net payoff to each agent is simply $x^h - c^h$. Suppose we take this as a simultaneous-move game where the actions are the participation decisions by each agent. Then the Nash equilibrium is $z^h = 0$ for all h, as

? **Mini Problems**

34 However, the intuitive criterion mentioned on page 360 indicates that all of these pooling equilibria should be rejected in favour of the separating equilibrium that places the a-types at $(z_0, \phi(\tau^a))$ and the b-types at $(0, \phi(\tau^b))$. Show why this is so using an argument similar to that on page 360.

long as a is strictly less than 1.[35] The problem is that each runs the risk of incurring cost c^h while getting consumption $x^h = 0$.

However, suppose we introduce a preliminary stage to the game where each agent has the opportunity to signal his or her intention as follows:

1. Each agent announces [YES] or [NO] to all the others.
2. Each agent then decides whether or not to participate.

Then there is an equilibrium in which the following occurs

1. Each agent h announces [YES] if and only if $c^h < a$.
2. Each agent selects $z^h = 1$ if and only if all agents have previously announced [YES].

In this equilibrium agents no longer run the risk of wasted effort since if there are genuinely high-cost individuals present that inhibit completion of the project, this will be announced at the signalling stage of the game.

Obviously there are also equilibria that contains worthless information—for example if everyone announced a decision to participate without checking their own costs first. However, it is clear from the example that it is possible for there to be a signalling equilibrium that imparts useful information, even though the signal is costless.

Example 11.3

For which type of occupations is this type of economic signalling by individuals and screening by firms appropriate? Riley (1979) provides an ingenious statistical test based on individual earnings, education, and occupational data available in the US Current Population Survey. He argues that it is possible to distinguish between screened and unscreened sectors, On the criteria that he suggests, the screened sector includes archivists, librarians, teachers, and school administrators; unscreened occupations include authors, designers, publicity writers, computer programmers, and data-processing repairs; this generally seems to accord with intuition. But the classification also assigns bank officers and public officials to the unscreened sector, which is rather less obvious.

11.4 Hidden actions

Now for a different version of the informational problem. We are going to consider an outline treatment of the 'hidden actions' paradigm in microeconomics. This issue pops up under a variety of names including the 'Principal-and-Agent' problem or (borrowed from the insurance industry) the problem of 'moral hazard'.

? Mini Problems

35 Show that this is true. [Hint: find the probability that h participates on the assumption that each of the other agents participates with given probability π.]

11.4.1 The issue

The main point can be encapsulated in the following brief description. Imagine that one economic actor undertakes a transaction with another in which the outcome is critically affected by a blend of luck and effort on the part of one of the two parties involved. This 'blending' is such that it is impossible to disentangle the separate contribution of luck and of effort to the outcome; it therefore means that it is impossible to set up a verifiable payment system based on effort; it also means that information about a state of the world is partially hidden.

In this thumbnail sketch we have an important component of the elementary theory of contracts. The contract serves as a payment schedule that takes account of the informational problem just described.

However, there is a slight terminological difficulty concerning the two economic actors in this story. The type of problem that we will discuss is essentially a 'master-and-servant' situation where the servant has a motive to pretend to be doing more than he really is in fulfilment of his duties. It is commonly known, perhaps less pejoratively, as the Principal-and-Agent problem; but here the term 'Agent' is rather narrowly defined. Contrast this to the general terms of previous usage of 'agent' as essentially equivalent to 'actor'—i.e. any individual, firm, or other organisation that takes action within one of our economic models. Following the usage of other authors I shall refer to Agent with a capital 'A' when I mean specifically the one in the Principal-and-Agent model, while I have used 'agent' (small 'a') for the general run of the *dramatis personae* in the economic stories considered elsewhere in the book.

11.4.2 Outline of the problem

Alf is hired by Bill to do a job of work. There is a single output q, and Bill the boss (i.e. the Principal) pays Alf, the Agent, a total wage payment w measured in terms of this output. The central problem is that, as they both know, the level of output depends on two factors

1. the amount of effort, z, that Alf decides to put into the job and
2. the state of the world ω (the weather?).

The idea is that effort is just an invisible input in production. The further difficulty is that, as they also both know, it may not be possible to determine the exact contribution of the random influences to output even *ex post*—after the state of the world ω has been realised.

The Principal (Bill) offers the Agent (Alf) a wage w for the work. In principle Alf and Bill may agree to the wage w being tied to (contingent on) q, z, or ω: the way that this is to be done will depend on the information structure of the problem—can z or ω actually be observed? Following the usage of section 11.2 we shall refer to w as a *wage schedule*; discussion of the specification of this schedule needs to be deferred until other parts of the model have been examined.

The time sequence is shown in Figure 11.17. Nature decides on a particular state of the world ([RED] or [BLUE]). Bill, the Principal cannot observe this at the time he draws up a

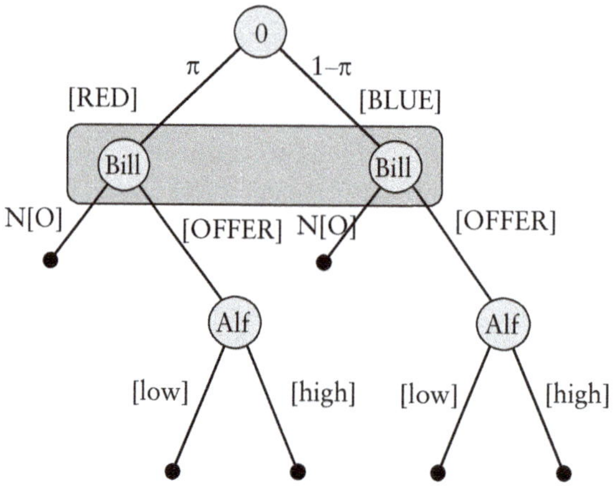

Figure 11.17 Principal-and-Agent

wage schedule. In the light of this wage schedule Alf (who cannot observe the state of the world either) decides whether or not to work hard. Again the payoffs at the last stage of the game will be discussed once we have set out the model details.

However, even before specifying the detail, it is intuitively clear that the possible lack of information will undermine the control that Bill can exercise over Alf. Being forced to use a second-best policy Bill will be able to capture less profit than would have been the case if had full information about Alf's activity. The *agency cost* is the expected net payoff for the Principal under full information less what it is in the second-best situation.

11.4.3 A simplified model

In order to examine the nuts and bolts of the economic problem we start with a simplified version and then (in section 11.4.4) move on to something that is richer and more interesting. The simple version is a 'two-by-two' setup:

- there are just two possible levels of production ('failure', 'success') that can be achieved:

$$q = \overline{q} \text{ or } \underline{q} \text{ where } \overline{q} > \underline{q}.$$

- there are also just two possible levels of effort ('shirk', 'work') by the Agent.

$$z = \overline{z} \text{ or } \underline{z} \text{ where } \overline{z} > \underline{z}.$$

The probability of $\overline{q}$ (success) is $\pi(z)$ where $\pi(\cdot)$ is an increasing function of effort, so that

$$\pi(\overline{z}) > \pi(\underline{z}). \tag{11.58}$$

So whether one gets failure or success depends both on effort and on a random component; working harder biases the distribution in favour of good outcomes. All of this is common knowledge.

Alf the agent has preferences represented by:

$$\mathcal{E}u^a\left(x^a, z\right) \tag{11.59}$$

where u^a is increasing in its first argument (the wage payment) and decreasing in the second argument (effort). If the Agent has no other source of income then

$$x^a = w. \tag{11.60}$$

For the moment we will suppose that Bill as the Principal is risk neutral and gets all the output that is not paid as wages to Alf. So Bill's utility is the expected value of his consumption $\mathcal{E}x^b$, where x^b is given by

$$x^b = q - w. \tag{11.61}$$

As with the discussion of section 11.2 how the two parties interact depends crucially on the availability of information.

Full information

We can be brief here. If Bill can observe exactly how hard Alf is working then we can deduce everything from some elementary reasoning based on the principles we have considered in previous chapters.

Assume that Bill the Boss has first move. He can therefore devise a take-it-or-leave-it contract for Alf the Agent. Because Bill can observe the effort that Alf actually makes, Bill can make the wage contingent on effort such that Alf is forced down on to his reservation utility $\underline{\upsilon}^a$, the utility that Alf could get in some alternative activity.

The participation constraint for this problem is therefore

$$u^a\left(w, z\right) \geq \underline{\upsilon}^a$$

where z is a given effort level. Because Bill can fully observe what Alf does and has the opportunity to set the terms of the transaction he can force Alf to a wage level so that this constraint binds:

$$u^a\left(w, z\right) = \underline{\upsilon}^a \tag{11.62}$$

from which we get $w = w\left(z\right)$ as the wage that will just induce Alf to participate and provide effort level z.

The Principal's aim is to choose the wage offer to maximise his expected payoff $\mathcal{E}x^b$ subject to the constraint (11.62). Formally we could represent this problem as the standard Lagrangean

$$\max_{\{w\}} \mathcal{E}q - w + \lambda\left[u^a\left(w, z\right) - \underline{\upsilon}^a\right] \tag{11.63}$$

but in the two-by-two case we can set out the problem even more simply. Knowing that Alf the Agent can only supply one of exactly two effort levels, Bill as the Principal would correspondingly offer only one of two wages—either $w\left(\underline{z}\right)$ or $w\left(\overline{z}\right)$. These two offers yield, respectively, the following expected payoffs for Bill

$$\overline{\mathcal{E}}q - w\left(\overline{z}\right) \tag{11.64}$$

$$\underline{\mathcal{E}}q - w\left(\underline{z}\right) \tag{11.65}$$

where $\overline{\mathcal{E}}$ denotes the expectation when the probability of success is that generated by high effort, $\pi(\overline{z})$ and $\underline{\mathcal{E}}$ is the corresponding expectation when the probability is that generated by low effort, $\pi(\underline{z})$.

Because Bill can observe and monitor Alf he can, in effect, choose the effort level that Alf will put in. Clearly Bill will make the choice simply on the basis of which of the two expressions (11.64), (11.65) is the greater. Bill will force the higher effort level if, and only if, the gain in expected output $\overline{\mathcal{E}}q - \underline{\mathcal{E}}q$ exceeds $w(\overline{z}) - w(\underline{z})$, the increment in wage needed to get the extra effort. The essence of the story is depicted in Figure 11.18, based on the Edgeworth-box diagram of Figure 8.21 (page 203). The 45° line through 0^a is Alf's certainty line; two families of a-indifference curves have been drawn in, the shallow ones for low effort level $\underline{z}$ (yielding probability to $\pi(\underline{z})$) and the steep ones for high effort $\overline{z}$; likewise there are two shaded areas indicating reservation utility in the low-effort and high-effort cases. Likewise the 45° line through 0^b is Bill's certainty line; Bill being risk neutral has straight-line indifference curves; again two sets have been drawn in corresponding to the two probabilities $\pi(\underline{z})$ and $\pi(\overline{z})$. Given that effort can be observed, Bill's wage offers to Alf can be tailored to z as shown: in this case Bill wants Alf to produce high effort level with the corresponding wage $w(\overline{z})$ (compare this with the answer to Exercise 8.15 on page 224).

Although we do not need it to characterise the solution to this simple problem, it is useful for future reference to check the FOC for the Lagrangean (11.63). Take a given effort level z and differentiate (11.63) with respect to w. We immediately find

$$\frac{1}{u_x^a(w, z)} = \lambda. \tag{11.66}$$

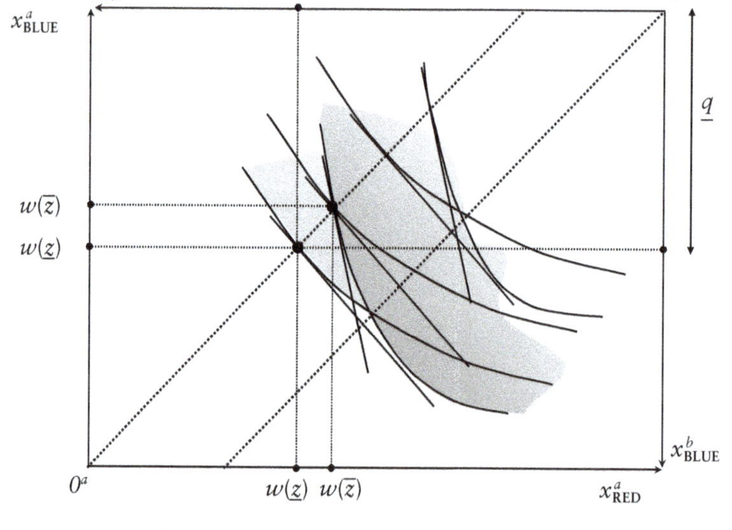

Figure 11.18 Full-information contracts

The interpretation of (11.66) accords with common sense: the marginal cost (measured in terms of consumption) of increasing Alf's utility exactly equals the price on the participation constraint, λ.

Hidden information

Now assume that Bill cannot observe effort z but that q, the combined outcome of effort and the random state of the world ω, is common knowledge. The fact that information is hidden means that it is impossible for Bill to condition the wage offer on the actual level; this limitation loosens his grip on power over Alf.

What Bill can do is condition the wage on the observed output: instead of a payment-for-effort scheme one substitutes a payment-by-results scheme, even though the results are not entirely of the Agent's making. So we now have a wage schedule that will yield $w(\underline{q})$ in the event of failure and $w(\overline{q})$ in the event of success.

If Bill wants Alf to choose the high-effort level $\bar{z}$ then he must ensure that Alf's expected utility at $\bar{z}$ is no less than the utility level $\underline{\upsilon}^a$, the best that he can do for himself elsewhere. In this case the participation constraint now becomes

$$\pi(\bar{z})\, u^a(\overline{w}, \bar{z}) + [1 - \pi(\bar{z})]\, u^a(\underline{w}, \bar{z}) \geq \underline{\upsilon}^a. \tag{11.67}$$

To ensure that Alf does not shirk, the structure of payments must be such that expected utility is higher when Alf works hard. This requires that the following incentive compatibility constraint be satisfied:

$$\pi(\bar{z})\, u^a(\overline{w}, \bar{z}) + [1 - \pi(\bar{z})]\, u^a(\underline{w}, \bar{z}) \tag{11.68}$$

$$\geq \pi(\underline{z}) u^a(\overline{w}, \underline{z}) + [1 - \pi(\underline{z})] u^a(\underline{w}, \underline{z})$$

or equivalently

$$\overline{\mathcal{E}}u^a(w, \bar{z}) \geq \underline{\mathcal{E}}u^a(w, \underline{z}).$$

So, the problem facing Bill, the Principal, is to maximise expected profit subject to the participation and incentive-compatibility constraints; this can be expressed as

$$\max_{\{\underline{w}, \overline{w}\}} \pi(z)\, [\overline{q} - \overline{w}] + [1 - \pi(z)]\, [\underline{q} - \underline{w}]$$

subject to (11.67) and (11.68). Assume that the boss, Bill, wants to ensure that Alf puts in serious effort ($z = \bar{z}$); then, to solve the problem, we set up the Lagrangean

$$\max_{\{\underline{w}, \overline{w}\}} \pi(\bar{z})[\overline{q} - \overline{w}] + [1 - \pi(\bar{z})][\underline{q} - \underline{w}]$$

$$+ \lambda[\pi(\bar{z}) u^a(\overline{w}, \bar{z}) + [1 - \pi(\bar{z})] u^a(\underline{w}, \bar{z}) - \underline{\upsilon}^a]$$

$$+ \mu[\pi(\bar{z}) u^a(\overline{w}, \bar{z}) + [1 - \pi(\bar{z})]\, u^a(\underline{w}, \bar{z})$$

$$- \pi(\underline{z}) u^a(\overline{w}, \underline{z}) - [1 - \pi(\underline{z})] u^a(\underline{w}, \underline{z})]$$

where, again, λ is the Lagrange multiplier on the participation constraint (11.67) and μ is the Lagrange multiplier on the incentive-compatibility constraint (11.68). Differentiating the Lagrangean:

$$
\begin{aligned}
&- [1 - \pi(\bar{z})] + \lambda[1 - \pi(\bar{z})]u_x^a(\underline{w}, \bar{z}) \\
&+ \mu[[1 - \pi(\bar{z})]u_x^a(\underline{w}, \bar{z}) - [1 - \pi(\underline{z})]u_x^a(\underline{w}, \underline{z})] \quad = 0
\end{aligned}
\tag{11.69}
$$

$$
- \pi(\bar{z}) + \lambda\pi(\bar{z})\, u_x^a(\overline{w}, \bar{z}) + \mu\left[\pi(\bar{z})\, u_x^a(\overline{w}, \bar{z}) - \pi(\underline{z})\, u_x^a(\overline{w}, \underline{z})\right] = 0 \tag{11.70}
$$

where u_x^a is the Agent's marginal utility of consumption.

If the function u^a is additively separable then the marginal utility of consumption $u_x^a(\overline{w}, \cdot)$ is independent of z and so, from the FOCs (11.69), (11.70), we get:[36]

$$
\frac{\pi(\bar{z})}{u_x^a(\overline{w}, \bar{z})} + \frac{1 - \pi(\bar{z})}{u_x^a(\underline{w}, \bar{z})} = \lambda \tag{11.71}
$$

$$
\frac{1}{u_x^a(\overline{w}, \bar{z})} = \lambda + \mu\left[1 - \frac{\pi(\underline{z})}{\pi(\bar{z})}\right]. \tag{11.72}
$$

The interpretation of (11.71) can be seen as a straightforward extension of the full-information case (11.66). The left-hand side of (11.71) can be expressed as $\bar{\mathcal{E}}(1/u_x^a(w, \bar{z}))$; so the price of the participation constraint is equal to the expected marginal cost of increasing Alf's utility. Solving for μ from (11.71) and (11.72) we can see that at the optimum $\mu > 0$—the price on the incentive-compatibility constraint is strictly positive in the hidden-information case.[37] From (11.72) we can then see that the marginal cost of utility in the 'success' state equals the price of the participation constraint (λ) plus the price of the incentive-compatibility constraint (μ) times an expression involving the *likelihood ratio* $\pi(\underline{z})/\pi(\bar{z})$.

The outcome is illustrated in Figure 11.19, based on Figure 11.18. Given that Bill wants Alf to exert high effort the participation constraint is represented by the shaded area labelled PC. The incentive-compatibility constraint is indicated by the shaded area labelled IC: notice that the boundary of this passes through the point where Alf's low-effort reservation indifference curve intersects his high-effort reservation indifference curve. The intersection of these two areas (heavily shaded) is the constraint facing Bill in the second-best case. He attains his highest indifference curve, subject to being in this area by offering the contract indicated by the point $(\overline{w}, \underline{w})$. Notice that, in doing so, Bill is offering Alf partial insurance against the consequences of state BLUE occurring.[38]

11.4.4 Principal-and-Agent: a richer model

It is time to generalise the Principal-and-Agent model of section 11.4.3 in three important ways:

? Mini Problems

36 Show how (11.71) and (11.72) are derived.

37 Show this.

38 Show what would happen if Alf were risk neutral.

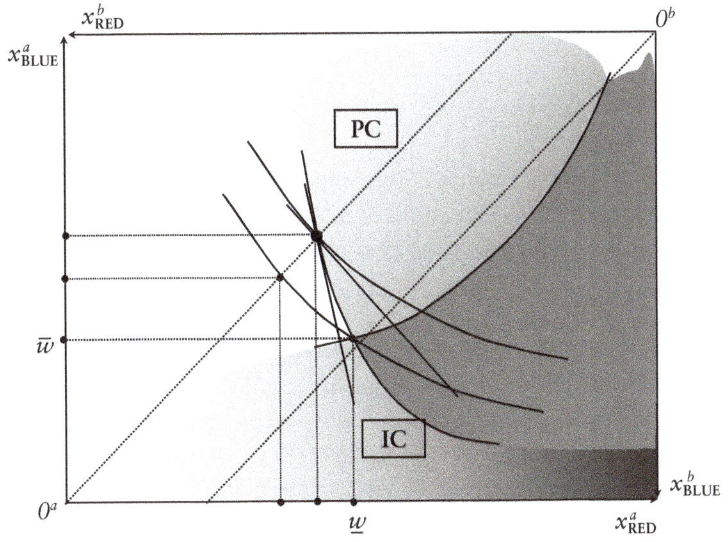

Figure 11.19 Second-best contracts

- We drop the artificial assumption that there are only two possible effort levels to allow for something similar to that in the conventional model of labour supply (section 5.3.1.)
- We likewise allow for the possibility that there is a large number of possible states of the world ω.
- We allow for a more general preference structure on the part of the Principal.

Principal and Agent: elements of the Problem

ω	state-of-the-world
z	effort
q	output
$\phi(\cdot)$	production function
$w(\cdot)$	wage schedule
$u^a(\cdot)$	Agent's cardinal utility
$u^b(\cdot)$	Boss's cardinal utility

However, despite these enrichments of the model we will find that many of the principles of the simple model in section 11.4.3 carry over.

In the generalised version of the Principal-and-Agent story we need to model the dependency of output on effort and the unseen random element. The dependency is represented by the following production function

$$q = \phi(z, \omega) \tag{11.73}$$

where we take z as lying in the interval $[0, 1]$ and $\omega \in \Omega$, some interval of values of the possible states of the world.

Bill the Boss has a von Neumann–Morgenstern utility function which depends solely on his own consumption. As in the simplified model, once he has paid Alf, he has the rest of the output available for his own consumption, so that his utility is

$$\mathcal{E}u^b(x^b) = \mathcal{E}u^b(q - w) \tag{11.74}$$

where $\mathcal{E}$ denotes expectation taken over the probability distribution of the states of the world ω. Alf the Agent has a utility function which depends on his own consumption and on effort z where now $0 \leq z \leq 1$. So his utility is again given by (11.59) and (11.60). Now let us consider the optimisation problems of these two parties.

Alf takes as given the wage schedule—not just a particular wage level—and selects his effort z so as to maximise his utility (11.59). This maximisation takes place subject to the counterpart to (11.67), the participation constraint:

$$\mathcal{E}u^a\,(w, z) \geq \underline{\upsilon}^a. \tag{11.75}$$

In the manner of a Stackelberg leader the Principal (Bill) takes as given the responses of the Agent (Alf) to the wage schedule. Working backward to the stage where he takes the decision, the Principal can build the Agent's responses into his problem of drawing up the wage schedule. We will pursue this optimisation problem under two information regimes, corresponding to those that we briefly reviewed in the simple model of section 11.4.3: where Alf's effort is observable, and where it is not observable.

Observable effort

Suppose Bill can monitor the effort level z being put in by Alf. This is equivalent to both parties, Principal and Agent, being able to determine unambiguously the precise contribution of ω to output. The two parties could then agree to conditioning the wage schedule upon the random element: they would then specify a wage schedule $w(\cdot)$ where $w(\omega)$ is the wage payment to be made if state of the world ω is realised.

Bill the Principal would choose $w(\cdot)$ so as to maximise his own utility. He arranges this by setting, in effect, a wage level for every possible state of the world that could occur (every $\omega \in \Omega$). Moreover, because Bill has complete freedom to specify the wage schedule, and because he can observe the effort level z, he can in effect treat Alf's effort as though it were his own control variable. However, once again, Bill has to do all this in the knowledge that, if he is too demanding, Alf can pack his bags and go and get $\underline{\upsilon}^a$ elsewhere. Bill's problem can be stated as 'choose $w(\cdot)$ to maximise (11.74) subject to (11.73) and the participation constraint (11.75)'. This can be represented as the Lagrangean:

$$\max_{\{w(\cdot),\, z\}} \mathcal{E}u^b\,(\phi(z, \omega) - w(\omega)) + \lambda\left[\mathcal{E}u^a\,(w(\omega), z) - \underline{\upsilon}^a\right]. \tag{11.76}$$

Since $w(\omega)$ may be specified separately for each $\omega \in \Omega$, the first-order conditions for an interior solution to (11.76) can be found in the usual way. We equate to zero the differential of (11.76) with respect to each $w(\omega)$, thus:

$$-u_x^b\left(q - w(\omega)\right) + \lambda u_x^a\left(w(\omega), z\right) = 0 \tag{11.77}$$

for all $\omega \in \Omega$, and we do likewise for the differential with respect to z, so as to give:

$$\mathcal{E}\left(u_x^b\left(\phi(z,\omega) - w(\omega)\right)\phi_z(z,\omega)\right) - \lambda\mathcal{E}u_z^a\left(w(\omega), z\right) = 0 \tag{11.78}$$

where the subscripts denote the appropriate partial derivatives. These two conditions immediately yield:

$$\frac{u_x^b\left(q - w(\omega)\right)}{u_x^a\left(w(\omega), z\right)} = \lambda \tag{11.79}$$

$$\frac{\mathcal{E}\left(u_x^b\left(\phi(z,\omega) - w(\omega)\right)\phi_z(z,\omega)\right)}{\mathcal{E}u_z^a\left(w(\omega), z\right)} = \lambda. \tag{11.80}$$

Combining (11.79) and (11.80) we get

$$\mathcal{E}\left(u_x^b\left(\phi(z,\omega) - w(\omega)\right)\phi_z(z,\omega)\right) - \mathcal{E}\left(\frac{u_z^a\left(w(\omega), z\right)}{u_x^a\left(w(\omega), z\right)}u_x^b\left(q - w(\omega)\right)\right) = 0. \tag{11.81}$$

Since the marginal utilities in (11.79) are positive, we see that the Lagrange multiplier λ is also positive, and thus constraint (11.75) is binding. What this means is that if Bill the boss has perfect information, he drives Alf the agent down on to his reservation utility $\underline{\upsilon}^a$.

Observe also that in the special case where the Principal is risk neutral (so that utility is a constant, independent of ω) the key equation (11.81) may be used to give the result

$$\mathcal{E}\phi_z(z,\omega) = \mathcal{E}\left(\frac{u_x^a\left(w(\omega), z\right)}{u_z^a\left(w(\omega), z\right)}\right) \tag{11.82}$$

or, put in plain language:

expected MRT	=	expected MRS

What we find therefore is that, under these circumstances where effort is observable, optimisation by the Principal (Bill the boss) ensures that the Agent (Alf) acts in a fashion that is familiar from chapters 7 and 9. The expected marginal willingness to supply effort (MRS) exactly equals the expected marginal product of effort (the MRT). This situation—although it forces Alf the agent down on to his reservation utility—is clearly *ex-ante* Pareto efficient. Once again we have the interesting condition of exploitative efficiency.

Unseen effort

Now suppose that it is not possible to observe effort. What this means is that you cannot distinguish the separate roles of z and ω in the production of output. It is equivalent to saying that you cannot directly and costlessly verify which state of the world has occurred: all you can see is a probability distribution of output q. Even though this probability distribution is driven by the weather we cannot introduce weather into the model. However, it is common knowledge that the worker's effort z will shift the distribution. To capture this write the density function of q as $f(q; z)$, where z acts as a shift parameter: the assumed impact of this parameter on the distribution of output is illustrated in Figure 11.20. Notice that we have assumed:

- The support of the distribution of output is bounded above and below.
- The bounds on the support $[\underline{q}, \overline{q}]$ are publicly known.
- The values $\underline{q}$ and $\overline{q}$ are not shifted by z.

Let us introduce the 'proportionate shift' in the probability distribution from a small increase in z:

$$\beta_z := \frac{f_z(q; z)}{f(q; z)}. \tag{11.83}$$

We see that β_z is negative for low values of q, and positive for high values of q, and that[39]

$$\mathcal{E}\beta_z = 0. \tag{11.84}$$

Alf the agent's maximand (11.59) can now be written as

$$\mathcal{E}u^a(w(q), z) = \int_{\underline{q}}^{\overline{q}} u^a(w(q), z) f(q; z) dq. \tag{11.85}$$

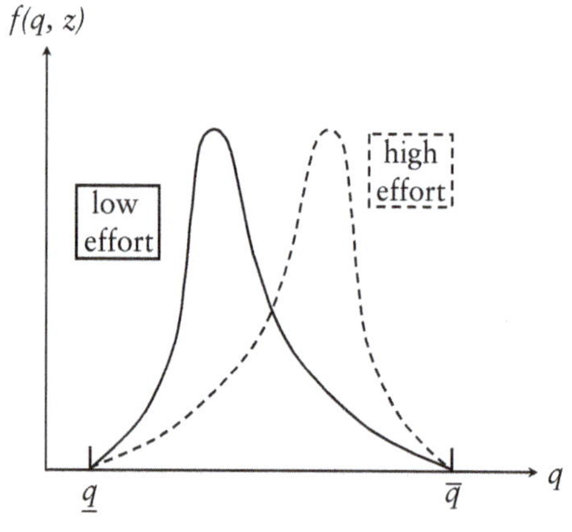

Figure 11.20 Effort shifts the frequency distribution

? Mini Problems

39 Use the standard property of a probability density function to explain why this is so.

Maximising this with respect to z gives the FOC:

$$\frac{\partial \mathcal{E}u^a\left(w(q),z\right)}{\partial z} = \mathcal{E}\left(u^a\left(w\left(q\right),z\right)\beta_z\right) + \mathcal{E}u^a_z\left(w,z\right) = 0. \tag{11.86}$$

The first term in (11.86) gives the marginal change in expected utility if the probability density were to be shifted in the direction of more favourable qs (as illustrated in Figure 11.20); the second term is the expected marginal utility of leisure. Equation (11.86) implicitly determines a particular value of z for any given payment schedule $w(\cdot)$: this behavioural condition acts as an effective constraint on the choice problem that the Principal has to solve in selecting $w(\cdot)$.

Bill the boss chooses the wage schedule $w(\cdot)$—a value $w(q)$ for each realisation of q—and manipulates Alf's effort z. Bill does this so as to maximise his own utility (11.74) subject to two constraints:

- Alf's participation constraint (11.75): Bill must take into account that Alf can exercise his outside option and refuse to accept any wage offer.
- Alf's first-order condition (11.86): Bill recognises that Alf can privately adjust effort z to suit himself.

We can imagine this as in Figure 11.21: Bill's preferences in (w, z)-space—to be found from (11.73) and (11.74)—are depicted by the indifference curves; the boundary of the opportunity set for Bill is given by the (w, z)-values satisfying Alf's FOC (11.86).[40]

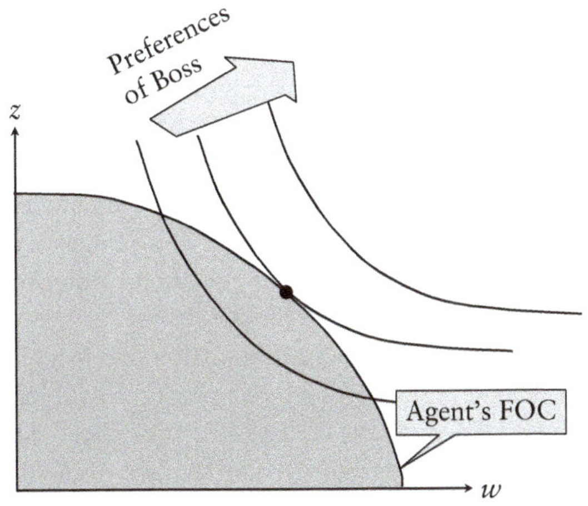

Figure 11.21 Principal-and-Agent: simple solution

? Mini Problems

40 We have simplified the solution by assuming that the attainable set has a regular shape. Draw a version of this diagram where the effort supplied by the Agent for a given wage rate is not unique. What problem could then arise in finding the solution to the Principal's problem?

Setting the problem out formally we see that Bill now tries to solve the problem:

$$\max_{\{w(\cdot),z\}} \mathcal{E}u^b(q - w(q)) + \lambda\left[\mathcal{E}u^a(w(q),z) - \underline{\upsilon}^a\right] + \mu\left[\frac{\partial \mathcal{E}u^a(w(q),z)}{\partial z}\right] \tag{11.87}$$

where λ and μ are the Lagrange multipliers for the participation constraint (11.75) and the behavioural constraint (11.86). In solving this problem we shall simplify the problem further by assuming that Alf's marginal utility of leisure is independent of income so that $u^a_{zx} \equiv 0$. So, let us derive the first-order conditions for the above problem. Differentiating (11.87) with respect to $w(q)$ and z, and using (11.85) and (11.86), we now find the following two FOCs for the boss's problem.[41]

First, for every output level q:

$$-u^b_x(q - w(q)) + \lambda u^a_x(w(q),z) + \mu u^a_x(w(q),z)\,\beta_z = 0. \tag{11.88}$$

Second, differentiating with respect to z, we must have:

$$\mathcal{E}\left(u^b(q - w(q))\,\beta_z\right) + \mu\left[\frac{\partial^2 \mathcal{E}u^a(w(q),z)}{\partial z^2}\right] = 0. \tag{11.89}$$

Contrast these two equations with (11.77) and (11.78), in the full-information case where z can be observed. The first term in (11.89) is positive because u^b is increasing in q; the term in [ ] must be negative in virtue of the second-order conditions in the agent's optimisation problem: so μ is positive. Hence the behavioural constraint (11.86) is binding at the optimum. Furthermore, (11.88) implies:

$$\frac{u^b_x(q - w(q))}{u^a_x(w(q),z)} = \lambda + \mu\beta_z \tag{11.90}$$

(cf. equation 11.79). So now we find that for high values of q (where $\beta_z > 0$) the ratio of marginal utilities lies above λ: the payment to Alf the agent from Bill the boss is relatively high, compared with the perfect information solution; conversely if q turns out low (where $\beta_z < 0$) then the payment to Alf from Bill is relatively low compared with the full-information solution. As in the adverse selection problem the presence of imperfect information again leads to an incentive scheme that has a built-in 'distortion'. The economic mechanism used to offset the inducement to misrepresentation offered by the lack of information will itself introduce an apparent distortion.

One implication of the Principal-and-Agent model is that—in contrast to the result where effort is observable—even if Bill were risk neutral he no longer provides effectively perfect insurance to Alf against the effects of the weather.[42] This can be seen from (11.90): putting u^b_1 equal to some constant we find that the optimal payment solution is still to pay Alf relatively well when q is high and poorly when q is low.

Mini Problems

41 Derive (11.88) and (11.89).

42 However if Alf is risk neutral and Bill is risk averse then the solution in (11.88) and (11.89) becomes equivalent to that in the risk-neutral case. Prove this.

Example 11.4

What is the economic logic behind the remuneration of corporate executives? It would not be surprising to find a strong relation with firms' stock-market performance or with sales. But the interconnection may be quite subtle. Based on a sample of 501 executives from Fortune 500 manufacturing firms, Murphy (1985) examines the relationship between the various components of executive remuneration (including salary, bonus, deferred compensation, value of stock options) and indicators of firms' performance. Modelling this relationship naively in terms of total financial reward (the sum of the components) is misleading: it understates the effects of performance on compensation. Murphy (1985) shows that bonus and deferred-payments components are strongly affected by inter-industry relative rates of return.

Summary

Information economics can be seen as a logical outgrowth of the theoretical developments in chapter 10. Game-theoretic reasoning can be used to sort out the logical structure of each of the variants of the fundamental problem that we have addressed. In particular, the perfect Bayesian equilibrium concept forms the intellectual basis for the solution of the entire collection of models used in this chapter. However, the *method* of solution often uses techniques that have become familiar from the earlier chapters featuring optimisation problems under full information: the Lagrangean approach usually provides the required tools with implicit prices on new constraints that allow for agents' behaviour when they cannot be fully controlled.

A common feature of all of the models that we have considered here is the way that the 'known unknowns' have to be pressed into a form suitable for economic analysis. Perhaps the most important example of this—although perhaps the most questionable—is the appeal to common knowledge to make certain features of the underlying probability distribution distinct and well known to all economic agents. On top of this, if the models are to work well it is nearly always necessary to introduce quite strong assumptions about the structure of preferences and technology. In virtually every case we have used the 'single-crossing condition' for different families of indifference curves in order to find a tractable solution and to be able to draw interpretable conclusions from the analysis.

Finally, let us remind ourselves of some common curiosities that emerge from imperfect-information models.

- The possible multiplicity of equilibria—as in the signalling models (section 11.3). It is not clear that intellectual devices to reduce this plethora are entirely convincing.
- More disturbing perhaps is the possible *lack* of equilibrium in some cases: see the model of the insurance market (section 11.2.6) and some signalling models (Exercise 11.5).

- The use of rationing and price distortions to force a second-best solution where imperfect information means that 'first best' just cannot be implemented.

We will see that some of these features will be particularly relevant for our discussion of the problem of economic design.

Reading notes

Good introductions to the economics of information and the theory of contracts are provided in Macho-Stadler and Pérez-Castrillo (1997) and in Salanié (1997). An overview of the issues is provided by Arrow (1986). The classic reference on adverse selection, screening, and the economics of insurance markets (on which subsection 11.2.6 is based) is Rothschild and Stiglitz (1976).

For a good retrospective overview of screening and signalling see Riley (2001) The classic papers on the economics of signalling are Akerlof (1970) and Spence (1973). The intuitive criterion is attributable to Cho and Kreps (1987). The case of costless signals—so called 'cheap-talk' models—is treated in Crawford and Sobel (1982). A good introduction is in Salanié (1997), pages 95, on which the example in section 11.3.2 is based.

For an introduction to the Principal-and-Agent model see Ross (1973) and for a thorough treatment refer to Laffont and Martimort (2002). The classic papers are Holmström (1979) and Mirrlees (1999); for detailed analysis of incentive schemes using the Principal-and-Agent approach see Grossman and Hart (1983) and Holmström and Milgrom (1987)—the methods developed there are examined using numerical simulations in Haubrich (1994). For an introductory diagrammatic treatment using the Edgeworth box try Ricketts (1986).

An overview of empirical approaches to some of these models is to be found in Chiappori and Salanié (2003).

Exercises

11.1 A firm sells a single good to a group of customers. Each customer either buys zero or exactly one unit of the good; the good cannot be divided or resold. However, it can be delivered as either a high-quality or a low-quality good. The quality is characterised by a non-negative number q; the cost of producing one unit of good at quality q is $C(q)$ where C is an increasing and strictly convex function. The taste of customer h is τ^h—the marginal willingness to pay for quality. Utility for h is

$$U^h(q, x) = \tau^h q + x$$

where τ^h is a positive taste parameter and x is the quantity of consumed of all other goods.

1. If F is the fee required as payment for the good write down the budget constraint for the individual customer.

2. If there are two types of customer show that the single-crossing condition is satisfied and establish the conditions for a full-information solution.
3. Show that the second-best solution must satisfy the no-distortion-at-the-top principle (page 344).
4. Derive the second-best optimum (Mussa and Rosen 1978).

11.2 An employee's type can take the value τ_1 or τ_2, where $\tau_2 > \tau_1$. The benefit of the employee's services to his employer is proportional to z, the amount of education that the employee has received. The cost of obtaining z years of education for an employee of type τ is given by

$$C(z, \tau) = ze^{-\tau}.$$

The employee's utility function is

$$U(y, z) = -e^{-y} - C(z, \tau)$$

where y is the payment received from his employer. The risk-neutral employer designs contracts contingent on the observed gross benefit, to maximise his expected profits.

1. If the employer knows the employee's type, what contracts will be offered? If he does not know the employee's type, which type will self-select the 'wrong' contract?
2. Show how to determine the second-best contracts. Which constraints bind? How will the solution to the second-best problem compare with that in part 1?

11.3 A large risk-neutral firm employs a number of lawyers. For a lawyer of type τ the required time to produce an amount x of legal services is given by

$$z = \frac{x}{\tau}$$

The lawyer may be a high-productivity a-type lawyer or a low-productivity b-type: $\tau^a > \tau^b > 0$. Let y be the payment to the lawyer. The lawyer's utility function is

$$y^{\frac{1}{2}} - z.$$

and his reservation level of utility is 0. The lawyer knows his type and the firm cannot observe his action z. The price of legal services is 1.

1. If the firm knows the lawyer's type what contract will it offer? Is it efficient?
2. Suppose the firm believes that the probability that the lawyer has low productivity is π. Assume $\tau^b \geq [1 - \pi]\,\tau^a$. In what way would the firm then modify the set of contracts on offer if it does not know the lawyer's type and cannot observe his action?

11.4 The analysis of section 11.2.6 was based on the assumption that the insurance market is competitive. Show how the principles established in section 11.2.4 for a monopolist can be applied to the insurance market:

1. In the case where full information about individuals' risk types is available.
2. Where individuals' risk types are unknown to the monopolist.

11.5 Good second-hand cars are worth v_1^a to the buyer and v_0^a to the seller where $v_1^a > v_0^a$. Bad cars are worth v_1^b to the buyer and v_0^b to the seller where $v_1^b > v_0^b$. It is common knowledge that the proportion of bad cars is π. There is a fixed stock of cars and effectively an infinite number of potential buyers

1. If there were perfect information about quality, why would cars be traded in equilibrium? What would be p^a and p^b, the equilibrium prices of good cars and of bad cars respectively?
2. If neither buyers nor sellers have any information about the quality of an individual car what is $\overline{p}$, the equilibrium price of cars?
3. If the seller is perfectly informed about quality and the buyer is uninformed show that good cars are only sold in the market if the equilibrium price is above v_0^a.
4. Show that in the asymmetric-information situation in part 3 there are only two possible equilibria
   - The case where $p^b < v_0^a$: equilibrium price is p^b.
   - The case where $\overline{p} \geq v_0^a$: equilibrium price is $\overline{p}$. (This is a version of the 'Lemons model'—Akerlof 1970.)

11.6 In an economy there are two types of worker: type-a workers have productivity 2 and type-b workers have productivity 1. Workers productivities are unobservable by firms but workers can spend their own resources to acquire educational certificates in order to signal their productivity. It is common knowledge that the cost of acquiring an education level z equals z for type-b workers and $\frac{1}{2}z$ for type-a workers.

1. Find the least-cost separating equilibrium.
2. Suppose the proportion of type-b workers is π. For what values of π will the no-signalling outcome dominate any separating equilibrium?
3. Suppose $\pi = \frac{1}{4}$. What values of z are consistent with a pooling equilibrium?

11.7 A worker's productivity is given by an ability parameter $\tau > 0$. Firms pay workers on the basis of how much education, z, they have: the wage offered to a person with education z is $w(z)$ and the cost to the worker of acquiring an amount of education z is $ze^{-\tau}$.

1. Find the first-order condition for a type τ person and show that it must satisfy
$$\tau = -\log\left(\frac{dw(z^*)}{dz}\right).$$
2. If people come to the labour market having the productivity that the employers expect on the basis of their education show that the optimal wage schedule must satisfy
$$w(z) = \log(z + k)$$
where k is a constant.
3. Compare incomes net of educational cost with incomes that would prevail if it were possible to observe τ directly.

11.8 The manager of a firm can exert a high effort level $\overline{z} = 2$ or a low effort level $\underline{z} = 1$. The gross profit of the firm is either $\Pi_1 = 16$ or $\Pi_2 = 2$. The manager's choice affects the probability of a particular profit outcome occurring. If he chooses $\overline{z}$, then Π_1 occurs with probability $\overline{\pi} = \frac{3}{4}$, but if he chooses $\underline{z}$ then that probability is only $\underline{\pi} = \frac{1}{4}$. The risk-neutral owner designs contracts which specify a payment y_i to the manager contingent on gross profit Π_i. The utility function of the manager is $u(y, z) = y^{1/2} - z$, and his reservation utility $\underline{v} = 0$.

1. Solve for the full-information contract.
2. Confirm that the owner would like to induce the manager to take action $\overline{z}$.
3. Solve for the second-best contracts in the event that the owner cannot observe the manager's action.
4. Comment on the implications for risk sharing.

11.9 The manager of a firm can exert an effort level $\overline{z} = \frac{4}{3}$ or $\underline{z} = 1$ and gross profits are either $\Pi_1 = 3z^2$ or $\Pi_2 = 3z$. The outcome Π_1 occurs with probability $\overline{\pi} = \frac{2}{3}$ if action $\overline{z}$ is taken, and with probability $\underline{\pi} = \frac{1}{3}$ otherwise. The manager's utility function is $u(y, z) = \log y - z$, and his reservation utility is $\underline{v} = 0$. The risk-neutral owner designs contracts which specify a payment y_i to the manager, contingent on obtaining gross profits Π_i.

1. Solve for the full-information contracts. Which action does the owner wish the manager to take?
2. Solve for the second-best contracts. What is the agency cost of the asymmetric information?
3. In part 1, the manager's action can be observed. Are the full-information contracts equivalent to contracts which specify payments contingent on effort?

11.10 A risk-neutral firm can undertake one of two investment projects each requiring an investment of z. The outcome of project i is x_i with probability π_i and 0 otherwise, where

$$\pi_1 x_1 > \pi_2 x_2 > z$$

$$x_2 > x_1 > 0$$

$$\pi_1 > \pi_2 > 0.$$

The project requires credit from a monopolistic, risk-neutral bank. There is limited liability, so that the bank gets nothing if the project fails.

1. If the bank stipulates repayment y from any successful project what is the expected payoff to the firm and to the bank if the firm selects project i?
2. What would be the outcome if there were perfect information?
3. Now assume that the bank cannot monitor which project the firm chooses. Show that the firm will choose project 1 if $y \leq \overline{y}$ where

$$\overline{y} := \frac{\pi_1 x_1 - \pi_2 x_2}{\pi_1 - \pi_2}.$$

4. Plot the graph of the bank's expected profits against y. Show that the bank will set $y = \overline{y}$ if $\pi_1 \overline{y} > \pi_2 x_2$ and $y = x_2$ otherwise.

5. Suppose there are N such firms and that the bank has a fixed amount M available to fund credit to the firms where

$$z < M < Nz.$$

Show that if $\pi_1 \bar{y} > \pi_2 x_2$ there will be credit rationing but no credit rationing otherwise (Macho-Stadler and Pérez-Castrillo 1997).

11.11 The tax authority employs an inspector to audit tax returns. The dollar amount of tax evasion revealed by the audit is $x \in \{x_1, x_2\}$. It depends on the inspector's effort level z and the random complexity of the tax return. The probability that $x = x_i$ conditional on effort z is $\pi_i(z) > 0$ $i = 1, 2$. The tax authority offers the inspector a wage rate $w_i = w(x)$, contingent on the result achieved and obtains the benefit $B(x - w)$. The inspector's utility function is

$$U(w, z) = u(w) - v(z)$$

and his reservation level of utility is $\underline{v}$. Assume

$$B'(\cdot) > 0,\ B''(\cdot) \leq 0,\ u'(\cdot) > 0,\ u''(\cdot) \leq 0,\ v'(\cdot) > 0,\ v''(\cdot) \geq 0.$$

Information is symmetric unless otherwise specified.

1. For each possible effort level find the first-order conditions characterising the optimal contract w_i $i = 1, \ldots, n$.
2. What is the form of the optimal contract when the tax authority is risk neutral and the inspector is risk averse? Comment on your solution and illustrate it in a box diagram.
3. How does this optimal contract change if the inspector is risk neutral and the tax authority is risk averse? Characterise the effort level that the tax authority will induce. State clearly any additional assumptions you wish to make.
4. As in part 2 assume that the tax authority is risk neutral and the tax inspector is risk averse. Effort can only take two possible values $\bar{z}$ or $\underline{z}$ with $\bar{z} > \underline{z}$. The effort level is no longer verifiable. Because the agency cost of enforcing $\bar{z}$ is too high the tax authority is content to induce $\underline{z}$. What is the optimal contract?

12 Design

The ill designed is most ill for the designer

Hesiod, *Opera et dies*

12.1 Introduction

The topic of design is not really new to our discussion of microeconomic principles and analysis. We have already seen examples of design in chapter 11, when we considered the rôle that participation and incentive-compatibility constraints play in shaping fee schedules and wage schedules. We have alluded to the design problem in chapter 9, when we mentioned the implementation problem associated with efficiency and other welfare criteria. Here we will focus more precisely on the issues that we glimpsed in those contexts.

The purpose of the discussion in this chapter is to understand the principles that apply to the design of systems that are intended to implement a particular allocation or social state. The design issue could be precisely focused on a very narrow context (a single market?) or implemented at the level of the whole economy. The 'designer'—the economic actor undertaking the design problem—could be just one firm or one person endowed with the appropriate amount of power, or 'the government' as a representative agent for all the persons in the economy under consideration. We will find that a lot of headway can be made by reusing concepts and methods from chapters 9–11. Indeed some of the analysis can be seen as an extension and generalisation of ideas that were introduced in the discussion of Principal and Agent.

The key problem can be summarised thus. In most of our previous work we have assumed the existence of an economic institution that sets and administers the rules of economic transactions: usually this was the market in some form. Occasionally we have noted cases where the shortcomings of the institution are evident—for example in the allocation of goods characterised by 'non-rivalness' or in the presence of externalities (see pages 244ff). Now we want to turn this mental experiment around. Can we establish the principles which would underpin a well-functioning economic system and thereby provide guidelines for designing such a system?

12.2 Social choice

If we are to consider the problem of economic design from scratch, then we had better be clear about the objectives of the exercise. What is it that the economic system is supposed to achieve? We need a representation of the workings of the economy that it is sufficiently flexible to permit general modelling of a variety of individual and social objectives.

We can do this simply and powerfully by revisiting the ideas that underlay the concepts of social welfare discussed in chapter 9. First we will reuse the very general description of a social state θ and the concept of a 'profile' of preferences defined over Θ, the set of all possible social states: remember that a profile is just an ordered list of preference relations, one for each household in the economy under consideration (see page 226). However, we will find it more convenient to work with the notation of utility functions rather than with the weak preference symbol $\succeq^h$ as in chapter 9, although this tweak is little more than cosmetic. In particular, let us use the 'reduced-form' representation of the utility function that expresses utility of household (agent) h as a direct function of the social state, $v^h(\theta)$ (see page 233). So in this notation a profile of preferences is an ordered list of utility functions,

$$\left[v^1, v^2, v^3, \ldots\right], \tag{12.1}$$

one for each member of the population; as a shorthand for a particular profile (12.1) we will again use the symbol $[v]$ and as a shorthand for the set of all possible profiles $[v]$ we use the symbol $\mathbb{V}$.

Two other key concepts from chapter 9 are relevant here: the constitution and the social welfare function. To these we need to add one new concept that fits neatly into the language of social choice, but that has wider applicability.

Definition 12.1

A *social choice function* is a mapping from the set of preference profiles $\mathbb{V}$ to the set of social states Θ.

So, using the utility representation agent h's preferences, $v^h(\cdot)$, the social-choice function in Definition 12.1 can be written as:

$$\theta^* = \Gamma\left(v^1, v^2, \ldots\right) \tag{12.2}$$

A few points to note about the social-choice function Γ:

- As a true function (rather than a correspondence) it selects a single member of Θ once a given profile of preferences is plugged in.
- The arguments of Γ are utility *functions*, not utility levels: this is like the constitution Σ that we defined in chapter 9 (page 226).
- Γ subsumes technology, markets, and the distribution of property in a summary of the process that transforms profiles of preferences into social states. So the expression (12.2) says 'you tell me what people's preferences are—the collection of their indifference maps—and then I will tell you what the social state should be'.
- Because its specification is similar in spirit to that of the constitution, it inherits some of the difficulties that we have come to associate with the constitution—see the discussion on pages 227–232.

On a grand scale we can consider the social-choice function as a kind of black box that transforms a profile of preferences into a social state. It is an intellectual device that focuses attention on consumer sovereignty as a principle governing the workings of the economy: it is as though the social-choice function lies ready for the collection of consumers to express their wishes and then brings forth an outcome θ in accordance with those wishes. On a smaller scale we can think of this apparatus as a convenient abstraction for describing a class of design problems that affect firms and other decision makers.

Social-choice functions: notation

θ	social state
Θ	set of all social states
$v^h(\cdot)$	'reduced-form' utility function for agent h
$[v] = [v^1, v^2, v^3, \ldots]$	profile of utility functions
$\mathbb{V}$	set of all possible profiles
Γ	social-choice function

To pave the way for a more detailed analysis, let us consider some possible properties of Γ. First we pick up on some essential concepts from the fundamental aggregation problem in social-welfare analysis (it is useful to compare these with the four axioms on page 227).

Definition 12.2

Suppose there is some θ^* such that for all h and all $\theta \in \Theta : v^h(\theta^*) \geq v^h(\theta)$. Then the social-choice function Γ is *Paretian* if

$$\theta^* = \Gamma\left(v^1, v^2, \ldots\right) \tag{12.3}$$

Definition 12.3

Suppose there are two profiles $[v]$ and $[\tilde{v}]$ such that

$$\theta^* = \Gamma\left(v^1, v^2, \ldots\right)$$

and, for all h :

$$v^h\left(\theta^*\right) \geq v^h(\theta) \Rightarrow \tilde{v}^h\left(\theta^*\right) \geq \tilde{v}^h(\theta). \tag{12.4}$$

Then the social-choice function Γ is *monotonic*[1] if

$$\theta^* = \Gamma\left(\tilde{v}^1, \tilde{v}^2, \ldots\right)$$

? Mini Problems

1 Suppose the social state is completely characterised by a consumption allocation $\theta := [\mathbf{x}^1, \mathbf{x}^2, \mathbf{x}^3, \ldots]$.

Definition 12.4

A social choice function is *dictatorial* if there is some agent whose preferences completely determine θ.

Definition 12.2 means that if there is some social state θ^* that is top-ranked by everyone, then Γ is Paretian if it always picks out θ^* from the set of social states Θ. The plain-language interpretation of monotonicity (Definition 12.3) is that the chosen social state is never dropped unless it becomes less attractive for some individual agent h. Definition 12.4 is intuitive: for example, if person 1 is a dictator then, when we replace the functions $v^2, v^3, \ldots, v^h, \ldots$ in (12.2) by any other utility functions and leave the function v^1 unchanged, we will find that θ remains unchanged. The dictatorship property seems as unappealing in the context of a social-choice function as it did in the context of a constitution.

A comparison of definitions 12.1–12.4 and the discussion of the constitution (page 227) suggests that there may be a counterpart to the Arrow Impossibility Theorem (Theorem 9.1) that applies to social-choice functions. This is indeed the case:

Theorem 12.1 (Dictatorial social-choice functions)

Suppose the number of social states is more than two and the social-choice function Γ is defined for all logically possible utility functions. Then, if Γ is Paretian and monotonic, it must be dictatorial.

The flavour of Theorem 12.1 is similar to Theorem 9.1 and, indeed, the proof is similar (check the reading notes to this chapter and Appendix C). But its implication may not be immediately striking. To appreciate this more fully let us introduce a crucial property that will enable us to build a bridge between the welfare-economic discussion of the constitution and the behavioural analysis of our discussion of the economics of information:

Definition 12.5

A social-choice function Γ is *manipulable* if there is a profile of preferences $[v]$ such that, for some household h and some other utility function $\hat{v}^h(\cdot) \neq v^h(\cdot)$:

$$v^h(\hat{\theta}) > v^h(\theta) \tag{12.5}$$

? Mini Problems

(a) In $\left(x_1^h, x_2^h\right)$-space draw the 'better-than' (actually, 'no-worse-than') set $B(\theta^*; v)$ when individual preferences are given by the profile

$$\left[v^1(\cdot), v^2(\cdot), v^3(\cdot), \ldots\right].$$

(b) Suppose agent h's preferences change from $v^h(\cdot)$ to $\tilde{v}^h(\cdot)$: interpret condition (12.4) using $B(\theta^*; v)$ and $B(\theta^*; \tilde{v})$

(c) State the monotonicity condition using this diagram.

where

$$\theta := \Gamma\left(v^1, v^2, \ldots, v^h, \ldots\right) \tag{12.6}$$

and

$$\hat{\theta} := \Gamma\left(v^1, v^2, \ldots, \hat{v}^h, \ldots\right) \tag{12.7}$$

The significance of this concept is worth thinking about carefully. If a social-choice function is manipulable, this does not mean that some household or individual is actually in a position to manipulate it—rather, under some circumstances someone *could* manipulate it. There is a close link with the idea of masquerading that we discussed in the context of adverse selection (page 339). For a manipulable social-choice function there may be a premium on false information for some agents in the economy: the form of the utility function is of course the quintessentially private information. If there were a way for h to reveal the false utility function $\hat{v}^h$, then the economic system would respond in such a way that h would be genuinely better off—notice that the inequality in expression (12.5) uses the *genuine* utility function v^h.[2]

However, monotonicity implies that the social-choice function cannot be manipulable.[3] This leads us on to a key result that is really no more than just a corollary of Theorem 12.1:

Theorem 12.2

If there are at least three social states and, for each household, any strict ranking of these alternative states is permissible, then the only Paretian, non-manipulable social-choice function is dictatorial.

? Mini Problems

2 Alf, Bill, and Charlie have appointments at 11:00, 11:20, and 12:00 respectively. Each of them is irritated by arriving too early (the longer Alf arrives in advance of his appointment, the more irritated he gets—the same is true for Bill and Charlie) and each is embarrassed by being late (and, for each of them, the embarrassment increases with the lateness). When they call for a taxi, they are told that there is only one taxi left (they'll have to share!) and it is only available from 10:00 to 13:00. So what time should they order the taxi for?

1. Draw a diagram similar to Figure 9.1 showing their preferences for the time that the taxi should come for them.
2. Suppose that they agree to take the simple average of the times that they each say they need to be at their appointments. Show that this arrangement is manipulable, in that at least one of them has an incentive to mis-state his preferences about the taxi time.
3. Suppose that, while they are making their minds up, the taxi firm calls back and offers to pick them up at 12:10, but at no other time. Explain why this solution to their problem is non-manipulable, but inefficient.
4. Suppose instead that they agree to take the median value of their stated times. Is this rule manipulable?

3 Use Definition 12.3 to produce a contradiction in the expressions (12.5)–(12.7).

Theorem 12.2 is a first attempt at capturing an essential concept that carries over from our consideration of information in chapter 11. It has profound consequences for the way in which economic systems can be designed if there is less than full information.

12.3 Markets and manipulation

To illustrate the power of misrepresentation and manipulation in a familiar setting let us rework the standard model of an exchange economy.

12.3.1 Markets: another look

Take the particularly interesting example of a social-choice function from chapter 7. Specify the details of the following:

- the technology of the firms;
- the resource endowments;
- the ownership rights of all the households.

Then we appear to have almost all the ingredients needed to construct the economy's excess-demand function (7.16); all that is missing is the profile of preferences represented by the list of utility functions (7.1). Once we plug those in, the general-equilibrium system is completely specified: the excess-demand functions determine the equilibrium prices; the prices determine the quantities in the allocation; the allocation is itself the social state. So the paraphernalia of the general-equilibrium model can be seen as a social-choice function Γ that will convert a set of preferences into a complete list of consumption bundles and net-output levels that constitute the social state θ.

There are two particularly interesting things about this:

1. Under well-defined circumstances the function Γ produces an outcome that has apparently desirable efficiency properties.[4]
2. It does not require explicit design.

However, this version of the market system incorporates an assumption that may be unwarranted: that each individual agent is effectively too small to matter. Let us look more closely at the market system in the context of the elementary model of a two-commodity exchange economy: this is illustrated in Figure 12.1, which represents a standard Edgeworth diagram box for the two-person case.

? Mini Problems

4 Suppose Γ is the social-choice function outlined above. If an individual agent's utility v^h is subject to a monotonic transformation how does this affect Γ?

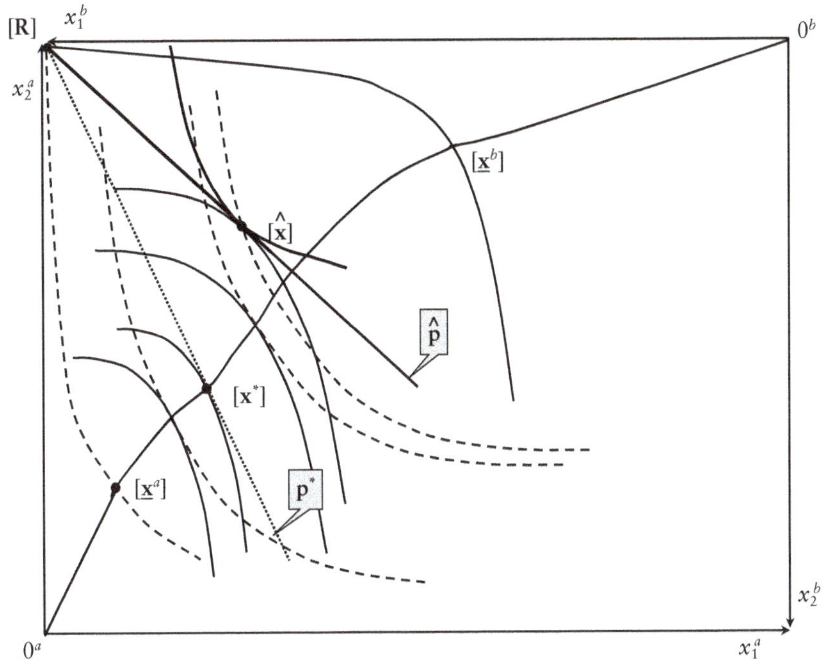

Figure 12.1 Manipulated trading

The trading game

$h = a, b$	households
$i = 1, 2$	goods
x_i^h	consumption by h of i
R_i^h	endowment of h with i

The initial property distribution is $\mathbf{R}^a = (0, R_2)$, $\mathbf{R}^b = (R_1, 0)$: Alf has all the commodity 2 and Bill all the commodity 1. Each person could survive on his endowment, but would benefit from trade with the other. Alf's indifference curves are represented by the contour map with broken lines with origin at 0^a; Bill's indifference curves are those with origin 0^b. The set of all Pareto-efficient allocations—the locus of all the points of tangency between the two sets of indifference curves—is drawn in as the irregularly shaped line joining 0^a and 0^b. The core of the two-person game is represented by the subset of this that is bounded by points $[\underline{\mathbf{x}}^a]$ and $[\underline{\mathbf{x}}^b]$; in the two-person case this corresponds to the set of allocations that could be regarded as full information equilibria where both persons tell the truth.[5]

? Mini Problems

5 Identify the reservation indifference curves for the two agents.

12.3.2 Simple trading

As we know from Chapter 7 (page 154), the two-person case is a paradigm for a $2N$-person case where $N > 1$ is a factor of replication, and if N is sufficiently large then the only points left in the core are those that are competitive equilibria—in this case the single equilibrium allocation at $[\mathbf{x}^*]$ with corresponding prices $\mathbf{p}^*$. Now, in such a competitive model, there is no point in misrepresenting one's preferences: if a person falsely states his marginal rate of substitution, all that happens is that he achieves a lower utility level than if he had selected a point on the boundary of his budget set at which his MRS equals the price ratio.

However, if a person has market power—if he perceives that he is 'large enough' to influence the prices at which the market will clear, this conclusion may no longer hold.

12.3.3 Manipulation: power and misrepresentation

Consider now a story about market power. Suppose Alf knows the trades that Bill is to make at each price and has the power to dictate the price. We can imagine an exercise in which various prices are tried out on Bill, and Bill's desired consumptions. Using this information Alf can exploit his position as monopolist of commodity 2 to force up the price. The outcome would be at a point such as $[\hat{\mathbf{x}}]$ with prices $\hat{\mathbf{p}}$ where the terms of trade have been moved in favour of Alf.[6]

Alternatively we can see this as a story of misrepresentation in which Alf lies about his marginal willingness to pay—he reveals a false indifference curve—to his trading partner. The story runs as follows. Each day of the week each trader comes to the market with the endowments represented by point $[\mathbf{R}]$. But there is an apparent change of tastes during the week:

- On Monday preferences are publicly declared to be as described by the indifference curves above. Haggling takes place between the two traders, with each telling the truth, and revealing to the other his demand functions. A competitive equilibrium is agreed upon, possibly by each side agreeing to abide by the rulings of an impartial arbitrating auctioneer. So each trader is acting as though he were a price taker at prices $\mathbf{p}^*$—the equilibrium is at point $[\mathbf{x}^*]$ in the accompanying figure.
- On Tuesday each trader arrives again with stocks $[\mathbf{R}]$, but Alf has now decided to lie—purely for material advantage of course. He realises that by trading at point $[\hat{\mathbf{x}}]$ rather than point $[\mathbf{x}^*]$ he will be better off: he can induce honest, trusting Bill to accept point $[\hat{\mathbf{x}}]$ by saying that his true preferences have changed, and once again securing agreement that a competitive equilibrium solution can be adopted. Alf misrepresents his indifference curve as shown by the heavily outlined curve passing through $[\hat{\mathbf{x}}]$. This curve is deliberately chosen by Alf to be tangential to a Bill indifference curve exactly at point $[\hat{\mathbf{x}}]$.

? Mini Problems

6 Use a diagram based on Figure 12.1 to draw Bill's offer curve. Show how Alf can maximise his utility using the offer curve as the boundary of his opportunity set and so will force a monopolistic solution at $[\hat{\mathbf{x}}]$.

12.3.4 A design issue?

It is clear from the example that misrepresentation can generate an inefficient outcome. It is also clear that the above example could be considered as a lesson in bad design. Imagine a public body or agency that regulates trade—if the rules of trade allow for actions that mimic the behaviour of a monopolist then the outcome will be suboptimal. We need to examine this issue in greater depth and generality.

12.4 Mechanisms

So far we have illustrated the point that social choices can be manipulated by individual economic agents to produce outcomes that are manifestly inefficient and therefore are likely to be considered undesirable by any reasonable system of social values. But in order to introduce misrepresentation by economic agents into the model we need a language of discourse and a method of analysis that is firmly rooted in the economics of information.

So our next step is to examine the engine that drives this general class of economic problem. To do this it is useful to pick up on the essentials of a game, first discussed in chapter 10, in order to use them as ingredients of the design problem. First, re-examine the description of a game in section 10.2.1. We can characterise these essentials as:

- The strategy sets of the agents $S^1, S^2, S^3, \ldots$. It is convenient to represent these collectively by their Cartesian product (see page 484 for a formal definition) S: each element of S is a profile of strategies $[s^1, s^2, s^3, \ldots]$.
- A convenient way of describing how the outcome of the game is determined from any given combination of strategies. Call this the *outcome function*. So, once the economic agents have each chosen a strategy, the social state is determined as $\theta = \gamma(s)$ where $s := [s^1, s^2, s^3, \ldots]$.
- The specification of the players' objectives. This consists of a profile of preferences $[v^1, v^2, v^3, \ldots]$. So, once the outcome (social state) θ has been determined, this leads to utility payoffs $v^1(\theta), v^2(\theta), v^3(\theta), \ldots$

If all three items in the above list are specified in detail then the game is fully described. Now the first two of these components give us exactly what is needed for a general description of the 'engine' that is at the core of this chapter:

Mechanism: notation

θ	social state
Θ	set of all social states
$[v^1, v^2, v^3, \ldots]$	profile of utility functions
$\mathbb{V}$	set of all possible profiles
s^h	strategy of agent h
$[s^1, s^2, s^3, \ldots]$	profile of strategies
S	set of all strategy profiles
γ	outcome function
Γ	social-choice function

Definition 12.6

A *mechanism* consists of the set of strategy profiles S and an outcome function γ from S to the set of social states Θ.

The mechanism is an almost completely specified game. The key thing that is missing is the collection of utility functions that will fully specify the maximand of and the actual payoff to each participating economic agent. So, once the objectives of the players are known—once we have plugged in a particular profile of utility functions—then we know the social state that will be determined by the game and the welfare implications for all the economic agents.

12.4.1 Implementation

The idea of a mechanism enables us to state the design problem precisely. The mechanism provides a link from the space of all possible profiles of preferences to a social state via the medium of an economic game. To the question 'can a social-choice function be made to work in practice?' the answer is 'yes, if it can be characterised as the equilibrium of a game.' First, let us sketch the implementation process: the idea can be expressed as the following sequence of steps:

- Specify a mechanism as a (strategy-set, outcome-function) pair (S, γ).
- Given their actual preferences $[v^1, v^2, v^3, \ldots]$, and using the mechanism as the rules of the game, the players determine their optimal strategies as the profile
$$\left[s^{*1}, s^{*2}, s^{*3}, \ldots\right].$$
- The outcome function determines the social state in the light of the profile of strategies
$$\theta^* = \gamma\left(s^{*1}, s^{*2}, s^{*3}, \ldots\right). \tag{12.8}$$
- Is this θ^* the one that the designer would have wished from the social-choice function Γ in (12.2)?

But this begs a number of important questions about the way in which the process is to be carried through. First, what of the players? The rôle of the n_h agents is fairly clear: their preferences form the argument of the mechanism; but there is an additional entity—the Designer—who remains as a shadowy presence in the background: we will see some specific examples of the designer below. Second, we spoke of an equilibrium: but what type of equilibrium? As we discussed in chapter 10 there is a range of equilibrium concepts that may be appropriate—which one is appropriate will depend on the timing and information structure built into the model and any restrictions that we may want to introduce on admissible strategies. The standard model paradigm is the Bayesian game of incomplete information (see section 10.7.1 on page 313) that formed the basis of most of chapter 11 and we will need to use both the conventional Nash equilibrium and also the more restrictive equilibrium in dominant strategies (page 277). Third, the game may have several equilibria: will they all lead to the desired θ^* as in (12.8)? If so we say that the mechanism *completely implements* the social-choice function Γ. Otherwise—if some equilibria yield θ^* but there is at least one equilibrium that leads to a social state other than θ^*—then the mechanism only *weakly implements* Γ.[7]

Drawing together this discussion for an important, but special interpretation of the concept, we may summarise thus:

Definition 12.7

The mechanism $(S, \gamma(\cdot))$ *weakly implements the social-choice function* Γ *in dominant strategies* if there is a dominant-strategy equilibrium of the mechanism, $\left[s^{*1}(\cdot), s^{*2}(\cdot), s^{*3}(\cdot), \ldots\right]$ such that

$$\gamma\left(s^{*1}\left(v^1\right), s^{*2}\left(v^2\right), s^{*3}\left(v^3\right), \ldots\right) = \Gamma\left(v^1, v^2, v^3, \ldots\right).$$

12.4.2 Direct mechanisms

Of course there may be a huge number of mechanisms that could conceivably be designed in order to implement a particular objective. For the purposes of effective design and clear exposition we might reason that it would be better to focus on those that are based on relatively simple games. So, let us consider a very simple game indeed.

The game consists in just announcing one's preferences: this means declaring everything that there is to be known about motivation in playing the game. It is a game of messages akin to those discussed in section 11.3 of chapter 11. In this game the strategy space—the message space—S is exactly the space of all the possible utility profiles $\mathbb{V}$;[8] the outcome function maps announced preferences directly into social states such that, for all profiles in $\mathbb{V}$,

$$\gamma\left(v^1, v^2, v^3, \ldots\right) = \Gamma\left(v^1, v^2, v^3, \ldots\right).$$

In other words, the mechanism is so simple that the outcome function *is* the social-choice function itself; unsurprisingly this device is conventionally known as a *direct mechanism*.

? Mini Problems

7 In the light of this discussion it is clear that the simple statement 'the social-choice function is implementable' could be made to mean a number of things. Consider the following four variants that differ in terms of the strength of the requirement of 'implementability':

There is a mechanism...

1. ...for which all the Nash equilibria yield θ^*.
2. ...with a unique Nash equilibrium that yields θ^*.
3. ...with a dominant-strategy equilibrium that yields θ^*.
4. ...with a Nash equilibrium that yields θ^*.

Arrange these descriptions of implementation in increasing order of strength.

8 Suppose each the taste parameter τ^h for agent h is a number in $[0, 1]$. Write down the exact expression for the combined strategy space. [Hint: check the definition on page 484.]

The trick is to design such a simple mechanism so as to ensure truth telling. But, what does it mean to ensure truth telling?

To make this clear we use the concept of a dominant strategy, introduced in chapter 10 (see page 277). We will say that the social-choice function Γ is *truthfully implementable* in dominant strategies if

$$s^{*h}\left(v^h\right) = v^h, h = 1, 2, \ldots, n_h$$

is a dominant-strategy equilibrium of the direct mechanism. Note that by specifying a dominant-strategy equilibrium we require that it is such that everyone finds that 'honesty is the best policy' irrespective of whether others are following the same rule or, indeed, whether others are even rational.

12.4.3 The revelation principle

The direct mechanism—or direct-revelation mechanism—is of mild interest in its own right: it is at least intriguing to think up tricks that will cause rational agents to reveal all the personal information that would otherwise be hidden from a designer. However, direct mechanisms are of fundamental importance in terms of the general problem of implementation. In the following, note that the pair (S, γ) represents any mechanism that you might think up, while $(\mathbb{V}, \Gamma)$ represents the direct mechanism just discussed in section 12.4.2:

Theorem 12.3 (Revelation principle)

If the social-choice function Γ is weakly implementable in dominant strategies by the mechanism (S, γ) then Γ is truthfully implementable in dominant strategies using the direct mechanism $(\mathbb{V}, \Gamma)$.

The idea of this is illustrated in Figure 12.2. The implementation story can be told in one of two ways:

1. The mechanism (S, γ) works this way. Given a particular choice of preference profile $[v]$ from $\mathbb{V}$ the agents select strategies

$$\left[s^{*1}\left(v^1\right), s^{*2}\left(v^2\right), s^{*3}\left(v^3\right), \ldots\right]$$

   that produce one or more equilibria, a subset of S: this is the left-hand arm of the diagram. The outcome function maps the equilibrium strategies into the set of social states Θ (right-hand arm). For some of the equilibria (all of them if it is complete implementation) this last step produces θ^* given by (12.2).

2. The direct mechanism $(\mathbb{V}, \Gamma)$ works this way. The social-choice function is used as a mechanism that, for a particular $[v]$ chosen from $\mathbb{V}$, produces θ^* (the bottom route in the diagram).

The revelation principle means that complex issues of implementation can be analysed in a particularly simple fashion. You can focus on situations involving the simplest

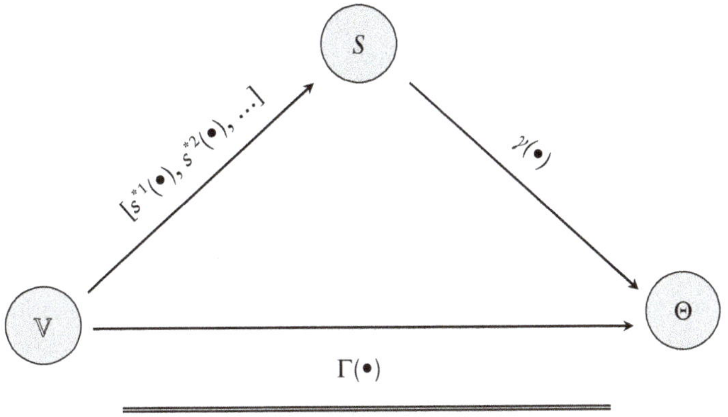

$$\Gamma(\bullet) = \gamma[s^{*1}(\bullet), s^{*2}(\bullet), \ldots]$$

Figure 12.2 The revelation principle

possible message—a statement of your personal preferences. If you want to establish whether a social-choice function is implementable in dominant strategies there is no point in going the pretty way round in the journey from $\mathbb{V}$ to Θ in Figure 12.2.

However, the direct-revelation mechanism is not necessarily the one that would be used in practice to resolve a design problem and the above result does nothing to clear up whether there are multiple equilibria in a mechanism that is used to implement Γ, or, indeed whether there are any equilibria at all.

12.5 The design problem

Equipped with the concept of the mechanism as a basic tool we can now continue the discussion we left in section 12.2: the issue of designing an economic system in order to fulfil a specific set of social objectives. We can build upon the results about social-choice functions by applying the concept of truthful implementation in section 12.4.

In particular, by combining the result on dictatorial social-choice functions and the revelation principle (Theorems 12.1 and 12.3) we have the following:

Theorem 12.4 (Gibbard–Satterthwaite)

If (i) the set of social states Θ contains at least three elements; (ii) the social choice function Γ is defined for the set $\mathbb{V}$ of all logically possible profiles of utility functions; and (iii) Γ is truthfully implementable in dominant strategies, then Γ must be dictatorial.

This is a key result. We can better understand the strength of it if we use the concept of manipulability of a social-choice function. By extension we can consider a mechanism to be manipulable if it is not one that ensures truthful revelation in dominant strategies. Having a mechanism that is non-manipulable or strategy proof seems like a particularly attractive property when we try to design a method of implementing the social objectives. But Theorem 12.4 makes clear that if all types of tastes are admissible and if the set of social choices is large enough to be interesting then the only way to achieve this is to allow one of the agents to act as dictator.

Another plain-language interpretation of the result can be seen in terms of cheating. We have already encountered particular situations in chapter 11 where individuals have an incentive to misrepresent information about themselves: high-valuation customers might want to pass themselves off as low valuation in order to take advantage of a more favourable fee schedule; an Agent would try to get away with low effort and pass off poor results as being due to the weather. However, the problem may be quite general: Theorem 12.4 implies that if the set of social states is large and the mechanism attempts to accommodate all types of agents without allowing any to act as a dictator then it will no longer be able to enforce truth telling: cheating may be endemic to the system.

The design issue reduces in large part to finding sensible ways around the rigours of Theorem 12.4. Is it generally possible to design a mechanism that would prevent this cheating or misrepresentation? A rereading of the conditions of the theorem suggests a number of possible avenues:

- Examine situations of choice between just two possible social states.
- Consider cases where only a restricted class of individual utility functions is admissible.
- Relax the stringent requirement of truth telling in terms of a dominant-strategy equilibrium.

We will first briefly consider the issues involved in the last of these ideas before looking at the others in greater detail.

Remember that our interpretation of truthful implementation by a mechanism has been quite restrictive: telling the truth about one's hidden information had to be the best option for each agent h, irrespective of what everyone else chose to do. This is a much stronger version of equilibrium than that typically used in strategic settings, for example those discussed in chapter 10. Suppose we consider a concept of equilibrium that is closer to what we used in discussing economic games: what if we require truth telling to be merely a Nash equilibrium rather than an equilibrium in dominant strategies?[9]

If we retain the requirement of merely weak implementation of the social-choice function, then the Nash-equilibrium approach could produce very unsatisfactory results: the difficulty is that the agents might coordinate on an equilibrium in which everyone is making a best response to everyone else's strategy, but where the outcome is very

? Mini Problems

9 We characterised the dominant-strategy version of truth telling (section 12.4.2) as 'honesty is always the best-policy'. What is the plain-language expression of the Nash-equilibrium version of truth telling?

unattractive.[10] Accordingly, we should consider the possibility of complete implementation using Nash equilibrium. Here each person knows his own preferences and the preferences of all the other players; but this information is unknown to the Designer. For this case an apparently attractive result is available:

Theorem 12.5 (Nash implementation)

If a social choice function is Nash implementable then it is monotonic.

However, this Nash-implementation result is in itself quite limiting. First, it may again imply that in economically interesting situations, the social-choice function has to be dictatorial. Second, monotonicity may have unattractive consequences for distribution (see Mini Problem 27 below). Thirdly there is a problem of consistency through time: it may be the case that individual agents would choose to renegotiate the outcome θ that has been generated by the mechanism.

12.6 Design: applications

The other approaches to dealing with the challenge of Theorem 12.4 can be usefully illustrated with a number of key economic applications. These are all of the type of Bayesian games of incomplete information that were modelled in chapter 11: in particular all of the applications can be seen as versions of the 'adverse selection' class of problems involving hidden characteristics—see pages 334 ff.

Remember that the second of the list of three mentioned on page 394 involved restricting the class of admissible utility functions. Accordingly, we will simplify the representation of individuals' preferences by using the same general form of utility function as was used in the adverse-selection models. We assume that all the economic agents in the game have the same general shape of utility function, but that they differ in some 'type' or

? Mini Problems

10 (a) Take the game represented in strategic form by Table 10.3 where there are two players Alf and Bill and exactly two strategies for each player. Suppose the payoff (3, 3) is the social state that is the outcome of the social-choice function that we want to implement. Let s_1^h and s_2^h represent the strategy of truth-telling and of lying for $h = a, b$. Explain why $\left(s_2^a, s_2^b\right)$ is an equilibrium, but is unsatisfactory.

	s_1^b	s_2^b
s_1^a	3, 3	0, 0
s_2^a	0, 0	0, 0

(b) Now slightly alter the payoff structure to that given above. Identify the Nash equilibria.

(c) Suppose that each player now has $N - 1$ ways rather than rather than 1 way of telling a lie, where $N > 2$, but that lies always produce the payoff (0, 0): adapt the table in part (b) to the case with N strategies and use this to argue that there may be an indefinitely large number of unsatisfactory Nash equilibria on which the game may focus.

'taste' parameter τ, a real number. The various values of parameter τ that may be imputed to an individual completely characterise the different objectives that the agent may have.

12.6.1 Auctions

An auction can be regarded as an exercise in posing the question 'tell me what your valuation is'. Someone sets up an event or an institution to extract payment from one or more potential buyers of an object, a collection of goods, ownership rights,... How do the mechanics work? How can the principles of design help us to understand the rules and likely outcomes?

Of course the problem that makes the analysis of auctions economically interesting is the nature of the concealed information: the seller usually does not know the characteristics of individual potential buyers, in particular their willingness to pay. In view of this it is appropriate to formulate the problem in terms of a Bayesian game and to use the revelation principle to simplify the analysis. There is a great variety of types of auction that differ in terms of the information available to participants, the timing, and the rules of conduct of the auction. We will first discuss the informational issues and then the rules.

The informational setup

There are several ways in which we might consider representing the unknown information that underlies an auction model. Here are the two leading examples:

- *The common-value problem.* There is a crock of gold, the value of which, once uncovered, will have the same value for everyone. At the time the auction takes place, however, individual agents have imperfect information about the value of the treasure and some may have better information than others.
- *The independent private values problem.* An alternative approach is that each person has his own personal valuation of the object that may differ from that of any other bidder and that would not change even if he were to know the other bidders' valuation: some may have a high regard for the work of a particular artist and therefore place a high monetary value on it; others may be much less impressed.

Of course there are interesting situations that combine elements of both types of unknown information.[11] However, to focus ideas, we will concentrate on the pure private-values case. We assume that a single indivisible object with known characteristics is for sale and that each potential bidder has a personal valuation τ of that object. Here τ can be taken as a taste or type parameter that corresponds to the agent's valuation of the good: it is a simple measure of the agent's willingness to pay.

? Mini Problems

11 Provide a brief argument that this is the case in the auction of a painting.

Example 12.1

Auctions with a substantial common-value element can produce some apparently strange results. Bazerman and Samuelson (1983) ran several instances of an experiment where they auctioned off jars of coins to students. Each jar had a value of \$8. The average bid was \$5.13. But the average *winning* bid was \$10.01. What was going on? See Exercise 12.7.

Types of auction

First a brief review of some terminology, summarised in Table 12.1: we will go round the table starting from the bottom left-hand corner:

- The *English auction* involves public announcements of bids that are gradually increased until only one bidder is left in the auction who wins the auction and pays the last price bid.
- The *Dutch auction* goes in the other direction. Starting from a high value, the announced price is gradually adjusted downwards until someone is ready to claim the object at that price.
- In the sealed-bid *first-price* auction all agents submit their bids in a way that is hidden from the others: the object goes to the agent who submitted the highest bid; the winner pays exactly the price that he or she bid.
- In the sealed-bid *second-price* counterpart the object again goes to the highest bidder; but the winner is required to pay the price that the 'runner up' had bid—the next highest price.

Fortunately we can simplify matters further by noting that in some cases these four possibilities effectively reduce to just two, corresponding to the two rows of the table. The Dutch open auction and the first-price sealed-bid auction are essentially equivalent mechanisms; for our information model the English open auction and the second price sealed-bid produce the same results. We will establish these assertions in each of the next two subsections before moving on to a more general approach to the auction mechanism.

First price

In strategic terms the Dutch auction is equivalent to the first-price auction with sealed bids: each bidder chooses a critical value at which to claim the object as the price

Open bid	Sealed bid
Dutch—descending price	first price
English—ascending price	second price

Table 12.1 Types of auction

descends or to submit in the sealed envelope, knowing that if the bid is successful he will be required to pay that price.

To consider equilibrium behaviour in a sealed-bid, independent private-values auction of an indivisible object where there are just two agents let us take a simple example. Alf and Bill are a pair of risk-neutral agents who take part in a sealed-bid, first-price auction. They have private values τ^a and τ^b, respectively, drawn from a distribution F on the support $[0, 1]$: i.e. the minimum possible value that either could place on the good is 0 and the maximum is 1. The problem is *symmetric* in that, although Alf and Bill may well have different realisations of the taste parameter τ, they face the same distribution and have the same objective function: this considerably simplifies the solution. Suppose that Alf assumes that Bill's bid will be determined by his type τ^b according to the function $\beta(\cdot)$: if Alf bids a price p^a then he gets the good if

$$p^a \geq \beta\left(\tau^b\right).$$

The probability that Alf's bid succeeds is

$$\pi\left(p^a\right) := \Pr\left(\tau^b \leq \beta^{-1}\left(p^a\right)\right) = F\left(\beta^{-1}\left(p^a\right)\right) \tag{12.9}$$

where β^{-1} denotes the inverse function. Because it is a first-price auction, the price you bid is the price you pay, if you win. Therefore, if Alf's bid succeeds and he gets the good, his benefit is $\tau^a - p^a$; otherwise he gets no net benefit. So, given that he is risk neutral, he seeks to maximise the expected net benefit $\pi\left(p^a\right)\left[\tau^a - p^a\right]$. Defining maximised expected net benefit as

$$\upsilon\left(\tau^a\right) := \max_{p^a} \pi\left(p^a\right)\left[\tau^a - p^a\right] \tag{12.10}$$

we immediately find the effect of an increase in the private value τ^a:[12]

$$\frac{\partial \upsilon\left(\tau^a\right)}{\partial \tau^a} = \pi\left(p^{a*}\right) \tag{12.11}$$

where p^{a*} is the optimal value of p^a. Because the problem is symmetric, in the Nash equilibrium each person has the same function β; so

$$p^{a*} = \beta\left(\tau^a\right) \tag{12.12}$$

and, from (12.9)–(12.11) Alf's expected net benefit is:[13]

$$\upsilon\left(\tau^a\right) = \int_0^{\tau^a} F(\tau)\, d\tau. \tag{12.13}$$

Alf's expected net benefit at the optimum can also be written as

$$\upsilon\left(\tau^a\right) = \pi\left(p^{a*}\right)\left[\tau^a - \beta\left(\tau^a\right)\right] \tag{12.14}$$

? Mini Problems

12 Why is this true?

13 Fill in the missing two lines to establish this point.

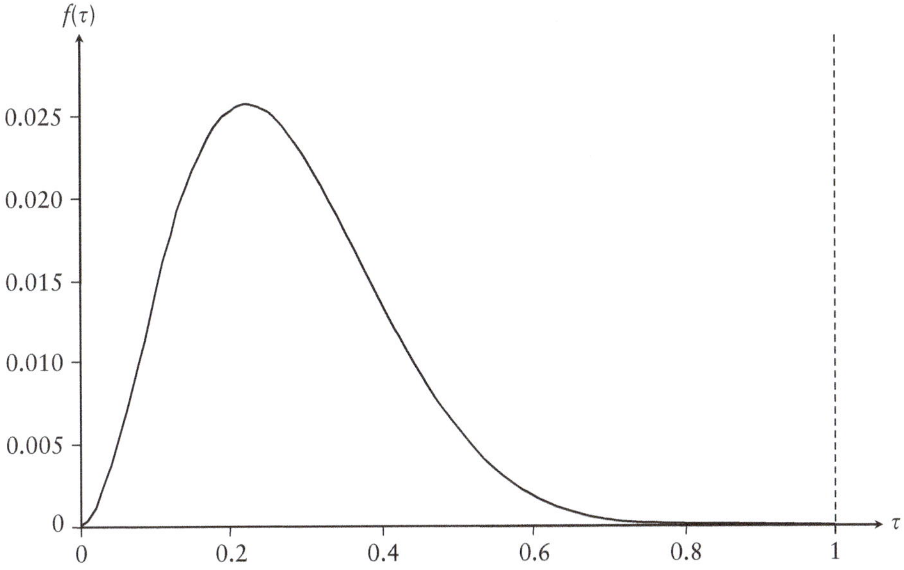

Figure 12.3 Distribution of tastes—Beta(2,7)

from which we can deduce that Alf's optimal bid in the first-price auction is given by[14]

$$\beta\left(\tau^a\right) = \tau^a - \frac{\int_0^{\tau^a} F(x)\,dx}{F\left(\tau^a\right)} \tag{12.15}$$

which, because we are using first-price auction rules, is the price that Alf will pay if he wins.

Because the problem is symmetric all of the above reasoning follows for Bill just by interchanging the a and b superscripts.[15] To illustrate this, suppose that tastes are distributed according to the beta distribution with parameters $(2, 7)$: the density function for this is in Figure 12.3 and the formal definition is given in Appendix A (page 516). Then the equilibrium bid function $\beta(\cdot)$ in equation (12.15) and the resulting probability of winning (12.9) as a function of individual values are as depicted in Figure 12.4.

Second price auction: a truth-telling mechanism?

Now take the English open-bid auction. In the case of the *private-values* information model, the dominant strategy in such an auction is to carry on bidding until the bid has reached one's true value of the object and then, if the price goes still higher, withdraw from the bidding; a successful bid need only be infinitesimally greater than the bid made by the last person to drop out. So in effect the successful bidder pays the price set by the 'runner-up' bid. If invited to submit a sealed bid, knowing that, if successful, one is only

? Mini Problems

14 Explain why, using (12.10).

15 Take a population of size $N > 2$. How does the above reasoning change for this case?

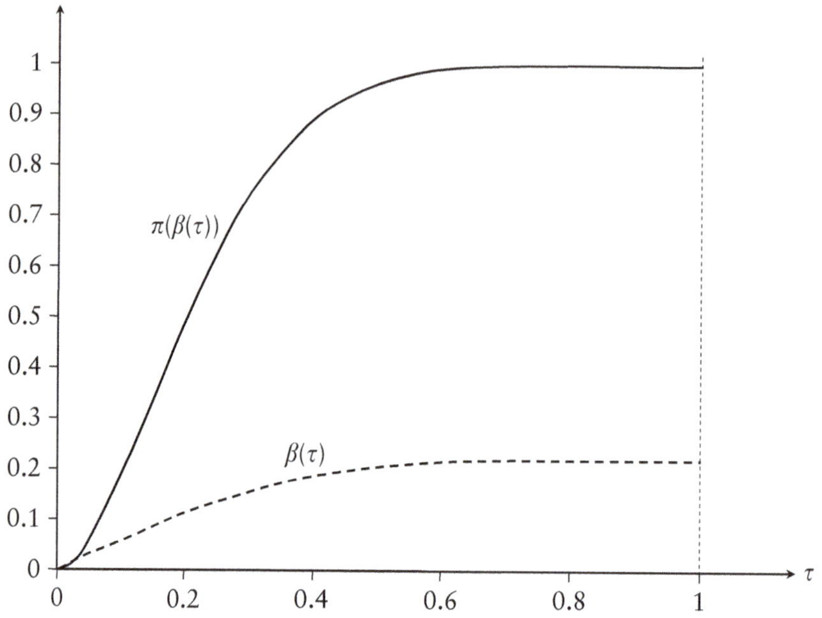

Figure 12.4 First-price auction: bid and probability of winning

required to pay the price of the next-highest bid, it is again a dominant strategy to bid one's true valuation.[16] So in the private-values case the English open-bid auction scheme works out as essentially the same as a second-price auction.[17]

The remarkable thing is that we have immediately found a simple mechanism that enforces truth telling in this particular imperfect information setting. However, this is a case where the mechanism only weakly implements the outcome with truth telling: there are other equilibria that will lead to dissimulation in the auction—and this may lead to collusive outcomes.[18]

? Mini Problems

16 Suppose your true valuation of the object is τ.

(a) Why is it pointless to submit a bid p that is less than τ?
(b) Why might it actually harm you to submit a bid p greater than τ?

17 Why might the English open-bid auction and the second-price sealed-bid auction not be equivalent if one were selling off the mineral rights on a plot of land?

18 In the independent private value model suppose there is a fixed number of bidders and that the private valuations for the good are distributed on the interval $[0, 1]$. Consider the following profile of strategies in the second-price auction: bidder 1 submits a price 1; all the others bid 0. (i) Show that this is an equilibrium of the auction mechanism. (ii) Show that collusion amongst the bidders in such an equilibrium may be self-enforcing. (iii) What practical arrangements might be necessary for such collusion to work?

Auctions: notation

τ^h	private value of agent h
p^h	price bid by agent h
P^h	payment required of h by the auction rules
π^h	probability that h wins the auction
$\beta(\cdot)$	bid function

Let us look again at the two-bidder example, just switching from first-price to second-price rules. Now, if Alf's bid succeeds and he gets the good his benefit is $\tau^a - \beta\left(\tau^b\right)$. Risk-neutral Alf again seeks to maximise expected net benefit $\pi\left(p^a\right)\left[\tau^a - p^b\right]$ where $p^b = \beta\left(\tau^b\right)$.[19] The optimal bid function in the second-price auction must be[20]

$$\beta\left(\tau^a\right) = \tau^a \qquad (12.16)$$

and the probability that Alf gets the good in equilibrium is $F(\tau^a)$. Finally the price that Alf will expect to pay, if successful in his bid, is

$$\tau^a - \frac{\int_0^{\tau^a} F(\tau)\, d\tau.}{F(\tau^a)} \qquad (12.17)$$

A natural question is to examine which of the two auction types—first or second price—is in some sense preferable. However, instead of addressing that comparison directly it is more useful to examine the fundamental design issues that underlie them and other types of auction.

Design issues

So far we have treated the rules governing an auction as though they were hardwired. Now we want to drop that assumption in order to think rather more broadly about some basic questions. What principles ought to be brought to bear in planning an auction? To answer this properly we would need first to think through the objectives of the design problem—who plays the role of Designer? In most cases it may be reasonable to suppose that the auctioneer acts in the seller's interest: so should we therefore make maximisation of the proceeds of the auction the sole target of the design problem?

We will return to this in a moment: before doing so, consider the way to write down an auction model. Rather than assuming the existence of a specific auction institution and a set of rules, we will describe it in fairly broad terms as a mechanism. In general we can characterise the auction by two rules, that are based on the signals that the bidders provide. Let the bid (the signal) by agent h be p^h. Then the two rules characterising the mechanism are as follows:

? Mini Problems

19 Could Alf's expected net benefit be negative?

20 Verify these conclusions by following an argument similar to that for the first-price case.

- The *allocation rule*

$$\pi^h\left(p^1,p^2,\ldots\right),\ h=1,2,3\ldots \tag{12.18}$$

gives the probability that any particular agent h will be awarded the object.

- The *payment rule*

$$P^h\left(p^1,p^2,\ldots\right),\ h=1,2,3\ldots \tag{12.19}$$

specifies who pays what when the auction is settled. It allows for the possibility that not only the winner has to pay up.

Armed with little more than this we can introduce a fundamental result. The only restriction that we need to impose a priori is that auctions are organised in such a way that the object goes to the highest bidder. Then we have:

Theorem 12.6 (Revenue equivalence)

If bidders are risk neutral and each has a taste type τ that is independently drawn from a common distribution with strictly positive density, then any auction mechanism in which (i) the object always goes to the highest bidder and (ii) any bidder with the lowest possible value gets zero net benefit, yields the same expected revenue and results in each bidder making the same expected payment as a function of his type.

The method for establishing this result is relatively simple (the proof is in Appendix C). The main steps in the argument are:

- In view of the revelation principle we can characterise the auction as an exercise in announcing a valuation.
- For the proposed mechanism to have a Bayesian Nash equilibrium the functions $\pi^h(\cdot)$ and $P^h(\cdot)$ it must satisfy the participation and incentive-compatibility constraints for every agent.
- Given that everyone is maximising expected net benefit, the requirement that the object goes to the highest bidder ensures that in equilibrium your expected net benefit, your bid, and the probability that you win are increasing functions of your true value of the object.
- The expected payment by the winner and the expected receipts of the seller can then be expressed in terms of these solution functions. But the solution is independent of the particular variant of the auction game.

Although Theorem 12.6 has been stated in terms of the private-information case it can be established for a wide class of models, as long as the bidders and the seller are interested only in expected payoffs, the object goes to the highest bidder and there is an appropriate constraint on the lowest-valuation bidders. The revenue equivalence theorem at first sight seems extraordinary, because of its apparent generality. However, it is a good idea to highlight some qualifications that are evident on a close reading of the result.

First, it is important to note the special conditions under which Theorem 12.6 holds. If, for example, there were just two possible taste types—every bidder is either τ° or τ' but nothing else—the requirement on the density condition is violated and it is possible to find a Bayesian Nash equilibrium that violates revenue equivalence.[21]

Second, the result is expressed only in terms of *expected* payoffs. If the seller were risk averse then he or she would be concerned with the entire probability distribution of the price that will emerge from the auction, not just its expected value. We can derive the distribution of price P from the underlying distribution of taste τ using (a) the rules that determine the price paid P (first price or second price) and (b) a result on order statistics (see page 514). As an example take the two-person auction discussed earlier, with the distribution of values depicted in Figure 12.5:

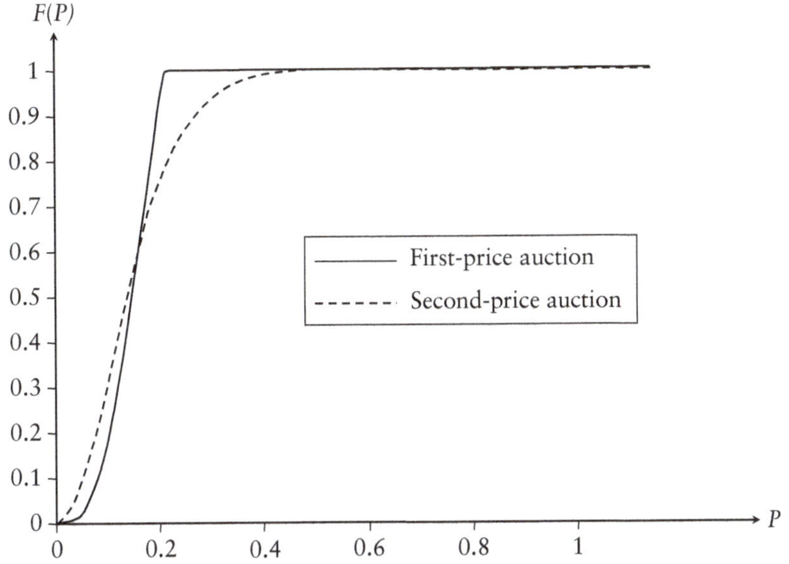

Figure 12.5 Distribution of price paid

? Mini Problems

21 Take an example where there are exactly two types with values $\tau = 0$ and $\tau = 1$. The potential buyers Alf and Bill each have independently a probability of 0.5 of being of either type. The auctioneer announces a price P; if just one of the buyers accepts he gets the object at price P. Otherwise the allocation is determined by spinning a coin and the price paid is either P (if both accept) or 0 (if neither accepts). If both accept then only the winner of the lottery has to pay.

(a) Suppose the announced price is $P = 0.5$. Alf assumes that Bill will only accept this price if and only if it turns out that $\tau^b = 1$. So, if Alf accepts the price, what is the probability that he gets the object?

(b) Show that Alf will accept the price $P = 0.5$ if it turns out that $\tau^a = 1$. Hence describe the equilibrium probabilities of winning and the net benefit as a function of τ.

(c) Show that such an equilibrium can be generated for *any* price P such that $0 < P < \frac{2}{3}$.

(d) Explain why this situation violates revenue equivalence.

- the solid curve represents the distribution function for the first-price auction. This is found by using the bid function in (12.15) for the higher of the two random variables τ^a, τ^b.
- the broken curve represents the distribution function for the second-price case. This is found by setting the price to the lower of the two random variables τ^a, τ^b.
- Clearly the curves intersect just once: the probability of prices at the extremes of the price range (towards zero or 1) is smaller under the first-price auction than under the second-price auction.
- Because of Theorem 12.6 the mean of the two distributions is the same: so comparing the two the risk-averse seller would clearly prefer the distribution with the lower dispersion of prices—the first-price auction.

Example 12.2

The auction of British third-generation mobile-phone licences in 2000 raised £22.5 billion ($34 billion). 'Not since the Praetorian Guard knocked down the entire Roman Empire to Didius Julianus in AD 195 had there been an auction quite as large.' Binmore and Klemperer (2002) examine the issues involved in designing the auction and the lessons that can be learned from it.

12.6.2 A public project

The second application of mechanism design concerns a special type of public good—one that fits well the working example used to discuss potential superiority in section 9.3.6 (page 253).

The main issue can be represented by a model of the economy in which agents consume quantities of just two goods. Good 1 is an indivisible project of fixed size: an airport, a bridge; good 2 is a basket of all other goods. The assumption is that there are only two values of the quantity of good 1, that make sense: $x_1 = 1$ where the good is provided and $x_1 = 0$ where it is not. To provide the resources for the project will require agents to give up some consumption of good 2.

In view of the restricted nature of the problem, the set of all social states can be represented very simply as $\Theta = \{\theta^\circ, \theta'\}$ where θ° and θ' mean 'NO-PROJECT', 'PROJECT' respectively. Production conditions for the two social states can be described as:

$$\begin{aligned} \theta^\circ &: \quad \phi(0) = 0 \\ \theta' &: \quad \phi(\overline{z}) = 1 \end{aligned} \tag{12.20}$$

where ϕ is the production function and $\overline{z}$ is the minimum amount of the private good that is required to produce the unit amount of the public good.

A public project: elements of the problem

τ^h	taste parameter of agent h
$\psi(\cdot)$	utility of good 1
y^h	income of agent h
z^h	required contribution from agent h
θ°	'NO-PROJECT' state
θ'	'PROJECT' state

A complete specification of the problem requires two further components:

- *Preferences.* Household's preferences are given by a function $U^h(\cdot)$ defined over (x_1, x_2^h)-space where, x_1 is common to all households and x_2^h is household h's private consumption of good 2. We take the special 'zero-income-effect' form of the utility function that we introduced in the discussion of a monopolist's design of a fee function—see equations (11.1 and 11.14). So in this case we have

$$U^h(x_1, x_2^h) = \tau^h \psi(x_1) + x_2^h \tag{12.21}$$

where ψ is an increasing concave function, common to all agents and τ^h is a taste parameter that captures household h's strength of desire for the public good. We may further simplify by normalising ψ such that

$$\psi(0) = 0; \;\; \psi(1) = 1. \tag{12.22}$$

- *An apportionment rule.* Some apportionment of the total required contribution $\bar{z}$ amongst the households. This rule could, but need not, involve equal division. However, the individual required contributions or levies $[z^1, z^2, z^3, \ldots]$ must satisfy

$$\bar{z} \leq \sum_{h=1}^{n_h} z^h. \tag{12.23}$$

If household h is endowed with an income y^h (denominated in units of good 2) then z^h, the amount of levy required from h, determines consumption of the private good:

$$x_2^h = y^h - z^h.$$

A full specification of state θ' requires a listing of all the individual required levies, which are public information. Given the list of individual levies and the utility functions we can work out each agent's compensating variation for the switch $\theta^\circ \to \theta'$, which we shall write as CV^h. Of course there will be winners, for whom this is positive, and losers, for whom the reverse is true—Figure 12.6 illustrates one of each in the special case where endowments and required contributions are identical across persons; individuals differ only in tastes—i.e. the function ψ in (12.21). Alf and Bill are each affected by the implementation of a large project that produces a public good of given size. In the absence of the project they are at points labelled θ° with coordinates $(0, y^a)$ and $(0, y^b)$; with it they are points labelled θ' with coordinates $(1, y^a - z^a)$ and $(1, y^b - z^b)$. From the

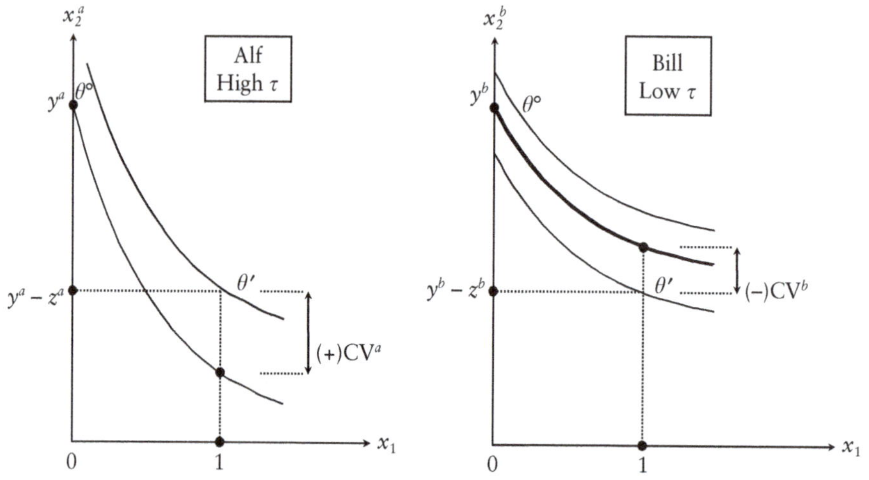

Figure 12.6 A fixed-size project

way in which Figure 12.6 is drawn it is clear that Alf's CV for the change in social state $\theta^\circ \rightarrow \theta'$ is positive and Bill's CV is negative.

If it is true that

$$\sum_{h=1}^{n_h} \mathrm{CV}^h > 0 \tag{12.24}$$

then it appears to be possible to obtain a potential Pareto improvement (see page 254) by switching from θ° to θ'. Indeed, if the population consisted only of Alf and Bill, then given the situation in Figure 12.6 the switch from θ° to θ' would generate a potential improvement.[22] Given the simplified structure of the utility function (12.21), the condition (12.24) is equivalent to[23]

$$\sum_{h=1}^{n_h} \tau^h > \bar{z}. \tag{12.25}$$

The design problem

We have again the same issues as in the previous application to auctions. Indeed we can reuse some of the same terminology and methods.

First the Designer and the objectives. In the present context it is reasonable to assume that the government acts as Principal in the problem, deciding on an appropriate implementation procedure that will affect its citizens, but relying on information from those citizens as agents. Unlike the seller in the auction application the government is not

? Mini Problems

22 Using the same preferences, but with different costs draw a diagram similar to Figure 12.6 to show a case where the reverse conclusion holds.

23 Calculate CV from (12.21) and show that (12.25) is equivalent to (12.24).

out to make money for itself but to maximise social welfare: we will assume that the welfare criterion to be used in connection with the project is consistent with the 'potential superiority' criterion in Definition 9.7.

Now for the problem of implementation. In order to make a choice from the set Θ that is consistent with the welfare criterion the government needs to know how large the CVs are, in other words, what agents' true values τ^h are: but how would the government get accurate information about preferences? If there were a list of agents perhaps it could do a house-to-house survey of people's willingness to pay, but of course this will not work. Irrespective of how the actual burden of cost will be resolved, the government knows that it cannot rely on the good nature of its citizens: it has to assume that each one will lie about his true value so as not to be saddled with so much of the share of the cost.

The recourse that the government has is to devise a mechanism—an incentive scheme—by which lying becomes pointless. Agents are invited to signal their tastes τ^h for the project by announcing values p^h: if h is telling the truth, of course, we have

$$p^h = \tau^h. \tag{12.26}$$

Pursuing the auction analogy it is as though a person submits a 'bid' for the project to go ahead. Corresponding to the expressions (12.18) and (12.19) that were used to define the auction mechanism we have here:

- The *decision rule*

$$\pi\left(p^1, p^2, \ldots\right) \tag{12.27}$$

  which determines whether the project goes ahead or not in the light of the announced bids. Here π takes exactly one of two values: 0 (for 'no go') or 1 (for 'go').

- The *payment rule*

$$P^h\left(p^1, p^2, \ldots\right),\; h = 1, 2, 3, \ldots \tag{12.28}$$

  specifies who pays what when the decision is made: this amount may include penalties as well as the cost allocations built into the project, as we will see.

Consider a system of contingent penalties, based on individual agents' declared bids p^h. Note, first of all, that misrepresentation does not matter very much if it is not 'decisive'. In the binary-choice case, suppose we were in the utopian situation where all agents tell the truth about their willingness to pay and that the sum of the compensating variations is strictly positive. Then it would not matter very much if one or two people lied a little bit, because we might still find that the sum of the bids covers the required amount $\bar{z}$ (the sum of the declared CVs was positive), so that the project would still go ahead: all that would happen is that the liars would get a bit of surplus good 2. But there is always the danger that the sum of the bids falls short of $\bar{z}$ (the sum of the declared CVs turns out negative). The trick is to punish anyone who might frivolously tip the balance in this way.

To make this idea of 'tipping the balance' more precise consider the following expressions:

$$\sum_{k=1}^{n_h}\left[p^k - z^k\right] \tag{12.29}$$

and

$$\Delta^h := \sum_{\substack{k=1 \\ k \neq h}}^{n_h} \left[p^k - z^k \right]. \tag{12.30}$$

The two expressions involve only things that can be directly observed and can be interpreted as follows:

- Expression (12.29) gives the equivalent to the sum-of-CV condition where one replaces the actual values τ^h by announced values or bids p^h: if it is non-negative then, analogous to (12.24), we can interpret this as meaning 'the announced willingness-to-pay for all the agents is large enough to cover the costs of the public good'.
- Expression (12.30) is the counterpart with agent h deleted: if it is non-negative then we can interpret this as 'the announced willingness-to-pay for all agents except h is large enough to cover their share of the cost of the public good' or, in a slight over-simplification, 'everyone except h says 'yes' to the project'.

A simple public-project mechanism relies just on these two quantities and can be characterised as a *pivotal mechanism* or a *tipping mechanism.* Take (12.29) as a criterion for going ahead with the project: 'no-go' if it is negative, 'go' otherwise. so that the decision criterion can be represented as

$$\pi\left(p^1, p^2, \ldots\right) = \begin{cases} 1 & \text{if} \sum_{k=1}^{n_h} p^k \geq \bar{z} \\ 0 & \text{otherwise} \end{cases} \tag{12.31}$$

Suppose we find that (12.29) is indeed negative, but that (12.30) is positive or zero: then, in a sense, agent h tips the balance, or is *pivotal*; without the announcement of his CV it looked as if the decision ought to have gone the other way. In these circumstances the appropriate penalty for the government to impose on h would be the apparent gains forgone by all the other households now that the project is 'no go'; in other words a penalty equal to Δ^h in (12.30). So in this mechanism the payment system (12.28) is as follows. Each agent h is required to pay:[24]

$$P^h\left(p^1, p^2, \ldots\right) = \begin{cases} z^h & \text{if } \pi = 1 \text{ and } h \text{ is not pivotal} \\ z^h - \Delta^h & \text{if } \pi = 1 \text{ and } h \text{ is pivotal} \\ 0 & \text{if } \pi = 0 \text{ and } h \text{ is not pivotal} \\ \Delta^h & \text{if } \pi = 0 \text{ and } h \text{ is pivotal} \end{cases} \tag{12.32}$$

where π is determined by (12.31). Note that the amount Δ^h plays the role of a penalty to be imposed on any pivotal agent.[25] Given the assumption of zero income effects then this mechanism becomes 'reversible': in Figure 12.6 we could take θ' as the status quo and apply the mirror-image criterion for 'go/no-go' of a switch back to θ°, with a mirror-image penalty for any 'pivotal' household.

? Mini Problems

24 Show that the penalty terms in (12.32) are never negative. What does this imply about total payments for the project? Show that this implies that the mechanism may be inefficient.

25 Show that a pivotal agent can always afford to pay the penalty if he or she is telling the truth.

Decision	Everyone else says... 'YES'	'NO'
'go'	Nil	$\sum$ costs imposed on everyone else
'no-go'	$\sum$ forgone gains of everyone else	Nil

Table 12.2 Penalty table for public projects

Then the complete contingent penalty system can be summarised as in Table 12.2, and it yields the following important result (for proof see Appendix C):

Theorem 12.7 (Clark–Groves)

A scheme which (a) approves a project if and only if (12.29) is non-negative, and (b) imposes a penalty of size (12.29) on any household h if (12.29) and (12.30) have opposite signs, will ensure that truthful revelation of CVs is a dominant strategy.

This result, which can be generalised,[26] is typical of a class of mechanisms that rely on restricting the form of the utility function and the set of states from which one can choose in order to get a mechanism that is non-manipulable or 'cheat-proof'.[27] The mechanism involved is essentially that of the second-price auction that we discussed in the previous application on page 400.

12.6.3 Contracting again

As we noted in the introduction to this chapter, one aspect of the design problem had already been glimpsed in the treatment of the economics of information in chapter 11. There a firm used its market power to design a truth-telling mechanism: it adjusted the fee schedule so as to ensure that, in situations where agents' characteristics were private information, the different customer types (high valuation or low valuation) revealed themselves through the quantities that they demanded. The general idea is clear: in cases where there is market power the monopolist or monopsonist can act as a designer who sets up trading rules; the designer's objectives are the profits generated by the trade.

We will now use this approach to consider an alternative interpretation of the Principal-and-Agent problem. This interpretation focuses on hidden characteristics on the part of

? Mini Problems

26 In the payment table you can add an amount to each payment that is an arbitrary function of each of the other agents declared ps. Why?

27 Suppose Alf's taste for the public project were to increase. What would happen to the decision as to whether the project goes ahead and on who pays for the project?

the Agent rather than hidden actions. Accordingly, instead of constructing a model where a Principal hires a worker who puts in unobservable effort—as in section 11.4—we simply adapt the adverse-selection model that was set out in chapter 11. One of the reasons that we treat the problem here rather than in chapter 11 is that it has such a close and powerful relationship to our next application (section 12.6.4) that is arguably a design issue par excellence.

Contracting with hidden information: elements of the problem

τ	talent of Agent
z	effort supplied
$\psi(\cdot)$	(dis)utility of effort
q	output produced by Agent
y	income offered to Agent
a	high-ability type
b	low-ability type
π	probability of a high-ability type

We are going to take the model of section 11.2 and adapt it in order to get some results on design that will have a familiar ring to them. Let us take the case of a single profit-maximising firm producing a single output: the firm as Principal hires an Agent—for example as a worker or manager—from a pool of individuals who may differ in their productivity (note that we are again using the convention of capitalisation when the Agent means specifically one half of the Principal-and-Agent double act). The behaviour of the Agent when employed is based on the elementary model of labour supply in chapter 5: he can supply an amount z of 'effort' where $0 \leq z \leq 1$ (the total amount of effort that can be supplied by the Agent is normalised to be 1). It is known that each potential employee in the pool has a constant marginal productivity—a 'talent'—that is given by a parameter τ: so the output from an Agent with talent τ who puts in an amount of effort z is given by

$$q = \tau z. \tag{12.33}$$

What of preferences? We can reuse the model introduced in chapter 11—see page 331: in this model utility is given by

$$\upsilon = \psi(z) + y \tag{12.34}$$

where y is the amount of income that the Agent gets and $\psi(\cdot)$ is a *decreasing* concave function representing the disutility of effort: the higher is z the lower is the Agent's utility for a given money income, but the marginal disutility of effort falls as z increases; $-\psi_z(z)$ is the marginal rate of substitution of money income for leisure. The indifference curves in (leisure, income)-space are shown in the left-hand panel of Figure 12.7. Using (12.33) and (12.34), for an Agent of type τ we can also express utility in

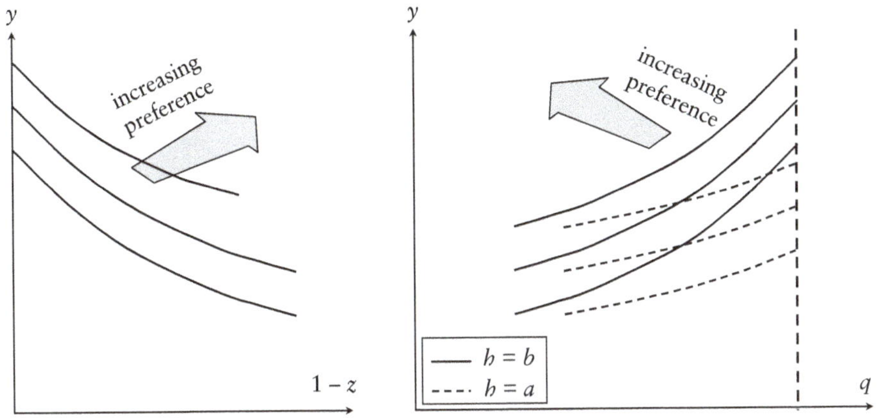

Figure 12.7 Indifference curves in (z, y)-space and (q, y)-space

(q, y)-space as[28]

$$\psi\left(\frac{q}{\tau}\right) + y.$$

Take two individuals a, b with different talents where $\tau^a > \tau^b$. In the right-hand panel of Figure 12.7 we can see that the indifference curves for an Agent with high talent ($h = a$) have unambiguously flatter indifference curves than those for the low-talent Agent ($h = b$); the figure also shows the 'single-crossing condition' that has to hold for this type of utility function (see page 334). The results that follow are not specific to this utility function, but they do require the single-crossing condition—see Exercise 12.8.

In this model the key point to notice is that all of the individuals who could potentially be employed as Agent by the Principal will have the same preferences (unlike the case of the monopolist with heterogeneous customers on pages 334–347) but the individuals differ from one another in terms of what they can produce from a given amount of effort.

Full information

Setting up the firm's optimisation problem is straightforward, since it has essentially the same shape as that in chapter 11. Suppose the firm (as Principal) hires person h as Agent with known talent τ^h (remember that everything is observable in the full-information case) and contracts to pay him a given amount of income y^h for a given amount of effort z^h. If the price of output is p then, given the simplified production function implied by (12.33) profits are:

$$p\tau^h z^h - y^h \tag{12.35}$$

which is exactly the payoff to the Principal given the contract $\left(q^h, y^h\right)$. The maximisation of profit (12.35) has to be subject to the constraint that the Agent gets as much utility as

? Mini Problems

28 What is the slope of an indifference curve in this diagram?

in any alternative occupation (where the alternative occupation includes doing nothing at all). We assume that this reservation utility for h is given by a number $\underline{\upsilon}^h$ that is common knowledge. So the participation constraint is

$$y^h + \psi\left(z^h\right) \geq \underline{\upsilon}^h. \tag{12.36}$$

We have seen this kind of problem before so we can jump straight to the full-information solution (compare page 335).[29] For any individual h with talent τ^h we must have:

$$-\psi_z\left(z^{*h}\right) = p \tag{12.37}$$

and

$$y^{*h} + \psi\left(z^{*h}\right) = \underline{\upsilon}^h. \tag{12.38}$$

This solution is illustrated in Figure 12.8. The broken curve labelled $\underline{\upsilon}^a$ and the solid curve labelled $\underline{\upsilon}^b$ are reservation indifference curves for an Agent with talent τ^a or τ^b, respectively, where $\tau^a > \tau^b$.[30] The solution for an Agent with talent τ^h must be on the reservation indifference curve $\underline{\upsilon}^h$—see equation (12.38)—exactly at the point where the indifference curve is tangential to a line with slope p—see equation (12.37) and Mini

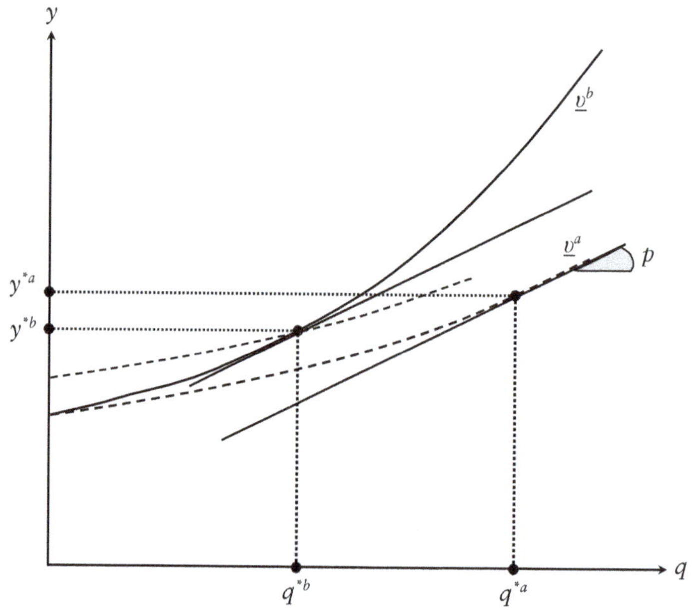

Figure 12.8 Two types of Agent: Full-information solution

? Mini Problems

29 Nevertheless it is useful to confirm this formally. Do so by setting up an appropriate Lagrangean and using the FOC to get (12.37) and (12.38).

30 Why do the two reservation indifference curves meet exactly on the vertical axis?

Problem 28. The interpretation is that the firm operates efficiently, adjusting the labour contract for any Agent h such that

$$\text{MRS}^h = \text{MRT}^h$$

and, having full knowledge of any Agent's options, exploits him by driving him down on to his reservation utility level $\underline{\upsilon}^h$.

Imperfect information

What if the productivity of workers cannot be independently observed or costlessly verified? How should the contract be designed then? Clearly productivity is no longer 'contractible' in this situation and we will have a variant of the second-best problem that was introduced on page 341. Corresponding to the situation described in chapter 11, where a monopolist did not know whether a customer was a high-valuation or a low-valuation person, we can model the situation in which the firm does not know the productivity of each potential employee at the time of signing the work contract. In order to distil the essence of the problem we can take the case of exactly two types: the *a*ble workers with talent τ^a and the *b*og-standard workers with talent τ^b where, again, $\tau^a > \tau^b$.

The problem can be characterised in terms of designing a direct mechanism (page 391) as a device for eliciting the truth. We can imagine the following situation: once again the contract can be written as a pair (q, y) (output is unambiguously observable); when a potential Agent applies for the job the Principal states the contracts that are available for each level of talent and then asks the applicant's ability level—τ^a or τ^b? Can the Agent be induced to tell the truth? In this imperfect-information case we have to take into account two constraints:[31]

- *The participation constraint.* In this case it will be relevant for the type-b Agent and is given by condition (12.36) with $h = b$.
- *The incentive-compatibility constraint.* Check Figure 12.8 once again. Notice that an able worker would strictly prefer the full-information contract offered to a bog-standard applicant rather than the full-information contract that would have been offered to an able person: if we draw the a-type's indifference curve that passes through the b-contract point $\left(q^{*b}, y^{*b}\right)$—the faint broken curve in the figure—we can see that it lies strictly above the a-type's reservation indifference curve: the able would rather get paid less, work less, and go and play golf. To prevent an a-type masquerading as a b-type the following would have to be satisfied:

$$y^a + \psi\left(\frac{q^a}{\tau^a}\right) \geq y^b + \psi\left(\frac{q^b}{\tau^a}\right). \tag{12.39}$$

? Mini Problems

31 Strictly speaking there are four constraints, not two, but two of the four are redundant. Following the reasoning on pages 342–3 explain why this is so using the model of indifference curves depicted in Figure 12.8.

An implication of this is that in equilibrium the a-types must have a higher (q, y)-combination than the b-types.[32]

If the proportion of the high-ability individuals in the pool of applicants is π, then the Principal assumes that a potential applicant is a-type with probability π, b-type with probability $1 - \pi$ So the firm seeks to maximise

$$\pi \left[pq^a - y^a\right] + [1 - \pi] \left[pq^b - y^b\right]$$

subject to (12.36) and (12.39). The Lagrangean representation of the problem is

$$\begin{aligned} \max_{\{q^a, q^b, y^a, y^b\}} \quad & \pi \left[pq^a - y^a\right] + [1 - \pi] \left[pq^b - y^b\right] \\ & + \lambda \left[y^b + \psi\left(\frac{q^b}{\tau^b}\right) - \underline{\upsilon}^b\right] \\ & + \mu \left[y^a + \psi\left(\frac{q^a}{\tau^a}\right) - y^b - \psi\left(\frac{q^b}{\tau^a}\right)\right] \end{aligned} \tag{12.40}$$

where λ and μ the Lagrange multipliers for, respectively, the participation constraint on the bog-standard workers and the incentive-compatibility constraint for the able workers. From the first-order conditions for the problem in (12.40) we derive the following for an interior solution:[33]

$$-\psi_z\left(\frac{q^a}{\tau^a}\right) = p\tau^a \tag{12.41}$$

$$-\psi_z\left(\frac{q^b}{\tau^b}\right) = p\tau^b + \frac{\pi}{1 - \pi}\left[\psi_z\left(\frac{q^b}{\tau^b}\right) - \frac{\tau^b}{\tau^a}\psi_z\left(\frac{q^b}{\tau^a}\right)\right]. \tag{12.42}$$

However, if ψ is concave and $0 < a < 1$ then[34] $a\psi_z(az) > \psi_z(z)$ and so (12.41), (12.42) imply

$$\text{MRS}^a = \text{MRT}^a$$

$$\text{MRS}^b < \text{MRT}^b.$$

Once again we have an example of the no-distortion-at-the-top principle (Theorem 11.2).

Contract design

As a consequence of conditions (12.41), (12.42) the firm, acting as Principal, could design the pair of contracts $(\tilde{q}^a, \tilde{y}^a)$ and $\left(\tilde{q}^b, \tilde{y}^b\right)$ in Figure 12.9 as a simple, truth-revealing

? Mini Problems

32 Use the answer to Mini Problem 31 and the indifference curve map in (q, y)-space to demonstrate this.

33 Write down the FOC and derive (12.41), (12.42).

34 Show this.

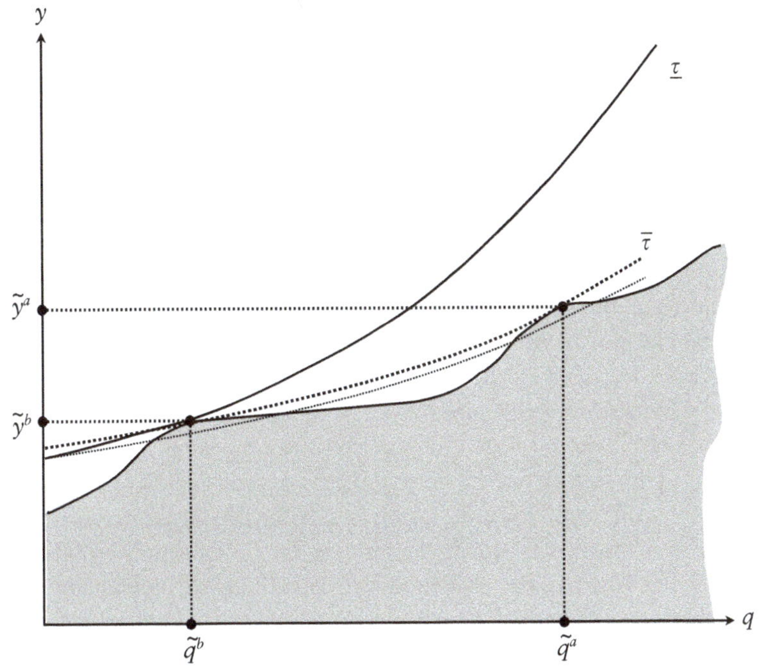

Figure 12.9 Two types of Agent: contract design

direct mechanism. Offering just these two contracts to potential applicants would ensure the following:[35]

- *Able applicants* would (just) prefer to take $(\tilde{q}^a, \tilde{y}^a)$ where they are paid exactly according to their marginal product. They get a higher money income than they would have done were a full-information solution possible, but they put in the same amount of effort.[36]
- *Bog-standard applicants* would be kept on their reservation utility level (just as they would have been under a full-information solution). However, the marginal return to effort for this type of applicants is set below their marginal product, in order to prevent misrepresentation by able applicants. So a typical b-type would produce less and earn less than under the full-information outcome.

As an alternative to just offering the pair of contracts the firm could offer a complete menu of (output, income) combinations for all potential applicants, knowing of course

? Mini Problems

35 Use a diagram similar to Figure 12.8 to illustrate the second-best contract. [Hint: check Figure 11.7.] Show the income and utility gain made by the able types compared with the situation under the full-information contract.

36 How will an increase in (i) p and (ii) π affect the payoffs to type-a and type-b applicants? Consider both the full-information equilibrium and the second-best equilibrium.

that an *a*-type would go for $\left(\tilde{q}^a, \tilde{y}^a\right)$ and a *b*-type for $\left(\tilde{q}^b, \tilde{y}^b\right)$—the attainable set facing a potential applicant would look something like that in Figure 12.9.[37]

12.6.4 Taxation

We can exploit the 'hidden characteristics' version of the Principal-and-Agent story in a particularly useful way. In chapters 7 and 9 we raised the possibility of the government as a kind of disembodied spirit that could adjust the distribution of property in order to produce a specific allocation of consumption bundles and a specific distribution of utility levels. By focusing on households' or individuals' ownership of property—assumed to be exogenously fixed endowments of resources and shares in firms—we appear to sidestep what is sometimes described as 'the incentives issue'. The issue is this: if you were to try to reach the desired allocation by imposing a tax on a people's labour *incomes*, say, then you would alter the effective wage rate and thus alter the supply of labour (there is a simple example of this in Exercise 5.7 on page 121); you will also have introduced a price distortion that is inefficient. However, trying to sidestep the incentives issue by focusing on property is perhaps illusory, for it glosses over the fundamental problem of appropriately identifying who are the well-endowed households or individuals from whom resources could be expropriated. To do this comprehensively would typically require the government to know essentially private information about individual economic agents. The problem of revealing private information, of course, places the issue firmly within the general approach to mechanism design that we have considered in this chapter.

The design issue

In order to keep the problem manageable and make the comparison with other applications relatively easy we will restrict the discussion to a narrowly defined example of taxation. What drives the example is the need for a government to raise revenue: this could be to fund transfers to support low-income households, to pay for publicly provided goods, or to meet some exogenous obligation. However, the revenue raising through taxation ought not to be capricious but should conform to some basic welfare-economic principles.

Our approach to the problem is to start with a very simple version of the model—so simple that its connections with the section 12.6.3 are obvious—and then show that the conclusions from this largely carry across to more interesting versions. Here is a brief summary of the main story that makes it easy to compare with the contracting model just considered:

- At the heart of the analysis is a two-commodity model—the commodities being leisure (i.e. the opposite of effort) and all other goods. Individuals work (i.e. they give up leisure) to provide themselves with means of acquiring other goods. Their preferences are given by the utility function (12.34) where z is effort and y is income (note that

? Mini Problems

37 Suppose it is common knowledge that there are three potential types of Agent, where $\tau^a > \tau^b > \tau^c$. What are the relevant constraints for the second-best problem? What is the Lagrangean? Show that the no-distortion-at-the-top principle still holds.

here and in what follows, in the language of public finance, 'income' means 'disposable income'). This is very close to the previous application of the contracting model.

- There is a community of individuals who differ in terms of their productive ability or talent τ. Higher-ability people produce more and thus earn more in terms of other goods: an individual with talent τ who puts in effort z will produce an amount q given by (12.33). Again this is similar to the contracting model: but instead of a single Agent with known *ex-ante* probability distribution of talents, we have a population of workers with a known distribution of abilities.
- There is an exogenously imposed constraint that requires the community to raise a fixed amount $K \geq 0$ of revenue: this is to be done by the government imposing a tax—driving a wedge between the market income generated by the individual worker and the amount of income that he or she has to spend on other goods.
- In each variant of the taxation model the designer is the government rather than a private firm acting as Principal. This follows the public-project application of section 12.6.2.
- The objective function is based on the welfare analysis of chapter 9. Social welfare is an additively separable function of individual utilities (see page 262).

Optimal taxation: elements of the problem

τ	productivity of worker
z	effort supplied
$\psi(\cdot)$	(dis)utility of effort
q	output produced (gross income earned) by worker
y	disposable income received by worker
a	high-productivity type
b	low-productivity type
π	proportion of high-productivity types
υ	individual utility
$\zeta(\upsilon)$	social evaluation of individual utility

A simple model

Consider first the economic opportunities facing the agents. As with previous applications we assume that every agent h has a well-defined best alternative that yields utility level $\underline{\upsilon}^h$. In this first attempt at the taxation model we assume that there are just two types of agent (household) in the economy: able workers with productivity τ^a and the others with basic talents, who have productivity τ^b; it is common knowledge that the proportion of type-a workers is π. So the output (income) being generated in the community is as follows:

$$\begin{aligned} q^a &= \tau^a z^a && \text{with proportion } \pi \\ q^b &= \tau^b z^b && \text{with proportion } 1-\pi \end{aligned}$$

Following standard practice we take a very simple interpretation of social welfare: the objective is the sum of a transformation of individual utilities:

$$\pi\zeta\left(v^a\right) + [1-\pi]\,\zeta\left(v^b\right)$$

where ζ is an increasing, concave function that incorporates a possible concern for inequality.[38] Using (12.34), this gives us

$$\pi\zeta\left(\psi\left(z^a\right) + y^a\right) + [1-\pi]\,\zeta\left(\psi\left(z^b\right) + y^b\right). \tag{12.43}$$

In the absence of taxation the incomes in (12.43) are determined just by output: $y^j = q^j$, $j = a, b$. Otherwise the government will determine what the income y^j of each type is; by an appropriate choice of income-tax schedule it can also determine the output q^j—or equivalently the effort z^j—of each type. This is the heart of the design problem in the income-tax setting. How it is to be done, of course, depends on the information that we assume to be available to the government: we again examine two standard cases.

The full-information case requires only that each agent is persuaded to participate in the production of output—so that condition (12.36) holds—and that the government's budget constraint be satisfied. This budget constraint is merely that the amount raised from the taxpayers must be at least as great as the exogenous revenue requirement:

$$\pi\left[q^a - y^a\right] + [1-\pi]\left[q^b - y^b\right] \geq K. \tag{12.44}$$

The solution to the full-information case in the two-type model is then given by:[39]

$$-\psi_z\left(\frac{q^j}{\tau^j}\right) = \tau^j,\ j = a, b. \tag{12.45}$$

which is of course MRS = MRT for each type.

However, the full-information solution is perhaps unreasonably demanding in its requirements: should we expect the government to know the *potential* earning capacity τ of each agent and to impose a tax based on this potential? It surely makes sense to look at the case where the value of the parameter τ is private to each individual, in other words the second-best solution. Comparison with the contracting model suggests that we only need to introduce an appropriate incentive-compatibility constraint. In designing the tax system—in effect setting up the output-income pairs (q, y)—the government must ensure that the a-type citizens are not to be encouraged to misrepresent themselves as b-types. This means that the utility available to a-types given the pair (q^a, y^a) must be at least as great as the utility available to them from the pair $\left(q^b, y^b\right)$; in other words we have constraint (12.39) again. Also (for the same reasons as in the answer to Mini Problem 32) the incentive compatibility condition requires that

$$\left(q^b, y^b\right) < \left(q^a, y^a\right). \tag{12.46}$$

? Mini Problems

38 How is this related to the function ζ used in the additive social-welfare function of chapter 9 (page 262)?

39 Show this by setting up a Lagrangean and using the first-order conditions.

Putting all the components together, the Lagrangean for this version of the optimal tax problem is then

$$\begin{aligned}\max_{\{q^a,q^b,y^a,y^b\}} \quad & \pi\zeta\left(y^a+\psi\left(\tfrac{q^a}{\tau^a}\right)\right)+[1-\pi]\zeta\left(y^b+\psi\left(\tfrac{q^b}{\tau^b}\right)\right) \\ & +\kappa\left[\pi\left[q^a-y^a\right]+[1-\pi]\left[q^b-y^b\right]-K\right] \\ & +\lambda\left[y^b+\psi\left(\tfrac{q^b}{\tau^b}\right)-\underline{\upsilon}^b\right] \\ & +\mu\left[y^a+\psi\left(\tfrac{q^a}{\tau^a}\right)-y^b-\psi\left(\tfrac{q^b}{\tau^a}\right)\right]\end{aligned} \tag{12.47}$$

where κ is the Lagrange multiplier for the government budget constraint (12.44) and λ, μ are the usual Lagrange multipliers for the constraints (12.36) and (12.39). Comparing (12.43) with (12.40) we can see that the structure of the present problem is very similar to the second-best contracting model with unknown talents. So it is unsurprising to find that the second-best equilibrium consists of the following conditions:[40]

$$-\psi_z\left(\frac{q^a}{\tau^a}\right)=\tau^a \tag{12.48}$$

$$-\psi_z\left(\frac{q^b}{\tau^b}\right)=\tau^b-\frac{\mu}{[1-\pi]\,\zeta_\upsilon\left(\upsilon^b\right)+\lambda}\left[\tau^b+\frac{\tau^b}{\tau^a}\psi_z\left(\frac{q^b}{\tau^a}\right)\right] \tag{12.49}$$

and

$$\pi\left[q^a-y^a\right]+[1-\pi]\left[q^b-y^b\right]-K=0 \tag{12.50}$$

—compare (12.48), (12.49) with (12.41), (12.42) in the contracting model. The right-hand side of (12.49) must be strictly less than τ^b if the incentive-compatibility constraint is binding.[41] So, from (12.48) and (12.49), we can once again infer

$$\text{MRS}^a=\text{MRT}^a$$

$$\text{MRS}^b<\text{MRT}^b,$$

a no-distortion-at-the-top result just as in the contracting model of section 12.6.3.[42]

A richer model

To reassure ourselves that this result is not a mere artefact of the simplified model just considered we now make a jump to a model that is closer to reality; but it does not involve a very big jump. Suppose there is a large number $N+1$ of talent types such that

$$\tau^0<\tau^1<\tau^2\ldots<\tau^N$$

? **Mini Problems**

40 Show this [Hint: follow the steps used in the answer to Mini Problem 33.]

41 Show this.

42 Carefully explain what happens if $\zeta_\upsilon(\cdot)$ is constant in (12.49): see also Exercise 12.11 at the end of the chapter.

with a known proportion π^j of the population belonging to type j such that $\sum_{j=0}^{N} \pi^j = 1$. One of the advantages of enriching the model in this way is that the redistribution aspect of tax can be made more interesting: if, for example $K = 0$ in (12.44), so that the taxation exercise is one of pure redistribution, then it is perfectly reasonable to suppose that $y^j > q^j$ for some types (a 'negative tax') and the question is which groups should pay for this income subsidy in the optimal design.

Let us think through how the design problem is changed. There is no point in going through the full-information story once more—we know that the best that can be done is achieved by (12.45) for $j = 0, 1, \ldots, N$. So let us again assume that the talent τ^j is private information. Here we can take advantage of a point established in the answer to Mini Problem 37: the two-type contracting model is easily extended to the three-type contracting model and thereby to as many types as you like. The key thing is that the incentive-compatibility constraint must hold for every adjacent pair of types: no one has the incentive to misrepresent himself as the type 'below'. So we now need to replace (12.39) with

$$y^j + \psi\left(\frac{q^j}{\tau^j}\right) \geq y^{j-1} + \psi\left(\frac{q^{j-1}}{\tau^j}\right) \tag{12.51}$$

for every $j = 1, 2, \ldots, N$. Following through the reasoning for the two-type model—see condition (12.46)—this implies that (q^j, y^j) increases with j.

Instead of the Lagrangean (12.47) we now have:

$$\begin{aligned} \max_{\{(q^j, y^j)\}} \quad & \sum_{j=0}^{N} \pi^j \zeta\left(y^j + \psi\left(\frac{q^j}{\tau^j}\right)\right) \\ & + \kappa\left[\sum_{j=0}^{N} \pi^j\left[q^j - y^j\right] - K\right] \\ & + \lambda\left[y^0 + \psi\left(\frac{q^0}{\tau^0}\right) - \underline{\upsilon}^0\right] \\ & + \sum_{j=1}^{N} \mu_j\left[y^j + \psi\left(\frac{q^j}{\tau^j}\right) - y^{j-1} - \psi\left(\frac{q^{j-1}}{\tau^j}\right)\right] \end{aligned} \tag{12.52}$$

where the only added complication is that we now have N incentive-compatibility constraints with corresponding Lagrange multipliers $\mu_1, \ldots, \mu_N$.

The great thing about this is that the shape of the conclusion remains unaltered despite the superficial increase in complexity. Checking out the reasoning that we have used several times before (see the answers to Mini Problems 33, 37, 40, and 41) it is clear that

$$\begin{aligned} \text{MRS}^N &= \text{MRT}^N \\ \text{MRS}^{N-1} &< \text{MRT}^{N-1} \\ \ldots \quad & \ldots \quad \ldots \\ \text{MRS}^1 &< \text{MRT}^1 \\ \text{MRS}^0 &< \text{MRT}^0. \end{aligned}$$

However, we can go yet one step further. Suppose that instead of a finite number of specific types we have the situation where the types are distributed continuously on an interval $[\underline{\tau}, \overline{\tau}]$ where the density at τ is given by $f(\tau)$. The objective function and the participation constraint can be 'translated' immediately into the notation of this continuous distribution model:

$$\int_{\underline{\tau}}^{\overline{\tau}} \zeta(\upsilon(\tau)) f(\tau)\, d\tau \tag{12.53}$$

and

$$\upsilon(\underline{\tau}) \geq \underline{\upsilon} \tag{12.54}$$

where

$$\upsilon(\tau) = y(\tau) + \psi\left(\frac{q(\tau)}{\tau}\right)$$

and $(q(\tau), y(\tau))$ is the output-income pair for a person of type τ. The incentive-compatibility constraint (12.51) can be written as[43]

$$\frac{d\upsilon(\tau)}{d\tau} \geq 0. \tag{12.55}$$

The constraint (12.55) has a simple interpretation: when the government designs the tax system it must ensure that the attainable utility level increases with talent; it also implies that the marginal tax rate can never be greater than 1.[44]

Now the Lagrangean (12.52) becomes

$$\begin{aligned} \max_{\{q(\tau),y(\tau)\}} \quad & \int_{\underline{\tau}}^{\overline{\tau}} \zeta(\upsilon(\tau)) f(\tau)\, d\tau \\ & +\kappa\left[\int_{\underline{\tau}}^{\overline{\tau}} [q(\tau) - y(\tau)] f(\tau)\, d\tau - K\right] \\ & +\lambda\left[\upsilon(\underline{\tau}) - \underline{\upsilon}\right] \\ & +\int_{\underline{\tau}}^{\overline{\tau}} \left[\mu(\tau) \frac{d\upsilon(\tau)}{d\tau}\right] f(\tau)\, d\tau \end{aligned} \tag{12.56}$$

where $\mu(\tau)$ is the Lagrange multiplier at talent level τ. Although a more sophisticated technique is required to find the full solution to (12.56) we can infer one point directly from the analogy with (12.52):

$$-\psi_z\left(\frac{q(\overline{\tau})}{\overline{\tau}}\right) = \overline{\tau} \tag{12.57}$$

? Mini Problems

43 Show how (12.55) can be derived from (12.51) by using a linear approximation for the derivative.

44 Show how this follows from the $(q(\tau), y(\tau))$ patterns that were identified for the previous versions of the model.

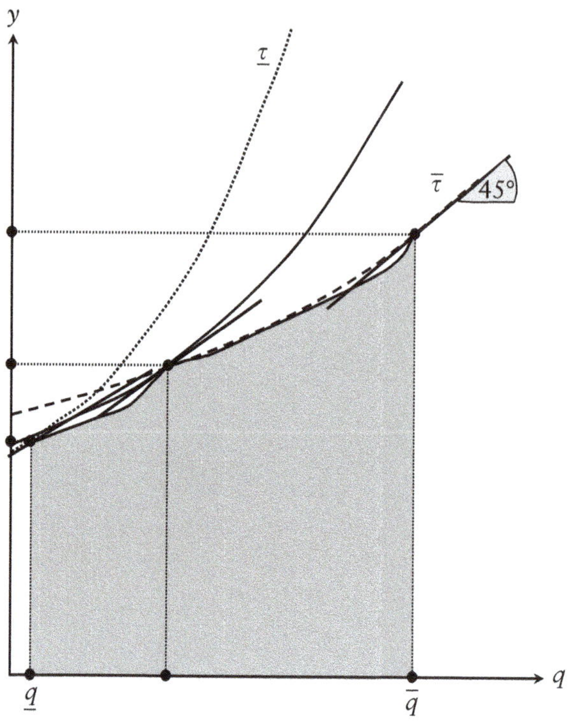

Figure 12.10 Output and disposable income under the optimal tax

exactly at $\tau = \bar{\tau}$ we must have MRS = MRT. Once again we see that the principle of 'no distortion at the top' applies. Figure 12.10 illustrates the relationship between output and income implied by the optimal tax system: the three indifference curves depicted there correspond to three different talent levels. The shaded area is the opportunity set presented to the agents by the tax system, the equilibria for the three different talent levels is where the indifference curve is tangential to the opportunity set. The implication of (12.57) is that at the topmost (q, y) pair the slope of the indifference curve and the slope of the boundary of the opportunity set must be exactly 1 (see the angle marked 45°).

The no-distortion-at-the-top principle has an implication that may at first seem surprising. The tax paid by someone on talent level τ is of course

$$T(\tau) := q(\tau) - y(\tau). \tag{12.58}$$

The result that the slope of the boundary of the opportunity set at the top is

$$\frac{dy}{dq} = 1$$

means that, whatever the attitude to inequality that is displayed in the objective function (12.53), the marginal tax rate $\frac{dT}{dq}$ at the top has to be zero!

Summary

The design problem consists in constructing an economic mechanism to implement the wishes of the government or the interests of a single economic agent. At the level of society it is an essential complement to the general considerations of welfare that were discussed in the early part of chapter 9; at the level of the individual firm it complements the market analysis of previous chapters. Right at the heart of the problem is the issue of misrepresentation of information. Putting it bluntly, selfish individuals may well try to cheat. Given the strong connection with the economics of information the issues raised are analysed using similar analytical tools: the fundamental equilibrium concept is the Bayesian Nash equilibrium. Recognising the possibility of misinformation, it is in the interests of the designer to neutralise this problem by explicitly incorporating it as a constraint in setting up the design problem.

The common threads that run through various design problems are evident from the solutions to the specific applications examined in section 12.6: the auction of an indivisible private good and the method of deciding on an indivisible public project have similar truth-revealing mechanisms; the Principal-and-Agent problem with private information about personal characteristics and the optimal tax problem have the same incentive-compatibility conditions. Other examples of this commonality of approach are shown in the Exercises (see in particular Exercise 12.9).

The principles of design learned here will prove to be essential in dealing with the questions addressed in chapter 13.

Reading notes

The original sources for the results reported in Theorems 12.1–12.4 are in Gibbard (1973) and Satterthwaite (1975); for an accessible proof see Benoit (2000) and Reny (2001) which dramatically illustrates its relation to Arrow's theorem (Theorem 9.1). For Theorem 12.5 see Maskin (1999) and Repullo (1987) For the related issue of strategic voting see Bowen (1945) and Vickrey (1960). For examples of misrepresentation of preferences in trading models see Hurwicz (1972, 1986).

The key statement of the revelation principle is attributable to Myerson (1979) and to Dasgupta et al. (1979), Harris and Townsend (1981).

On auctions see Klemperer (1999, 2002) and Vickrey (1961).

For the key references on pivotal mechanisms and their effectiveness for implementing the public-project problem in dominant strategies see Clarke (1971), Groves (1977), Groves and Loeb (1975), and Green and Laffont (1997).

For an exposition of the standard optimal-income tax model go to Salanié (2003). A nice exposition of the optimal tax problem with two talent (ability) levels is to be found in Bolton and Dewatripont (2005): 62-8). The classic reference is Mirrlees (1971), but this is tough going on first reading.

Exercises

12.1 In a two-good exchange economy there are two persons a and b with utility functions, respectively:

$$\tau^a \left[1 - e^{-x_1^a}\right] + x_2^a$$

$$\tau^b x_1^b + x_2^b$$

where x_i^h is the amount of good i consumed by person h, and $\tau^h > 0$ is a taste parameter for person h ($h = a, b$), where $\tau^b < \tau^a$. Person b owns the entire stock of good 1, R_1; a and b each own half of the stock of good 2, R_2.

1. Assuming that both persons act as price takers:
   (a) Find the offer curve for person a,
   (b) Describe the competitive equilibrium allocation. What would have happened if $\tau^b > \tau^a$?
2. Now suppose that person b can act as a simple monopolist in the supply of good 1 while person a continues to act as a price taker. Show that b will set a price strictly greater than τ^b; comment on the outcome in terms of efficiency.
3. Now suppose that person b can set a fee (fixed charge) for the right to purchase good 1 as well as setting the unit price of good 1. For any given price of good 1 what is the maximum fee that person b can set so that a is still willing to trade? Find b's optimal fee and price of good 1; comment on the outcome in terms of efficiency.

12.2 Consider a collective choice problem where the set of options is given by the interval $\Theta := \left[\underline{\theta}, \overline{\theta}\right]$. Three agents, Alf, Bill, and Charlie are to select a particular $\theta \in \Theta$. They all have single-peaked preferences over Θ (see the formal statement in Definition C.2 or the graphical representation in Figure 9.1) and θ^h is the element of Θ at which agent h has peak preference, $h = a, b, c$. The mechanism designer does not know the preferences of the agents and sets out to design a direct revelation mechanism. Show that the following mechanism is manipulable:

- The designer chooses θ' such that that $\underline{\theta} < \theta' < \overline{\theta}$.
- If θ' is efficient, given the preferences announced by the three agents, then it is selected.
- Otherwise the selected alternative is min $\left\{\theta^a, \theta^b, \theta^c\right\}$.

12.3 Two voters are to select one element from $\left\{\theta', \theta'', \theta'''\right\}$. Each voter has a strict preference over the alternatives. Show that the following rule is manipulable: if θ' is efficient, then it is selected; if θ' is not efficient, but θ'' is, then θ'' is selected; if neither θ' nor θ'' is efficient, then θ''' is selected.

12.4 Two firms are considering whether to undertake a joint project. It is common knowledge that the value of the project to firm 1 must be either 200 or 700 and that the value to firm 2 must be either 400 or 700. However, information about the precise value is private to the firm. The firms would like to undertake the project if the sum of their values exceeds the cost of the project which is known to be 1000. The firms use the pivotal mechanism in (12.32).

1. Find the amount each firm will have to pay as a function of its announcement.
2. Show that the mechanism cannot be manipulated.
3. Check that there will always be enough money if they decide to undertake the project.

12.5 There is a fixed number of bidders N in a first-price (Dutch) auction.

1. Suppose the values are drawn from the same rectangular distribution with support $[\underline{\tau}, \overline{\tau}]$. What is the density function and the distribution function for τ?
2. Agent h assumes that all the other agents' bids are determined by their type: so that a rival with value τ bids $\beta(\tau)$ where β is a strictly increasing function. On this assumption show that, if agent h bids a price p, the probability that he wins the auction is
$$\left[\frac{\varphi(p) - \underline{\tau}}{\overline{\tau} - \underline{\tau}}\right]^{N-1},$$
where $\varphi(\cdot)$ is the inverse function of $\beta(\cdot)$.
3. Suppose the agent is risk neutral and that $\underline{\tau} = 0, \overline{\tau} = 1$. Again assuming that the other agents' bids are determined by the same bid function $\beta(\cdot)$, show that the agent's best response is determined by the following equation:
$$[p - \varphi(p)][N - 1]\frac{d\varphi(p)}{dp} + \varphi(p) = 0. \tag{12.59}$$
4. Show that condition (12.59) implies
$$\varphi(p) = \frac{N}{N-1}p \tag{12.60}$$
and that the equilibrium bid function takes the form
$$\beta(\tau) = \frac{N-1}{N}\tau. \tag{12.61}$$
5. Use the result that the expected value of the kth smallest member of a sample of size N drawn from a rectangular distribution on [0, 1] is
$$\frac{k}{N+1} \tag{12.62}$$
to show that the expected price received by the seller in the special case $\underline{\tau} = 0, \overline{\tau} = 1$ is
$$\beta(\tau) = \frac{N-1}{N+1}.$$
6. Use this to find the optimal bid function and the expected price received by the seller for a rectangular distribution with support $[\underline{\tau}, \overline{\tau}]$.

12.6 Suppose that in the model of Exercise 12.5 a second-price (English) auction were used rather than a first-price auction:

1. What is the optimal bid function?
2. Use the result in (12.62) to determine the expected price paid by the winner.

3. Use the results on order statistics (page 514) to draw the distribution of the price paid to the seller in the case of the first- and the second-price auction.

12.7 Alf and Bill are bidding in a conventional English auction for an object of unknown market value: Alf's valuation of the object is τ^a, Bill's valuation is τ^b and the true value is expected to be $\tau^a + \tau^b$, but at the time of the auction neither bidder knows the other's valuation. However, it is common knowledge that τ^a and τ^b are drawn from a rectangular distribution with support $[\underline{\tau}, \overline{\tau}]$.

1. What is the expected value of the object?
2. From Alf's point of view, what is the expected value of the object, conditional on his winning the object?
3. Show that the price $2\min\left\{\tau^a, \tau^b\right\}$ is an equilibrium.
4. Suppose Alf followed a policy of bidding $\tau^a + \mathcal{E}\tau^b$ and believed that Bill was following the same type of policy. Why might this bidding policy lead to an unfavourable outcome for the winner (a phenomenon known as 'the winner's curse')(Klemperer 1998)?

12.8 A Principal hires an Agent to manage a firm. The Agent produces an outcome q given by

$$q = \phi(z, \tau)$$

where z is effort and τ is the talent of the Agent that may or may not be observable by the Principal; the function ϕ is twice differentiable increasing in both arguments, concave in z, and has a positive cross-derivative. The Principal contracts to pay the Agent an amount of income y in return for output q. The Principal's utility is

$$q - y$$

and the Agent's utility is

$$\vartheta(y) - z$$

where ϑ is an increasing, strictly concave function such that $\vartheta(0) = 0$.

1. Using the production function ϕ show that the indifference curves in (q, y)-space for Agents of different types must satisfy the single-crossing condition.
2. If the Principal can costlessly observe the talent of any potential Agent at the time of hiring and knows that the utility available to any Agent in alternative employment is 0, find the conditions that characterise the full-information solution.
3. It is known that there are exactly two types of Agent and the proportion of high-talent agents is π. Write down the incentive-compatibility constraint for the second-best problem.
4. Find the conditions that characterise the second-best equilibrium and show that the no-distortion-at-the-top principle holds.

12.9 Consider a good that is produced by a monopoly that is known to have constant marginal cost c and a fixed cost C_0; marginal cost is given by

$$c = \tfrac{1}{\tau} \qquad (12.63)$$

where τ is a parameter that characterises the firm's efficiency. If the monopoly sells a quantity q of output in the market then the price that it can command is given by $p(q)$ where $p(\cdot)$ is a known, decreasing function. A government authority wants to regulate the behaviour of the monopoly. The regulation specifies an output level q and a subsidy (fee) F that is intended to ensure that the firm does not make a loss. The authority has been instructed to take into account the interests of both consumers and the owners of the firm. Consumers' interests are assumed to be given by consumer's surplus; the firms' interests are assumed to be given by profits including the subsidy F.

1. If the authority places a weight 1 on consumer's surplus and a weight β (where $0 < \beta \leq 1$) on profits show that the authority's objective function can be expressed as

$$V(q, R) := \int_0^q p(x)\,dx - [1-\beta]R - \beta C_0 - \beta\tau q$$

   where R is total revenue for the firm.
2. If the parameters of the cost function C_0 and τ are common knowledge
   (a) What is the relevant participation constraint and Lagrangean for the problem?
   (b) How will the authority set q and F?
   (c) Interpret this full-information result.
   [Hint: In formulating the answer to this and the next part exploit the close similarity with the contracting model of section 12.6.3.]
3. Assume that C_0 is known but marginal cost is unknown; however it is known that the efficiency of the firm is either τ^a or τ^b where

$$\tau^a > \tau^b$$

   and marginal cost is again given by (12.63). The authority wants to use the same kind of regulatory regime but it does not know for certain which type of firm, low cost (i.e. τ^a or high efficiency) or high cost (i.e. τ^b or low efficiency), it is dealing with.
   (a) What is the incentive-compatibility constraint that the authority should take into consideration?
   (b) What form does the participation constraint now take?
   (c) If the authority faces a low-cost type firm with probability π and it intends to maximise expected welfare what is the Lagrangean for the problem?
   (d) Find and interpret the second-best solution (Baron and Myerson 1982).

12.10 An economy consists of two equal-sized groups of people. The gifted, with an ability parameter $\tau = 2$ and the deprived, for whom $\tau = 1$. All persons have a utility function given by

$$U(x, z) = \log x + \log(1 - z)$$

where x is consumption and z is effort in the labour market, $0 \leq z \leq 1$. Consumption is given by

$$x = w + T$$

where w is the market wage given by

$$w(z, \tau) = \tau z$$

and T is a transfer from the government (if positive) or a tax (if negative). The government would like to set $T = \Delta > 0$ for deprived individuals and $T = -\Delta$ for gifted people.

1. If utility is observable and each person chooses z so as to maximise utility, draw the graph of utility against earnings for a gifted person and for a deprived person, for a given value of Δ. What is the optimum value of earnings for each type of person?
2. Assume utility is not observable. The government plans the following transfer scheme

$$T = \begin{cases} \Delta & \text{if } w \leq w^* \\ -\Delta & \text{if } w > w^* \end{cases}$$

   where w^* is the optimum earnings for deprived people in part 1. Show that gifted people may find it in their interest to pretend to be deprived. In the diagram for part 1 plot the utility of someone carrying out this pretence.
3. Use the above diagram to show the case where a gifted person is just indifferent between acting as though utility were observable and pretending to be deprived.
4. Show that deprived people's utility could be increased by restricting the amount that they are allowed to earn.

12.11 The government has to raise a fixed sum K through income tax. It is known that there are two types of worker a and b in the economy and that the output (gross income) produced by each is given by

$$q^j = \tau^j z^j, j = a, b$$

where z^j is the amount of effort supplied by a person of type j and $\tau^a > \tau^b$. It is also known that workers have preferences given by the function

$$\upsilon^j = q^j - T^j + \psi\left(z^j\right)$$

where T^j is the tax on a worker of type j and ψ is a decreasing concave function. The government has no interest in the inequality of utility outcomes and so just seeks to maximise

$$\pi \upsilon^a + [1 - \pi]\, \upsilon^b$$

where π is the proportion of a-type workers.

1. What is the government's budget constraint?
2. Write the government's objective function in terms of q^a, q^b, π, and K.

3. If the value of τ^j for each worker is private and unknown to the government, write down the Lagrangean for the government's optimisation problem.
4. Show that the second-best solution in this case is identical to the full-information solution.
5. Set up the problem in an alternative, equivalent way where the government's budget constraint is modelled as a separate constraint in the Lagrangean. What must be the value of the Lagrange multiplier on this constraint at the optimum?

13 Government and the Individual

Frankly, I'd like to see the government get out of the war altogether and leave the whole field to private industry—Milo Minderbinder

(Joseph Heller, *Catch-22*)

13.1 Introduction

Until now we have taken for granted that the principles and analysis of microeconomics should relate to the individual: decisions should be at the individual level; individuals' or households' interests are those that are considered to be paramount; unorganised individuals are the decision makers in the market place. But there is no compelling economic reason why this should be so. Although this is not the place for an extensive discussion of the interesting questions raised by the economics of institutions, it is appropriate to examine a number of issues that may not be well suited to approaches that entirely focused on the individual. In this chapter we will put chapter 9's welfare concepts to work in a number of areas where we have earlier noted some difficulties; we do this having now benefited from the strategic and informational analysis in chapters 10–12. There are two main themes from earlier discussions that need to be followed through.

First, we will examine the issue of market failure—sections 13.2–13.6. Can the desired social state be achieved through the market mechanism or is explicit intervention required? If the first is true, then maybe everything can indeed be left to Milo Minderbinder and unfettered private enterprise; an essentially individual-focused approach would indeed be appropriate. Otherwise the question of correcting market failure will require application of the lessons of economic design from chapter 12.

Second, we will look at how resources—agents' incomes—'ought to be' distributed. This is addressed in section 13.7. It is an issue that requires more than application of basic criteria such as efficiency; we need a full welfare approach. In order to find a way of shaping the economy to achieve this desired goal we again need the analysis from the chapter on design.

13.2 Market failure?

We begin with the economic mechanism that underpinned much of the first half of this book. We re-examine the rôle that can be played by the market and its possible limitations in achieving the outcomes that one might desire for the economy. Put crudely, why and how do markets 'fail?'

To address this question properly we need to use the welfare-economic analysis that was introduced earlier in the book. Specifically we will build on the idea of the *efficiency* of an allocation of consumptions and net outputs: this concept can be a powerful tool in the design of economic policy prescription. The key questions to be addressed are those that were raised in chapter 9 (page 244). They are:

1. *The characterisation problem.* What combination of goods will result in a Pareto-efficient allocation? We already know the answer to this question, not only for private goods, but in several other interesting cases. But we will need to refer back regularly to the answer in order to deal properly with question 2.

2. *The implementation problem.* In other words, what mechanism could be used to support the efficient allocation characterised in question 1?

In some cases the answer to the second question follows almost as a matter of course from the first. In chapter 9 we established that, under certain conditions, the workings of the market would ensure an efficient allocation. The key requirements for characterising an efficient allocation $([\mathbf{x}^*], [\mathbf{q}^*])$, distilled from equations (9.11)–(9.15), can be written as

$$\frac{U_j^h(\mathbf{x}^{*h})}{U_i^h(\mathbf{x}^{*h})} = \frac{\kappa_j}{\kappa_i}, \tag{13.1}$$

$$\frac{\Phi_j^f(\mathbf{q}^{*f})}{\Phi_i^f(\mathbf{q}^{*f})} = \frac{\kappa_j}{\kappa_i}, \tag{13.2}$$

where

- the left-hand side of (13.1) is the MRS of good i for good j in when household h consumes $\mathbf{x}^{*h}$ (page 79);
- the left-hand side of (13.2) is the MRT of good i into good j when firm f's activity is given by net output $\mathbf{q}^{*f}$ (page 41);
- the right-hand side of both equations is just the ratio of shadow prices, reflecting the relative scarcity of the two goods, that emerges from taking account of the materials balance condition in deriving the efficiency condition.

From this characterisation of efficiency it is but a step to replace the shadow-price ratios $\frac{\kappa_j}{\kappa_i}$ in (13.1) and (13.2) with market prices to see the suggested implementation; we

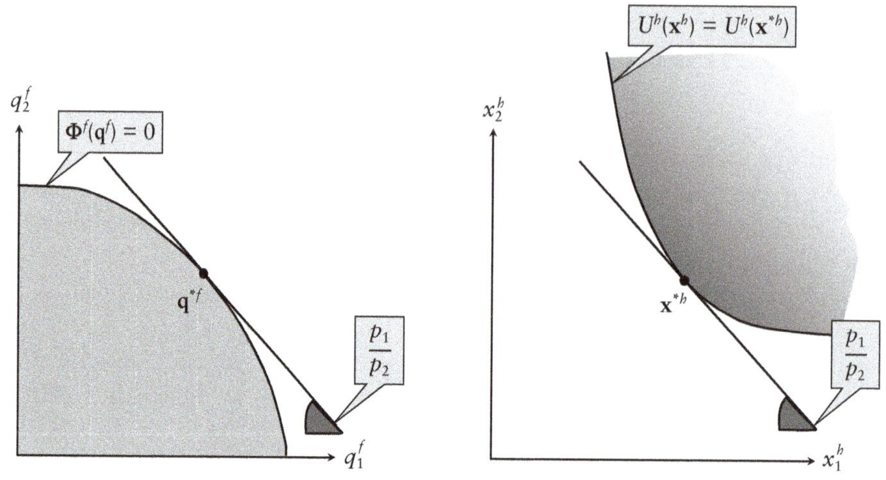

Figure 13.1 Implementation through the market

then get, for any pair of goods i and j

$$\frac{U_j^h(\mathbf{x}^{*h})}{U_i^h(\mathbf{x}^{*h})} = \frac{p_j}{p_i}, \tag{13.3}$$

$$\frac{\Phi_j^f(\mathbf{q}^{*f})}{\Phi_i^f(\mathbf{q}^{*f})} = \frac{p_j}{p_i}. \tag{13.4}$$

Equation (13.3) is clearly the FOC for a utility-maximisation problem for household h given prices $\mathbf{p}$; equation (13.4) is the necessary FOC for a profit-maximisation problem for firm f given prices $\mathbf{p}$. If the necessary conditions are also sufficient conditions—and as we shall see, this qualification is important—then allowing firms and households to maximise given the prices $\mathbf{p}$ is sufficient to implement the allocation. In effect we have a rerun of the decentralisation argument that we first encountered in the Robinson Crusoe economy (page 136); it is also the logic underlying the support theorem (page 239). The allocation is illustrated in Figure 13.1—compare this with Figures 6.8 and 7.15.

But, beyond the cases where the conditions for this result apply, how can implementation be achieved? Should we look to market intervention—a kind of tweaking of the price system? Should we consider regulation—allowing profit/utility maximisation to take place subject to the imposition of some side constraints? Or does the answer lie in some more arcane form of non-market administration?

We will examine the issues in the following four cases:

- increasing returns or 'non-convexities'—section 13.3;
- 'externalities' or 'spillovers'—section 13.4;
- non-rival goods—section 13.5;
- public goods—section 13.6.

13.3 Non-convexities

We begin with the problem that prevented decentralisation on Crusoe's island (page 136) and that re-emerged in chapters 7 and 9. Although there are other examples of non-convexity that we can choose we shall examine just one of the most obvious and relevant cases, that of increasing returns in production. This is an issue that is typical of large infrastructure projects and public utilities. However, it is purely an issue of the technology set—or of the cost structure if you like—and should not be confused with 'public goods'; the issue of public goods is dealt with separately in section 13.6 below.

We need to think about non-convexity both in the small—at the level of individual firms—and in the large—the overall technology set that describes the production possibilities for the economy as a whole. The technology set of an economy may prove to be non-convex for either of two reasons

- Interactions amongst individual firms (positive externalities).
- Technology sets of individual firms are non-convex—in other words, for some firms in isolation, production possibilities display increasing returns to scale.

If neither of these phenomena is present then we can be sure that the aggregate technology set must be convex—see Theorem 6.1 on page 131.

Recall that the support theorem presupposed rather stringent requirements of convexity—not only of aggregate production possibilities, but also at the level of the individual firm and of each household's 'better-than' set—see the argument relating to the figures on page 239. Given the examples of fixed cost or other indivisibilities that casual observation suggests are commonplace in the world around us, it seems like a good idea to examine more closely the problem of characterising economic efficiency in the presence of non-convexities.

We will do this in three stages: first we will consider the possibilities if there is a large number of small firms each with increasing returns to scale; then we will look at how the interactions generated by externalities might be handled; finally we look at the general problem of 'large' non-convexities (section 13.3.3) and the regulation problems to which they give rise (section 13.3.4).

13.3.1 Large numbers and convexity

Let us start by thinking about non-convexities at the firm level that are in some sense 'sufficiently small'. We know from the discussion of Theorem 9.5 that, if there are non-convexities in individual firms' technology sets, then an arbitrary efficient allocation $([\hat{\mathbf{x}}], [\hat{\mathbf{q}}])$ may not be capable of being supported by a competitive equilibrium—see the case illustrated in Figure 9.5. However, where there are many small firms each with increasing returns to scale we may not need to be concerned about the implementation role of the price mechanism. There are two reasons for this.

First, on aggregating up the individual firms' production possibilities (the technology sets Q^f) the overall effect may nevertheless be to produce a convex aggregate technology set Q: the non-convexity of one firm's technology set may be offset by the convexity of that for another firm (see Mini Problem 2 in chapter 6). The fact that production possibilities overall have the appropriate property will permit the existence of separating prices as in Figure 7.15.

Second, even if the aggregation procedure over a finite number of firms does not produce an overall technology set Q that is convex one may nevertheless be able to appeal to a 'large-numbers' argument used in chapter 7. This follows along the lines of the example on page 171: in the limit the aggregation of an infinite number of infinitesimally small firms will produce a Q that is convex, even if each firm has an increasing-returns technology. Clearly it is a matter of judgement as to whether this argument is appropriate for modelling a particular economy.

For each of these two arguments, even though the price mechanism may not support any and every arbitrarily chosen allocation (as in the example of Figure 9.5), it may nevertheless do the job well enough. The competitive-equilibrium allocation is efficient and can yield individual utilities that are sufficiently close to those obtainable under $([\hat{\mathbf{x}}], [\hat{\mathbf{q}}])$.

13.3.2 Interactions and convexity

Consider now the case where the non-convexity arises from positive externalities amongst firms. In some respects we know how this can be resolved. If firms do interact in this way, then competitive equilibrium may still be possible. Each firm acting as a price taker can make non-negative profits in equilibrium although, as we have seen in the discussion in chapter 3, the relationship between overall supply and the supply curve of each firm will be a bit different from the case of no interaction, and the supply curve may actually slope the 'wrong way'—see page 57. However, although competitive equilibrium may exist, the market mechanism will not in general produce an efficient outcome because of the production externalities involved.[1] These and other related issues are dealt with in section 13.4.

Example 13.1

The Italian shoe industry in the Marche region provides an interesting example of beneficial externalities (Rabellotti and Schmitz 1999). Typically there is high concentration of relatively small producers within a small area and strong social ties amongst economic agents, creating a common code of behaviour. In addition to the strong market interconnections involving trade in goods and services, there are important informational linkages and a network of local institutions supporting the local enterprises. Is there a case for subsidising these institutions?

? Mini Problems

1 Suggest a policy which might be used to ensure efficiency in this case.

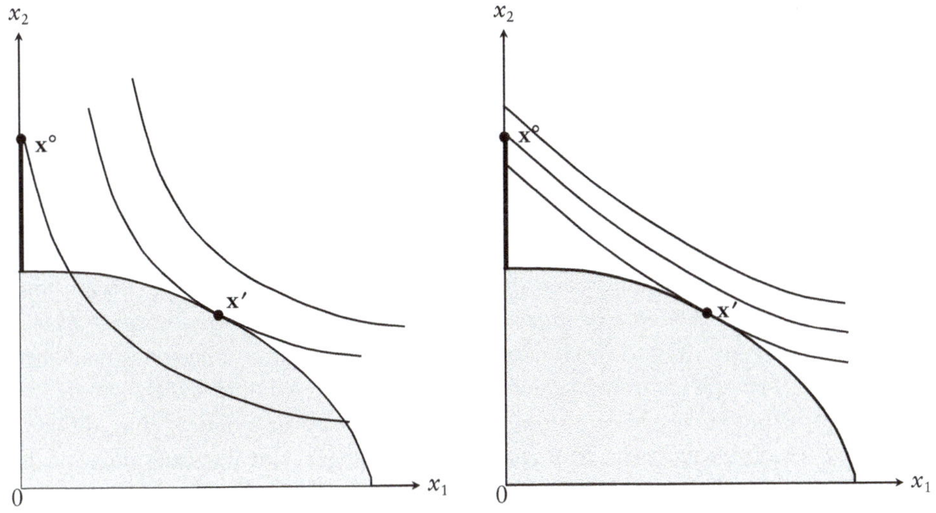

Figure 13.2 Non-convexities in production and efficiency: Two cases

13.3.3 The infrastructure problem

If we cannot appeal to a large-numbers argument then the implementation problem becomes more difficult: we cannot just rely on the marginal conditions (13.3), (13.4) for guidance. Furthermore, the implications can be quite dramatic as can be seen with the aid of an example that, as a convenient short-hand description, may be called the *infrastructure* problem.

Consider the situation in Figure 13.2. Good 1 is a commodity where the production requires a large initial investment: something like electricity, water supply, the telephone service, rail travel. Good 2 is a 'basket' of all other consumer goods which is again used as *numéraire*. The production function for the economy as a whole is given by

$$\Phi(\mathbf{q}) \leq 0$$

and there are zero resource stocks of good 1 and good 2 so that the materials balance condition requires

$$x_1 \leq q_1$$

$$x_2 \leq q_2.$$

However, Φ is not a concave function and the associated attainable set is shown as the shaded area in each of the two halves of the figure:[2] notice in particular that this set includes the little spike on the vertical axis, with its peak at the point $\mathbf{x}^\circ$. The significance of this spike is to represent the assumption that electricity (or whatever) is subject to

? Mini Problems

2 Identify the technically efficient points in this diagram.

substantial initial setup costs: if there were no electricity produced then an amount equal to x_2^0 of consumption of good 2 is available. However, the moment you want even one kilowatt-hour of electricity a substantial amount of good 2—equal to the height of the 'spike'—has to be sacrificed; thereafter additional units of electricity require further sacrifice of good 2.

Now consider the two sets of indifference curves illustrated in the two halves of Figure 13.2: these can be taken to represent two different versions of the preferences of a 'representative citizen', so that social welfare is just this person's utility function. This will imply that the 'willingness-to-pay' criterion that we have used in previous discussions of economic welfare (see the treatment of potential superiority on page 255) is unambiguous: we just need to check whether this one representative person is made better or worse off by moving from one point to another on the attainable set.

By construction each set of contours has a tangency at point $\mathbf{x}'$ but different curvatures. The fact that each set of contours has a tangency at the same point of the attainable set suggests the same set of shadow prices for the two cases. However, despite the fact that shadow prices are the same for the two versions of the contours, the welfare implications are dramatically different. Notice that the left-hand diagram has a single Pareto efficient point at $\mathbf{x}'$: simple inspection reveals that it would be impossible to get to a higher indifference curve. By contrast, in the right-hand diagram the corresponding point is not Pareto efficient: although it would yield some sort of 'local maximum' of utility, one clearly does better at point $\mathbf{x}^\circ$: in this case Pareto efficiency implies that none of good 1 should be produced.

This example illustrates the two-stage procedure that has to be adopted in order to characterise the efficient allocation in the presence of non-convexities:

1. Find the relevant part of the feasible set by searching for a global maximum of welfare: in the present case this means finding the global maximum of the representative person's utility.

2. If the good is to be produced in positive amounts, then production should take place such that

$$\frac{\Phi_1(\mathbf{q}')}{\Phi_2(\mathbf{q}')} = \frac{p_1}{p_2} = \frac{U_1(\mathbf{x}')}{U_2(\mathbf{x}')}, \tag{13.5}$$

   the marginal rate of transformation exactly equals the marginal rate of substitution for the representative consumer—just as in the elementary competitive model.[3]

Notice that, while standard efficiency conditions are enough to characterise stage 2, stage 1 explicitly involves the introduction of an assumption about the social-welfare function.

Also notice that leaving things to the market has a demonstrably disastrous effect here. Suppose the situation is as in the left-hand panel of Figure 13.2 and that someone has

? Mini Problems

3 (a) Show how the compensating variation can be used as a measure of welfare in Figure 13.2. (b) Why might it be problematic to extend this idea to an economy with heterogeneous consumers?

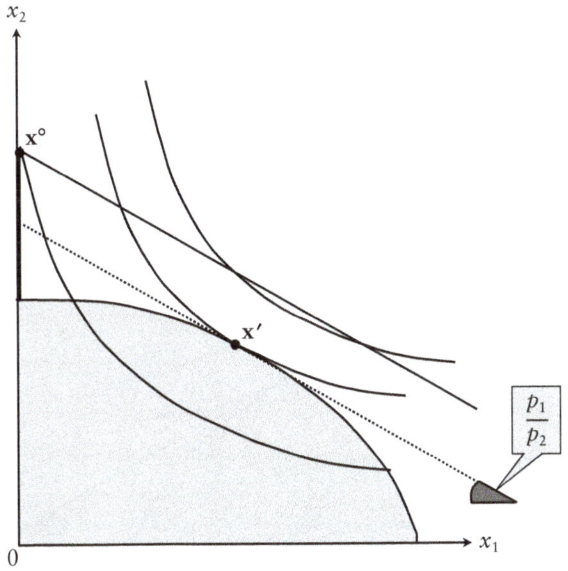

Figure 13.3 Non-convexity: effect of the competitive market

estimated customers' willingness to pay for good 1 at the optimum (at point $\mathbf{x}'$). The willingness to pay for an extra unit of good 1 is represented by the relative prices $\frac{p_1}{p_2}$ as shown in Figure 13.3. But what would happen if a price-taking firm or firms maximised profits at those prices? Profit maximisation would be achieved at $\mathbf{x}^\circ$, not $\mathbf{x}'$.[4] In effect it is a rerun of the version of the Robinson Crusoe story that we considered on page 136; but here it means that the electric power grid or the rail service never gets built, even though it is clearly desirable that it should.[5]

13.3.4 **Regulation**

So, leaving the infrastructure to the free market in this case produces a disastrous outcome. But simply transferring ownership or restricting competition will not do—for

? Mini Problems

4 Explain why this will occur.

5 Suppose the attainable set is given by

$$\Phi(x_1, x_2) \leq 0$$

where

$$\Phi(x_1, x_2) = \begin{cases} x_1^2 + x_2^2 - 1, & x_1 > 0, x_2 \geq 0 \\ x_2 - 1 - k, & x_1 = 0, x_2 \geq 0 \end{cases}$$

Interpret this in terms of Figure 13.2. Let $p_1 = p_2 = 1$. If there is a single price-taking firm producing good 1, plot profit as a function of x_1. For what value of k will a price-taking firm produce zero amount of good 1?

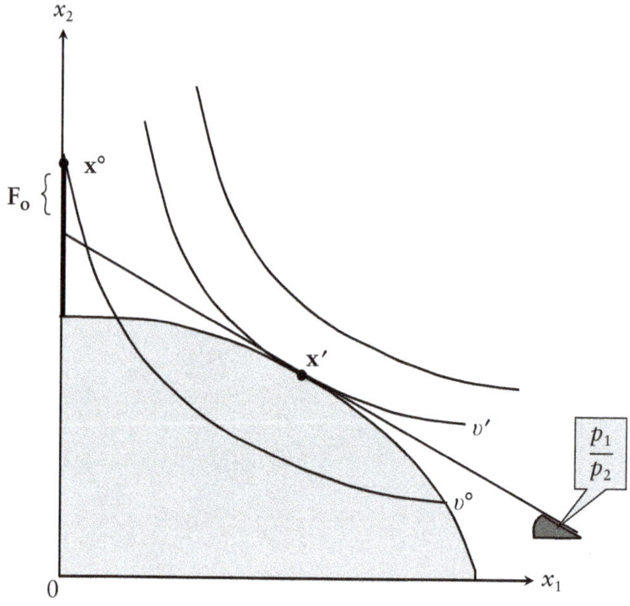

Figure 13.4 Non-convexity: an efficient fee schedule

example nationalisation cannot be the complete answer to the problem. Just creating a simple monopoly, whether public or private, will also be suboptimal.[6]

However, one may be able to do much better by adapting the analysis of information and monopoly power in chapter 11 (pp. 329–347).

Full information

We begin with the full-information approach: the utility functions of the households are assumed to be common knowledge. Suppose a firm or an agency is empowered to charge an entrance fee for the right to consume good 1: clearly this will only work for certain types of good or service that might be modelled by good 1.[7] By assigning the production of good 1 to such a firm it is possible to construct an efficient fee schedule: this can be of the type of non-linear fee schedules that we considered in chapter 11 (see Figure 11.2).

Examine Figure 13.4. The kinked line passing through $\mathbf{x}^\circ$ and $\mathbf{x}'$ is the required fee schedule.[8] It consists of a fixed fee F_0 and a variable charge at the price p_1; note that $\frac{p_1}{p_2}$ is the marginal cost of producing good 1 in terms of good 2. This fee schedule clearly satisfies the FOCs in (13.5) that characterise the efficiency condition. It will also enable the

? Mini Problems

6 Why is this so? See Exercise 3.1 on 'natural monopoly'

7 What types?

8 Will such a regulated firm produce more of good 1 than a non-regulated monopolist? [Hint: check Exercise 3.4.]

firm to break even.[9] The firm can construct such a schedule given that it knows the customers' demand functions and, if we were to extend the argument to the case where there are different types of consumers, it can introduce a more complex version of the same charging structure as long as it can identify the type of each consumer (see the argument on pages 334—337).

However, this form of fee schedule is not the only way of setting up an efficient payment system for the firm or agency. Suppose the government allows the firm to charge the price p_1 (equal to marginal cost of production) and then underwrites its losses by paying the firm a subsidy equal in value to F_0. By the same reasoning the firm covers its costs: the subsidy can be financed by levying a tax on the population and it is clear that there is a welfare increase because the representative consumer is assured of the utility level υ' rather than υ°. The implementation in terms of a tax-financed subsidy combined with price regulation apparently produces the same effect as allowing the firm the freedom to set a fee. With some extra caveats the argument can also be applied to the heterogeneous-consumer case.[10]

Private information

The assumption of perfect information underlying these proposed efficient solutions may be particularly inappropriate. There are at least two respects in which this may be a poor way to model the situation facing such a firm or public agency.

First, the firm may face different types of customers. If so, it then has the now familiar problem of misrepresentation. High-valuation types will try to masquerade as low-valuation types in order to acquire a more favourable contract for themselves, with a lower fixed charge. The analysis is essentially that outlined in section 11.2.4: it retains the essentially private and individualistic approach to finding the efficient solution.

Second, in attempting to regulate the firm, the government may not be fully informed about the firm's circumstances. Common sense suggests that in order to regulate it effectively the government must have some information about the firm's cost function: otherwise how will it know whether or not the subsidy paid to cover F_0 is in fact an overpayment? However, imagine the situation confronting the government that is to award the right to supply good 1 subject to the price regulation and subsidy scheme that we have discussed. Although the government may be informed about the distribution of cost structures of the possible candidate firms, the specific information about the costs of any one particular firm may be unobservable to the government. In other words the shape of $\Phi(\cdot)$ in Figure 13.4 may be information that is private to the firm. Figure 13.5 illustrates the case where there are two possibilities for the (x_1, x_2)-tradeoff: the larger, lightly shaded area corresponds to that in Figure 13.4 and the other depicts a case in which less of the infrastructure good 1 is obtained for any given sacrifice of good 2. If there were perfect information about which of the two cases was true, then one could achieve

? Mini Problems

9 Show this.

10 Suppose, following Mini Problem 3, that $\sum_h \mathrm{CV}^h$ were proposed as the objective function for the government, where CV^h is the compensating variation of household h. Why might this prove unsatisfactory as a welfare criterion?

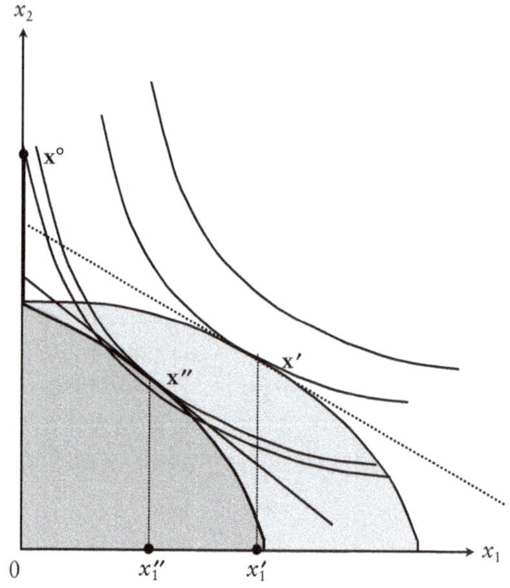

Figure 13.5 Nonconvexity: uncertain tradeoff

an efficient outcome either at $\mathbf{x}'$ (if the true situation were as in Figure 13.4) or at $\mathbf{x}''$ (if the true situation were as in the new, smaller, attainable set): in either case one uses the marginal-cost-price-plus-subsidy method of ensuring that a producer of known cost operates efficiently. However, under imperfect information about the producer's type, this approach is not going to be implementable.[11]

This conclusion about imperfect information should come as no surprise: it is just what we had in the case of the contracting model of section 12.6.3, for example. It can be handled using the principles of design that are by now fairly familiar. The designer here is of course the government and it attempts to maximise expected social welfare, where the expectation is taken over the various types of monopoly producer that the regulator may be confronting. This is a 'second-best' maximisation problem because the regulator has to incorporate an incentive-compatibility constraint that ensures that a low-cost producer would not find it profitable to masquerade as a high-cost producer: the detail of how it works in a specific model is contained in Exercise 12.9. The outcome will be a multi-part payment schedule that is contingent on output. Maximised social welfare will be lower than the full information solution, but then that is just what we have come to expect from this type of model.

The non-convexity problem that undermines the operation of the unfettered free market can be solved without abandoning the approach that focuses on individual profit

? Mini Problems

11 Show that the low-cost (high-efficiency) type of firm would like to pretend to the regulator that it is a high-cost type—see also Exercise 12.9.

maximisation. However, it usually requires some external intervention (the government regulator) to ensure that the producers stay solvent as well as operate efficiently.

Example 13.2

The importance of information issues in regulation is well illustrated by the California water utility industry. Wolak (1994) examines the impact on consumers resulting from the asymmetric-information nature of the regulation problem. The optimal regulatory outcomes are modelled econometrically for the two regimes discussed above—the full-information case where the regulator can observe the cost information and the private-information case where the water utility has superior information about its production process. There are indeed significant cost increases introduced by private information in the regulatory process; these are associated with significant losses in welfare arising from the lower output levels and higher prices under the private-information regime.

13.4 Externalities

Externalities imply a particular type of interdependence amongst economic agents; but we must be careful what kind of interdependence. Take the standard multi-market model of the economy introduced in chapter 7. In a market economy there are bound to be interdependencies induced by the forces of competition. The demand for ice-cream goes up in the summer; as a result the wages of ice-cream vendors increase; as a result the wages of other workers increase; as a result up go the marginal costs of apple-growers, bicycle-repair firms, car-parks... All of this is part of the routine functioning of the market mechanism.

However, the type of interdependency that is relevant here does not operate through the regular channels of the market: if it did then the economic issues involved would be much simpler. Instead the interdependency works by shifting one or more of the basic components of the model that we set for examining economic efficiency: the production function Φ^f or the utility function U^h of other agents in the economy.

The externality problem emerges in a number of guises; we had a glimpse of this in chapter 3 and in chapter 9 where the method for analysing efficiency was developed. Some of the standard versions of the externality issue are:

- *Networking effects.* Firms benefit from each others' investment in certain capital and human resources that facilitate cooperation or otherwise lower other firms' costs. This is the kind of phenomenon that in the aggregate may give rise to the increasing returns or 'non-convexity' problem mentioned in section 13.3.2.
- *Civic action.* 'Good citizenship' activity by some consumers may benefit others—painting the house, for example.
- *Common-ownership resources.* Suppose firms have access to a resource where the ownership rights are vague or undefined—fishing grounds beyond territorial waters,

common land. A typical firm may use the common-ownership resource as an input in a way that takes no account of indirect fact on other firms' costs in accessing the resource—as the fishing grounds get depleted or the land is overgrazed. The phenomenon is epitomised as the 'tragedy of the commons'.

- *Pollution.* Actions by firms or consumers may directly affect others profits or utility.

The first pair of items in this list are clearly activities that provide benefits to others and intuition suggests that individual agents pursuing their private interests may in some sense 'underprovide' the beneficial good. The last two items on the list are examples of negative or detrimental externality and the same intuitive reasoning suggests that private interests responding to market signals will lead to overindulgence in the market activity that is producing the externality. However, is the intuition likely to be right here, or has it missed a key point about the market mechanism?

We will address this by examining first the production case and then consumption: the essential difference between them concerns not only the nature of the agents' objectives and constraints but also the informational questions associated with the particular externality, as we shall see. Dealing first with production externalities enables us to develop a method of analysis and set of criteria for other types of externality and for introducing the issue of public goods.

13.4.1 Production externalities: the efficiency problem

The essence of the problem can be expressed in the form of a two-commodity model of a closed economy. Firm f's production of good 1 causes a spillover effect that impinges on the production costs of other firms: the greater the activity, the larger is this effect. We will again assume that there is a single individual whose preferences are represented by a standard quasiconcave utility function. Equation (9.29) states the basic principle of the efficiency condition with the production externality; for the consumer the relevant condition for a private good is (13.1); combining the two one has:

$$\frac{\Phi_1^f}{\Phi_2^f} = \frac{U_1}{U_2} + e_{21}^f, \tag{13.6}$$

where e_{21}^f is the marginal valuation of the externality. The other two terms in (13.6) have essentially the same interpretation as in equations (13.1)–(13.4): they are the marginal cost of producing good 1 in terms of good 2 (left-hand side) and the consumer's marginal willingness to pay for good 1 in terms of good 2 (right-hand side).

We can exploit the efficiency condition (13.6) to provide a method of implementation in a market economy.

13.4.2 Corrective taxes

That the consumer(s) are maximising utility in a free market (13.6) could be interpreted as a simple rule for setting corrective taxes. We simply need to redefine the components as

$$\frac{\tilde{p}_1}{\tilde{p}_2} = \frac{p_1}{p_2} - t \tag{13.7}$$

where the $\tilde{p}$s denote producer prices, the ps are consumer prices, and t is a tax on the output of polluters. If we arrange things so that

$$t = -e^f_{21}$$

then we have a corrective tax that imposes the value of the marginal externality on the one generating it. Note that, by definition, this tax is positive if the externality is deleterious (as in the case of pollution), but that t is negative (a subsidy to the firm producing good 1) if the externality is beneficial.[12]

It is clear that although there could be informational problems with this neat solution, including the question of defining the boundaries between taxable and non-taxable commodities and the problem of enforcement, it has the advantage of simplicity in that it requires only a relatively minor modification of the market mechanism.

13.4.3 Production externalities: private solutions

However, does the government need to get involved at all with corrective taxes or subsidies? Perhaps if the interests of the various firms involved in an externality are correctly modelled, then outside intervention by the government may be irrelevant.

Internalisation through reorganisation

In some cases, where the production externality impinges only on one or a few other firms, an industrial organisation solution can be sought. A merger of the 'victim' firm with the firm generating the externality would change the nature of the problem. What had been two separate decision-making entities relying on market signals become two component plants of a single firm. A rational manager of the combined firm would recognise the interdependencies amongst the plants and allow for this in making decisions on net outputs for the combined firm. The merger has thus 'internalised' the externality. Of course this leaves open the question of whether a large organisation would be efficiently organised internally to take account of the richer information that becomes available from the merger of the erstwhile separate firms.

Internalisation through a pseudo-market

However, changes in the industrial structure may not be necessary to do the job of internalisation. It could be that self-interested but enlightened managers of the firm can extend the operation of the market.

To see the argument here take the case where there are just two firms: firm 1 is a polluter and firm 2 the victim. We assume that both firms are fully informed about technological possibilities and production activities, including the impact of the externality: this informational assumption is important. We also assume that there is no legal or other restraint on the activities of firm 1, the polluter. So it would appear that firm 2 would have to suffer a loss of profits that, *ceteris paribus*, becomes larger as firm 1 increases its output.

? Mini Problems

12 Does this imply that the 'polluter pays'? [See Mini Problems 20 and 22 in chapter 9.]

The key to the private solution is for firm 2 (the victim) to make an offer of a side payment or bribe to firm 1. The bribe is an amount that is made conditional upon the amount of output that firm 1 generates: the greater the pollution, the smaller is the bribe; so we model the bribe as a decreasing function $\beta(\cdot)$ having as argument the polluter's output. The scheme can be implemented because we assume that the pollution activity is common knowledge. How should β be determined? We can treat it as one more control variable for firm 2, and so the optimisation problem is

$$\max_{\{\mathbf{q}^2,\beta\}} \sum_{i=1}^{n} p_i q_i^2 - \beta - \mu_2 \Phi^2\left(\mathbf{q}^2, q_1^1\right). \tag{13.8}$$

The first-order conditions are:

$$p_i - \mu_2 \Phi_i^2\left(\mathbf{q}^2, q_1^1\right) = 0 \tag{13.9}$$

$$-1 + \mu_2 \frac{d\Phi^2\left(\mathbf{q}^2, q_1^1\right)}{dq_1^1}\frac{dq_1^1}{d\beta} = 0. \tag{13.10}$$

Using the definition of the externality we can write (13.10) as

$$-1 + \mu_2 \Phi_2^2\left(\mathbf{q}^2, q_1^1\right) e_{21}^1 \frac{dq_1^1}{d\beta} = 0 \tag{13.11}$$

which, in view of (13.9), implies

$$\frac{d\beta}{dq_1^1} = \mu_2 \Phi_2^2\left(\mathbf{q}^2, q_1^1\right) e_{21}^1 = p_2 e_{21}^1. \tag{13.12}$$

Solving (13.12) gives $\beta\left(q_1^1\right)$, the optimal bribe as a function of the polluter's output. In other words the FOCs yield a differential equation that defines the optimal bribe function $\beta(\cdot)$ for firm 2, the victim firm.[13]

Now look at the problem from the point of view of firm 1. Once the victim firm makes its offer of a conditional bribe, firm 1 should take account of it. So its profits must look like this

$$\max_{\{\mathbf{q}^1\}} \sum_{i=1}^{n} p_i q_i^1 + \beta(q_1^1) - \mu_1 \Phi^1\left(\mathbf{q}^1\right) \tag{13.13}$$

—there is explicit recognition in (13.13) that the size of the side payment will depend upon q_1^1, which is under firm 1's direct control. The first-order conditions for firm 1's problem are then given by

$$p_1 q_i^1 + \frac{d\beta(q_1^1)}{dq_1^1} - \mu_1 \Phi_1^1\left(\mathbf{q}^1\right) = 0 \tag{13.14}$$

$$p_2 - \mu_1 \Phi_2^1\left(\mathbf{q}^1\right) = 0 \tag{13.15}$$

? Mini Problems

13 Interpret (13.12) in words as a 'marginal rule' for firm 2.

which, taking into account (13.12), imply

$$\frac{\Phi_1^1}{\Phi_2^1} = \frac{p_1}{p_2} + e_{21}^1. \tag{13.16}$$

Remarkably we seem to have come to the same efficient solution as would have been reached by an optimally designed pollution tax—see equations (13.6) and (13.7). What is more this apparently efficient outcome can be obtained even if the legal system assigned rights to the victim rather than the perpetrator. It appears, therefore, that if there is perfect information, and that costless enforcement and meaningful negotiation is possible, then an efficient outcome can be attained through a purely private mechanism. In effect the set of markets has been augmented by the creation of a pseudo-market in pollution rights, and the appropriate pricing of these rights plays the central role in implementing the efficient allocation. This extension of the market has effectively internalised the externality by placing an implicit price on it that the producer of the externality cannot afford to ignore.

However, there may yet be problems:

- If a polluter is allowed to sell rights to pollute indefinitely, then it is possible that the process might go on until firm 2 goes out of business. In which case the feasible set will look like that illustrated in Figure 13.6. However, if this occurs it is then clear that reliance on the extended market mechanism will not work for the very same reason that we encounter in section 13.3: the pricing of pollution rights leads one to

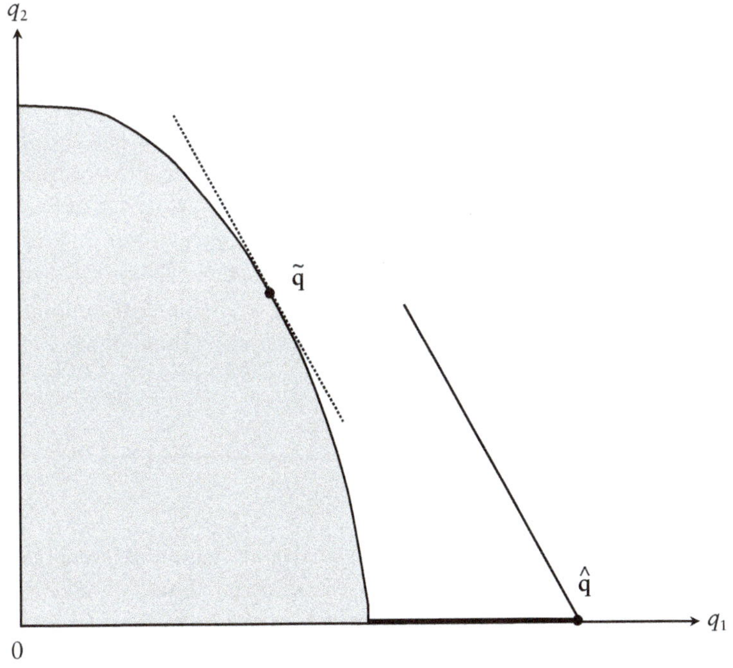

Figure 13.6 A fundamental nonconvexity

point $\hat{q}$ rather than the efficient point $\tilde{q}$. One may have transformed the externality-type problem of market failure into a non-convexity-type problem.

- The argument implicitly supposes that transactions costs are negligible. The bribe is negotiated and paid with no more fuss than a conventional market transaction; the quid pro quo of the reduction in the polluting activity is verified with no more fuss than checking the quality of goods in the market. But it is not hard to think of situations where this assumption just will not do. For example, where there are many potential perpetrators and victims, isolating the particular polluter involved, implementing the bribe and monitoring the actions contingent on the bribe may be difficult.

- Each firm is supposed to be well informed about the cost functions of others in order to implement the optimal bribe function. This assumption could seem rather unsatisfactory in view of the regulation problem highlighted in section 13.3.4: will a competitor know a rival's costs better than the government?

Example 13.3

Although the trading of pollution rights is essentially an 'individual' activity—in that individual agents decide whether and how much to trade—and although the (extended) market determines prices there is still an important role for 'government' where the quote marks indicate that the government may in fact be some loose informal arrangement of agents. Someone has to determine the allocation of rights here. An appropriate example here is the Kyoto protocol, which came into force in February 2005 and incorporates a provision for a market in pollution rights at country level. The agreement has an explicit recognition of 'emissions trading'. This works by allowing countries to trade agreed allowances of greenhouse gas emissions: polluting countries can buy unused credits from those which are allowed to emit more than they actually do. Countries are also able to gain credits for activities (such as tree planting and soil conservation) that enhance the environment's capacity to absorb carbon. An important question, though, is whether the initial distribution of rights is appropriate in that it does not lead to an inequitable distribution of market power—see Maeda (2003), who provides some interesting simulations.

13.4.4 Consumption externalities

We can use some of the production-externality analysis to handle external effects in consumption as well. Now, in contrast to the case considered above, we take the situation where production takes place without externality, but there may be interdependencies between agents' utility functions. Good 1 is some commodity that affects the utility of other people either negatively (tobacco?) or positively (deodorant?) and good 2 is just a basket of other goods. Using the basic efficiency principles from equation (9.34) and

(13.2) we get

$$\frac{U_1^h}{U_2^h} = \frac{\Phi_1}{\Phi_2} - e_{21}^h \tag{13.17}$$

where e_{21}^h is the marginal externality generated by h in consuming good 1 (valued in terms of good 2) obtained from equation (9.33): at an efficient allocation each household's marginal willingness to pay for good 1 should just equal the marginal cost of producing good adjusted by the value of the marginal externality. Again we might think of a modified market solution using a corrective tax. So, reasoning as before, equation (13.17) would lead to

$$\frac{p_1}{p_2} = \frac{\tilde{p}_1}{\tilde{p}_2} + t \tag{13.18}$$

where $\frac{p_1}{p_2}$ again represents the consumer' price ratio, $\frac{\tilde{p}_1}{\tilde{p}_2}$ is the producer's price ratio and

$$t = -e_{21}^h \tag{13.19}$$

is the required corrective tax.[14]

Let us follow through on the example used in the efficiency discussion on page 248. The implication of (13.18) and (13.19) is that if smoking generates a negative externality ($e_{21}^h < 0$) then there should be a positive corrective tax on smoking equal to the value of the marginal externality. The tax can be seen as a way of incorporating in the firm's cost computations the social costs of a negative externality along with the private cost of supplying the consumer with the good that generates the externality.

However, it is clear that in the case of consumption externalities the problems of information and measurement could be fairly intractable. In some cases (as with smoking) it may be true that there is independent information on the damage to other peoples' health: if so then the value of the marginal externality is common knowledge. But in many cases the problems of getting reliable information about consumption externalities will be at least as great as the problems associated with getting information about firms' costs in the production-externality model. Given the heterogeneity of tastes it may be impossible for someone to provide accurate and verifiable information about the externality; it may even be impossible to determine in which direction (positive or negative) the externality works! In the light of this people may have an incentive to misrepresent their preferences.[15] This is a problem that emerges more sharply in the analysis of public goods—section 13.6 below.

13.4.5 Externalities: assessment

Can all the various types of externality be satisfactorily handled through the workings of private interests? This central question, which we have addressed in this section, resolves into the following two questions: can the externality be internalised? If so, how?

? Mini Problems

14 On this basis should deodorant and perfume be subsidised?

15 Provide an example to show this based on Mini Problem 14.

In some cases the answer appears to be positive, but the workings of the market need to be adjusted appropriately. These cases cover situations where the efficient outcome can be sustained by a corrective tax that drives a wedge between consumer and producer prices. Some versions of internalisation rely on explicitly superseding the conventional market mechanism by merging separate production entities. Internalisation may be trickier in situations where agents voluntarily set up their own extended market or where the problem of imperfect information means that it is impossible to prevent agents from misrepresenting their preferences or misrepresenting their costs.

13.5 Public consumption

Check out Table 9.2 (page 234) once more. It gives four special cases on the public-private spectrum of goods. We have examined two of these (those on the left of the table, corresponding to 'Rival' goods); it is now time to look at the analysis of the case in the top-right-hand corner, marked with an enigmatic '?'.

This special case is 'public consumption' in the sense that the good lacks the rivalness property—making it available for an extra person to consume the good or service without using up extra resources. But it is not truly 'public' because we assume that it is excludable. It is an interesting halfway house on the way to discussing the topic of public goods in section 13.6. Fortunately we can deal with the issues that it raises in comparatively short order.

13.5.1 Non-rivalness and efficiency conditions

So, let us think through the provision of a good that exhibits the characteristic of non-rivalness but yet is excludable—pay-for-view TV, for example. The excludability property means that you can charge for the good; and so an efficient allocation could be implementable through some type of market mechanism. How should the price be set and can we rely on the free market to set it?

Let good 1 be the non-rival good and good 2 a basket of all other goods. The argument of section 9.3.4 implies that the efficient allocation must satisfy[16]

$$\sum_{h=1}^{n_h} \frac{U_1^h(\mathbf{x}^h)}{U_2^h(\mathbf{x}^h)} = \frac{\Phi_1}{\Phi_2}. \tag{13.20}$$

This immediately suggests an implementation method. Because the good is assumed to be excludable we can introduce a charge p^h for each agent h that is the price (for that agent) for the right to consume good 1, denominated in terms of good 2. The condition (13.20) then gives

$$\sum_{h=1}^{n_h} p^h = \frac{\Phi_1}{\Phi_2}. \tag{13.21}$$

? Mini Problems

16 Explain why.

Each consumer is set a price that corresponds to his marginal willingness to pay for the service supplied; each could be cut off (excluded) if he does not pay; the sum of these prices totals the marginal cost of supply of the service.[17]

Two difficulties with this allocation rule suggest themselves:

- The assumption of perfect excludability in this case is a strong one—things will go wrong if individual consumers' marginal willingness to pay cannot be readily observed.
- It is often the case that this type of good is to be supplied not by a collection of competitive firms but by just one, or a few, large producers. So there may also be a problem of monopoly supply that requires regulation, as discussed in section 13.3.4.

However, there is a commonly-encountered institution that, it could be argued, is designed precisely to supply such non-rival goods.

13.5.2 Club goods

The club can be seen as a device that does exactly that job. Through its membership rules it implements an effective exclusion mechanism. Let us analyse a simple version of a club that provides good 1.

First we introduce the idea of the size of the club and its relation to the good or service that the club provides. If there are N members then the amount x_1 of good 1 produced by the club is given by a production function ϕ such that

$$x_1 = \phi(z, N) \tag{13.22}$$

where z is the input of good 2 (the composite good consisting of all other goods). Let us make conventional assumptions about ϕ: it is increasing and strictly concave in z; it is decreasing or constant in N.[18] This latter assumption allows both for the pure non-rivalness case and for the case where the services provided by the club are subject to congestion.[19]

Agent h's preferences are assumed to be represented by the following utility function

$$U^h(x_1, x_2^h). \tag{13.23}$$

The membership fee of the club must be set to cover the cost of producing the good. We will simplify the exposition by assuming

1. The cost of the club is allocated equally amongst its members.
2. All members of the club are identical in their preferences and incomes.

? Mini Problems

17 What is the marginal unit of the product that is being supplied in the TV example?

18 It is sometimes convenient to work instead with the club's cost function. The cost of providing an amount x_1 of good 1 is $C(x_1, N)$ measured in terms of good 2. Explain the relationship between C and ϕ. Show that the above assumptions on ϕ imply that C is increasing and convex in x_1 and is non-decreasing in N.

19 Explain why.

The boundary of agent h's budget constraint is then

$$\frac{z}{N} + x_2^h = y^h \tag{13.24}$$

where y^h is the same for all h. The agent's utility can then be written

$$U^h\left(\phi(z, N), y^h - \frac{z}{N}\right). \tag{13.25}$$

For any agent who is interested in joining the club it must be true that

$$U^h\left(\phi(z, N), y^h - \frac{z}{N}\right) \geq U^h\left(0, y^h\right) \tag{13.26}$$

—utility from club membership (allowing for the membership fee) must be at least as great as utility if the agent stays out of the club.

What is the optimal amount of x_1, the good or service provided by the club? We can answer this by finding the amount of input z that maximises the utility of a representative club member. Differentiating (13.25) with respect to z the first-order condition for a maximum for a club of given size N is

$$U_1^h\left(\phi(z, N), y^h - \frac{z}{N}\right)\phi_z(z, N) - \frac{1}{N}U_2^h\left(\phi(z, N), y^h - \frac{z}{N}\right) = 0. \tag{13.27}$$

Therefore, rearranging and summing over all the h in the club, we have

$$\sum_{h=1}^{N} \frac{U_1^h\left(\phi(z, N), y^h - \frac{z}{N}\right)}{U_2^h\left(\phi(z, N), y^h - \frac{z}{N}\right)} = \frac{1}{\phi_z(z, N)} \tag{13.28}$$

in other words[20]

$$\sum_h \text{MRS}^h = \text{MRT} \tag{13.29}$$

—compare equation (9.36) and (13.20). An efficient allocation characterised by (13.28) will be implementable because of the excludability assumption: condition (13.26) ensures that any agent h would rather pay the membership fee z/N than be excluded from the club.[21]

Clearly we have a story of the private provision of something that has essentially public characteristics. But the assumption of perfect excludability may be unreasonably strong: more of this in the next section.

? Mini Problems

20 Show how (13.28) can be generalised to a heterogeneous membership.

21 (a) If there is congestion, find the condition for the optimal membership of the club. [Hint: assume that membership can be (approximately) treated as a continuous variable and differentiate with respect to N.] (b) Show that this condition can be interpreted as 'marginal cost = average cost'. (c) Show that at the optimum this can be interpreted as setting the membership fee equal to the marginal cost of admitting the marginal member.

13.6 Public goods

We have encountered public goods at a number of points. In chapter 9 we discussed the issue of efficiency in an economy with public goods; in chapter 12 we saw how to do a kind of 'auction' of an indivisible public project in order to find a simple mechanism in this special case. However, beyond this special case, what of the general problem of providing public goods? Can we find a suitable mechanism for doing this? Could it be implemented by an individualistic approach?

13.6.1 The issue

Recall that a public good has two key characteristics—it is both (1) completely non-rival and (2) completely non-excludable (check Table 9.2 on page 234 and the accompanying discussion).

The first of these two properties is at the heart of the question of allocative efficiency with public goods. From Theorem 9.6 and the discussion of section 13.5 we know that the efficiency rule is to choose the quantities of goods on the boundary of the economy's attainable set such that (13.29) holds. The sum-of-MRS rule follows directly from the non-rivalness property.

The second property is central to the implementation question. Here we have a potentially serious problem, simply because, by assumption, the good is non-excludable. The intrinsic non-excludability will make the design issue quite tricky: the intuition here is that the problem contains in extreme form the feature that we considered on page 446. Unlike the club story that we have just analysed it is impossible to run a membership scheme: you cannot keep non-payers out of the club.

To see the nature of the problem in more detail let us look at a couple of simplistic mechanisms that can fail catastrophically.

13.6.2 Voluntary provision

The essential points can be established in a model that is very similar to that considered in section 12.6.2. We have a two-commodity world, in which there are n_h agents (households): commodity 1 is a pure public good and commodity 2 is purely private. An important difference here is that we are no longer considering a fixed-size project but the general problem of allocating the two goods, public and private.

Each agent has an exogenously given income y^h, denominated in units of the private good 2. We imagine that the public good is to be financed voluntarily: each household makes a contribution z^h which leaves an amount

$$x_2^h = y^h - z^h$$

of the private good available for h's own consumption. Good 1 is produced from good 2 according to the following production function:

$$x_1 = \phi(z) \tag{13.30}$$

where z is the total input of the good 2 used in the production process, derived simply by summing the contributions as in (12.23). What contribution will each household make and how much of the public good will be provided? The answer will depend not only on the model of each agent's preferences but also on the agent's assumption about the actions of others.

We again suppose that agent (household) h has preferences given by (13.23). Each agent realises that the total output of the public good depends upon his or her own contribution and upon that made by others. Suppose that everyone assumes that what others choose to do is independent of his own contribution: in other words h takes the contribution of the others as a constant, $\bar{z}$, where

$$\bar{z} := \sum_{\substack{k=1 \\ k\neq h}}^{n_h} z^k \tag{13.31}$$

so that

$$z = \bar{z} + z^h.$$

The constant-$\bar{z}$ assumption appears to be rational for h but, as we will see, there is a catch when we consider h's wider interests.

Combining equations (13.30) to (13.31), agent h's optimisation problem becomes:

$$\max_{x_2^h} U^h(\phi(\bar{z} + y^h - x_2^h),\, x_2^h). \tag{13.32}$$

The first-order condition for an interior solution is:

$$-U_1^h(x_1, x_2^h)\phi_z(\bar{z} + y^h - x_2^h) + U_2^h(x_1, x_2^h) = 0 \tag{13.33}$$

and a simple rearrangement of (13.33) gives:

$$\frac{U_1^h(x_1, x_2^h)}{U_2^h(x_1, x_2^h)} = \frac{1}{\phi_z(z)} \tag{13.34}$$

where

$$z := \sum_{h=1}^{n_h} z^h. \tag{13.35}$$

The condition (13.34) has the simple interpretation

$$\text{MRS}^h = \text{MRT}.$$

However, by contrast, Pareto efficiency requires (13.29) to be satisfied, which, in terms of the simple two-good model used here, means

$$\sum_{h=1}^{n_h} \frac{U_1^h(x_1, x_2^h)}{U_2^h(x_1, x_2^h)} = \frac{1}{\phi_z(z)}. \tag{13.36}$$

The implication of the contrasting individual optimisation condition (13.34) and the efficiency condition (13.36) can be illustrated in Figure 13.7. This figure represents the production possibilities in this two-commodity model, with the public good on the

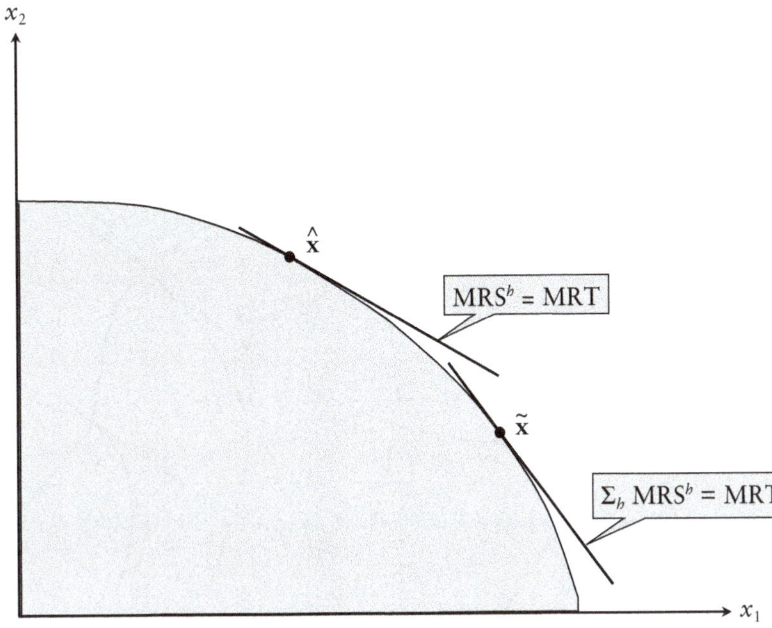

Figure 13.7 Myopic rationality underprovides public good

horizontal axis and the total amount of the private good on the vertical axis.[22] If agents are myopically rational they choose a consumption bundle satisfying (13.34) that yields the aggregate consumption vector such as $\hat{\mathbf{x}}$ in Figure 13.7. But if there were some way of implementing the efficient outcome—satisfying equation (13.36)—then the aggregate consumption bundle would be at point $\tilde{\mathbf{x}}$ where the slope of the tangent is steeper. Clearly voluntarism leads to an underprovision of the public good.

What is going on here can be understood in strategic terms by reference to the Cournot model of quantity competition discussed in chapter 10 (page 287). Figure 13.8 represents Alf's and Bill's contributions to a public good where $n_h = 2$. Alf's indifference curves are given by the U-shaped family where the direction of increasing preference is upwards.[23]

? Mini Problems

22 Assume that all n_h agents are identical and that agent h has the utility function

$$U^h(x_1, x_2^h) = 2\sqrt{x_1} + x_2^h.$$

Assume that production conditions are such that 1 unit of private good can always be transformed into 1 unit of the public good. What is the condition for efficiency? How much of the public good should be produced? How much would be produced if it were left to individual contributions under the above assumptions?

23 Explain why this is so, given the model of utility in (13.23) and (13.32) where U^h is a conventional quasiconcave function.

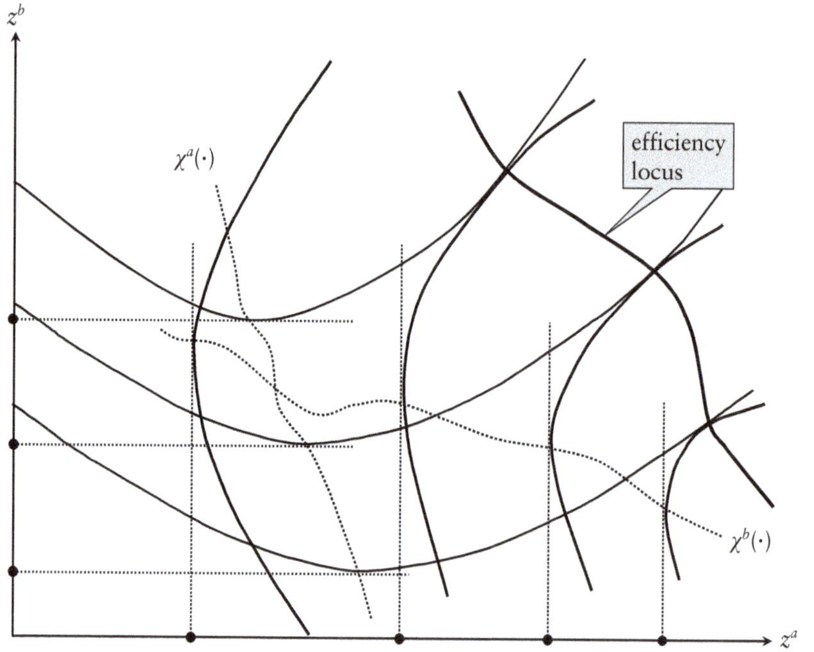

Figure 13.8 The Cournot-Nash solution underprovides

Bill's indifference curves work similarly: they are C-shaped and the direction of increasing preference is to the right. Using the logic of the argument on page 238 we can construct the efficiency locus as the path connecting all the points of tangency between an a-indifference curve and a b-indifference curve: allocations corresponding to these values of $\left(z^a, z^b\right)$ are Pareto efficient.

But now consider the myopic optimisation problem of each of the two agents. In effect they play a simple simultaneous-move game to decide their contributions to the public good. If Alf chooses z^a on the assumption that z^b is fixed, he selects a point that is just at the bottom of one of the U-shaped indifference curves: the locus of all such points is given by the reaction function χ^a that enables one to read off the best-response value of Alf's contribution to any given level of Bill's contribution. A similar derivation and interpretation applies to Bill's reaction function χ^b and, of course, the same remarks about the slight inexactitude of the term 'reaction function' apply to this simultaneous move game as in the context of Cournot quantity-competition on page 288. In the light of this argument the point of intersection of the curves χ^a and χ^b in Figure 13.8 represents the Nash equilibrium of the public-good contribution game: each agent is simultaneously making the best response to the other's contribution. A glance at the figure is enough to see that the Nash-equilibrium contributions fall short of the contributions required to provide a Pareto-efficient outcome.

There are other ways in which the story of voluntary provision of the public good could have been dressed up, but typically they have the same sort of suboptimal Cournot–Nash outcome. Each agent would like to 'free ride' on the contributions provided by others rather than providing the socially responsible contribution himself. This conclusion seems rather depressing:[24] what might be the way forward?

13.6.3 Personalised prices?

In the light of the discussion of other aspects of market failure such as the non-convexity issue (section 13.3) we might want to consider a direct public means of providing the public good—perhaps a benevolent government agency that produces the public good and is empowered to requisition the amounts z^h in order to do so. But this would presume that an important part of the problem had already been solved. In order to do this job the agency would need to know each household's preferences, not just the distribution of preferences in the population.

There is an alternative approach that avoids making this assumption of frightening omniscience on the part of the government agency. It builds directly on the representation of an efficient allocation with public goods given in Figure 9.9.Instead of assuming that the government is all-knowing, imagine that the agency which produces the public good is empowered only to fix a discriminatory 'subscription price' that is specific to each household h, in the manner of a discriminating monopolist. Once again p^h measures the cost per unit of good 1 in terms of good 2. The agency announces the set of personalised prices and then household h announces how much of the public good it would wish to purchase. The decision problem of household h is therefore:

$$\max_{(x_1, x_2^h)} U^h(x_1, x_2^h) \tag{13.37}$$

subject to the following budget constraint:

$$p^h x_1 + x_2^h = y^h. \tag{13.38}$$

Clearly the household will announce intended purchases (x_1, x_2^h) such that

$$\frac{U_1^h}{U_2^h} = p^h. \tag{13.39}$$

Apparently all the agency needs to do to ensure efficiency—equation (13.36) above—is to select the personalised prices appropriately. This means selecting all the p^h simultaneously such that

$$\sum_{h=1}^{n_h} p^h = \frac{1}{\phi_z}. \tag{13.40}$$

Condition (13.40)—known as the *Lindahl solution* to the public goods problem—embodies the principle that the sum of households' marginal willingness to pay (here the sum of the personalised prices p^h) equals the marginal cost of providing

? Mini Problems

24 Could we rely on a version of the Folk Theorem (Theorem 10.3) to ensure an efficient supply of public goods?

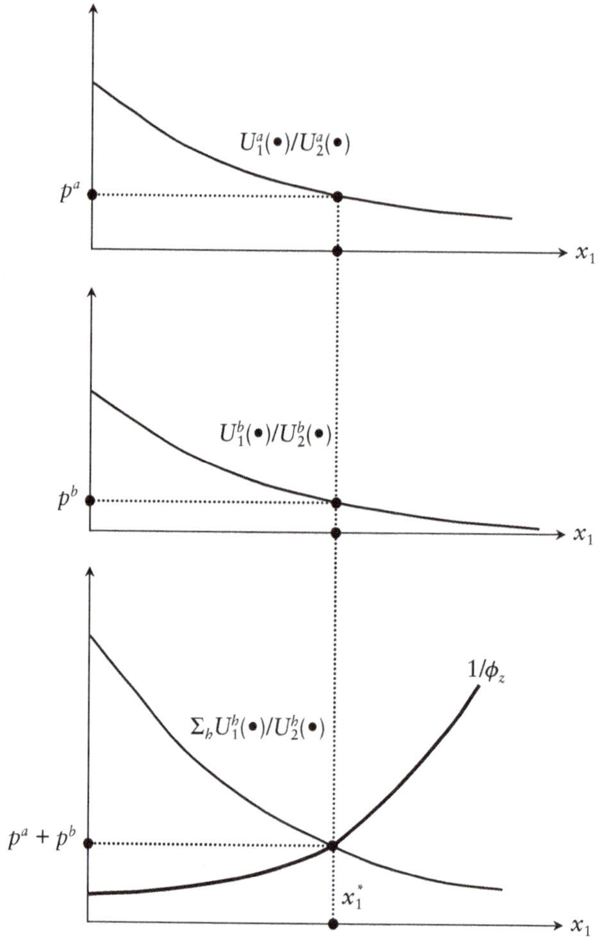

Figure 13.9 Lindahl solution

the public good (13.36). It can be illustrated in the two-good, two-person case as in Figure 13.9, derived from Figure 9.9. This can be interpreted as an illustration of aggregating individual demands for a public good: for each person an individual subscription price is set equal to that individual's MRS_{21}^h (equation 13.39). By contrast to the case of private goods (where for a given, unique price each household's demanded quantity is summed) we find that for a unique quantity each household's subscription price is summed. One adds up everyone's marginal willingness to pay, and the aggregated subscription price matches the production price of the public good (equation 13.40). If this sounds like club goods again then this impression is correct—Figure 13.9 could have been used to illustrate the optimal charging rule for the non-rival excludable good in equation (13.21).

However, now, with true public goods, there are two rather obvious problems. The first is that the procedure may be computationally rather demanding, since one might have to iterate through several personalised price schemes and provision levels for a large number of people all the potential beneficiaries of the public good and not just those who self-select by applying to join the club. The second problem is more fundamental. Why should each household reveal its true marginal rate of substitution to the agency? After all, there may be no way of checking whether the agent (the household) is telling lies or not, and the higher the marginal rate of substitution one admits to, the higher the subscription price one will be charged. So, once a household realises this, what will be the outcome?

The household then realises that it can effectively choose the price that confronts it by announcing a false marginal rate of substitution. It seems reasonable to suppose that it will do this to maximise its own utility subject to the actions of all other households assumed to be given. Once again we assume that equation (13.31) holds: household h assumes that the net contribution of everyone else is fixed. So household h in effect chooses both x_2^h and x_1 so as to maximise expression (13.23) subject to

$$x_1 = \phi(\bar{z} + p^h x_1) \tag{13.41}$$

and the budget constraint (13.38).

However, this is exactly the problem above where each household made its own voluntary contribution. Because there is no incentive for any household to reveal its true preference and no way of checking the preferences independently, the inefficiency persists: the subscription mechanism is open to manipulation. Evidently we have re-encountered the problem of misrepresentation in the economics of information and design (page 388 in chapter 12) or indeed the problem of 'chiselling' in the oligopoly problem (page 291 in chapter 10).

Is this conclusion inescapable?

13.6.4 Public goods: market failure and the design problem

The strategic problem that we 'rediscovered' at the end of the previous section arises from two key features at the heart of the public goods issue. First, joint interests diverge from individual interests because of the definition of the public good, by now a familiar problem.[25] In this respect it is like the cartel in oligopoly (page 290): by adhering to a collusive tacit agreement the producers maximise joint profits; but each is tempted to break the cartel and pursue higher profits individually. Of course the individual firms could set up some institution to police the agreement; the counterpart in the present case is, of course, the government. However, the second feature of the public goods issue may

? Mini Problems

25 Imagine a simple two-person economy in which each person is endowed with 1 unit of a private good. Each person has a simple binary choice, whether or not to contribute their whole endowment of private good to the production of a public good. If both persons contribute this will produce 1.2 units of a public good that will be enjoyed by both persons. If one person contributes but the other does not this will produce 0.5 units of the public good. The payoff to each person is simply the sum of the person's private good (if any) and the public good (if any). Set this decision problem out as a strategic form (normal form) game and show that it is exactly the form of the Prisoner's Dilemma (page 280).

or may not be present in the oligopoly setting: we assume in the public goods setting that the policing institution is not well informed about the objectives and constraints of the individual agents. This is what leads to the endemic problem of misrepresentation that we saw in section 13.6.3. In view of this it is useful to review the principles of design from chapter 12.

Let us think again about the implications of the Gibbard–Satterthwaite Theorem (page 393). Recall the essence of the result: for any mechanism Γ in an economy with a finite number of agents:

- if there is more than a single pair of alternatives,
- and if Γ is defined for possible profiles of utility functions,
- and if Γ is non-manipulable in the sense that it is implementable in dominant strategies,

then Γ must be dictatorial.

It is clearly this result (Theorem 12.4) that underlies the problem that we have encountered with the implementation of public goods via voluntarism or the attempt at subscription-price taxation. So, following through the three main parts of the theorem that we have repeated here, perhaps it might be possible to make some progress on the implementation problem if we were to relax one or more of these conditions.

- First, what if we reconsider the nature of the voluntary model in the light of, for example, the public-project mechanism of chapter 12? The key point is that in the public-project story (pages 404 ff) there are just two possible social states. So, perhaps a possible solution to the difficulties of sections 13.6.2 and 13.6.3 is to recast the public goods decision problem: instead of considering the possibility that the amount of public goods x_1 can take any real value, we could focus on a fixed-size project so that x_1 becomes a binary variable. Although this is obviously restrictive, the insight provided by the pivotal mechanism is important: it provides a way of internalising the externality that each agent imposes on the others though a signalling procedure that is similar to that discussed in section 11.3.2 (page 361). Can the lesson of the pivotal mechanism be extended to other cases so as to find a way of internalising the externality associated with the public good?
- Second, we could focus attention on a specific class of utility functions rather than admitting all types of preferences over public and private goods.
- Third, we could consider weakening dominant-strategy truthful implementation to, say, Nash implementation: agent h reveals his true preferences just as long as everyone else does the same.

Some elements of these approaches will become evident in the mechanisms discussed in section 13.6.5.

13.6.5 Public goods: alternative mechanisms

Our examination of alternative mechanisms for providing public goods is driven by two motivations. First, it would be interesting to find a device for assisting the cooperation of individual agents in achieving either an efficient outcome or, at least, one that is an improvement on what arises from the pursuit of myopic interests. Second, there is the question of private rather than public approach that has run as a theme through this chapter. Relying automatically on the institution of government for the provision of public goods seems somewhat restrictive: is it not possible to find a method of coordinated individual action that would take into account more than just their myopic interests?

The rôle of government

Suppose we are prepared to assume that the government has a lot of knowledge and expertise at implementation. Then the public project can provide the foundation for more sophisticated mechanisms: using a more complex penalty and taxation scheme the pivotal mechanism could be applied to situations other than the simple fixed-size project, although this is likely to be administratively complex. However, the government may also have a rôle to play in modifying other types of individualistic equilibria: by making it in individual agents' interest to consider the outcomes for others, implementation of an efficient solution may be possible; there is an example of this kind of thing in Exercise 13.6. The government may also have a role to play in setting up the institutions required for essentially private, individualistic, but non-market forms of provision. This is illustrated in the following two applications.

Money-back guarantees

The first attempt has a pleasantly parochial feel to it and may be familiar from the office or neighbourhood. Everyone is encouraged to provide voluntary contributions for the public good so as to achieve a given target value z^*, sometimes known as the 'provision point'. If the target is not reached then no public good is produced; but if the target is reached or surpassed then any excess is returned to the contributors on a pro-rata basis. The money-back guarantee aspect of the scheme is central: without it the target becomes a mere aspiration for exhortation, devoid of economic incentive.

To model the scheme let the utility of agent be given by the zero-income-effect form

$$U\left(x_1, x_2^h\right) = \psi(x_1) + x_2^h \tag{13.42}$$

—compare equation (12.21) on page 405. Under the rules of the money-back guarantee the individual's utility is thus given by

$$U^h\left(x_1, x_2^h\right) = \begin{cases} \psi(\phi(z^*)) + \pi^h[z - z^*] + y^h - z^h & \text{if } z \geq z^* \\ y^h & \text{otherwise} \end{cases} \tag{13.43}$$

where $z := \sum_h z^h$ denotes the total contribution and $\pi^h := z^h/z$ is agent h's proportion of the total. Clearly if the public good is valuable to the individual agent h, then h will voluntarily contribute under this scheme.[26]

However, there are two interconnected problems with this approach. First, who decides the provision point and how? To fix z^* appropriately one would have to have

? Mini Problems

26 Show that under these circumstances contributing for the public good is a Nash equilibrium.

prior information about preferences for the public good; perhaps the government has this information, but otherwise it comes close to assuming away a major part of the problem. Second, if the provision point is not exogenously fixed, then one will immediately revert to the underprovision outcome of voluntarism.[27]

Lotteries

A common method of financing the provision of public goods is a national or local lottery. Suppose that there is a fixed prize K and that agents are invited to buy lottery tickets that will be used to fund a public good. The prize, of course, also has to be paid for out of the sum provided by the lottery tickets. Therefore the total amount of the public good provided is given by

$$x_1 = \phi(z - K), \tag{13.44}$$

where z is the sum of all the agents' lottery-ticket purchases. The lottery is fair, so that if agent h purchases an amount z^h of lottery tickets, the probability of h winning is

$$\pi^h = \frac{z^h}{z}. \tag{13.45}$$

Assume that agent h makes the Cournot assumption so that the total input provided for public good production is

$$z = \bar{z} + z^h, \tag{13.46}$$

where $\bar{z}$ is the sum of everyone else's ticket purchases. Again we take the utility function for agent h to be given by (13.42). So expected utility is

$$\mathcal{E}U^h\left(x_1, x_2^h\right) = \psi^h(x_1) + \pi^h K + y^h - z^h, \tag{13.47}$$

where x_1 and π^h are given by (13.44)–(13.46). The first-order conditions for the maximum of (13.47) are straightforward and yield[28]

$$\psi_x^h(x_1) = \frac{\beta(K)}{\phi_z(z - K)}, \tag{13.48}$$

where

$$\beta(K) := 1 - \frac{\bar{z}}{z^2}K < 1.$$

The left-hand side of (13.48) is MRS; the right-hand side is $\beta(K)$ times MRT. From this we can deduce that, although the lottery will not provide the efficient amount of the public good given by (13.36), it will attenuate the problem of underprovision that arises from simple voluntary initiative by individuals. A higher prize K will result in more public good being provided through this mechanism.[29] Why does this happen? Setting up a

? Mini Problems

27 Show that each agent h would wish to argue for a smaller contribution.

28 Show this.

29 Show how to represent the case of voluntary provision as a special case of this model. Use the example of Mini Problem 22 to evaluate condition (13.48) and to illustrate that z will increase fixed-prize lottery introduces an offsetting externality: each time you buy a lottery ticket you affect everyone else's chances of winning the prize.[30]

Example 13.4

Will the lottery method of funding for public goods work in practice? Obviously the answer depends on what we mean by 'work'. Here are two interpretations:

1. One way is to check this out in the laboratory. Morgan and Sefton (2000) use this method to check out the Morgan (2000) model. It appears that public goods provision is indeed higher under lottery funding than under pure voluntarism. The purchase of lottery tickets varies with the size of the fixed prize and with the perceived value of the public good.
2. Alternatively we could look at the effect of introducing a national or state lottery. Does this establish the desired funding for public goods or does it just divert funds from elsewhere? For example the UK National Lottery was set up in 1993 with the intention that this would make a new contribution to the funding of designated 'good causes' such as the Arts and National Heritage. It was intended that this net *additionality* should be guaranteed through the transparency of the funding system: citizens participating in the lottery should be supremely aware of the destination of the funds generated by their ticket purchase. Bailey and Connolly (1997) show that this idea of additionality is difficult to establish in both theory and in practice.

Public goods mechanisms: assessment

In strategic terms the problem with public goods is essentially a version of the problem of the Prisoner's Dilemma (see Mini Problems 24 and 25). The intractability of this game form gives us an idea as to why the implementation problem is comparatively tricky in this case. The analysis of design issues from chapter 12 can be of some assistance—for example the insights from the pivotal mechanism. By changing the form of the perceived budget constraint there is a way in which the government as an external agent can induce a certain amount of cooperative behaviour by self-interested agents that otherwise might not be present. But this type of device cannot do everything in all circumstances. Furthermore, the models that use it nearly always focus upon a special class of utility functions which may limit their attraction as suitable parables for what might be done in practice.

? Mini Problems

with K. [Hint: make use of the assumption that all agents are identical to write the FOC as a function of z; then draw graphs of MRS and $\beta(K)$MRT.]

30 But, be careful here! Suppose the prize itself is related to the amount of lottery tickets bought. Specifically let K be equal to a proportion a of ticket sales. What will then be the equilibrium behaviour of each agent?

13.7 Optimal allocations?

As a final topic we turn to an issue which could be called, rather grandly, the optimal distribution of income. The basic question is how should the resources in the economy be deployed in the best possible way given the preferences that are imputed to society and the limitations imposed by the technology?

We use the approach to the social-welfare function developed in section 9.5 of chapter 9. Specifically we will suppose:

- The choice of an appropriate social state effectively amounts to the choice of an allocation of pure private goods.
- The social welfare function is individualistic and self-interested (W is a function of individual utility levels, and each U^h is a function only of household h's consumption).
- Utility is interpersonally comparable so that social welfare can be interpreted in terms of the distribution of income as well as its aggregate.

Of course specification of the social-welfare function is not sufficient to determine what the social state should be. As with other types of optimisation problem we also need to specify the feasible set.

Specification of the feasible set in this case is difficult because it is not self-evident what the limitations are on the freedom of action of the government. Contrast this with the optimisation problem of the monopoly used as an extended example in chapter 11 (pp. 329–347). In the chapter 11 case we could contrast two sharply defined informational regimes. These regimes corresponded clearly to two contrasting assumptions that could reasonably be made about the firm in relation to its market:

- *The full-information solution* where each potential customer could be correctly identified as to his/her type.
- *The second-best solution* where the distinction between types could not be made and the profit-maximising firm had to build in an incentive-compatibility constraint in order to prevent customers of one type masquerading as the other so as to get a better deal for themselves.

The distinction between full-information and second-best approaches is again crucial to the present analysis, but we may need to extend the meaning of the term 'second best'. It could once again be principally a question of incomplete information; but it may also be that the government or other agency is not allowed to use certain information in seeking to achieve a redistribution of resources or income.

The consequence for the structure of the optimisation problem is that we have to consider a number of side constraints on agents that are analogous to the side constraints that we built in to model the short-run optimisation problem of the firm.

13.7.1 Optimum with lump-sum transfers

Consider what is meant by lump-sum transfers. It is as though there were some means of transferring resource endowments or shares in firms from agent to agent costlessly as though they were the title deeds in the game *Monopoly*. Can we achieve so-called 'first-best' solutions with such transfers? The answer is probably yes, but the range of application is likely to be very limited and some of these 'solutions' could well be unattractive for a variety of reasons.[31]

However, if lump-sum transfers of income are possible, then the solution to the social optimum problem is immediate. To analyse this case we can use either a diagram representing the utility possibility set, or one like Figure 9.12 in terms of incomes (see page 261). If it is costless to transfer incomes between agents then, given that there are n_h agents ('households') and that total income is K, the set of possible income distributions is given by:

$$Y^* := \left\{ (y^1, y^2, \ldots) : \sum_{h=1}^{n_h} y^h = K \right\}. \tag{13.49}$$

In the two-person case this is simply a line at 45°. Likewise it is easy to see that, if all commodities are costlessly transferable, then the set of feasible income distributions is that defined in (13.49). Then, as we have already noted, the optimal distribution of income is going to be on the 45° ray through the origin. These are just two ways of motivating the idea that there is a fixed-sized 'cake' of national income to be shared out.

Let us briefly consider two problems that will often—if not always—arise.

- Not all resources may be costlessly transferable.
- Even with goods which are transferable, it may not be possible to transfer them on a lump-sum basis.

If the property distribution is changed in a market economy, then the total income in the community is also likely to change since the equilibrium price vector will also change. Consider Figure 13.10 (drawn using the same axes as Figure 9.12) and suppose the economy is initially at point $\hat{\mathbf{y}}$. The incomes of the households are determined, (i) by $\mathbf{d}$, the property distribution of resources and shares in firms, and (ii) by the equilibrium prices at $\hat{\mathbf{y}}$. Now imagine all the possible income distributions corresponding to changes in the property distribution away from that which was in force at $\hat{\mathbf{y}}$: we may do this by using the equivalent-variation concept, and taking as our starting point the household utility levels that were attained at point $\hat{\mathbf{y}}$. Each $\mathbf{d}$ determines a particular equilibrium price vector, and thus each $\mathbf{d}$ fixes a market-determined income for household h, $y^h(\mathbf{d})$. We may thus construct the set of all feasible (market-determined) income distributions:

$$Y := \{(y^1(\mathbf{d}), y^2(\mathbf{d}), \ldots) : \mathbf{d} \in D\}. \tag{13.50}$$

? Mini Problems

31 Suppose all the world consists of one jurisdiction and the government has a complete register of all the citizens. The government wants to finance the provision of a given amount of public good. (a) If the required taxes were divided equally among the citizens, would this be lump-sum? (b) If the required taxes were assigned to the citizens at random would this be lump-sum?

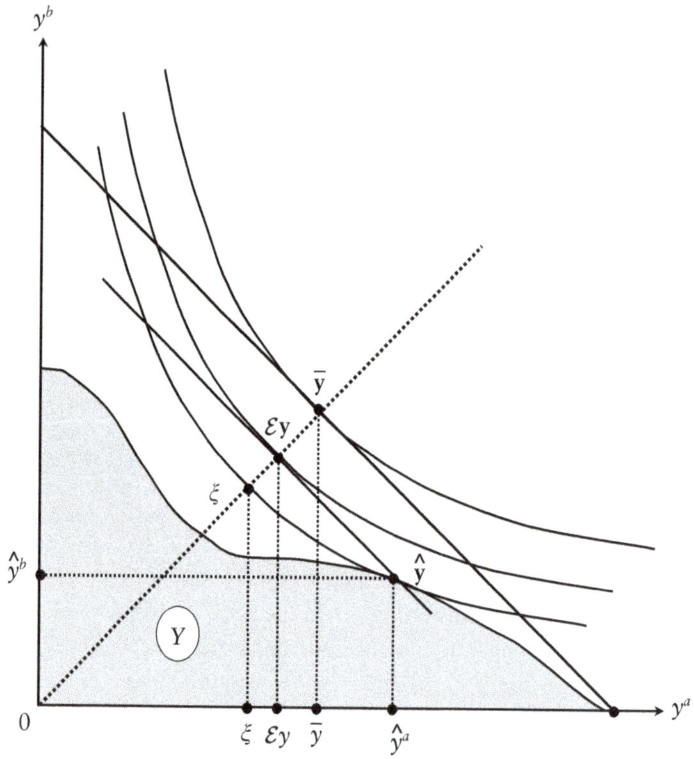

Figure 13.10 Opportunities for redistribution

This is illustrated by the shaded area in Figure 13.10. As we saw in Figure 9.12 the apparent welfare loss from being at point $\hat{\mathbf{y}}$ is given by the ratio of the distance $\mathcal{E}y - \xi$ to mean income $\mathcal{E}y$. But, by construction, $\hat{\mathbf{y}}$ is in fact a welfare optimum on the assumption that Y represents the set of feasible income distributions: the frontier of Y is tangential to a contour of the social welfare function at that point. Whether $\hat{\mathbf{y}}$ is an optimum in some wider sense depends on what we are prepared to assume about the scope for intervention in the economy. For example, as we have seen, if lump-sum transfers of income are possible, then the optimum would be at point $\bar{\mathbf{y}}$ and the set of all possible income distributions will be the set bounded by the 45° line through this point.

However, if such transfers are not practical policy then the 'true' attainable set may be somewhere intermediate between that determined by the market (as shown by Y) and that which would have been relevant had lump-sum income transfers been attainable.

Of course it is impossible to specify the attainable set without the structure of possible interventionist policies being specified. So one cannot in general state that equality of incomes is a welfare-maximising condition. One simple result is available, however.[32]

? Mini Problems

32 Prove this using an elementary geometrical argument.

Theorem 13.1

Given identical individuals, an equal distribution of income is welfare maximising for all symmetric concave social-welfare functions if Y is symmetric and convex.

To say more about the possibilities for redistribution we need to examine the second-best issue more closely.

13.7.2 Second-best approaches

Our treatment of the second-best approach to optimal allocation will focus on two things. First, we will consider the kind of constraints that ought to be modelled. Second, we will examine an example of the way in which the government's optimisation problem can be set up under such constraints.

Administrative costs and information

Clearly a major part of the 'second-best' approach is the nature of information as it relates to taxes and government transfers. Broadly speaking we can imagine that the government may have some information about personal characteristics—including income-generating attributes as in the income-tax problem and some information about transactions. We have examples of a second-best approach to the problem of income redistribution when personal characteristics are hidden in the chapter on 'design': namely the optimal-tax model of section 12.6.4 and Exercise 12.10 on income support. But we have yet to consider the way in which information about transactions might be used.

In addition there is the related question of administrative complexity. This is of enormous practical importance when considering the constraints on redistribution but it is difficult to model convincingly. One way of doing this is to impose some additional restriction on the form of the policy instrument by which the tax or transfer is to be administered: for example restricting the functional form of the income-tax schedule (see Exercise 13.7) or requiring that taxes that are conditioned on transactions are simple modifications of market prices rather than taking some complex, non-linear form. Let us look at this a little further.

Commodity taxation

In Chapter 9 we introduced the idea of measuring economic waste (page 241). This idea can be used to underpin practical policy making. A principal example of this concerns the design of commodity taxes. There is an attraction to standard linear commodity taxes—such as sales taxes or the value-added tax—in that they have only minimal information requirements.[33] Given that one restricts attention to this type of

? Mini Problems

33 Here linear is used in the strict sense—i.e. the taxes are proportional to the amounts purchased. What complications would arise if one introduced a small amount of non-linearity—e.g. a low tax rate for purchases of good i below $\bar{x}_i$ units and a higher rate for $\bar{x}_i$ units and above?

tax—whether for reasons of information requirements or otherwise—the obvious question that arises is: which commodities should bear the higher rates of tax? One approach would be to adjust the rates so as to minimise waste while meeting the overall revenue requirements. But what is the rationale for this and would it produce an 'acceptable' tax structure?[34]

To analyse this consider the second-best optimisation problem for the government. Let us assume that the government has information about consumers' transactions but not about their wealth or income. It needs to raise taxes, perhaps to fund public goods or because of some external constraint, such as foreign debt. The constraint represented by this revenue requirement is to be incorporated into the second-best problem. To simplify things let us suppose that distributional questions are irrelevant: the government just needs to raise the target amount of revenue in the most efficient way possible. So the problem can be modelled as 'minimise waste subject to the revenue constraint'.

Use the notation of section 9.3.2 but adapt it so that there are now $n+1$ goods. We assume that there is a representative consumer who supplies labour (commodity 0) and purchases commodities $(1, 2, \ldots, n)$. Consider the constraints facing the consumer and the government:

- *The consumer.* The only income-yielding resource is one unit of commodity 0. The consumer's budget constraint is

$$\sum_{i=1}^{n} p_i x_i \leq y \tag{13.51}$$

  where p_i is the price of commodity i. The consumer actually chooses quantities of all $n+1$ goods including x_0 (leisure) so that income in (13.51) is given by

$$y := p_0 [1 - x_0] + \bar{y} \tag{13.52}$$

  where $\bar{y}$ is the consumer's lump-sum income, if any.[35]

- *The government.* Details about the consumer's income are assumed to be unknown to the government, but some transactions carried out by the consumer are observable and taxable. Goods $1, \ldots, n$ are taxable. So consumer prices are given by

$$p_i = \tilde{p}_i + t_i, \tag{13.53}$$

  where $\tilde{p}_i$ is the producer price of commodity i (assumed to be fixed) and t_i is the specific tax imposed on commodity i. Good 0 is assumed to be non-taxable.[36] If a given

? Mini Problems

34 Suppose that the price distortion is caused by an *ad valorem* tax t on good 1, and that $\Delta p_i \approx 0$ for $i = 2, 3, \ldots, n$. Identify the tax revenue received by the government, and the total burden imposed on the consumer.

35 How, if at all, would the problem change if $\bar{y} = 0$?

36 Why is it essential that one assume good zero to be untaxable?

revenue K is to be raised in taxation, then the government's budget constraint is:

$$\sum_{j=1}^{n} t_j x_j \geq K. \tag{13.54}$$

Let the consumer's preferences be represented by the indirect utility function $V(\cdot)$ which is assumed to be common knowledge. Since there is assumed to be a single representative consumer social welfare is represented by the consumer's utility. The government's second-best problem is therefore to choose $(t_1, t_2, \ldots, t_n)$ so as to maximise $V(\mathbf{p}, \bar{y})$ where $\mathbf{p} := (p_0, p_1, p_2, \ldots, p_n)$, subject to (13.54). This is equivalent to solving

$$\max_{\{t_1, t_2, \ldots, t_n, \lambda\}} V(\mathbf{p}, \bar{y}) + \lambda \left[\sum_{j=1}^{n} t_j x_j - K \right] \tag{13.55}$$

where p_j is given by (13.53). The first-order conditions for the problem are:

$$V_i(\mathbf{p}, \bar{y}) + \lambda x_i + \lambda \sum_{j=1}^{n} t_j \frac{\partial x_j}{\partial p_i} = 0, \; i = 1, 2, \ldots, n \tag{13.56}$$

and the 'equality' part of (13.54). This yields[37]

$$\sum_{j=1}^{n} t_j \frac{\partial x_j}{\partial p_i} = -\left[\frac{\lambda - \mu}{\lambda} \right] x_i \tag{13.57}$$

where μ is the consumer's marginal utility of income. From the Slutsky equation (4.21) we know that

$$\frac{\partial x_j}{\partial p_i} = H_i^j(\mathbf{p}, \upsilon) - x_i \frac{\partial x_j}{\partial \bar{y}} \tag{13.58}$$

where υ is utility, $H^j(\cdot)$ is the individual's compensated demand function for good j—see equation (4.10) on page 82—and H_i^j is its derivative respect to p_i, the consumer's substitution effect. Substituting (13.58) into (13.57) and rearranging we obtain[38]

$$\frac{\sum_{j=1}^{n} t_j H_j^i}{x_i} = -\kappa \tag{13.59}$$

where

$$\kappa := \left[\frac{\lambda - \mu}{\lambda} \right] - \sum_{j=1}^{n} t_j \frac{\partial x_j}{\partial \bar{y}}. \tag{13.60}$$

Note that κ is a constant independent of the particular commodity i under consideration.

The rule (13.59) says that at the optimum tax policy should bring about the same proportional reduction in *compensated demand* for each commodity i. So how should second-best taxes be structured? The answer depends on which commodities are inelastic in demand. But it is important to remember that this rule has been derived solely on the

? Mini Problems

37 Explain why. [Hint: use Roy's identity.]

38 Show this. [Hint: Use the symmetry of substitution effects.]

basis of efficiency within the second-best context: in practice this can lead to relatively high tax rates on goods that are likely to form a large part of the expenditure of poorer people—see Example 13.5.

Example 13.5

Atkinson and Stiglitz (1972) computed optimal taxes by broad commodity groups assuming that consumer preferences were appropriately represented by the Linear Expenditure System (the specification of this demand system is set out in Exercise 4.6 on page 96).Obviously the size of these estimates depends on the nature of the government budget constraint. They capture this using λ and μ, the Lagrange multipliers in the government's and the individual's optimisation problems respectively (see equations 13.55 and 13.57 above). The larger is the ratio $\frac{\lambda}{\mu}$, the greater is the marginal cost of the government's budget constraint: i.e. larger values correspond to higher values of the exogenous revenue requirement K. Atkinson and Stiglitz's estimates are summarised in Table 13.1 for three different values of the ratios of the ratio $\frac{\lambda}{\mu}$. Note that, in every case, food (in the first two rows) is taxed much higher than durable goods, reflecting the compensated-demand elasticities of the different types of commodities.

	$\frac{\lambda}{\mu} = 1.025$	$\frac{\lambda}{\mu} = 1.05$	$\frac{\lambda}{\mu} = 1.075$
Meat, fish, dairy products and fats	11.1	27.8	63.2
Fruits and vegetables	8.2	18.6	33.4
Drink and Tobacco	10.1	24.1	48.5
Household running expenses	5.3	11.4	18.2
Durable goods	5.6	11.8	19.0
Other goods and services	6.2	13.4	22.0

Table 13.1 Optimal commodity tax rates

13.8 Conclusion: economic prescriptions

How should the economy be organised? It is natural to look to microeconomic principles for guidance and the various welfare approaches that we have used here and in Chapter 9 give us the necessary analytical tools.

General principles

Simple, general criteria can sometimes provide useful prescriptions. For example we can get a lot of mileage out of the concept of efficiency. The naive 'MRS and MRT' rules can be extended—with some modifications—to difficult cases such as externalities, public goods, or decreasing-cost industries. However, the characterisation problem that we have considered here really just opens the door on to a much more interesting and intractable economic problem—that of implementing efficient allocations in the presence of these types of economic phenomena.

Welfare analysis

The full welfare approach is obviously more ambitious. Clearly the discussion of the specification of a social-welfare function and the nature of a welfare optimum has been on an extremely limited basis. For example, in discussing the optimal distribution of income we have, for the sake of interpretable results, swept aside difficulties that would be essential to practical policy making. Most notably we assumed that we were in a pure private goods economy and that social welfare was individualistic. Each of these assumptions can be relaxed, at a cost.

Dropping individualism may seem anathema, although it is something that policy makers do all the time in practice. But the implication for economic analysis of such a pragmatic approach is not entirely obvious.

It may be more rewarding to address the problem of extending the analysis beyond a pure private-good economy. Obviously the problems of inefficiency arising from the presence of production or consumption externalities will mean that the National Income theorem (Theorem 9.12) is no longer applicable: prices will have to be 'corrected' if a social optimum is to be attained. The marginal benefit to *each household* of any change in the level of public-good supply needs to be taken into account in determining the optimum: even if people are similar in tastes, differences in income between persons and the possible lack of a satisfactory preference revelation mechanism will make this information difficult to obtain.

A final word

This chapter has provided a small snapshot of the prescriptive role of economics. The techniques that we have examined address some of the really big issues in the organisation of the economy—which things can be safely left to individual decision making, which can be achieved by individual decision making with some guidance or adjustment, which need to be cared for by the government or some other representation of the collective will. They enable us to understand what is involved in implementing social objectives: turning 'what should be done' into 'how it can be done'. But this is far from easy. All the more reason then for making good use of microeconomic principles and analysis.

Reading notes

The standard reference on market 'failure' is Bator (1958). Hotelling (1938) provides an early treatment of the non-convexity ('increasing returns') issue. On the analysis of regulation of firms see Baron and Myerson (1982), Demsetz (1968), and Laffont and Tirole (1993).

The classic treatment of the market approach to externalities is in Meade (1952) and Buchanan and Stubblebine (1962). The corrective taxes discussed in the context of externalities are commonly known as Pigovian taxes after the contribution by Pigou (1926). The seminal paper on the internalisation of externalities is Coase (1960) and the issue of information in connection with this approach is discussed in Farrell (1987). Starrett (1972) showed the problem of the fundamental non-convexity that can arise when pollution rights are traded.

The economics of club goods owes much to Buchanan (1965); for further analysis see Cornes and Sandler (1996).

A nice introduction to the Prisoner's Dilemma interpretation of public goods problems and related issues is given in Daniel et al. (2005)

The classic reference on the pseudo-tax pricing of public goods is Lindahl (1919). On the shortcomings of the private provision of public goods see Andreoni (1988) and Bergstrom et al. (1986). For approaches that relax the dominant-strategy requirement for the implementation of public goods see Groves and Ledyard (1977) (Nash equilibria) and d'Aspremont and Gérard-Varet (1979) (a Bayesian approach). The provision-point mechanism and money-back guarantees are dealt with in Bagnoli and Lipman (1989) and Palfrey and Rosenthal (1984). The use of the lottery as a public-goods allocation mechanism is considered by Morgan (2000).

On the commodity-tax problem the classic reference is Ramsey (1927); for the same principles applied to the regulation of a monopoly see Boiteux (1956).

Exercises

13.1 A *local public good* is one that is specific to a particular municipality: within the municipality good 1 is provided as a public good, but the consumer has to be resident there to benefit from good 1. Residence in a municipality also determines liability to provide for the public good. Residents can choose which municipality to live in (Tiebout 1956). Suppose that exactly one unit of private good 2 is required to produce one unit of the local public good 1 and that, in a given municipality of N people, total output is determined by a production function

$$q = \phi(N)$$

where ϕ is a strictly concave function. Each individual in a municipality gets utility $U(x_1, x_2)$ where x_1 is the amount of the local public good, x_2 is the individual's consumption of the private good, and U is a utility function with the usual properties.

1. What are the transformation curve and the production-possibility set for a single municipality of size N?
2. If the residents of the municipality could choose both the proportion of total output devoted to the local public good and the size of the municipality, explain how these would be determined. Show that if individuals are paid their marginal product then the amount required to finance the public good is exactly the difference between the wage bill and the total output.

3. If the size of a municipality N can take any value between 1 and $\overline{N}$ inclusive, where $\overline{N}$ is the total population in the economy, use your answer to part 1 to explain what the production possibility set is when N is allowed to vary. Hence show that the optimal size of municipality could be multivalued.
4. Assuming that there is an interior solution to the optimal value of N sketch the relationship between utility and size of municipality.
5. In an economy there are two municipalities with identical production conditions. Individuals can migrate costlessly from one community to another if they would achieve higher utility by doing so. Using the diagram from part 4 show that this migration mechanism may lead to multiple equilibria, some of which will be unstable.
6. Show that the stable equilibria in part 5 may be inefficient.

13.2 (A continuation of Exercise 4.13 on page 98) There is a single firm producing good 1 with costs as described in Exercise 4.13; all consumers are identical with preferences given as in Exercise 4.12. The government allows the firm to charge what price it likes but offers to pay the firm a subsidy equal to the consumer's surplus generated by the price that it charges.

1. Is the regulation mechanism efficient?
2. Does the government as regulator need to know (a) the cost function, (b) the utility function?
3. Show that this mechanism allows the firm to exploit consumers completely (Loeb and Magat 1979).

13.3 The government of the tiny island of Mugg is considering whether it would be a good idea to install piped gas. Once the gas-distribution system is installed each unit of gas (commodity 1) costs a fixed amount m of other goods (commodity 2); there is additionally a fixed cost F incurred in setting up a distribution system on the island. Before the system is installed Mugg enjoys a total amount R_2 of commodity 2. The residents of Mugg are assumed to be identical in every respect and their tastes are represented by the utility function

$$a\left[1 - e^{-x_1}\right] + x_2$$

where (x_1, x_2) represent the quantities consumed of the two goods and a is a non-negative parameter.

1. What is the maximum number of units of gas that could be afforded on Mugg?
2. Draw the production-possibility set; draw the indifference curves in two cases: where a is large and where a is small.
3. Use the diagram to show that whether it is a Pareto improvement to install the gas system depends on the value of a.
4. If the installation of gas on Mugg is Pareto improving, describe the Pareto-efficient allocation of goods and suggest a scheme by which the publicly owned corporation MuggGas could implement this allocation if it knows the willingness to pay of the residents.

13.4 Take the model of the Island of Mugg (Exercise 13.3) again. Suppose that the government of Mugg has a horror of public enterprise and decides to delegate the decision on installation and supply by selling off MuggGas.

1. Will this generate an improvement on the no-gas situation?
2. Will it generate an efficient allocation?
3. How would your answers be affected if MuggGas were split into a number of private companies, or if consumers were allowed to resell gas to each other?

13.5 In an economy there are two firms each producing a single output from a single non-produced resource according to

$$q_1 = \sqrt{z}$$

$$q_2 = \max\left(\sqrt{R - z} - aq_1, 0\right)$$

where q_i is the amount produced of good i, z is the amount of the resource used in the production of good 1, R is the total stock of the resource, and a is a parameter.

1. What phenomenon does this model represent?
2. Draw the production-possibility set.
3. Assuming that all consumers are identical, sketch a set of indifference curves for which (a) an efficient allocation may be supported by a pseudo market in externalities; (b) a pseudo market is not possible.
4. What role does the parameter a play in the answer to the previous parts?

13.6 In a large economy all agents have a utility function of the form

$$\psi(x_1) + x_2^h$$

where x_1 is the amount provided of a public good and x_2^h is agent h's consumption of a private good. All agents are endowed with the same amount of private good $R_2^h = 1$. Each individual can choose whether to contribute to the public good:

$$z_2^h = \begin{cases} 1 & \text{'contribute'} \\ 0 & \text{'not contribute'} \end{cases}$$

The unit contribution costs an amount c^h to agent h; the individual costs are unobservable but the distribution function $F(\cdot)$ of costs is known. The production of the public good is given by

$$x_1 = \phi(a)$$

where a is the proportion of contributing individuals.

1. Show that an efficient outcome implies that there is cost level c^0 such that

$$z_2^h = \begin{cases} 1 & c^h \le c^0 \\ 0 & c^h > c^0 \end{cases}$$

2. The government introduces a tax-subsidy scheme based on individual actions as follows. Each contributor receives a subsidy s and each non-contributor has to pay t. Given c^0 and the distribution of costs F what is the condition for a balanced budget if agents behave as in part 1?

3. Under the conditions of part 2 what is the utility of someone with $c^h < c^0$? Of someone with $c^h > c^0$?
4. By requiring that someone with $c^h = c^0$ be indifferent between contributing and non-contributing show that this tax-subsidy scheme induces an efficient equilibrium.
5. How much of the public good is provided and what is the tax rate and subsidy rate (Gradstein 1998)?

13.7 An economy consists of individuals whose income is only from labour: each person is endowed with a specific level of ability which is reflected in his or her market wage w, and chooses ℓ, the amount of time he or she works $0 \leq \ell \leq 1$. The minimum value of w in the population is w_0, and the mean value is γw_0, where $\gamma > 1$. The government imposes a tax-transfer scheme such that a person with pretax cash income y has after-tax cash income of $x = [1 - t][y - y_0] + y_0$.

1. Interpret the parameters t and y_0.
2. Assume that every individual's preferences can be represented by the utility function in Exercise 5.7. What is optimal labour supply as a function of w, t, and y_0?
3. If the government wants to ensure that everyone works what constraint will this impose on the values of t and y_0? Assuming that everyone does work, and that the tax raised is used solely for the purposes of redistribution, show that this implies that t and y_0 must satisfy the constraint:

$$y_0 = a\gamma w_0 \frac{1-t}{1-at}$$

4. If the government seeks to maximise the after-tax cash income of the poorest person (the welfare function with $\varepsilon = \infty$ in Exercise 9.5) subject to the above constraints show that the optimal tax rate is

$$t^* = \frac{1}{a}\left[1 - \sqrt{\frac{\gamma - a\gamma}{\gamma - 1}}\right]$$

Interpret this result (Broome 1975).

REFERENCES

Akerlof, G. A. (1970). The market for "lemons", quality uncertainty and the market mechanism. *Quarterly Journal of Economics 84*, 488–500.

Allais, M. (1953). Le comportement de l'homme rationnel devant le risque: Critique des postulats et axiomes de l'école américaine. *Econometrica 21*, 503–46.

Allen, R. G. D. (1936). Professor Slutsky's theory of consumer choice. *Review of Economic Studies 3*, 120–9.

Amiel, Y., J. Creedy, and S. Hurn (1999). Attitudes towards inequality. *Scandinavian Journal of Economics 101*, 83–96.

Andreoni, J. (1988). Privately provided public goods: the limits to altruism. *Journal of Public Economics 35*, 57–73.

Arrow, K. J. (1951). *Social Choice and Individual Values*. New York: John Wiley.

——(1970). *Essays in the Theory of Risk-Bearing*. Amsterdam: North-Holland.

——(1986). The economics of agency. In J. Pratt and R. Zeckhauser (eds.), *Principals and Agents: Structure of Business*. Boston: Harvard Business School Press.

——and G. Debreu (1954). Existence of equilibrium in a competitive economy. *Econometrica 22*, 265–90.

——and F. H. Hahn (1971). *General Competitive Analysis*. Edinburgh: Oliver and Boyd.

Atkinson, A. B. (1970). On the measurement of inequality. *Journal of Economic Theory 2*, 244–63.

——(1998). *Poverty in Europe*. Yrjö Jahnsson Lectures. Oxford: Blackwell Publishers.

——and J. E. Stiglitz (1972). The structure of indirect taxation and economic efficiency. *Journal of Public Economics 1*, 97–119.

Attanasio, O., and G. Weber (1993). Consumption growth, the interest rate and aggregation. *Review of Economic Studies 60*, 631–49.

Bagnoli, M., and B. Lipman (1989). Provision of public goods: fully implementing the core through private contributions. *Review of Economic Studies 56*, 583–602.

Bailey, S., and S. Connolly (1997). The national lottery: a preliminary assessment of net additionality. *Scottish Journal of Political Economy 44*, 100–12.

Bandera, V. N. (1970). Market orientation of state enterprises during NEP. *Soviet Studies 22*, 110–21.

Baron, D., and R. B. Myerson (1982). Regulating a monopoly with unknown costs. *Econometrica 50*, 911–30.

Barsky, R. B., F. T. Juster, M. S. Kimball, and M. D. Shapiro (1997). Preference parameters and behavioral heterogeneity: An experimental approach in the health and retirement survey. *Quarterly Journal of Economics 112*, 537–79.

Bator, F. M. (1958). The anatomy of market failure. *Quarterly Journal of Economics 72*, 351–78.

Bazerman, M. H., and W. F. Samuelson (1983). I won the auction but I don't want the prize. *Journal of Conflict Resolution 27*, 618–34.

Becker, G. S. (1965). The economics of the allocation of time. *Economic Journal 75*, 493–517.

Beesley, M. E., and C. D. Foster (1965). The Victoria line: social benefits and finances. *Journal of the Royal Statistical Society, Series A 128*, 67–88.

Bell, D. E. (1982). Regret in decision-making under uncertainty. *Operations Research 30*, 961–81.

——(1988). Disappointment in decision-making under uncertainty. In D. E. Bell, H. Raiffa, and A. Tversky (eds.),

Decision Making: Descriptive, Normative and Prescriptive Interactions. Cambridge: Cambridge University Press.

Benoit, J.-P. (2000). The Gibbard–Satterthwaite theorem: a simple proof. *Economics Letters 69*, 319–22.

Bergstrom, T., L. Blume, and H. Varian (1986). On the private provision of public goods. *Journal of Public Economics 29*, 25–49.

Bernouilli, D. (1954). Exposition of a new theory on the measurement of risk (1738, translated Louise Sommer). *Econometrica 22*, 23–36.

Bertrand, J. (1883). Théorie mathématique de la richesse sociale. *Journal des savants*, 499–508.

Binmore, K., and P. Klemperer (2002). The biggest auction ever: the sale of the British 3G telecom licences. *Economic Journal 112*, C74–C96.

Black, D. (1948). On the rationale of group decision making. *Journal of Political Economy 56*, 23–4.

____(1958). *The Theory of Committees and Elections*. Cambridge: Cambridge University Press.

Blundell, R., and I. Walker (1982). Modelling the joint distribution of household labour supplies and commodity demands. *Economic Journal 92*, 351–64.

Boadway, R. W., and N. Bruce (1984). *Welfare Economics*. Oxford: Basil Blackwell.

Boiteux, M. (1956). Sur la gestion des monopoles publics astreints à l'équilibre budgétaire. *Econometrica 24*, 22–40.

Bolton, P., and M. Dewatripont (2005). *Contract Theory*. Cambridge, Mass.: MIT Press.

Bopp, A. (1983). The demand for kerosene: a modern Giffen good. *Applied Economics 15*, 459–67.

Border, K. (1985). *Fixed Point Theorems with Applications to Economics and Game Theory*. Cambridge: Cambridge University Press.

Bowen, H. (1945). The interpretation of voting in the allocation of economic resources. *Quarterly Journal of Economics 58*, 27–48.

Bresnahan, T. J. (1987). Competition and collusion in the American automobile industry: the 1955 price war. *Journal of Industrial Economics 35*, 457–82.

Broome, J. (1975). An important theorem on income tax. *Review of Economic Studies 42*, 649–52.

Browne, M. J. (1992). Evidence of adverse selection in the individual health insurance market. *Journal of Risk and Insurance 59*, 13–33.

Buchanan, J. M. (1965). An economic theory of clubs. *Economica 32*, 1–14.

____and C. Stubblebine (1962). Externality. *Economica 29*, 371–84.

Central Statistical Office (1991). *Retail Prices 1914-1990*. London: HMSO.

Chamberlin, E. H. (1933). *The Theory of Monopolistic Competition*. Cambridge, Mass.: Harvard University Press.

Chiang, A. C. (1984). *Fundamental Methods of Mathematical Economics* (3rd edn.). New York: McGraw-Hill.

Chiappori, P.-A., and B. Salanié (2003). Testing contract theory: A survey of some recent work. In M. Dewatripoint, L. P. Hansen, and S. Turnovsky (eds.), *Advances in Economics and Econometrics: Theory and Applications*. Cambridge: Cambridge University Press.

Cho, I.-K., and D. M. Kreps (1987). Signaling games and stable equilibrium. *Quarterly Journal of Economics 102*, 179–221.

Clarke, E. H. (1971). Multi-part pricing of public goods. *Public Choice 11*, 17–33.

Coase, R. H. (1960). The problem of social cost. *Journal of Law and Economics 2*, 1–44.

Cook, P. (1972). A one-line proof of the Slutsky equation. *American Economic Review 62*, 139.

Cornes, R., and T. Sandler (1996). *The Theory of Externalities, Public Goods and Club Goods* (second edn.). Cambridge: Cambridge University Press.

Cournot, A. (1838). *Recherches sur les principes mathémathiques de la théorie des richesses*. Paris: M. Rivière et Cie.

Crawford, V. P. (2002). Introduction to experimental game theory. *Journal of Economic Theory 104*, 1–15.

—— and J. Sobel (1982). Strategic information transmission. *Econometrica 50*, 1431–51.

Cutler, D. M., and S. J. Reber (1998). Paying for health insurance: the trade-off between competition and adverse selection. *Quarterly Journal of Economics 113*, 433–66.

Daniel, G., M. Arce, and T. Sandler (2005). The dilemma of the prisoner's dilemmas. *Kyklos 58*, 3–24.

Dasgupta, P., P. J. Hammond, and E. Maskin (1979). The implementation of social choice rules: some general results on incentive compatibility. *Review of Economic Studies 46*, 185–216.

d'Aspremont, C., and L.-A. Gérard-Varet (1979). Incentives and incomplete information. *Journal of Public Economics 11*, 25–45.

Deaton, A. S., and J. Muellbauer (1980). *Economics and Consumer Behavior*. Cambridge: Cambridge University Press.

Debreu, G. (1954). Representation of a preference ordering by a numerical function. In R. Thrall, C. Coombs, and R. Davis (eds.), *Decision Processes*. New York: John Wiley.

—— (1960). Topological methods in cardinal utility theory. In K. Arrow, S. Karlin, and P. Suppes (eds.), *Mathematical Methods in the Social Sciences*. Stanford, Calif.: Stanford University Press.

—— and H. Scarf (1963). A limit theorem on the core of an economy. *International Economic Review 4*, 235–46.

de la Fuente, A. (1999). *Mathematical Models and Methods for Economists*. Cambridge: Cambridge University Press.

Demsetz, H. (1968). Why regulate utilities? *Journal of Law and Economics 9*, 55–65.

Dixit, A. K. (1980). The role of investment in entry-deterrence. *Economic Journal 90*, 95–106.

—— (1990). *Optimization in Economic Theory* (2nd edn.). Oxford: Oxford University Press.

—— and S. Skeath (2004). *Games of Strategy* (2nd edn.). New York: Norton.

—— and J. E. Stiglitz (1977). Monopolistic competition and optimum product diversity. *American Economic Review 67*, 297–308.

Dupuit, J. (1844). De la mesure de l'utilité des travaux publics. *Annales des ponts et chaussées*. Paris: Éditions Scientifiques et Médicales Elsevier.

Dwyer, G. P., and C. M. Lindsey (1984). Robert Giffen and the Irish potato. *American Economic Review 74*, 188–92.

Eads, G., M. Nerlove, and W. Raduchel (1969). A long-run cost function for the local service airline industry. *Review of Economic and Statistics 51*, 258–70.

Edgeworth, F. Y. (1881). *Mathematical Psychics: An Essay on the Application of Mathematics to the Moral Sciences*. London: Kegan Paul.

Ellsberg, D. (1961). Risk, ambiguity,and the Savage axioms. *Quarterly Journal of Economics 75*, 643–69.

Farrell, J. (1987). Information and the Coase theorem. *Journal of Economic Perspectives 1*, 113–29.

—— and M. Rabin (1996). Cheap talk. *Journal of Economic Perspectives 10*, 103–18.

Farrell, M. J. (1959). The convexity assumption in the theory of competitive markets. *Journal of Political Economy 67*, 377–91.

Fishburn, P. C. (1970). *Utility Theory for Decision Making*. New York: John Wiley.

Fisher, F. M., and J. Monz (1992). *Aggregate Production Functions and Related Topics*. Cambridge, Mass.: MIT Press.

Fixler, D. (1993). The Consumer Price Index: underlying concepts and caveats. *Monthly Labor Review 116*(12/Dec.), 3–10.

Friedman, J. (1971). A non-cooperative equilibrium for supergames. *Review of Economic Studies 38*, 1–12.

Friedman, M., and L. J. Savage (1948). The utility analysis of choices involving risk. *Journal of Political Economy 56*, 1–23.

Fudenberg, D. and E. Maskin (1979). The folk theorem in repeated games with discounting or with incomplete information. *Econometrica 54*, 533–56.

—— and J. Tirole (1991). *Game Theory*. Cambridge, Mass.: MIT Press.

Fuss, M., and D. McFadden (1980). *Production Economics: A Dual Approach to Theory and Applications*. Amsterdam: North-Holland.

Gardner, R. (2003). *Games for Business and Economics* (2nd edn.). New York: John Wiley.

Garner, T. I., D. S. Johnson, and M. F. Kokoski (1996). An experimental Consumer Price Index for the poor. *Monthly Labor Review 119*(9/Sept.), 32–42.

Gerstner, E., and J. D. Hess (1987). Why do hot dogs come in packs of 10 and buns in 8s or 12s? A demand-side investigation. *Journal of Business 60*, 491–517.

Gibbard, A. (1973). Manipulation of voting schemes: a general result. *Econometrica 41*, 587–601.

Gibbons, R. (1992). *A Primer in Game Theory*. Hemel Hempstead: Harvester-Wheatsheaf.

Gorman, W. M. (1980). A possible procedure for analysing quality differentials in the egg market. *Review of Economic Studies 47*, 843–56.

Gradstein, M. (1998). Provision of public goods in a large economy. *Economics Letters 61*(2), 229–34.

Green, J., and W. P. Heller (1981). Mathematical analysis and convexity with applications to economics. In K. J. Arrow and M. D. Intiligator (eds.), *Handbook of Mathematical Economics*, vol. i, ch. 1. Amsterdam: North-Holland Elsevier.

—— and J.-J. Laffont (1997). *Incentives in Public Decision-Making*. Amsterdam: North-Holland.

Griffin, J. M., and W. Xiong (1997). The incentive to cheat: an empirical analysis of OPEC. *Journal of Law and Economics 40*, 289–316.

Grossman, S. J. and O. D. Hart (1983). An analysis of the principal-agent problem. *Econometrica 51*(1), 7–46.

Groves, T. (1977). Incentives in teams. *Econometrica 41*, 617–31.

—— and J. Ledyard (1977). Optimal allocation of public goods: a solution to the free rider problem. *Econometrica 45*, 783–809.

—— and M. Loeb (1975). Incentives and public inputs. *Journal of Public Economics 4*, 311–26.

Hahn, F. H. (1982). Stability. In K. J. Arrow and M. D. Intriligator (eds.), *Handbook of Mathematical Economics*, vol. ii, ch. 16. Amsterdam: North Holland.

Harberger, A. C. (1971). Three basic postulates for applied welfare economics. *Journal of Economic Literature 9*, 785–97.

Harris, M., and M. Townsend, R. (1981). An alternative approach to aggregate surplus analysis. *Econometrica 49*, 33–64.

Harsanyi, J. C. (1955). Cardinal welfare, individualistic ethics and interpersonal comparisons of utility. *Journal of Political Economy 63*, 309–21.

—— (1967). Games with incomplete information played by 'Bayesian' players. *Management Science 14*, 159–82, 320–34, 486–502.

—— (1973). Games with randomly disturbed payoffs: a new rationale for mixed-strategy equilibrium points. *International Journal of Game Theory 2*, 1–23.

Haubrich, J. (1994). Risk aversion, performance pay, and the principal-agent model. *Journal of Political Economy 102*, 258–76.

Hayashi, F. (2000). *Econometrics*. Princeton: Princeton University Press.

Hicks, J. R. (1946). *Value and Capital* (2nd edn.). Oxford: Oxford University Press.

——(1956). *A Revision of Demand Theory*. Oxford: Oxford University Press.

Hoffman-Jørgensen, J. (1994). *Probability with a View toward Statistics*, volume i. London: Chapman and Hall.

Holmström, B. (1979). Moral hazard and observability. *Bell Journal of Economics 10*, 74–91.

——and P. Milgrom (1987). Aggregation and linearity in the provision of intertemporal incentives. *Econometrica 55*, 303–28.

Hotelling, H. (1932). Edgeworth's taxation paradox and the nature of demand supply functions. *Journal of Political Economy 40*, 577–616.

——(1938). The general welfare in relation to problems of taxation and utility rates. *Econometrica 6*, 242–69.

Houthakker, H. S. (1950). Revealed preference and the utility function. *Economica 17*, 159–74.

Huber, J. R. (1971). Effect on Japan's entry into world commerce after 1858. *Journal of Political Economy 79*, 614–28.

Hurwicz, L. (1972). On informationally decentralized systems. In R. Radner and C. McGuire (eds.), *Decision and Organization*, pp. 297–336. Amsterdam: North Holland.

——(1986). On informational decentralization and efficiency in resource allocation mechanisms. In S. Reiter (ed.), *Studies in Mathematical Economics*. Mathematics Association of America.

Intriligator, M. D. (1971). *Mathematical Optimization and Economic Theory*. Englewood Cliffs, NJ: Prentice Hall.

Jewitt, I. (1988). Justifying the first-order approach to principal-agent problems. *Econometrica 56*(5), 1177–90.

Kaldor, N. (1939). Welfare propositions of economics and intertemporal comparisons of utility. *Economic Journal 49*, 549–51.

Keenan, D. C., and A. Snow (1999). A complete characterization of potential compensation tests in terms of Hicksian welfare measures. *Canadian Journal of Economics 32*, 215–33.

Kleiber, C., and S. Kotz (2003). *Statistical Size Distributions in Economics and Actuarial Sciences*. Hoboken, NJ: John Wiley.

Klemperer, P. (1998). Auctions with almost common values: the 'wallet game' and its applications. *European Economic Review 42*, 757–69.

——(1999). Auction theory: a guide to the literature. *Journal of Economic Surveys 13*, 227–86.

——(2002). What really matters in auction design. *Journal of Economic Perspectives 16*(1), 169–89.

——(2004). *Auctions: Theory and Practice*. Princeton: Princeton University Press.

Koopmans, T. C. (1957). *Three Essays on the State of Economic Science*. New York: McGraw-Hill.

Kreps, D. M. (1990). *Game Theory and Economic Modelling*. Oxford: Clarendon Press.

——and J. Sheinkman (1983). Quantity precommitment and Bertrand competition yield Cournot outcomes. *Bell Journal of Economics 14*, 326–37.

Laffont, J. J., and D. Martimort (2002). *The Theory of Incentives: The Principal Agent Model*. Princeton: Princeton University Press.

——and J. Tirole (1993). *A Theory of Incentives in Procurement and Regulation*. Cambridge: Cambridge University Press.

Lancaster, K. (1966). A new approach to consumer theory. *Journal of Political Economy 74*, 132–7.

Lenin, V. I. (1965 [1921]). *The Tax in Kind: The Significance of the New Policy and its Conditions*, vol. xxxii. Moscow: Progress Publishers.

Leontief, W. W. (1947a). Introduction to a theory of the internal structure of functional relationsips. *Econometrica 15*, 361–73.

____(1947b). A note on the interrelations of subsets of independent variables of a continuous function with continuous first derivatives. *Bulletin of the American Mathematical Society 53*, 343–50.

Lichtenstein, S., and P. Slovic (1983). Reversal of preference between bids and choices in gambling decisions. *Journal of Experimental Psychology 89*, 46–55.

Lindahl, E. (1919). Positive Lösung, die Gerechtigkeit der Besteuerung, reprinted as "Just taxation - a positive solution". In R. A. Musgrave and A. T. Peacock (eds.), *Classics in the Theory of Public Finance*. London: Macmillan.

Loeb, M., and W. A. Magat (1979). A decentralized model for utility regulation. *Journal of Law and Economics 22*, 399–404.

Loomes, G., and R. Sugden (1982). Testing different stochastic specifications of risky choice. *Economic Journal 92*, 805–24.

________(1983). A rationale for preference reversal. *American Economic Review 73*, 428–32.

McDonough, T., and J. Eisenhauer (1995). Sir Robert Giffen and the great potato famine: a discussion of the role of a legend in neoclassical economics. *Journal of Economic Issues 29*, 747–59.

Machina, M. J. (1982). Expected utility analysis without the independence axiom. *Econometrica 50*, 277–323.

____(1987). Choice under uncertainty: problems solved and unsolved. *Journal of Economic Perspectives 1*, 121–54.

____(1989). Dynamic consistency and non-expected utility models of choice under uncertainty. *Journal of Economic Literature 27*, 1622–68.

Macho-Stadler, I., and D. Pérez-Castrillo (1997). *An Introduction to the Economics of Information: Incentives and Contracts*. Oxford: Oxford University Press.

Maeda, A. (2003). The emergence of market power in emission rights markets: The role of the initial permit distribution. *Journal of Regulatory Economics 24*, 293–314.

Mailath, G. J. (1998). Do people play Nash equilibrium? Lessons from evolutionary game theory. *Journal of Economic Literature 36*, 1347–74.

Marschak, J. (1950). Rational behavior, uncertain prospects and measurable utility. *Econometrica 18*, 111–41.

Marshall, A. (1890). *Principles of Economics* (8th (1920) edn.). London: Macmillan and Co., Ltd.

Maskin, E. (1999). Nash equilibrium and welfare optimality. *Review of Economic Studies 66*, 23–38.

Meade, J. E. (1952). External economies and diseconomies in a competitive situation. *Economic Journal 62*, 54–67.

Menezes, C., C. Geiss, and J. Tressler (1980). Increasing downside risk. *American Economic Review 70*, 921–31.

Mirrlees, J. A. (1971). An exploration in the theory of the optimal income tax. *Review of Economic Studies 38*, 135–208.

____(1999). The theory of moral hazard and unobservable behaviour: Part I. *Review of Economic Studies 66*, 3–21.

Morgan, J. (2000). Public goods and lotteries. *Review of Economic Studies 67*, 761–84.

____and M. Sefton (2000). Funding public goods with lotteries: experimental evidence. *Review of Economic Studies 67*, 785–810.

Moulin, H. (2003). *Fair Division and Collective Welfare*. Cambridge, Mass.: MIT Press.

Murphy, K. J. (1985). Corporate performance and managerial remuneration: an empirical analysis. *Journal of Accounting and Economics 7*, 11–42.

Mussa, M., and S. Rosen (1978). Monopoly and product quality. *Journal of Economic Theory 18*, 301–17.

Myerson, R. B. (1979). Incentive compatibility and the bargaining problem. *Econometrica 47*, 61–73.

——(1999). Nash equilibrium and the history of economic theory. *Journal of Economic Literature* 37, 1067–82.

Nash, J. F. (1951). Non-cooperative games. *Annals of Mathematics* 54, 286–95.

Nerlove, M. (1963). Returns to scale in the electricity supply. In *Measurement in Economics: Studies in Mathematical Economics and Econometrics in Memory of Yehuda Grunfeld*. Stanford, Calif.: Stanford University Press.

O'Donoghue, J., and C. Wilkie (1998). Harmonised indices of consumer prices. *Economic Trends* (532/Feb.), 34–43.

Oi, W. (1971). A Disneyland dilemma: two-part tariffs for a Mickey-Mouse monopoly. *Quarterly Journal of Economics* 85, 77–96.

Okun, A. M. (1975). *Equality and Efficiency: The Big Trade-off*. Washington: Brookings Institution.

Osborne, M. J. (2004). *An Introduction to Game Theory*. Oxford: Oxford University Press.

Ostaszewski, A. (1993). *Mathematics in Economics: Models and Methods*. Oxford: Blackwell.

Palfrey, T. R., and H. Rosenthal (1984). Participation and the provision of discrete public goods: a strategic analyis. *Journal of Public Economics* 24, 171–93.

Pigou, A. C. (1926). *A Study of Public Finance*. London: Macmillan.

——(1952). *The Economics of Welfare* (4th edn.). London: Macmillan.

Pollack, R. A. (1989). *The Theory of the Cost-of-Living Index*. New York: Oxford University Press.

Pratt, J. W. (1964). Risk-aversion in the small and in the large. *Econometrica* 32, 122–36.

Rabellotti, R., and H. Schmitz (1999). The internal heterogeneity of industrial districts in Italy, Brazil and Mexico. *Regional Studies* 33, 97–108.

Radford, R. A. (1945). The economic organisation of a P.O.W. camp. *Economica* 12, 189–201.

Ramsey, F. P. (1927). A contribution to the theory of taxation. *Economic Journal* 37, 47–61.

Rasmusen, E. (2001). *Games and Information: An Introduction to Game Theory* (3rd edn.). Oxford: Blackwell.

Reny, P. J. (2001). Arrow's theorem and the Gibbard–Satterthwaite theorem: a unified approach. *Economics Letters* 70, 99–105.

Repullo, R. (1987). A simple proof of Maskin's theorem on Nash implementation. *Social Choice and Welfare* 4, 39–41.

Ricketts, M. (1986). The geometry of principal and agent: yet another use for the Edgeworth box. *Scottish Journal of Political Economy*, 228–47.

Riley, J. G. (1979). Testing the educational screening hypothesis. *Journal of Political Economy* 87, S227–S252.

——(2001). Silver signals: twenty-five years of screening and signaling. *Journal of Economic Literature* 39, 432–78.

Rosen, S. (1999). Potato paradoxes. *Journal of Political Economy* 107, S294–S313.

Ross, S. A. (1973). The economic theory of agency: the principal's problem. *American Economic Review* 63, 193–7.

Rothschild, M., and J. E. Stiglitz (1970). Increasing risk: I. A definition. *Journal of Economic Theory* 2, 225–43.

——(1976). Equilibrium in competitive insurance markets: an essay on the economics of imperfect intonation. *Quarterly Journal of Economics* 90, 629–49.

Roy, R. (1947). La distribution de revenu entre les divers biens. *Econometrica* 15, 205–25.

Rubinstein, A. (1982). Perfect equilibriuim in a bargaining game. *Econometrica* 50, 97–109.

Salanié, B. (1997). *The Economics of Contracts: A Primer*. Cambridge, Mass.: MIT Press.

——(2003). *The Economics of Taxation*. Cambridge, Mass.: MIT Press.

Samuelson, L. (2002). Evolution and game theory. *Journal of Economic Perspectives* 16(2), 47–66.

Samuelson, P. A. (1938). A note on the pure theory of consumer's behaviour. *Economica* 5, 353–4.

____(1948). Consumption theory in terms of revealed preference. *Economica* 15, 243–53.

____(1954). The pure theory of public expenditure. *Review of Economics and Statistics* 36, 387–9.

____(1955). Diagrammatic exposition of a pure theory of public expenditure. *Review of Economics and Statistics* 37, 350–6.

____(1983). *Foundations of Economic Analysis* (enlarged edn.). Cambridge, Mass.: Harvard University Press.

Sandmo, A. (1983). Ex-post welfare economics and the theory of merit goods. *Economica* 50, 19–33.

Satterthwaite, M. A. (1975). Strategy-proofness and Arrow's conditions. *Journal of Economic Theory* 10, 187–217.

Schmalensee, R. (1985). Econometric diagnosis of competitive localisation. *International Journal of Industrial Organisation* 3, 57–70.

Schweizer, U. (1982). A Langrangian approach to the limit theorem on the core of an economy. *Zeitschrift für Nazionalökonomie*, 23–30.

Scitovsky, T. (1941). A note on welfare propositions in economics. *Review of Economic Studies* 9, 89–110.

Selten, R. (1965). Spieltheoretische Behandlung eines Oligopolmodells mit Nachfrageträgheit. *Zeitschrift für die gesamte Staatswissenschaft* 12, 310–24.

____(1975). Reexamination of the perfectness concept for equilibrium points in extensive games. *International Journal of Game Theory* 4, 25–55.

____(1978). The chain-store paradox. *Theory and Decision* 9, 127–59.

Sen, A. K. (1970). *Collective Choice and Social Welfare*. Edinburgh: Oliver and Boyd.

____(1973). Behaviour and the concept of preference. *Economica* 40, 241–7.

____(1983). Poor, relatively speaking. *Oxford Economic Papers* 35, 153–69.

Shephard, R. W. (1953). *Cost and Production Functions*. Princeton: Princeton University Press.

Shy, O. (1995). *Industrial Organisation: Theory and Applications*. Cambridge, Mass.: MIT Press.

Simon, C. P., and L. Blume (1994). *Mathematics for Economists*. New York: Norton.

Slesnick, D. T. (1998). Empirical approaches to the measurement of welfare. *Journal of Economic Literature* 36, 2108–65.

Slutsky, E. (1915). Sulla teoria del bilancio del consumatore. *Giornale degli economisti* 51, 1–26.

Spanos, A. (1999). *Probability Theory and Statistical Inference*. Cambridge: Cambridge University Press.

Spence, A. M. (1973). Job market signalling. *Quarterly Journal of Economics* 87, 366–74.

____(1977). Entry, capacity, investment and oligopolistic pricing. *Bell Journal of Economics* 2, 534–44.

Ståhl, I. (1972). *Bargaining Theory*. Stockholm: EFI: The Economic Research Institute.

Starrett, D. A. (1972). Fundamental nonconvexities in the theory of externalities. *Journal of Economic Theory* 4, 180–99.

Stone, J. R. N. (1954). Linear expenditure systems and demand analysis:. *Economic Journal* 64, 511–27.

Sugden, R. (1986). New developments in the theory of choice under uncertainty. *Bulletin of Economic Research* 38, 1–24.

Sundaram, R. K. (2002). *A First Course in Optimization Theory*. Princeton: Princeton University Press.

Sutton, J. (1986). Non-cooperative bargaining theory: an introduction. *Review of Economic Studies* 53, 709–24.

Suzumura, K. (1983). *Rational Choice, Collective Decisions and Social Welfare.* Cambridge: Cambridge University Press.

Sydsæter, K., and P. J. Hammond (1995). *Mathematics for Economic Analysis* (3rd edn.). Englewood Cliffs, NJ: Prentice-Hall International.

——A. Strøm, and P. Berck (1999). *Economists' Mathematical Manual* (3rd edn.). Berlin: Springer.

Tiebout, C. M. (1956). A pure theory of local expenditures. *Journal of Political Economy 64*, 416–24.

Tirole, J. (1988). *The Theory of Industrial Organization.* Cambridge, Mass.: MIT Press.

Tullock, G. (1967). The welfare economics of tariffs, monopolies and theft. *Western Economic Journal 5*, 224–32.

Varian, H. R. (1974). Equity, envy and efficiency. *Journal of Economic Theory 9*, 63–91.

——(1980). A model of sales. *American Economic Review 70*, 651–6.

Vega-Redondo, F. (2003). *Economics and the Theory of Games.* Cambridge: Cambridge University Press.

Vickrey, W. (1945). Measuring marginal utility by reaction to risk. *Econometrica 13*, 319–33.

——(1960). Utility, strategy and social decision rules. *Quarterly Journal of Economics 74*, 507–35.

——(1961). Counterspeculation auctions and sealed tenders. *Journal of Finance 16*, 8–37.

Vives, X. (1999). *Oligopoly Pricing: Old Ideas and New Tools.* Cambridge, Mass.: MIT Press.

von Neumann, J., and O. Morgenstern (1944). *Theory of Games and Economic Behavior.* Princeton: Princeton University Press.

von Stackelberg, H. (1934). *Marktform und Gleichgewicht.* Vienna: Julius Springer.

Walras, L. (1954). *Elements of Pure Economics.* London: Allen and Unwin.

Willig, R. D. (1976). Consumer's surplus without apology. *American Economic Review* 66(4), 589–97.

Wolak, F. (1994). An econometric analysis of the asymmetric information, regulator-utility interaction. *Annales d'économie et de statistiques 34*, 13–69.

World Bank (2005). *Equity and Development: World Development Report 2006.* New York: World Bank and Oxford University Press.

Zhang, X. (1998). Modeling economic transition: A two-tier price computable general equilibrium model of the Chinese economy. *Journal of Policy Modeling 20*, 483–511.

APPENDIX A

Mathematics Background

A.1 Introduction

This appendix is intended to be a brief review of some of the main concepts and results that are used intensively in the body of the book. However, it does not pretend to be comprehensive or exhaustive in its treatment of the mathematical topics covered. The emphasis of the book is on economic results not on mathematical technique, and so in what follows we usually state lemmas, theorems, and corollaries without formal proof. For more detail and further discussion you are invited to check out the references given in section A.9.

The symbol conventions used in this book include the following:

Symbol	*Context*	*Meaning*
$:=$	Definitions and equations	'LHS is defined by RHS'
$\geq$	Vector expressions	'every component of LHS is greater than or equal to corresponding component of RHS'
$\succeq$	Vector expressions	'vector on LHS is as good as, or better than, the vector on RHS'
$\mathbb{R}^n$	Vector spaces	n-dimensional real space
$\log(x)$	functions	natural logarithm of x
$\exp(x)$	functions	e^x
$f_i(x_1, x_2, \ldots)$	Differentiable functions	Partial differential with respect to ith argument
#	Sets	number of elements in the set
$\Rightarrow$	Logical expressions	'expression on LHS implies expression on RHS'
$\Longleftrightarrow$	Logical expressions	'expression on LHS is true if and only if expression on RHS is true'

A.2 Sets

We use the standard operators:

Membership	$x \in A$	'x is a member of A'
Equality	$A = B$	$x \in A$ if and only if $x \in B$
Subset	$A \subset B$	$x \in B$ if $x \in A$
Intersection	$A \cap B$	$A \cap B = \{x : x \in A \text{ and } x \in B\}$
Union	$A \cup B$	$A \cup B = \{x : x \in A \text{ or } x \in B\}$

In addition the operator '\' is often useful. If $B \subset A$ then

$$A \backslash B = \{x : x \in A \text{ and not } x \in B\}.$$

Where relevant, the notation $\#A$ is used to denote the number of elements of A. The symbol $\varnothing$ is used to denote the empty set—the set with no elements.

The *Cartesian product* of sets A and B is the set of all ordered pairs with the first element of the pair taken from A and the second element from B

$$A \times B = \{(x, y) : x \in A,\ y \in B\}.$$

A *binary relation* on a set A is subset R of the Cartesian product $A \times A$, the set of pairs $\{(x, y) : x, y \in A\}$; but, rather than writing, for example, '$(x, y) \in R$' to characterise the relationship between two elements x, y of A it is common to write 'xRy'. Examples of binary relations include the ordinary mathematical operator '$\geq$' and the weak preference relation '$\succcurlyeq$'.

A.2.1 Sets in $\mathbb{R}^n$

The symbol $\mathbb{R}$ stands for the set of real numbers: the numbers that are in one-to-one correspondence with the points on an infinite line (the real line). Let $X \subset \mathbb{R}$

Definition A.1

The *infimum* or *greatest lower bound* of X is given by

$$\inf(X) := \max\left(y \in \mathbb{R} : y \leq x \text{ for all } x \in X\right).$$

Definition A.2

The *supremum* or *least upper bound* of X is given by

$$\sup(X) := \min\left(y \in \mathbb{R} : y \geq x \text{ for all } x \in X\right).$$

If X has a smallest element $\underline{x}$ then $\inf(X) = \underline{x}$; otherwise $\inf(X)$ does not belong to X. Likewise if X has a largest element $\overline{x}$ then $\sup(X) = \overline{x}$; otherwise $\sup(X)$ does not belong to X.

By extension to the notation for the set of real numbers the following conventions are used

- $\mathbb{R}^n$ is n-dimensional real space, the set of all vectors $(x_1, x_2, \ldots, x_n)$ where each x_i is a real number. $\mathbb{R}^n$ is just the n-fold Cartesian product

$$\mathbb{R}^n = \underbrace{\mathbb{R} \times \mathbb{R} \times \ldots \times \mathbb{R}}_{n \text{ terms}}.$$

- $\mathbb{R}_+$ is the subset of $\mathbb{R}$ consisting of non-negative numbers.

In what follows we assume $A, X \subset \mathbb{R}^n$. For any $\mathbf{x}$, $\mathbf{x}' \in X$ let

$$\|\mathbf{x} - \mathbf{x}'\| := \sqrt{\sum_{i=1}^{n} [x_i - x_i']^2}. \quad \text{(A.1)}$$

Definition A.3

A set $A \subset X$ is *open in* X if, for every $\mathbf{x} \in A$, there is some $\delta > 0$ such that

$$\mathbf{x}' \in X \text{ and } \|\mathbf{x} - \mathbf{x}'\| < \delta \text{ imply } \mathbf{x}' \in A.$$

Definition A.4

A set $A \subset X$ is *closed in* X if $X \backslash A$ is open in X.

Definition A.5

A set A is *bounded* if, for every $\mathbf{x} \in A$, there is some $\delta > 0$ such that

$$\sqrt{\sum_{i=1}^{n} [x_i]^2} < \delta.$$

Definition A.6

A set A is *compact* if it is bounded and closed in $\mathbb{R}^n$.

A.3 Functions

By a *mapping* from a set D to a set R, written

$$f : D \mapsto R,$$

we mean a rule that sets up an association between the elements of D and the element of R; the set D is known as the *domain* of the mapping and the set R is the *range*. A *function* is a mapping that associates with each $x \in D$ a single element $f(x) \in R$. A *correspondence* is a mapping that associates with each $x \in D$ a set of points $f(x) \subset R$.

Consider a function $f : D \mapsto R$ where D is a set of vectors in $\mathbb{R}^n$ and R is a subset of the real line $\mathbb{R}$.

A.3.1 Linear and affine functions

Consider a function $f : D \mapsto R$ where D and R are sets of real numbers; f is an *affine function* (affine transformation) if and only if it can be written in the form

$$f(x) = ax + b, \tag{A.2}$$

where a and b are real numbers. The affine function f in (A.2) is a linear function (transformation) if and only if $b = 0$.

If D is a set of vectors in $\mathbb{R}^n$ and R is a set of vectors in $\mathbb{R}^m$ then $\mathbf{f} : D \mapsto R$ is an affine function or transformation if and only if it can be written in the form

$$\mathbf{f}(\mathbf{x}) = \mathbf{A}\mathbf{x} + \mathbf{b}, \tag{A.3}$$

where $\mathbf{A}$ is an $m \times n$ matrix

$$\begin{bmatrix} a_{11} & a_{12} & \cdots & a_{1n} \\ a_{21} & a_{22} & \cdots & a_{2n} \\ \vdots & & & \vdots \\ a_{m1} & a_{m2} & \cdots & a_{mn} \end{bmatrix}$$

and $\mathbf{b} \in \mathbb{R}^m$. Written out in detail (A.3) becomes

$$f^1(\mathbf{x}) = \sum_{j=1}^{n} a_{1j}x_j + b_1$$

$$f^2(\mathbf{x}) = \sum_{j=1}^{n} a_{2j}x_j + b_2$$

$$\vdots$$

$$f^m(\mathbf{x}) = \sum_{j=1}^{n} a_{mj}x_j + b_m$$

where $\mathbf{f} := (f^1, f^2, \ldots, f^m)$. Again $\mathbf{f}$ in (A.3) is also a linear function or transformation if and only if $\mathbf{b} = 0$.

The special case where $m = n$ is of particular interest. In this case both D and R are subsets of $\mathbb{R}^n$ and A is an $n \times n$ square matrix. Define the $[n-1] \times [n-1]$ submatrix A_{ij} as the matrix formed by deleting the ith row and jth column from A. Then we can define the *determinant* of A for the cases where $n = 1, 2, 3$ as follows:

$$\text{case 1}: \ \det A = a_{11}$$

$$\text{case 2}: \ \det A = a_{11}a_{22} - a_{12}a_{21}$$

$$\text{case 3}: \ \det A = a_{11}\det A_{11} - a_{12}\det A_{12} + a_{13}\det A_{13}.$$

In the general case we have

Definition A.7

The determinant of the $n \times n$ square matrix A is given by

$$\det A = a_{11}\det A_{11} - a_{12}\det A_{12} + \ldots + [-1]^{n+1}\det A_{1n}.$$

A.3.2 Continuity

Consider a function $f : D \mapsto R$ where D and R are sets of real numbers, and let $y \in D$.

Definition A.8

The function f is *continuous* at y if and only if the following holds: For any number $\varepsilon > 0$ there exists some $\delta > 0$ such that for all x satisfying $y - \delta < x < y + \delta$, the value of $f(x)$ satisfies $f(y) - \varepsilon < f(x) < f(y) + \varepsilon$.

There is an alternative approach to continuity that is more easily expressed for more general functions defined in n-dimensional real space. It uses the concept of a limit. In what follows we assume that $D \subset \mathbb{R}^n$ and $R \subset \mathbb{R}^m$. By a *sequence* in D we mean an assignment of elements of D to the set of natural numbers, written $\{\mathbf{x}_1, \mathbf{x}_2, \ldots\}$ or $\{\mathbf{x}_i\}_{i=1}^{\infty}$ where $\mathbf{x}_i \in D$, $i = 1, 2, \ldots$ Denote by $N_\delta(\mathbf{x}')$ a *δ-neighbourhood* of $\mathbf{x}'$:

$$N_\delta(\mathbf{x}') := \{\mathbf{x} : \|\mathbf{x} - \mathbf{x}'\| < \delta\}.$$

Then we can introduce the following intuitive concept:

Definition A.9

$\tilde{\mathbf{x}} \in D$ is the *limit* of the sequence $\{\mathbf{x}_1, \mathbf{x}_2, \ldots\}$, written

$$\lim_{i \to \infty} \mathbf{x}_i = \tilde{\mathbf{x}}$$

or

$$\lim \mathbf{x}_i = \tilde{\mathbf{x}},$$

if and only if for every neighbourhood $N_\delta(\tilde{\mathbf{x}})$ of $\tilde{\mathbf{x}}$ there is an i^* such that $\mathbf{x}_i \in N_\delta(\tilde{\mathbf{x}})$ for all $i > i^*$.

We may call $\tilde{\mathbf{x}}$ a *limit point* of D if there is a sequence $\{\mathbf{x}_i\}$ such that, for all i, $\mathbf{x}_i \in D$ and $\lim \mathbf{x}_i = \tilde{\mathbf{x}}$. From Definitions A.3 and A.4 it is clear that if D is a closed set then it contains all its limit points.

Now use the concept of a limit as the basis of an alternative definition of continuity:

Definition A.10

The function $\mathbf{f} : D \mapsto R$ is *continuous at a point* $\mathbf{c} \in D$ if the following are satisfied for all sequences x_i such that $\lim x_i = c$:

1. $\lim \mathbf{f}(\mathbf{x}_i)$ exists;
2. $\lim \mathbf{f}(\mathbf{x}_i) = \mathbf{f}(\mathbf{c})$.

The function is (everywhere) *continuous* if it is continuous at every point of its domain—see Figure A.1 part (a).

Now consider a correspondence $f : D \mapsto R$ where R is closed.

Definition A.11

The *graph* of f is the set $\{(x, y) \in D \times R : y = f(x)\}$.

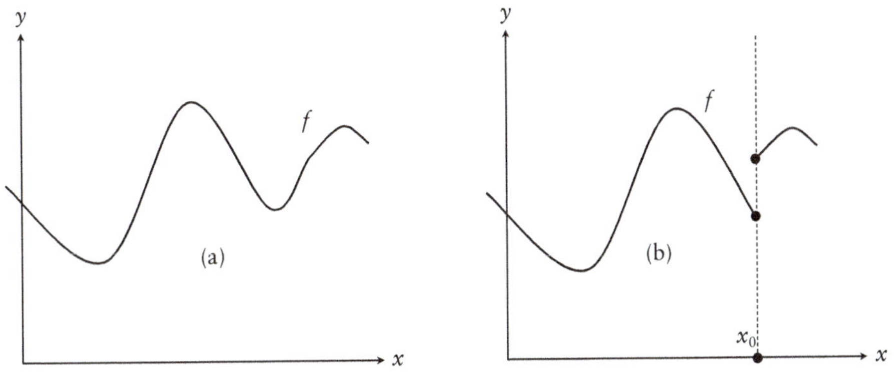

Figure A.1 (a) A continuous function (b) An upper-hemicontinuous correspondence

Definition A.12

The correspondence f is *upper hemicontinuous* if it has a closed graph and the image of every compact set is bounded.

Note that in part (b) of Figure A.1 the upper-hemicontinuous correspondence f is multivalued at point x_0.

A.3.3 Homogeneous functions

Unless otherwise stated all functions are assumed to be from $X \subset \mathbb{R}^n$ to $\mathbb{R}$. The symbol $\mathbf{x}$ denotes $(x_1, x_2, \ldots, x_n)$.

Definition A.13

A *homogeneous function* f has the following property. For any positive scalar t:

$$f(t\mathbf{x}) = t^r f(\mathbf{x}) \tag{A.4}$$

For obvious reasons such a function is said to be 'homogeneous of degree r'; the case $r = 1$ is sometimes referred to as 'linearly homogeneous'.

Assume that f is differentiable. Then, differentiating (A.4) with respect to x_i, where i is any number from 1 to n, we get

$$tf_i(t\mathbf{x}) = t^r f_i(\mathbf{x}) \tag{A.5}$$

where

$$f_i(\mathbf{y}) := \frac{\partial f(\mathbf{y})}{\partial y_i},$$

for any $\mathbf{y} \in X$. Rearranging (A.5) we have:

$$f_i(t\mathbf{x}) = t^{r-1} f_i(\mathbf{x}), \tag{A.6}$$

and so:

Lemma A.1

For a differentiable function $f : X \mapsto \mathbb{R}$ that is homogeneous of degree r each of its first derivatives is a function that is homogeneous of degree $r - 1$.

Lemma A.1 has a tremendous significance for economics. To see why consider any collection of vectors $\mathbf{x}, \mathbf{x}', \mathbf{x}'', \mathbf{x}''', \ldots$ such that each is a scale transformation of any one of the others:

$$\mathbf{x}' = t'\mathbf{x}$$

$$\mathbf{x}'' = t''\mathbf{x}$$

$$\ldots$$

We can imagine all these as being in the same 'direction': they are all points along the same ray through the origin. Then, noting that (A.5) is true for arbitrary i, j, we have

$$\frac{f_i(\mathbf{x})}{f_j(\mathbf{x})} = \frac{f_i(\mathbf{x}')}{f_j(\mathbf{x}')} = \frac{f_i(\mathbf{x}'')}{f_j(\mathbf{x}'')} = \ldots, 1 \leq i, j \leq n. \tag{A.7}$$

So:

Corollary A.1

For any pair (i, j), the homogeneous function f has the same slope for all vectors in a given direction.

Given that slopes often have the interpretation of relative prices in economics it is clear that this property implies that the relevant relative prices of i and j would be independent of scale transformations of the quantities of i and j.

Now, differentiating (A.4) with respect to t, we get

$$f_1(t\mathbf{x})x_1 + f_2(t\mathbf{x})x_2 + \ldots + f_n(t\mathbf{x})x_n = rt^{r-1}f(\mathbf{x}). \tag{A.8}$$

Taking the case where $t = 1$ in (A.8), we immediately get the following:

Lemma A.2

For a differentiable function $f : X \mapsto \mathbb{R}$ that is homogeneous of degree r:

$$\forall \mathbf{x} \in X := \sum_{i=1}^{n} f_i(\mathbf{x})x_i = rf(\mathbf{x}).$$

A.3.4 Homothetic functions

Homothetic functions have a more general structure than homogeneous functions.

Definition A.14

Let $\varphi : \mathbb{R} \mapsto \mathbb{R}$ be given by

$$g := \varphi(f) \tag{A.9}$$

where f is a homogeneous function $X \mapsto \mathbb{R}$; then g is a homothetic function $X \mapsto \mathbb{R}$.

Now suppose that is a differentiable and monotonic function. Using (A.4) and (A.9) we have, for any scalar t and any $\mathbf{x} \in X$:

$$\begin{aligned} g(t\mathbf{x}) &= \varphi\left(f(t\mathbf{x})\right) \\ &= \varphi\left(t^r f(\mathbf{x})\right) \\ &= \varphi\left(t^r \varphi^{-1}(g(\mathbf{x}))\right) \end{aligned} \tag{A.10}$$

where $\varphi^{-1}(\cdot)$ denotes the inverse function corresponding to φ. Differentiating (A.10) with respect to x_i we get

$$g_i(t\mathbf{x}) = \varphi_1\left(t^r\varphi^{-1}(g(\mathbf{x}))\right)t^r\frac{1}{\varphi_1\left(f(\mathbf{x})\right)}g_i(\mathbf{x})$$

$$= \frac{\varphi_1\left(t^r f(\mathbf{x})\right)t^r}{\varphi_1\left(f(\mathbf{x})\right)}g_i(\mathbf{x}) \tag{A.11}$$

where φ_1 denotes the first derivative of φ. However, (A.11) is also true for any other component j:

$$g_j(t\mathbf{x}) = \frac{\varphi_1\left(t^r f(\mathbf{x})\right)t^r}{\varphi_1\left(f(\mathbf{x})\right)}g_j(\mathbf{x}) \tag{A.12}$$

and so (A.11) and (A.12) together imply

$$\frac{g_i(\mathbf{x})}{g_j(\mathbf{x})} = \frac{g_i(t\mathbf{x})}{g_j(t\mathbf{x})}.$$

Corollary A.2

For any pair (i, j), the homothetic function g has the same slope for all vectors in a given direction.

A.4 Differentiation

A.4.1 Function of one variable

Let f be a function from $\mathbb{R}$ to $\mathbb{R}$:

Definition A.15

The *derivative of* f is

$$\frac{df(x)}{dx} = \lim_{\Delta x \to 0}\frac{f(x+\Delta x) - f(x)}{\Delta x}$$

where the limit exists.

Some useful examples of derivatives:

$f(x)$	$\frac{df(x)}{dx}$
$x^t, t \neq 0$	tx^{t-1}
$\log x$	$\frac{1}{x}$
e^x	e^x
t^x	$t^x \log t$

The following result can often get you out of difficulty.

Theorem A.1 (L'Hôpital's rule)

Let $I = (x_0, x_1) \subset \mathbb{R}$ be an interval and let $\xi \in I$. Suppose f and g are differentiable on $I \backslash \{\xi\}$ such that $\lim_{x\to\xi} f(x) = \lim_{x\to\xi} g(x) = 0$ and $\frac{dg(x)}{dx} \neq 0$ for $x \in I\backslash\{\xi\}$. If

$$\lim_{x\to\xi}\frac{\frac{df(x)}{dx}}{\frac{dg(x)}{dx}} = z$$

then

$$\lim_{x \to \xi} \frac{f(x)}{g(x)} = z.$$

A.4.2 Function of several variables

Let f be a function from $\mathbb{R}^n$ to $\mathbb{R}$:

$$y = f(x_1, x_2, \ldots, x_n) = f(\mathbf{x}).$$

Consider a variation in the ith component of $\mathbf{x}$:

$$f(x_1, x_2, \ldots, x_{i-1}, x_i + \Delta x_i, x_{i+1}, \ldots, x_n).$$

Definition A.16

The *derivative of f with respect to x_i* is given by

$$\frac{\partial f(\mathbf{x})}{\partial x_i} := \lim_{\Delta x_i \to 0} \frac{f(x_1, x_2, \ldots, x_{i-1}, x_i + \Delta x_i, x_{i+1}, \ldots, x_n) - f(x_1, x_2, \ldots, x_n)}{\Delta x_i}$$

where the limit exists.

In the main text we have often used $f_i(\mathbf{x})$ as a shorthand for $\frac{\partial f(\mathbf{x})}{\partial x_i}$. Now consider a simultaneous variation of all n components of $\mathbf{x}$.

$$y + \Delta y = f(x_1 + \Delta x_1, x_2 + \Delta x_2, \ldots, x_n + \Delta x_n).$$

In the limit we may write:

$$dy = \frac{\partial f(\mathbf{x})}{\partial x_1} dx_1 + \frac{\partial f(\mathbf{x})}{\partial x_2} dx_2 + \ldots + \frac{\partial f(\mathbf{x})}{\partial x_n} dx_n.$$

This is the *total differential* of f.

A.4.3 Function-of-a-function rule

Suppose f and φ are continuously differentiable functions from $\mathbb{R}^n$ to $\mathbb{R}$ and from $\mathbb{R}$ to $\mathbb{R}$, respectively, and that g is a composite function of f and φ thus:

$$y = f(\mathbf{x})$$

$$g(\mathbf{x}) = \varphi(y) = \varphi\big(f(\mathbf{x})\big)$$

then the partial derivative of g with respect to x_i is

$$\frac{\partial g(\mathbf{x})}{\partial x_i} = \frac{d\varphi(y)}{\partial y} \frac{\partial f(\mathbf{x})}{\partial x_i}$$

—the 'function-of-a-function rule'. The result carries over to the case where φ takes a vector argument. Let $f^1, \ldots, f^m$ be continuously differentiable functions from $\mathbb{R}^n$ to $\mathbb{R}$, and φ a continuously differentiable function from $\mathbb{R}^m$ to $\mathbb{R}$, and g is a composite function of $\mathbf{f}$ and φ thus:

$$\mathrm{y} = \mathbf{f}(\mathbf{x})$$

$$g(\mathbf{x}) = \varphi(\mathrm{y}) = \varphi\left(\mathbf{f}(\mathbf{x})\right).$$

Then we have:

$$\frac{\partial g(\mathbf{x})}{\partial x_i} = \sum_{j=1}^{m} \frac{\partial \varphi(\mathbf{y})}{\partial y_j} \frac{\partial f^j(\mathbf{x})}{\partial x_i}$$

A.4.4 The Jacobian derivative

Consider a set of m differentiable functions $f^j : \mathbb{R}^n \mapsto \mathbb{R}$, $j = 1, \dots, m$; this could be represented equivalently as a vector-valued function $\mathbf{f} : \mathbb{R}^n \mapsto \mathbb{R}^m$ where $\mathbf{f}(\mathbf{x}) = (f^1(\mathbf{x}), \dots, f^m(\mathbf{x}))$. Use a subscript notation as shorthand for partial derivatives thus:

$$f_i^j(\mathbf{x}) := \frac{\partial f^j(\mathbf{x})}{\partial x_i}$$

Suppose we have a relationship $\mathbf{y} = \mathbf{f}(\mathbf{x})$ where $\mathbf{y} \in \mathbb{R}^m$. The effect of a change $\Delta\mathbf{x}$ in the variables $\mathbf{x}$ can be expressed thus:

$$\Delta\mathbf{y} = \mathbf{f}(\mathbf{x} + \Delta\mathbf{x}) - \mathbf{f}(\mathbf{x}) \simeq \frac{\partial \mathbf{f}(\mathbf{x})}{\partial \mathbf{x}} \Delta\mathbf{x} \tag{A.13}$$

$$= \begin{bmatrix} f_1^1(\mathbf{x}) & f_2^1(\mathbf{x}) & \dots & f_n^1(\mathbf{x}) \\ f_1^2(\mathbf{x}) & f_2^2(\mathbf{x}) & \dots & f_n^2(\mathbf{x}) \\ \dots & \dots & \dots & \dots \\ f_1^m(\mathbf{x}) & f_2^m(\mathbf{x}) & \dots & f_n^m(\mathbf{x}) \end{bmatrix} \begin{bmatrix} \Delta x_1 \\ \Delta x_2 \\ \dots \\ \Delta x_n \end{bmatrix} \tag{A.14}$$

where the expression $\frac{\partial \mathbf{f}(\mathbf{x})}{\partial \mathbf{x}}$ in (A.13), expressed in full as the $n \times m$ matrix on the right-hand side of (A.14), is known as the *Jacobian* matrix.

A.4.5 The Taylor expansion

The following approximation result can also be restated in the case of many variables.

Theorem A.2

Let f be differentiable n^{+1} times on an open interval D. Then, for x and $x + h \in D$:

$$f(x+h) \simeq f(x) + \frac{df(x)}{dx} + \frac{1}{2!}\frac{d^2 f(x)}{dx^2}h^2 + \frac{1}{3!}\frac{d^3 f(x)}{dx^3}h^3 + \dots + \frac{1}{n!}\frac{d^n f(x)}{dx^n}h^n + \dots$$

where $n! = n \times [n-1] \times \dots \times 3 \times 2$.

A.4.6 Elasticities

Point elasticities: the simple case

Assume that we have a relationship between y and x given by

$$y = f(x) \tag{A.15}$$

where f is a differentiable function of one variable.

Definition A.17

The *elasticity* of y with respect to x is given by

$$\eta := \frac{x}{y}\frac{dy}{dx}. \tag{A.16}$$

Note that there is no single standard notation for elasticities. Furthermore, there is not even a standard sign convention: for example if y is a decreasing function of x for $x, y > 0$ then obviously (A.16) is negative; but it is quite common to find the elasticity expressed as a positive number—i.e. $|\eta|$ rather than η. Check carefully and use common sense to determine the convention that is being used in any particular instance.

Remark A.1

An equivalent way of writing (A.16) is

$$\eta = \frac{d \log y}{d \log x}. \tag{A.17}$$

To establish this let us define

$$u := \log x$$
$$v := \log y.$$

Note that dv/du is exactly (A.17) and that we may write the inverses

$$x = \mathrm{e}^u$$
$$y = \mathrm{e}^v \;;$$

from (A.15) we have

$$\mathrm{e}^v = f\left(\mathrm{e}^u\right)$$
$$v = \log\left(f\left(\mathrm{e}^u\right)\right). \tag{A.18}$$

Differentiating (A.18) we have

$$\begin{aligned}\frac{dv}{du} &= \frac{1}{f\left(\mathrm{e}^u\right)}\frac{df\left(\mathrm{e}^u\right)}{du}\\ &= \frac{1}{f(x)}\frac{df\left(\mathrm{e}^u\right)}{du} = \frac{1}{f(x)}\frac{df(x)}{dx}\frac{d\mathrm{e}^u}{du}\\ &= \frac{1}{f(x)}\frac{df(x)}{dx}\mathrm{e}^u = \frac{x}{f(x)}\frac{df(x)}{dx}\\ &= \frac{x}{y}\frac{dy}{dx}\end{aligned}$$

which is exactly (A.16).

Multivariate functions

This does not introduce any major new complication of substance, but one has to be careful about notation. Let $f^1, \ldots, f^m$ be functions from $\mathbb{R}^n$ to $\mathbb{R}$:

$$y_1 = f^1(x_1, x_2, \ldots, x_n)$$
$$y_2 = f^2(x_1, x_2, \ldots, x_n)$$
$$\ldots$$
$$y_m = f^m(x_1, x_2, \ldots, x_n) \tag{A.19}$$

then

Definition A.18

The *elasticity* of y_j with respect to x_i is given by

$$\eta_{ij} := \frac{x_i}{y_j}\frac{\partial y_j}{\partial x_i}. \tag{A.20}$$

Remark A.2

An equivalent way of writing (A.20) is

$$\eta_{ij} = \frac{d \log y_j}{d \log x_i}. \tag{A.21}$$

Where $i \neq j$ one sometimes uses the term 'cross-elasticity' and where $i = j$ one uses terms such as 'own-price elasticity.'

A.5 Mappings and systems of equations

A.5.1 Fixed-point results

In a number of settings it is useful to be able to appeal to a class of results that refer to the mapping of a set into itself. They are typically used to establish whether a system of equations has a solution. To make this precise consider a set $A \subset \mathbb{R}^n$ and a mapping $f : A \mapsto A$; f may be a system of equations that describes an economic process.

First let us assume that the mapping is a well-defined function—i.e. each element of A is mapped by f into a unique element of A. Suppose there were a member of A such that

$$\mathbf{x}^* = f(\mathbf{x}^*). \tag{A.22}$$

Such a value $\mathbf{x}^*$ is known as a *fixed point* of the mapping f. If a fixed point exists then the process described by f has an 'equilibrium' in A: the point $\mathbf{x}^*$ reproduces itself.

In what follows we will assume that A is a convex, compact set.

Theorem A.3 (Brouwer)

If the function $f : A \mapsto A$ is continuous then there exists $\mathbf{x}^* \in A$ such that (A.22) is satisfied.

The result is illustrated in Figure A.2 using the simplest possible example where the convex, compact set A is the closed interval $[0, 1]$; the elements of A are scalars, x. The function f transforms any value x from A on the horizontal axis into a value $\hat{x}$ in A on the vertical axis. The value marked x^* is clearly the required fixed point.

Now suppose that the map of A into itself is not single-valued—i.e. one has a correspondence rather than a function. In this case the fixed-point concept (A.22) generalises in a natural way to:

$$\mathbf{x}^* \in f(\mathbf{x}^*) \tag{A.23}$$

and one needs to use the following result.

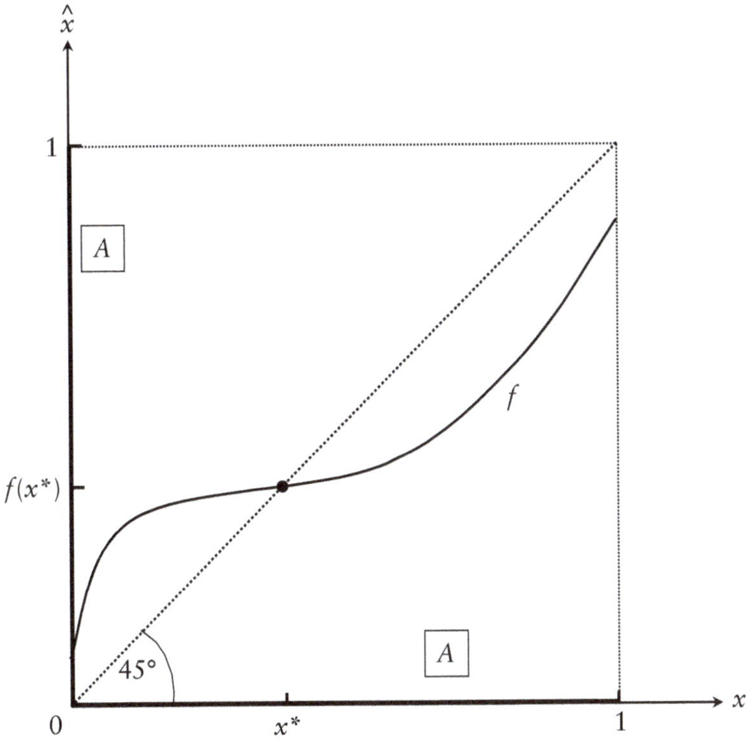

Figure A.2 Continuous mapping with a fixed point

Theorem A.4 (Kakutani)

Let $C(A)$ be the set of all non-empty closed convex subsets of A. If the correspondence $f : A \mapsto C(A)$ is upper-hemicontinuous then there exists $\mathbf{x}^* \in A$ such that (A.23) is satisfied.

The result is illustrated in Figure A.3, again for the case where $A = [0, 1]$. Here values of x from A on the horizontal axis are mapped into possibly multiple values $\hat{x}$ in A on the vertical axis: in particular the image of $\mathbf{x}^*$ is a proper interval of points, a closed convex subset of A.

A.5.2 Implicit functions

It is often the case that the conditions characterising the solution to an optimisation problem lead to an expression that appears to contain an implicit relationship between a vector of unknown variables and a vector of given parameters. The question is whether one can solve this relationship in order to obtain the variables as a function of the parameters. To address this we need the concept of *solvability* as follows.

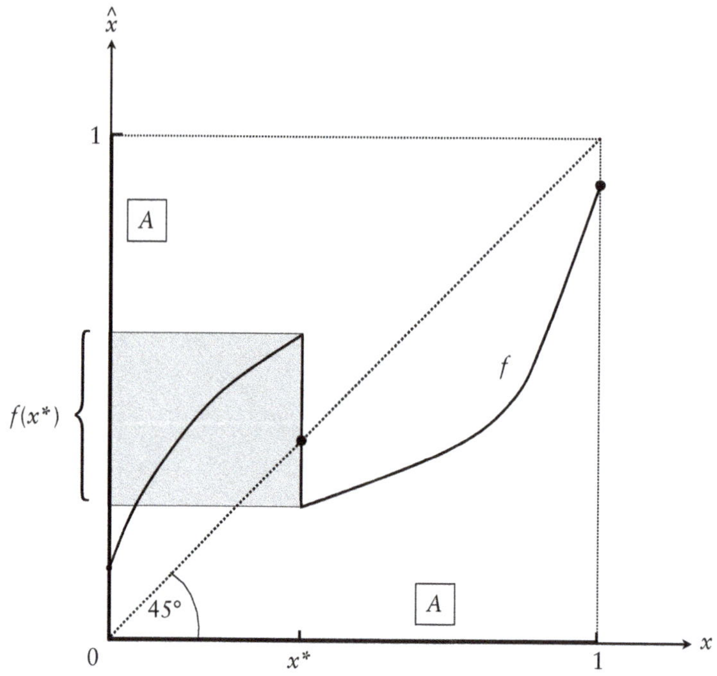

Figure A.3 Upper hemicontinuous mapping with a fixed point

Suppose the variables in question are $\mathbf{x} \in \mathbb{R}^n$ and the parameters are $\mathbf{p} \in \mathbb{R}^m$. The relationship between them is given by a set of n functions $f^1, \ldots, f^n$ such that

$$f^1(\mathbf{x}; \mathbf{p}) = 0$$
$$f^2(\mathbf{x}; \mathbf{p}) = 0$$
$$\vdots$$
$$f^n(\mathbf{x}; \mathbf{p}) = 0.$$

This set of relationships can be written more compactly as

$$\mathbf{f}(\mathbf{x}; \mathbf{p}) = 0.$$

If there are points $\mathbf{x}^\circ \in X \subset \mathbb{R}^n$ and $\mathbf{p}^\circ \in P \subset \mathbb{R}^m$ (where X and P are open sets) and functions $g^1, \ldots, g^n \; P \mapsto X$ such that

$$x_1^\circ = g^1(\mathbf{p}^\circ)$$
$$x_2^\circ = g^2(\mathbf{p}^\circ)$$
$$\ldots$$
$$x_n^\circ = g^n(\mathbf{p}^\circ)$$

and

$$\mathbf{f}(\mathbf{g}(\mathbf{p}); \mathbf{p}) = 0$$

for all $\mathbf{p} \in P$, then we say that f is *solvable* at $(\mathbf{x}^\circ; \mathbf{p}^\circ)$. The following result makes use of the Jacobian matrix, introduced in section A.4.4.

Theorem A.5 (Implicit function)

If f is continuously differentiable in the neighbourhood of $(\mathbf{x}^\circ; \mathbf{p}^\circ)$ and the determinant of the Jacobian matrix $\frac{\partial \mathbf{f}(\mathbf{x};\mathbf{p})}{\partial \mathbf{x}}$ is non-zero then f is solvable at $(\mathbf{x}^\circ; \mathbf{p}^\circ)$.

A.6 Convexity and concavity

A.6.1 Convex sets

The idea of convexity is quite intuitive, but it is useful to see how it can be made precise. Although the concept can be expressed more generally, we will confine ourselves to discussion of subsets of $\mathbb{R}^n$. The symbol a will denote a scalar.

Definition A.19

The set A is *convex* if, for every $\mathbf{x}, \mathbf{x}' \in A$ it is always true that $\mathbf{x}_a \in A$, where

$$\mathbf{x}_a := a\mathbf{x} + [1 - a]\mathbf{x}', \; 0 \leq a \leq 1.$$

Let $\bar{A}$ and A^0 denote respectively the boundary and the interior of a set $A \subset \mathbb{R}^n$.

Definition A.20

The set A is *strictly convex* if, for every $\mathbf{x}, \mathbf{x}' \in A$ it is always true that $\mathbf{x}_a \in A^0$, where

$$\mathbf{x}_a := a\mathbf{x} + [1 - a]\mathbf{x}', \; 0 < a < 1.$$

Note that, by contrast to definition A.19, definition A.20 states that the points lying along the line between $\mathbf{x}$ and $\mathbf{x}'$ (*excluding* the endpoints) must lie in the *interior* of the set. This rules out $\bar{A}$ being made up, in part, of line segments—see Figure A.4.

Define the sum of two sets A, B in $\mathbb{R}^n$ as follows:

$$A + B = \{\mathbf{x} + \mathbf{y} : \mathbf{x} \in A, \mathbf{y} \in B\}. \tag{A.24}$$

Then we have:

Theorem A.6 (Addition of convex sets)

If A and B are convex sets then $A + B$ is a convex set.

Proof

Let $\mathbf{z}, \mathbf{z}' \in A + B$; then, from (A.24), there are $\mathbf{x}, \mathbf{x}' \in A$ and $\mathbf{y}, \mathbf{y}' \in B$ such that $\mathbf{z} = \mathbf{x} + \mathbf{y}$ and $\mathbf{z}' = \mathbf{x}' + \mathbf{y}' \in A + B$. Then, by (A.24), $\mathbf{x} + \mathbf{y} \in A + B$ and $\mathbf{x}' + \mathbf{y}' \in A + B$. By Definition A.19 $a\mathbf{x} + [1 - a]\mathbf{x}' \in A$, $a\mathbf{y} + [1 - a]\mathbf{y}' \in B$, where $0 \leq a \leq 1$. So, from (A.24), $a[\mathbf{x} + \mathbf{y}] + [1 - a][\mathbf{x}' + \mathbf{y}'] \in A + B$. Therefore $a\mathbf{z} + [1 - a]\mathbf{z}' \in A + B$. ■

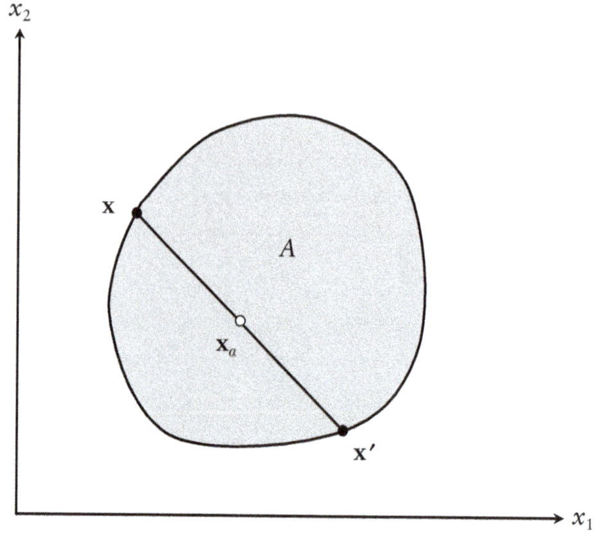

Figure A.4 A strictly convex set in $\mathbb{R}^2$

A.6.2 Hyperplanes

A hyperplane is a set in $\mathbb{R}^n$ defined thus

$$H(\mathbf{p}, c) := \left\{ \mathbf{x} \in \mathbb{R}^n : \sum_{i=1}^{n} p_i x_i = c \right\}. \tag{A.25}$$

In $\mathbb{R}^2$ (the case relevant to many of our examples and questions) this is just a straight line; in $\mathbb{R}^3$ it is a plane. Clearly a hyperplane is itself a convex set. A hyperplane divides the space into two halves: points $\mathbf{x}$ that lie 'above' it such that $\sum_{i=1}^{n} p_i x_i > c$ and points $\mathbf{x}$ that lie 'below' it such that $\sum_{i=1}^{n} p_i x_i < c$—see Figure A.5.

A.6.3 Separation results

The theorems on separating and supporting hyperplanes can be expressed in a number of ways—see Theorems A.8 and A.9. The fundamental result is as follows:

Theorem A.7 (Separation of convex set and a point)

Let $A \subset \mathbb{R}^n$ be a closed convex set and let $\mathbf{y} \in \mathbb{R}^n \backslash A$. Then there is $\mathbf{p} \in \mathbb{R}^n$, $\mathbf{p} \neq \mathbf{0}$ and $c \in \mathbb{R}$ such that $\sum_{i=1}^{n} p_i y_i > c$ and $\forall \mathbf{x} \in A$ $\sum_{i=1}^{n} p_i x_i < c$.

Proof

Let $\mathbf{x}^*$ be the closest point in A to $\mathbf{y}$, i.e. the point such that

$$\forall \mathbf{x} \in A : \sum_{i=1}^{n} [y_i - x_i^*]^2 \leq \sum_{i=1}^{n} [y_i - x_i]^2$$

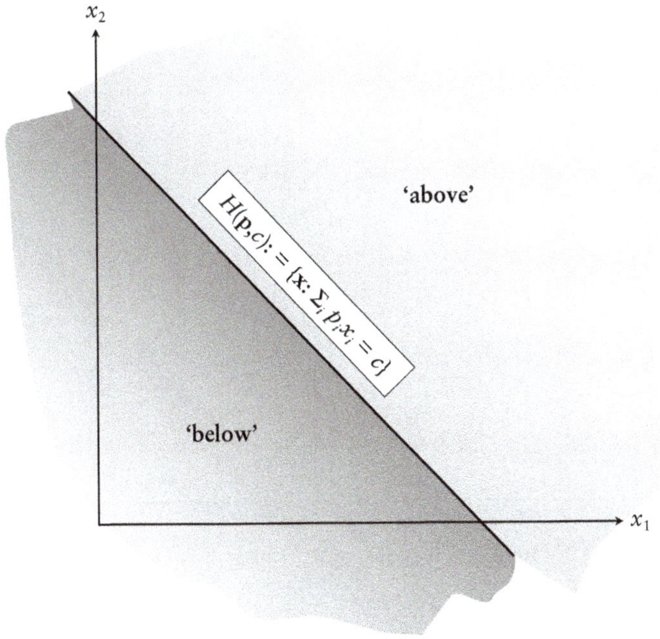

Figure A.5 A hyperplane in $\mathbb{R}^2$

—see Figure A.6. Given that $\mathbf{y}$ does not lie in A one must have

$$\sum_{i=1}^{n} [y_i - x_i^*]^2 > 0. \tag{A.26}$$

Let

$$\mathbf{p} := \mathbf{y} - \mathbf{x}^* \tag{A.27}$$

and

$$c' := \sum_{i=1}^{n} p_i x_i^*. \tag{A.28}$$

From (A.26) we have

$$\sum_{i=1}^{n} [y_i - x_i^*] y_i - \sum_{i=1}^{n} [y_i - x_i^*] x_i^* > 0$$

and so, on rearranging,

$$\sum_{i=1}^{n} p_i y_i - \sum_{i=1}^{n} p_i x_i^* > 0$$

which implies $\sum_{i=1}^{n} p_i y_i > c'$.

Now suppose there is some $\mathbf{x} \in A$ such that

$$\sum_{i=1}^{n} p_i x_i > c'. \tag{A.29}$$

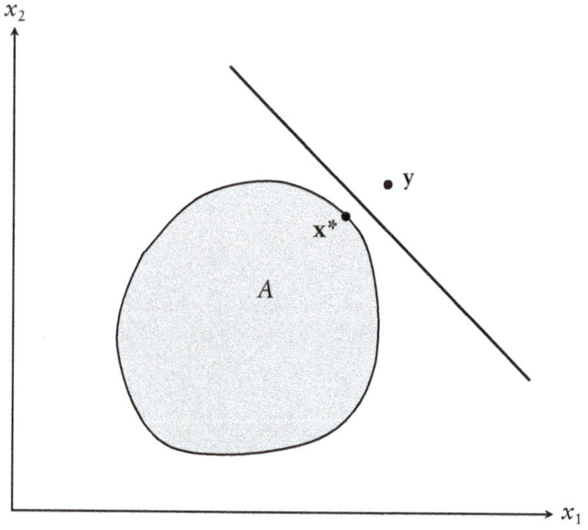

Figure A.6 A hyperplane separating A and y

Let $\mathbf{x}_a := a\mathbf{x}+[1-a]\mathbf{x}^*$, $0 < a < 1$. Clearly $\mathbf{x}_a \in A$ (by definition A.19) and the distance from y to $\mathbf{x}_a$ is

$$\sum_{i=1}^{n}[y_i - x_{ai}]^2 = \sum_{i=1}^{n}[y_i - x_i^*]^2 - 2a\sum_{i=1}^{n}[y_i - x_i^*][x_i - x_i^*] + a^2\sum_{i=1}^{n}[x_i - x_i^*]^2$$

which—using (A.27) and (A.28)—becomes:

$$\sum_{i=1}^{n}[y_i - x_i^*]^2 - 2a\left[\sum_{i=1}^{n}p_i x_i - c'\right] + a^2\sum_{i=1}^{n}[x_i - x_i^*]^2. \tag{A.30}$$

However, as $a \to 0$, (A.30) has the sign of $\sum_{i=1}^{n} p_i x_i - c'$. But if (A.29) is true then this would imply that, for a sufficiently small:

$$\sum_{i=1}^{n}[y_i - x_{ai}]^2 < \sum_{i=1}^{n}[y_i - x_i^*]^2$$

which is an impossibility.

Finally choose $c := c' + \delta$ where δ is sufficiently small that $\sum_{i=1}^{n} p_i y_i > c$. ■

Theorem A.8 (Separating hyperplane)

Let $A, B \subset \mathbb{R}^n$ be closed convex sets with no points in common. Then there is $\mathbf{p} \in \mathbb{R}^n$, $\mathbf{p} \neq 0$ and $c \in \mathbb{R}$ such that $\sum_{i=1}^{n} p_i x_i < c \; \forall \mathbf{x} \in A$ and $\sum_{i=1}^{n} p_i x_i > c \; \forall \mathbf{x} \in B$.

Theorem A.9 (Supporting hyperplane)

Let $A, B \subset \mathbb{R}^n$ be closed convex sets with only boundary points in common. Then there is $\mathbf{p} \in \mathbb{R}^n$, $\mathbf{p} \neq 0$, and $c \in \mathbb{R}$ such that $\sum_{i=1}^{n} p_i x_i \leq c \; \forall \mathbf{x} \in A$ and $\sum_{i=1}^{n} p_i x_i \geq c \; \forall \mathbf{x} \in B$.

The supporting hyperplane is illustrated as the straight line in Figure A.7.

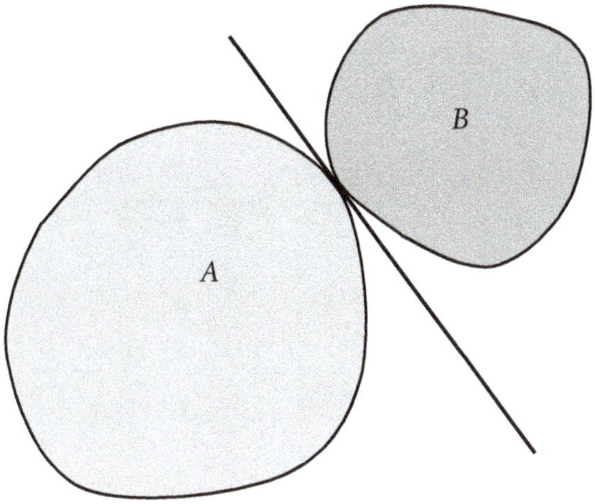

Figure A.7 Supporting hyperplane

A.6.4 Convex and concave functions

Let us use the idea of convexity to characterise a class of functions. As in section A.3.3 we will assume that all functions are from $X \subset \mathbb{R}^n$ to $\mathbb{R}$. The main definitions are really quite easy since they seem to accord closely with common sense.

Definition A.21

The function f is *convex* if and only if the set

$$\{(\mathbf{x}, y) : \mathbf{x} \in X,\ y \geq f(\mathbf{x})\}$$

is convex.

Definition A.22

The function f is *strictly convex* if and only if the set

$$\{(\mathbf{x}, y) : \mathbf{x} \in X,\ y \geq f(\mathbf{x})\}$$

is strictly convex.

The definition of (strict) convexity is a natural one since it means that the function is convex if the set of points 'above its graph' is (strictly) convex—see Figure A.8. The next definition is even easier.

Definition A.23

The function f is *concave* if and only if the function $-f$ is convex.

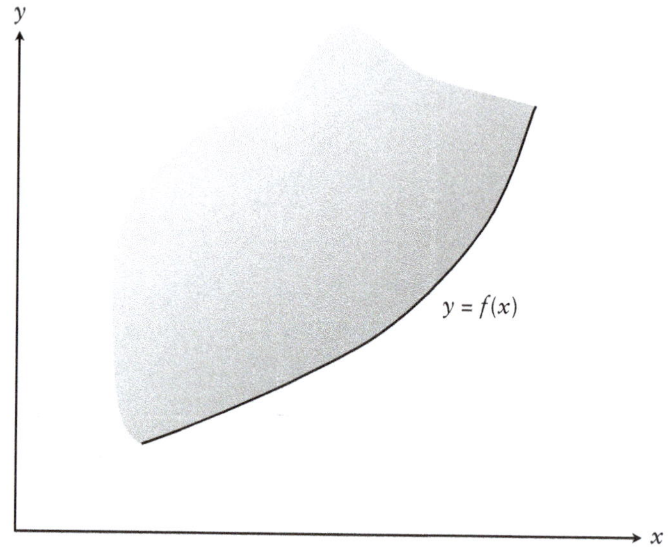

Figure A.8 A strictly convex function of one variable

If you turn the graph of a convex function upside down you get a concave function and vice versa. A similar definition applies for strict concavity. Finally note the following:

Remark A.3

(a) Definition A.21 is equivalent to:

$$\text{for all } \mathbf{x}, \mathbf{x}' \in X, 0 \leq a \leq 1 : af(\mathbf{x}) + [1-a]f(\mathbf{x}') \geq f(a\mathbf{x} + [1-a]\mathbf{x}').$$

(b) Definition A.22 is equivalent to:

$$\text{for all } \mathbf{x}, \mathbf{x}' \in X, 0 < a < 1 : af(\mathbf{x}) + [1-a]f(\mathbf{x}') > f(a\mathbf{x} + [1-a]\mathbf{x}').$$

Also, from definition A.23:

Remark A.4

(a) A function is *concave* if:

$$\text{for all } \mathbf{x}, \mathbf{x}' \in X, 0 \leq a \leq 1 : af(\mathbf{x}) + [1-a]f(\mathbf{x}') \leq f(a\mathbf{x} + [1-a]\mathbf{x}').$$

(b) A function is *strictly concave* if:

$$\text{for all } \mathbf{x}, \mathbf{x}' \in X, 0 < a < 1 : af(\mathbf{x}) + [1-a]f(\mathbf{x}') < f(a\mathbf{x} + [1-a]\mathbf{x}').$$

These alternative equivalent forms are often particularly convenient in practical application.

Finally two very powerful results that underpin important parts of the discussion in chapters 2 and 4.

Theorem A.10

Let f be a twice-differentiable function. Then f is concave if and only if, for all $\mathbf{x} \in X$ and for any vector $\mathbf{w} \in \mathbb{R}^n$,

$$\sum_{i=1}^{n}\sum_{j=1}^{n} w_i w_j \frac{\partial^2 f(\mathbf{x})}{\partial x_i \partial x_j} \leq 0.$$

This property is used to characterise the substitution properties for both the firm and the household's optimisation problems.

Theorem A.11 (Continuity of concave function)

Let f be a concave function on an open set $X \subset \mathbb{R}^n$. Then f is continuous on X.

For a proof see de la Fuente (1999: 253). Since solution functions are typically concave (or, a continuous transformation of a concave function) we can also be sure that they are continuous.

A.6.5 Quasiconcave functions

Unfortunately the above intuitive characterisation does not extend so neatly to a broader class of functions that are of tremendous importance in economics. To introduce this broader class consider the *contours* of a real-valued function f.

Definition A.24

The y_0-*contour* of the function f is the set of points

$$\{\mathbf{x} : \mathbf{x} \in X,\ y_0 = f(\mathbf{x})\}.$$

Clearly the y_0-contour is the boundary of the set

$$B(y_0) := \{\mathbf{x} : \mathbf{x} \in X,\ y_0 \leq f(\mathbf{x})\}. \tag{A.31}$$

—see Figure A.9. It is also clear that

- If f is a concave function then $B(y_0)$ must be a convex set.
- If f is a strictly concave function then $B(y_0)$ must be a strictly convex set.
- There are functions for which the contours look like those of a concave function but which are not themselves concave. An example here would be $\varphi(f(\mathbf{x}))$ where f is a concave function and is an arbitrary monotonic transformation.

These remarks lead us to the definition:

Definition A.25

A function f is *(strictly) concave contoured* if all the sets $B(y_0)$ in (A.31) are (strictly) convex.

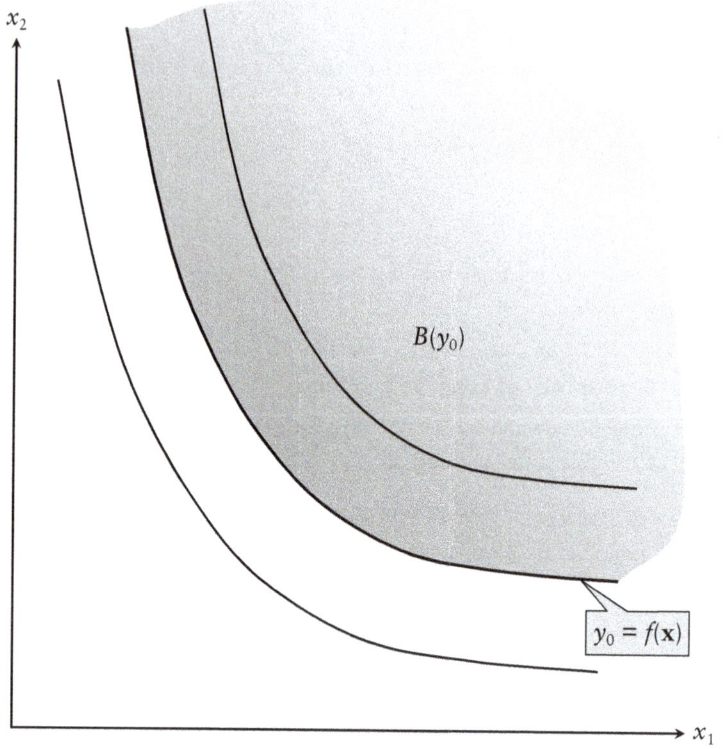

Figure A.9 A strictly concave-contoured (strictly quasiconcave) function

A synonym for (strictly) concave contoured is *(strictly) quasiconcave*. Try not to let this (unfortunately necessary) jargon confuse you. Take, for example, a 'conventional' looking utility function such as

$$U(\mathbf{x}) = x_1 x_2. \tag{A.32}$$

According to definition A.25 this function is strictly quasiconcave: if you draw the set of points $B(\upsilon) := \{(x_1, x_2) : x_1 x_2 \geq \upsilon\}$ you will get a strictly convex set. Furthermore, although U in (A.32) is not a concave function, it is a simple transformation of the strictly concave function

$$\hat{U}(\mathbf{x}) = \log x_1 + \log x_2, \tag{A.33}$$

and has the same shape of contour map as $\hat{U}$. But when we draw those contours on a diagram with the usual axes we would colloquially describe their shape as being 'convex to the origin'! There is nothing seriously wrong here: the definition, the terminology, and our intuitive view are all correct; it is just a matter of the way in which we visualise the function. Finally, the following complementary property is sometimes useful:

Definition A.26

A function f is *(strictly) quasiconvex* if $-f$ is (strictly) quasiconcave.

A.6.6 The Hessian property

Consider a twice-differentiable function f from $D \subset \mathbb{R}^n$ to $\mathbb{R}$. Let $f_{ij}(\mathbf{x})$ denote $\frac{\partial^2 f(\mathbf{x})}{\partial x_i \partial x_j}$. The symmetric matrix

$$\begin{bmatrix} f_{11}(\mathbf{x}) & f_{12}(\mathbf{x}) & \dots & f_{1n}(\mathbf{x}) \\ f_{21}(\mathbf{x}) & f_{22}(\mathbf{x}) & \dots & f_{2n}(\mathbf{x}) \\ \dots & \dots & \dots & \dots \\ f_{n1}(\mathbf{x}) & f_{n2}(\mathbf{x}) & \dots & f_{nn}(\mathbf{x}) \end{bmatrix}$$

is known as the *Hessian matrix* of f.

Definition A.27

The Hessian matrix of f at $\mathbf{x}$ is *negative semidefinite* if, for any vector $\mathbf{w} \in \mathbb{R}^n$, it is true that

$$\sum_{i=1}^{n} \sum_{j=1}^{n} w_i w_j f_{ij}(\mathbf{x}) \leq 0.$$

A twice-differentiable function f from D to $\mathbb{R}$ is concave if and only if f is negative semidefinite for all $\mathbf{x} \in D$.

Definition A.28

The Hessian matrix of f at $\mathbf{x}$ is *negative definite* if, for any vector $\mathbf{w} \in \mathbb{R}^n$, $\mathbf{w} \neq \mathbf{0}$, it is true that

$$\sum_{i=1}^{n} \sum_{j=1}^{n} w_i w_j f_{ij}(\mathbf{x}) < 0.$$

A twice-differentiable function f from D to $\mathbb{R}$ is strictly concave if f is negative definite for all $\mathbf{x} \in D$; but the reverse is not true—a strictly concave function f may have a negative semidefinite Hessian.

If the Hessian of f is negative definite for all $\mathbf{x} \in D$ we will say that f has the *Hessian property*.

A.7 Maximisation

Because a lot of economics is concerned with optimisation we will briefly overview the main techniques and results. However, this only touches the edge of a very big subject: you should consult the references in section A.9 for more details.

A.7.1 The basic technique

The problem of maximising a function of n variables

$$\max_{\mathbf{x} \in X} f(\mathbf{x}) \tag{A.34}$$

$X \subset \mathbb{R}^n$ is straightforward if the function f is differentiable and the domain X is unbounded. We adopt the usual first-order condition (FOC)

$$\frac{\partial f(\mathbf{x})}{\partial x_i} = 0, \ i = 1, 2, \dots, n \tag{A.35}$$

and then solve for the values of $(x_1, x_2, \ldots, x_n)$ that satisfy (A.35). However, the FOC is, at best, a *necessary* condition for a maximum of f. The problem is that the FOC is essentially a simple hill-climbing rule: 'if I'm really at the top of the hill then the ground must be flat just where I'm standing.' There are a number of difficulties with this:

- The rule only picks out 'stationary points' of the function f. As Figure A.10 illustrates, this condition is satisfied by a minimum (point C) as well as a maximum (point A), or by a point of inflection (E). To eliminate points such as C and E we may look at the second-order conditions which essentially require that at the top of the hill (a point such as A) the slope must be (locally) decreasing in every direction.
- Even if we eliminate minima and points of inflection the FOC may pick out multiple 'local' maxima. In Figure A.10 points A and D are each local maxima, but obviously A is the point that we really want. This problem may be sidestepped by introducing a priori restrictions on the nature of the function f that eliminate the possibility of multiple stationary points—for example by requiring that f be strictly concave.
- If we have been careless in specifying the problem then the hill-climbing rule may be completely misleading. We have assumed that each x-component can range freely from $-\infty$ to $+\infty$. But suppose—as if often in the case in economics—that the definition of the variable is such that only non-negative values make sense. Then it is clear from Figure A.10 that A is an irrelevant point and the maximum is at B. In climbing the hill we have reached a logical 'wall' and we can climb no higher.
- Likewise if we have overlooked the requirement that the function f be everywhere differentiable the hill-climbing rule represented by the FOC may be misleading. If we draw the function

$$f(x) = \begin{cases} x & x \leq 1 \\ 2 - x & x > 1 \end{cases}$$

it is clear that it is continuous and has a maximum at $x = 1$. But the FOC as stated in (A.35) is useless because the differential of f is undefined exactly at $x = 1$.

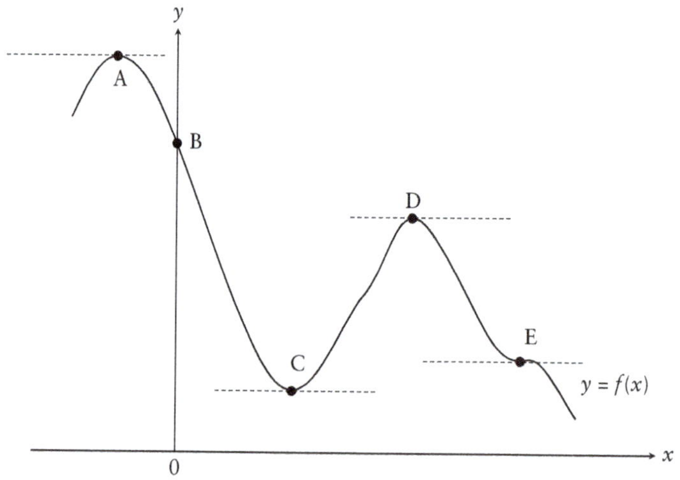

Figure A.10 Different types of stationary point

If we can sweep these difficulties aside then we can use the solution to the system of equations provided by the FOC in a powerful way. To see what is usually done, slightly rewrite the maximisation problem (A.34) as

$$\max_{\mathbf{x}\in\mathbb{R}^n} f(\mathbf{x};\mathbf{p}) \tag{A.36}$$

where $\mathbf{p}$ represents a vector of *parameters*, a set of numbers that are fixed for the particular maximisation problem in hand but which can be used to characterise the different members of a whole class of maximisation problems and their solutions. For example, $\mathbf{p}$ might represent prices (outside the control of a small firm and therefore taken as given) and $\mathbf{x}$ might represent the list of quantities of inputs and outputs that the firm chooses in its production process; profits depend on both the parameters and the choice variables.

We can then treat the FOC (A.35) as a system of n equations in n unknowns (the components of $\mathbf{x}$). Without further regularity conditions such a system is not guaranteed to have a solution nor, if it has a solution, will it necessarily be unique. However, if it does then we can write it as a function of the given parameters $\mathbf{p}$:

$$\left.\begin{aligned} x_1^* &= x_1^*(\mathbf{p}) \\ x_2^* &= x_2^*(\mathbf{p}) \\ &\dots \\ x_n^* &= x_n^*(\mathbf{p}) \end{aligned}\right\} \tag{A.37}$$

We may refer to the functions $x_1^*(\cdot)$ in (A.37) as the *response functions* in that they indicate how the optimal values of the choice variables ($\mathbf{x}^*$) would change in response to changes in values of the given parameters $\mathbf{p}$.

A.7.2 Constrained maximisation

By itself the basic technique in section A.7.1 is of limited value in economics: optimisation is usually subject to some side constraints which have not yet been introduced. We now move on to a simple case of constrained optimisation that, although restricted in its immediate applicability to economic problems, forms the basis of other useful techniques. We consider the problem of maximising a differentiable function of n variables

$$\max_{\mathbf{x}\in\mathbb{R}^n} f(\mathbf{x};\mathbf{p}) \tag{A.38}$$

subject to the m equality constraints

$$\left.\begin{aligned} G^1(\mathbf{x};\mathbf{p}) &= 0 \\ G^2(\mathbf{x};\mathbf{p}) &= 0 \\ &\dots \\ G^m(\mathbf{x};\mathbf{p}) &= 0 \end{aligned}\right\} \tag{A.39}$$

There is a standard technique for solving this kind of problem: this is to incorporate the constraint in a new maximand. To do this introduce the *Lagrange multipliers* $\lambda_1, \dots, \lambda_m$, a set of non-negative variables, one for each constraint. The constrained maximisation problem in the n

variables $x_1, \ldots, x_n$, is equivalent to the following (unconstrained) maximisation problem in the $n+m$ variables $x_1, \ldots, x_n, \lambda_1, \ldots, \lambda_m$: maximise

$$\mathcal{L}(\mathbf{x}, \boldsymbol{\lambda}; \mathbf{p}) := f(\mathbf{x}; \mathbf{p}) - \sum_{j=1}^{m} \lambda_j G^j(\mathbf{x}; \mathbf{p}) \tag{A.40}$$

where $\mathcal{L}$ is the *Lagrangean* function. By introducing the Lagrange multipliers we have transformed the constrained optimisation problem into one that is of the same format as in section A.7.1, namely

$$\max_{\mathbf{x}, \boldsymbol{\lambda}} \mathcal{L}(\mathbf{x}, \boldsymbol{\lambda}; \mathbf{p}). \tag{A.41}$$

The FOC for solving (A.41) are found by differentiating (A.40) with respect to each of the $n+m$ variables and setting each to zero.

$$\frac{\partial \mathcal{L}(\mathbf{x}^*, \boldsymbol{\lambda}^*; \mathbf{p})}{\partial x_i} = 0, \; i = 1, \ldots, n \tag{A.42}$$

$$\frac{\partial \mathcal{L}(\mathbf{x}^*, \boldsymbol{\lambda}^*; \mathbf{p})}{\partial \lambda_j} = 0, \; j = 1, \ldots, m \tag{A.43}$$

where the '*' means that the differential is being evaluated at a solution point $(\mathbf{x}^*, \boldsymbol{\lambda}^*)$. So the FOC consist of the n equations

$$\frac{\partial f(\mathbf{x}^*; \mathbf{p})}{\partial x_i} = \sum_{j=1}^{m} \lambda_j^* \frac{\partial G^j(\mathbf{x}^*; \mathbf{p})}{\partial x_i}, \; i = 1, \ldots, n \tag{A.44}$$

plus the m constraint equations (A.39) evaluated at $\mathbf{x}^*$. We therefore have a system of $n+m$ equations (A.44, A.39) in $n+m$ variables.

As in section A.7.1, if the system of equations does have a unique solution $(\mathbf{x}^*, \boldsymbol{\lambda}^*)$, then this can be written as a function of the parameters $\mathbf{p}$:

$$\left.\begin{aligned} x_1^* &= x_1^*(\mathbf{p}) \\ x_2^* &= x_2^*(\mathbf{p}) \\ &\ldots \\ x_n^* &= x_n^*(\mathbf{p}) \end{aligned}\right\} \tag{A.45}$$

$$\left.\begin{aligned} \lambda_1^* &= \lambda_1^*(\mathbf{p}) \\ \lambda_2^* &= \lambda_2^*(\mathbf{p}) \\ &\ldots \\ \lambda_m^* &= \lambda_m^*(\mathbf{p}) \end{aligned}\right\} \tag{A.46}$$

Once again the functions $x_1^*(\cdot)$ in (A.45) are the response functions and have the same interpretation. The Lagrange multipliers in (A.46) also have an interesting interpretation which is handled in A.7.4 below.

If the equations (A.44, A.39) yield more than one solution, but f in (A.38) is quasiconcave and the set of $\mathbf{x}$ satisfying (A.39) is convex, then we can appeal to the commonsense result in Theorem A.12 below.

A.7.3 More on constrained maximisation

Now modify the problem in section A.7.2 in two ways that are especially relevant to economic problems.

- Instead of allowing each component x_i to range freely from $-\infty$ to $+\infty$. We restrict to some interval of the real line. So we will now write the domain restriction $\mathbf{x} \in X$ where we will take X to be the non-negative orthant of $\mathbb{R}^n$ so that

$$x_i \geq 0,\ i = 1, \ldots, n. \tag{A.47}$$

  The results below can be adapted to other specifications of X.

- We replace the equality constraints in (A.39) by the corresponding inequality constraints

$$\left.\begin{array}{c} G^1(\mathbf{x}; \mathbf{p}) \leq 0 \\ G^2(\mathbf{x}; \mathbf{p}) \leq 0 \\ \cdots \\ G^m(\mathbf{x}; \mathbf{p}) \leq 0 \end{array}\right\} \tag{A.48}$$

  This is reasonable in economic applications of optimisation. For example, the appropriate way of stating a budget constraint is 'expenditure must not exceed income' rather than '... must *equal* ...'.

So the problem is now

$$\max_{\mathbf{x} \in X} f(\mathbf{x}; \mathbf{p})$$

subject to (A.48). The solution to this modified problem is similar to that for the standard Lagrangean—see Intriligator (1971: 49-60). Again we transform the problem by forming a Lagrangean (as in A.40):

$$\max_{\mathbf{x} \in X, \boldsymbol{\lambda} > 0} \mathcal{L}(\mathbf{x}, \boldsymbol{\lambda}; \mathbf{p}). \tag{A.49}$$

However, instead of (A.42, A.43) we now have the following FOCs:

$$\frac{\partial \mathcal{L}(\mathbf{x}^*, \boldsymbol{\lambda}^*; \mathbf{p})}{\partial x_i} \leq 0,\ i = 1, \ldots, n \tag{A.50}$$

$$x_i^* \frac{\partial \mathcal{L}(\mathbf{x}^*, \boldsymbol{\lambda}^*; \mathbf{p})}{\partial x_i} = 0,\ i = 1, \ldots, n \tag{A.51}$$

and

$$\frac{\partial \mathcal{L}(\mathbf{x}^*, \boldsymbol{\lambda}^*; \mathbf{p})}{\partial \lambda_j} \geq 0,\ j = 1, \ldots, m \tag{A.52}$$

$$\lambda_j^* \frac{\partial \mathcal{L}(\mathbf{x}^*, \boldsymbol{\lambda}^*; \mathbf{p})}{\partial \lambda_j} = 0,\ j = 1, \ldots, m. \tag{A.53}$$

This set of equations and inequalities is conventionally known as the *Kuhn–Tucker conditions*. They have important implications relating the values of the variables and the Lagrange multipliers at the optimum.

From the pair of conditions (A.50) and (A.51) we find

$$\frac{\partial f(\mathbf{x}^*; \mathbf{p})}{\partial x_i} \leq \sum_{j=1}^{m} \lambda_j^* \frac{\partial G^j(\mathbf{x}^*; \mathbf{p})}{\partial x_i},\ i = 1, \ldots, n \tag{A.54}$$

with (A.44) holding if the non-negativity constraint i (A.47) is slack at the optimum ($x_i^* > 0$). Note that if, for some i, the non-negativity constraint (A.47) is binding at the optimum ($x_i^* = 0$) we could have strict inequality in (A.54). Figure A.11 illustrates this possibility for a case where the objective function is strictly concave: note that the conventional condition of 'slope = 0' (A.42) (which would appear to be satisfied at point A) is irrelevant here since a point such as A would

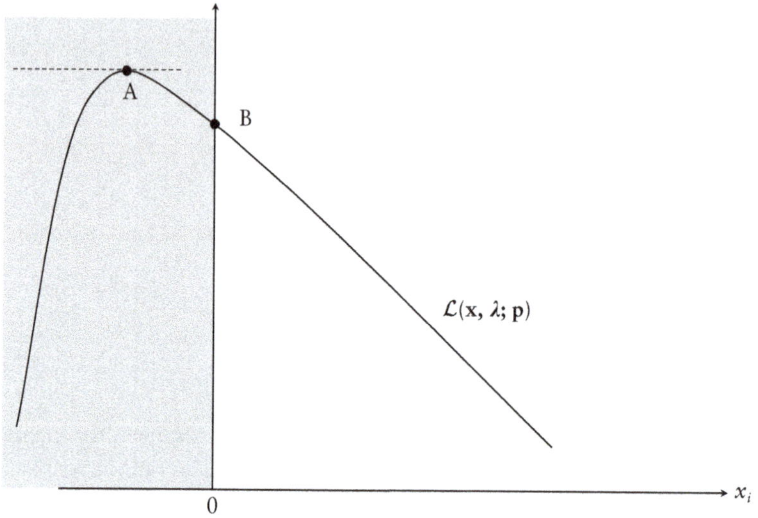

Figure A.11 A case where $x_i^* = 0$ at the optimum

violate the constraint $x_i \geq 0$; at the optimum (point B) the Lagrangean has a strictly decreasing slope. Similar interpretations will apply to the Lagrange multipliers. From the pair of conditions (A.52) and (A.53) we can see the following:

1. If the Lagrange multiplier associated with constraint j is strictly positive at the optimum ($\lambda_j^* > 0$), then it must be *binding* ($G^j(\mathbf{x}^*; \mathbf{p}) = 0$).
2. Conversely one could have an optimum where one or more Lagrange multiplier ($\lambda_j^* = 0$) is zero in which case the constraint may be *slack*—i.e. not binding—($G^j(\mathbf{x}^*; \mathbf{p}) < 0$).

So, for each j at the optimum, there is at most one inequality condition: if there is a strict inequality on the Lagrange multiplier then the corresponding constraint must be satisfied with equality (case 1); if there is a strict inequality on the constraint then the corresponding Lagrange multiplier must be equal to zero (case 2). These facts are conventionally known as the *complementary slackness condition*. However, note that one can have cases where both the Lagrange multiplier is zero ($\lambda_j^* = 0$) and the constraint is binding ($G^j(\mathbf{x}^*; \mathbf{p}) = 0$).

Again if the system (A.54, A.48) yields a unique solution it can be written as a function of the parameters $\mathbf{p}$ which in turn determines the response functions; but if it yields more than one solution, but f in (A.38) is quasiconcave and the set of $\mathbf{x}$ satisfying (A.48) is convex, then we can use the following.

Theorem A.12

If $f : \mathbb{R}^n \mapsto \mathbb{R}$ is quasiconcave and $A \subset \mathbb{R}^n$ is convex then the set of values $\mathbf{x}^*$ that solve the problem

$$\max f(\mathbf{x}) \text{ subject to } \mathbf{x} \in A$$

is convex.

A.7.4 Envelope theorem

We now examine how the solution, conditional on the given set of parameter values $\mathbf{p}$, changes when the values $\mathbf{p}$ are changed. Let $v(\mathbf{p}) = \max_{\mathbf{x}\in X} f(\mathbf{x}; \mathbf{p})$ subject to (A.39). Using the response functions in (A.37) we obviously have

$$v(\mathbf{p}) = f(\mathbf{x}^*(\mathbf{p}); \mathbf{p}). \tag{A.55}$$

The maximum-value function v has an important property:

Theorem A.13

If the objective function f and the constraint functions G^j are all differentiable then, for any k:

$$\frac{\partial v(\mathbf{p})}{\partial p_k} = \frac{\partial f(\mathbf{x}^*; \mathbf{p})}{\partial p_k} - \sum_{j=1}^{m} \lambda_j \frac{\partial G^j(\mathbf{x}^*; \mathbf{p})}{\partial p_k}.$$

Proof

Evaluating the constraints (A.39) at $\mathbf{x} = \mathbf{x}^*(\mathbf{p})$ we have

$$G^j(\mathbf{x}^*(\mathbf{p}); \mathbf{p}) = 0 \tag{A.56}$$

and differentiating (A.56) with respect to p_k and rearranging gives:

$$\sum_{i=1}^{n} \frac{\partial G^j(\mathbf{x}^*; \mathbf{p})}{\partial x_i} \frac{\partial x_i^*(\mathbf{p})}{\partial p_k} = -\frac{\partial G^j(\mathbf{x}^*(\mathbf{p}); \mathbf{p})}{\partial p_k}. \tag{A.57}$$

Differentiate (A.55) with respect to p_k

$$\frac{\partial v(\mathbf{p})}{\partial p_k} = \frac{\partial f(\mathbf{x}^*(\mathbf{p}); \mathbf{p})}{\partial p_k} + \sum_{i=1}^{n} \frac{\partial f(\mathbf{x}^*(\mathbf{p}); \mathbf{p})}{\partial x_i} \frac{\partial x_i^*(\mathbf{p})}{\partial p_k}. \tag{A.58}$$

Using (A.44) evaluated at $\mathbf{x} = \mathbf{x}^*(\mathbf{p})$ (A.58) becomes

$$\frac{\partial v(\mathbf{p})}{\partial p_k} = \frac{\partial f(\mathbf{x}^*(\mathbf{p}); \mathbf{p})}{\partial p_k} + \sum_{j=1}^{m} \lambda_j \sum_{i=1}^{n} \frac{\partial G^j(\mathbf{x}^*(\mathbf{p}); \mathbf{p})}{\partial x_i} \frac{\partial x_i^*(\mathbf{p})}{\partial p_k}. \tag{A.59}$$

Using (A.57) in (A.59) gives the result. ■

The envelope theorem has some nice economic corollaries. One of the most important of these concerns the interpretation of the Lagrange multiplier(s). Suppose we modify any one of the constraints (A.39) to read

$$G^j(\mathbf{x}; \mathbf{p}) = \delta_j \tag{A.60}$$

where δ_j could have any given value. This does not really make the problem any more general because we could have redefined the parameter list as $\bar{\mathbf{p}} := (\mathbf{p}, \delta_j)$ and used a modified form of the jth constraint $\bar{G}^j$ defined by

$$\bar{G}^j(\mathbf{x}; \bar{\mathbf{p}}) := G^j(\mathbf{x}; \mathbf{p}) - \delta_j = 0. \tag{A.61}$$

In effect we can just treat δ as an extra parameter which does not enter the function f. Then

Corollary A.3

$$\frac{\partial v(\mathbf{p})}{\partial \delta_j} = \lambda_j.$$

The result follows immediately from Theorem A.13 using the definition of δ_j in (A.61) and the fact that $\frac{\partial f(\mathbf{x}^*;\mathbf{p})}{\partial \delta} = 0$. So λ_j is the 'value' that one would put on a marginal change in the jth constraint (represented as a small displacement of δ_j).

A similar result is available for the case where the relevant constraints are inequality constraints—as in section A.7.3 rather than section A.7.2. In particular, notice the nice intuition if constraint j is slack at the optimum. We know then that the associated Lagrange multiplier is zero (see page 510), and the implication of Corollary A.3 is that the marginal value placed on the jth constraint is zero: you would not pay anything to relax an already-slack constraint.

A.7.5 A point on notation

For some maximisation problems in microeconomics it is convenient to use a special notation. Consider the problem of choosing s from a set S in order to maximise a function φ. To characterise the set of values that do the job of maximisation one uses:

$$\arg\max_s \varphi(s) := \left\{s \in S : \varphi(s) \geq \varphi(s'), s' \in S\right\}$$

where the function φ may, of course, incorporate side constraints.

A.8 Probability

For the basic definition of a random variable and the meaning of probability see, for example, Spanos (1999). We will assume that the random variable X is a scalar. This is not essential to most of the discussion that follows, but it makes the exposition easier. The case where the random variable is a vector is discussed in standard books on probability and statistics—see section A.9 below.

The *support* of a random variable is defined to be the smallest closed set whose complement has probability zero. For the applications in this book we can take the support to be either an interval on the real line or a finite set of real numbers. For the exposition that follows we take the support of X to be the interval $S := [\underline{x}, \overline{x}]$.

A convenient general way of characterising the distribution of a random variable is the *distribution function* F of X. This is a non-decreasing function

$$F(x) := \Pr(X \leq x) \tag{A.62}$$

where $0 \leq F(x) \leq 1$ for all x and $F(\overline{x}) = 1$; the symbol Pr stands for 'probability'. In words $F(x)$ in (A.62) gives the probability that the random variable X has a value less than or equal to a given value x. For the present purposes we will take two important sub-cases

1. *Continuous distributions.* Here we assume that $F(\cdot)$ is everywhere continuously differentiable. In this sub-case we can define the *density function* f as

$$f(x) := \frac{dF(x)}{dx}.$$

By the definition of f we have

$$\int_{\underline{x}}^{\overline{x}} f(x)\, dx = 1. \tag{A.63}$$

2. *Discrete distributions*. There is a finite set of possible states of the world

$$\Omega := \{1, 2, \ldots, \varpi\} \tag{A.64}$$

and the density associated with state ω is a non-negative number π_ω. If the states are labelled in increasing order of payoff x_ω then the distribution is characterised by the vector of probabilities

$$\left.\begin{array}{c} \pi := (\pi_1, \pi_2, \ldots \pi_\varpi) \\ \text{such that } \pi_1 + \pi_2 + \ldots + \pi_\varpi = 1 \end{array}\right\} \tag{A.65}$$

and the distribution function takes the form of a step function:

$$F(x) = \begin{cases} 0 & \text{if } x < x_1 \\ \sum_{j=1}^{\omega} \pi_j & \text{if } x_{\omega-1} \le x < x_\omega,\ \omega = 2, \ldots \varpi \\ 1 & \text{if } x \ge x_\varpi \end{cases}$$

Although there are many economically interesting 'hybrid' cases these two categories are sufficient for the types of models that we will need to use. Section A.8.3 contains some simple examples of F.

A.8.1 Statistics

For our purposes a *statistic* is just a mapping from the set of all probability distributions to the real line. Some standard statistics of the distribution are useful for summarising its general characteristics.

Definition A.29

The *median* of the distribution is the smallest value x_{med} such that

$$F(x_{\text{med}}) = 0.5.$$

Definition A.30

The *expectation* of a random variable X with distribution function F is

$$\mathcal{E}x := \int x\, dF(x).$$

Definition A.31

The *variance* of a random variable X with distribution function F is

$$\text{var}(x) := \int x^2 dF(x) - [\mathcal{E}x]^2 .$$

From the given distribution of the random variable we can derive distributions of other useful concepts. For example, the variance can be written equivalently in terms of the distribution of the random variable X^2 as

$$\text{var}(x) = \left[\mathcal{E}x^2\right] - [\mathcal{E}x]^2 .$$

Often one is interested in the distribution of a general transformation of the random variable represented by some function $\varphi(\cdot)$: for example the distribution of utility if utility is a function of wealth and wealth is a random variable. The property of concave functions given in Remark A.4 (page 502) also gives us:

Corollary A.4 (Jensen's inequality)

If $\varphi(\cdot)$ is a continuous, monotonic, concave function defined on the support of F then:

$$\int \varphi(x)\, dF(x) \le \varphi\left(\int x dF(x)\right)$$

or, equivalently

$$\mathcal{E}\varphi(x) \le \varphi(\mathcal{E}x) . \tag{A.66}$$

Now consider a collection of N variables with the same distribution F. Order them in such a way that

$$X_{[1]} \le X_{[2]} \le \ldots \le X_{[N]}.$$

Then $X_{[k]}, k = 1, 2, \ldots, N$ is known as the kth *order statistic* of the sample of size N. Because of the special order imposed on them the statistics $X_{[k]}$ are not distributed according to the distribution function F but according to the derived distribution $F_{[k]}(\cdot)$ given by

$$F_{[k]}(x) = \sum_{j=k}^{N} \binom{N}{j} F(x)^j \left[1 - F(x)\right]^{N-j} . \tag{A.67}$$

The expectation of the kth order statistic can be derived from (A.67) as

$$\mathcal{E}X_{[k]} = \int x dF_{[k]}(x) = \frac{n!}{[k-1]!\,[n-k]!} \int xF(x)^{k-1} \left[1 - F(x)\right]^{n-k} dF(x) . \tag{A.68}$$

A.8.2 Bayes's rule

Let E_1, E_2, E_3 be subsets of S (the support of the distribution) and let $\bar{E}_i := S \backslash E_i$ be the complement of E_i in S. Write $\Pr(E_i)$ as equivalent to $\Pr(X \in E_i)$. By definition of probability, if $E_1 \cap E_2 = \varnothing$ then

$$\Pr(E_1 \cap E_2) = \Pr(E_1) + \Pr(E_2)$$

and

$$\Pr(E_i) + \Pr\left(\bar{E}_i\right) = \Pr(S) = 1.$$

Definition A.32

The *conditional probability* of E_2 given E_1 is the probability that $X \in E_2$ given that $X \in E_1$:

$$\Pr(E_2|E_1) := \frac{\Pr(E_2 \cap E_1)}{\Pr(E_1)} .$$

By definition of the complement of E_1 we have

$$\begin{aligned}\Pr(E_1) &= \Pr(E_1 \cap E_2) + \Pr(E_1 \cap \bar{E}_2) \\ &= \Pr(E_1|E_2)\Pr(E_2) + \Pr(E_1|\bar{E}_2)\Pr(\bar{E}_2). \end{aligned} \tag{A.69}$$

From definition A.32 and (A.69) we get *Bayes's rule*:

$$\Pr(E_2|E_1) = \frac{\Pr(E_1|E_2)\Pr(E_2)}{\Pr(E_1|E_2)\Pr(E_2) + \Pr(E_1|\bar{E}_2)\Pr(\bar{E}_2)}.$$

A.8.3 Probability distributions: examples

A number of standard statistical distributions are often useful in simple economic models. We review here just a few of the more useful:

Elementary discrete distribution

$$F(x) = \left\{ \begin{array}{ll} 0, & x < x_0 \\ \pi_0, & x_0 \leq x < x_1 \\ 1, & x \geq x_1 \end{array} \right\}$$

This example puts a probability mass of π_0 on the value x_0 and a probability mass of $1 - \pi_0$ on the value x_1.

Rectangular distribution

The density is assumed to be uniform over the interval $[x_0, x_1]$ and zero elsewhere:

$$f(x) = \left\{ \begin{array}{ll} \dfrac{1}{x_1 - x_0} & \text{if } x_0 \leq x \leq x_1 \\ 0 & \text{elsewhere} \end{array} \right\}$$

$$F(x) = \left\{ \begin{array}{lll} 0 & \text{if} & x < x_0 \\ \dfrac{x - x_0}{x_1 - x_0} & \text{if} & x_0 \leq x < x_1 \\ 1 & \text{if} & x \geq x_1 \end{array} \right\}$$

Normal distribution

This has the whole real line as its support. The variable x is distributed with the density

$$f(x) = \frac{1}{\sqrt{2\pi}\sigma} e^{-\frac{1}{2\sigma^2}[x-\mu]^2}$$

where μ, σ are parameters with $\sigma > 0$. The mean of the distribution is μ and the variance is σ^2.

Lognormal distribution

This has the set of non-negative reals as its support. If the logarithm of x is distributed normally, then x itself is distributed with the density

$$f(x) = \frac{1}{\sqrt{2\pi}\sigma x} e^{-\frac{1}{2\sigma^2}\log[x-\mu]^2}$$

where μ, σ are parameters with $\sigma > 0$. The parameter μ determines location: e^{μ} is the median of the distribution. The parameter σ is a measure of dispersion. In contrast to the normal distribution the lognormal is distribution skewed to the right.

Beta distribution

A useful example of a single-peaked distribution with bounded support is given by the density function

$$f(x) = \frac{x^a [1 - x]^b}{B(a, b)}$$

where $0 \leq x \leq 1$, a, b are positive parameters and $B(a, b) := \int_0^1 x^a [1 - x]^b \, dx$. The corresponding distribution function is found by integration of f.

A.9 Reading notes

For an overall review of concepts and methods there are several suitable books on mathematics designed for economists such as Chiang (1984), de la Fuente (1999), Ostaszewski (1993), Simon and Blume (1994), or Sydsæter and Hammond (1995). A useful summary of results is to be found in the very short, but rather formal, book by Sydsæter et al. (1999).

On optimisation in economics see Dixit (1990) and Sundaram (2002). For more on applications of convexity and fixed-point theorems see Green and Heller (1981) and (for the mathematically inclined) the very thorough treatment by Border (1985).

A useful introduction to the elements of probability theory for economists is given in Spanos (1999); for a more advanced treatment see Hoffman-Jørgensen (1994). For more information on specific distribution functions with applications to economics see Kleiber and Kotz (2003).

APPENDIX B

Answers to Mini Problems

B.1 Introduction

1. The answer depends on the exact shape of the pencil. Suppose it has an octagonal section. Then there is an equilibrium corresponding to each one of its eight 'faces'. Each of these equilibria is stable. There is also an equilibrium at the blunt end of the pencil—this is stable under small shocks. There is also an unstable equilibrium at its sharp end: you could in principle balance the pencil on its point, but the slightest perturbation would take it back to one of the eight 'face' equilibria.

B.2 The firm

1. Sales maximisation, or maximisation of managerial utility subject to a profit constraint, for example.

2. We need to introduce time and/or uncertainty into the model, or some return from the firm which is not measured in money (for example the supposed power that comes from owning a newspaper).

3. Figure B.1 illustrates the $Z(q)$ set for the minimum size of operation of the firm. Points $\mathbf{z}^0$ and $\mathbf{z}'$ represent situations where the headquarters is in location 1, 2 respectively. The minimum viable size of office and of headquarters constitute indivisibilities in the production technology.

4. Write $r_{ij} := \log(z_j/z_i)$ for the log-input price ratio and $m_{ij} := \phi_j(\mathbf{z})/\phi_i(\mathbf{z})$ for the log-MRTS$_{ij}$. Then the definition in equation (2.6) can be written

$$\sigma_{ij} = -\frac{\partial r_{ij}}{\partial m_{ij}}. \tag{B.1}$$

But it is clear that $r_{ji} = \log(z_i/z_j) = -\log(z_j/z_i) = -r_{ij}$ and $m_{ji} = -m_{ij}$. So we have $dr_{ji} = -dr_{ij}$ and $dm_{ji} = -dm_{ij}$, which means that

$$\sigma_{ji} = -\frac{\partial r_{ji}}{\partial m_{ji}} = -\frac{-\partial r_{ij}}{-\partial m_{ij}} = -\frac{\partial r_{ij}}{\partial m_{ij}} \tag{B.2}$$

as required.

5. (a) It is sufficient to differentiate the relationship with respect to z_i and with respect to z_1:

$$\frac{\hat{\phi}_i(\mathbf{z})}{\hat{\phi}_1(\mathbf{z})} = \frac{\Psi_1(q)\,\phi_i(\mathbf{z})}{\Psi_1(q)\,\phi_1(\mathbf{z})} \tag{B.3}$$

where Ψ_1 is the derivative of Ψ and

$$q = \phi(\mathbf{z}).$$

Then the result follows immediately from (B.3). However, a stronger result is also available: if the MRTS property holds for all $\mathbf{z}$ then this alone implies that $\hat{\phi} = \Psi(\phi)$—see Lemma C.1 in Appendix C. (b) This follows using the same method as part (a). Again, a stronger result is also available: if the MRTS property holds for all $\mathbf{z}$ then this alone implies that $\phi(\mathbf{z}^\circ, \mathbf{z}') = \Psi(\psi(\mathbf{z}^\circ), \mathbf{z}')$—see Theorem C.1 in Appendix C.

6. In the following let t be any positive scalar. Note that (by definition) in all cases where ϕ is homogeneous, it is also homothetic.

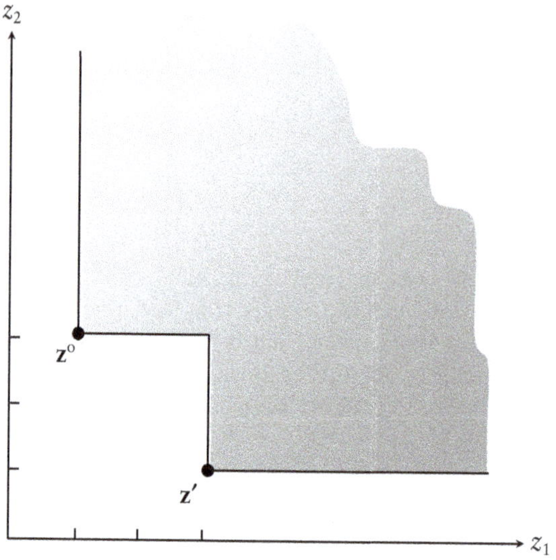

Figure B.1 Labour input in two locations

1. $\phi(t\mathbf{z}) = [tz_1]^{0.1}[tz_2]^{0.2} = t^{0.3}z_1^{0.1}z_2^{0.2} = t^{0.3}\phi(\mathbf{z})$. So ϕ is homogeneous of degree 0.3.
2. $\phi(t\mathbf{z}) = \log(tz_1) + 2\log(tz_2) = 3\log(t) + \log(z_1) + 2\log(z_2) = 3\log(t) + \phi(\mathbf{z})$. So ϕ is not homogeneous. However, we can write $\phi(\mathbf{z}) = \log\left(\hat{\phi}(\mathbf{z})\right)$ where $\hat{\phi}(\mathbf{z}) := z_1 z_2^2$; since the function $\hat{\phi}$ is homogeneous it is clear that ϕ is homothetic. Notice that the production function here can be obtained from the production function in case 1 just by applying the transformation $10\log(\cdot)$. So the contour map of the isoquants in this case is exactly the same as in case 1; but, of course, the q-values on the isoquants will be different in the two cases.
3. $\phi(t\mathbf{z}) = [tz_1]^{0.5} + 2[tz_2]^{0.5} = t^{0.5}\left[z_1^{0.5} + 2z_2^{0.5}\right] = t^{0.5}\phi(\mathbf{z})$. So ϕ is homogeneous of degree 0.5.
4. $\phi(t\mathbf{z}) = \exp\left([tz_1]^{0.5}[tz_2]^{0.5}\right) = \exp\left(tz_1^{0.5}z_2^{0.5}\right) = \left[\exp\left(z_1^{0.5}z_2^{0.5}\right)\right]^t = \phi(\mathbf{z})^t$. So ϕ is not homogeneous. However, we can write $\phi(\mathbf{z}) = \exp\left(\hat{\phi}(\mathbf{z})\right)$ where $\hat{\phi}(\mathbf{z}) := z_1^{0.5}z_2^{0.5}$; since the function $\hat{\phi}$ is homogeneous it is clear that ϕ is homothetic.
5. $\phi(t\mathbf{z}) = \left[tz_1 - k\right]^{0.5} + \left[tz_2 - k\right]^{0.5}$. It is clear that ϕ does not satisfy the standard definition of homotheticity. However, on examining Figure B.2 it is also clear that if the origin were shifted from $(0, 0)$ to (k, k) then the contours with respect to the new axes would be homothetic. We might say that such a function is 'homothetic to the point (k, k)'.
6. Not homothetic. There is no transformation of ϕ which would yield a homogeneous function.

7. Increasing returns: $r > 1$; constant returns $r = 1$; decreasing returns: $r < 1$.
8. In what follows, assume that $t > 1$.

1. ϕ is homogeneous of degree 0.3, so decreasing returns to scale.
2. $\phi(t\mathbf{z}) = 3\log(t) + \phi(\mathbf{z})$ which is greater or less than $t\phi(\mathbf{z})$ according as

$$3\log(t) + \phi(\mathbf{z}) \gtrless t\phi(\mathbf{z})$$

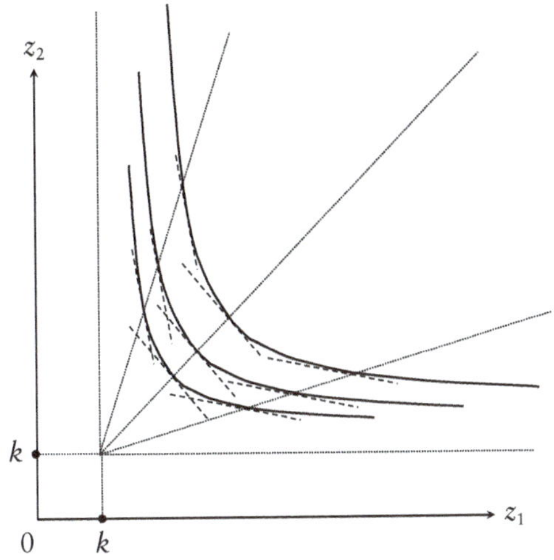

Figure B.2 A function homothetic to point (k, k)

i.e. according as $\phi(\mathbf{z}) \lesseqgtr \underline{q}$ where

$$\underline{q} := \frac{3\log(t)}{t-1}$$

So we have increasing returns for output below $\underline{q}$, decreasing returns above $\underline{q}$.

3. Decreasing returns to scale for same reason as in part 1.

4. $\phi(t\mathbf{z}) = \phi(\mathbf{z})^t$ which is greater or less than $t\phi(\mathbf{z})$ according as

$$\phi(\mathbf{z})^t \gtrless t\phi(\mathbf{z})$$

i.e. according as

$$\phi(\mathbf{z}) \gtrless t^{\frac{1}{t-1}}.$$

So we have decreasing returns for low output, increasing returns for high output.

5. Along the diagonal we have $\phi(t\mathbf{z}) = 2\left[tz_1 - k\right]^{0.5}$ which is greater or less than $t\phi(\mathbf{z})$ according as

$$\left[tz_1 - k\right]^{0.5} \gtrless t\left[z_1 - k\right]^{0.5}$$

$$tz_1 - k \gtrless t^2 z_1 - t^2 k$$

$$\left[t^2 - t\right] z_1 \lesseqgtr \left[t^2 - 1\right] k$$

$$z_1 \lesseqgtr \frac{t^2 - 1}{t^2 - t} k.$$

So we have increasing returns for low input, decreasing returns for high input .

6. It is clear that $t^{0.1} z_1^{0.1} + t^{0.2} z_2^{0.2} < t z_1^{0.1} + t z_2^{0.2}$ so we have decreasing returns to scale.

9. For case 2 see Figure 6.3.

10. Case 1 in Figure 2.1 corresponds to case 1 in Figure 2.8. As an example consider the production function $q = \sqrt{z_1 z_2}$. Case 4 (bottom right) in Figure 2.1 corresponds to case 2 in

Figure 2.8. Example $q = \min\{a_1z_1, a_2z_2\}$. The other two panels represent non-concave production functions and so cannot be constant returns to scale.

11. First let us note that (2.12) can be thought of as a form of (A.49); but it is a *minimisation* problem. Minimising $\mathcal{L}$ is the same as maximising $-\mathcal{L}$; so to write out the Kuhn–Tucker conditions we just need to reinterpret the notation and put in an appropriate minus sign. The direct 'translation' (A.50) to (A.53) in the firm's cost-minimisation problem then yields the following FOCs:

$$-\frac{\partial \mathcal{L}(\mathbf{z}^*, \lambda^*; \mathbf{w}, q)}{\partial z_i} \leq 0,\ i = 1, \ldots, m, \tag{B.4}$$

$$-z_i^* \frac{\partial \mathcal{L}(\mathbf{z}^*, \lambda^*; \mathbf{w}, q)}{\partial z_i} = 0,\ i = 1, \ldots, m, \tag{B.5}$$

$$-\frac{\partial \mathcal{L}(\mathbf{z}^*, \lambda^*; \mathbf{w}, q)}{\partial \lambda} \geq 0, \tag{B.6}$$

$$-\lambda^* \frac{\partial \mathcal{L}(\mathbf{z}^*, \lambda^*; \mathbf{w}, q)}{\partial \lambda} = 0. \tag{B.7}$$

Evaluating (B.4)–(B.7) using the right-hand side of (2.12) we have

$$-w_i + \lambda \phi(_i\mathbf{z}^*) \leq 0,\ i = 1, \ldots, m, \tag{B.8}$$

$$-z_i^* \left[w_i - \lambda \phi_i(\mathbf{z}^*)\right] = 0,\ i = 1, \ldots, m, \tag{B.9}$$

$$-q + \phi(\mathbf{z}^*) \geq 0, \tag{B.10}$$

$$-\lambda^* \left[q - \phi(\mathbf{z}^*)\right] = 0. \tag{B.11}$$

It is clear that the complementary slackness condition immediately gives us the results that (from B.8, B.9)

$$\lambda^* \phi_i(\mathbf{z}^*) < w_i \tag{B.12}$$

only if $z_i^* = 0$ and that (from B.10, B.11)

$$q < \phi(\mathbf{z}^*) \tag{B.13}$$

only if $\lambda^* = 0$.

12. In non-trivial cases we must have at least one input i which is utilised in positive amounts and for which the input price w_i is positive. Applying (2.13) gives the result.

13. If $\phi(\mathbf{z}) > q$ then you could cut all the inputs a little bit and still meet the output target; cutting the inputs would, of course, reduce costs, so you could not have been at a cost-minimising point.

14. (a) The equilibrium is a corner solution, illustrated in Figure B.3. (b) If the firm were not using any of input j and its valuation of j at the margin were strictly less than the market price then it would not want to use any j. (ii) The firm would go on substituting i for j up until the point where its valuation of j exactly equals the price of j in the market.

15. (a) The Lagrangean is

$$\mathcal{L}(\mathbf{z}, \mu; \mathbf{w}, q) := w_1z_1 + w_2z_2 + \mu \left[\log q - \frac{1}{4}\log z_1 - \frac{3}{4}\log z_2\right]$$

where μ is a Lagrange multiplier. Note that this is equivalent to the following

$$w_1z_1 + w_2z_2 + \lambda\left[q - z_1^{0.25} z_2^{0.75}\right].$$

The reason is that the constraint $q \leq z_1^{0.25} z_2^{0.75}$ holds whenever the constraint $\log q \leq \frac{1}{4}\log z_1 + \frac{3}{4}\log z_2$ holds. However, if we transform the problem in this way we will have a different value for the Lagrange multiplier.

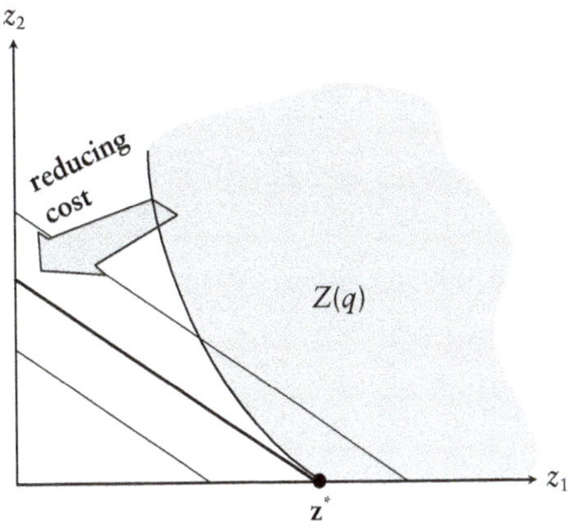

Figure B.3 Cost minimisation: a corner solution

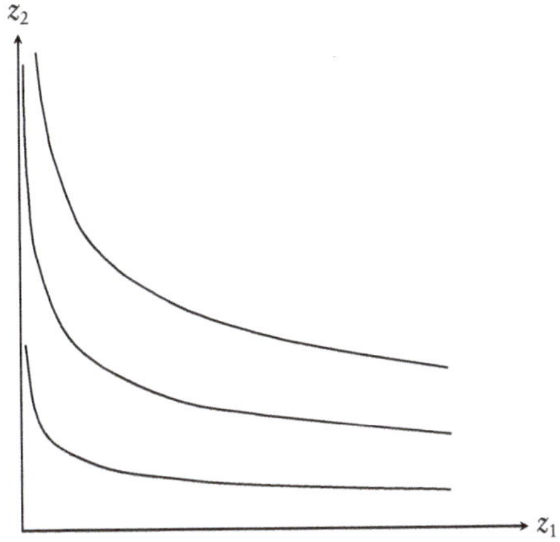

Figure B.4 Cobb–Douglas isoquants

(b) The isoquants have the shape depicted in Figure B.4. It is clear that they do not touch the axis at any finite input. To confirm this note that, for given q, the equation of the isoquant is

$$z_2 = q^{4/3} z_1^{-1/3}.$$

Clearly if q is positive and finite then $z_1 \to 0$ implies $z_2 \to \infty$; likewise $z_2 \to 0$ implies $z_1 \to \infty$.

(c) Given that there are no corner solutions we can write the FOC as equalities

$$\frac{\partial \mathcal{L}}{\partial z_1} = 0; \ \frac{\partial \mathcal{L}}{\partial z_2} = 0; \ \frac{\partial \mathcal{L}}{\partial \mu} = 0.$$

Carrying out the differentiation we have

$$w_1 - \frac{1}{4}\frac{\mu^*}{z_1^*} = 0 \tag{B.14}$$

$$w_2 - \frac{3}{4}\frac{\mu^*}{z_2^*} = 0 \tag{B.15}$$

$$\log q - \frac{1}{4}\log z_1^* - \frac{3}{4}\log z_2^* = 0 \tag{B.16}$$

where the asterisks denote the optimal (cost-minimising) values. Rearranging (B.14) and (B.15) we have

$$\log z_1^* = \log\left(\frac{1}{4}\mu^*\right) - \log w_1 \tag{B.17}$$

$$\log z_2^* = \log\left(\frac{3}{4}\mu^*\right) - \log w_2 \tag{B.18}$$

and so, substituting into (B.16), we get

$$\log q + \log k - \log\mu^* + \frac{1}{4}\log w_1 + \frac{3}{4}\log w_2 = 0 \tag{B.19}$$

where

$$k := 0.25^{-0.25} \times 0.75^{-0.75} \simeq 1.755. \tag{B.20}$$

Rearranging (B.19) we find the optimised Lagrange multiplier:

$$\mu^* = k w_1^{0.25} w_2^{0.75} q. \tag{B.21}$$

So from (B.17) and (B.18) we get the cost-minimising values

$$z_1^* = \frac{1}{4}\frac{\mu^*}{w_1} \tag{B.22}$$

$$z_2^* = \frac{3}{4}\frac{\mu^*}{w_2}. \tag{B.23}$$

(d) By definition minimised cost is $w_1 z_1^* + w_2 z_2^*$; multiplying (B.22) by w_1, (B.23) by w_2 and then adding, it is clear that minimised cost is just μ^*. But we have already computed μ^* as a function of the given values q, w_1 and w_2. So (B.21) yields the cost function

$$C(\mathbf{w}, q) = 1.755\, w_1^{0.25} w_2^{0.75} q. \tag{B.24}$$

16. The firm might not be buying any of input i at the optimum. Therefore its costs are unaffected by a small increase in w_i.

17. Note first from Remark A.4 on page 502 that function f is concave if for all $\mathbf{x}, \mathbf{x}' \in X, 0 \leq a \leq 1$:

$$af(\mathbf{x}) + [1-a]f(\mathbf{x}') \leq f(a\mathbf{x} + [1-a]\mathbf{x}'). \tag{B.25}$$

Now consider any two input price vectors $\mathbf{w}$ and $\mathbf{w}'$ and let a be any number between zero and 1 inclusive. We can form another input-price vector as the combination $\overline{\mathbf{w}} := a\mathbf{w} + [1-a]\mathbf{w}'$; if $\mathbf{z}^*$ is the cost-minimising input vector for $\overline{\mathbf{w}}$ then, for any q, by definition:

$$C(\overline{\mathbf{w}}, q) = \sum_{i=1}^{m} \overline{w}_i z_i^* = \sum_{i=1}^{m} \left[a w_i + [1-a] w_i'\right] z_i^*.$$

A simple rearrangement gives

$$C(a\mathbf{w} + [1-a]\mathbf{w}', q) = a\sum_{i=1}^{m} w_i z_i^* + [1-a]\sum_{i=1}^{m} w_i' z_i^*. \tag{B.26}$$

By definition of cost minimisation we have, for prices $\mathbf{w}$, $C(\mathbf{w}, q) \leq \sum_{i=1}^m w_i z_i^*$ and, for prices $\mathbf{w}'$, $C(\mathbf{w}', q) \leq \sum_{i=1}^m w_i' z_i^*$. Therefore, substituting these two inequalities in (B.26) we have

$$C(a\mathbf{w} + [1-a]\mathbf{w}', q) \geq aC(\mathbf{w}, q) + [1-a]C(\mathbf{w}', q). \tag{B.27}$$

But checking this against the property of a concave function given in (B.25) we can see that (B.27) implies that C is concave in $\mathbf{w}$.

18. Minimised cost may be written as

$$C(\mathbf{w},q) = \sum_{i=1}^{m} w_i z_i^* = \sum_{i=1}^{m} w_i H^i(\mathbf{w},q)\,. \tag{B.28}$$

Differentiating (2.20) as suggested, we have

$$\frac{\partial}{\partial w_i}\left(\sum_{j=1}^{m} H^j(\mathbf{w},q)\right) = z_i^* + \sum_{j=1}^{m} w_j H_i^j(\mathbf{w},q) \tag{B.29}$$

where $H_i^j(\mathbf{w},q) := \frac{\partial H^j(\mathbf{w},q)}{\partial w_i}$. However, condition (2.15) implies, for a given q,

$$0 = \sum_{j=1}^{m} \phi_j(\mathbf{z}^*) H_i^j(\mathbf{w},q)\,. \tag{B.30}$$

Using the assumption that $z_j^* > 0$ (2.13) and (B.30) imply

$$0 = \lambda^* \sum_{j=1}^{m} w_j H_i^j(\mathbf{w},q)\,. \tag{B.31}$$

From this we immediately see that the last term in (B.29) must be zero and the result follows. See also the remarks on the envelope theorem in section A.7.4 on page 511.

19. Let there be increasing returns to scale over the output levels $\bar{q}$ to $t\bar{q}$ where $t > 1$, and let $\bar{\mathbf{z}}$ be cost minimising for $\bar{q}$ at input prices $\mathbf{w}$. Now consider the input vector $\hat{\mathbf{z}} := t\bar{\mathbf{z}}$, and let $\hat{q} := \phi(\hat{\mathbf{z}})$. Given increasing returns to scale we know that

$$\hat{q} = \phi(t\bar{\mathbf{z}}) > t\phi(\bar{\mathbf{z}}) = t\bar{q}. \tag{B.32}$$

However, by definition of the cost function,

$$C(\mathbf{w},\hat{q}) \le \sum_{j=1}^{m} w_j \hat{z}_j \tag{B.33}$$

which, by definition of $\hat{\mathbf{z}}$, yields

$$C(\mathbf{w},\hat{q}) \le t\left[\sum_{j=1}^{m} w_j \bar{z}_j\right] = t\,[C(\mathbf{w},\bar{q})]\,. \tag{B.34}$$

From (B.32) and (B.34) we immediately get

$$\frac{C(\mathbf{w},\hat{q})}{\hat{q}} \le \frac{C(\mathbf{w},\bar{q})}{\bar{q}} \tag{B.35}$$

which shows that average cost must be falling as output is increased from $\bar{q}$ to $t\bar{q}$. The decreasing return to scale case follows similarly.

20. Differentiate average cost $C(\mathbf{w},q)/q$ with respect to q:

$$\frac{\partial}{\partial q}\left(\frac{C(\mathbf{w},q)}{q}\right) = \frac{1}{q}\left[C_q(\mathbf{w},q) - \frac{C(\mathbf{w},q)}{q}\right]. \tag{B.36}$$

The term in [ ] is MC-AC, which proves the result.

21. From (2.12) and (2.13) the maximised value of the Lagrangean is.

$$\mathcal{L}^*(\mathbf{w},q) := \sum_{i=1}^{m} w_i z_i^*(\mathbf{w},q) - \lambda^*(\mathbf{w},q)\,[\phi(\mathbf{z}^*(\mathbf{w},q)) - q] \tag{B.37}$$

at the optimum. Given that production is efficient here (see 2.15) we have also

$$C(\mathbf{w},q) = \mathcal{L}^*(\mathbf{w},q). \tag{B.38}$$

Differentiating (B.37) with respect to q, and using (2.15) and (2.13), we have

$$\begin{aligned}\frac{\partial}{\partial q}\mathcal{L}^*(\mathbf{w},q) &= \sum_{i=1}^{m} w_i \frac{\partial}{\partial q} z_i^*(\mathbf{w},q) - \lambda^*(\mathbf{w},q)\left[\frac{\partial}{\partial q}\phi(\mathbf{z}^*(\mathbf{w},q)) - 1\right] \\ &= \lambda^*(\mathbf{w},q)\sum_{i=1}^{m}\phi_i(\mathbf{z}^*)\frac{\partial}{\partial q}z_i^*(\mathbf{w},q) \\ &\quad -\lambda^*(\mathbf{w},q)\left[\sum_{i=1}^{m}\phi_i(\mathbf{z}^*)\frac{\partial}{\partial q}z_i^*(\mathbf{w},q) - 1\right] \\ &= \lambda^*(\mathbf{w},q).\end{aligned}$$

This and (B.38) establishes the result. For a more general treatment see section A.7.4.

22. Presumably similar new firms would set up to exploit these profits.

23. We want AC to be at first falling and then rising: by virtue of question 19 this requires first increasing returns to scale and then decreasing returns to scale.

24. The boundary should look rather like that in panel 1 of Figure 2.1, but with a finite number of kinks: draw it by overlaying one smooth curve with another and then erasing the redundant arc segments. Conditional input demand is locally constant with respect to input price wherever the isocost line is on a kink, and falls steadily with input price elsewhere.

25. Because C is homogeneous of degree 1 in $\mathbf{w}$, so too is C_q: therefore the first-order condition $p = C_q(\mathbf{w}, q^*)$—which is used to derive the supply function—reveals that if both $\mathbf{w}$ and p are multiplied by some positive scalar t, optimal output q^* remains unchanged; this implies that S is homogeneous of degree zero in $(\mathbf{w}, p)$. We know that $H^i(\mathbf{w}, q)$ is homogeneous of degree zero in $\mathbf{w}$; so the homogeneity of degree zero of S implies that $H^i(\mathbf{w}, S(\mathbf{w}, p))$ also has this property; this means that $D^i(\mathbf{w}, p)$ is homogeneous of degree zero in $(\mathbf{w}, p)$.

26. Differentiate (2.36) with respect to p

$$\frac{\partial}{\partial p}C_q(\mathbf{w}, S(\mathbf{w},p)) = 1;$$

using the function-of-a-function rule, we get

$$C_{qq}(\mathbf{w}, S(\mathbf{w},p))S_p(\mathbf{w},p) = 1. \tag{B.39}$$

So, rearranging and using (2.33), we find (2.37).

27. Shephard's Lemma tells us that

$$H^i(\mathbf{w},q) = C_i(\mathbf{w},q). \tag{B.40}$$

Differentiating (B.40) with respect to q:

$$H^i_q(\mathbf{w},q) = C_{iq}(\mathbf{w},q) = C_{qi}(\mathbf{w},q). \tag{B.41}$$

28. Differentiate (2.36) with respect to w_j:

$$C_{qj}(\mathbf{w}, S(\mathbf{w},p)) + C_{qq}(\mathbf{w}, S(\mathbf{w},p))\, S_j(\mathbf{w},p) = 0$$

which will give us the derivative of the supply function, S_j. This and the answer to question 27 then give the result.

29. Because C is concave, for any m-vector $\mathbf{x}$ it must be true that

$$\sum_{i=1}^{m}\sum_{j=1}^{m} x_i x_j C_{ij} \le 0 \tag{B.42}$$

(see Theorem A.10). So take the case where $\mathbf{x}$ has 1 for the ith component, and 0 elsewhere: $\mathbf{x} = (0, 0, \ldots, 0, 1, 0 \ldots, 0)$. It is immediate that (B.42) implies that $C_{ii} \le 0$.

30. No. See page 87 for an explanation.

31. Differentiating (B.24) with respect to z_1 and z_2 respectively the conditional demand functions are found as

$$H^1(\mathbf{w},q) = \frac{\partial C(\mathbf{w},q)}{\partial w_1} = 0.439\left[\frac{w_2}{w_1}\right]^{0.75} q \tag{B.43}$$

$$H^2(\mathbf{w},q) = \frac{\partial C(\mathbf{w},q)}{\partial w_2} = 1.316\left[\frac{w_1}{w_2}\right]^{0.25} q \tag{B.44}$$

which we knew anyway from the answer to Mini Problem 15. Therefore, differentiating (B.43) and (B.44) we get

$$H^1_2(\mathbf{w},q) = \frac{H^1(\mathbf{w},q)}{\partial w_2} = \frac{\partial^2 C(\mathbf{w},q)}{\partial w_1 \partial w_2} = 0.329\, w_2^{-0.25} w_1^{-0.75} q \tag{B.45}$$

$$H^2_1(\mathbf{w},q) = \frac{H^2(\mathbf{w},q)}{\partial w_1} = \frac{\partial^2 C(\mathbf{w},q)}{\partial w_2 \partial w_1} = 0.329\, w_2^{-0.25} w_1^{-0.75} q \tag{B.46}$$

$$H^1_1(\mathbf{w},q) = \frac{H^1(\mathbf{w},q)}{\partial w_1} = \frac{\partial^2 C(\mathbf{w},q)}{\partial^2 w_1^2} = -0.329\, w_2^{0.75} w_1^{-1.75} q < 0 \tag{B.47}$$

$$H^2_2(\mathbf{w},q) = \frac{H^2(\mathbf{w},q)}{\partial w_2} = \frac{\partial^2 C(\mathbf{w},q)}{\partial w_2^2} = -0.329\, w_1^{0.25} w_2^{-1.25} q < 0 \tag{B.48}$$

Clearly (B.45) and (B.46) are the same, which verifies part (a) of the theorem; (B.47) and (B.48) verify part (c) of the theorem.

32. Yes: the ordinary demand curve must always be flatter than the conditional demand curve (although this is not the case in consumer theory). The reason for this result is that, whether C_{iq} is negative (the inferior case) or non-negative (the normal case), we must have

$$-\frac{C_{iq}(\mathbf{w},q^*)^2}{C_{qq}(\mathbf{w},q^*)} \geq 0 \tag{B.49}$$

so that, from (2.43):

$$D^i_i(\mathbf{w},p) \leq H^i_i(\mathbf{w},q^*) \tag{B.50}$$

with strict inequality in (B.49) and (B.50) if changing the price of input i has a non-zero effect on marginal cost.

33. In macro models one often considers capital to be fixed, with labour (and possibly raw materials) variable.

34. Observe that because $w_m \bar{z}_m$ is a constant (in the short run) it drops out of the expressions involving derivatives.

35. At the point $q = \bar{q}$, the input level $\bar{z}_m$ is cost minimising; therefore costs will be invariant to small changes in $\bar{z}_m$. Differentiate (2.49) with respect to q so as to yield, in the neighbourhood of $q = \bar{q}$:

$$\tilde{C}_q\left(\mathbf{w},q,H^m(\mathbf{w},q)\right) + \frac{\partial \tilde{C}(\mathbf{w},q,H^m(\mathbf{w},q))}{\partial \bar{z}_m} H^m_q(\mathbf{w},q) = C_q(\mathbf{w},q). \tag{B.51}$$

Given that $\partial\tilde{C}/\partial\bar{z}_m = 0$ at $q = \bar{q}$ the result follows.

36. From (2.32), in the long run the demand for input m is given by

$$z_m = H^m(\mathbf{w},q).$$

So the long-run cost curve can be written as

$$C(\mathbf{w},q) = \tilde{C}(\mathbf{w},q,H^m(\mathbf{w},q)). \tag{B.52}$$

The counterpart of (A.39) is the short-run constraint

$$z_m - \bar{z}_m = 0$$

and it is clear that the differential of the left-hand side of this constraint with respect to q is zero. So, applying Theorem A.13 we have

$$\frac{\tilde{C}(\mathbf{w}, q, \bar{z}_m)}{\partial q} = \frac{\tilde{C}(\mathbf{w}, q, H^m(\mathbf{w}, q))}{\partial q}. \tag{B.53}$$

In other words, using (B.51):

$$\frac{\tilde{C}(\mathbf{w}, q, \bar{z}_m)}{\partial q} = \frac{C(\mathbf{w}, q)}{\partial q}. \tag{B.54}$$

37. Writing short-run costs as $V(w_1, \ldots, w_{m-1}, q, \bar{z}_m) + w_m \bar{z}_m$ where the first term represents variable costs and the second term fixed costs we can see that short-run marginal cost q is $V_q(w_1, \ldots, w_{m-1}, q, \bar{z}_m)$ which is independent of w_m. Hence we have $\partial \tilde{C}_q / \partial w_m = 0$, and so differentiating (2.50) with respect to w_m we get

$$\tilde{C}_{q\bar{z}_m}(\mathbf{w}, \bar{q}, \bar{z}_m)\, H^m_m(\mathbf{w}, \bar{q}) = C_{qm}(\mathbf{w}, \bar{q}). \tag{B.55}$$

Use Shephard's Lemma for the right-hand side to obtain:

$$\tilde{C}_{q\bar{z}_m}(\mathbf{w}, \bar{q}, \bar{z}_m) = \frac{H^m_q(\mathbf{w}, \bar{q})}{H^m_m(\mathbf{w}, \bar{q})}. \tag{B.56}$$

Substitute this into (2.53) and the result follows.

38. Differentiating equation (2.52) with respect to w_i as suggested we get

$$\tilde{H}^i_i(\mathbf{w}, \bar{q}, \bar{z}_m) + \tilde{H}^i_{\bar{z}_m}(\mathbf{w}, \bar{q}, \bar{z}_m) H^m_i(\mathbf{w}, \bar{q}) = H^i_i(\mathbf{w}, \bar{q}). \tag{B.57}$$

Differentiating (2.52) with respect to w_m we get

$$\tilde{H}^i_{\bar{z}_m}(\mathbf{w}, \bar{q}, \bar{z}_m) + H^m_m(\mathbf{w}, \bar{q}) = H^i_m(\mathbf{w}, \bar{q}). \tag{B.58}$$

(Compare the answer to problem 37 in order to see why $\partial \tilde{H}^i / \partial w_m = 0$.) Substituting from (B.58) into (B.57) gives the answer.

39. If 'ideal size' means the situation where the firm is just breaking even in the long run then redraw the short-run average cost curve so that it is tangential to the long-run AC curve exactly at its minimum point.

40. $\Phi(\mathbf{q})$ becomes $q_{m+1} - \phi(-q_1, -q_2, \ldots, -q_m)$ where $q_i = -z_i \leq 0, i = 1, 2, \ldots, m$ (the inputs) and $q_{m+1} = q \geq 0$ (the output).

41. The convention is that $\Phi(\mathbf{q}) \leq 0$ denotes feasibility and $\Phi(\mathbf{q}) > 0$ infeasibility. Consider a net output vector $\mathbf{q}^*$ which is just feasible: $\Phi(\mathbf{q}^*) = 0$; by definition, raising output (increasing a positive component of $\mathbf{q}^*$) or cutting an input (increasing a negative component of $\mathbf{q}^*$ towards zero) must be infeasible: it must make Φ positive. In other words Φ should be increasing in each of its arguments.

42. If, for some $\mathbf{y}$, $\Phi(\mathbf{y}) = 0$ then $\Phi(t\mathbf{y}) = 0$ for all $t > 0$—see also page 129.

43. Using (2.65) condition (2.30) becomes just $\sum_{i=1}^{n} p_i q_i \geq 0$.

44. In Figure B.5 both goods 1 and 2 are outputs. Clearly

$$\frac{p_1}{p_2} > \frac{\Phi_1(\mathbf{q}^*)}{\Phi_2(\mathbf{q}^*)} \tag{B.59}$$

and the market price of good 1 is so high relative to that of 2 that the firm specialises in the production of good 1: $q_2^* = 0$.

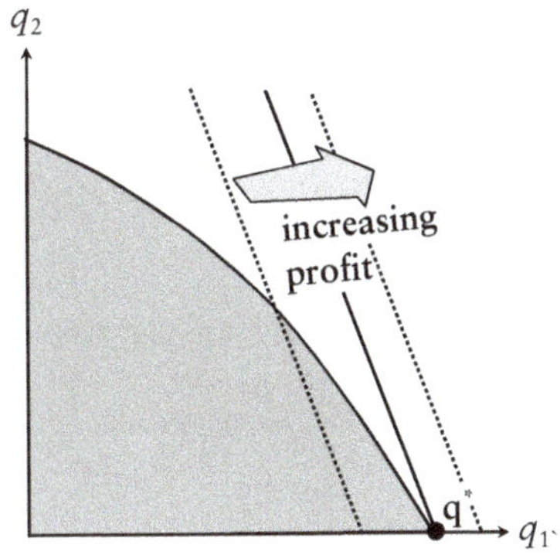

Figure B.5 Profit maximisation: corner solution

B.3 The firm and the market

1. Consider the cost function

$$a + bq_1 + cq_1^2.$$

Marginal cost is

$$b + 2cq_1$$

and this will form the supply curve in the region where MC $\geq$ AC, i.e. where $q_1 \geq \sqrt{a/c}$.

2. There will be $n_f + 1$ blobs with output values given by the set

$$\left\{16\frac{i}{n_f} : i = 0, 1, \ldots, n_f\right\}.$$

As $n_f \to \infty$, this set becomes dense in the interval $[0, 16]$.

3. If demand increases then (at the original quantity supplied) the price would initially have to rise to clear the market. This rise in price would induce each firm to increase its output which shifts down the marginal cost curves for all the other firms: output goes on increasing, and marginal cost and price goes on falling until equilibrium is reached at a lower market price and a higher aggregate output level.

4. This will shift up the average cost curve for each firm and (for normal inputs) marginal cost curve too.

5. If there were fewer than n_f firms at least one could set up and make non-negative profits; if there were more than n_f firms one of them would have to go out of business.

6. If the firm perceived itself in a situation of strategic interaction with rivals or potential rivals.

7. (a) We have $q = Ap^{\eta}$, so AR is $[q/A]^{1/\eta}$, MR$= [1 + 1/\eta]$AR. (b) Draw downward-sloping straight lines that intersect on the vertical axis. The point of intersection of MR curve on the horizontal axis is halfway between the origin and the point of intersection of the AR curve.

8. If the elasticity condition is not satisfied then $\partial\Pi/\partial q < 0$ for all $q > 0$: profits get larger as output approaches zero (but does not reach zero). Profits jump to 0 if q actually reaches zero. So there is no true maximum.

9. From the FOC we would get

$$p_q^1\left(q^1\right)q^1 + p^1\left(q^1\right) = C_q\left(\mathbf{w}, q^1\right), q^{2*} = 0$$

or

$$p_q^2\left(q^2\right)q^2 + p^2\left(q^2\right) = C_q\left(\mathbf{w}, q^2\right), q^{1*} = 0.$$

10. Assume that $\eta^1 < \eta^2$. Suppose that the firm ignored the possibility of splitting the market and just implemented the simple monopolistic solution (3.10) with same price p in both submarkets. Now consider the possibility of transferring some product from market 2 to market 1. The impact on profits of a small transfer is given by

$$p_q^1\left(q^1\right)q^1 - p_q^2\left(q^2\right)q^2 = p\left[\frac{1}{\eta^1} - \frac{1}{\eta^2}\right].$$

Given the assumption on elasticities this is obviously positive. Therefore profits will be increased by abandoning the common-price rule for the two markets—see also Exercise 3.5.

11. The good must not be easy to resell by the consumers. Otherwise they could, in effect, set up rival firms that would undermine the fixed charge.

B.4 The consumer

1. If all goods were indivisible then, instead of X being a connected set, we might take it to be a lattice of points. For the (food, refrigerator) example, X is a set of horizontal straight lines.

2. See Figures B.6 and B.7.

3. You could get sudden 'jumps' in preference in parts of X. This might be reasonable if certain parts of X have a special significance. See Mini Problem 1 on page 180.

4. The standard answer is 'no' , and does not rely upon changing preferences: the behaviour could be accounted for by transitive but cyclical preferences (see page 73 of the text). But this requires a rather special restriction on the alternatives from which you make a choice (Sen 1973).

5. In Figure B.8 good 1 is booze and good 2 is other goods. Clearly $\mathbf{x}' \succ \mathbf{x}^\circ$; but in view of the lexicographic assumption $\mathbf{x}'' \succ \mathbf{x}'$ even though $\mathbf{x}''$ contains a lot less of other goods. In the case of n goods lexicographic preferences imply:

$$\mathbf{x}' \succcurlyeq \mathbf{x}^\circ \text{ if } x_1' \geq x_1^\circ$$

$$\mathbf{x}' \succ \mathbf{x}^\circ \text{ if } x_1' > x_1^\circ$$

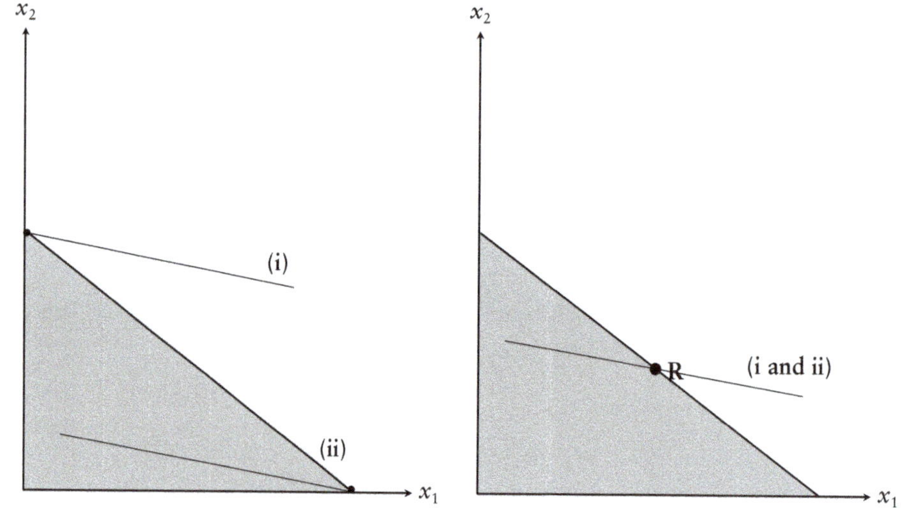

Figure B.6 Price changes (i) and (ii) in two cases

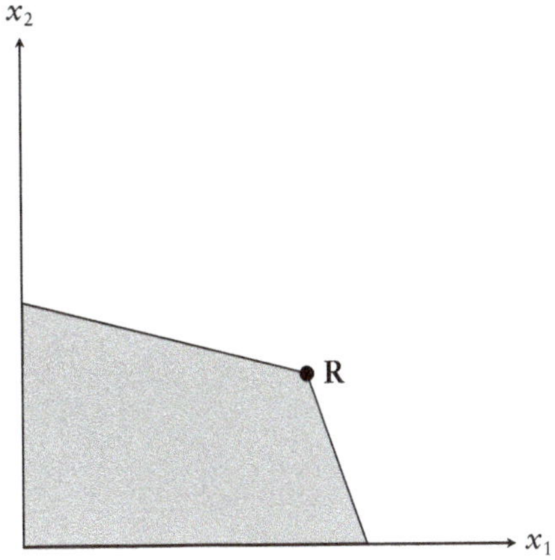

Figure B.7 Prices differ for buying and selling

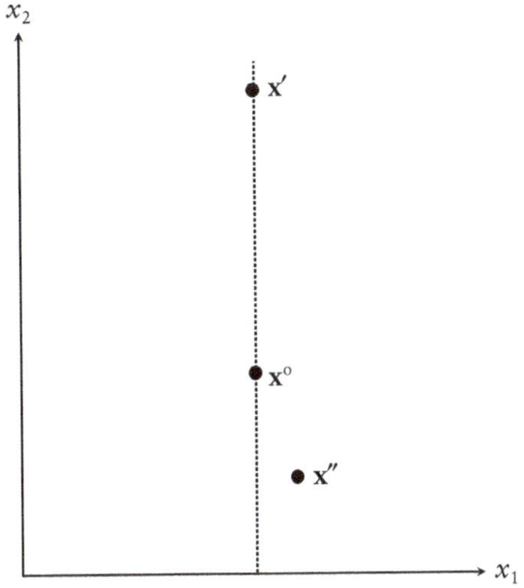

Figure B.8 Lexicographic preferences

$$\mathbf{x}' \succ \mathbf{x}^\circ \text{ if } x_1' = x_1^\circ \text{ and } x_2' > x_2^\circ$$

$$\mathbf{x}' \succ \mathbf{x}^\circ \text{ if } x_1' = x_1^\circ, x_2' = x_2^\circ, \text{ and } x_3' > x_3^\circ$$

... etc. continuity is violated

6. Yes. No.

7. Draw a budget constraint so that the bliss point is in the interior of the budget set. Consider a point to the 'north-east' of the bliss point: you see immediately that by moving away from the boundary of the set you move to a higher indifference curve. If the person could afford the bundle at the bliss point then he would buy this bundle and leave the rest of the income unspent.

8. All the results go through except that the optimal commodity demands $\mathbf{x}^*$ may no longer be well-defined functions of $\mathbf{p}$ and υ (or of $\mathbf{p}$ and y): at certain sets of prices there may be multiple solutions, and we have demand correspondences which will, however, be upper hemicontinuous.

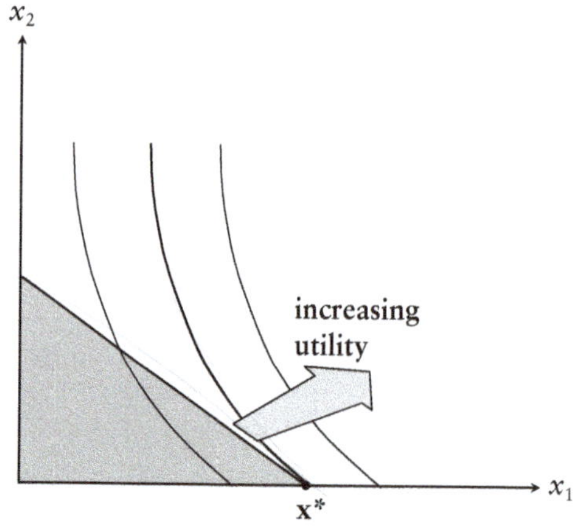

Figure B.9 Utility maximisation: corner solution

9. Indifference curves with the direction of preference as in Figure 4.8, but concave to the origin rather than convex.

10. Using the function-of-a-function rule. $\tilde{U}_i(\mathbf{x}) = \varphi_u(U(\mathbf{x}))U_i(\mathbf{x})$. Likewise for $\tilde{U}_j(\mathbf{x})$. So

$$\frac{\tilde{U}_j(\mathbf{x})}{\tilde{U}_i(\mathbf{x})} = \frac{\varphi_u(U(\mathbf{x}))U_j(\mathbf{x})}{\varphi_u(U(\mathbf{x}))U_i(\mathbf{x})} = \frac{U_j(\mathbf{x})}{U_i(\mathbf{x})}.$$

With a change of notation this is exactly the same as part (a) of Mini Problem 5 in chapter 2.

11. (a) Notice that the second expression can be obtained from the first by applying the transformation $\hat{U}(\mathbf{x}) = \varphi(U(\mathbf{x}))$ where $\varphi(\upsilon) = \frac{1}{4}\log(\upsilon)$ which is clearly monotonic increasing. Parts (b) to (e) follow exactly from Mini Problem 15 in chapter 2 with just a change of notation.

12. Some consumer purchases have close analogies with the computer example on page 36: houses, cars, central heating systems, for example. Also where the consumer is rationed (either by the intervention of some public agency, or through some additional market constraint such as unemployment), consumer behaviour can exhibit features similar to the short run.

13. The solution is essentially as for Mini Problem 11 in chapter 2. The counterparts to conditions (B.8–B.11) are

$$U_i(\mathbf{x}^*) - \mu^* p_i \leq 0,\ i = 1, \ldots, n, \tag{B.60}$$

$$x_i^* \left[U_i(\mathbf{x}^*) - \mu^* p_i\right] = 0,\ i = 1, \ldots, n, \tag{B.61}$$

$$y - \sum_{i=1}^{n} p_i x_i^* \geq 0, \tag{B.62}$$

$$\mu^* \left[y - \sum_{i=1}^{n} p_i x_i^*\right] = 0. \tag{B.63}$$

The complementary slackness condition immediately gives us the results that $U_i(\mathbf{x}^*) < \mu^* p_i$ only if $x_i^* = 0$ and that $y > \sum_{i=1}^{n} p_i x_i^*$ only if $\mu^* = 0$.

14. The corner solution equilibrium is illustrated in Figure B.9.

15. (a) If I do not have any of good j and my marginal willingness to pay for good j (my personalised price for j) is strictly less than the market price then I do not buy any j. (b) I go on trading i for j up until the point where my willingness to pay for j exactly equals the cost to me in the market.

16. (a) Given that MRS=price ratio we have

$$\frac{[x_2^*]^3}{3x_1^*[x_2^*]^2} = \frac{p_1}{p_2} \tag{B.64}$$

rearranging we get

$$\frac{x_2^*}{x_1^*} = 3\frac{p_1}{p_2}. \tag{B.65}$$

From the budget constraint we have

$$p_1x_1^* + p_2x_2^* = y \tag{B.66}$$

and so, combining (B.65) and (B.66) we have:

$$\frac{y - p_1x_1^*}{p_2x_1^*} = 3\frac{p_1}{p_2}$$

which, on rearranging, gives

$$y - p_1x_1^* = 3p_1x_1^*$$

and so

$$x_1^* = \frac{y}{4p_1}. \tag{B.67}$$

Using (B.66) again we get

$$x_2^* = \frac{3y}{4p_2}. \tag{B.68}$$

(b) Making the suggested substitution in the utility function we have

$$\begin{aligned} U(x_1, x_2) &= x_1x_2^3 \\ &= x_1\left[\frac{y - p_1x_1}{p_2}\right]^3. \end{aligned}$$

This is now an expression with just one unknown, x_1. To maximise this, differentiate and set the differential equal to zero:

$$\left[\frac{y - p_1x_1^*}{p_2}\right]^3 - 3x_1^*\frac{p_1}{p_2}\left[\frac{y - p_1x_1^*}{p_2}\right]^2 = 0,$$

which, on simplifying gives:

$$\frac{y - p_1x_1^*}{p_2} - 3x_1^*\frac{p_1}{p_2} = 0.$$

Rearranging this we immediately get (B.67) and so, of course, (B.68) follows.

(c) Using the logarithmic form of the utility function in Mini Problem 11 (this is not essential but it makes the manipulation slightly easier) the Lagrangean is

$$\mathcal{L}(\mathbf{x}, \mu; \mathbf{p}, y) = \frac{1}{4}\log x_1 + \frac{3}{4}\log x_2 + \mu\left[y - p_1x_1 - p_2x_2\right]. \tag{B.69}$$

There can only be an interior solution for the same reason as in the answer to part (b) of Mini Problem 15 in chapter 2. Differentiating (B.69) with respect to x_1 and x_2 and setting to zero we get two FOCs:

$$\frac{1}{4x_1^*} - \mu^*p_1 = 0 \tag{B.70}$$

$$\frac{3}{4x_2^*} - \mu^*p_2 = 0. \tag{B.71}$$

The third FOC is (B.66). Multiplying (B.70) by x_1^*, (B.71) by x_2^* and summing we have

$$\frac{1}{4} + \frac{3}{4} - \mu^* \left[p_1 x_1^* + p_2 x_2^* \right] = 0 \tag{B.72}$$

which, using (B.66), implies

$$\mu^* = \frac{1}{y}. \tag{B.73}$$

Substituting this value for μ^* in (B.70) and (B.71) we get (B.67) and (B.68).

17. In Figure B.10 the quantity discount corresponds to the 'horizontal' part of the boundary of the budget set. For the given prices the consumer is indifferent between the bundles $\mathbf{x}^*$ and $\mathbf{x}^{**}$: if the price p_1 were a little higher the equilibrium would be just to the left of $\mathbf{x}^*$; if it were a little lower the equilibrium would be just to the right of $\mathbf{x}^{**}$. Demand is discontinuous at this point.

18. Part (a) follows directly from equation (4.13), the budget constraint, which is binding at the optimum given the greed assumption. (b) Can also be deduced from the binding budget constraint: multiplying each p_i and y by some factor t clearly leaves (4.13) unaltered, since the t will cancel on both sides; therefore the optimal commodity demands $\mathbf{x}^*$ will remain unchanged. Also consider equation (4.9). We know that C is homogeneous of degree 1: so if all prices are increased by a factor t the cost function tells us that income has to be increased by the same factor to be able to attain the same utility level as before. Also the left-hand side is homogeneous of degree zero in $\mathbf{p}$ because it is the first derivative of C with respect to p_i. So rescaling prices and income by t leaves $D^i(\mathbf{p}, y)$ unaltered.

19. For very finely defined commodity specifications we might find quite a few inferior goods (Co-op margarine, sliced white bread...); for more broadly defined commodities we would expect them to be non-inferior goods (edible fats, bread...).

20. (a) The Slutsky equations for the effect of the price of good j on the demand for good i and vice versa are:

$$D_j^i(\mathbf{p}, y) = H_j^i(\mathbf{p}, \upsilon) - x_j^* D_y^i(\mathbf{p}, y) \tag{B.74}$$

$$D_i^j(\mathbf{p}, y) = H_i^j(\mathbf{p}, \upsilon) - x_i^* D_y^j(\mathbf{p}, y). \tag{B.75}$$

Although the substitution term (first term on the right-hand side) has to be equal in equations (B.74) and (B.75), the income effects could be very different. So it is possible for the left-hand side

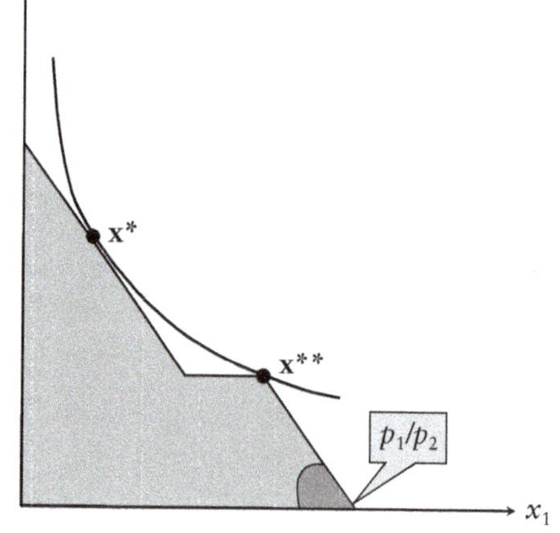

Figure B.10 Quantity discount

to be negative in one case and positive in the other. (b) In the two-good case the result is obvious from the indifference curve diagram: we know that if the price of good 1 goes up then, along an indifference curve, the demand for good 1 must fall; but to keep on the same indifference curve good 2 would have to rise. However, the result can be generalised. Differentiate equation (4.13) with respect to y:

$$\sum_{i=1}^{n} p_i D^i_y(\mathbf{p}, y) = 1 \tag{B.76}$$

—a convenient adding-up property for the income effects.

Alternatively differentiate it with respect to p_j:

$$x^*_j + \sum_{i=1}^{n} p_i D^i_j(\mathbf{p}, y) = 0. \tag{B.77}$$

Using the Slutsky equation (4.21), we get

$$x^*_j + \sum_{i=1}^{n} p_i \left[H^i_j(\mathbf{p}, \upsilon) - x^*_j D^i_y(\mathbf{p}, y) \right] = 0 \tag{B.78}$$

which, in view of the adding-up property of the income effects (B.76), yields:

$$\sum_{i=1}^{n} p_i H^i_j(\mathbf{p}, \upsilon) = 0. \tag{B.79}$$

Now, because the own-price substitution effect must be negative, equation (B.79) implies that at least one of the cross-price substitution effects must be positive. In other words at least one pair of goods i, j must be net substitutes.

21. In Figure B.11 the income effect is from $\mathbf{x}^*$ to $\circ$ and the substitution effect from $\circ$ to $\mathbf{x}^{**}$.

22. The first term on the right-hand side of equation (4.23) must be negative; so if D^i_y is positive or zero, the left-hand side must be negative.

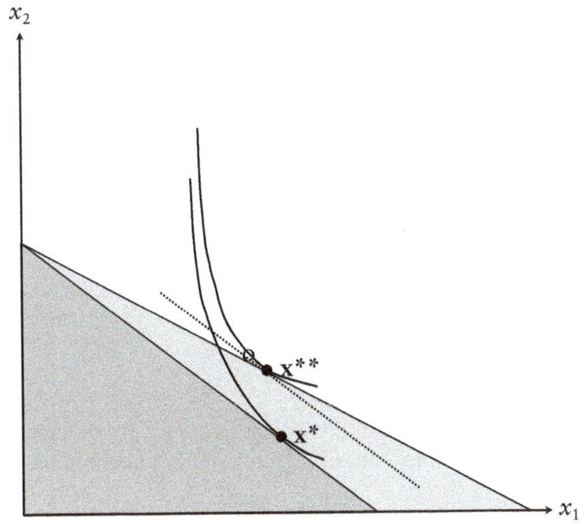

Figure B.11 Giffen good

23. Using (B.67) and (B.68) maximised utility is

$$\frac{1}{4}\log x_1^* + \frac{3}{4}\log x_2^* = \frac{1}{4}\log\left(\frac{y}{4p_1}\right) + \frac{3}{4}\log\left(\frac{3y}{4p_2}\right).$$

Simplifying this we have

$$V(\mathbf{p}, y) = -\log k + \log y - \frac{1}{4}\log p_1 - \frac{3}{4}\log p_2 \qquad \text{(B.80)}$$

where k is the constant defined in (B.20).

- Differentiating (B.80) with respect to p_1 and p_2 respectively we have

$$V_1(\mathbf{p}, y) = -\frac{1}{4p_1} < 0 \qquad \text{(B.81)}$$

$$V_2(\mathbf{p}, y) = -\frac{3}{4p_2} < 0. \qquad \text{(B.82)}$$

- Differentiating (B.80) with respect to y we have

$$V_y(\mathbf{p}, y) = \frac{1}{y} \qquad \text{(B.83)}$$

which is exactly μ^* in (B.73).

- Dividing (B.81) and (B.82) by (B.83) and multiplying by -1 we get

$$-\frac{V_1(\mathbf{p}, y)}{V_y(\mathbf{p}, y)} = \frac{y}{4p_1}$$

$$-\frac{V_2(\mathbf{p}, y)}{V_y(\mathbf{p}, y)} = \frac{3y}{4p_2}$$

which are just (B.67) and (B.68).

- If p_1, p_2, and y are all multiplied by the same positive number t then (B.80) gives

$$\begin{aligned} V(t\mathbf{p}, ty) &= -\log k + \log ty - \frac{1}{4}\log tp_1 - \frac{3}{4}\log tp_2 \\ &= V(\mathbf{p}, y) + \log t - \frac{1}{4}\log t - \frac{3}{4}\log t \\ &= V(\mathbf{p}, y). \end{aligned}$$

Furthermore, in this cardinalisation we can see that V is convex in $\mathbf{p}$ because, from (B.81) and (B.82) we have

$$\begin{aligned} V_{11}(\mathbf{p}, y) &= \frac{1}{4p_1^2} > 0 \\ V_{22}(\mathbf{p}, y) &= \frac{3}{4p_2^2} > 0 \\ V_{12}(\mathbf{p}, y) &= 0. \end{aligned}$$

24. If you do not consume commodity i then you are not hurt by an increase in p_i, so V_i would be zero for this good; but you must be consuming something, so there must be some good whose price rise would hurt you.

25. V_y is the marginal increase in maximal utility that you would get if your income were to rise: it is the 'price' of income in utility terms; this is exactly what is meant by the optimised Lagrange multiplier.

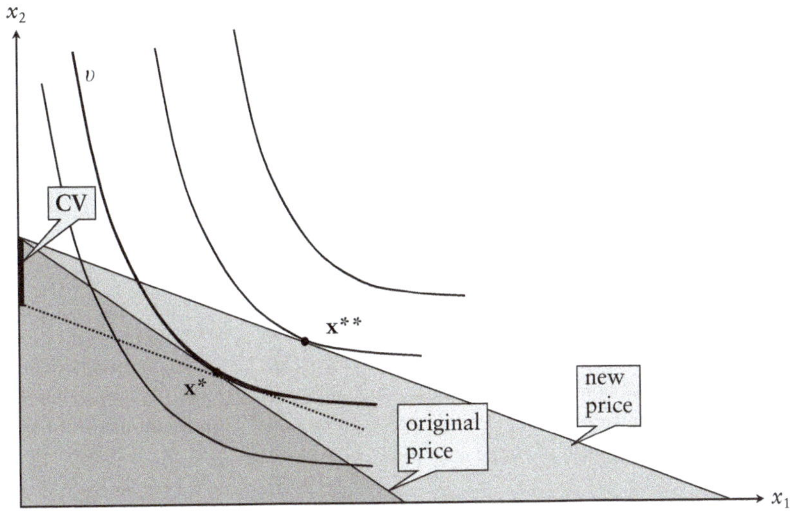

Figure B.12 The compensating variation measured in terms of good 2

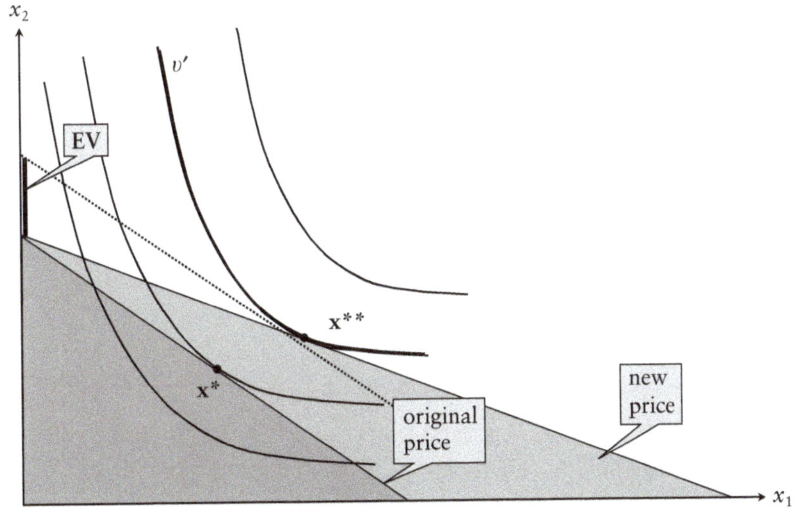

Figure B.13 The equivalent variation measured in terms of good 2

26. Differentiation of (4.27) yields

$$V_i\,(\mathbf{p}, C(\mathbf{p}, \upsilon)) + V_y\,(\mathbf{p}, C(\mathbf{p}, \upsilon))\; C_i(\mathbf{p}, \upsilon) = 0. \tag{B.84}$$

Using Shephard's Lemma gives the result immediately.

27. From (4.27) we see that

$$V\,(t\mathbf{p}, C(t\mathbf{p}, \upsilon)) = \upsilon\;; \tag{B.85}$$

for any $t > 0$ and, because C is homogeneous of degree 1 in prices, we have

$$V(t\mathbf{p}, ty) = \upsilon = V(\mathbf{p}, y). \tag{B.86}$$

28. By definition we have:

$$\upsilon = V(\mathbf{p}', C(\mathbf{p}, \upsilon) - CV) = V(\mathbf{p}', C(\mathbf{p}', \upsilon)) \tag{B.87}$$

from which the result follows.

29. Take (4.31): on the right-hand side we subtract the cost of getting reference level utility after the price change from the original cost. If there has simply been a price fall then the cost must have fallen, and so the expression is positive, the same sign as the welfare change.

30. See Figures B.12 and B.13

31. Use equation (4.23) and apply reasoning similar to the answer to question 22.

32. Compare equations (4.37) and (4.40). By definition of the optimal commodity demands and the cost function the denominators on the right-hand side must be equal; but by definition of the cost function the numerator of (4.37) must be less than or equal than the numerator of (4.40). A similar argument can be applied in the case of (4.38) and (4.41).

B.5 The consumer and the market

1. Substitute in $\partial y/\partial p_j$ using equation (5.1).

2. Reflect Figure 5.1 about the vertical axis and shift the origin to $(R_1, 0)$—see B.14. Then, to obtain Figure 5.2, rescale the vertical axis to plot p_1 rather than x_2.

3. Suppose the person is paid at the rate w_0 for working hours up to ℓ_0 and at the rate $w_1 > w_0$ for working hours in excess of ℓ_0. The budget constraint is.

$$y = \left\{ \begin{array}{ll} w_0\ell + y_0 & \ell \leq \ell_0 \\ w_1[\ell - \ell_0] + w_0\ell_0 + y_0 & \ell > \ell_0 \end{array} \right\}. \tag{B.88}$$

Figure B.15 illustrates this

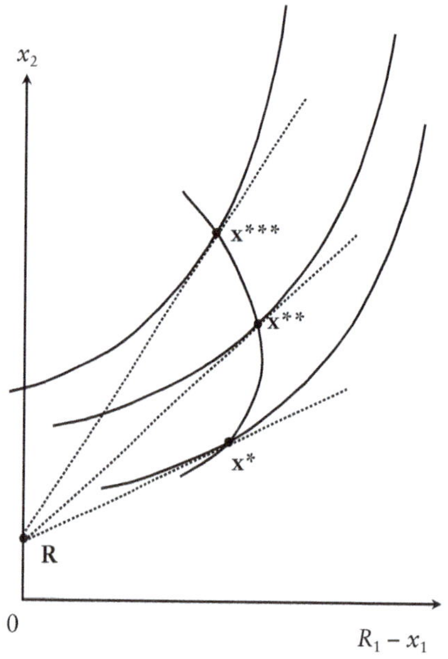

Figure B.14 Supply of good 1

(a) The left-hand panel gives the (x_1, x_2) view. The horizontal axis measures 'leisure' so that labour is just measured on the same axis, but in the opposite direction. Assuming that $y_0 = 0$, the endowment point is marked in as **R**.

(b) The right-hand panel gives the (ℓ, y) view. Note the natural upper bound on ℓ.

(c) In either view it is clear from the indifference curve that has been drawn in that the consumer's optimum may be non-unique and that labour supply may be discontinuous (consider what happens in Figure B.15 if w_1 is a little higher or lower.)

4. (a) Equation (5.13) generalises to

$$U(x_1, \ldots, x_n) = \sum_{i=1}^{n} \delta^{i-1} u(x_i). \tag{B.89}$$

If $n \to \infty$ one may need to have $\delta < 1$ to ensure that the right-hand side of (B.89) converges. (b) Differentiation of the utility function and rearrangement shows that

$$\frac{U_{11}(\mathbf{x}_1, \mathbf{x}_2)}{U_{12}(\mathbf{x}_1, \mathbf{x}_2)} = \frac{u_1(\mathbf{x}_1)}{u_2(\mathbf{x}_1)}$$

$$\frac{U_{21}(\mathbf{x}_1, \mathbf{x}_2)}{U_{22}(\mathbf{x}_1, \mathbf{x}_2)} = \frac{u_1(\mathbf{x}_2)}{u_2(\mathbf{x}_2)}$$

where u_i denotes the derivative of u with respect to its ith argument $i = 1, 2$. From this it is clear that the MRS is the same if $\mathbf{x}_1 = \mathbf{x}_2$. Here δ can be expressed as either the MRS of bread today for bread tomorrow or as the MRS of jam today for jam tomorrow; either way it is still the pure rate of pure time preference.

5. The specific version of (B.89) required is given by

$$u(x_{\text{BREAKFAST}}) + \delta u(x_{\text{LUNCH}}) + \delta^2 u(x_{\text{TEA}}). \tag{B.90}$$

It is immediate from this that $\text{MRS}_{\text{BREAKFASTTEA}}$ is independent of consumption at LUNCH.

6. It is the distance between the two blobs on the vertical axis.

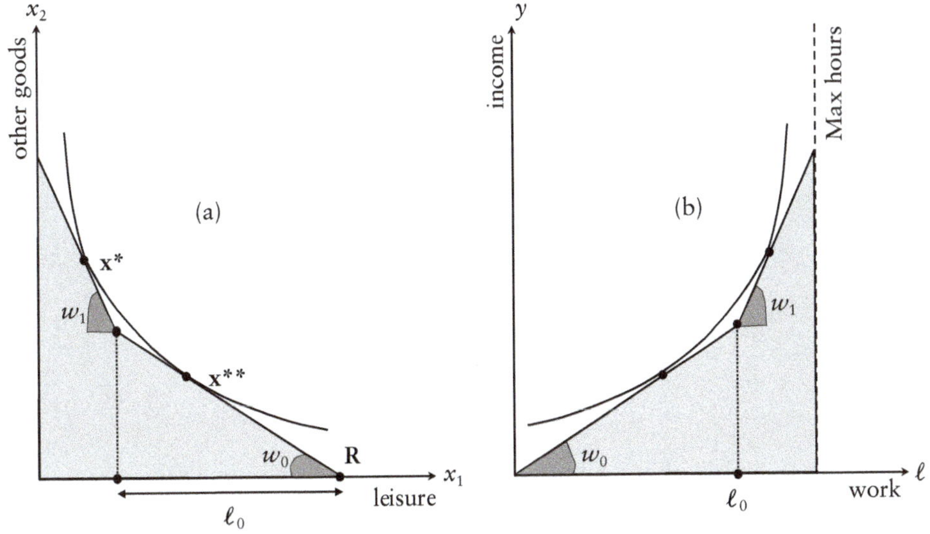

Figure B.15 Budget constraint with overtime

7. The Lagrangean is

$$u(x_1) + \delta u(x_2) + \mu \left[\bar{y} - x_1 - \frac{x_2}{1+r} \right]. \tag{B.91}$$

The FOCs for an interior maximum of (B.91) are

$$u_x(x_1^*) - \mu = 0$$

$$\delta u_x(x_2^*) - \mu \frac{1}{1+r} = 0$$

On rearranging we get

$$\frac{u_x(x_1^*)}{u_x(x_2^*)} = [1+r]\delta \tag{B.92}$$

If $\delta > 1/[1+r]$ then RHS of (B.92) is greater than 1 and, because $u_x(\cdot)$ is a decreasing function we must have $x_1^* < x_2^*$.

8. Suppose that x^0 and x^1 are two points on the boundary of A, that $\mathbf{z}^0$ is the minimum cost combination of inputs to produce $\mathbf{x}^0$, and that $\mathbf{z}^1$ is the minimum cost combination required to produce $\mathbf{x}^1$. If the technology is convex, then the vector $\mathbf{x}^t := t\mathbf{x}^0 + [1-t]\mathbf{x}^1$ (where $0 < t < 1$) can be produced from the input combination $\mathbf{z}^t := t\mathbf{z}^0 + [1-t]\mathbf{z}^1$. But $\sum w_j z_j^t = t \sum_j w_j z_j^0 + [1 - t] \sum_j w_j z_j^1 = ty + [1-t]y = y$; so $\mathbf{z}^t$ can certainly be purchased, and $\mathbf{x}^t$ must lie in A.

9. Every input is always essential so any such change is bound to shift the cost of any given output bundle.

10. In the (wool, meat) example the different breeds correspond to inputs $z_1, \ldots z_m$, b_{1j} is the wool yield of breed j and b_{2j} is the wool yield of breed j.

11. (a) To get x_1 you need x_1/b_{11} units of input 1; to get x_2 you need x_2/b_{21} units of input 1. Therefore cost is

$$w_1 \max \left\{ \frac{x_1^0}{b_{11}}, \frac{x_2^0}{b_{21}} \right\}$$

(b)

$$w_2 \min \left\{ \frac{x_1^0}{b_{11}}, \frac{x_2^0}{b_{21}} \right\} < w_1 \max \left\{ \frac{x_1^0}{b_{11}}, \frac{x_2^0}{b_{21}} \right\}.$$

(c) The condition in (b) and

$$w_1 \min \left\{ \frac{x_1^0}{b_{11}}, \frac{x_2^0}{b_{21}} \right\} < w_2 \max \left\{ \frac{x_1^0}{b_{11}}, \frac{x_2^0}{b_{21}} \right\}.$$

(d) We need

$$\begin{bmatrix} x_1 \\ x_2 \end{bmatrix} = \begin{bmatrix} z_1 b_{11} + z_2 b_{12} \\ z_1 b_{21} + z_2 b_{22} \end{bmatrix}. \tag{B.93}$$

Solving this we have

$$z_1 = \frac{b_{22}x_1 - b_{12}x_2}{b_{11}b_{22} - b_{12}b_{21}} \tag{B.94}$$

$$z_2 = \frac{b_{11}x_2 - b_{21}x_1}{b_{11}b_{22} - b_{12}b_{21}}. \tag{B.95}$$

Cost of this bundle is

$$\frac{w_1 [b_{22}x_1 - b_{12}x_2] + w_2 [b_{11}x_2 - b_{21}x_1]}{b_{11}b_{22} - b_{12}b_{21}}.$$

12. If $R_3 > 0$ the household's budget y increases and the frontier moves outwards at all points: consumption of goods 1 and 2 increases.

13. Given the linear technology in equation (5.20) it is clear that if the person's income increases then the attainable set expands along the rays shown in Figure 5.5; if the indifference curves are homothetic then the utility-maximising output bundle $\mathbf{x}^*$ remains at the same relative position on the figure—it too is moved out radially. So, in view of the linearity of the model, the inputs that are purchased will always increase proportionately. But if the indifference curves are non-homothetic then as income expands $\mathbf{x}^*$ will move along a facet and eventually may switch between facets. When such a switch occurs one input j is no longer purchased and another input is substituted. In this case as income increases the demand for good j at first increases and then, when the switch occurs, a further increase in income causes the demand for j to fall to zero.

14. Apply an induction argument.

15. There are several interpretations. One is the problem of obtaining a coherent ordering for a group of persons $\{a, b, \ldots\}$ from their individual orderings $\succcurlyeq^a$, $\succcurlyeq^b$ ... See chapter 9.

16. The services of a wide congestion-free bridge are non-rival. The perfume or aftershave that you wear may be providing a non-excludable service to other consumers.

17. Given the specified tastes my demand for cider falls continuously with an increase in price until the price of cider equals that of beer; if the price of cider increases further the demand for cider jumps to zero (I buy only beer). But this jump for each consumer is just like the jump in supply considered in chapter 3. Therefore in a large number of consumers the demand for cider at this critical price is effectively continuous—see also Exercise 5.9.

18. There is a class of such definitions that may involve some type of generalised mean of incomes:

$$\hat{y} := \varphi^{-1}\left(\sum_h \varphi\left(y^h\right)\right)$$

where φ is a monotonic increasing function and φ^{-1} is its inverse.

B.6 A simple economy

1. In Figure B.16 good 1 is input, good 2 is output.

2. See Figure B.17. The combined set

$$Q = \{\mathbf{q}^\circ + \mathbf{q}' : \mathbf{q}^\circ \in Q^\circ, \mathbf{q}' \in Q'\}$$

will be identical to Q'.

3. See Figures B.18 and B.19.

4. See answer to Mini Problem 40 in chapter 2: rewrite $q \leq \phi(z_1, z_2)$ as $-\phi(-q_1, -q_2) + q_3 \leq 0$ where $q_1 := -z_1$, $q_2 := -z_2$, $q_3 := q$. Figure B.20 illustrates this—compare this with Figure 2.7.

5. If Q^1 and Q^2 are the technology sets for processes 1 and 2 then because there are no externalities $Q^1 + Q^2$ is the technology set for the combined processes. From Theorem A.6 convexity of Q^1 and Q^2 implies convexity of $Q^1 + Q^2$.

6. Each constraint restricts you to a triangle. So the attainable set is the polygon shown in Figure B.21.

7. If we concentrate on interior solutions we do not have to worry about constraint (6.8). The Lagrangean is

$$U(\mathbf{x}) + \lambda[\mathbf{q} + \mathbf{R} - \mathbf{x}] - \mu\Phi(\mathbf{q}).$$

Differentiating with respect to x_i we get:

$$U_i(\mathbf{x}) - \lambda = 0. \tag{B.96}$$

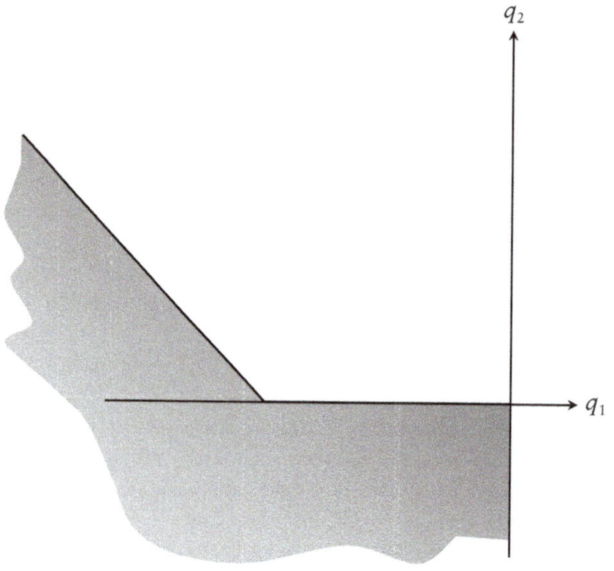

Figure B.16 Indivisibility in production

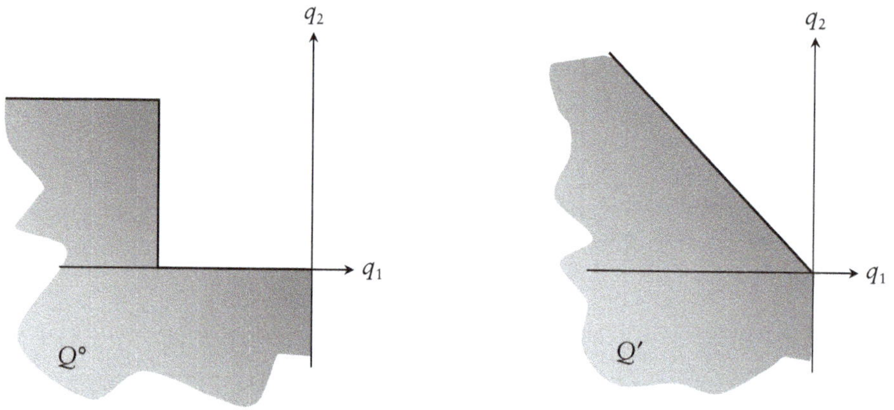

Figure B.17 Combination of technology sets

Differentiating with respect to q_i we find:

$$\lambda - \mu \Phi_i(\mathbf{q}) = 0. \tag{B.97}$$

A simple rearrangement gives the result.

8. Shift the line corresponding to constraint 4 outwards. Do this for the case (a) where the equilibrium is on this facet, (b) where the equilibrium is elsewhere.

9. Draw an elongation rightwards of the attainable set.

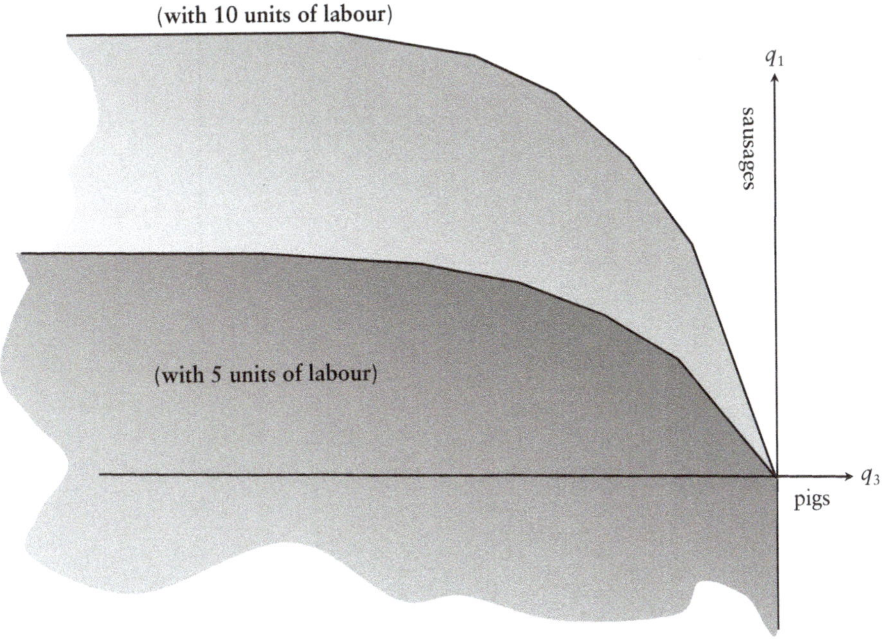

Figure B.18 Answer to 2a

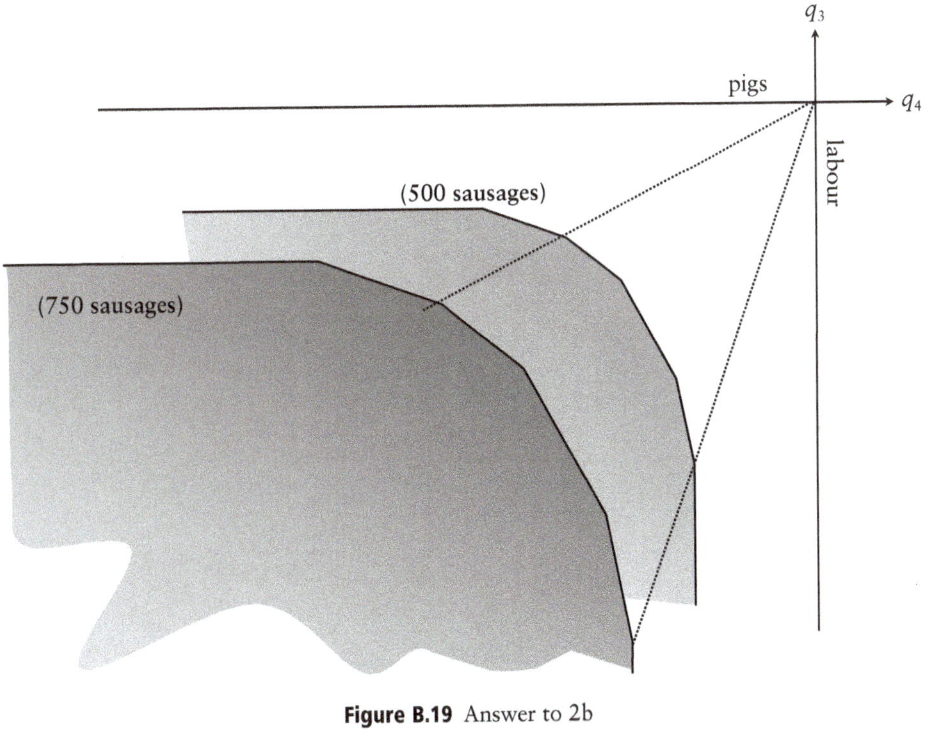

Figure B.19 Answer to 2b

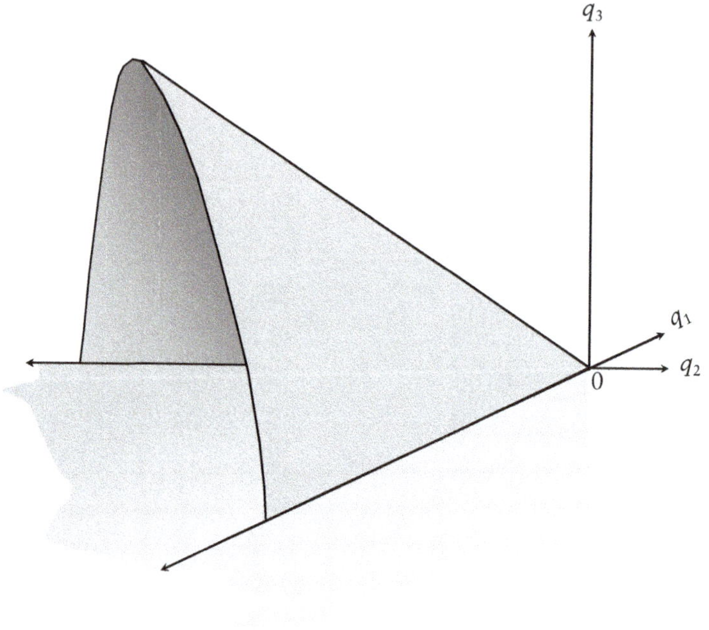

Figure B.20 2-input, 1-output production function

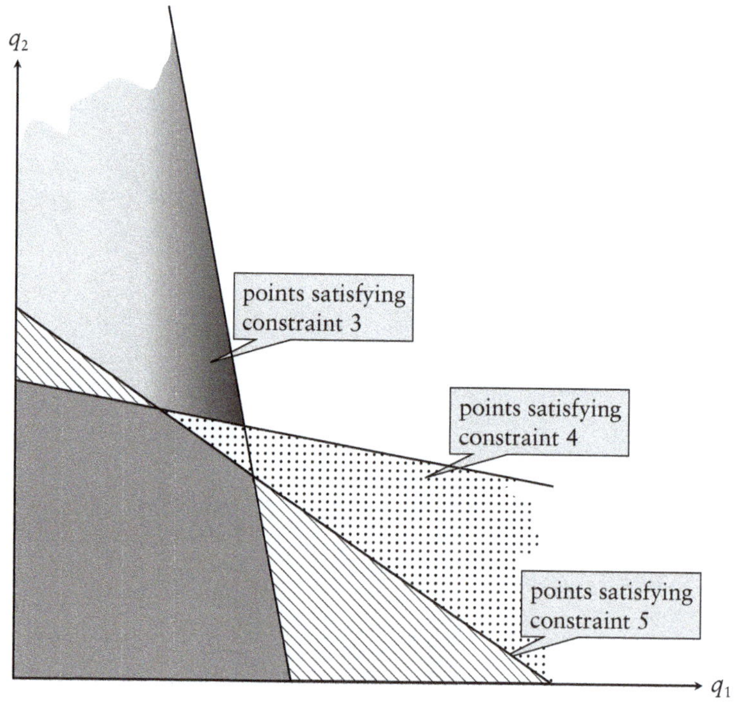

Figure B.21 The attainable set

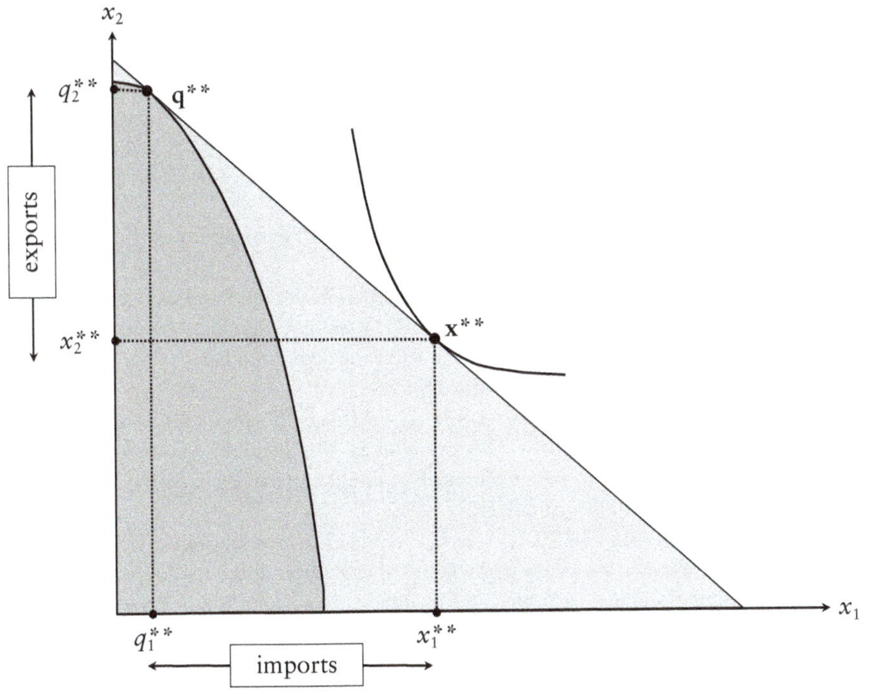

Figure B.22 Imports and exports

10. Use the same argument as on page 42. Labelling goods $1, \ldots, m$ as inputs and $m+1, \ldots, n$ as outputs, [Revenue – Cost] can be written:

$$\sum_{i=m+1}^{n} p_i q_i - \sum_{i=1}^{m} p_i [-q_i] \tag{B.98}$$

which immediately gives the result.

11. There may be costs of monitoring Friday. Also if Crusoe cannot costlessly observe all inputs and outputs there may be inefficiency. See models in chapter 11.

12. Introduce a set of notional or shadow prices such as ρ in Figure 5.4. Then household production is carried out to maximise 'profit' at input prices $\mathbf{w}$, output prices $\boldsymbol{\rho}$; household consumption maximises $U(\mathbf{x})$ subject to $\sum \rho_j x_j \leq y$.

13. If there are fixed costs there may be a non-convexity in the attainable set with trade.

14. See Figure B.22: $q_1^{**} - x_1^{**}$ is imports; $q_2^{**} - x_2^{**}$ is exports.

15. The standard budget set (see Figure 4.2) is convex.

B.7 General equilibrium

1. Suppose firm 1 sells q units of good 1 to firm 2. Then $q_1^1 = (+)q$ and $q_1^2 = -q$; firm 1 would have an entry $(+)p_1 q$ in its revenue account; firm 2 would have an entry $(-)p_1 q$ as a component of its costs. If the two firms merge the net output of good 1 becomes $q_1^1 + q_1^2 = 0$; nil profit is made by the merged firm on good 1; transactions in good 1 are now purely internal to the merged firm.

2. Substituting from equation (7.3) we see that the last term in (7.8) becomes

$$\sum_{f=1}^{n_f} s_h^f \sum_{i=1}^{n} p_i q_i^f.$$

Simple rearrangement then gives the result.

3. Alf's budget constraint is $p_1 x_1^a + p_2 x_2^a \leq p_1 R_1^a + p_2 R_2^a$; the first-order condition simplifies to $U_1^a(\mathbf{x}^a)/U_2^a(\mathbf{x}^a) = p_1/p_2$.

4. Alf sells some of his endowment of good 2 to Bill and buys some of Bill's endowment of good 1.

5. The point marked [**R**] is a horizontal distance R_1^a from the left-hand axis and R_1^b from the right-hand axis: in the two-person case $R_1^a + R_1^b = R_1$. A similar argument applies to R_2. If there is a gift from outside the economy then this must affect the size of the box.

6. We could end up at a point off the contract curve.

7. Pick some point off the contract curve: now move along Alf's indifference curve (in the direction of the contract curve): notice that Bill's utility must rise; therefore you would reach a point at which one of the pair would be better off and (because the point lies in the box) which can be attained by pooling Alf's and Bill's resources.

8. From the remark on page 147 it is clear that competitive equilibrium in an exchange economy must lie at the intersection of the consumers' offer curves: in the two-person case this can easily be drawn within the Edgeworth box. At this intersection (point [**x***] in Figure 7.2) each person's indifference curve is tangential to the same line. Therefore [**x***] must lie in the set of allocations that represent common tangencies of the two persons' indifference curves, the contract curve. Clearly it must lie on or above the reservation indifference curve for each person or the trade would not be offered. See Figure B.23.

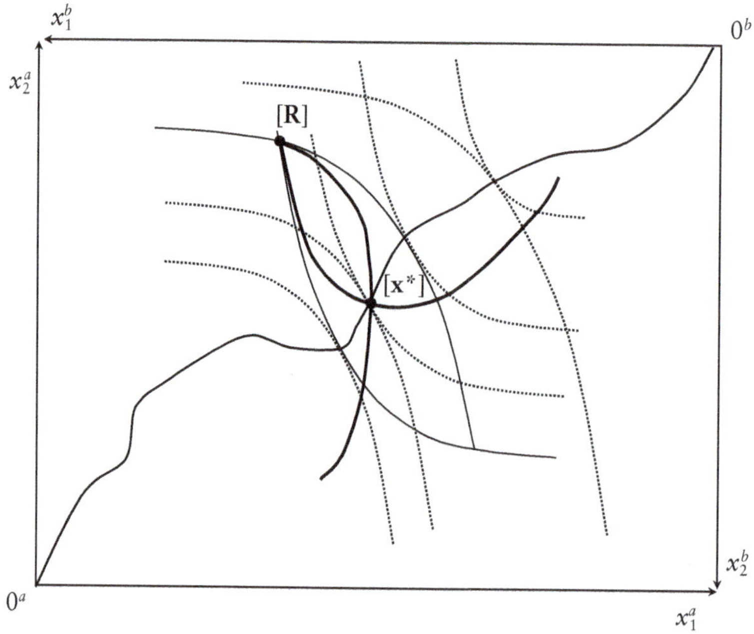

Figure B.23 The offer curves and equilibrium

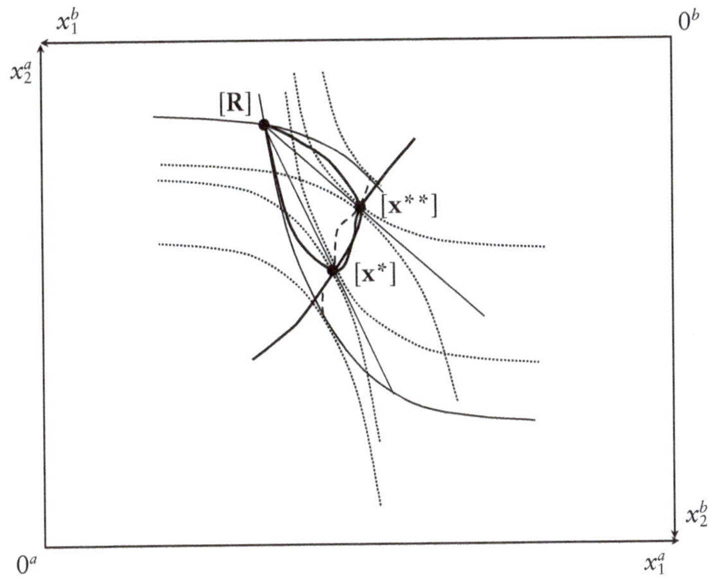

Figure B.24 Offer curves and multiple equilibria

9. See Figure B.24. Note that there is a third intersection of the two offer curves between [**x***] and [**x****]! The economic issues concerning an equilibrium of the sort corresponding to this third intersection are discussed further in sections 7.4.3 and 7.4.4.

10. Using (7.14) and (7.15) we find the total consumption of the Alf-Arthur-Bill coalition to be

$$\begin{aligned} 2\hat{\mathbf{x}}^a + \underline{\mathbf{x}}^b &= 2 \cdot \frac{1}{2}\left[\mathbf{R}^a + \underline{\mathbf{x}}^a\right] + \mathbf{R}^b + \mathbf{R}^a - \underline{\mathbf{x}}^a \\ &= \mathbf{R}^a + \underline{\mathbf{x}}^a + \mathbf{R}^b + \mathbf{R}^a - \underline{\mathbf{x}}^a \\ &= 2\mathbf{R}^a + \mathbf{R}^b. \end{aligned}$$

11. Clearly Ben would be unhappy about the situation in Table 7.1; it would be in his interests to propose a coalition with Alf and Arthur that would give them slightly more than they would have enjoyed in (7.15) and himself correspondingly less than his treacherous brother would have enjoyed in (7.14). This could always be done in any proposed allocation that did not treat agents of a given type (each of the pair of twins in our example) equally in the allocation.

12. It might happen that one side can exert monopoly power.

13. Let L_1 be the line from [**R**] to [$\tilde{\mathbf{x}}$]; if it is not a tangent to the indifference curves at [$\tilde{\mathbf{x}}$] then it must cut the Alf indifference curve through [$\tilde{\mathbf{x}}$] again somewhere: call the point where it does so [$\mathbf{x}'$] and let L_2 be the line from [$\mathbf{x}'$] to [$\tilde{\mathbf{x}}$]. Notice that at any point in L_2 the Alf tribe would be at a higher utility level than at [$\tilde{\mathbf{x}}$]. Define β as the ratio

$$\frac{\text{length}(L_2)}{\text{length}(L_1)}.$$

Given that there are N of the a-tribe and N of the b-tribe let m be an integer between $[1-\beta]N$ and N. A coalition of N a-types and m b-types will then secure a consumption allocation for a-type members of the coalition at a point [$\hat{\mathbf{x}}$] in the interior of L_2 (they are better off than at [$\tilde{\mathbf{x}}$]) and for b-members of the coalition at the point [$\tilde{\mathbf{x}}$] (they are no worse off). If a coalition of N of the a-tribe and m of the b-tribe is formed, will the proposed consumptions $\hat{\mathbf{x}}^a$ and $\tilde{\mathbf{x}}^b$ for individual a- and b-members respectively be feasible? Total consumption is $N\hat{\mathbf{x}}^a + m\tilde{\mathbf{x}}^b$ so that the condition for feasibility is

$$N\hat{\mathbf{x}}^a + m\tilde{\mathbf{x}}^b \leq N\mathbf{R}^a + m\mathbf{R}^b$$

$$N\left[\hat{\mathbf{x}}^a - \mathbf{R}^a\right] \leq m\left[\mathbf{R}^b - \tilde{\mathbf{x}}^b\right]. \tag{B.99}$$

But, using the property

$$\tilde{\mathbf{x}}^a + \tilde{\mathbf{x}}^b = \mathbf{R}^a + \mathbf{R}^b$$

condition (B.99) can be rewritten

$$N\left[\hat{\mathbf{x}}^a - \mathbf{R}^a\right] \leq m\left[\tilde{\mathbf{x}}^a - \mathbf{R}^a\right] \tag{B.100}$$

$$\hat{\mathbf{x}}^a - \mathbf{R}^a \leq \frac{m}{N}\left[\tilde{\mathbf{x}}^a - \mathbf{R}^a\right]. \tag{B.101}$$

However, condition (B.101) is satisfied by construction of $[\hat{\mathbf{x}}]$ at a point $\frac{m}{N}$ along the line L_1.

14. Costs of forming and enforcing coalitions; information costs.

15. Household h's offer curve is given by the graph of $\left(x_1^h(\mathbf{p}), x_2^h(\mathbf{p})\right)$ in a two-good economy (see Figures B.23 and B.24) or, more, generally the graph of $\left(x_1^h(\mathbf{p}), \ldots, x_n^h(\mathbf{p})\right)$. From (7.16) it is clear that the vector of excess demands in an exchange economy is found just by summing $\left(x_1^h(\mathbf{p}), \ldots, x_n^h(\mathbf{p})\right)$ over h and then subtracting $\mathbf{R}$.

16. If there is a good which actually no one wants to buy (used toothbrushes?) there could just be an unutilised stock of this 'good' in equilibrium.

17. Each firm's supply function is homogeneous of degree zero in all prices, and each household's demand function is homogeneous of degree zero in all prices and income (Theorem 4.6); and in this model income in turn is homogeneous of degree 1 in prices.

18. If each household is greedy, then in equilibrium it must be on the boundary of its budget set:

$$\sum_{i=1}^{n} p_i x_i^h = y^h. \tag{B.102}$$

Substituting in for y^h from equation (7.9) and summing (B.102) over all households h we get

$$\sum_{i=1}^{n} p_i x_i = \sum_{i=1}^{n} p_i \left[R_i + \sum_{f=1}^{n_f} q_i^f\right] \tag{B.103}$$

(remember that the sum over h of ς_h^f is 1). Simple rearrangement of (B.103) and using the definitions of excess demand E_i gives the result.

19. See Figure B.25.

20. Given the normalisation of prices ($p_2 = 1 - p_1$) and Walras's Law:

$$E_2 = -\frac{p_1 E_1}{1 - p_1}.$$

If E_1 stays positive as $p_1 \to 1$, the result immediately follows.

21. Examine Figure 7.12. A perturbation might shift the system from the neighbourhood of one equilibrium allocation to another: in the process, prices may change dramatically. This could be bad news for people whose incomes are derived mainly from one commodity.

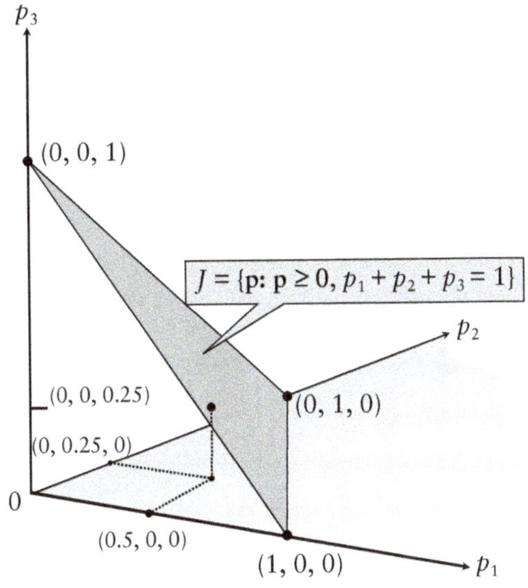

Figure B.25 Normalised prices, $n = 3$

22. Squaring equation (7.24) and differentiating, we get

$$2\Delta(t)\frac{d\Delta(t)}{dt} = 2\sum_{i=1}^{n}\left[p_i(t) - p_i^*\right]\frac{dp_i(t)}{dt}. \tag{B.104}$$

Using the adjustment $dp_i(t)/dt = E_i(\mathbf{p})$ and applying Walras's Law in (B.104) gives the result.

23. If aggregate demand satisfies WARP, then for two distinct price vectors, $\mathbf{p}$ and $\hat{\mathbf{p}}$, we have

$$\sum_{i=1}^{n} p_i x_i(\mathbf{p}) < \sum_{i=1}^{n} p_i x_i(\hat{\mathbf{p}}). \tag{B.105}$$

By profit maximisation we must have

$$\sum_{i=1}^{n} p_i q_i(\mathbf{p}) \geq \sum_{i=1}^{n} p_i q_i(\hat{\mathbf{p}}). \tag{B.106}$$

Subtracting (B.106) from (B.105) and subtracting the value of resources from both sides of the inequality we get:

$$\sum_{i=1}^{n} p_i E_i(\mathbf{p}) < \sum_{i=1}^{n} p_i E_i(\hat{\mathbf{p}}). \tag{B.107}$$

24. We would have a series of adjustments in which individuals' endowments change during the process.

25. For household h let

$$B^h := \left\{\mathbf{x}^h : U^h(\mathbf{x}^h) \geq U^h(\mathbf{x}^{*h})\right\}. \tag{B.108}$$

Clearly B^h is convex if U^h is quasiconcave. Also, from (7.33) $B = \sum_h B^h$; so, by Theorem A.6 B is also convex.

26. For diagrams showing this see Figure 9.4 and 9.5.

B.8 Uncertainty and risk

1. If the continuity axiom is violated in this way then there will be a 'hole' in each indifference curve exactly at the point where it intersects the 45° ray.

2. Risk neutral—straight-line contours. Risk lover—contours bend the 'wrong' way.

3. The behaviour is inconsistent with the continuity axiom. However, there is a large literature on the preference-reversal phenomenon and it has been argued that the transitivity axiom is problematic here (Loomes and Sugden 1983).

4. 'Disappointment' refers to the relationship between different outcomes on the same gamble. 'Regret' requires a comparison between two different gambles (Sugden 1986).

5. Given that the function u in (8.1) is defined up to an affine transformation, we could always replace u by $u/\sum\pi_\omega$.

6. The slope of the indifference curve is given by

$$-\frac{\pi_{\text{RED}}u_x(x_{\text{RED}})}{\pi_{\text{BLUE}}u_x(x_{\text{BLUE}})}.$$

Putting $x_{\text{RED}} = x_{\text{BLUE}}$ shows that where the indifference curve intersects the diagonal it has slope

$$-\frac{\pi_{\text{RED}}}{\pi_{\text{BLUE}}}.$$

Draw a line through $(x_{\text{RED}}, x_{\text{BLUE}})$ with this slope. Let (z, z) be the point where this line intersects the diagonal. By construction

$$\frac{z - x_{\text{BLUE}}}{z - x_{\text{RED}}} = -\frac{\pi_{\text{RED}}}{\pi_{\text{BLUE}}}$$

and so

$$\pi_{\text{BLUE}}[z - x_{\text{BLUE}}] + \pi_{\text{RED}}[z - x_{\text{RED}}] = 0.$$

Given that the probabilities sum to 1 this equation implies

$$z = \pi_{\text{RED}}x_{\text{RED}} + \pi_{\text{BLUE}}x_{\text{BLUE}}.$$

Therefore z is the expected value of $(x_{\text{RED}}, x_{\text{BLUE}})$.

7. According to the standard theory expounded here the answer must be 'no' if the person is risk neutral or risk averse. Of course one could assume that the act of participating in the lottery itself yielded pleasure.

8. Consider a prospect $P_0 := (x^0_{\text{RED}}, x^0_{\text{BLUE}})$ and let

$$R := \pi_{\text{RED}}x^0_{\text{RED}} + \pi_{\text{BLUE}}x^0_{\text{BLUE}} \tag{B.109}$$

for arbitrary positive values of $\pi_{\text{RED}}, \pi_{\text{BLUE}}$ such that $\pi_{\text{BLUE}} = 1 - \pi_{\text{RED}}$. Define $\bar{P} := (R, R)$ and draw a line from P_0 through $\bar{P}$ to intersect the indifference curve again at $P_1 := (x^1_{\text{RED}}, x^1_{\text{BLUE}})$. By construction $U(P_0) = U(P_1)$ and quasiconcavity implies

$$U(\bar{P}) \geq U(P_0).$$

However, using (B.109) and the definitions of $\bar{P}$ and P_0, the last equation implies

$$u\left(\pi_{\text{RED}}x^0_{\text{RED}} + \pi_{\text{BLUE}}x^0_{\text{BLUE}}\right) \geq \pi_{\text{RED}}u\left(x^0_{\text{RED}}\right) + \pi_{\text{BLUE}}u\left(x^0_{\text{BLUE}}\right).$$

Given that this holds for arbitrary weights $\pi_{\text{RED}}, \pi_{\text{BLUE}}$ this implies that u is concave.

9. Figure B.26 provides an example—for more see Friedman and Savage (1948: 297).

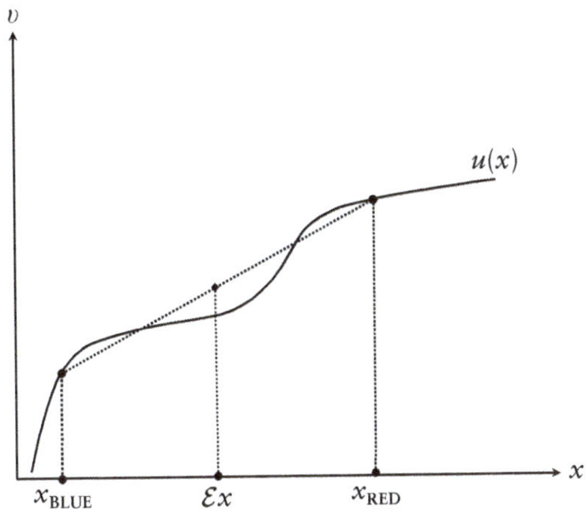

Figure B.26 Ambiguous risk attitude

10. Let a new function $\hat{u}$ be defined as in (8.2). Clearly, for any value of x, we have

$$\hat{u}_x(x) = bu_x(x)$$

$$\hat{u}_{xx}(x) = bu_{xx}(x).$$

So

$$\hat{a}(x) := -\frac{\hat{u}_{xx}(x)}{\hat{u}_x(x)} = a(x).$$

11. Expanding the left-hand side of (8.4) we have

$$u(\mathcal{E}x) + u_x(\mathcal{E}x)[\xi - \mathcal{E}x] + \frac{1}{2}u_{xx}(\mathcal{E}x)[\xi - \mathcal{E}x]^2 \ldots$$

Similarly the right-hand side, expanded around $\mathcal{E}x$, becomes:

$$u(\mathcal{E}x) + u_x(\mathcal{E}x)\mathcal{E}[x - \mathcal{E}x] + \frac{1}{2}u_{xx}(\mathcal{E}x)\mathcal{E}[x - \mathcal{E}x]^2 \ldots$$

Equating these we get

$$u_x(\mathcal{E}x)[\xi - \mathcal{E}x] + \frac{1}{2}u_{xx}(\mathcal{E}x)[\xi - \mathcal{E}x]^2 \ldots = \frac{1}{2}u_{xx}(\mathcal{E}x)\mathcal{E}[x - \mathcal{E}x]^2 \ldots$$

For small risks ξ is close to $\mathcal{E}x$ and we may neglect terms in $[\xi - \mathcal{E}x]^r$ for $r \geq 2$. So, noting that $\text{var}(x) = \mathcal{E}[x - \mathcal{E}x]^2$, we have

$$u_x(\mathcal{E}x)[\xi - \mathcal{E}x] \simeq \frac{1}{2}u_{xx}(\mathcal{E}x)\text{var}(x).$$

Dividing the equation in thc question by $u_x(\mathcal{E}x)$ and using the definition of a we get Theorem 8.2.

12. It is immediate from Definition 8.2 that

$$\varrho(x) = xa(x). \tag{B.110}$$

Differentiating:

$$\frac{d\varrho(x)}{dx} = a(x) + x\frac{da(x)}{dx}.$$

13. Given the cardinal utility (felicity) function u, let a new function $\hat{u}$ be defined as

$$\hat{u} = \varphi(u) \tag{B.111}$$

where φ is a differentiable function with first derivative positive and second derivative negative. Applying the function-of-a-function rule of differentiation, for any value of x we have

$$\hat{u}_x(x) = \varphi_u(u)\, u_x(x)$$

$$\hat{u}_{xx}(x) = \varphi_{uu}(u)\, u_x(x)^2 + \varphi_u(u)\, u_{xx}(x)\,.$$

So

$$\hat{a}(x) := -\frac{\hat{u}_{xx}(x)}{\hat{u}_x(x)} = -\frac{\varphi_{uu}(u)}{\varphi_u(u)} u_x(x) + a(x).$$

Given that $\varphi_u(\cdot)$ and $u_x(\cdot)$ are positive and $\varphi_{uu}(\cdot)$ is negative we must have

$$\hat{a}(x) > a(x).$$

Using (B.110) and multiplying the last equation by x gives

$$\hat{\varrho}(x) > \varrho(x).$$

14. Using equation (8.4) we have

$$\hat{u}(\hat{\xi}) = \mathcal{E}\hat{u}(x)$$

$$= \mathcal{E}\varphi(u(x))\,. \tag{B.112}$$

By Jensen's inequality (A.66), if φ is a concave function then

$$\mathcal{E}\varphi(\upsilon) \le \varphi(\mathcal{E}\upsilon)\,. \tag{B.113}$$

Using (B.112) and (B.113) we have

$$\hat{u}(\hat{\xi}) \le \varphi(\mathcal{E}u(x)) \tag{B.114}$$

so that, using (8.4) and (B.111), we have

$$\hat{u}(\hat{\xi}) \le \varphi(u(\xi)) = \hat{u}(\xi). \tag{B.115}$$

Given that $\hat{u}$ is monotonic, this implies $\hat{\xi} \le \xi$.

15. Constant absolute risk aversion means

$$-\frac{u_{xx}(x)}{u_x(x)} = a. \tag{B.116}$$

Define the function φ as the logarithm of the first derivative of u so that

$$\varphi(x) := \log(u_x(x))\,. \tag{B.117}$$

Then (B.116) implies

$$\frac{d\varphi(x)}{dx} = -a. \tag{B.118}$$

Integrating both sides, (B.118) has as a solution

$$\varphi(x) = -ax + \text{constant}$$

which implies

$$u_x(x) = e^{\varphi(x)} = be^{-ax} \tag{B.119}$$

where b is an arbitrary positive constant. Integrating B.119 we get

$$u(x) = a - \frac{b}{a}e^{-ax} \tag{B.120}$$

where a is an arbitrary constant.

16. For part (a) see Figure B.27 depicting two sets of indifference curves in state-space. Notice that, for either set of indifference curves, where the indifference curves intersect any given 45° line, the slope of the indifference curves is the same. Also note that, by inspection of the slopes where they intersect the 45° ray through the origin, the solid indifference curves represent higher $\pi_{\text{RED}}/\pi_{\text{BLUE}}$ than the dashed indifference curves. For part (b) see Figure B.28.

17. CRRA means

$$-x\frac{u_{xx}(x)}{u_x(x)} = \varrho. \tag{B.121}$$

As in Mini problem 15 we define φ as the logarithm of u_x—see (B.117) above—(B.121) implies

$$\frac{d\varphi(x)}{dx} = -\frac{\varrho}{x}. \tag{B.122}$$

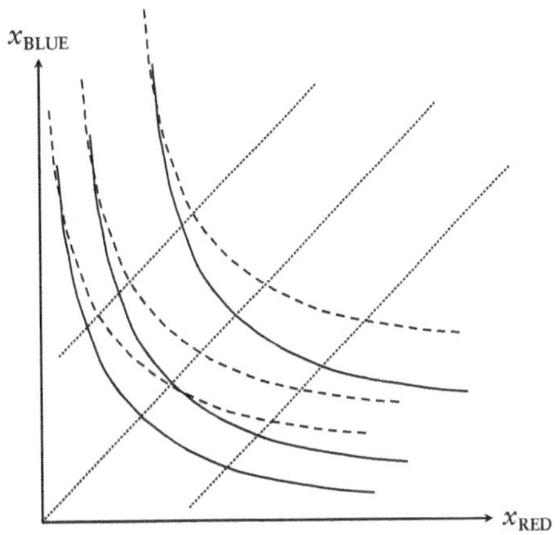

Figure B.27 CARA: changing π

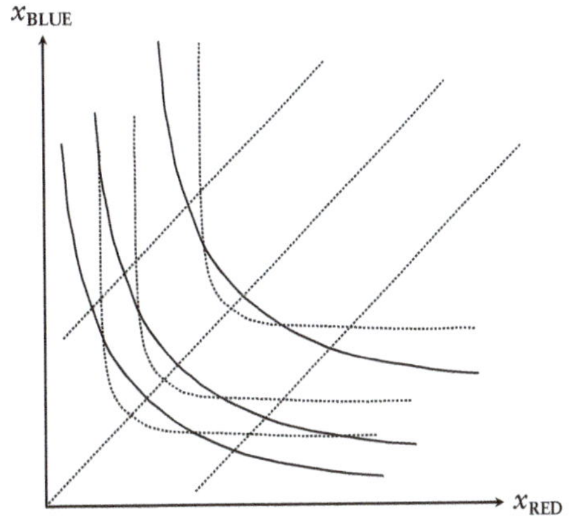

Figure B.28 CARA: $a = 2$ and $a = 5$

Noting that

$$\frac{d\log x}{dx} = \frac{1}{x},$$

integrating both sides of (B.122) we find the solution

$$\varphi(x) = -\varrho \log x + \text{constant}$$

which implies

$$u_x(x) = bx^{-\varrho} \tag{B.123}$$

where b is an arbitrary positive constant. Integrating (B.123) we get

$$u(x) = a + \frac{b}{1-\varrho}x^{1-\varrho} \tag{B.124}$$

where a is an arbitrary constant.

18. The argument generally follows the answer to Mini Problem 16 but now, for either set of indifference curves the slope is the same along any ray through the origin, rather than along all the 45° lines. For part (a) see the right-hand panel of Figure 8.13. For part (b) see the left-hand panel of Figure 8.13.

19. (a) The area contained in an isosceles right-angled triangle. (b) π_{BLUE} is determined implicitly from equation (B.125). (c) Straight lines—see the discussion of Mini Problem 20. See Machina (1982: 305) or Marschak (1950: 115).

20. By definition of probability we have

$$\pi_{\text{RED}} + \pi_{\text{GREEN}} + \pi_{\text{BLUE}} = 1 \tag{B.125}$$

so that

$$\pi_{\text{GREEN}} = 1 - \pi_{\text{RED}} - \pi_{\text{BLUE}}. \tag{B.126}$$

In this case the bilinear form (8.11) can be written

$$\pi_{\text{RED}}\upsilon_{\text{RED}} + \pi_{\text{GREEN}}\upsilon_{\text{GREEN}} + \pi_{\text{BLUE}}\upsilon_{\text{BLUE}}$$

which, in view of (B.126), can be written

$$a_0 + a_1\pi_{\text{RED}} + a_2\pi_{\text{BLUE}}$$

where

$$a_0 := \upsilon_{\text{GREEN}}$$

$$a_1 := \upsilon_{\text{RED}} - \upsilon_{\text{GREEN}}$$

$$a_2 := \upsilon_{\text{BLUE}} - \upsilon_{\text{GREEN}}.$$

So indifference curves in the space of probabilities have the form:

$$a_1\pi_{\text{RED}} + a_2\pi_{\text{BLUE}} = \text{const.}$$

The slope of the indifference curve is given by

$$\frac{d\pi_{\text{BLUE}}}{d\pi_{\text{RED}}} = -\frac{a_1}{a_2} = \frac{\upsilon_{\text{RED}} - \upsilon_{\text{GREEN}}}{\upsilon_{\text{GREEN}} - \upsilon_{\text{BLUE}}}.$$

The above equation shows that if $\upsilon_{\text{RED}} > \upsilon_{\text{GREEN}} > \upsilon_{\text{BLUE}}$, the slope $\frac{d\pi_{\text{BLUE}}}{d\pi_{\text{RED}}}$ is positive. Also, if υ_{BLUE} increases, then the slope also increases.

21. If there is a large number of traders and all the individuals are appropriately 'small' in the sense of section 7.5.2 (page 169) then once again prices may play their decentralising rôle—see the 'second thoughts' discussion in Arrow (1970), essay 2.

22. (a) The sides of the box will be of equal length and the two 45° lines collapse into one. (b) the slope of the a-indifference curves where they cross the 45° line through 0^a equals the slope of the b-indifference curves where they cross the 45° line through 0^b.

23. Bond 1 has a zero rate of return and is indistinguishable from money. Bond 7 pays a return of −100 per cent in state BLUE—i.e. you lose all your money invested if state BLUE occurs.

24. As $\bar{y}$ the set A expands proportionately—each vertex moves along a ray through the origin and the slopes of the facets stay constant. If the indifference curves in the state-space diagram were homothetic then it is clear that the point indicating the optimal portfolio mix would also move outward along a ray through the point P^* as A expands. But if preferences were non-homothetic then the optimal portfolio mix will shift and it may be that one eventually switches to another facet of A.

25. (a) We have

$$\mathcal{E}\left(ru_y\left(\bar{y}+\beta^* r\right)\right) \leq 0 \tag{B.127}$$

for the case where $\beta^* = 0$—see Figure B.29. We also have

$$\mathcal{E}\left(ru_y\left(\bar{y}+\beta^* r\right)\right) \geq 0 \tag{B.128}$$

for the case where $\beta^* = \bar{y}$—see Figure B.30.

26. From Definition 8.1 we have

$$a(x) = -\frac{u_{xx}(x)}{u_x(x)}.$$

Differentiating this with respect to x we have

$$\frac{da(x)}{dx} = -\frac{u_{xxx}(x)}{u_x(x)} + \left[\frac{u_{xx}(x)}{u_x(x)}\right]^2.$$

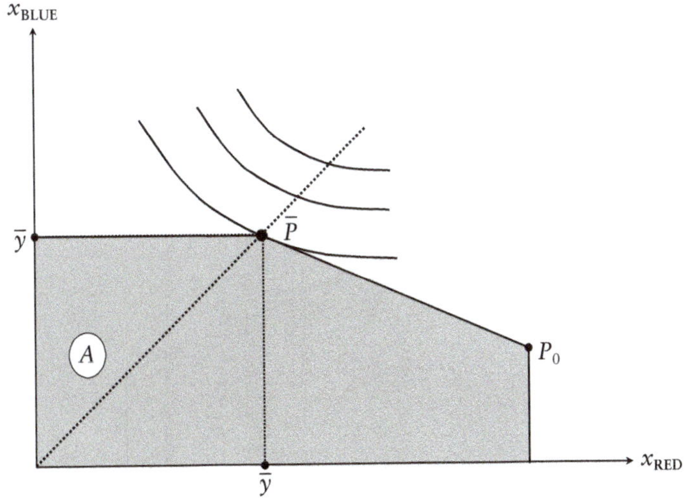

Figure B.29 Portfolio choice: playing safe

So, the condition for decreasing absolute risk aversion is

$$u_{xxx}(x) > \frac{u_{xx}(x)^2}{u_x(x)}.$$

27. Differentiating (8.27) with respect to t we obtain

$$\mathcal{E}\left(ru_y\left(\bar{y}+\beta^* tr\right)\right)+\mathcal{E}\left(t\beta^* u_{yy}\left(\bar{y}+\beta^* tr\right)r^2\right)+\mathcal{E}\left(tu_{yy}\left(\bar{y}+\beta^* tr\right)r^2\frac{\partial\beta^*}{\partial t}\right)=0. \quad \text{(B.129)}$$

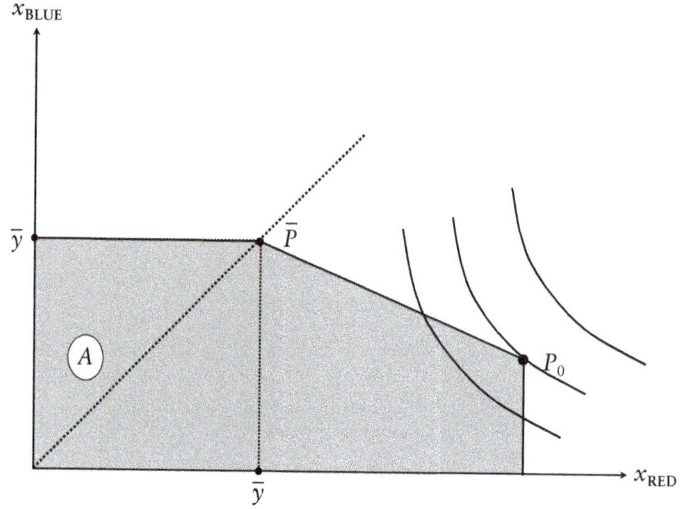

Figure B.30 Portfolio choice: plunging in the risky asset

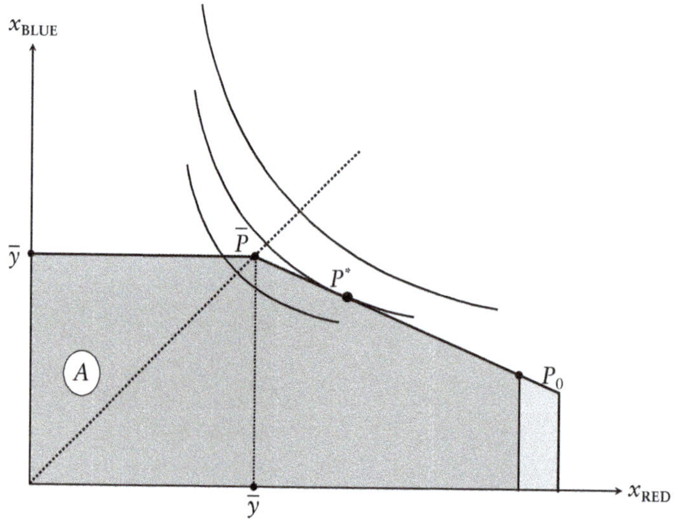

Figure B.31 Effect of an increase in spread

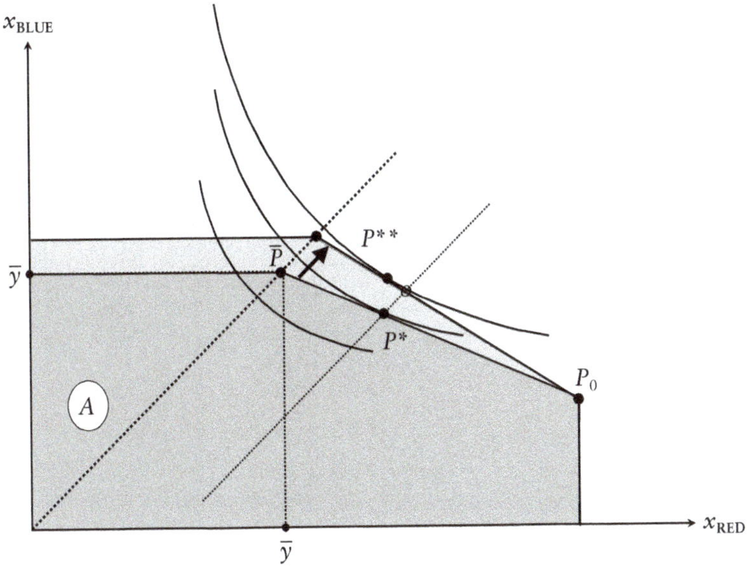

Figure B.32 A cut in the premium

The first term in (B.129) is zero because of the FOC (8.27); so (B.129) can be written

$$\mathcal{E}\left(u_{yy}\left(\bar{y}+\beta^{*}tr\right)r^{2}\right)\left[t\beta^{*}+t\frac{\partial\beta^{*}}{\partial t}\right]=0. \tag{B.130}$$

Given that $\mathcal{E}\left(u_{yy}\left(\bar{y}+\beta^{*}tr\right)r^{2}\right)>0$ for any distribution where $\beta^{*}>0$ we immediately get $\frac{1}{\beta^{*}}\frac{\partial\beta^{*}}{\partial t}=-1$. The solution is illustrated in Figure B.31 where $t>1$ is the proportion by which the line through $\bar{P}$ and P_0 has extended.

$$x_{\text{RED}}-\bar{y}=\beta^{*}tr'$$

$$x_{\text{BLUE}}-\bar{y}=\beta^{*}tr^{\circ}.$$

28. The change is depicted in Figure B.32: clearly risk taking increases.

B.9 Welfare

1. Utility is ordinal, and so $\succeq$ will be invariant if utilities are transformed by some monotonic function φ. See the answer to part (a) in Mini problem 6 on efficiency below.

2. Quasi-transitivity does not get us very far—see Sen (1970).

3. In 9.1 the preferences are

Alf	Bill	Charlie
θ''	θ	θ'
θ'	θ'	θ
θ	θ''	θ''

If they vote as between pairs of states then the ordering is clearly $\theta'\succ\theta\succ\theta''$ where '$\succ$' denotes strict preference.

4. Given the independent 'single-peaked' rankings of each of the two characteristics we only get single peaked rankings over the social states if the set of alternatives can be represented along a straight line in the space of the two characteristics. This is a serious restriction on the applicability of the 'single-peak' criterion.

5. (a) The votes cast for $[\theta, \theta', \theta'', \theta''']$ are $[8, 7, 7, 8]$. (b) The votes cast for $[\theta, \theta'']$ (when other states have been excluded) are $[4, 5]$: inspection of the voting points yields the result.

6. (a) Scale and origin changes clearly leave the shape of the diagram unaltered. (b) Although the curvature and slope of part of the frontier will change, horizontal and vertical segments will still remain; in (a) and (b) the set of Pareto-efficient states is unaltered. (c) Points to the 'north-east' in the diagram.

7.

$$\frac{\partial \mathcal{L}}{\partial x_i^1} = U_i^1\left(\mathbf{x}^1\right) - \kappa_i \leq 0 \tag{B.131}$$

8. (a) Replace (9.11) by

$$\lambda_h U_i^h\left(\mathbf{x}^h\right) \leq \kappa_i \tag{B.132}$$

(b) Replace (9.13) by

$$\mu_f \Phi_i^f(\mathbf{q}^f) \geq \kappa_i \tag{B.133}$$

9. Take a contour and 'convexify' it by laying a ruler or straight edge as a tangent at two points. Figure B.33 illustrates it for the case of a single firm; Figure 7.17 illustrates it for a single consumer.

10. (a) Potential earnings that may be inherent in someone's innate talents—see chapters 11 and 12 for an account of the issues to which this gives rise.

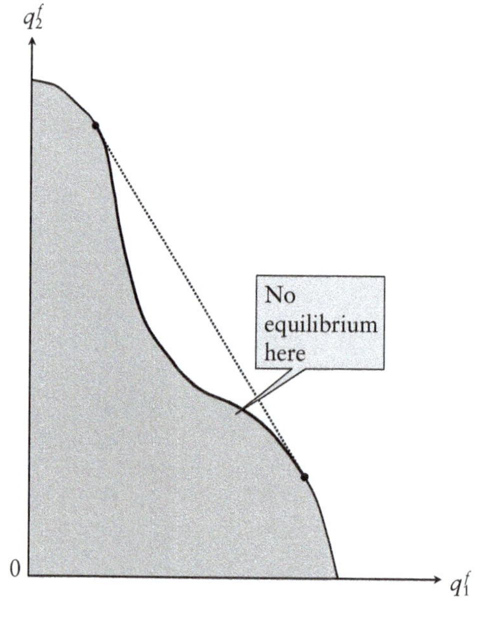

Figure B.33 Points that cannot be supported in an equilibrium

(b) The income tax is effectively a tax on working time. We can think of this as introducing a distortion such as the 'price wedge' δ discussed in section 9.3.2.

11. Some resources such as human capital or 'labour power' may be regarded as inalienably the right of their possessor even if they could be costlessly observed. See Exercise 9.6 as an example of what may happen in such cases.

12. Notice the slope of the two tangents representing consumer and producer prices and the welfare loss in Figure B.34. We are on the bottom indifference curve at the point marked with a '•', whereas we could be on the middle indifference curve marked with a '∘'.

13. From equations (7.8) and (7.9) we have

$$y^h = \sum_{i=1}^{n} p_i R_i^h + \sum_{f=1}^{n_f} \varsigma_f^h \Pi^f(\mathbf{p}). \tag{B.134}$$

Substitute this in (9.20) and use Theorem 2.7 in chapter 2, from which we know that the effect of a change in price p_i on the profits of firm f is given by $q_i^f(\mathbf{p})$ where the function $q_i^f(\cdot)$ is the counterpart of (2.72). Then using the facts that

$$\sum_{h=1}^{n_h} \varsigma_f^h = 1,$$

$$\sum_{h=1}^{n_h} R_i^h = R_i,$$

$$\sum_{f=1}^{n_f} q_i^f = q_i$$

gives (9.21).

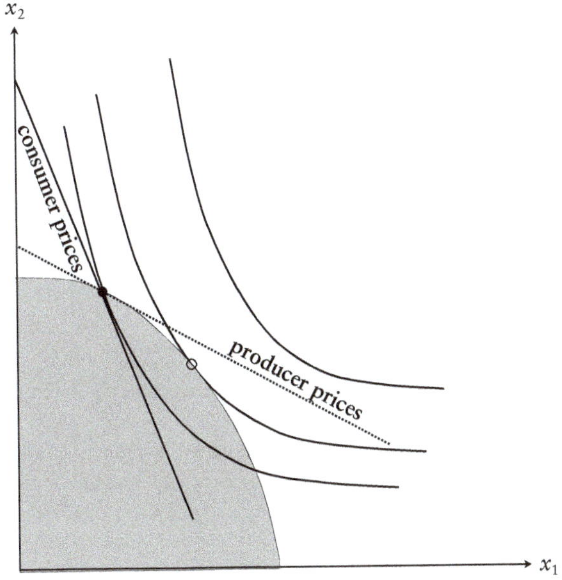

Figure B.34 Utility loss through price distortion

14. A Taylor expansion of (9.21) gives

$$\Lambda(\Delta\mathbf{p}) \approx \Lambda(\mathbf{z}) + \sum_{i=1}^{n} \frac{\partial \Lambda(\mathbf{z})}{\partial z_i}\Delta p_i + \frac{1}{2}\sum_{i=1}^{n}\sum_{j=1}^{n} \frac{\partial^2 \Lambda(\mathbf{z})}{\partial z_i \partial z_j} + \Delta p_i \Delta p_i \ldots \tag{B.135}$$

evaluated at $\mathbf{z} = \mathbf{0}$. Because $\Lambda(0) = 0$ the expression (B.135), when evaluated, provides the following approximation.

$$\Lambda(\Delta\mathbf{p}) \approx \sum_{i=1}^{n}\left[\sum_{h=1}^{n_h} x_i^h - R_i - q_i\right]\Delta p_i - \frac{1}{2}\sum_{i=1}^{n}\sum_{j=1}^{n}\sum_{h=1}^{n_h} C_{ij}^h(\mathbf{p}, \upsilon^h)\Delta p_i \Delta p_j. \tag{B.136}$$

Because of the materials balance condition, the first term in (B.136) vanishes. So, applying Shephard's Lemma again, we find (9.23).

15. We follow the same reasoning as in the answer to Mini Problem 14 but allow for the possibility that $\frac{\partial q_i(\tilde{\mathbf{p}})}{\partial \tilde{p}_j} \neq 0$ where $\tilde{\mathbf{p}}$ denotes producer prices. The counterpart of (B.136) is

$$\Lambda(\Delta\mathbf{p}) \approx \sum_{i=1}^{n}\left[\sum_{h=1}^{n_h} x_i^h - R_i - q_i\right]\Delta p_i$$
$$-\frac{1}{2}\sum_{i=1}^{n}\sum_{j=1}^{n}\left[\sum_{h=1}^{n_h} C_{ij}^h(\mathbf{p}, \upsilon^h) - \frac{\partial q_i(\tilde{\mathbf{p}})}{\partial \tilde{p}_j}\right]\Delta \tilde{p}_i \Delta \tilde{p}_j$$

and so the counterpart of (9.23) is:

$$\Lambda(\Delta\mathbf{p}) \approx -\frac{1}{2}\sum_{i=1}^{n}\sum_{j=1}^{n}\sum_{h=1}^{n_h} H_j^{hi}(\mathbf{p}, \upsilon^h)\Delta p_i \Delta p_j + \frac{1}{2}\sum_{i=1}^{n}\sum_{j=1}^{n} \frac{\partial q_i(\tilde{\mathbf{p}})}{\partial \tilde{p}_j}\Delta \tilde{p}_i \Delta \tilde{p}_j.$$

16. (a) Use the notation of chapter 3, so that p is the price of good 1, etc. From (3.11) we get

$$\frac{p - C_q(\mathbf{w}, q)}{p} = -\frac{1}{\eta}. \tag{B.137}$$

Waste is measured by the area of the triangle in Figure 9.6 $\frac{1}{2}\Delta p_1 \Delta x_1$. Given that $\Delta x_1 = -\eta \Delta p_1 \frac{x_1}{p_1}$, in this case we see that Δp_1 is $p - C_q$ and the change in quantity is $\Delta x_1 = -\eta\left[p - C_q\right] q/p$. So, using (B.137), the measure of waste is given by

$$-\frac{\eta}{2p}\left[p - C_q\right]^2 q$$
$$= -\frac{\eta}{2}\left[\frac{p - C_q}{p}\right]^2 pq$$
$$= -\frac{1}{2\eta}pq.$$

Clearly the loss increases as $[-\eta]$ falls. The intuitive reason for this is that, given $\eta < -1$, the less elastic is consumer demand, the more the monopolist can profitably force price above marginal cost according to (3.11).

17. Yes. Consider a t-fold increase in the inputs of each firm: given decreasing returns to scale then output of each firm taken in isolation would increase by some factor $t' < t$. If there were no externality, then total output would also increase by t'. Under the conditions stated total output will increase by *less* than t'.

18. Reverse the inequality in (9.24). Everything else stays the same except that e_{21}^f is now negative.

19. Notice that q_1^f is now an argument in all firms' production functions.

20. The first term on the left-hand side of (9.29) represents the price that the polluter gets for good 1 (measured in terms of good 2); the term on the right-hand side is the price that consumers will be paying for good 1 (in terms of good 2): the difference is the tax on the polluter, which of course is just the marginal valuation of the externality. However, the apparently simple answer may neglect some serious implementation problems—see chapter 13, section 13.4.

21. Notice that x_1^h now enters the utility function of every household.

22. As in answer 20. Again, check section 13.4.

23. If households $1, \ldots h^*$ are non satiated, and the rest are satiated with good 1, then we have $U_1^h > 0, h = 1, \ldots h^*$, and $U_1^h = 0, h = h^* + 1, \ldots, n_h$. Equation (9.35) still holds (the last $n_h - h^*$ terms are zero) and so too does equation (9.36) if there is some good i in which no one is satiated.

24. Suppose everyone has the same income y^* and that the competitive equilibrium occurs at prices $\mathbf{p}^*$ yielding a bundle $\mathbf{x}^{*h}$ for household h. Because everyone is utility maximising in a competitive equilibrium it must be true that:

$$U^h(\mathbf{x}^{*h}) \geq U^h(\mathbf{x}^h) \tag{B.138}$$

for all $\mathbf{x}^h$ such that

$$\sum_{i=1}^{n} p_i x_i^h \leq y^*. \tag{B.139}$$

Suppose household h were instead to have $\mathbf{x}^{*\ell}$—the bundle of household ℓ. Since everyone has the same income and faces the same prices $\mathbf{x}^{*\ell}$ must also satisfy (B.139), and so (B.138) implies

$$U^h(\mathbf{x}^{*h}) \geq U^h(\mathbf{x}^{*\ell}). \tag{B.140}$$

Nobody wants anyone else's bundle in equilibrium, and so the equilibrium allocation is fair.

25. If all utilities are subjected to a uniform transformation welfare orderings can change. To see this, suppose $W = \sum_h \log(U^h)$, and let state θ yield utilities 2 and 4 for Alf and Bill and let state θ' yield utilities 1 and 6 for Alf and Bill. Now let U^h be replaced by $a + \beta U^h$.

Welfare in state θ is $\log(a + 2\beta) + \log(a + 4\beta) = \log(a^2 + 6a\beta + 8\beta^2)$
Welfare in state θ' is $\log(a + \beta) + \log(a + 6\beta) = \log(a^2 + 7a\beta + 6\beta^2)$

This social welfare function ranks state θ over state θ' if $2\beta > a$ and θ' over θ otherwise. See also the answers to Mini Problems 1 and 6.

26. Using Roy's identity $V_i^h = -x_i^* V_y^h$. Substituting this in (9.51) gives the left-hand side of (9.52). Writing M for $W_h V_y^h$ gives the right-hand side of (9.52).

27. We just need the following reinterpretation. Suppose there are n_1 households of type 1 and n_2 households of type 2 and that each person in a type-2 household with household income y^h gets the same level of welfare as if he were living alone with income y^h/β where $\beta > 1$. Then we can say that there are hn_h persons in the economy with 'equivalised' incomes y_*^h, such that $y_*^h = y^h$ for type-1 persons, $y_*^h = y^h/\beta$ for type-2 persons. Mean equivalised income is

$$\frac{n_1\bar{y}^1 + 2n_2\bar{y}^2/\beta}{n_1 + 2n_2}$$

where $\bar{y}^j$ is the mean household income of type j.

28. In the case where all households are of the same type, each 'probability' is just $1/n_h$. In the two-type example in Mini Problem 27 the 'probability' is $1/[n_1 + 2n_2]$ for type-1 persons and $2/[n_1 + 2n_2]$ for type-2 persons.

29. (a) Let $\hat{\zeta} = \varphi(\zeta)$. Then by definition we have

$$\hat{\iota}(y) = -\zeta_y(y)\frac{\varphi_{\zeta\zeta}(\zeta(y))}{\varphi_\zeta(\zeta(y))} + \iota(y).$$

Clearly if φ is increasing and concave the first term on the right-hand side is non-negative and the result follows. (b) Follows from the answer to Mini Problem 13 on page 193.

B.10 Strategic behaviour

1. If Alf makes his move but can hide the announcement until after Bill has made his move then Bill's information set is exactly the same as in Figure 10.1. Therefore Bill's problem is exactly the same as in the simultaneous move game.

2. The game form, known as 'Battle of the Sexes' is depicted in Table B.1 and in Figure B.35.

3. Compare Figure B.36 with Figure 10.1. Now it is as though Bill moves first but then conceals his move until Alf has made his move (see the answer to Mini Problem 1). It is clear that the two versions are equivalent in economic terms.

4. For each agent it is clear that the payoff is higher if he chooses strategy 1 rather than 2, irrespective of what the other agent does. $\left[s_1^a, s_1^b\right]$ is the dominant-strategy solution, yielding the payoff $(3, 3)$. This payoff is clearly the highest attainable for each player from any cell in the table: but this property is not true of the dominant-strategy solution to the game in Table 10.1.

5. We are implicitly assuming that it is common knowledge that both players are individually rational. Alf knows that Bill would never choose a dominated strategy and so Alf can eliminate such strategies from consideration when making his own decision. Likewise Bill can eliminate from consideration any of Alf's dominated strategies because he knows Alf to be rational. There is an example of this in Exercise 10.1.

6. It depends on whether there is reason for one player to believe the other. In the case of Table 10.3 if player b were to announce an intention to play [left] this is likely to be believed by player a in that it is clearly in the interest of both of them to be at $(3, 3)$ rather than $(2, 2)$. For more on this see Mini Problem 10 in chapter 12 (page 395) and the discussion of 'cheap talk' in Farrell and Rabin (1996).

		s_1^b [West]	s_2^b [East]
s_1^a	[West]	2,1	0,0
s_2^a	[East]	0,0	1,2

Table B.1 'Battle of the sexes'—strategic form

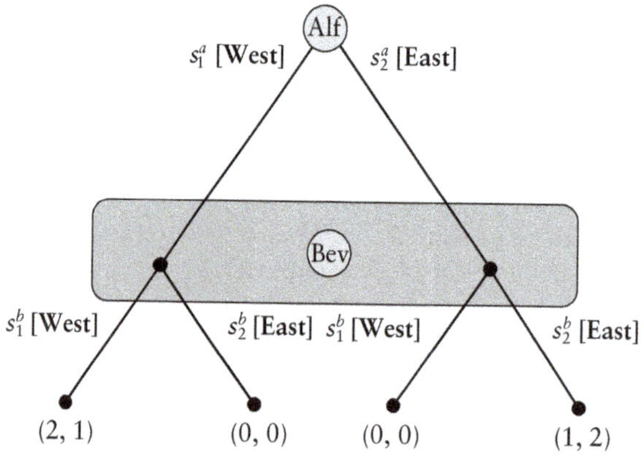

Figure B.35 Battle of the sexes: extensive form

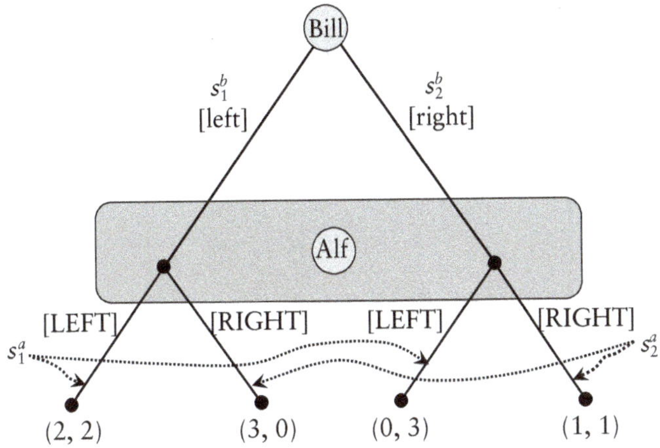

Figure B.36 Extensive form: alternative representation

7. (a) Utility must be in the following (ascending) order: 0 'death', 1 'ignominy', 2 'embarrassment', 3 'hero'.

(b) Unlike the game in Table 10.4 we might think it unlikely that one lad will be convinced by the other's pre-play announcement.

(c) The game then becomes the same as that introduced in Table 10.1, the Prisoner's Dilemma, which is analysed in section 10.3.4: there would be just one Nash equilibrium, which is inefficient.

8. Measure payoffs in terms of (−) the length of the sentence. Then for the two bad guys (labelled *a* and *b* as usual) the strategic form of the game is as in Table B.2; the dilemma is immediate—whatever you believe the other person to be doing, given that you are held in separate locations it is always in your interest to confess rather than stay shtumm. 'Confess' exactly fits the definition of a dominant strategy on page 277. Moreover, even if this trick of the authorities is well known and the bad guys communicate to each other the desirability of their both staying shtumm, the moment they are separated again the dilemma re-emerges.

9. In Figure B.37 the possible outcomes are illustrated by dots; Nash equilibria are circled.

10. The answer is immediate from Figure 10.2. With the transformations suggested all one is doing is transforming each of the two utility axes—the problem remains unaltered.

11. The two prisoners cannot sign a meaningful and binding agreement without introducing an additional player to the game—an enforcement agent.

12. Here strategies are actions and the game is completely described by Table B.3. The underlined payoffs indicate the best responses. For example '<u>1</u>' in the top left-hand cell means that [H] is *a*'s best response if *b* chooses [h]. It is clear that there is no situation where each agent is simultaneously making the best reply to the other. Therefore there is no Nash equilibrium in pure strategies.

		s_1^b [shtumm]	s_2^b [confess]
s_1^a	[shtumm]	−2, −2	−20, −1
s_2^a	[confess]	−1, −20	−10, −10

Table B.2 The Prisoner's Dilemma

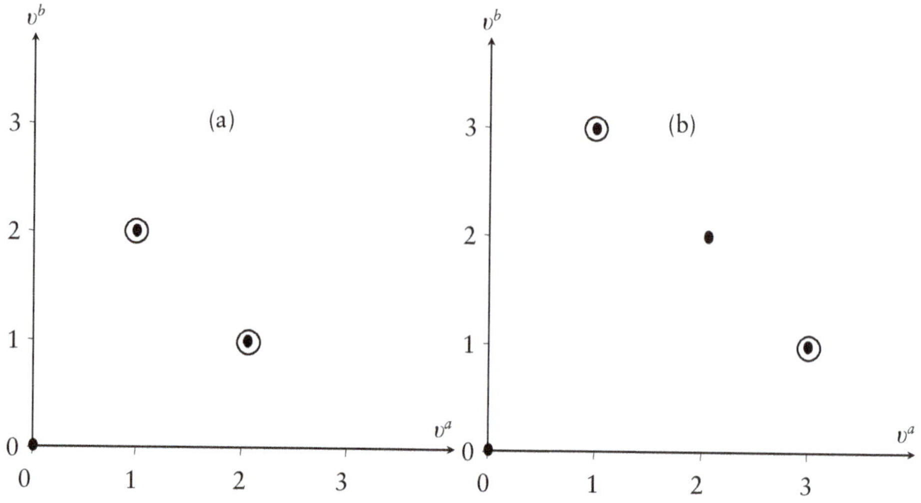

Figure B.37 (a) Battle of sexes (b) Chicken

		s_1^b [h]	s_2^b [t]
s_1^a	[H]	$\underline{1}, -1$	$-1, \underline{1}$
s_2^a	[T]	$-1, \underline{1}$	$\underline{1}, -1$

Table B.3 Matching pennies

13. If Alf believes that Bill will use strategy s_1^b with probability π^b and strategy s_1^b with probability $1 - \pi^b$ then, from the top row of Table 10.5, Alf's payoff from using strategy s_1^a is $\pi^b \cdot 2 + \left[1 - \pi^b\right] \cdot 0 = 2\pi^b$; likewise, from the bottom row of Table 10.5, his payoff from using strategy s_2^a is $\pi^b \cdot 0 + \left[1 - \pi^b\right] \cdot 1 = 1 - \pi^b$. So if Alf randomises between s_1^a and s_2^a with probabilities $(\pi^a, 1 - \pi^a)$ his expected payoff is

$$\pi^a \left[2\pi^b\right] + [1 - \pi^a]\left[1 - \pi^b\right]$$
$$= 3\pi^b\pi^a - \pi^a + 1 - \pi^b$$

By similar reasoning, if Bill believes that Alf will use strategies s_1^a and s_2^a with probabilities $(\pi^a, 1 - \pi^a)$ then his payoff from using strategy s_1^b is $\pi^a \cdot 2 + [1 - \pi^a] \cdot 1 = \pi^a + 1$, and his payoff from using strategy s_2^b is $\pi^a \cdot 3 + [1 - \pi^a] \cdot 0 = 3\pi^a$. So if Bill randomises between s_1^b and s_2^b with probabilities $\left(\pi^b, 1 - \pi^b\right)$ his expected payoff is

$$\pi^b [\pi^a + 1] + \left[1 - \pi^b\right][3\pi^a]$$
$$= \pi^b + 3\pi^a - 2\pi^a\pi^b.$$

14. From (10.8), if $\pi^a = 0$ Alf's expected utility is $1 - \pi^b$ and if $\pi^a = 1$ Alf's expected utility is $\left[3\pi^b - 1\right] + 1 - \pi^b = 2\pi^b$. These correspond to the utility levels Alf gets if he presses one or other

of the two radio buttons. So Alf is indifferent to which of the two buttons s_1^a or s_2^a he presses if

$$1 - \pi^b = 2\pi^b$$
$$\pi^b = \frac{1}{3}.$$

From (10.9), if $\pi^b = 0$ Bill's expected utility is $3\pi^a$ and if $\pi^b = 1$ Bill's expected utility is $[1 - 2\pi^a] + 3\pi^a = 1 + \pi^a$. So Bill is indifferent to which of the two buttons s_1^b or s_2^b he presses if

$$3\pi^a = 1 + \pi^a$$
$$\pi^a = \frac{1}{2}.$$

15. Suppose b plays [h] with probability π^b and [t] with probability $1 - \pi^b$. If a plays [H] the expected payoff is

$$1 \cdot \pi^b - 1 \cdot \left[1 - \pi^b\right] = 2\pi^b - 1.$$

If a plays [T] the expected payoff is

$$-1 \cdot \pi^b + 1 \cdot \left[1 - \pi^b\right] = 1 - 2\pi^b.$$

So, if a plays [H] with probability π^a and [T] with probability $1 - \pi^a$ the expected payoff is

$$\pi^a \left[2\pi^b - 1\right] + [1 - \pi^a]\left[1 - 2\pi^b\right] = 4\pi^a\pi^b - 2\pi^a + 1 - 2\pi^b. \tag{B.141}$$

Clearly, for a given value of π^b, the expression on the right-hand side of (B.141) is increasing in π^a if $\pi^b > 0.5$ and is decreasing if $\pi^b < 0.5$. So the best-response correspondence χ^a is given by

$$\chi^a\left(\pi^b\right) = \begin{cases} 1 & \text{if } \pi^b > 0.5 \\ [0,1] & \text{if } \pi^b = 0.5 \\ 0 & \text{if } \pi^b < 0.5. \end{cases}$$

The same argument can be used for player b from which it is clear that the mixed-strategy equilibrium is given by $\left[\pi^a, \pi^b\right] = [0.5, 0.5]$.

16. We follow the same track as Mini Problem 13. If Alf believes that Bill will use strategy s_1^b with probability π^b and strategy s_1^b with probability $1 - \pi^b$ then, from the top row of Table 10.1, Alf's payoff from using strategy s_1^a is $\pi^b \cdot 2 + \left[1 - \pi^b\right] \cdot 0 = 2\pi^b$; likewise, from the bottom row of Table 10.1, his payoff from using strategy s_2^a is $\pi^b \cdot 3 + \left[1 - \pi^b\right] \cdot 1 = 1 + 2\pi^b$. So if Alf randomises between s_1^a and s_2^a with probabilities $(\pi^a, 1 - \pi^a)$ his expected payoff is

$$\pi^a \left[2\pi^b\right] + [1 - \pi^a]\left[1 + 2\pi^b\right]$$
$$= 1 + 2\pi^b - \pi^a.$$

But this is everywhere decreasing in π^a: the optimum for Alf is clearly to put $\pi^a = 0$, in other words adopt only strategy s_2^a. Because the game is symmetric, the same logic works for Bill: his optimum puts $\pi^b = 0$ so that he adopts only strategy s_2^b. The outcome is exactly the same as when we considered pure strategies only.

17. Consider what happens horizontally on the diagram assuming that you represent firm 1: given q^2 constant, increasing your own output from zero at first increases profits and then, as the market becomes saturated with your output (the price is declining as your output increases), profits must decrease. Now consider what happens vertically: cutting q^2 while keeping your own output constant must always increase your profits because the price will rise as q^2 falls.

18. For any given $q^2 \geq \overline{q}^2$ the market price would be so low that firm 1 would choose $q^1 = 0$; the situation would become a monopoly for firm 2.

19. If there is some $\overline{q}$ such that a monopolist setting $q > \overline{q}$ would make negative profits then it is reasonable to assume that the set of strategies is convex and compact—the interval $[0, \overline{q}]$ would do. From (10.12) the requirement that payoff functions be continuous is clearly satisfied if the inverse demand function is continuous (innocuous?) and cost functions are continuous in output (not so innocuous). The requirement that payoff functions be quasiconcave imposes conditions on the second derivative of the demand function and the cost functions.

20. The isoprofit contours are given by

$$p(q)\, q^f - C^f\left(q^f\right) = \text{const} \tag{B.142}$$

$f = 1, 2$. The slope of firm 1's isoprofit curve is therefore found from

$$p_q(q)\, q^1 \left[1 + \frac{dq^2}{dq^1}\right] + p(q) - C_q^1\left(q^1\right) = 0 \tag{B.143}$$

so that

$$\frac{dq^2}{dq^1} = \frac{C_q^1(q^1) - p(q)}{p_q(q)\, q^1} - 1. \tag{B.144}$$

The slope of firm 2's isoprofit curve is found from

$$p_q(q)\, q^2 \left[1 + \frac{dq^2}{dq^1}\right] + p(q)\frac{dq^2}{dq^1} - C_q^2\left(q^2\right)\frac{dq^2}{dq^1} = 0 \tag{B.145}$$

so that

$$\frac{dq^2}{dq^1} = \frac{p_q(q)\, q^2}{C_q^2(q^2) - p_q(q)\, q^2 - p(q)}. \tag{B.146}$$

If (10.18) and (10.19) are satisfied then (B.144) and (B.146) become

$$\frac{dq^2}{dq^1} = \frac{C_q^1(q^1) - p(q) - p_q(q)\, q^1}{p_q(q)\, q^1} = \frac{q^2}{q^1} \tag{B.147}$$

$$\frac{dq^2}{dq^1} = \frac{q^2}{q^1}. \tag{B.148}$$

The last two equations demonstrate that at the joint-profit-maximising solution the slopes of the two isoprofit curves (B.144) and (B.146) become identical and equal to $\frac{q^2}{q^1}$, the slope of the ray through the origin.

21. Under the stated conditions firm 2's profits must fall if market demand is downward sloping. If firm 2's output is kept constant and firm 1 increases its output then the increase in total output must reduce the market price and so reduce firm 2's profits.

22. The possible payoffs are shown in Figure B.38 where the labelling convention is the same as for Table 10.7. The profit frontier has slope 45°. However, suppose that the firms adopt the joint-profit-maximising strategy and then agree on some other point on the frontier as a division of the profit. It is clear each firm would still have the incentive to try to increase its own output (and thereby its profit) if it thought that the other firm's output were fixed.

23. We could solve this in the manner of section 3.6.1 (page 59)—by finding the monopolist's optimal output and then inferring what the price must be. From (10.20) for a quantity q price in the market is given by

$$p = \beta_0 - \beta q \tag{B.149}$$

and so profits are

$$\Pi = [\beta_0 - \beta q]\, q - cq.$$

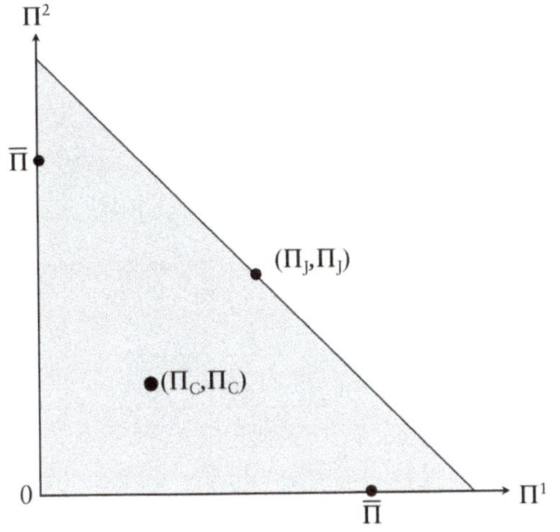

Figure B.38 Payoff possibilities

Differentiating this expression with respect to q one has

$$\beta_0 - c - 2\beta q = 0$$

which implies the monopolist's optimal quantity as

$$q_M = \frac{\beta_0 - c}{2\beta}$$

or, equivalently, using (B.149) optimal price is

$$p_M = \frac{\beta_0 + c}{2}. \tag{B.150}$$

However, in the present context it is more natural to model the monopolist as choosing price directly. Putting (10.20) into the expression for profits we get

$$\Pi = [p - c]\,\frac{p - \beta_0}{\beta}.$$

Differentiating this expression with respect to p one has

$$\frac{p - \beta_0}{\beta} + \frac{p - c}{\beta} = 0$$

from which (B.150) follows immediately.

24. The number ε is not well defined in (10.21); it is just small and positive. This means that firm 1 could always find a 'better' response than $p^2 - \varepsilon$ just by halving the value of ε.

Write Π_m for the total profit being made in the industry when the price is set equal to mc, $m = 1, \ldots, 4$ (of course $\Pi_1 = 0$). Following the rules of the Bertrand game, the situation is then as set out in Table B.4. Now that prices have to be integers there is a well-defined best response: if you anticipate the competitor will set price equal to mc you set price equal to $[m-1]\,c$, as long as $m > 1$; if you anticipate that the competitor will set price equal to c you cannot do better than just match the price.

25. Clearly by choosing to be player b you can guarantee that you will get, rather than pay, the dollar. There is an obvious counterpart of first-mover advantage (page 309): but here of course the advantage lies in moving *second*.

		s_1^2 $p=c$	s_2^2 $p=2c$	s_3^2 $p=3c$	s_4^2 $p=4c$
s_1^1	$p=c$	$0,0$	$0,0$	$0,0$	$0,0$
s_2^1	$p=2c$	$0,0$	$\frac{1}{2}\Pi_2, \frac{1}{2}\Pi_2$	$\Pi_2, 0$	$\Pi_2, 0$
s_3^1	$p=3c$	$0,0$	$0, \Pi_2$	$\frac{1}{2}\Pi_3, \frac{1}{2}\Pi_3$	$\Pi_3, 0$
s_4^1	$p=4c$	$0,0$	$0, \Pi_2$	$0, \Pi_3$	$\frac{1}{2}\Pi_4, \frac{1}{2}\Pi_4$

Table B.4 Bertrand model with integer prices

		s_1^b [h-h]	s_2^b [h-t]	s_3^b [t-h]	s_4^b [t-t]
s_1^a	[H]	$1,-1$	$1,-1$	$-1,1$	$-1,1$
s_2^a	[T]	$-1,1$	$1,-1$	$-1,1$	$1,-1$

Table B.5 Matching pennies: sequential version

26. The distinction is essentially about when information becomes available during the game. It is likely that one firm will choose its quantity before the other in the duopoly game, as far as 'real' time is concerned. Nevertheless since the other firm does not observe this choice at the moment of choosing its own quantity, it is as if they were choosing quantities simultaneously, measured in 'playing' time.

27. See Table B.5.

28. If it were known that Alf had played [LEFT] then Bill would do better to play [right] (he would get a payoff of 3 rather than 2) and if it were known that Alf had played [RIGHT] then Bill would also do better to play [right]; knowing this it seems clear that Alf would choose to play [RIGHT] (to avoid the Alf payoff of 0 that would be the consequence of a [LEFT],[right] sequence).

29. The possible payoffs are illustrated in Figure B.37 (a). If the players move sequentially then it is clear that the outcome will be either (2,1) or (1,2) depending on who gets to move first. If they have to move simultaneously there is a coordination problem. Independent randomisation by the two agents does not help much—it produces an outcome pair $\left(\frac{2}{3}, \frac{2}{3}\right)$. But if the two agents implement a correlated random strategy they could guarantee an expected outcome of $\left(\frac{3}{2}, \frac{3}{2}\right)$—see Exercise 10.4 on page 323.

30. Take the left-hand successor node of the node marked #. It belongs in an information set along with two other nodes (the shaded area); but these other two nodes are not successor nodes to #.

31. The Doomsday machine is an extreme version of a *commitment device*. If Bill could set up such a device on Sunday then indeed the 'play [left] whatever' threat becomes credible: Alf would know that Bill cannot change his mind on Monday night.

32. (a) Consider the situation on Friday. Clearly the argument on page 275 applies and [RIGHT],[right] is the dominant-strategy equilibrium for this subgame, whatever may have happened the day before. Now consider the situation on Thursday; the action of neither agent will have an effect on the outcome of the following day's game: only Thursday's payoff is involved. Again [RIGHT],[right] is the dominant-strategy equilibrium. It is clear that the subgame-perfect equilibrium requires Alf to play [RIGHT] on both days and Bill to play [right] on both days.

(b) Just apply the same argument as in part (a) for each day working backwards Wednesday,..., Sunday. The subgame-perfect equilibrium must be as before: [RIGHT],[right] is played on every day.

(c) We can see that such a strategy cannot be Alf's best response to anything that Bill has done up to Wednesday by considering an alternative Alf strategy that has the same actions from Sunday to Tuesday but involves playing [RIGHT] on Wednesday. A switch to this alternative strategy clearly increases Alf's payoff on Wednesday, whatever Bill may have done from Sunday to Wednesday; it leaves Alf's payoffs from Sunday to Tuesday unaltered; it will leave Alf's payoffs on Thursday and Friday unaltered or increased (if Bill changes his actions on those days). We could apply the same argument to any other subperiod (one day or more) where Alf plays [LEFT]. So the Nash equilibrium involves [RIGHT],[right] being played on every day.

(d) It is clear that the discount rate played no role in the solution of parts (a)–(c); so, doubling it will make no difference.

33. The difference in utility per period is $\overline{\upsilon}^a - \upsilon^{*a}$; this applies for every period $t+1, t+2, \ldots$ Discounting this stream back to period $t+1$ using the constant discount factor δ gives the value

$$V := \frac{1}{1-\delta}\left[\upsilon^{*a} - \underline{\upsilon}^a\right].$$

Evaluating this in period t gives

$$\delta V = \frac{\delta}{1-\delta}\left[\upsilon^{*a} - \underline{\upsilon}^a\right].$$

34. Rearranging (10.23) we get the condition for Alf that

$$\delta \geq \frac{\overline{\upsilon}^a - \upsilon^{*a}}{\overline{\upsilon}^a - \underline{\upsilon}^a}.$$

Applying this to Bill also we see that the condition required is

$$\delta \geq \underline{\delta} := \max_h \left\{\frac{\overline{\upsilon}^h - \upsilon^{*h}}{\overline{\upsilon}^h - \underline{\upsilon}^h}\right\}.$$

35. Yes. Check the definition of $\underline{\delta}$ in the answer to Mini Problem 34: it is clear that this critical value could change if utility is subjected to a non-linear transformation (one that is not just a simple change of the origin or the slope). Changing the critical value could affect the existence of a subgame-perfect equilibrium.

36. If firm 1's strategy involved selecting an output of zero, then clearly firm 2's best response is $q^2_{\mathrm{M}} = \chi^2(0)$; likewise if firm 1 were to believe that firm 2's strategy involves producing output q^2_{M} whatever firm 1 does then it is clear that firm 1's best response to this involves choosing output 0. So the strategy pair yielding $(0, q^2_{\mathrm{M}})$ is a Nash equilibrium. But it is not credible because if firm 1 goes first and produces an output $q^1 > 0$ then firm 2, following, would want to reconsider its output decision. So we do not have subgame perfection.

37. With the modified payoffs the incumbent becomes relatively strong. The game can be expressed in strategic form as in Table B.6. The strategy combination $\left[s^b_1, s^a_2\right]$—or equivalently $\left[s^b_2, s^a_2\right]$—is a subgame-perfect equilibrium.

38. (i) The window-cleaning fluid is a variable cost. (ii) The ladder is a fixed cost, but not a sunk cost (you could sell it again, good as new). (iii) The leaflets are fixed costs that are also sunk costs.

		s^b_1 [left-left]	s^b_2 [left-right]	s^b_3 [right-left]	s^b_4 [right-right]
s^a_1	[LEFT]	0, 1	0, 1	2, 0	2, 0
s^a_2	[RIGHT]	**1, 2**	**1, 2**	1, 2	1, 2

Table B.6 Strong incumbent

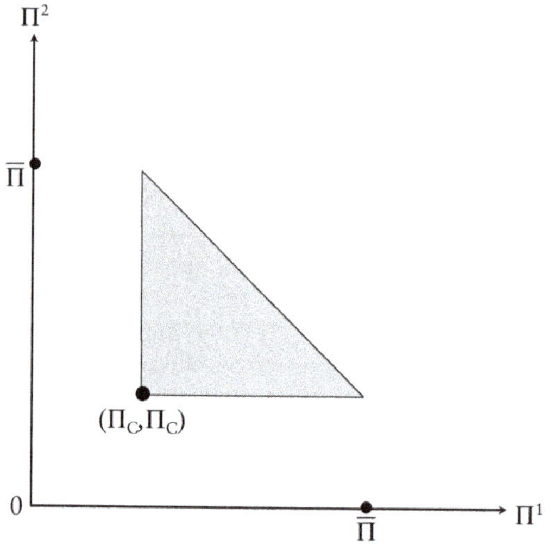

Figure B.39 Payoffs consistent with Nash equilibrium in a repeated Cournot game

39. Note first that the bottom right-hand subgame in Figure 10.12 is irrelevant since the same payoffs arise whatever move Bill makes. If Bill is the incumbent then putting $\Pi_M = 2$, $\Pi_J = 1$, $\Pi_F = 0$ and making similar equivalences for Alf completes the demonstration.

40. See Figure B.39.

In the case of Bertrand competition the Nash equilibrium of the stage game involves setting price equal to marginal cost (see page 293) which, of course, results in zero profits. This is the minimax outcome. So the minimax outcome is implementable as a Nash equilibrium in all the subgames that follow on from a defection from the cooperative solution.

41. Assign the numbers 0 to type [HEALTHY] and 1 to type [ILL] and let the joint probability distribution have the property

$$F\left(\tau^h|\tau^{-h}\right) = \begin{cases} \pi, & 0 \leq \tau^h < 1. \\ 1 & \tau^h = 1. \end{cases}$$

42. Define $K := \pi^2\Pi_J + [1 - \pi^2]\Pi_M$ and $K^* := \pi^2\Pi_J^* + [1 - \pi^2]\Pi_M^*$. Then expected payoff to firm 1 is

$$\begin{aligned} \mathcal{E}\Pi^1 &= \pi^0\left[\pi^1 K^* + \left[1 - \pi^1\right]K\right] + \left[1 - \pi^0\right]K \\ &= \pi^0\pi^1 K^* + \left[1 - \pi^0 + \pi^0 - \pi^0\pi^1 K\right] \\ &= K + [K^* - K]\,\pi^0\pi^1. \end{aligned}$$

This is increasing in π^1 if $K^* > K$, i.e. if

$$\pi^2\Pi_J^* + \left[1 - \pi^2\right]\Pi_M^* > \pi^2\Pi_J + \left[1 - \pi^2\right]\Pi_{M.}$$

Rearranging this gives

$$\pi^2 < \frac{\Pi_M^* - \Pi_M}{\Pi_M^* - \Pi_M + \Pi_J - \Pi_J^*}$$

a small further rearrangement gives (10.37). Note that the sign of γ in (10.38) follows from the assumptions made that $\Pi_M^* > \Pi_M$ and $\Pi_J^* < \Pi_J$.

Define $H := \pi^2\Pi_J + [1 - \pi^2]\underline{\Pi}$ and $H^* := [1 - \pi^2]\underline{\Pi}$. Then the expected payoff to firm 2 is

$$\begin{aligned}\mathcal{E}\Pi^2 &= \pi^0\pi^1 H^* + \pi^0 H - \pi^1\pi^0 H + H - \pi^0 H \\ &= H + [H^* - H]\pi^0\pi^1 \\ &= \pi^2\left[\Pi_J - \underline{\Pi} - \pi^0\pi^1\Pi_J\right] + \underline{\Pi}.\end{aligned}$$

This increases with π^2 if and only if

$$\Pi_J - \pi^1\pi^0\Pi_J - \underline{\Pi} > 0.$$

This is equivalent to

$$\pi^1 < \frac{\Pi_J - \underline{\Pi}}{\pi^0\Pi_J}.$$

If π^0 is small then π^1 is bound to be less than the right-hand side of this expression and so $\mathcal{E}\Pi^2$ must increase with π^2. Hence the solution involves setting $\pi^2 = 1$; this implies that $\mathcal{E}\Pi^1$ must be decreasing in π^1 so that solution is $\pi^1 = 0$.

43. Yes, if (10.40) holds. The mixed-strategy equilibrium is characterised by

$$\left(\pi^{*1}, \pi^{*2}\right) := \left(\frac{1}{\pi^0}\left[1 - \frac{\underline{\Pi}}{\Pi_J}\right], \frac{1}{1+\gamma}\right).$$

B.11 Information

1. Consider the demand for good 1 in the simplest case of the fee schedule, where there is a uniform price p for good 1 and no entry fee. Given the special type of 'zero-income-effect' (or 'quasi-linear') utility function that we are using (11.1), from (11.5) and (11.6) it is clear that we get

$$x_1^* = \varphi(p) \tag{B.151}$$

where φ is the inverse of the marginal-utility function ψ_x. From (B.151) we can see that $\partial x_1^*/\partial y = 0$.

2. Clearly, for any given x_1, the higher the payment level specified in the package, the higher the firm's profits, as long as the consumer still accepts the 'take-it-or-leave-it' offer. So, once the firm has chosen the quantity in the package, it specifies a payment amount that just forces the consumer on to his 'reservation utility level'—i.e. where the consumer is only just willing to accept the package.

3. Suppose that for some (x_1, x_2) and $(\hat{x}_1, \hat{x}_2)$ we have the crossing points of the two persons' indifference curves given by

$$\begin{aligned}\upsilon^\circ &= x_2 + \tau^\circ\psi(x_1) \\ &= \hat{x}_2 + \tau^\circ\psi(\hat{x}_1)\end{aligned}$$

such that

$$\begin{aligned}\upsilon' &= x_2 + \tau'\psi(x_1) \\ &\hat{x}_2 + \tau'\psi(\hat{x}_1).\end{aligned}$$

where $\tau' > \tau^\circ$. Then

$$\begin{aligned}0 &= x_2 - \hat{x}_2 + \tau^\circ[\psi(\hat{x}_1) - \psi(x_1)] \\ 0 &= x_2 - \hat{x}_2 + \tau'[\psi(\hat{x}_1) - \psi(x_1)].\end{aligned}$$

This is only true if

$$\left[\tau' - \tau^\circ\right]\left[\psi\left(\hat{x}_1\right) - \psi\left(x_1\right)\right] = 0.$$

But if ψ is strictly increasing this implies $\hat{x}_1 = x_1$ which, in turn, implies $\hat{x}_2 = x_2$.

4. Differentiating (11.18) we get

$$\begin{aligned}\frac{\partial U\left(\mathbf{x}^*\right)}{\partial \tau} &= \psi\left(x_1^*\right) + \left[\tau\psi_x\left(x_1^*\right) - p\left(x_1^*; \tau\right)\right]\frac{\partial x_1^*}{\partial \tau} \\ &= \psi\left(x_1^*\right) > 0.\end{aligned}$$

5. See Figure B.40. Note that the firm has enough information—and the power—to switch individuals on to the low entry-fee contract (solid line) or the high entry-fee contract (broken line).

6. Differentiating (11.22) we get:

$$\begin{aligned}\frac{\partial F_0^h}{\partial \tau^h} &= \psi\left(\varphi\left(\frac{c}{\tau^h}\right)\right) + \left[\tau^h\psi_x\left(x_1^h\right) - c\right]\frac{\partial \varphi\left(c/\tau^h\right)}{\partial \tau^h} \\ &= \psi\left(\varphi\left(\frac{c}{\tau^h}\right)\right) > 0. \end{aligned} \quad \text{(B.152)}$$

On differentiating (11.17) we find

$$\frac{\partial x_1^*\left(F; \tau\right)}{\partial \tau} = -\frac{1}{\psi_{xx}\left(x_1^*\right)}\frac{p}{\tau^2} > 0. \quad \text{(B.153)}$$

7. Follows from the assumption of zero income effects of the good under consideration.

8. (a) The budget constraint is

$$y^h = \begin{cases} y_0^h + w^h\ell^h - F^h & \text{if } \ell^h > 0 \\ y_0^h & \text{otherwise.}\end{cases}$$

(b) Flipping Figure 11.4 and drawing in the budget constraint we have Figure B.41. The firm pays each worker his marginal product: $w^a = w$ and $w^b = w$ (the slope of the budget constraint in each

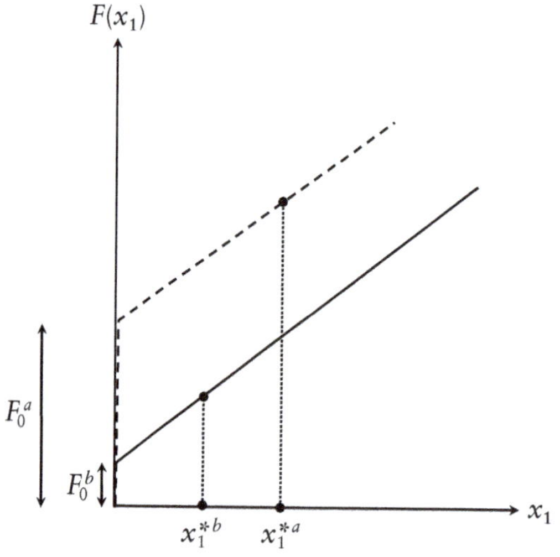

Figure B.40 Full-information contracts: fee schedule

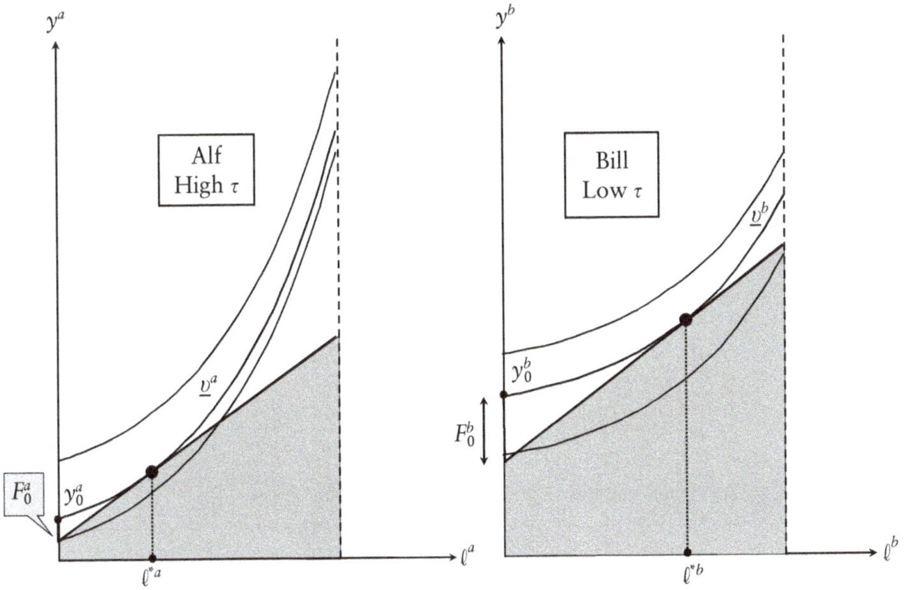

Figure B.41 Full-information contracts: Labour supply for each type

part of the figure). It sets the up-front fees F^a and F^b so as to keep Alf and Bill on their reservation utility levels.

9. If there were full information so that the firm can sort out the two customer types then it could set

$$z^a = F_0^a + px_1^{*a}$$

$$z^b = F_0^b + px_1^{*b}$$

and these two packages would then completely exploit the a-types and the b-types respectively. But if the two customer types cannot be separated out beforehand then obviously an a-type would be better off picking up the package $\left(x_1^{*b}, F_0^b + px_1^{*b}\right)$ and the firm can do nothing to stop this. But if the firm sets

$$z^a = F_{00}^a + px_1^{*a}$$

then the a-type would be (just) willing to go for the (x_1^{*a}, z^a) package rather than the $\left(x_1^{*b}, z^b\right)$ package.

10. If an a-type did so, then it would immediately reveal its hidden information and (under Version 1 of the story) would then be liable to render the contract invalid.

11. In this case hard-working Bill has an incentive to misrepresent himself as an a-type: see Figure B.42. Bill realises that if he were able to use the a-type budget constraint unrestrictedly he could achieve the topmost indifference curve depicted on the right-hand side of the figure and supply an amount ℓ^{*b} of work.

12. From (11.18) the condition that the b-type stays on the same utility level is given by

$$y^b + \tau^b\psi\left(x_1^b\right) + \tau^b\psi_x\left(x_1^b\right)dx_1^b - [p+dp]\left[x_1^b + dx_1^b\right] - F_0^b + dF_0^b = y^b + \tau^b\psi\left(x_1^b\right) - px_1^b - F_0^b$$

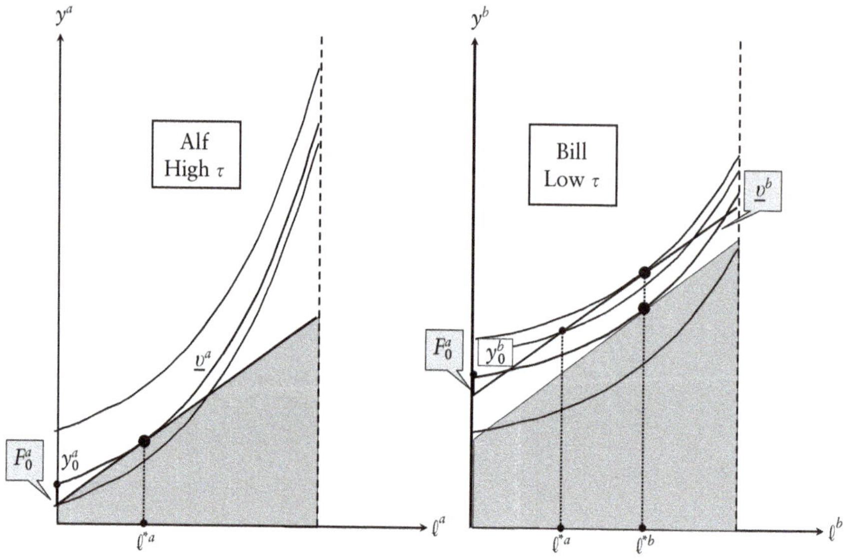

Figure B.42 Bill masquerades as an a-type in labour supply

which, on simplification, yields

$$\frac{dF_0^b}{dp} = \left[p + dp - \tau^b \psi_x\left(x_1^b\right)\right] \frac{dx_1^b}{dp} + x_1^b.$$

Using (11.15) we get

$$\frac{dF_0^b}{dp} = x_1^b.$$

13. Given that the a-type is mimicking a b-type's consumption we have

$$\frac{dU^a\left(\hat{\mathbf{x}}^a\right)}{dp} = \tau^a \psi_x\left(x_1^b\right) \left.\frac{dx_1^b}{dp}\right|_{U^b\left(\mathbf{x}^b\right)=\underline{\upsilon}^b} - p \left.\frac{dx_1^b}{dp}\right|_{U^b\left(\mathbf{x}^b\right)=\underline{\upsilon}^b} - x_1^b + \frac{dF_0^b}{dp}.$$

Using (11.24) and simplifying this becomes

$$\frac{dU^a\left(\hat{\mathbf{x}}^a\right)}{dp} = \left[\tau^a \psi_x\left(x_1^b\right) - \tau^b \psi_x\left(x_1^b\right)\right] \left.\frac{dx_1^b}{dp}\right|_{U^b\left(\mathbf{x}^b\right)=\underline{\upsilon}^b}.$$

Using (11.15) then gives the result.

14. Conditions (11.23) and (11.30) imply that

$$\tau^a \psi\left(x_1^a\right) - F^a > \tau^b \psi\left(x_1^b\right) - F^b.$$

Therefore, if '>' were to hold in (11.29), then also one would have $\tau^a \psi\left(x_1^a\right) - F^a > 0$.

15. Assuming that '>' holds then, given (11.23), we have

$$\begin{aligned} \tau^a \psi\left(x_1^a\right) - F^a &> \tau^a \psi\left(x_1^b\right) - F^b \\ &> \tau^b \psi\left(x_1^b\right) - F^b. \end{aligned}$$

In view of (11.32) this would imply that $\tau^a \psi\left(x_1^a\right) - F^a > 0$.

16. In view of (11.23) and (11.33) we obtain

$$\tau^a \psi\left(x_1^a\right) - F^a > \tau^b \psi\left(x_1^b\right) - F^b$$

and so, from (11.32):

$$\tau^a \psi\left(x_1^a\right) - F^a > 0.$$

17. If the incentive-compatibility constraint (11.31) were binding as well as (11.33) then:

$$\tau^a \psi\left(x_1^a\right) - F^a = \tau^a \psi\left(x_1^b\right) - F^b$$

$$\tau^b \psi\left(x_1^b\right) - F^b = \tau^b \psi\left(x_1^a\right) - F^a$$

which implies

$$\psi\left(x_1^a\right) = \psi\left(x_1^b\right)$$

$$x_1^a = x_1^b.$$

18. λ: the 'price' of the participation constraint is exactly one unit of good 2 because the utility function is linear in good 2. μ: the 'price' of the incentive-compatibility constraint increases the more of the potentially masquerading a-types there are.

19. $\pi < 1$ implies

$$\frac{c}{\left[1 - \frac{\pi}{1-\pi}\left[\frac{\tau^a}{\tau^b} - 1\right]\right]\tau^b} > \frac{c}{\tau^a}.$$

Since $\psi_x(\cdot)$ is monotonic decreasing (11.35) and (11.36) imply that $\tilde{x}_1^b < \tilde{x}_1^a$; for this to make sense requires

$$\pi\tau^a < \tau^b.$$

The result $\tilde{x}_1^a = x_1^{*a}$ follows from the fact that preferences are such that good 1 has a zero income effect: since there is no distortion for an a-type in either the full-information or the second-best solution, MRS_{21}^a is the same in both cases which means, for this type of preferences, that the quantity of good 1 consumed must be the same. The result $\tilde{x}_1^b < x_1^{*b}$ follows from the fact that for both the full-information and second-best solutions a low-valuation b-type is kept exactly on his reservation indifference curve: given that MRS_{21}^b is higher in the second-best case the quantity of good 1 consumed must be lower because of the pure substitution effect involved.

20. Denote by $\tilde{\upsilon}^a$ the utility level that would be achieved by an a-type if he/she were to masquerade as a b-type. Now check the attainable set constructed by the firm in the right-hand panel of Figure 11.8. Note that it is bounded above by two lines that are tangent to (i) an a-type's indifference curve at utility level $\tilde{\upsilon}^a$ at the point where $x_1^a = \tilde{x}_1^a$, and (ii) a b-type's reservation indifference curve (labelled $\underline{\upsilon}^b$) at the point where $x_1^b = \tilde{x}_1^b$. The point $\underline{x}_1$ is chosen as the intersection of those two lines.

21. See Figure B.43; part (1) illustrates the fee schedule and part (2) the attainable set that confronts a consumer of either type. Note that there are two levels of quantity discount giving two 'steps' in the fee schedule and that the price (slope of boundary of attainable set) is not unique—you could increase the price and offset it with larger quantity discounts, for example.

22. By analogy to Figure 11.7 the optimal contract must resemble that in Figure B.44. Combining the a-type and b-type schedules the analogy to the right-hand side of Figure 11.8 is that shown in Figure B.45. There is a kink at point $\underline{\ell}$; to the right of ℓ the firm pays exactly the worker's marginal product w; but for $\ell < \underline{\ell}$ the firm pays less than the marginal product. This shape of the attainable set is the same as for the overtime example in Mini Problem 3 of chapter 5 (see Figure B.15 on page 537).

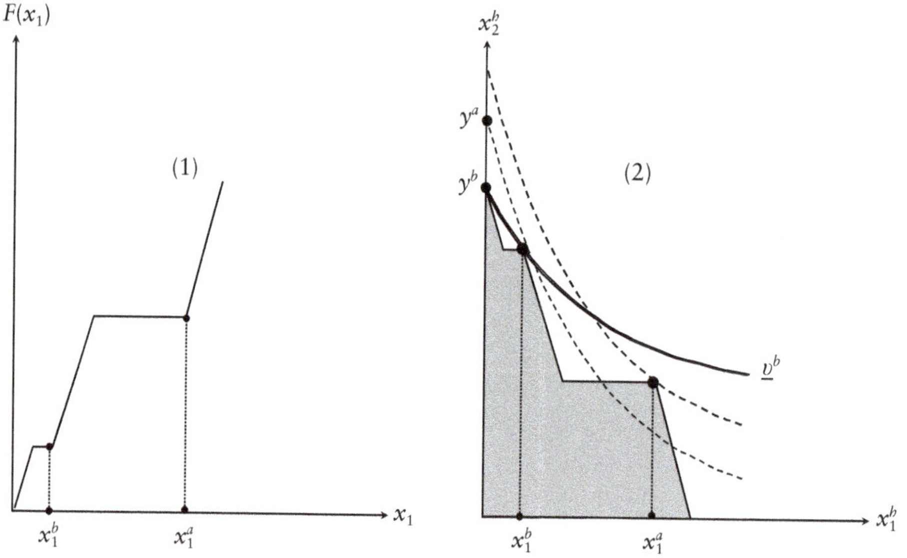

Figure B.43 Second best contract: quantity discount

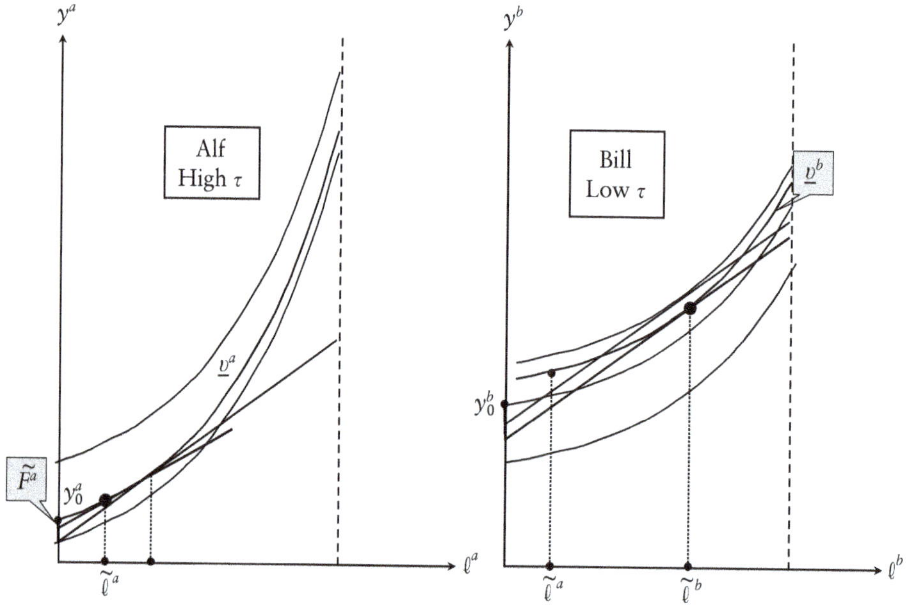

Figure B.44 Second-best labour contracts

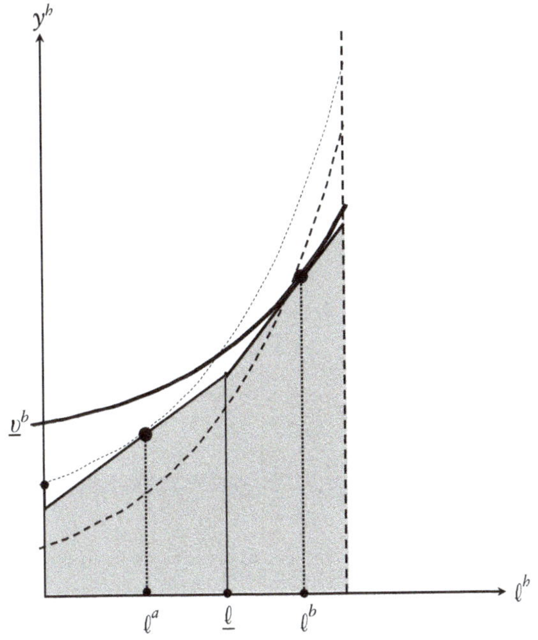

Figure B.45 Second-best labour contract: attainable set

23. Because of special structure of the von Neumann–Morgenstern utility function. See page 189.

24. Suppose there are two prospects that lie both on a given b-type indifference curve and on a given a-type indifference curve. Then we have

$$\pi^b u\left(x^{\circ}_{\text{BLUE}}\right) + \left[1 - \pi^b\right] u\left(x^{\circ}_{\text{RED}}\right) = \pi^b u\left(x'_{\text{BLUE}}\right) + \left[1 - \pi^b\right] u\left(x'_{\text{RED}}\right)$$

$$\pi^a u\left(x^{\circ}_{\text{BLUE}}\right) + \left[1 - \pi^a\right] u\left(x^{\circ}_{\text{RED}}\right) = \pi^a u\left(x'_{\text{BLUE}}\right) + \left[1 - \pi^a\right] u\left(x'_{\text{RED}}\right)$$

where the superscripts $^{\circ}$ and $'$ refer to the two prospects. But simplifying these two equations we get

$$\left[\frac{1-\pi^b}{\pi^b} - \frac{1-\pi^a}{\pi^a}\right] u\left(x^{\circ}_{\text{RED}}\right) = \left[\frac{1-\pi^b}{\pi^b} - \frac{1-\pi^a}{\pi^a}\right] u\left(x'_{\text{RED}}\right).$$

Since $\pi^a > \pi^b$ this must mean that $x^{\circ}_{\text{RED}} = x'_{\text{RED}}$ and therefore also $x^{\circ}_{\text{BLUE}} = x'_{\text{BLUE}}$. In other words the two prospects must be identical: the indifference curves intersect only once. If the individuals differed in terms of risk aversion it is easy to see that the single-crossing property could be violated—see the left-hand panel of Figure 8.13 (page 411).

25. As in Mini Problem 9 firms would offer a choice between given insurance 'packages' represented by points P_1 and P_2.

26. No. If you superimpose the line $P_0\overline{P}$ carefully on Figure 11.12 it is clear that it passes below the b-contour through $\tilde{P}^b$. So none of the low-risk b-types would accept any contract on $P_0\overline{P}$.

27. For a given utility level υ and a given value of the talent parameter τ the equation of an indifference curve in (z, y)-space is given by

$$y = \upsilon + C(z, \tau). \qquad \text{(B.154)}$$

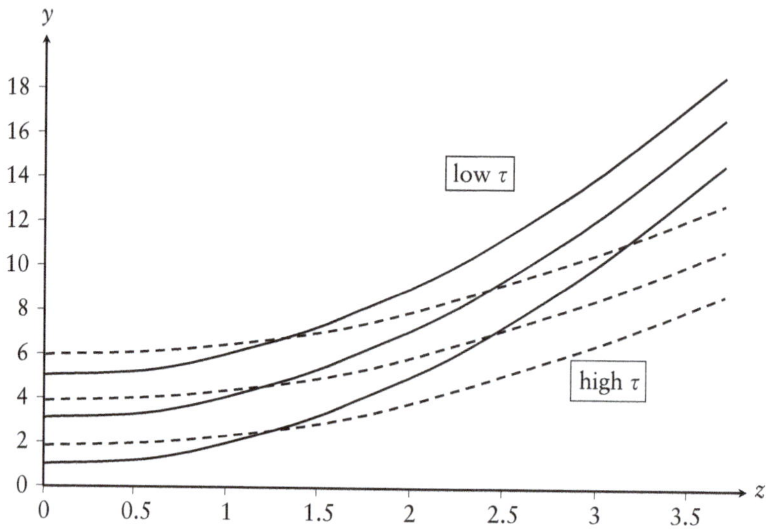

Figure B.46 Indifference curves for quadratic cost

Clearly the slope of the indifference curve is:

$$\frac{dy}{dz} = C_z(z, \tau).$$

Consider the indifference curve for someone with a higher parameter value $\tau' > \tau$ that passes through the point (z_0, y_0) that satisfies (B.154). By (11.47d) this curve has a slope that is less than the slope of the original indifference curve for every z. It therefore lies above the original curve for $z < z_0$ and below the original curve for $z > z_0$. See Figure B.46.

28. Rearranging (11.51) we have

$$C\left(z^a, \tau^b\right) - C\left(z^b, \tau^b\right) \geq \phi\left(\tau^a\right) - \phi\left(\tau^b\right). \tag{B.155}$$

The right-hand side of this is strictly positive because $\phi(\cdot)$ is strictly increasing and $\tau^a > \tau^b$. However, given (11.47b) the left-hand side is positive if and only if $z^a > z^b$.

29. Using (11.52) in (11.50) and (11.51) and then rearranging we get

$$C\left(z^a, \tau^a\right) - C\left(0, \tau^a\right) \leq \phi\left(\tau^a\right) - \phi\left(\tau^b\right)$$

$$C\left(z^a, \tau^b\right) - C\left(0, \tau^b\right) \geq \phi\left(\tau^a\right) - \phi\left(\tau^b\right).$$

Using (11.47a) then gives the result.

30. See Figure B.47. From the definition z_0 is where the net payoff to a b-type in the separating equilibrium exactly equals net payoff to a b-type if he mimicked an a-type's education.

$$\phi\left(\tau^b\right) = \phi\left(\tau^a\right) - C\left(z_0, \tau^b\right).$$

Also z_1 is where the net payoff to an a-type in the separating equilibrium exactly equals payoff to an a-type if he had zero education:

$$\phi\left(\tau^b\right) = \phi\left(\tau^a\right) - C\left(z_1, \tau^a\right).$$

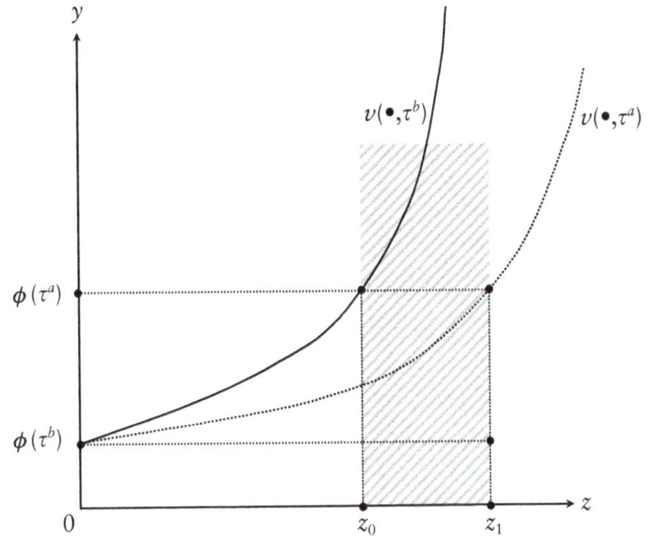

Figure B.47 Bounds on education (1)

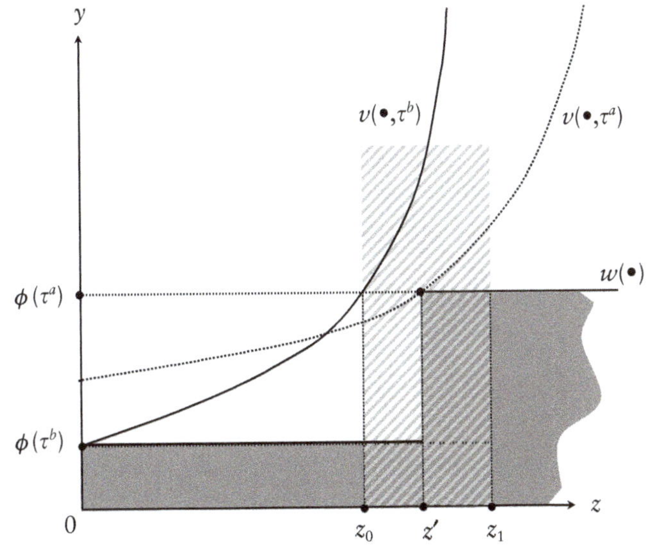

Figure B.48 A simple set of beliefs

31. See Figure B.48.

32. It would be in the interests of both types of worker to prevent signalling if the amount of income that each group would get in the no-signalling case exceeds the highest net income that it could get under signalling. Figure B.49 illustrates this. The indifference curves through the point $(0, \mathcal{E}\phi(\tau))$ show situations equivalent to the no-signalling case. The type-b indifference curve must always lie above the indifference curve for a type-b person under signalling. However, given this

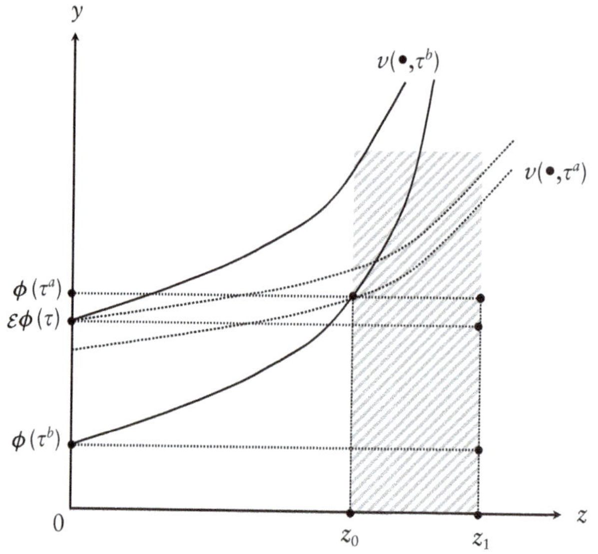

Figure B.49 No-signalling dominates

value of $\mathcal{E}\phi(\tau)$, it is clear that the type-a indifference curve through $(0, \mathcal{E}\phi(\tau))$ also lies above the one passing through the point $(z_0, \phi(\tau^a))$, the highest type-a indifference curve possible under signalling.

33. If the net income for b-type people in the pooling equilibrium is to exceed what they could get with zero education then it must be true that

$$[1-\pi]\phi(\tau^a) + \pi\phi\left(\tau^b\right) - C\left(z^*, \tau^b\right) \geq \phi\left(\tau^b\right) - C\left(0, \tau^b\right).$$

Using (11.47a) and rearranging this implies

$$C\left(z^*, \tau^b\right) \leq [1-\pi]\left[\phi(\tau^a) - \phi\left(\tau^b\right)\right].$$

Given (11.47b) the result then follows. Figure B.50 illustrates the determination of z_2.

34. Take the pooling equilibrium given by $(z^*, \mathcal{E}\phi(\tau))$ in Figure B.51 and define z' to be the education level such that

$$\mathcal{E}\phi(\tau) - C\left(z^*, \tau^b\right) = \phi(\tau^a) - C\left(z', \tau^b\right).$$

Suppose one were to observe an out-of-equilibrium choice $(z, \phi(\tau^a))$ where $z > z'$. Could this be some over-optimistic b-type trying to convince firms that he is an a-type? No, because the b-type indifference curve through $(z, \phi(\tau^a))$ lies below the b-type indifference curve at the pooling equilibrium. The intuitive criterion therefore suggests that firms' beliefs are $\tilde{\pi}(z) = 0$ so that $w(z) = \phi(\tau^a)$. But if this were done then any a-type would migrate from the pooling equilibrium: the a-type indifference curve through $(z, \phi(\tau^a))$ lies above the a-type indifference curve at the pooling equilibrium. So the pooling equilibrium cannot be consistent with the intuitive criterion.

35. Consider the choice facing agent h. If π is the probability that any other agent decides to participate then the payoff to h is

$$\begin{array}{ll} a - c^h & \text{with probability } [\pi]^{N-1} \\ -c^h & \text{otherwise} \end{array}$$

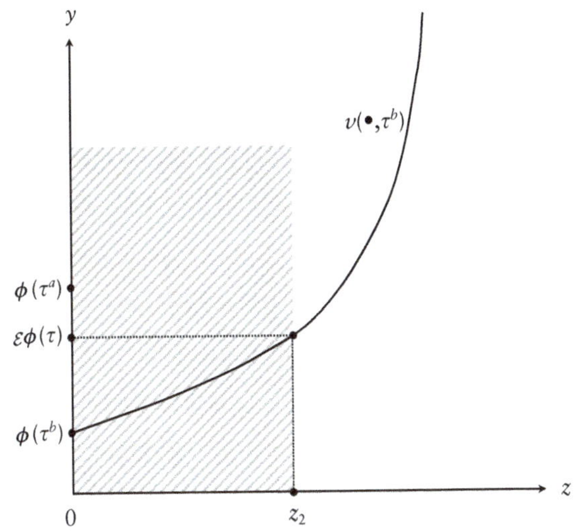

Figure B.50 Bounds on education (2)

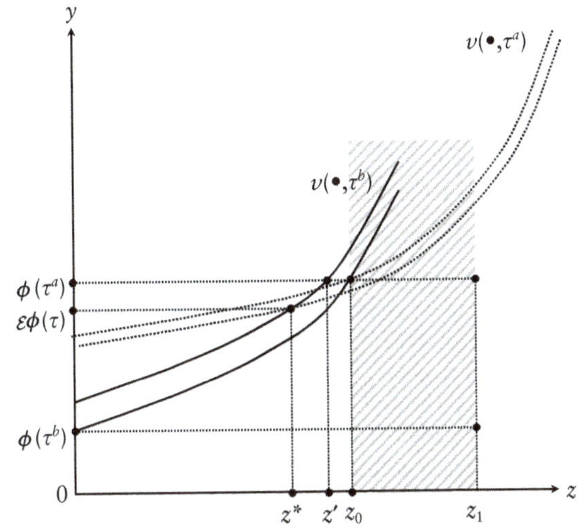

Figure B.51 Equilibrium under the intuitive criterion

so that the expected payoff is

$$c - c^h \qquad \text{(B.156)}$$

where $c := a\,[\pi]^{N-1}$. In view of the assumed distribution of cost in the population, the probability that (B.156) is positive is c; but this probability is the probability that agent h actually participates. So we must have

$$\pi = a\,[\pi]^{N-1}$$

which, if $a < 1$, can only be satisfied if $\pi = 0$.

36. From (11.70) and (11.69):

$$\mu = \frac{\pi(\bar{z}) - \lambda\pi(\bar{z})u_x^a(\overline{w},\bar{z})}{\pi(\bar{z})u_x^a(\overline{w},\bar{z}) - \pi(\underline{z})u_x^a(\overline{w},\underline{z})} \qquad \text{(B.157)}$$

$$\mu = \frac{[1-\pi(\bar{z})] - \lambda[1-\pi(\bar{z})]u_x^a(\underline{w},\bar{z})}{[1-\pi(\bar{z})]u_x^a(\underline{w},\bar{z}) - [1-\pi(\underline{z})]u_x^a(\underline{w},\underline{z})}. \qquad \text{(B.158)}$$

Using the assumption that the marginal of consumption is independent of z we get $u_x^a(\overline{w},\bar{z}) = u_x^a(\overline{w},\underline{z})$ and so (B.157) and (B.158) become

$$\mu = \frac{\frac{\pi(\bar{z})}{u_x^a(\overline{w},\bar{z})} - \lambda\pi(\bar{z})}{\pi(\bar{z}) - \pi(\underline{z})} \qquad \text{(B.159)}$$

$$\mu = \frac{\lambda[1-\pi(\bar{z})] - \frac{1-\pi(\bar{z})}{u_x^a(\underline{w},\bar{z})}}{\pi(\bar{z}) - \pi(\underline{z})}. \qquad \text{(B.160)}$$

Rearranging (B.159) we immediately get (11.72). Combining (B.159) and (B.160) to eliminate μ we get

$$\frac{\pi(\bar{z})}{u_x^a(\overline{w},\bar{z})} - \lambda\pi(\bar{z}) = \lambda[1-\pi(\bar{z})] - \frac{1-\pi(\bar{z})}{u_x^a(\underline{w},\bar{z})}$$

from which a simple rearrangement gives (11.71).

37. Eliminating λ between (11.71) and (11.72) we get

$$\mu\left[1 - \frac{\pi(\underline{z})}{\pi(\bar{z})}\right] + \frac{1-\pi(\bar{z})}{u_x^a(\underline{w},\bar{z})} = \frac{1-\pi(\bar{z})}{u_x^a(\overline{w},\bar{z})}.$$

Rearranging this gives

$$\mu = \left[\frac{1-\pi(\bar{z})}{1-\frac{\pi(\underline{z})}{\pi(\bar{z})}}\right]\left[\frac{1}{u_x^a(\overline{w},\bar{z})} - \frac{1}{u_x^a(\underline{w},\bar{z})}\right]. \qquad \text{(B.161)}$$

We know that, by nature of a constrained optimisation problem, the Lagrange multiplier must satisfy $\mu \geq 0$. So, could (B.161) be zero? By assumption $\pi(\underline{z}) < \pi(\bar{z})$ and for non-trivial cases $\pi(\bar{z}) < 1$. So the only way that (B.161) could be zero is if $u_x^a(\overline{w},\bar{z}) = u_x^a(\underline{w},\bar{z})$, which in turn implies $\overline{w} = \underline{w}$. But this means that the incentive-compatibility constraint would be violated: by paying only the same wage irrespective of output—irrespective of anything—Bill cannot persuade Alf to supply high effort.

38. In the case of risk neutrality condition (11.71) becomes

$$\frac{\pi(\bar{z}) + 1 - \pi(\bar{z})}{u_x^a(\overline{w},\bar{z})} = \lambda$$

which implies

$$\frac{1}{u_x^a(\overline{w},\bar{z})} = \lambda \qquad \text{(B.162)}$$

given (11.58) equations (B.162) and (11.72) imply $\mu = 0$. This is illustrated in Figure B.52.

39. By definition we have

$$\mathcal{E}\beta_z = \int_{\underline{q}}^{\overline{q}} \frac{f_z(q,z)}{f(q;z)} f(q;z)dq$$

$$= \int_{\underline{q}}^{\overline{q}} f_z(q;z)dq = \frac{\partial}{\partial z}\left(\int_{\underline{q}}^{\overline{q}} f(q;z)dq\right).$$

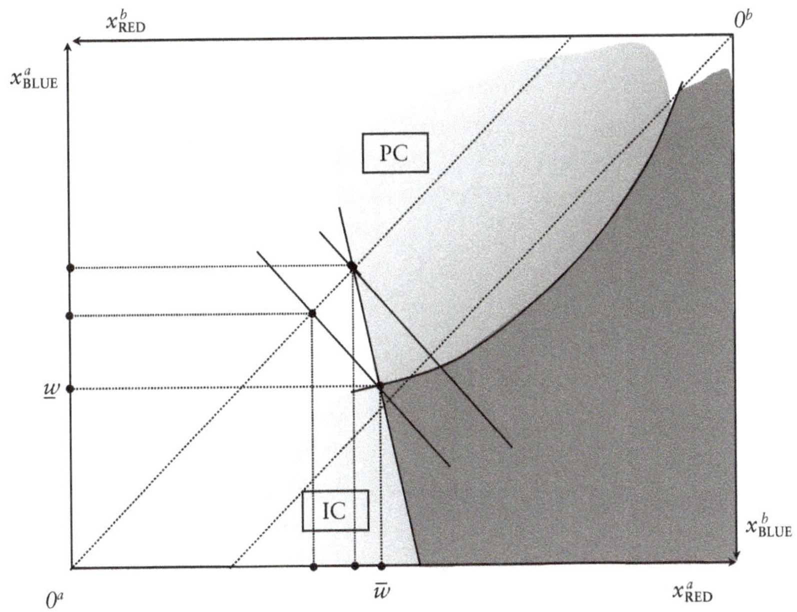

Figure B.52 Second-best contracts: Alf risk-neutral

From the standard property of the density function (A.63) we know that the expression in the parentheses is identically 1 so that differentiating it with respect to z (or anything else) produces the answer zero.

40. See Figure B.53. The boundary of the shaded area again characterises the Agent's FOC. However, it is clear that if the Agent were offered, say, wage w° then he would choose z' and not z° (less effort and so higher utility for the Agent). Under these circumstances a point of common tangency—such as that marked with the symbol $\circ$ —is clearly no longer a solution. For more on the first-order approach see Jewitt (1988).

41. Write (11.87) out in full as

$$\max_{\{w(\cdot),z\}} \int_{\underline{q}}^{\overline{q}} u^b\left(q - w(q)\right) f(q; z) dq \tag{B.163}$$

$$+ \lambda \left[\int_{\underline{q}}^{\overline{q}} u^a\left(w(q), z\right) f(q; z) dq - \underline{\upsilon}^a \right]$$

$$+ \mu \left[\int_{\underline{q}}^{\overline{q}} \left[u^a\left(w(q), z\right) \beta_z + u^a_z\left(w(q), z\right) \right] f(q; z) dq \right].$$

We can treat each integral as though it were a summation over all the values of q and then differentiate (B.163) with respect to any specific value of $w(q)$ as though it were a separate variable. This gives (11.88). Differentiating (11.87) with respect to z we use (11.86) to note that the term involving $\lambda\,[\cdot]$ is zero.

42. If Alf is risk neutral then the marginal utility u^a_x is non-stochastic, independent of q. Multiply (11.88) by $f(q)$ and integrate from $\underline{q}$ to $\overline{q}$ (i.e. take expectations); using (11.84) we get:

$$-\mathcal{E}u^b_x\left(q - w(q)\right) + \lambda u^a_x = 0. \tag{B.164}$$

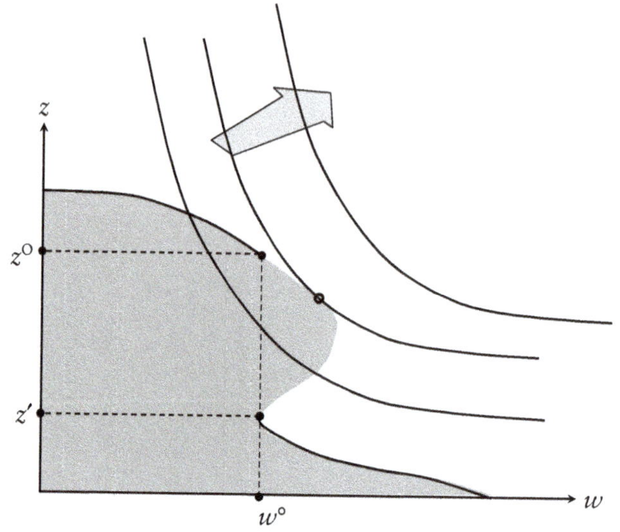

Figure B.53 Principal-and-Agent: failure of first-order approach

If Bill is risk averse then (B.164) can only be true if $w(\cdot)$ has been designed such that $u^b\ (q - w(q))$ is independent of q. Using this in (11.89), the first term becomes $u^b \mathcal{E}\beta_z$ which is zero, in view of (11.84). Hence $\mu = 0$ and, from (B.164),

$$\frac{u_x^b}{u_x^a} = \lambda$$

which is the condition obtained under full information.

B.12 Design

1. (a) In Figure B.54 the lightly shaded set is the original $B(\theta^*; v)$. (b) Clearly $B(\theta^*; \tilde{v}) \subset B(\theta^*; v)$ for condition (12.4) to be satisfied. (c) The chosen allocation remains at point θ^* when preferences switch from v to $\tilde{v}$.

2. Here the object of choice can be seen as a point from an interval on the real line.

   1. See Figure B.55. Note that, given the specification in the question, all three agents have single-peaked preferences.
   2. A straight average would give 11:33 for the taxi time. But if Bill and Charlie told the truth and Alf stated a preferred time of 10:00 (the earliest the taxi could arrive) then this averaging rule would get them to order the taxi at 11:07, which Alf would obviously prefer to the truth-telling outcome of 11:33 under this averaging rule. Likewise Charlie has an incentive to state a time after 12:00.
   3. None of them can influence the time by mis-stating information; but all could be made better off if the taxi company were to bring the time forward to, say 12:05: so the 12:10 proposed solution is inefficient.
   4. The median value is not manipulable. If Charlie overstates his late departure time it does not change the median. Similarly, it does not help Alf to claim to want to go earlier.

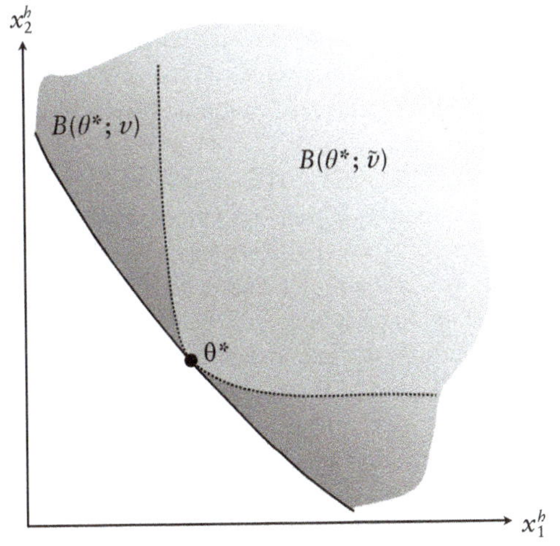

Figure B.54 Implications of monotonicity

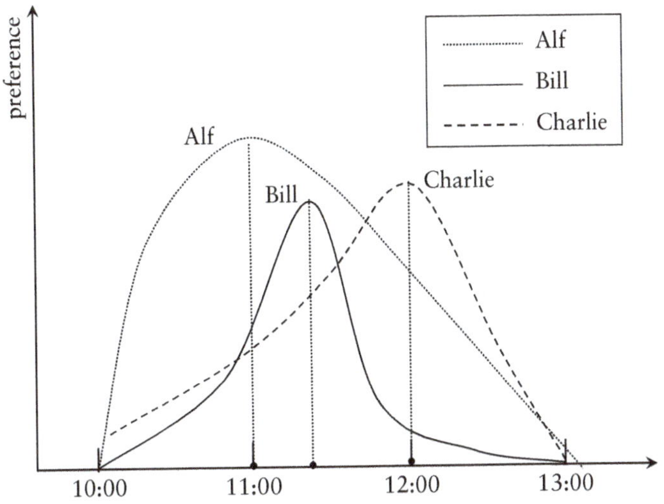

Figure B.55 Alf, Bill, Charlie, and the taxi

3. Let $\theta, \hat{\theta} \in \Theta$. $v^h(\hat{\theta}) > v^h(\theta)$. Let $\hat{v}^h(\cdot) \neq v^h(\cdot)$ and $\hat{v}^k(\cdot) = v^k(\cdot)$, $k \neq h$. We know that

$$\hat{\theta} = \Gamma\left(\hat{v}^1, \hat{v}^2, \ldots, \hat{v}^h, \ldots\right)$$

Now let preferences change from $[\hat{v}]$ to $[v]$. For all $k \neq h$ it is immediate that $\hat{\theta}$ maintains its position (tastes have remained unchanged for those individuals). But for h we are given $v^h(\hat{\theta}) > v^h(\theta)$. So monotonicity requires

$$\hat{\theta} = \Gamma\left(v^1, v^2, \ldots, v^h, \ldots\right)$$

contrary to the definition of a manipulable social choice function.

4. It will have no effect at all. The reason is that Γ is concerned only with market outcomes and because individual and household demands depend on only on ordinal preferences. Transforming υ^b as suggested has no effect on anyone's preference map.

5. The curve through $[\underline{\mathbf{x}}^a]$ and [**R**] is Alf's reservation indifference curve; that through $\left[\underline{\mathbf{x}}^b\right]$ and [**R**] is Bill's reservation indifference curve.

6. Figure B.56 is adapted from Figure 12.1. The straight lines through [**R**] indicate alternative prices that Alf (as a monopolist) might try out on Bill (a price taker). The locus of tangency points with the Bill indifference curves traces out Bill's offer curve. The offer curve is then treated by Alf as an attainable set A. Alf maximises profits with a trade that induces consumption at point $[\hat{\mathbf{x}}]$—note the representative Alf indifference curve that has been drawn in as a broken curve. Prices charged are given by $\hat{p}_1/\hat{p}_2$—the slope of the line joining [**R**] and $[\hat{\mathbf{x}}]$; this slope is of course equal to Bill's MRS, but is different from Alf's MRS (the slope of the dotted line through $[\hat{\mathbf{x}}]$).

7. 4, 1, 2, 3.

8. Using the Cartesian product notation we have $S = \underbrace{[0, 1] \times [0, 1] \times \ldots \times [0, 1]}_{n_h}$.

9. 'Tell the truth just as long as everyone else is telling the truth.'

10. (a) By inspection it is clear that s_2^a is a best response to s_2^b and that s_2^b is a best response to s_2^a. (b) All four strategy combinations are now Nash equilibria. (c) The resulting payoffs are now given by Table B.7.

All N^2 strategy combinations are now Nash equilibria: once focused on a particular combination of lies there is no incentive for anyone to switch to truth telling. Clearly this holds for N arbitrarily large.

11. The private-values argument is provided by the example in the text. However, if the painting is easily resold then there may be an important common-value element: the work of an as-yet-unknown artist may be like the crock of gold example.

12. It follows from the envelope theorem—Theorem A.13.

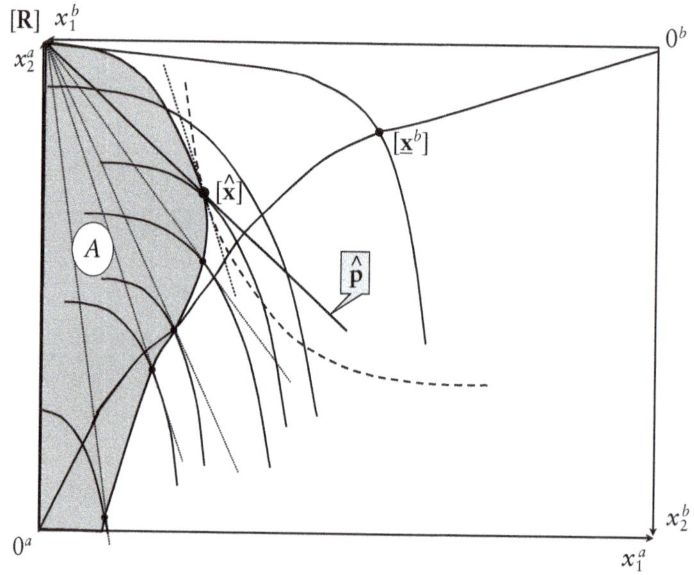

Figure B.56 Monopolistic trading

	s_1^b	s_2^b	...	s_N^b
s_1^a	3, 3	0, 0	...	0, 0
s_2^a	0, 0	0, 0	...	0, 0
...	...	...	...	...
s_N^a	0, 0	0, 0	...	0, 0

Table B.7 Lots of uninteresting Nash equilibria

13. From (12.9) and (12.12) we get

$$\pi\left(p^{a*}\right) = F\left(\tau^a\right) \tag{B.165}$$

so that, from (12.11),

$$\frac{\partial \upsilon\left(\tau^a\right)}{\partial \tau^a} = F\left(\tau^a\right).$$

Integrating from 0 (the lowest possible value of τ) we get (12.13).

14. By definition of the optimum (12.10) immediately gives (12.14) on substituting in the optimal bid function β. Rearrange this to give

$$\beta\left(\tau^a\right) = \tau^a - \frac{\upsilon\left(\tau^a\right)}{\pi\left(p^{a*}\right)}.$$

Substituting in from (12.13) and using the formula for $\pi\left(p^{a*}\right)$ from Mini Problem 13 gives the result.

15. The probability in (12.9) is now

$$\pi\left(p^a\right) = \left[F\left(\varphi\left(p^a\right)\right)\right]^{N-1} \tag{B.166}$$

and (12.13) becomes

$$\upsilon\left(\tau^a\right) = \int_0^{\tau^a} \left[F\left(\tau\right)\right]^{N-1} d\tau. \tag{B.167}$$

16. (a) If $p' > \tau$ you lose the auction, but then you would have lost it anyway, so you are no better or worse off than if you had bid truthfully. Otherwise, if $\tau > p \geq p'$ you win the auction and pay p'—but that would have happened if you had bid truthfully. But if $\tau \geq p' > p$ your underbidding will cause you to lose the auction and forgo a potential gain of $\tau - p'$. (b) Suppose the highest bid other than yours is p'. If $p < p'$ then you do not win the auction and you are no better or worse off than bidding truthfully. Otherwise, if $p' \leq \tau$ you pay no more than your true valuation, but you do not improve your chance of winning—again no better or worse off than for a truthful bid; but if $p' > \tau$ you win the object but you are forced to pay a price that is greater than your true valuation—you make a loss.

Conclusion: in this second-price sealed-bid auction bidding $p = \tau$ is a weakly dominant strategy.

17. In the case cited one is dealing with a common-value problem: the private-values assumption used in the argument is not satisfied. Each potential bidder may have private information about the common value of the mineral rights that are being auctioned. Under an English open-bid auction each person's bid may be used as a signal to the other bidders: so a rational agent may update the information that is used in his bidding strategy. However, if the auction involved sealed bids this updating is impossible.

18. (i) Under the rules of the second-price auction the object goes to bidder 1 who bid 1, but the price P is zero. If all other bidders are believed to be bidding zero bidder 1 cannot improve on the outcome by changing his bid—if he changes it by a small amount he still wins and gets exactly

the same net benefit $\tau^1 - P = \tau^1$; if he drops the bid to zero he may lose the object and get zero net benefit. Now consider bidder 2: if he believes that bidder 1 is bidding 1 and bidders 3, 4,... are bidding zero, he cannot improve on the outcome by raising his bid a little—he still will not get the object and his net benefit remains at zero—and if he raises his bid to 1 he may get the object but his net benefit is still at most zero. The same applies to every other bidder. So it is an equilibrium. (ii) By this argument it is clear that collusion in such arrangement would be self-enforcing. (iii) To make the collusive arrangement work it would be necessary to have a means of communication in advance and, possibly, side payments from bidder 1 to make the other bidders interested in the collusion.

19. Yes if $\beta\left(\tau^b\right)$ is high.

20. Because the problem is symmetric and because truth telling is a weakly dominant strategy (12.16) follows, with the function $\beta(\cdot)$ common to both agents. Alf wins the auction if his bid is higher than Bill's. In equilibrium both are bidding their true valuations so the probability that Alf wins is the same as the probability that the realisation of Bill's taste parameter is less than the realised value of Alf's τ^a, i.e. $F(\tau^a)$—see (B.165) in the answer to Mini Problem 13. If Alf wins the auction then he pays the price bid by Bill, which in equilibrium is Bill's true value. The expectation of this price is

$$\frac{1}{F(\tau^a)}\int_0^{\tau^a} \tau f(\tau)\, d\tau \tag{B.168}$$

where $f(\tau)$ is the density function $\frac{dF(\tau)}{d\tau}$. On integrating this expression by parts we get (12.17).

21. (a) The probability that Bill has $\tau^b = 0$ (in which case Alf certainly wins) is 0.5; otherwise if $\tau^b = 1$ Alf and Bill would have an equal chance of winning at price P; so the combined probability of Alf winning is 0.75.

(b) Suppose $\tau^a = 1$. If Alf accepts the price 0.5; there is probability 0.75 that he gets the good in which case he gets net benefit $\tau^a - P = 1 - 0.5 = 0.5$; otherwise net benefit would be 0. If Alf does not accept then there is the probability 0.25 that he gets the good anyway (if $\tau^b = 0$ and the good is awarded by lottery to Alf). Therefore Alf's expected net benefit from accepting price $P = 0.5$ is $0.75 \cdot 0.5 = 0.375$ and the expected net benefit of refusing is 0.25, so he accepts. Letting $\upsilon(\tau)$ be the equilibrium net benefit for type τ and $\pi^*(\tau)$ the probability that a type-τ person gets the good we have

$$\begin{aligned} \upsilon(0) &= 0, & \pi^*(0) &= 0.25 \\ \upsilon(1) &= 0.375, & \pi^*(1) &= 0.75. \end{aligned}$$

(c) By the same argument for some other price P a person with $\tau^h = 1$ $(h = a, b)$ would accept paying price P for the object as long as

$$0.75 \cdot [1 - P] > 0.25$$

i.e. as long as $P < \frac{2}{3}$. In equilibrium at price P we would have:

$$\begin{aligned} \upsilon(0) &= 0, & \pi^*(0) &= 0.25 \\ \upsilon(1) &= 0.75\,[1 - P] & \pi^*(1) &= 0.75. \end{aligned}$$

(d) There is evidently a multiplicity of equilibria corresponding to different prices set by the auctioneer. The value to the seller is obviously strictly increasing in P. So the seller would not be indifferent between the outcomes to these alternative auctions—see Klemperer (2004).

22. See Figure B.57.

23. Using the definition on page 90. We have

$$\upsilon^h\left(\theta^\circ\right) = \tau^h \psi(0) + y^h \tag{B.169}$$

$$\upsilon^h\left(\theta'\right) = \tau^h \psi(1) + y^h - z^h \tag{B.170}$$

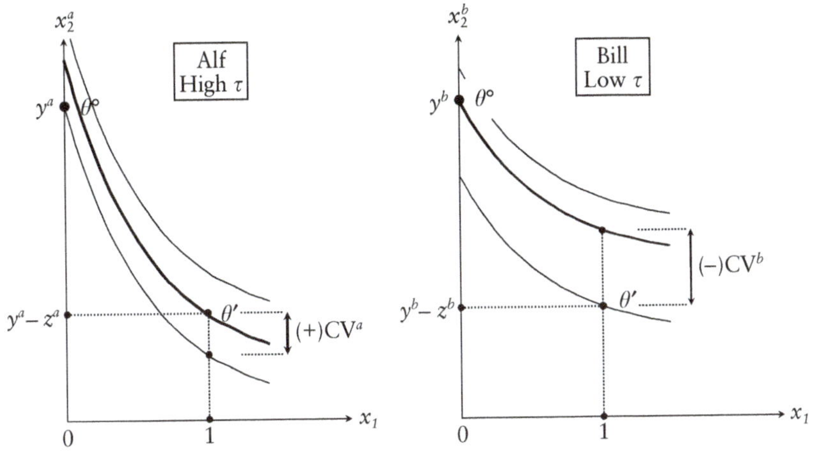

Figure B.57 A fixed-size project (2)

where y^h is the income of agent h. Therefore

$$\begin{aligned} CV^h &= \tau^h [\psi(1) - \psi(0)] - z^h \\ &= \tau^h - z^h \end{aligned}$$

where the last step follows from the normalisation of $\psi(\cdot)$.

24. Suppose the project goes ahead but agent h is pivotal. This means that $\Delta^h < 0$: collectively the agents other than h are reportedly suffering a negative impact from the project. The condition

$$\sum_{k=1}^{n_h} \left[p^k - z^k\right] > 0$$

can be written as

$$\begin{aligned} \Delta^h + p^h - z^h &> 0 \\ p^h &> z^h - \Delta^h. \end{aligned}$$

So if condition (12.26) is satisfied, the pivotal agent h can pay his own contribution (z^h) and the compensation to everyone else ($-\Delta^h$) and still make a net gain ($\tau^h > z^h - \Delta^h$).

Suppose now the project does not go ahead but agent h is pivotal. This means that $\Delta^h > 0$: collectively the agents other than h are reportedly prevented from gaining a positive impact from the project. The condition

$$\sum_{k=1}^{n_h} \left[p^k - z^k\right] < 0$$

can be written as

$$z^h - p^h > \Delta^h \tag{B.171}$$

If condition (12.26) is satisfied, then the left-hand side of (B.171) is the true loss (as measured by the compensating variation) to agent h if the project were to go ahead; condition (B.171) means that this is strictly greater than the required compensation to the other agents ($\Delta^h > 0$) under the payment rule.

25. Take the case $\pi = 1$, which means

$$\sum_{k=1}^{n_h} p^k \geq \bar{z}.$$

If h is pivotal then

$$\sum_{\substack{k=1 \\ k \neq h}}^{n_h} \left[p^k - z^k\right] < 0.$$

So the penalty payment is $-\Delta^h > 0$ in this case. If $\pi = 0$, which means

$$\sum_{k=1}^{n_h} p^k < \bar{z},$$

then, if h is pivotal, we have

$$\sum_{\substack{k=1 \\ k \neq h}}^{n_h} \left[p^k - z^k\right] \geq 0$$

and the penalty payment is $\Delta^h \geq 0$. Adding up over the h means that if there is a pivotal agent total payments may exceed $\bar{z}$. But this excess cannot be returned to the agents themselves because this would affect behaviour.

26. There is nothing that agent h can do about $p^k, k \neq h$, so it would just be treated as a constant in h's decision process. See the last part of section C.9.2 of Appendix C.

27. If, in the original situation, the decision on the project would have been negative (θ°), then clearly the critical question is by how much Alf's willingness to pay has increased: if it is large enough to tip the balance of the sum-of-reported-CV rule then we switch to θ'. However, if we would already have been at θ' then *nothing* would change—not even the apportionment of the costs!

28.

$$\frac{dy}{dq} = -\frac{1}{\tau}\psi_z\left(\frac{q}{\tau}\right).$$

29. For any individual h that is employed as Agent the Lagrangean is

$$p\tau^h z^h - y^h + \lambda^h\left[y^h + \psi\left(z^h\right) - \underline{\upsilon}^h\right] \tag{B.172}$$

where λ^h is the Lagrange multiplier for the participation constraint (12.36) in the case of agent h. Differentiating (B.172) with respect to z^h, y^h, and λ^h respectively and setting them to zero we get:

$$p\tau^h + \lambda^h\psi_z\left(z^{*h}\right) = 0 \tag{B.173}$$

$$-1 + \lambda^{*h} = 0 \tag{B.174}$$

$$y^{*h} + \psi\left(z^{*h}\right) - \underline{\upsilon}^h = 0 \tag{B.175}$$

from which (12.37) and (12.38) follow.

30. The two types of agent differ only in their productivity. Therefore when effort is zero (so that output is zero) they must enjoy the same level of utility for any given level of income.

31. In Figure 12.8 the reservation utility levels are given by

$$y^a + \psi\left(\frac{q^a}{\tau^a}\right) = \underline{\upsilon}^a$$

$$y^b + \psi\left(\frac{q^b}{\tau^b}\right) = \underline{\upsilon}^b.$$

If $\psi(0) = 0$ and both a and b indifference curves pass through the same point $(0, y_0)$ then $\underline{\upsilon}^a = \underline{\upsilon}^b$. The four constraints (two participation constraints and two incentive-compatibility constraints are then:

$$y^a + \psi\left(\frac{q^a}{\tau^a}\right) \geq \underline{\upsilon}^a \tag{B.176}$$

$$y^b + \psi\left(\frac{q^b}{\tau^b}\right) \geq \underline{\upsilon}^b \tag{B.177}$$

$$y^a + \psi\left(\frac{q^a}{\tau^a}\right) \geq y^b + \psi\left(\frac{q^b}{\tau^a}\right) \tag{B.178}$$

$$y^b + \psi\left(\frac{q^b}{\tau^b}\right) \geq y^a + \psi\left(\frac{q^a}{\tau^b}\right). \tag{B.179}$$

Given $\tau^a > \tau^b$ it is clear that if '>' holds in (B.177) then (B.178) implies that '>' holds in (B.176). This cannot hold if the firm is profit maximising—it would wish to reduce y^a and/or y^b in the menu of contracts on offer, thus increasing profit while making sure that potential Agents of either type still participated; therefore '=' holds in (B.177). If '>' were to hold in (B.178) then, using the fact that $\tau^a > \tau^b$, we see that '>' would hold in (B.176). Again this cannot hold if the firm is profit maximising—it could reduce y^a without violating the participation or incentive-compatibility constraints for the a types. So (B.178) must hold with equality. In view of this and the fact that $\tau^a > \tau^b$ it must be true that '>' holds in (B.176). Finally notice that by virtue of the single-crossing condition (page 411) it must be the case that if '=' holds in (B.178) it cannot be the case that '=' holds in (B.179). This last point is illustrated in Figure B.58 below where (B.178) is depicted by the heavy broken a-type curve passing through $\left(\tilde{q}^b, \tilde{y}^b\right)$ and $(\tilde{q}^a, \tilde{y}^a)$; on this curve the a-type gets just as much utility as if he were to masquerade as a b-type and claim the contract $\left(\tilde{q}^b, \tilde{y}^b\right)$; but if we drew an a-type indifference curve through $(\tilde{q}^a, \tilde{y}^a)$ it is clear that because of the single-crossing condition this curve must lie strictly below the b-type indifference curve passing through $\left(\tilde{q}^b, \tilde{y}^b\right)$; in other words we have automatically '>' in (B.179).

The upshot is that constraints (B.176) and (B.179) are never binding (condition '>' holds) and so can be dropped from the optimisation problem.

32. See Figure B.58 below. Because of the incentive-compatibility constraint the solution for the a-types must lie on the a-indifference curve that passes through the (q, y) combination for the b-types: but it cannot lie to the left, because then the b-types would prefer the a-contract, in contradiction to the arguments in the answer to Mini Problem 31; so it must lie to the right.

33. Differentiating (12.40) with respect to q^a, q^b, y^a, y^b respectively the FOC are

$$\pi p + \frac{\mu}{\tau^a}\psi_z\left(\frac{q^a}{\tau^a}\right) = 0$$

$$[1-\pi]p + \frac{\lambda}{\tau^b}\psi_z\left(\frac{q^b}{\tau^b}\right) - \frac{\mu}{\tau^a}\psi_z\left(\frac{q^b}{\tau^a}\right) = 0$$

$$-\pi + \mu = 0$$

$$-[1-\pi] + \lambda - \mu = 0$$

which imply the following values for the Lagrange multipliers:

$$\mu = \pi$$

$$\lambda = 1.$$

Substituting these values in the FOC we get

$$p + \frac{1}{\tau^a}\psi_z\left(\frac{q^a}{\tau^a}\right) = 0$$

$$[1-\pi]p + [1-\pi]\frac{1}{\tau^b}\psi_z\left(\frac{q^b}{\tau^b}\right) + \pi\left[\frac{1}{\tau^b}\psi_z\left(\frac{q^b}{\tau^b}\right) - \frac{1}{\tau^a}\psi_z\left(\frac{q^b}{\tau^a}\right)\right] = 0$$

which, rearranged, gives (12.41), (12.42).

34. Define $x := -z$ as 'leisure' and a function v such that

$$v(x) := \psi(z)$$

$$-v_x(-z) = \psi_z(z) < 0$$

$$v_{xx}(-z) = \psi_{zz}(z) < 0.$$

If $0 < a < 1$ then $-az > -z$ and so

$$v_x(-az) < v_x(-z)$$

$$av_x(-az) < v_x(-z)$$

therefore

$$a\psi_z(az) > \psi_z(z).$$

35. See Figure B.58. Second-best output and income values are given by $\tilde{q}^a, \tilde{q}^b, \tilde{y}^a, \tilde{y}^b$. Note that $\tilde{y}^a > y^{*a}$ and that the able types are on an indifference curve that lies strictly above $\underline{\upsilon}^a$: this curve passes through the b-type's second-best contract $\left(\tilde{q}^b, \tilde{y}^b\right)$ but is below the indifference curve that passes through the b-type's first-best contract $\left(q^{*b}, y^{*b}\right)$.

36. Consider first the effects of p. In the full-information equilibrium it is clear from (12.37) or Figure 12.8 that the increase in product price will change the contract so that an Agent of any type is induced to provide higher output for an increased amount of income (the slope of the tangent

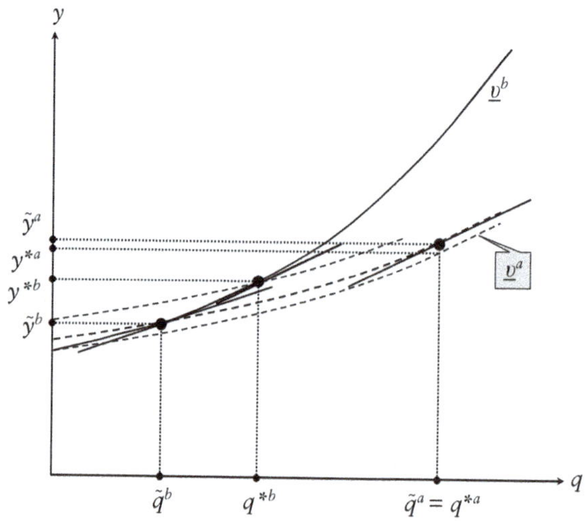

Figure B.58 Two types of Agent: Second-best solution

increases); however, the Agent will be kept on the same indifference curve—none of the price increase is 'passed on' in the form of a utility increase. The conclusion also applies to an a-type in the second-best equilibrium—see equation (12.41) and Figure B.58. The conclusion on utility also applies to a b-type in the second-best equilibrium. However, on differentiating (12.42) we have

$$\frac{dq^b}{dp} = \frac{1-\pi}{\pi\left[\frac{1}{\tau^a}\right]^2 \psi_{zz}\left(\frac{q^b}{\tau^a}\right) - \left[\frac{1}{\tau^b}\right]^2 \psi_{zz}\left(\frac{q^b}{\tau^b}\right)} \tag{B.180}$$

the denominator of which is of ambiguous sign. We know that $\psi_{zz}(\cdot)$ is negative; if $\psi_{zz}(\cdot)$ is constant or decreasing then the right-hand side of (B.180) is positive; clearly, in order to maintain the b-type on the same utility level, y^b has to move in the same direction as q^b. It is also clear from Figure B.58 that because of the incentive-compatibility constraint (captured by the a-indifference curve that passes through the b-contract) the utility level achieved by an a-type rises or falls according as y^b and q^b rise or fall.

Now consider the effect of changing π. This is irrelevant to the full-information equilibrium and, in the second-best equilibrium, it leaves unaffected the output of an a-type and the utility level of a b-type. Now consider the effect on a b-type's output. Differentiating (12.42), using (12.41), and rearranging we get

$$\frac{dq^b}{d\pi} = \frac{\psi_z\left(\frac{q^a}{\tau^a}\right) - \psi_z\left(\frac{q^b}{\tau^a}\right)}{\pi\frac{1}{\tau^a}\psi_{zz}\left(\frac{q^b}{\tau^a}\right) - \tau^a\left[\frac{1}{\tau^b}\right]^2 \psi_{zz}\left(\frac{q^b}{\tau^b}\right)} \tag{B.181}$$

the numerator is negative because ψ_z is a decreasing function; the sign of the denominator is determined in exactly the same way as for (B.180); so $\frac{dq^b}{d\pi}$ will be negative if $\psi_{zz}(\cdot)$ is constant or decreasing. The conclusions on a-type utility levels then follow as before.

37. Given $\tau^a > \tau^b > \tau^c$. The participation constraints are as in (12.36). The incentive-compatibility constraint (12.39) still applies as does its counterpart that stops b-types masquerading as c-types. Drawing together these points we have:

$$y^a + \psi\left(\frac{q^a}{\tau^a}\right) > \underline{\upsilon}^a \tag{B.182}$$

$$y^b + \psi\left(\frac{q^b}{\tau^b}\right) > \underline{\upsilon}^b \tag{B.183}$$

$$y^c + \psi\left(\frac{q^c}{\tau^c}\right) = \underline{\upsilon}^c \tag{B.184}$$

$$y^a + \psi\left(\frac{q^a}{\tau^a}\right) = y^b + \psi\left(\frac{q^b}{\tau^a}\right) \tag{B.185}$$

$$y^b + \psi\left(\frac{q^b}{\tau^b}\right) = y^c + \psi\left(\frac{q^c}{\tau^b}\right). \tag{B.186}$$

By the reasoning in the answer to Mini Problem 31 above participation constraints (B.182) and (B.183) must be slack and participation constraint (B.184) must bind: furthermore, it is clear from Figure B.59 that if (B.185) and (B.186) hold, then an a-type has no incentive to masquerade as a c-type.

If the proportions of each type are π^a, π^b, π^c then the constraints (B.184)–(B.186) yield the Lagrangean:

$$\pi^a\left[pq^a - y^a\right] + \pi^b\left[pq^b - y^b\right] + \pi^c\left[pq^c - y^c\right]$$
$$+\lambda\left[y^c + \psi\left(\frac{q^c}{\tau^c}\right) - \underline{\upsilon}^c\right]$$

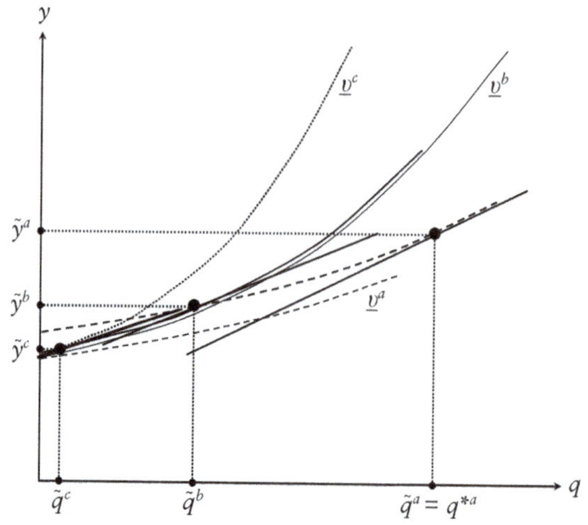

Figure B.59 Three types of Agent: Second-best solution

$$+\mu^b\left[y^b+\psi\left(\frac{q^b}{\tau^b}\right)-y^c-\psi\left(\frac{q^c}{\tau^b}\right)\right]$$

$$+\mu^a\left[y^a+\psi\left(\frac{q^a}{\tau^a}\right)-y^b-\psi\left(\frac{q^b}{\tau^a}\right)\right]$$

where μ^a and μ^b are the Lagrange multipliers for constraints (B.185) and (B.186) respectively. Differentiating the Lagrangean with respect to q^a and with respect to y^a we get, for an interior solution:

$$\pi^a p+\frac{\mu^a}{\tau^a}\psi_z\left(\frac{q^a}{\tau^a}\right)=0$$

$$-\pi^a+\mu^a=0$$

and so, once again we have (12.41): the no-distortion-at-the-top principle holds. Evaluating the rest of the conditions for the second-best equilibrium it is easy to see that

$$\mathrm{MRS}^b<\mathrm{MRT}^b$$

$$\mathrm{MRS}^c<\mathrm{MRT}^c.$$

—the solution is shown in Figure B.59.

38. ζ in (9.55) has income as its argument whereas ζ is a function of utility; however, utility here is denominated in income units—the function ψ in the definition of utility (12.34) can be taken as the dollar evaluation of the disutility of effort.

39. The Lagrangean is

$$\begin{aligned}\max_{\{q^a,q^b,y^a,y^b\}}\quad & \pi\zeta\left(y^a+\psi\left(\tfrac{q^a}{\tau^a}\right)\right)+[1-\pi]\,\zeta\left(y^b+\psi\left(\tfrac{q^b}{\tau^b}\right)\right)\\ & +\kappa\left[\pi\left[q^a-y^a\right]+[1-\pi]\left[q^b-y^b\right]-K\right]\\ & +\lambda^a\left[y^a+\psi\left(\tfrac{q^a}{\tau^a}\right)-\underline{\upsilon}^a\right]\\ & +\lambda^b\left[y^b+\psi\left(\tfrac{q^b}{\tau^b}\right)-\underline{\upsilon}^b\right].\end{aligned}\qquad\text{(B.187)}$$

The FOCs are

$$\pi\zeta_{\upsilon}\left(\upsilon^{a}\right)\left[\frac{1}{\tau^{a}}\psi_{z}\left(\frac{q^{a}}{\tau^{a}}\right)+\lambda^{a}\right]+\kappa\pi=0 \quad (B.188)$$

$$[1-\pi]\zeta_{\upsilon}\left(\upsilon^{b}\right)\left[\frac{1}{\tau^{b}}\psi_{z}\left(\frac{q^{b}}{\tau^{b}}\right)+\lambda^{b}\right]+\kappa[1-\pi]=0 \quad (B.189)$$

$$\pi\zeta_{\upsilon}\left(\upsilon^{a}\right)-\kappa\pi+\lambda^{a}=0 \quad (B.190)$$

$$[1-\pi]\zeta_{\upsilon}\left(\upsilon^{b}\right)-\kappa[1-\pi]+\lambda^{b}=0. \quad (B.191)$$

Substituting from (B.190) and (B.191) into (B.188) and (B.189) immediately gives the result.

40. The FOC for an interior solution to (12.47) are

$$\pi\zeta_{\upsilon}\left(\upsilon^{a}\right)\frac{1}{\tau^{a}}\psi_{z}\left(\frac{q^{a}}{\tau^{a}}\right)+\kappa\pi+\frac{\mu}{\tau^{a}}\psi_{z}\left(\frac{q^{a}}{\tau^{a}}\right)=0 \quad (B.192)$$

$$\left[[1-\pi]\zeta_{\upsilon}\left(\upsilon^{b}\right)+\lambda\right]\frac{1}{\tau^{b}}\psi_{z}\left(\frac{q^{b}}{\tau^{b}}\right)+\kappa[1-\pi]-\frac{\mu}{\tau^{a}}\psi_{z}\left(\frac{q^{b}}{\tau^{a}}\right)=0 \quad (B.193)$$

$$\pi\zeta_{\upsilon}\left(\upsilon^{a}\right)-\kappa\pi+\mu=0 \quad (B.194)$$

$$[1-\pi]\zeta_{\upsilon}\left(\upsilon^{b}\right)-\kappa[1-\pi]+\lambda-\mu=0 \quad (B.195)$$

$$\pi\left[q^{a}-y^{a}\right]+[1-\pi]\left[q^{b}-y^{b}\right]-K=0 \quad (B.196)$$

Substituting from (B.194) and (B.195) into (B.192) and (B.193) gives the result.

41. We can use a simple proof by contradiction. From inspection of (12.49) it is clear that $\zeta_{\upsilon}\left(\upsilon^{b}\right)>0$, $\lambda\geq 0$ and so if the incentive-compatibility constraint is binding (such that $\mu>0$) the right-hand side of (12.49) must be less than τ^{b} if

$$\tau^{b}+\frac{\tau^{b}}{\tau^{a}}\psi_{z}\left(\frac{q^{b}}{\tau^{a}}\right)$$

is positive. Suppose the opposite, that the above expression is ≤ 0; then

$$\psi_{z}\left(\frac{q^{b}}{\tau^{b}}\right)<\psi_{z}\left(\frac{q^{b}}{\tau^{a}}\right)\leq-\tau^{a}$$

which implies

$$-\psi_{z}\left(\frac{q^{b}}{\tau^{b}}\right)>\tau^{a}>\tau^{b}$$

—a contradiction.

42. If

$$\zeta_{\upsilon}\left(\upsilon^{a}\right)=\zeta_{\upsilon}\left(\upsilon^{b}\right)=1$$

then the FOCs (B.192)–(B.195) become

$$\frac{1}{\tau^{a}}\psi_{z}\left(\frac{q^{a}}{\tau^{a}}\right)[\pi+\mu]+\kappa\pi=0 \quad (B.197)$$

$$[[1-\pi]+\lambda]\frac{1}{\tau^{b}}\psi_{z}\left(\frac{q^{b}}{\tau^{b}}\right)+\kappa[1-\pi]-\frac{\mu}{\tau^{a}}\psi_{z}\left(\frac{q^{b}}{\tau^{a}}\right)=0 \quad (B.198)$$

$$\pi-\kappa\pi+\mu=0 \quad (B.199)$$

$$[1-\pi]-\kappa[1-\pi]+\lambda-\mu=0 \quad (B.200)$$

from which we get

$$\mu = [\kappa - 1]\,\pi$$

$$\lambda = \kappa - 1$$

$$\mu = \lambda\pi$$

and so

$$-\psi_z\left(\frac{q^b}{\tau^b}\right) = \tau^b - \frac{[\kappa-1]\,\pi}{\kappa - \pi}\left[\tau^b + \frac{\tau^b}{\tau^a}\psi_z\left(\frac{q^b}{\tau^a}\right)\right].$$

However, comparison with Exercise 12.11 (page 428) reveals that $\kappa = 1$: in this case the government is indifferent from whom it raises the taxes and an increase in the external revenue requirement K would have a dollar-for-dollar impact on the objective function; we get the full-information solution.

43. Expression (12.51) can be written

$$y\left(\tau^j\right) + \psi\left(\frac{q\left(\tau^j\right)}{\tau^j}\right) \geq y\left(\tau^{j-1}\right) + \psi\left(\frac{q\left(\tau^{j-1}\right)}{\tau^j}\right). \tag{B.201}$$

Letting $\tau := \tau^j$ and $d\tau := \tau^j - \tau^{j-1}$ we have

$$y(\tau) + \psi\left(\frac{q(\tau)}{\tau}\right) \geq y(\tau - d\tau) + \psi\left(\frac{q(\tau - d\tau)}{\tau}\right) \tag{B.202}$$

which, for small $d\tau$, gives

$$y(\tau) + \psi\left(\frac{q(\tau)}{\tau}\right) \geq y(\tau) - y'(\tau)\,d\tau + \psi\left(\frac{q(\tau)}{\tau}\right) - \psi_z\left(\frac{q(\tau)}{\tau}\right)d\tau \tag{B.203}$$

which, on rearranging and dividing by $d\tau$ (a positive number) yields

$$y'(\tau) + \psi_z\left(\frac{q(\tau)}{\tau}\right) \geq 0. \tag{B.204}$$

44. We know that in the two-type and the N-type case $(q(\tau), y(\tau))$ must increase with τ. The same reasoning applies here. This implies that in the optimal design it is impossible to have a situation where q is increasing at the same time as y is decreasing. From the definition of personal tax in (12.58) we have

$$dT(\tau) = dq(\tau) - dy(\tau). \tag{B.205}$$

$$\frac{dT}{dq} = 1 - \frac{dy}{dq} \tag{B.206}$$

Since $\frac{dy}{dq}$ is positive, $\frac{dT}{dq}$ must be less than 1.

B.13 Government and the individual

1. If the overall non-convexity arises from positive externalities then a subsidy to each firm's output (proportional to the size of the externality) may be appropriate: see Mini Problem 20 in chapter 9 and section 13.4 below.

2. Technically efficient points consist of the point $\mathbf{x}^\circ$ and the 'north-east' boundary of the smooth curve (except for the point directly below $\mathbf{x}^\circ$).

3. Figure B.60 shows the CV as a measure of the utility gain from introducing the infrastructure project, using units of good 2 as a measure of value (b). If consumers differ in their preferences then there may be winners and losers in the move from $\mathbf{x}^\circ$ to $\mathbf{x}'$. In this case how one treats (or

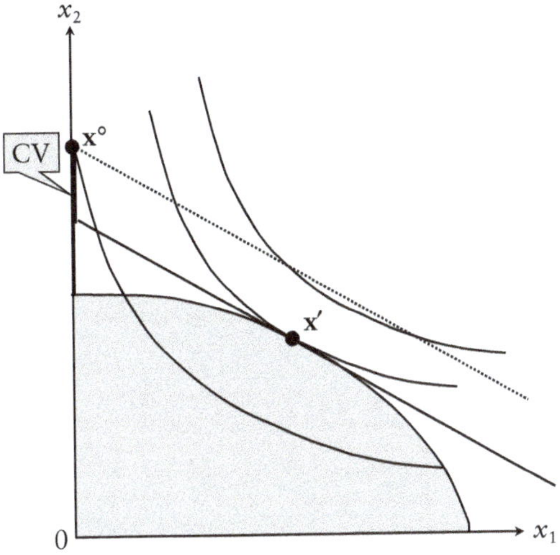

Figure B.60 Compensating variation measure of welfare

fails to treat) distributional issues is crucial (see Exercise 9.9): just adding the CVs up may be problematic. Getting the information may also be problematic because in this situation people may misrepresent their CV—see the argument in the following section 13.3.4.

4. The line through $\mathbf{x}'$ is one of a family of parallel isoprofit lines. The direction of increasing profit is 'north-east'—see Figure 2.18 on page 43. The highest one of the family isoprofit lines that you can reach over the attainable set is at the peak of the spike, $\mathbf{x}^\circ$.

5. The main part of the diagram is contained by a quarter-circle from $(1, 0)$ to $(0, 1)$. The spike is of height $1 + k$: the fixed cost of producing good 1 is k. Profits are as in Figure B.61: note the graph consists of the isolated point at $1 + k$ on the vertical axis and the curve. There would be a global maximum at $x_1 = 0$ if $k > \sqrt{2} - 1 \simeq 0.414$.

6. A simple monopoly will set price above marginal cost and thus marginal willingness to pay will be above marginal cost. This will incur a welfare loss as analysed on page 243.

7. Goods or services where resale can be prevented by virtue of their physical characteristics or legal constraint—see Mini Problem 11 in chapter 3.

8. It may be higher or lower depending on the position of the demand curve i.e. the shape of the indifference curves—compare cases 3a and 3c in Exercise 3.4.

9. The firm is assured of the profits obtainable at $\mathbf{x}^\circ$, the status quo. The isoprofit lines depicted in Figures 13.3 and 13.4 are of the form

$$p_1 x_1 + p_2 x_2 = \text{const.}$$

Clearly the difference in the constant term between the isoprofit line through $\mathbf{x}^\circ$ and that through $\mathbf{x}'$ is exactly F_0. So the assurance of an entry fee F_0 is just sufficient to assure the firm of the same level of profit at $\mathbf{x}'$ as it would have received at $\mathbf{x}^\circ$.

10. This proposal is effectively the 'potential superiority' criterion again. It takes no account of distributional issues and it assumes that the possible losses of one agent could just be offset by the gains to another. See page 254 and Exercise 9.9 on page 268.

11. See Figure B.62. If the low-cost (high-efficiency) firm were correctly identified it would produce at $\mathbf{x}'$. However, it knows that a high-cost type would produce an amount x_1''; if it mimics this

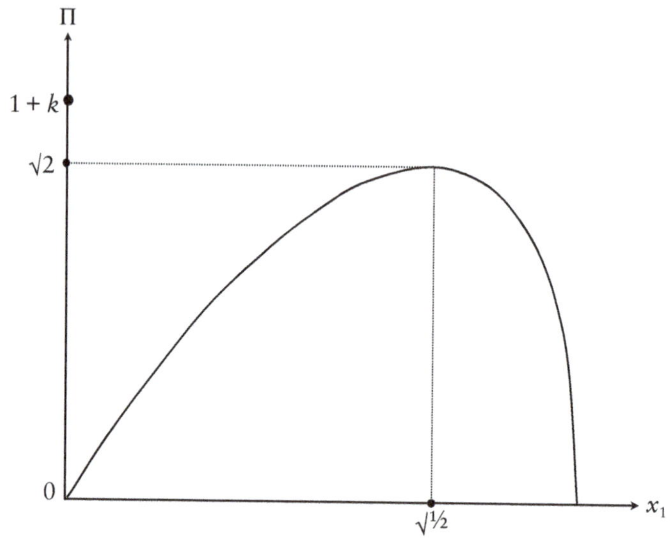

Figure B.61 Profits in the non-convexity example

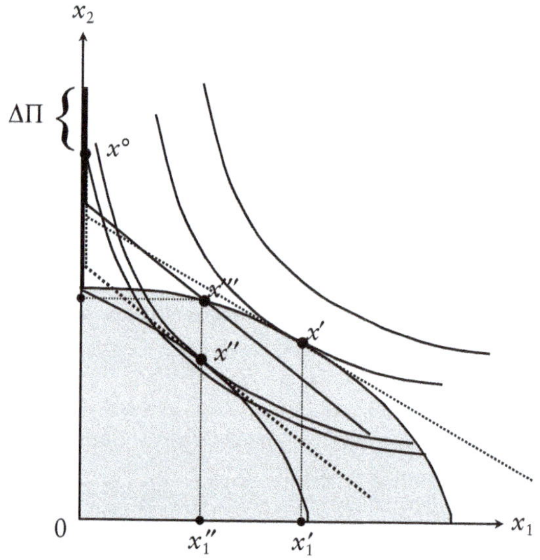

Figure B.62 High-efficiency type masquerades as low-efficiency type

behaviour it will be producing at point $\mathbf{x}'''$. Given the subsidy offered to a high-cost firm it could therefore make the increase in profits shown by ΔΠ. (To see this, just shift the payment schedule for a high-cost firm up from $\mathbf{x}''$ to $\mathbf{x}'''$.)

12. No, because nothing is being said about ownership and legal liability. It is certainly consistent with that principle, but it is also consistent with, for example, a subsidy on good 2.

13. Marginal cost of bribe equals marginal benefit in reduction of pollution.

14. In principle, why not? If deodorant is commodity 1 then it may be common knowledge that $e^h_{21} > 0$ for all consumers. Then (13.19) requires that there be a negative corrective tax—i.e. a subsidy—on good 1. But see Mini Problem 15.

15. Check the definition of e^h_{21} in equation (9.33). For some specific commodity 1 it will be the case that

$$\frac{\partial U^\ell}{\partial x^h_1} > 0 \tag{B.207}$$

for some pairs of agents h and ℓ, while for others the reverse is true. Agent ℓ may like h's perfume but strongly dislike the awful stuff used by h'. Worse still agent ℓ may appreciate all types of perfume worn by everyone else, but agent ℓ' could be completely perfume intolerant. The sign of (B.207) could be difficult to verify on a case-by-case basis. Knowing this, even if it were true that all in the population were perfume appreciators—so (B.207) is true, $e^h_{21} > 0$ and there is a case for a subsidy—individuals might even to try to pretend that they were actually being *harmed* by the perfume. Misrepresenting their preferences might be seen as a way to avoid having to pay the tax required to fund the subsidy on the socially beneficial good 1.

16. Although section 9.3.4 deals with public goods (those that are both non-rival and non-excludable) condition (9.36) is valid irrespective of whether or not the good is excludable. Combining this with (9.13) and (9.14) gives (13.20).

17. Hours of TV broadcasting service.

18. From (13.22) we must have

$$x_1 = \phi\left(C(x_1, N), N\right). \tag{B.208}$$

Note that it is assumed that $\phi_z > 0$ and $\phi_{zz} < 0$. Therefore, differentiating (B.208) twice with respect to x_1 we get

$$1 = \phi_z\left(C(x_1, N), N\right) C_1(x_1, N)$$
$$0 = \phi_{zz}\left(C(x_1, N), N\right) [C_1(x_1, N)]^2 + \phi_z\left(C(x_1, N), N\right) C_{11}(x_1, N).$$

From this we have

$$C_1(x_1, N) = \frac{1}{\phi_z\left(C(x_1, N), N\right)} > 0$$
$$C_{11}(x_1, N) = -\frac{\phi_{zz}\left(C(x_1, N), N\right)}{\phi_z\left(C(x_1, N), N\right)} [C_1(x_1, N)]^2 > 0.$$

It is also assumed that, for any N:

$$\phi\left(C(x_1, N+1), N+1\right) \le \phi\left(C(x_1, N+1), N\right).$$

But, from (B.208) we get

$$x_1 = \phi\left(C(x_1, N+1), N+1\right) \tag{B.209}$$

and so

$$\phi\left(C(x_1, N+1), N\right) - \phi\left(C(x_1, N), N\right) = -\left[\phi\left(C(x_1, N+1), N+1\right) - \phi\left(C(x_1, N+1), N\right)\right] \ge 0$$

so that $\phi(C(x_1, N))$ must be non-decreasing in N.

19. Use the terminology of Mini Problem 18. If good 1 is completely non-rival then it costs no more to serve $N+1$ people than it costs to serve N; so $C(x_1, N+1) = C(x_1, N)$. If there is congestion then an additional person raises the cost of providing any given level of service x_1: $C(x_1, N+1) > C(x_1, N)$.

20. The heterogeneity among the membership can be handled by having different membership fees for different agents. Let the membership fee for agent h be z^h. For each member of the club the following must hold:

$$U^h\left(\phi\left(z,N\right),y^h-z^h\right)\geq U^h\left(0,y^h\right). \tag{B.210}$$

Now consider a small variation in all the membership fees $(z^1,z^2,\ldots,z^N)$. The effect on agent h's utility is

$$U_1^h\left(\phi\left(z,N\right),y^h-z^h\right)\phi_z\left(z,N\right)\sum_{k=1}^{N}dz^k-U_2^h\left(\phi\left(z,N\right),y^h-z^h\right)dz^h=0 \tag{B.211}$$

so that

$$U_1^h\left(\phi\left(z,N\right),y^h-z^h\right)\phi_z\left(z,N\right)\sum_{k=1}^{N}dz^k=U_2^h\left(\phi\left(z,N\right),y^h-z^h\right)dz^h. \tag{B.212}$$

Rearranging and summing over h in the club we get

$$\sum_{h=1}^{N}\frac{U_1^h\left(\phi\left(z,N\right),y^h-z^h\right)}{U_2^h\left(\phi\left(z,N\right),y^h-z^h\right)}=\frac{1}{\phi_z\left(z,N\right)} \tag{B.213}$$

which is the counterpart of (13.28).

21. (a) Differentiating (13.25) with respect to N we have

$$U_1^h\left(\phi\left(z,N\right),y^h-\frac{z}{N}\right)\phi_N\left(z,N\right)+\frac{z}{N^2}U_2^h\left(\phi\left(z,N\right),y^h-\frac{z}{N}\right)=0.$$

Using (13.27) we then get

$$\frac{1}{N}U_2^h\left(\phi\left(z,N\right),y^h-\frac{z}{N}\right)\frac{\phi_N\left(z,N\right)}{\phi_z\left(z,N\right)}+\frac{z}{N^2}U_2^h\left(\phi\left(z,N\right),y^h-\frac{z}{N}\right)=0$$

and so, on rearrangement, the condition is

$$-\frac{\phi_N\left(z,N\right)}{\phi_z\left(z,N\right)}=\frac{z}{N}. \tag{B.214}$$

(b) The term on the left of (B.214) is the marginal cost of increasing N, evaluated in terms of extra input z. The term on the right is just average cost.

(c) The right-hand side of (B.214) is the membership fee for the club. So (B.214) can be interpreted as stated.

22. The MRS for each agent is

$$\frac{1}{\sqrt{x_1}}.$$

So the efficiency condition is

$$n_h\frac{1}{\sqrt{x_1}}=1$$

$$x_1=\left[n_h\right]^2.$$

23. Suppose there are two persons, Alf and Bill. Alf's utility can be written

$$U^a(\phi(z^a+z^b),y^a-z^a).$$

Given that U^a is increasing in both arguments and ϕ is an increasing function it is clear that U^a is everywhere increasing in z^b and that the first argument of U^a is increasing in z^a but the second

		s_1^b [yes]	s_2^b [no]
s_1^a	[YES]	1.2, 1.2	0.5, 1.5
s_2^a	[NO]	1.5, 0.5	1, 1

Table B.8 A simple public-goods game

argument of U^a is decreasing in z^a. Now consider the slope of the indifference curve in $\left(z^a, z^b\right)$-space. Differentiating Alf's utility:

$$U_1^a(\phi(z), y^a - z^a)\phi_z(z^a + z^b)dz^b + U_1^a(\phi(z), y^a - z^a)\phi_z(z^a + z^b)dz^a - U_2^a(\phi(z), y^a - z^a)dz^a$$

$$\frac{dz^b}{dz^a} = 1 - \frac{U_2^a(\phi(z), y^a - z^a)}{U_1^a(\phi(z), y^a - z^a)\phi_z(z)}$$

where $z = z^a + z^b$. Given that U is quasiconcave the ratio $\frac{U_2^a}{U_1^a}$ is everywhere decreasing in x_1^a, increasing in x_2^a; therefore it is everywhere decreasing in z^a; therefore $\frac{dz^b}{dz^a}$ is negative for low values of z^a, where

$$\frac{U_2^a}{U_1^a} > \phi_z(z)$$

and positive for high values of z^a. This establishes the U-shape.

24. In principle it could, but the requirements of the Folk Theorem would be quite demanding. One needs very long-lived individuals and everyone must be able to observe the actions (contributions in this case) of all others at each stage of the game.

25. Evaluate the payoffs in terms of 'private + public'.

- If neither person contributes obviously there is no public good and both get a payoff of $1 + 0$.
- If, say a contributes and b does not, a gets a payoff of $0 + 0.5$ and b gets $1 + 0.5$.
- If both contribute then both get $0 + 1.2$.

So the game looks like that in Table B.8 which is exactly the same form as that in Table 10.1, up to a monotonic transformation of the payoffs, which we know is irrelevant.

26. Equation (13.43) can be written.

$$U^h\left(x_1, x_2^h\right) = \begin{cases} \psi\left(\phi\left(z^*\right)\right) - \frac{z^h}{z} z^* + y^h & \text{if } z \geq z^* \\ y^h & \text{otherwise} \end{cases}$$

Therefore if

$$\psi\left(\phi\left(z^*\right)\right) > \frac{z^h}{z} z^*$$

and $\left(z^1, z^2 \ldots, z^h, \ldots\right)$ satisfy $\sum_h z^h = z^*$ no one will have an incentive to deviate.

27. Note that if $z \geq z^*$

$$\frac{\partial U^h}{\partial z^h} = -\frac{z^*}{z} + \frac{z^h z^*}{z^2} < 0$$

and so everyone would like to argue for a lower contribution.

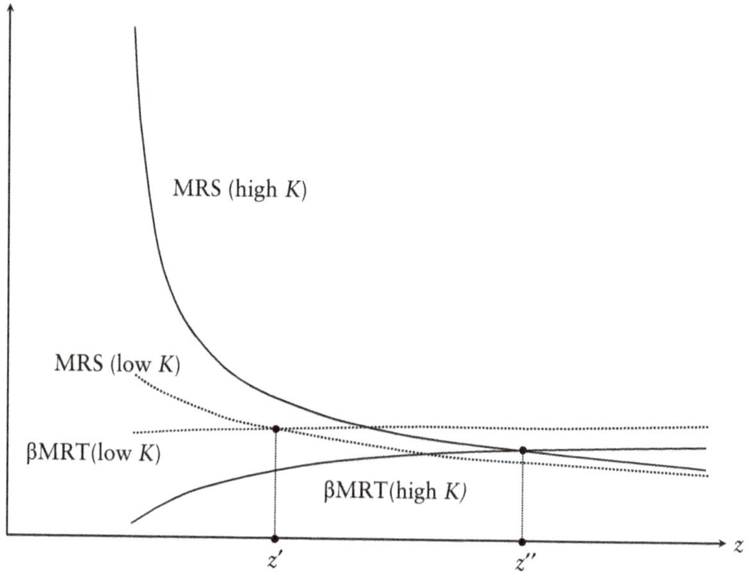

Figure B.63 Public good provision under lottery

28. Differentiating (13.47) with respect z^h to we get the FOC for an interior solution:

$$0 = \psi_x^h(x_1)\,\phi_x(z-K) + \frac{1}{z}K - \frac{z^h}{z^2}K - 1. \tag{B.215}$$

Rearranging and using (13.46) we have

$$\psi_x(x_1)\,\phi_x(z-K) = \left[1 - \frac{\bar{z}}{z^2}K\right] \tag{B.216}$$

from which the result follows.

29. Evaluating (13.34) with the utility function (13.42) we immediately get (13.48) for the special case $K = 0$: note that $\beta(0) = 1$.

Using the assumption that 1 unit of private good can always be transformed into 1 unit of the public good, from (13.45)–(13.47) expected utility is

$$2\sqrt{\bar{z} + z^h - K} + \frac{z^h}{\bar{z} + z^h}K + y^h - z^h. \tag{B.217}$$

The FOC gives us

$$\frac{1}{\sqrt{z-K}} = 1 - \frac{\bar{z}}{z^2}K \tag{B.218}$$

If they are all identical then $z = \gamma\bar{z}$, where $\gamma := n_h/[n_h - 1]$ and so the FOC becomes

$$\frac{1}{\sqrt{z-K}} = 1 - \frac{K}{\gamma z} \tag{B.219}$$

which corresponds to (13.48) for this model. Plotting the LHS and the RHS of this relationship in Figure B.63 it is clear that for low K we get z' and for high K we get z'' where $z' < z''$.

30. Using the relationship $K = az$ the amount of the public good is

$$x_1 = [1 - a]\,z$$

and expected utility is

$$\psi^h(\phi([1-a]z)) + a\pi^h z + y^h - z^h$$
$$= \psi^h(\phi([1-a]z)) - [1-a]z^h + y^h. \qquad \text{(B.220)}$$

Maximising this with respect to z^h yields the FOC

$$\psi_x^h(\phi([1-a]z))\frac{\partial\phi([1-a]z)}{\partial z} - [1-a]z^h = 0$$

which leads to exactly the same first-order conditions as for voluntary provision—see the answer to Mini Problem 29 above.

31. Under the stringent conditions imposed, the answers to both parts is yes. But it does not require too much effort to think of a number of practical difficulties with introducing either form of tax system. Clearly tax scheme (b) would be regarded as inequitable by many.

32. Suppose, to the contrary, that $\mathbf{y}^*$ maximises a concave social-welfare function where $\mathbf{y}$ is not perfectly equal. Let $\mathbf{y}^{**}$ be some vector, distinct from $\mathbf{y}^*$, that is formed from a permutation of $\mathbf{y}^*$; by symmetry of Y we have $\mathbf{y}^{**} \in Y$; by symmetry of the social-welfare function welfare at these two vectors is identical. Now consider $\bar{\mathbf{y}} := a\mathbf{y}^* + [1-a]\mathbf{y}^{**}$; by convexity we have $\bar{\mathbf{y}} \in Y$; by concavity of the social-welfare function, welfare at is at least as great as at $\mathbf{y}^*$. Hence, for any distribution of income that is unequal we can always find an equalising redistribution that yields an income distribution vector for which social welfare is at least as high.

33. If one has proportional taxes, they can be levied on aggregate purchases across all consumers; this could be administered, for example, through producers or retailers so that the tax authority does not have to concern itself with individual transactions. With even a 'small' amount of non-linearity one would have to keep track of every agent's purchases.

34. Tax revenue is given by the lightly shaded rectangle in Figure 9.6; total burden on consumers is this rectangle plus the dark triangle.

35. The problem remains unaffected.

36. Suppose we could introduce a tax on the consumption of good zero. Then the counterpart of the consumer prices equation is (13.53)

$$p_0 = \tilde{p}_0 + t_0 \qquad \text{(B.221)}$$

and the definition of income (13.52) now becomes

$$y := \tilde{p}_0 - [\tilde{p}_0 + t_0]x_0 + \bar{y}. \qquad \text{(B.222)}$$

So the consumer's budget constraint (13.51) becomes

$$\sum_{i=1}^{n}[\tilde{p}_i + t_i]x_i \le \tilde{p}_0 - [\tilde{p}_0 + t_0]x_0 + \bar{y}.$$

Rearranging, this gives us

$$\sum_{i=0}^{n}[\tilde{p}_i + t_i]x_i \le \tilde{p}_0 + \bar{y}.$$

Now suppose we introduce the same, proportionate tax rate t on all commodities $0, 1, \ldots, n$. Then the budget constraint becomes

$$\sum_{i=0}^{n}\tilde{p}_i[1+t]x_i \le \tilde{p}_0 + \bar{y}$$

which is equivalent to

$$\sum_{i=0}^{n} \tilde{p}_i x_i \leq \frac{\tilde{p}_0 + \bar{y}}{1+t}.$$

But the right-hand side is obviously equivalent to taxing the consumer's endowment of good 0 (one unit, worth $\tilde{p}_0$) and lump-sum income. By assuming that all goods are taxable we have made an important assumption about information: we have backed ourselves into a situation where we are assuming that endowments are observable and taxable. If this were true, it would mean that the government could raise its revenue without any waste at all!

37. From Roy's identity (4.28) we know that

$$V_i(\mathbf{p}, \bar{y}) = -V_{\bar{y}}(\mathbf{p}, \bar{y}) x_i \tag{B.223}$$

and, substituting (B.223) into (13.56) we get, for all $i = 1, 2, \ldots, n$

$$[\lambda - \mu] x_i + \lambda \sum_{j=1}^{n} t_j \frac{\partial x_j}{\partial p_i} = 0, \tag{B.224}$$

where μ is the Lagrange multiplier in the consumer's primal problem (see page 89).

38. From (13.57) and (13.58) we get

$$\sum_{j=1}^{n} t_j \left[H_i^j - x_i \frac{\partial x_j}{\partial \bar{y}} \right] = -\left[\frac{\lambda - \mu}{\lambda} \right] x_i \tag{B.225}$$

which yields

$$\sum_{j=1}^{n} t_j H_i^j = x_i \left[\sum_{j=1}^{n} t_j \frac{\partial x_j}{\partial \bar{y}} - \left[\frac{\lambda - \mu}{\lambda} \right] \right]. \tag{B.226}$$

Use the symmetry of the substitution effect, so that $H_i^j = H_j^i$. Then (B.226) can be expressed as

$$\sum_{j=1}^{n} t_j H_j^i = -\kappa x_i \tag{B.227}$$

where κ is given by (13.60). Writing (B.227) in a slightly different form we get the result.

APPENDIX C

Selected Proofs

The proofs provided in this appendix are intended to satisfy the curiosity of the reader who needs to know how and why certain results come about. They should be seen as a supplement to the argument of the main text, rather than a focus of interest in their own right. Following through a proof, line by line, is not a substitute for understanding the intuition underlying key economic principles. Where a proof is too long or intricate to warrant setting out here I give a pointer to the literature either in this appendix or in the chapter where the result appears. In some cases I show how a simpler, related result can be established.

The proofs presented here follow the main chapter sequence, although sometimes the order within the chapter is not respected where it is useful to build one proof upon another.

C.1 The firm

Although Lemma C.1 and Theorem C.1 that follow are only used in a minor way in chapter 2, the Theorem is the foundation of several other results that we need elsewhere.

Lemma C.1

Let $\phi(\cdot)$ and $\hat{\phi}(\cdot)$ be production functions that are everywhere differentiable and where both $\phi_1(\mathbf{z}) > 0$, $\hat{\phi}_1(\mathbf{z}) > 0$ for all $\mathbf{z}$. Then

$$\hat{\phi}(\mathbf{z}) = \Psi(\phi(\mathbf{z})) \tag{C.1}$$

where Ψ is a differentiable, strictly increasing function, if and only if, for all $\mathbf{z}$

$$\frac{\hat{\phi}_i(\mathbf{z})}{\hat{\phi}_1(\mathbf{z})} = \frac{\phi_i(\mathbf{z})}{\phi_1(\mathbf{z})},\ i = 2, \ldots, m \tag{C.2}$$

Proof

For the 'only if' part it is sufficient to differentiate (C.1) with respect to z_i and with respect to z_1:

$$\frac{\hat{\phi}_i(\mathbf{z})}{\hat{\phi}_1(\mathbf{z})} = \frac{\Psi_1(q)}{\Psi_1(q)}\frac{\phi_i(\mathbf{z})}{\phi_1(\mathbf{z})} \tag{C.3}$$

where Ψ_1 is the derivative of Ψ and

$$q = \phi(\mathbf{z});$$

then (C.2) follows immediately from (C.3).

For the 'if' part suppose (C.2) is true and that (C.1) holds for $m-1$. Let $z_m = a$, a constant. Then

$$\hat{\phi}(z_1, \ldots, z_{m-1}, a) = \Psi(\phi(z_1, \ldots, z_{m-1}, a), a) \tag{C.4}$$

where the second argument of Ψ allows for the possibility that the relationship between $\hat{\phi}$ and ϕ may depend on the value of a. This implies that for the case where there are m variable inputs

$$\hat{\phi}(\mathbf{z}) = \Psi(\phi(\mathbf{z}), z_m) \tag{C.5}$$

where, as before,

$$\mathbf{z} = z_1, \ldots, z_{m-1}, z_m.$$

Differentiate (C.5) with respect to z_m and with respect to z_1

$$\frac{\hat{\phi}_m(\mathbf{z})}{\hat{\phi}_1(\mathbf{z})} = \frac{\phi_m(\mathbf{z})}{\phi_1(\mathbf{z})} + \frac{\Psi_2(q, z_m)}{\Psi_1(q, z_m)}. \tag{C.6}$$

But, in view of (C.2) we must have $\Psi_2(q, z_m) = 0$ in (C.2), so that Ψ is actually independent of z_m in (C.5). Therefore, if (C.1) holds for $m-1$, it also holds for m. In the case $m = 1$, because ϕ is monotonic it has an inverse and we have

$$z_1 = \phi^{-1}(q)$$

$$\hat{\phi}(z_1) = \hat{\phi}\left(\phi^{-1}(q)\right) = \Psi(\phi(z_1)) \tag{C.7}$$

where $\Psi = \hat{\phi}(\phi^{-1})$ Therefore (C.1) holds for all m. ■

Now let $\mathbf{z}$ be an m-vector of inputs and use $\mathbf{z}^{\circ}$ to denote the first k components and $\mathbf{z}'$ to denote the remaining $m-k$ components, so that

$$\mathbf{z} = \left[\mathbf{z}^{\circ}, \mathbf{z}'\right].$$

Theorem C.1 (Leontief decomposition)

There exist functions ψ and Ψ such that

$$\phi(\mathbf{z}) = \Psi\left(\psi\left(\mathbf{z}^{\circ}\right), \mathbf{z}'\right) \tag{C.8}$$

if and only if, for every $\mathbf{z}$:

$$\frac{\phi_i(\mathbf{z})}{\phi_1(\mathbf{z})} \text{ is independent of } \mathbf{z}' \; i = 2, \ldots, k.$$

Proof

For the 'only if' part it is sufficient to differentiate (C.1) with respect to z_i and with respect to z_1:

$$\frac{\phi_i(\mathbf{z})}{\phi_1(\mathbf{z})} = \frac{\Psi_1(\psi(\mathbf{z}^{\circ}))\, \psi_i(\mathbf{z}^{\circ})}{\Psi_1(\psi(\mathbf{z}^{\circ}))\, \psi_1(\mathbf{z}^{\circ})} = \frac{\psi_i(\mathbf{z}^{\circ})}{\psi_1(\mathbf{z}^{\circ})} \tag{C.9}$$

where Ψ_1 is the derivative of Ψ.

For the 'if' part, let $\mathbf{z}'$ be fixed at some constant $\mathbf{a}$ so that $\mathbf{z} = \left[\mathbf{z}^{\circ}, \mathbf{a}\right]$ and define ψ such that

$$\psi\left(\mathbf{z}^{\circ}\right) := \phi\left(\mathbf{z}^{\circ}, \mathbf{a}\right).$$

Then, the assumption that $\phi_i(\mathbf{z})/\phi_1(\mathbf{z})$ is independent of $\mathbf{z}'$ implies

$$\frac{\phi_i\left(\mathbf{z}^{\circ}, \mathbf{a}\right)}{\phi_1\left(\mathbf{z}^{\circ}, \mathbf{a}\right)} = \frac{\psi_i\left(\mathbf{z}^{\circ}\right)}{\psi_1\left(\mathbf{z}^{\circ}\right)} \; i = 2, \ldots, k \tag{C.10}$$

By Lemma C.1 this implies that

$$\phi\left(\mathbf{z}^{\circ}, \mathbf{a}\right) = \Psi\left(\psi\left(\mathbf{z}^{\circ}\right), \mathbf{a}\right) \tag{C.11}$$

for the given value $\mathbf{a}$. But if we repeat the argument for any other given value of $\mathbf{z}'$ we have (C.8). ■

C.1.1 Marginal cost and the Lagrange multiplier

The numbering of inputs is arbitrary, so label them such that $z_i^* > 0$ for $i = 1, \ldots, m^*$ and $z_i^* = 0$ for $i = m^* + 1, \ldots, m$, where $m^* \leq m$. Then (2.22) can be rewritten

$$C(\mathbf{w}, q) = \sum_{i=1}^{m*} w_i z_i^* + \lambda^*(\mathbf{w}, q)\,[q - \phi(\mathbf{z}^*)]$$

$$= \sum_{i=1}^{m*} w_i H^i(\mathbf{w}, q) + \lambda^*(\mathbf{w}, q)\,[q - \phi(\mathbf{H}(\mathbf{w}, q))] \qquad \text{(C.12)}$$

where $\mathbf{H} := (H^1, H^2, \ldots, H^m)$ is the vector of conditional demand functions. Differentiating (C.12) with respect to q we get

$$C_q(\mathbf{w}, q) = \sum_{i=1}^{m*} [w_i - \lambda^*(\mathbf{w}, q)\phi_i(\mathbf{z}^*)]\, H_q^i(\mathbf{w}, q)$$

$$+ \lambda_q^*(\mathbf{w}, q)\,[q - \phi(\mathbf{z}^*)]$$

$$+ \lambda^*(\mathbf{w}, q) \qquad \text{(C.13)}$$

where H_q^i and λ_q^* may be multivalued if $\mathbf{z}^*$ is multivalued at $(\mathbf{w}, q)$. Using equations (2.13) and (2.15) the first two terms on the right-hand side of (C.13) are zero and we get equation (2.23). ■

C.1.2 Properties of the cost function (Theorem 2.2)

We establish each of the principal properties in separate subsections.

Homogeneous of degree 1 in prices

Let $\mathbf{z}^*$ be a solution to the following problem: choose $\mathbf{z}$ to minimise

$$\sum_{i=1}^{n} w_i z_i \qquad \text{(C.14)}$$

over the set

$$Z(q) := \{\mathbf{z} : \mathbf{z} \geq 0,\ \phi(\mathbf{z}) \geq q\} \qquad \text{(C.15)}$$

where $\mathbf{w} \in \mathbb{R}_+^m$.

By definition the cost function is the minimised value of (C.14) and may be written

$$C(\mathbf{w}, q) = \sum_{i=1}^{n} w_i z_i^*. \qquad \text{(C.16)}$$

Now consider the problem of choosing $\mathbf{z}$ to minimise $\sum_{i=1}^{n} [tw_i]\, z_i$ over (C.15) where t is an arbitrary positive number. The constraint set is independent of t and so $\mathbf{z}^*$ is a solution to the modified problem as well. Therefore, applying the general relationship (C.16) to the input-price vector $t\mathbf{w}$ we get:

$$C(t\mathbf{w}, q) = \sum_{i=1}^{n} [tw_i]\, z_i^* = t \sum_{i=1}^{n} w_i z_i^* = tC(\mathbf{w}, q). \qquad \text{(C.17)}$$

Shephard's Lemma (equation 2.21)

Note that the argument in the answer to Mini Problem 18 of chapter 2 relies on all the inputs being positive and unique. The following general method does not require those restrictions.

Consider an arbitrary small variation in input prices $d\mathbf{w}$ for which the ith component is $dw_i > 0$ and all other components are zero. Let $Z^*(\mathbf{w}, q)$ be the set of cost-minimising input vectors for input prices $\mathbf{w}$ and output level q (in the 'conventional' case this set will have just one element) and let $\mathbf{z}^* \in Z^*(\mathbf{w}, q)$ and $\mathbf{z}^* + d\mathbf{z} \in Z^*(\mathbf{w} + d\mathbf{w}, q)$. By definition of cost minimisation

$$C(\mathbf{w} + d\mathbf{w}, q) \leq \sum_{j=1}^{m} [w_j + dw_j] z_j^* \tag{C.18}$$

$$= C(\mathbf{w}, q) + dw_i z_i^* \tag{C.19}$$

and

$$C(\mathbf{w}, q) \leq \sum_{j=1}^{m} w_j \left[z_j^* + dz_j^*\right]$$

$$= \sum_{j=1}^{m} [w_j + dw_j] \left[z_j^* + dz_j^*\right] - \sum_{j=1}^{m} dw_j \left[z_j^* + dz_j^*\right]$$

$$= C(\mathbf{w} + d\mathbf{w}, q) - dw_i \left[z_i^* + dz_i^*\right]. \tag{C.20}$$

Conditions (C.19) and (C.20) imply respectively:

$$\frac{C(\mathbf{w} + d\mathbf{w}, q) - C(\mathbf{w}, q)}{dw_i} \leq z_i^* \tag{C.21}$$

$$\frac{C(\mathbf{w} + d\mathbf{w}, q) - C(\mathbf{w}, q)}{dw_i} \geq z_i^* + dz_i^*. \tag{C.22}$$

Clearly as $dw_i \to 0$ the left-hand side of (C.21) and (C.22) becomes $C_i(\mathbf{w}, q)$ and the right-hand side is z_i^*.

Strictly increasing in at least one w_i

In view of (2.3) a positive q requires that at least one input is positive. Now, for given q let $\mathbf{z}^*$ be cost minimising for $\mathbf{w}'$ and let $\mathbf{z}^{**}$ be cost minimising for $\mathbf{w}''$, where $\mathbf{w}', \mathbf{w}'' \in \mathbb{R}_+^m$. Suppose $\mathbf{w}'' \geq \mathbf{w}'$ with $w_i'' > w_i'$ for some i where $z_i^{**} > 0$. Then

$$C(\mathbf{w}'', q) = \sum_{i=1}^{n} w_i'' z_i^{**} > \sum_{i=1}^{n} w_i' z_i^{**}.$$

Also, by cost minimisation

$$C(\mathbf{w}', q) = \sum_{i=1}^{n} w_i' z_i^* \leq \sum_{i=1}^{n} w_i' z_i^{**} \tag{C.23}$$

which implies $C(\mathbf{w}', q) < C(\mathbf{w}'', q)$. This is only possible if C is strictly increasing in at least one w_i.

Non-decreasing in every w_i

Suppose $\mathbf{w}', \mathbf{w}'' \in \mathbb{R}_+^m$ and $\mathbf{w}' \leq \mathbf{w}''$. Then

$$C(\mathbf{w}'', q) = \sum_{i=1}^{n} w_i'' z_i^{**} \geq \sum_{i=1}^{n} w_i' z_i^{**}$$

and using (C.23)

$$C(\mathbf{w}', q) = \sum_{i=1}^{m} w_i' z_i^* \leq \sum_{i=1}^{m} w_i' z_i^{**}$$

we find $C(\mathbf{w}', q) \leq C(\mathbf{w}'', q)$.

Increasing in q

For a given vector of input prices $\mathbf{w} \in \mathbb{R}^m_+$ let $\mathbf{z}^*$ be cost minimising for q° and $\mathbf{z}^{**}$ be cost minimising for q' where $q' > q^\circ$. By definition $\mathbf{z}^*$ is on the q°-isoquant and $\mathbf{z}^{**}$ is on the q'-isoquant. Consider a ray from the origin to $\mathbf{z}^{**}$; by the continuity of ϕ this must cut the q°-isoquant; call the point where it does so $\hat{\mathbf{z}}$. By construction it is clear that

$$\sum_{i=1}^{m} w_i \hat{z}_i < \sum_{i=1}^{m} w_i z_i^{**}. \tag{C.24}$$

Furthermore, by definition of the cost function

$$C(\mathbf{w}, q') = \sum_{i=1}^{m} w_i z_i^{**} \tag{C.25}$$

$$C(\mathbf{w}, q^\circ) \leq \sum_{i=1}^{m} w_i \hat{z}_i. \tag{C.26}$$

From (C.24)–(C.26) it is clear that $C(\mathbf{w}, q^\circ) < C(\mathbf{w}, q')$.

Concavity in $\mathbf{w}$

For arbitrary $\mathbf{w}'$ and $\mathbf{w}''$ and for any t such that $0 \leq t \leq 1$ define

$$\mathbf{w} := t\mathbf{w}' + [1-t]\,\mathbf{w}''$$

and let $\mathbf{z}^*$ be cost minimising for $(\mathbf{w}, q)$. By definition of $\mathbf{w}$:

$$C(\mathbf{w}, q) = t\sum_{i=1}^{m} w_i' z_i^* + [1-t]\sum_{i=1}^{m} w_i'' z_i^*.$$

By definition of minimum cost:

$$C(\mathbf{w}', q) \leq \sum_{i=1}^{m} w_i' z_i^*$$

$$C(\mathbf{w}'', q) \leq \sum_{i=1}^{m} w_i'' z_i^*.$$

Therefore

$$tC(\mathbf{w}', q) + [1-t]\,C(\mathbf{w}'', q) \leq C(t\mathbf{w}' + [1-t]\,\mathbf{w}'', q).$$

Continuity in $\mathbf{w}$

Because C is concave in $\mathbf{w}$, continuity follows from Theorem A.11 in Appendix A. ■

C.1.3 Firm's demand and supply functions (Theorem 2.4)

We first show that, under the specified conditions, $\mathbf{z}^*$ is unique, given $\mathbf{w}$ and q. Suppose $\phi(\cdot)$ is strictly concave contoured and let there be two distinct solutions $\mathbf{z}^*, \mathbf{z}^{**}$ to the problem: then we would have

$$\phi\left(\frac{1}{2}[\mathbf{z}^* + \mathbf{z}^{**}]\right) > \phi(\mathbf{z}^*)$$

by definition of the strictly concave-contoured property and

$$q = \phi(\mathbf{z}^*)$$

by definition of $\mathbf{z}^*$ and q. Hence there is some $\hat{\mathbf{z}}$ lying on the q-isoquant ($\phi(\hat{\mathbf{z}}) = q$) where $\hat{\mathbf{z}} := \frac{1}{2}t[\mathbf{z}^* + \mathbf{z}^{**}]$ where $0 < t < 1$. But the outlay on inputs at $\hat{\mathbf{z}}$ would be

$$\sum_{i=1}^{m} \tfrac{1}{2}t[w_i z_i^* + w_i z_i^{**}] = tC(\mathbf{w}, q).$$

If $\mathbf{w} > 0$ then $tC(\mathbf{w}, q) < C(\mathbf{w}, q)$; but this implies that $\hat{\mathbf{z}}$ would have a lower input cost than $\mathbf{z}^*$ or $\mathbf{z}^{**}$: a contradiction.

Now let us write the unique z_i^* as a function $H^i(\mathbf{w}, q)$ for given $\mathbf{w}$ and q; we investigate whether H^i is continuous under the above conditions. Let $(\mathbf{w}^1, \mathbf{w}^2, \mathbf{w}^3, \ldots)$ be a sequence of input-price vectors which converge to $\mathbf{w}$:

$$\lim_{t\to\infty} \mathbf{w}^t = \mathbf{w} > 0 \tag{C.27}$$

and write

$$\bar{z}_i := \lim_{t\to\infty} H^i(\mathbf{w}^t, q); \tag{C.28}$$

we need to prove that $\bar{\mathbf{z}} = \mathbf{z}^*$. The fact that $\mathbf{z}^*$ is cost minimising for $(\mathbf{w}, q)$ implies

$$\sum_{i=1}^{m} w_i \bar{z}_i \geq \sum_{i=1}^{m} w_i z_i^*$$

where one has equality if and only if $\bar{\mathbf{z}} = \mathbf{z}^*$. We will now show that it is impossible to have $\bar{\mathbf{z}} \neq \mathbf{z}^*$. If this were to be true then there would be some a, where $0 < a < 1$, such that

$$\sum_{i=1}^{m} w_i \bar{z}_i = \frac{1}{a} \sum_{i=1}^{m} w_i z_i^* \tag{C.29}$$

Consider any member of the above sequence of input prices. By cost minimisation we have

$$\sum_{i=1}^{m} w_i^t H^i(\mathbf{w}^t, q) \leq \sum_{i=1}^{m} w_i^t z_i^*. \tag{C.30}$$

Subtracting (C.30) from (C.29) we have

$$\sum_{i=1}^{m} \left[w_i \bar{z}_i - w_i^t H^i\left(\mathbf{w}^t, q\right) \right] \geq \sum_{i=1}^{m} \left[\frac{w_i}{a} - w_i^t \right] z_i^*. \tag{C.31}$$

Now consider what happens to (C.31) in the limit. From (C.27) and (C.28) we get

$$0 \geq \left[\frac{1}{a} - 1 \right] \sum_{i=1}^{m} w_i z_i^*. \tag{C.32}$$

Given $a < 1$ this implies

$$\sum_{i=1}^{m} w_i z_i^* \leq 0. \tag{C.33}$$

an impossibility in view of the requirement that $\mathbf{w} > 0$. Therefore $\bar{\mathbf{z}} = \mathbf{z}^*$. ■

C.1.4 Firm's demand and supply functions (continued)

It is instructive to look at the proof in a slightly different version of Theorem 2.4 which brings out more clearly the way in which the solution function is derived from the FOC (2.13).

Theorem C.2

(a) If there is some transform of the production function which has the Hessian property, then the conditional input demand functions are always well defined and continuous.

(b) If the production function has the Hessian property, then input demand functions are always well defined and continuous.

Consider the proof of part (b) first since it is slightly more straightforward. Write the firm's maximisation problem as

$$\max p\phi(\mathbf{z}) - \sum_{i=1}^{m} w_i z_i$$

where we have substituted in $q = \phi(\mathbf{z})$ from the conditions for technical efficiency (2.15). Assuming that attention is restricted to inputs that are actually purchased, the first-order conditions give us:

$$\begin{aligned}\phi_1(\mathbf{z}) &= \frac{w_1}{p}\\ &\dots\\ \phi_m(\mathbf{z}) &= \frac{w_m}{p}\end{aligned} \tag{C.34}$$

a system of m equations in m unknowns $\mathbf{z}$. From the implicit function theorem (Theorem A.5) we may solve for the unknowns in terms of the parameters $w_1/p, \dots, w_m/p$ if the matrix

$$\mathbf{M} = \begin{bmatrix} \frac{\partial\phi_1}{\partial z_1} & \frac{\partial\phi_1}{\partial z_2} & ,\dots, & \frac{\partial\phi_1}{\partial z_m}\\ \frac{\partial\phi_2}{\partial z_1} & \frac{\partial\phi_2}{\partial z_2} & ,\dots, & \frac{\partial\phi_2}{\partial z_m}\\ \dots & \dots & \dots & \dots\\ \frac{\partial\phi_m}{\partial z_1} & \frac{\partial\phi_m}{\partial z_2} & ,\dots, & \frac{\partial\phi_m}{\partial z_m}\end{bmatrix} \tag{C.35}$$

is non-singular. But ϕ_i of course is simply $\partial\phi(\mathbf{z})/\partial z_i$ and so the (i,j)-th element of the matrix $\mathbf{M}$ is just ϕ_{ij}. $\mathbf{M}$ is the Hessian matrix of second partial derivatives (see page 505). But if we assume the Hessian condition to hold, $\mathbf{M}$ is negative definite and so is non-singular. Hence there exist continuous functions $\psi^1, \dots, \psi^m$ such that we may write

$$z_i = \psi^i\left(\frac{w_1}{p}, \dots, \frac{w_m}{p}\right) \tag{C.36}$$

as a solution to (C.34). A change in notation gives (2.34).

The method of proof of (a) is similar to the above. Minimising $\sum_{i=1}^{m} w_i z_i$ subject to $\varphi(\mathbf{z}) \geq q$ is clearly equivalent to minimising $\sum_{i=1}^{m} w_i z_i$ subject to $\hat{\phi}(\mathbf{z}) \geq \hat{q}$ where $\hat{\phi}(\mathbf{z}) := \varphi(\phi(\mathbf{z}))$, $\hat{q} := \varphi(q)$, and φ is an increasing function. In view of the premiss of the theorem we may select ψ such that $\hat{\phi}(\mathbf{z})$ has the Hessian property. The FOCs for this modified problem yield:

$$\begin{aligned}\lambda_0\hat{\phi}_i(\mathbf{z}) &= w_i, \quad i = 1, \dots, m\\ \hat{\phi}(\mathbf{z}) &= \hat{q}\end{aligned} \tag{C.37}$$

where λ_0 is the Lagrange multiplier, cf. equations (2.13) and (2.15). This is a system of $m+1$ equations in $m+1$ unknowns $z_1, \dots, z_m, \lambda_0$. Consider the matrix:

$$\hat{\mathbf{M}} := \begin{bmatrix} \lambda_0\hat{\phi}_{11} & \dots & \lambda_0\hat{\phi}_m & \hat{\phi}_1\\ \lambda_0\hat{\phi}_{m1} & \dots & \lambda_0\hat{\phi}_{mm} & \hat{\phi}_m\\ \hat{\phi}_1 & \dots & \hat{\phi}_m & 0\end{bmatrix}. \tag{C.38}$$

$\hat{\mathrm{M}}$ is non-singular because $\hat{\phi}$ has the Hessian property so that the $m \times m$ is non-singular, and $\hat{\phi}_i$ are not all zero. Hence by the implicit function theorem there exist continuous solutions of the form (2.32). ■

C.1.5 Properties of profit function (Theorem 2.7)

For the properties of non-decreasingness, continuity, homogeneity of degree one, and concave in $\mathbf{p}$ see the proof of Theorem 2.2. To show (2.71) consider an arbitrary small variation in prices $d\mathbf{p}$ such that $dp_i > 0$ and $dp_j = 0, j \neq i$. Let $Q^*(\mathbf{p})$ be the set of profit-maximising net output vectors for input prices $\mathbf{p}$ and let $\mathbf{q}^* \in Q^*(\mathbf{p})$ and $\mathbf{q}^* + d\mathbf{q} \in Q\left(\mathbf{p} + d\mathbf{p}\right)$. By definition of profit maximisation

$$\begin{aligned}\Pi\left(\mathbf{p} + d\mathbf{p}\right) &\leq \sum_{j=1}^{n}\left[p_j + dp_j\right] q_j^* \\ &= \Pi\left(\mathbf{p}\right) + dp_i q_i^*\end{aligned} \tag{C.39}$$

and

$$\begin{aligned}\Pi\left(\mathbf{p}\right) &\leq \sum_{j=1}^{n} p_j\left[q_j^* + dq_j^*\right] \\ &= \sum_{j=1}^{n}\left[p_j + dp_j\right]\left[q_j^* + dq_j^*\right] - \sum_{j=1}^{n} dp_j\left[q_j^* + dq_j^*\right] \\ &= \Pi\left(\mathbf{p} + d\mathbf{p}\right) - dp_i\left[q_i^* + dq_i^*\right].\end{aligned} \tag{C.40}$$

Conditions (C.39) and (C.40) imply respectively:

$$\frac{\Pi\left(\mathbf{p} + d\mathbf{p}\right) - \Pi\left(\mathbf{p}\right)}{dp_i} \leq q_i^* \tag{C.41}$$

$$\frac{\Pi\left(\mathbf{p} + d\mathbf{p}\right) - \Pi\left(\mathbf{p}\right)}{dp_i} \geq q_i^* + dq_i^*. \tag{C.42}$$

Clearly as $dp_i \to 0$ the left-hand side of (C.41) and (C.42) becomes $\Pi_i\left(\mathbf{p}\right)$ and the right-hand side is q_i^*. ■

C.2 The consumer

C.2.1 The representation theorem (Theorem 4.1)

We establish here a modified form of the theorem that also requires the greed assumption.

For any $\mathbf{x} \in X$ we construct the sets illustrated in Figure 4.5. Let $\mathbf{1}$ denote the n-vector $(1, 1, \ldots, 1)$. By virtue of the greed assumption there is some real number m sufficiently large such that the vector $m\mathbf{1} \succ \mathbf{x}$—this is the vector $\mathbf{x}^M$ (check the notation defined on page 74). Likewise there must be a non-negative real number ℓ such that the vector $\ell\mathbf{1} \prec \mathbf{x}$—this is vector $\mathbf{x}^L$. By continuity there is some real number $U(\mathbf{x})$ such that

$$\ell < U(\mathbf{x}) < m$$

and

$$U(\mathbf{x})\mathbf{1} \sim \mathbf{x}. \tag{C.43}$$

Now consider some other $\mathbf{x}' \in X$ where

$$U(\mathbf{x}')\mathbf{1} \sim \mathbf{x}' \tag{C.44}$$

If $U(\mathbf{x}') > U(\mathbf{x})$ then $U(\mathbf{x}')\mathbf{1} > U(\mathbf{x})\mathbf{1}$ and, by Axiom 4.6 it is clear that $U(\mathbf{x}')\mathbf{1} \succ U(\mathbf{x})\mathbf{1}$ so that $\mathbf{x}' \succ \mathbf{x}$. So we have

$$U(\mathbf{x}') > U(\mathbf{x}) \text{ if and only if } \mathbf{x}' \succ \mathbf{x}$$

$$U(\mathbf{x}') = U(\mathbf{x}) \text{ if and only if } \mathbf{x}' \sim \mathbf{x}. \blacksquare$$

For a demonstration of the general result see Debreu (1954).

C.2.2 Existence of ordinary demand functions (Theorem 4.5)

Noting that in the case of the firm strict convexity of input requirement sets means that the production function is strictly concave contoured it is immediate that the proof of Theorem 4.5 follows from Theorem 2.4. ■

C.2.3 Quasiconvexity of the indirect utility function

We use Definition A.26 and the fact that the cost function is concave in prices. Consider any $\mathbf{p}$ and $\mathbf{p}'$ such that

$$\upsilon = V(\mathbf{p}, y) = V(\mathbf{p}', y) \tag{C.45}$$

and, for any $a \in [0, 1]$, let

$$\overline{\mathbf{p}} := a\mathbf{p} + [1 - a]\mathbf{p}' \tag{C.46}$$

$$\overline{y} := C(\overline{\mathbf{p}}, \upsilon). \tag{C.47}$$

Because C is concave in $\mathbf{p}$ we have

$$C(\overline{\mathbf{p}}, \upsilon) \geq aC(\mathbf{p}, \upsilon) + [1 - a]C(\mathbf{p}', \upsilon). \tag{C.48}$$

In view of (C.45) the right-hand side of (C.48) is just y. Hence $\overline{y} \geq y$, and so, because V is increasing in income:

$$V(\overline{\mathbf{p}}, \overline{y}) \geq V(\overline{\mathbf{p}}, y). \tag{C.49}$$

In view of (C.47) the left-hand side of (C.49) is just υ; so (C.45) and (C.49) imply

$$aV(\mathbf{p}, y) + [1 - a]V(\mathbf{p}', y) \geq V(\overline{\mathbf{p}}, y). \qquad \blacksquare$$

C.3 The consumer and the market

C.3.1 Composite commodity (Theorem 5.1):

Using the definitions

$$\bar{p} := p_2 + p_3 \tag{C.50}$$

$$a := \frac{p_2}{\bar{p}}$$

rewrite the cost function as:

$$\bar{C}\left(p_1, \bar{p}, \upsilon\right) := C\left(p_1, a\bar{p}, [1 - a]\bar{p}, \upsilon\right). \tag{C.51}$$

From (C.50) and (C.51), given that both C and $\bar{p}$ are concave, homogeneous of degree 1, and non-decreasing in prices, $\bar{C}$ is also concave, homogeneous of degree 1, and non-decreasing in prices. Given that C is increasing in utility, so too is $\bar{C}$. Also, differentiating (C.51) with respect to p_1 and $\bar{p}$ respectively gives:

$$\bar{C}_1(p_1,\bar{p},\upsilon) = C_1(p_1,a\bar{p},[1-a]\bar{p},\upsilon) = x_1^*$$
$$\bar{C}_p(p_1,\bar{p},\upsilon) = aC_2(p_1,a\bar{p},[1-a]\bar{p},\upsilon) + [1-a]C_3(p_1,a\bar{p},[1-a]\bar{p},\upsilon)$$
$$= ax_2^* + [1-a]x_3^* = \bar{x}.$$

So $\bar{C}$ is actually the cost function that would be derived from maximising $\overline{U}(x_1,\bar{x})$. ■

C.3.2 The representative consumer (Theorem 5.2)

Consider the effect on demand of a small redistribution of income from person 1 to person 2: $dy^1 = -dy^2 > 0$, $dy^h = 0, h = 3,\ldots,n_h$. Clearly, $\bar{y}$ remains unchanged. So, differentiating equation (5.27), we get:

$$\frac{\partial D^{1i}(\mathbf{p},y^1)}{\partial y^1} = -\frac{\partial D^{2i}(\mathbf{p},y^2)}{\partial y^1}. \tag{C.52}$$

But households 1 and 2 were chosen arbitrarily and y^1 and y^2 could be arbitrary values. So (C.52) means that the income effect is independent of the household h and of income. This implies

$$\frac{\partial D^{hi}(\mathbf{p},y)}{\partial y} = b_i(\mathbf{p}) \tag{C.53}$$

where b_i is some function of prices. So, if (5.27) is to hold, the income effect for each household h, must be independent of y^h. Integrate (C.53) over y to get

$$D^{hi}(\mathbf{p},y) = a_i^h(\mathbf{p}) + b_i(\mathbf{p})y \tag{C.54}$$

where a_i^h is a function of prices that may be specific to each household: (C.54) implies that all households' demands must be linear in income and have the same slope with respect to income. ■

C.4 A simple economy

C.4.1 Decentralisation (Theorem 6.2)

The core of this proof is the demonstration of the existence of a supporting hyperplane. A hyperplane is defined in (A.25); separating and supporting hyperplanes are defined in section A.6.3. Given the assumptions about the attainable set and the utility function it is clear that a maximum to the problem (6.16) exists: let $(\mathbf{q}^*,\mathbf{x}^*)$ denote the values of $(\mathbf{q},\mathbf{x})$ that achieve this maximum. Define the attainable set $A(\mathbf{R};\Phi)$ as in (6.19) and the 'better-than-$\mathbf{x}^*$' set $B(\mathbf{x}^*)$ as in (6.20): it is clear that both $A(\mathbf{R};\Phi)$ and $B(\mathbf{x}^*)$ are closed in X and convex. By definition, the point $\mathbf{x}^*$ belongs to both sets. It is also clear that no point in $\mathbf{x}^\circ \in A(\mathbf{R};\Phi)$ also lies in the interior of $B(\mathbf{x}^*)$; if it did then, by the greed axiom we would have $U(\mathbf{x}^\circ) > U(\mathbf{x}^*)$; this would mean that $\mathbf{x}^\circ$ would be both attainable and strictly preferred to $\mathbf{x}^*$, a contradiction of the definition of $\mathbf{x}^*$.

So $A(\mathbf{R};\Phi)$ and $B(\mathbf{x}^*)$ can have only boundary points in common (these can only be points, like $\mathbf{x}^*$, that solve the problem 6.16). Then, using Theorem A.9 (with modified notation) there is $\boldsymbol{p} \in \mathbb{R}^n$, $\boldsymbol{p} \neq \mathbf{0}$ and a real number y such that

$$\text{For all } \mathbf{x} \in A(\mathbf{R};\Phi): \sum_{i=1}^{n} p_i x_i \leq y \tag{C.55}$$

and

$$\text{For all } \mathbf{x} \in B(\mathbf{x}^*): \sum_{i=1}^{n} p_i x_i \geq y. \tag{C.56}$$

Define

$$\begin{aligned} y &:= \sum_{i=1}^{n} \rho_i x_i^* \\ &= \sum_{i=1}^{n} \rho_i \left[q_i^* + R_i \right]. \end{aligned}$$

Then it is clear from (C.56) that $\mathbf{x}^*$ solves the problem (6.18) given the shadow prices ρ in (C.56). But it is also true that $\mathbf{q}^* = \mathbf{x}^* - \mathbf{R}$ solves the problem (6.17) given the shadow prices ρ in (C.55). ■

C.5 General equilibrium

C.5.1 Competitive equilibrium and the core (Theorem 7.1)

If there is an allocation $\hat{\mathbf{a}}$ that blocks $\mathbf{a}^*$ then it must be possible to find a coalition K such that its members can achieve $\hat{\mathbf{a}}$ from their own resources. This requires:

$$\forall i : \sum_{h \in K} \hat{x}_i^h \leq \sum_{h \in K} R_i^h \tag{C.57}$$

which implies

$$\sum_{h \in K} \sum_{i=1}^{n} p_i \hat{x}_i^h \leq \sum_{h \in K} \sum_{i=1}^{n} p_i R_i^h. \tag{C.58}$$

However, if $\mathbf{a}^*$ is a competitive equilibrium allocation with associated prices $\mathbf{p}^*$, everyone maximises utility at $\mathbf{a}^*$ given $\mathbf{p}^*$. So if $U^h(\hat{\mathbf{x}}^h) \geq U^h(\mathbf{x}^{*h})$ it must be the case that $\hat{\mathbf{x}}^h$ is at least as expensive as $\mathbf{x}^{*h}$ (which of course costs $\sum_{i=1}^{n} p_i R_i^h$); if $U^h(\hat{\mathbf{x}}^h) > U^h(\mathbf{x}^{*h})$ then $\hat{\mathbf{x}}^h$ must be strictly more expensive than $\mathbf{x}^{*h}$. So if $\mathbf{a}^*$ were a competitive allocation and $\hat{\mathbf{a}}$ were to block $\mathbf{a}^*$ then we would find:

$$\sum_{h \in K} \sum_{i=1}^{n} p_i \hat{x}_i^h > \sum_{h \in K} \sum_{i=1}^{n} p_i R_i^h \tag{C.59}$$

which is a direct contradiction of (C.58). ■

C.5.2 Existence of competitive equilibrium (Theorem 7.4)

The proof relies on the setting up of a continuous function Γ from the set of normalised prices J (which is convex and compact) into J itself. This function can be thought of as a notional 'price adjustment' for any given price vector selected from J, and is constructed so that no such 'adjustment' takes place if the vector selected happens to be an equilibrium price vector. Choose an arbitrary positive number Δ, and define δ_i, $i = 1, \ldots, m$ thus

$$\delta_i := \begin{cases} \min\{E_i, \Delta\} \text{ if } E_i \geq 0 \\ \max\{E_i, -p_i\} \text{ if } E_i < 0. \end{cases} \tag{C.60}$$

Now consider a set of functions $\Gamma_i(\cdot)$ defined by

$$\Gamma_i(\mathbf{p}) := \frac{p_i + \delta_i}{1 + \sum_{j=1}^{n} \delta_j}. \tag{C.61}$$

The mapping $\mathbf{\Gamma} := (\Gamma_1, \ldots, \Gamma_n)$ generates a vector of 'adjusted' prices $\hat{\mathbf{p}}$ where $\hat{p}_i = \Gamma_i(\mathbf{p})$. We require E_i to be continuous and bounded below to ensure that $\Gamma_i(\cdot)$ is continuous; if E were not bounded below the situation depicted in Figure 7.11 could arise. It is clear that (C.61) ensures that

$\hat{p}_i \geq 0$ and $\sum_{j=1}^{n} \hat{p}_j = 1$: so $\hat{\mathbf{p}} \in J$. So, by construction, Γ is a continuous function from the convex set J into itself.

From Brouwer's theorem (Theorem A.3) there must exist a fixed point of the mapping $\mathbf{\Gamma}$, in other words some $\mathbf{p}^* \in J$ such that

$$\mathbf{p}^* = \Gamma(\mathbf{p}^*). \tag{C.62}$$

The vector $\mathbf{p}^*$ must satisfy the conditions given in (7.17) for equilibrium price vector; see page 158. For, suppose that for some $i : E_i(\mathbf{p}^*) > 0$, then (from C.60) $\delta_i > 0$. If $p_i^* > 0$ then Walras's Law (7.18) implies that there is some j for which $p_j E_j(\mathbf{p}) < 0$ so that (from C.60) $\delta_j > 0$; otherwise we must have $\delta_j = 0$ for some j. In either case we clearly would not have $\mathbf{p}^* = \Gamma(\mathbf{p}^*)$ thus violating the definition of $\mathbf{p}^*$ in (C.62). Again, suppose $E_i(\mathbf{p}^*) < 0$ and $p_i^* > 0$. Then (C.60) implies $\delta_i < 0$, and Walras's law implies that for some j we have $E_j(\mathbf{p}^*) > 0$, so that $\delta_j > 0$. So again, we would find $\mathbf{p}^* \neq \Gamma(\mathbf{p}^*)$, in violation of (C.62). Hence $\mathbf{p}^*$ is indeed the required equilibrium price vector. ■

C.5.3 Uniqueness of competitive equilibrium (Theorem 7.5)

If $\mathbf{p}^*$ is an equilibrium price vector then, from (7.17), $E_i(\mathbf{p}^*) \leq 0$ for all i. Also, from Walras's Law, equation (7.18) holds for any price vector $\mathbf{p}$. Combining these two facts

$$\sum_{i=1}^{n} p_i E_i(\mathbf{p}^*) \leq \sum_{i=1}^{n} p_i E_i(\mathbf{p}) \tag{C.63}$$

where the right-hand side of (C.63) is zero. If all firms maximise profits at any price $\mathbf{p}$ then this implies

$$\sum_{i=1}^{n} p_i y_i(\mathbf{p}) \geq \sum_{i=1}^{n} p_i y_i(\mathbf{p}^*). \tag{C.64}$$

Equations (C.63), (C.64), and the materials balance condition (7.6) imply that, for any price $\mathbf{p}$:

$$\sum_{i=1}^{n} p_i x_i(\mathbf{p}) \geq \sum_{i=1}^{n} p_i x_i(\mathbf{p}^*). \tag{C.65}$$

In particular, if $\mathbf{p}^{**}$ is another distinct equilibrium price vector, then

$$\sum_{i=1}^{n} p_i^{**} x_i(\mathbf{p}^{**}) \geq \sum_{i=1}^{n} p_i^{**} x_i(\mathbf{p}^*). \tag{C.66}$$

If WARP holds with reference to the equilibrium $\mathbf{p}^*$ then (C.66) implies

$$\sum_{i=1}^{n} p_i^* x_i(\mathbf{p}^{**}) > \sum_{i=1}^{n} p_i^* x_i(\mathbf{p}^*). \tag{C.67}$$

Together (C.66) and (C.67) imply

$$\sum_{i=1}^{n} [p_i^{**} + p_i^*] x_i(\mathbf{p}^{**}) > \sum_{i=1}^{n} [p_i^* + p_i^{**}] x_i(\mathbf{p}^*). \tag{C.68}$$

But if $\mathbf{p}^{**}$ is an equilibrium price vector and WARP holds then, by the same reasoning,

$$\sum_{i=1}^{n} [p_i^* + p_i^{**}] x_i(\mathbf{p}^*) > \sum_{i=1}^{n} [p_i^{**} + p_i^*] x_i(\mathbf{p}^{**}) \tag{C.69}$$

—a contradiction. ■

C.5.4 Valuation in general equilibrium (Theorem 7.6)

Follows immediately from the proof of Theorem 6.2 above. ■

C.6 Uncertainty and risk

C.6.1 Expected utility (Theorem 8.1)

Let there be a finite number of states of the world, $\Omega := \{1, 2, \ldots, \varpi\}$ If U is differentiable then Axiom 8.2 implies that for any commodity i the MRTS of consumption in state of the world ω for consumption in state of the world ω' is independent of consumption in any other state of the world ω', for example, where $\omega \neq \omega' \neq \varpi$. From Theorem C.1 this means that

$$U(\mathbf{x}_1, \mathbf{x}_2, \ldots \mathbf{x}_\varpi) = \Psi(\psi(\mathbf{x}_1, \mathbf{x}_2, \ldots, \mathbf{x}_{\varpi-1}), \mathbf{x}_\varpi) \tag{C.70}$$

Given that Ψ is a continuous monotonic function and that a utility function is defined up to an arbitrary monotonic transformation we can rewrite the right-hand side of (C.70) as

$$\psi(\mathbf{x}_1, \mathbf{x}_2, \ldots, \mathbf{x}_{\varpi-1}) + u(\mathbf{x}_\varpi). \tag{C.71}$$

Repeated application of this argument implies that U can be written in the additively separable form

$$\sum_{\omega=1}^{\varpi} v(\mathbf{x}_\omega; \omega) \tag{C.72}$$

where the function $v(\cdot; \omega)$ may be different in each state of the world ω.

Now consider the implications of Axiom 8.3. For simplicity we can take the case where there are just two states of the world, $\omega = 1, 2$. Take an arbitrary consumption vector $\mathbf{x}$ and consider a small variation $d\mathbf{x}$ that would leave the individual's utility unchanged under perfect certainty. Given the form (C.72) and the differentiability assumption this implies

$$\sum_{i=1}^{n} v_i(\mathbf{x}; 1)\, dx_i + \sum_{i=1}^{n} v_i(\mathbf{x}; 2)\, dx_i = 0. \tag{C.73}$$

Suppose the individual is indifferent between (i) $\mathbf{x} + d\mathbf{x}$ if $\omega = 1$ occurs, $\mathbf{x}$ if $\omega = 2$ occurs, and (ii) $\mathbf{x}$ if $\omega = 1$ occurs, $\mathbf{x} + d\mathbf{x}$ if $\omega = 2$ occurs. Then

$$v(\mathbf{x} + \mathbf{dx}; 1) + v(\mathbf{x}; 2) = v(\mathbf{x}; 1) + v(\mathbf{x} + \mathbf{dx}; 2)$$

which may be written

$$\sum_{i=1}^{n} v_i(\mathbf{x}; 1)\, dx_i = \sum_{i=1}^{n} v_i(\mathbf{x}; 2)\, dx_i. \tag{C.74}$$

Together (C.73) and (C.74) imply

$$\sum_{i=1}^{n} v_i(\mathbf{x}; 1)\, dx_i = 0$$

$$\sum_{i=1}^{n} v_i(\mathbf{x}; 2)\, dx_i = 0$$

which means that for arbitrary i, j:

$$\frac{v_i(\mathbf{x}, 1)}{v_j(\mathbf{x}, 1)} = \frac{v_i(\mathbf{x}, 2)}{v_j(\mathbf{x}, 2)}$$

$$\frac{v_i(\mathbf{x}, 1)}{v_i(\mathbf{x}, 2)} = \frac{v_j(\mathbf{x}, 1)}{v_j(\mathbf{x}, 2)} = k_{12} \tag{C.75}$$

where k_{12} is a constant, independent of i and j. However, if this holds for some $\mathbf{x}$ and $\mathbf{x}+\mathbf{dx}$ Axiom 8.3 requires it to hold for all such $\mathbf{x}$ and $\mathbf{x}+\mathbf{dx}$ and (C.75) can only be satisfied for arbitrary $\mathbf{x}$ if

$$v_i(\mathbf{x},\omega) = \pi_\omega u_i(\mathbf{x})$$

where π_ω is a constant, dependent on ω, u is a differentiable function $X \to \mathbb{R}$ and u_i denotes the partial derivative with respect to its ith component. Therefore

$$v(\mathbf{x},\omega) = \pi_\omega u(\mathbf{x}) + a_\omega$$

so that U can be written in the form

$$\sum_{\omega=1}^{\varpi} \left[\pi_\omega u(\mathbf{x}_\omega) + a_\omega\right]. \tag{C.76}$$

Finally Axiom 8.1 requires that utility be independent of the labelling of the states so that a_ω is constant, independent of ω.

C.6.2 Lottery preference representation (Theorem 8.4)

The result is established in Lemmas C.2 to C.6.

Lemma C.2 (Compound lotteries)

For any lottery $\boldsymbol{\pi}$ and any positive number k, if $\boldsymbol{\pi} \succcurlyeq \boldsymbol{\pi}_i$ for all $i = 1,\ldots,k$ then, for any $\lambda_i \geq 0$, $i = 1,\ldots,k$ such that $\sum_{i=1}^{k} \lambda_i = 1$

$$\boldsymbol{\pi} \succcurlyeq \sum_{i=1}^{k} \lambda_i \boldsymbol{\pi}_i \tag{C.77}$$

Proof

Suppose (C.77) is true for some value k. Introduce an additional lottery $\boldsymbol{\pi}_{k+1}$ such that

$$\boldsymbol{\pi} \succcurlyeq \boldsymbol{\pi}_{k+1} \tag{C.78}$$

and a number $\lambda_{k+1} \geq 0$ and define

$$\mu_i := \frac{\lambda_i}{1+\lambda_{k+1}}.$$

We then have

$$\sum_{i=1}^{k+1} \mu_i \boldsymbol{\pi}_i = \frac{1}{1+\lambda_{k+1}} \sum_{i=1}^{k} \lambda_i \boldsymbol{\pi}_i + \frac{\lambda_{k+1}}{1+\lambda_{k+1}} \boldsymbol{\pi}_{k+1}. \tag{C.79}$$

Using Axiom 8.5, (C.77) and (C.79) imply

$$\frac{1}{1+\lambda_{k+1}} \boldsymbol{\pi} + \frac{\lambda_{k+1}}{1+\lambda_{k+1}} \boldsymbol{\pi}_{k+1} \succcurlyeq \frac{1}{1+\lambda_{k+1}} \sum_{i=1}^{k} \lambda_i \boldsymbol{\pi}_i + \frac{\lambda_{k+1}}{1+\lambda_{k+1}} \boldsymbol{\pi}_{k+1}.$$

Using Axiom 8.5 again, (C.78) implies

$$\frac{1}{1+\lambda_{k+1}} \boldsymbol{\pi} + \frac{\lambda_{k+1}}{1+\lambda_{k+1}} \boldsymbol{\pi} \succcurlyeq \frac{1}{1+\lambda_{k+1}} \boldsymbol{\pi} + \frac{\lambda_{k+1}}{1+\lambda_{k+1}} \boldsymbol{\pi}_{k+1}.$$

Combining these two we have

$$\boldsymbol{\pi} \succcurlyeq \sum_{i=1}^{k+1} \mu_i \boldsymbol{\pi}_i.$$

Therefore if (C.77) holds for $k > 0$ lotteries it holds for $k + 1$ lotteries; given that it is trivially true for $k = 1$ the result is proved. ■

Lemma C.3

There are well-defined best and worst lotteries $\overline{\pi}$ and $\underline{\pi}$ respectively.

Proof

Given that ϖ is finite there must be one (or more) best payoff from the set of payoffs $(x_1, x_2, \ldots, x_\varpi)$. So let $\overline{\pi}$ be the primitive lottery that yields this payoff with probability 1 and let $\pi_{[\omega]}$ be the lottery that assigns probability 1 to payoff ω. By construction

$$\overline{\pi} \succcurlyeq \pi_{[\omega]}$$

and so, by Lemma C.2

$$\overline{\pi} \succcurlyeq \sum_{\omega=1}^{\varpi} \lambda_\omega \pi_{[\omega]}. \tag{C.80}$$

Note that any lottery π can be written in the form on the right-hand side of (C.80) with suitable choice of weights λ_ω: this establishes the existence of $\overline{\pi}$. The existence $\underline{\pi}$ is established in the same way. ■

Lemma C.4

Given $\lambda, \lambda' \in [0, 1]$, $\lambda' > \lambda$ if and only if

$$\hat{\pi}(\lambda') \succ \hat{\pi}(\lambda) \tag{C.81}$$

where $\hat{\pi}(\lambda)$ is the compound lottery that is a weighted average of the best and worst lotteries:

$$\hat{\pi}(\lambda) := \lambda\overline{\pi} + [1 - \lambda]\underline{\pi}. \tag{C.82}$$

Proof

First note that if $\pi \succ \pi'$ and $\lambda \in (0, 1)$, then Axiom 8.5 implies

$$\pi = \lambda\pi + [1 - \lambda]\pi \succ \lambda\pi + [1 - \lambda]\pi' \succ \lambda\pi' + [1 - \lambda]\pi' = \pi'$$

so that we have

$$\pi \succ \lambda\pi + [1 - \lambda]\pi' \succ \pi'. \tag{C.83}$$

Now suppose $\lambda < \lambda'$. We may write

$$\hat{\pi}(\lambda') = \mu\overline{\pi} + [1 - \mu]\hat{\pi}(\lambda) \tag{C.84}$$

where

$$\mu := \frac{\lambda' - \lambda}{1 - \lambda'}.$$

By (C.83)

$$\overline{\pi} \succ \hat{\pi}(\lambda). \tag{C.85}$$

Expressions (C.84) and (C.85) together imply (C.81).

Now suppose that (C.81) is true, then it must be the case that $\lambda' > \lambda$—otherwise, by the argument leading to (C.81) we would have a contradiction. ■

Lemma C.5

For any lottery π there is a unique $\lambda_\pi \in [0, 1]$ such that

$$\hat{\pi}(\lambda_\pi) \sim \pi. \tag{C.86}$$

Proof

For any π define the following unique values:

$$\lambda_{\text{inf}} := \inf \{\lambda : \hat{\pi}(\lambda) \succ \pi\} \tag{C.87}$$

$$\lambda_{\text{sup}} := \sup \{\lambda : \pi \succ \hat{\pi}(\lambda)\}. \tag{C.88}$$

Note that, by Axiom 8.6, the sets in (C.87) and (C.88) are not empty. Clearly

$$\pi \succcurlyeq \hat{\pi}(\lambda_{\text{inf}}) \tag{C.89}$$

for otherwise $\pi(\lambda_{\text{inf}}) \succ \pi$ and by Axiom 8.6 there exists $\lambda \in (0, 1)$ such that

$$\lambda\hat{\pi}(\lambda_{\text{inf}}) + [1 - \lambda]\underline{\pi} \succ \pi$$

which implies

$$\lambda'\overline{\pi} + [1 - \lambda']\underline{\pi} \succ \pi$$

where $\lambda' := \lambda_{\text{inf}}\lambda < \lambda_{\text{inf}}$, a contradiction of the definition of λ_{inf}. Likewise

$$\hat{\pi}(\lambda_{\text{sup}}) \succcurlyeq \pi. \tag{C.90}$$

Together (C.89) and (C.90) rule out $\lambda_{\text{sup}} < \lambda_{\text{inf}}$. We cannot have $\lambda_{\text{inf}} < \lambda_{\text{sup}}$ because this would imply that there is some λ' such that $\lambda_{\text{inf}} < \lambda' < \lambda_{\text{sup}}$ so that $\hat{\pi}(\lambda') \succ \pi$ and $\pi \succ \hat{\pi}(\lambda')$, a contradiction. We therefore have $\lambda_{\text{inf}} = \lambda_{\text{sup}} =: \lambda_\pi$, let us say. Given that both (C.89) and (C.90) hold we must have (C.86). ■

Lemma C.6

Let v be a utility function representing $\succcurlyeq$. Then

1. $v(\pi) = \varphi(\lambda_\pi)$ where λ_π is defined in Lemma C.5 and φ is a monotonic increasing function.
2. v is linear in π.

Proof

Take two arbitrary lotteries π and π'.

From Lemma C.5 $\pi \succcurlyeq \pi'$ if and only if $\hat{\pi}(\lambda_\pi) \succcurlyeq \hat{\pi}(\lambda_{\pi'})$ and so, using Lemma C.4 $\pi \succcurlyeq \pi'$ if and only if $\lambda_\pi \geq \lambda_{\pi'}$. From Lemma C.5 we have

$$\pi \sim \hat{\pi}(\lambda_\pi). \tag{C.91}$$

Using Axiom 8.5 (C.91) implies:

$$\mu\pi + [1 - \mu]\pi' \sim \mu\hat{\pi}(\lambda_\pi) + [1 - \mu]\pi'. \tag{C.92}$$

We also have

$$\pi' \sim \hat{\pi}(\lambda_{\pi'}). \tag{C.93}$$

Using Axiom 8.5 (C.93) implies:

$$\mu\hat{\pi}(\lambda_\pi) + [1 - \mu]\pi' \sim \mu\hat{\pi}(\lambda_\pi) + [1 - \mu]\hat{\pi}(\lambda_{\pi'}). \tag{C.94}$$

But, using the definition in (C.82) we have

$$\mu\hat{\pi}(\lambda_\pi) + [1 - \mu]\hat{\pi}(\lambda_{\pi'}) = \hat{\pi}(\mu\lambda_\pi + [1 - \mu]\lambda_{\pi'}). \tag{C.95}$$

So, using (C.92), (C.94), and (C.95) it is clear that

$$\mu v(\pi) + [1 - \mu]v(\pi') = v(\mu\pi + [1 - \mu]\pi'). \blacksquare \tag{C.96}$$

Note that Lemma C.6 implies that the utility of the lottery must be expressible in the form

$$\sum_{\omega=1}^{\varpi} \pi_\omega u_\omega$$

where u_ω are positive weights. Assigning $u_\omega = u(\mathbf{x}_\omega)$—where clearly $u(\cdot)$ is defined up to an affine transformation.—completes the proof.

C.6.3 Risk taking and wealth (Theorem 8.7)

From the FOC of the portfolio problem (8.18) we know that at an interior solution β^* we must have $\frac{\partial \beta^*}{\partial \bar{y}}$ given by (8.22). Given decreasing absolute risk aversion we have

$$ra(\bar{y} + \beta r) \leq ra(\bar{y}) \tag{C.97}$$

for r positive, negative or zero, with strict inequality if r is non-zero. Using Definition 8.1 (C.97) becomes

$$-ru_{yy}(\bar{y} + \beta r) \leq a(\bar{y})\, ru_y(\bar{y} + \beta r)\,. \tag{C.98}$$

Taking expectations of both sides (C.98) yields

$$-\mathcal{E}\left(ru_{yy}(\bar{y} + \beta r)\right) \leq a(\bar{y})\,\mathcal{E}\left(ru_y(\bar{y} + \beta r)\right). \tag{C.99}$$

The case '=' in (C.99) is very special: it only applies if there is a degenerate distribution where r is always zero; but this is ruled out if the risky asset is distinct from the safe asset. Hence we only need consider case '<' in (C.99). By the FOC for an interior maximum (8.19) the right-hand side of (C.99) is 0. Hence we have

$$-\mathcal{E}\left(ru_{yy}(\bar{y} + \beta r)\right) < 0. \tag{C.100}$$

This is the numerator of (8.22); we already know that the denominator of (8.22) is negative, so $\frac{\partial \beta^*}{\partial \bar{y}} > 0$. ■

C.7 Welfare

C.7.1 Arrow's theorem (Theorem 9.1)

First a reminder of notation and a few extensions. Θ is the set of all social states and θ, θ°, θ', and so on are used to denote elements of Θ: in what follows we assume that Θ has at least three elements. The expression $\theta \succeq^h \theta'$ denotes that state θ is no worse than social state θ' according to household (agent) h with preferences $\succeq^h$. A profile of preferences for the population of n_h households is written as

$$[\succeq] := \left[\succeq^1, \succeq^2, \ldots, \succeq^h, \ldots,\right]$$

and the corresponding set of social preferences is written $\succeq$, without the enclosing [ ]. Where we need to distinguish between different profiles of preferences that may be imputed to the population we will write them as $[\succeq_1]$ and $[\succeq_2]$.

Definition C.1

A subset K of the population $\{1, 2, \ldots, n_h\}$ is *decisive* if, for all profiles and for any pair of states (θ°, θ'):

$$\left(\forall h \in K : \theta^\circ \succ^h \theta'\right) \Rightarrow \theta^\circ \succ \theta'.$$

The proof proceeds by establishing three lemmas.

Lemma C.7

If preference profiles $[\succeq_1]$ and $[\succeq_2]$ are such that

$$\forall h \in K : \theta \succ_1^h \theta^\circ \text{ and } \theta' \succ_2^h \theta'' \tag{C.101}$$

$$\forall h \notin K : \theta^\circ \succ_1^h \theta \text{ and } \theta'' \succ_2^h \theta' \tag{C.102}$$

then

$$\theta \succ_1 \theta^\circ \Longleftrightarrow \theta' \succ_2 \theta''. \tag{C.103}$$

$$\theta \sim_1 \theta^\circ \Longleftrightarrow \theta' \sim_2 \theta''. \tag{C.104}$$

Proof

Suppose $\theta \succ_1 \theta^\circ$. By Axiom 9.1 there exists a profile $[\succeq]$ such that the following are true

$$\forall h \in K : \theta' \succ^h \theta \succ^h \theta^\circ \succ^h \theta'' \tag{C.105}$$

$$\forall h \notin K : \theta^\circ \succ^h \theta'' \succ^h \theta' \succ^h \theta \tag{C.106}$$

Noting that both $\theta \succ_1^h \theta^\circ, h \in K$ (C.101) and $\theta \succ_1 \theta^\circ$ then, by Axiom 9.3 (independence of irrelevant alternatives) given that $\theta \succ^h \theta^\circ$ (C.105) it must also be true that $\theta \succ \theta^\circ$. Axiom 9.2 (Pareto unanimity) implies $\theta' \succ \theta$ and $\theta^\circ \succ \theta''$ so that, by transitivity implies $\theta' \succ \theta''$. By the same reasoning as above, if $\theta' \succ \theta''$ then Axiom 9.3 implies $\theta' \succ_2 \theta''$. If $\theta \sim_1 \theta^\circ$ but $\theta' \succ_2 \theta''$ then we have a contradiction: by Axiom 9.3 $\theta' \succ_2 \theta''$ would imply $\theta \succ_1 \theta^\circ$. ■

Lemma C.8

If, for all profiles, it is true that

$$\left(\forall h \in K : \theta^\circ \succ^h \theta'\right) \text{ and } \left(\forall h \notin K : \theta' \succ^h \theta^\circ\right) \Longrightarrow \theta^\circ \succ \theta' \tag{C.107}$$

then K is decisive.

Proof

Let the profile $[\succeq]$ be such that $\theta^\circ \succ^h \theta'$, $\forall h \in K$. Choose some θ such that

$$\forall h \in K : \theta^\circ \succ^h \theta \succ^h \theta' \tag{C.108}$$

$$\forall h \notin K : \theta \succ^h \theta^\circ \succ^h \theta'; \tag{C.109}$$

so, by construction

$$\forall h \in K : \theta^\circ \succ^h \theta \text{ and } \forall h \notin K : \theta \succ^h \theta^\circ. \tag{C.110}$$

From Lemma C.7 conditions (C.107) and (C.110) imply

$$\theta^\circ \succ \theta.$$

Axiom 9.2 and the transitivity of $\succeq$ then imply that $\theta^\circ \succ \theta'$.

However, given that (C.107) implies $\theta^\circ \succ \theta'$ Lemma C.7 means that for any other pair of states (θ'', θ''')

$$\left(\forall h \in K : \theta'' \succ^h \theta'''\right) \Longrightarrow \theta'' \succ \theta'''. ■ \tag{C.111}$$

Lemma C.9

If K is decisive and contains more than one element then there is a subset of K that is decisive.

Proof

Let K be partitioned into two non-empty subsets K_1 and K_2 such that

$$\forall h \in K_1 : \theta \succ^h \theta^\circ \succ^h \theta' \tag{C.112}$$

$$\forall h \in K_2 : \theta^\circ \succ^h \theta' \succ^h \theta \tag{C.113}$$

$$\forall h \notin K : \theta' \succ^h \theta \succ^h \theta^\circ . \tag{C.114}$$

If K is decisive then $\theta^\circ \succ \theta'$. Furthermore, one of the following must hold

Case 1 $\theta \succ \theta^\circ$. By transitivity we have $\theta \succ \theta'$ then in view of Lemma C.8 K_1 is decisive.

Case 2 $\theta \sim \theta^\circ$. Same argument as for Case 1.

Case 3 $\theta^\circ \succ \theta$. In view of Lemma C.8 K_2 is decisive. ■

It is easy to find a decisive group: by Axiom 9.2 the whole population collectively is decisive. The implication of Lemma C.9 is that one can carry on considering ever smaller decisive subsets until we arrive at a subset consisting of a single household h that is decisive, i.e. such that for all $\theta, \theta' \in \Theta : \theta \succ^h \theta' \Rightarrow \theta \succ \theta'$. But this means that h is a dictator, in violation of Axiom 9.4.

C.7.2 Black's theorem (Theorem 9.2)

In this case we can represent the set of social states as a subset Θ of the real line; this permits the following definition.

Definition C.2

$\succeq^h$ is *single peaked* if there is a $\theta^h \in \Theta$ such that (i) $\theta < \theta^\circ \leq \theta^h$ implies $\theta^\circ \succ^h \theta$ and (ii) $\theta^h \geq \theta' > \theta''$ implies $\theta' \succ^h \theta''$.

■ **Lemma C.10**

If the profile $[\succeq]$ consists of single-peaked preferences then majority voting yields a unique Condorcet winner.

Proof

Let F be the distribution function of the peak values: $F(\theta)$ is the proportion of the population with a peak $\leq \theta$. Let θ^* be the median of the distribution (i.e. such that $F(\theta^*) = \frac{1}{2}$)—see Definition A.29 on page 513. Take any $\theta < \theta^*$. Consider households for which $\theta^h \geq \theta^*$: there are at least $\frac{1}{2}[n_h + 1]$ of these. Clearly, by definition of single-peakedness for all households in this group $\theta^h \succ^h \theta$. By contrast consider households for which $\theta^h < \theta^*$: there are at most $\frac{1}{2}[n_h - 1]$ of those. So a simple vote on θ versus θ^* will unambiguously select θ^*. A symmetric argument follows for any $\theta > \theta^*$. ■

Lemma C.10 establishes that there is a best alternative. The following proof of Theorem 9.2 then requires a slightly stronger form of single-peakedness—no household is indifferent as between any two distinct alternatives.

Proof

Because n_h is odd and indifference is ruled out for each $\succeq^h$ on any pair of states in Θ voting between pairs always produces a decisive majority. Suppose $\theta \succ \theta'$ and $\theta' \succ \theta''$. From

Lemma C.10 we know that the set $\{\theta, \theta', \theta''\}$ must have a unique best alternative if the profile consists of single-peaked preferences: this has to be θ because, by assumption, θ' and θ'' are outvoted by θ and θ' respectively We have thus established that $\theta \succ \theta'$ and $\theta' \succ \theta''$ together imply $\theta \succ \theta''$. ■

C.7.3 The support theorem (Theorem 9.5)

As with Theorem 6.2 the core of this proof is the demonstration of the existence of a separating hyperplane. If $\hat{\mathbf{a}} := ([\hat{\mathbf{x}}], [\hat{\mathbf{q}}])$ is the Pareto-efficient allocation, then define the set

$$B(\hat{\mathbf{x}}) := \left\{ \sum_h \mathbf{x}^h : U^h(\mathbf{x}^h) \geq U^h(\hat{\mathbf{x}}^h) \right\} \tag{C.115}$$

analogous to the definition in equation (7.33). Since all goods are private goods $\hat{\mathbf{x}} = \sum_h \hat{\mathbf{x}}^h$ and $B(\hat{\mathbf{x}})$ represents the set of aggregate consumption vectors which correspond to allocations that are Pareto superior to, or are equivalent to $\hat{\mathbf{a}}$. By virtue of the assumption of concave-contoured utility functions this set is convex; by virtue of the assumption of greed any $\hat{\mathbf{x}} \geq \hat{\mathbf{x}}$ must belong to $B(\hat{\mathbf{x}})$, and any $\hat{\mathbf{x}} > \hat{\mathbf{x}}$ must be an interior point. Also define the set of attainable aggregate consumption vectors

$$A := \{\mathbf{x} : \mathbf{x} \leq \mathbf{q} + \mathbf{R}; \mathbf{q} \in Q\}$$

where $\mathbf{R}$ is the vector of resource endowments for the economy. Since it is assumed that each firm's technology set is convex and there are no externalities, A is convex. By definition of a Pareto-efficient allocation $\hat{\mathbf{x}} \in \bar{B}(\hat{\mathbf{x}})$, and $\hat{\mathbf{x}} \in A$, but no vector in A could also belong to the interior of $\bar{B}(\hat{\mathbf{x}})$ for, if it did, then there would be some feasible allocation in which some greedy consumer could be made better off, without anyone else being made worse off. So there is a separating hyperplane (A.25) such that, for all $\mathbf{x} \in A$:

$$\sum_{i=1}^{n} p_i x_i \leq y \tag{C.116}$$

and, for all $\mathbf{x} \in B(\mathbf{x}^*)$:

$$\sum_{i=1}^{n} p_i x_i \geq y \tag{C.117}$$

where $y := \sum_{i=1}^{n} p_i \hat{x}_i$ since $\hat{\mathbf{x}}$ lies on the boundary of both sets. From (C.116) we have

$$\sum_i p_i [x_i - \hat{x}_i] \geq 0 \text{ for all } \mathbf{x} \geq \hat{\mathbf{x}} \tag{C.118}$$

which reveals immediately that $\mathbf{p} \geq 0$.

It remains to be shown that the semi-positive vector $\mathbf{p}$ plays the rôle of a genuine competitive equilibrium price vector. Using (C.117) and the definition of A we have

$$\sum_{i=1}^{n} p_i [q_i + R_i] \leq \sum_{i=1}^{n} p_i [\hat{q}_i + R_i] \text{ for all } \mathbf{q} \in Q. \tag{C.119}$$

In view of the absence of externalities we have $\mathbf{q} = \sum_f \mathbf{q}^f$ and so the inequality (C.119) implies

$$\sum_{i=1}^{n} \sum_{f=1}^{n_f} p_i q_i^f \leq \sum_{i=1}^{n} \sum_{f=1}^{n_f} p_i \hat{q}_i^f \text{ for all } \mathbf{q}^f \in Q^f. \tag{C.120}$$

But this implies $\sum_{i=1}^{n} p_i \hat{q}_i^f \geq \sum_{i=1}^{n} p_i q_i^f$ for any firm f: in other words, given prices $\mathbf{p}$, firm f would maximise profits at $\mathbf{q}^f$.

Next observe that an analogous argument yields the result:

$$U^h(\tilde{\mathbf{x}}^h) \geq U^h(\hat{\mathbf{x}}^h) \Rightarrow \sum_{i=1}^{n} p_i \tilde{x}_i^h \geq y^h \text{ for all } h \tag{C.121}$$

where

$$y^h := \sum_{i=1}^{n} p_i \hat{x}_i^h > 0.$$

In other words: any bundle that yields h at least as much utility as $\hat{\mathbf{x}}^h$ must cost at least as much as $\hat{\mathbf{x}}^h$ when valued at prices $\mathbf{p}$. So, consider any arbitrary $\mathbf{x}^h$ that h could afford at these prices, i.e. such that $\sum_{i=1}^{n} p_i x_i^h \leq y^h$. Take some positive scalar t. Obviously $t \sum_{i=1}^{n} p_i x_i^h < y^h$. for all $t < 1$. So, in view of (C.121) we have, for any $t < 1$:

$$t \sum_i p_i x_i < y^h \Rightarrow U^h(t\mathbf{x}^h) < U^h(\hat{\mathbf{x}}^h) \tag{C.122}$$

and in the limit, as $t \longrightarrow 1$ we see that we indeed have the result that, given prices $\mathbf{p}$, $\hat{\mathbf{x}}^h$ maximises $U^h(\mathbf{x}^h)$ over the budget set $\left\{\mathbf{x}^h : \mathbf{x}^h \geq 0, \sum_{i=1}^{n} p_i x_i^h \leq y^h\right\}$. Hence the allocation $\hat{\mathbf{a}}$ and the associated price vector $\mathbf{p}$ is indeed a competitive equilibrium since each household is maximising utility, each firm is maximising profits, and the allocation satisfies the materials balance condition (7.7). ■

C.7.4 Potential superiority (Theorem 9.10)

The state θ is *potentially superior* to θ' if there exists $\theta^* \in \hat{\Theta}(\theta)$ such that θ^* is Pareto superior to θ'. Let $\mathbf{p}$ be the prices in state θ and let $y^h = C^h\left(\mathbf{p}, \upsilon^h(\theta)\right)$ be h's income in state θ. By definition 9.7 there exists some feasible θ^* such that

$$\sum_{h=1}^{n_h} C^h\left(\mathbf{p}, \upsilon^h(\theta^*)\right) \leq \sum_{h=1}^{n_h} y^h \tag{C.123}$$

and

$$\forall h : \upsilon^h(\theta^*) \geq \upsilon^h(\theta') \tag{C.124}$$

with strict inequality for at least one h. Condition (C.124) implies

$$\sum_{h=1}^{n_h} C^h\left(\mathbf{p}, \upsilon^h(\theta^*)\right) > \sum_{h=1}^{n_h} C^h\left(\mathbf{p}, \upsilon^h(\theta')\right) \tag{C.125}$$

and so, from (C.123):

$$\sum_{h=1}^{n_h} y^h > \sum_{h=1}^{n_h} C^h\left(\mathbf{p}, \upsilon^h(\theta')\right) \tag{C.126}$$

$$\sum_{h=1}^{n_h} C^h\left(\mathbf{p}, \upsilon^h(\theta)\right) > \sum_{h=1}^{n_h} C^h\left(\mathbf{p}, \upsilon^h(\theta')\right) \tag{C.127}$$

which implies that $\sum_{h=1}^{n_h} \mathrm{CV}^h(\theta' \rightarrow \theta) > 0$. This establishes necessity.

For the sufficiency part let

$$y^{*1} := C^1\left(\mathbf{p}, \upsilon^h(\theta')\right) + \sum_{h=1}^{n_h} \mathrm{CV}^h(\theta' \rightarrow \theta), \tag{C.128}$$

$$y^{*h} := C^h\left(\mathbf{p}, \upsilon^h(\theta')\right),\ h = 2, 3, \ldots, n_h. \tag{C.129}$$

Note that

$$\sum_{h=1}^{n_h} y^{*h} = \sum_{h=1}^{n_h} C^h\left(\mathbf{p}, \upsilon^h(\theta')\right) + \sum_{h=1}^{n_h} \mathrm{CV}^h(\theta' \to \theta)$$

$$= \sum_{h=1}^{n_h} C^h\left(\mathbf{p}, \upsilon^h(\theta)\right). \tag{C.130}$$

So this produces a social state θ^* which is superior to θ' and accessible from θ. ■

C.8 Strategic behaviour

C.8.1 Nash equilibrium in pure strategies with infinite strategy sets (Theorem 10.2)

Let the Cartesian product of all the agents' strategy sets be

$$S := S^1 \times S^2 \times \ldots \times S^h \times \ldots$$

Also, let $\beta^h(\cdot)$ be the best-response correspondence for agent h defined by (10.5) so that

$$\beta^h\left([s]^{-h}\right) = \arg\max_{s^h} \upsilon^h\left(s^h, [s]^{-h}\right) \tag{C.131}$$

is the set of h-strategies that maximise υ^h given the strategies of all other agents. Using Theorem A.12 it is clear that, given the quasiconcavity of υ^h and the convexity of S^h, the set $\beta^h\left([s]^{-h}\right)$ is convex. Consider any sequence of strategy profiles

$$\{[s_1], [s_2], \ldots, [s_i], \ldots\}$$

where $[s_i] \in S$ for all i such that

1. the sequence converges to a limit:

$$\lim [s_i] = [\tilde{s}] \in S \tag{C.132}$$

2. and for every profile i in the sequence:

$$s_i^h \in \beta^h\left([s_i]^{-h}\right). \tag{C.133}$$

Condition (C.133) implies that

$$\text{for all } s_0^h \in S^h: \ \upsilon^h\left(s_i^h, [s]^{-h}\right) \geq \upsilon^h\left(s_0^h, [s]^{-h}\right) \tag{C.134}$$

—see equation (10.4) on page 277. By the continuity of υ^h it is therefore the case that

$$\text{for all } s_0^h \in S^h: \ \upsilon^h\left(\tilde{s}^h, [\tilde{s}]^{-h}\right) \geq \upsilon^h\left(s_0^h, [\tilde{s}]^{-h}\right) \tag{C.135}$$

so that

$$\tilde{s}^h \in \beta^h\left([\tilde{s}]^{-h}\right). \tag{C.136}$$

Now consider a correspondence $\beta : S \mapsto S$ given by

$$\beta := \beta^1 \times \beta^2 \times \ldots \times \beta^h \times \ldots \tag{C.137}$$

The expression $\beta([s])$ gives the profile of strategies that are best responses to an arbitrarily given profile of strategies $[s]$. By definition the correspondence β maps a convex, compact set S into itself. The graph of β is closed because, from (C.132) and (C.136), the set $\{([s], \beta([s])) : [s] \in S\}$ contains all its limit points. Also, given that S is assumed to be compact, it is true that the image under β of every compact set is bounded. So, from Definition A.12 the correspondence β is upper-hemicontinuous. One may therefore apply Kakutani's theorem (Theorem A.4) to establish that there is some $[s^*] \in S$ such that

$$[s^*] \in \beta([s^*]).$$ ■

C.8.2 Existence of Nash equilibrium (Theorem 10.1)

For a finite set of pure strategies S^h let $\boldsymbol{\pi}^h$ denote the vector of probabilities characterising a mixed strategy for agent h, where $\boldsymbol{\pi}^h$ has dimension $\#S^h$, and write Δ^h for the set of all such probability vectors. Clearly Δ^h is a convex, compact set and so the Cartesian product

$$\Delta := \Delta^1 \times \Delta^2 \times \ldots \times \Delta^h \times \ldots$$

is also convex and compact. Write $v^h\left(\boldsymbol{\pi}^h, [\boldsymbol{\pi}]^{-h}\right)$ for the expected utility of agent h if he uses the probability vector $\boldsymbol{\pi}^h$ given that all other agents are using $[\boldsymbol{\pi}]^{-h}$. Also, let $\beta^h(\cdot)$ be the best-response correspondence for agent h defined by (10.5) so that

$$\beta^h\left([\boldsymbol{\pi}]^{-h}\right) = \arg\max_{\boldsymbol{\pi}^h} v^h\left(\boldsymbol{\pi}^h, [\boldsymbol{\pi}]^{-h}\right). \tag{C.138}$$

Define the correspondence $\beta : \Delta \mapsto \Delta$ as in (C.137). Then by the same argument as in the proof of Theorem 10.2 (section C.8.1) β is an upper-hemicontinuous mapping of a convex compact set Δ into convex subsets itself of Δ.

From Theorem A.4 the correspondence β has a fixed point $[\boldsymbol{\pi}^*]$. This is the mixed-strategy equilibrium. ■

Note that in the above result the profile $[\boldsymbol{\pi}^*]$ may include components such as $\boldsymbol{\pi}^{*h} = (0, 0, \ldots, 0, 1, 0 \ldots)$—i.e. pure strategies—as a special case.

C.8.3 The Folk Theorem

We establish here a result that is somewhat weaker than Theorem 10.3. The notation used is taken from section 10.5.3 (page 301 onwards), slightly generalised to allow for more than two players.

Theorem C.3

Given a stage game with Nash-equilibrium payoffs $[\underline{\upsilon}] := [\underline{\upsilon}^1, \underline{\upsilon}^2, \ldots]$ that lie in the interior of $\mathbb{U}^*$ there is a non-negative $\underline{\delta}$ such that a repeated game with discount factor $\delta \in (\underline{\delta}, 1]$ has a subgame-perfect equilibrium yielding payoffs that strictly dominate $[\underline{\upsilon}]$.

Denote the actions for the stage game by $[q] := [q^1, q^2, \ldots]$ and let the actions that yield the Nash equilibrium of the stage game be $[\underline{q}]$. Suppose that there is some given profile of actions $[\hat{q}]$ that yields payoffs $[\hat{\upsilon}]$ where $\hat{\upsilon}^h > \underline{\upsilon}^h$, $h = 1, 2, \ldots$ Let the maximum payoff available to agent h in the stage game be $\overline{\upsilon}^h > \hat{\upsilon}^h$ and define

$$\underline{\delta} := \frac{\overline{\upsilon}^h - \hat{\upsilon}^h}{\overline{\upsilon}^h - \underline{\upsilon}^h}.$$

Note that, by construction, $0 < \underline{\delta} < 1$.

For the repeated game with discount factor δ payoffs are given by the sum (10.22). Consider the trigger strategy s^h_{T} defined as follows:

Observed actions in $0, \ldots, t$	action by h at $t+1$
$[\hat{q}]$	$\hat{q}^h$
Anything else	$\underline{q}^h$

The strategy profile $[s_{\mathrm{T}}]$ is a Nash equilibrium as long as

$$[1-\delta]\,\bar{\upsilon}^h + \delta\underline{\upsilon}^h < \hat{\upsilon}^h$$

This is satisfied as long as $\underline{\delta} < \delta \leq 1$. Given that in every subgame off the equilibrium path $[s_{\mathrm{T}}]$ specifies the actions $[\underline{q}]$ that form the Nash equilibrium of the stage game we see that $[s_{\mathrm{T}}]$ induces a Nash equilibrium in all subgames. Hence it is subgame perfect. ■

Note that the proof introduced the assumption that there was a given action profile $[\hat{q}]$ that would yield the payoffs $[\hat{\upsilon}]$. If this assumption is not satisfied for a particular game then it is possible to introduce a coordinated randomisation between two or more action profiles that would do the job. The coordination is important here, in that independent randomisations may not produce a point on the frontier of $\mathbb{U}^*$—see Exercise 10.4 (page 323) for an example.

C.9 Design

C.9.1 Revenue equivalence (Theorem 12.6)

We take the case where the tastes τ are distributed according to the distribution function F with support $[\underline{\tau}, \bar{\tau}]$; it is assumed that the density $f(\tau)$ is strictly positive everywhere in $[\underline{\tau}, \bar{\tau}]$.

Suppose all bidders $\ell \neq h$ are following an optimal strategy $p^\ell = \beta(\tau^\ell)$. Using the general description of the auction mechanism given in (12.18) and (12.19), the probability that h wins and the expected payment that h faces are

$$\pi\left(p^h\right) := \mathcal{E}\pi^h\left(\beta\left(\tau^1\right), \beta\left(\tau^2\right), \ldots, \beta\left(\tau^{h-1}\right), p^h, \beta\left(\tau^{h+1}\right), \ldots\right)$$

$$P\left(p^h\right) := \mathcal{E}P^h\left(\beta\left(\tau^1\right), \beta\left(\tau^2\right), \ldots, \beta\left(\tau^{h-1}\right), p^h, \beta\left(\tau^{h+1}\right), \ldots\right)$$

where the expectation is taken over the joint distribution of $\tau^\ell, \ell \neq h$. The utility from bidding p^h is

$$V\left(p^h; \tau^h\right) = \pi\left(p^h\right)\tau^h - P\left(p^h\right).$$

Let υ be defined by

$$\upsilon(\tau) := V(\beta(\tau); \tau).$$

Because υ is a maximum-value function we can apply the envelope theorem:

$$\frac{d\upsilon(\tau)}{d\tau} = \pi(\beta(\tau)). \tag{C.139}$$

For (C.139) to be defined everywhere on $[\underline{\tau}, \bar{\tau}]$ we require strictly positive density. Consider two values $\tau' < \tau''$; let $\tau^\circ := t\tau' + [1-t]\tau''$ for some t such that $0 < t < 1$ and let $p^\circ := \beta(\tau^\circ)$. Clearly

$$\upsilon\left(\tau^\circ\right) = t\pi\left(p^\circ\right)\tau' + [1-t]\pi\left(p^\circ\right)\tau'' - P\left(p^\circ\right). \tag{C.140}$$

Because υ is a maximum-value function, we have

$$\pi\left(p^\circ\right)\tau' - P\left(p^\circ\right) \leq V\left(\beta\left(\tau'\right); \tau'\right) \tag{C.141}$$

$$\pi\left(p^\circ\right)\tau'' - P\left(p^\circ\right) \leq V\left(\beta\left(\tau''\right); \tau''\right). \tag{C.142}$$

From (C.140)–(C.142) we have

$$\upsilon(\tau^{\circ}) \leq t\upsilon(\tau') + [1-t]\,\upsilon(\tau'').$$

In other words $\upsilon(\cdot)$ is convex so that $\frac{d\upsilon(\tau)}{d\tau}$ is non-decreasing in τ.

We have a Bayesian Nash equilibrium if, for all h such that $\tau^h \geq \underline{\tau}^h$:

$$\upsilon\left(\tau^h\right) \geq V\left(p^h, \tau^h\right), \text{ for all } \tau^h \geq \underline{\tau}^h :$$

$$\upsilon\left(\underline{\tau}^h\right) = 0$$

or equivalently

$$\pi\left(\beta\left(\tau^h\right)\right)\tau^h - P\left(\beta\left(\tau^h\right)\right) \geq \pi\left(p^h\right)\tau^h - P\left(p^h\right) \tag{C.143}$$

$$\pi\left(\beta\left(\underline{\tau}^h\right)\right)\underline{\tau}^h - P\left(\beta\left(\underline{\tau}^h\right)\right) = 0. \tag{C.144}$$

Condition (C.143) is an incentive-compatibility constraint; condition (C.144) is a participation constraint. To satisfy (C.143) $\pi(\cdot)$ must be a non-decreasing function; so, given that $\frac{d\upsilon(\cdot)}{d\tau}$ is non-decreasing, equation (C.139) implies that $\beta(\cdot)$ must be non-decreasing. However, if the auction goes to the highest bidder then $\beta(\cdot)$ cannot be constant over some interval: if $\tau' < \tau''$ were such that $\beta(\tau') = \beta(\tau'')$ then a bidder with taste τ'' would be able to increase expected payoff by raising the bid slightly to win the auction. So $\beta(\cdot)$ is a strictly increasing function.

A consequence of this is that in equilibrium if a bidder with taste parameter τ wins then all the other bidders must have values less than τ. So the probability of a person with taste τ winning must be

$$\pi^*(\tau) := \pi(\beta(\tau)) = [F(\tau)]^{N-1}. \tag{C.145}$$

Using (C.145) and integrating (C.139), the utility that an agent gets if $\tau \geq \underline{\tau}$ is therefore

$$\upsilon(\tau) = \int_{\underline{\tau}}^{\tau} \frac{d\upsilon(x)}{dx}dx = \int_{\underline{\tau}}^{\tau} \pi(\beta(x))\,dx = \int_{\underline{\tau}}^{\tau} [F(x)]^{N-1}\,dx.$$

At the optimum

$$\upsilon(\tau) = \pi(\beta(\tau))\,\tau - P(\beta(\tau)).$$

So, $P^*(\tau)$, the expected equilibrium payment by a participating agent with taste τ is:

$$\begin{aligned} P(\beta(\tau)) &= \pi^*(\tau)\,\tau - \upsilon(\tau) \\ &= \tau[F(\tau)]^{N-1} - \int_{\underline{\tau}}^{\tau} [F(x)]^{N-1}\,dx. \end{aligned} \tag{C.146}$$

The expected revenue to the seller is given by N times the expected value of (C.146)

$$\begin{aligned} &N\int_{\underline{\tau}}^{\bar{\tau}} \tau[F(\tau)]^{N-1} f(\tau)\,d\tau - N\cdot\int_{\underline{\tau}}^{\bar{\tau}}\left[\int_{\underline{\tau}}^{\tau}[F(x)]^{N-1}dx\right] f(\tau)\,d\tau \\ &= N\int_{\underline{\tau}}^{\bar{\tau}}\left[\tau - \frac{1-F(\tau)}{f(\tau)}\right]\frac{dF(\tau)^N}{d\tau}d\tau \\ &= N\int_{\underline{\tau}}^{\bar{\tau}}\left[\tau - \frac{1-F(\tau)}{f(\tau)}\right]\pi^*(\tau) f(\tau)\,d\tau \\ &= N\int_{\underline{\tau}}^{\bar{\tau}} \tau\pi^*(\tau) f(\tau)\,d\tau - N\int_{\underline{\tau}}^{\bar{\tau}} [1-F(\tau)]\,\pi^*(\tau)\,d\tau. \end{aligned} \tag{C.147}$$

But expression (C.147) is independent of the auction type and the associated bid function.

C.9.2 The Clark–Groves mechanism (Theorem 12.7)

The payment rule (12.32) can be written

$$P^h\left(p^1,p^2,\ldots\right) = \pi\left(p^1,p^2,\ldots\right)\left[z^h - \Delta^h\right] + \max\left(\Delta^h,0\right) \tag{C.148}$$

where π is determined by (12.31) and Δ^h is given by (12.30). Given (12.21), (12.22), and income y^h the utility of agent h is then given by

$$\begin{aligned}
\tau^h\psi(x_1) + x_2^h &= \tau^h\psi(\pi) + y^h - P^h \\
&= \tau^h\pi - \pi\left[z^h - \Delta^h\right] - \max\left(\Delta^h,0\right) + y^h \\
&= \pi\left(p^1,p^2,\ldots,p^h,\ldots\right)\left[\tau^h - z^h + \Delta^h\right] - \max\left(\Delta^h,0\right) + y^h \\
&= \pi\left(p^1,p^2,\ldots,p^h,\ldots\right)\left[\sum_{k=1}^{n_h}\left[p^k - z^k\right] + \tau^h - p^h\right] - \max\left(\Delta^h,0\right) + y^h.
\end{aligned}$$

There are two cases to consider

1. Suppose $\tau^h - z^h + \Delta^h \geq 0$, then declaring $p^h = \tau^h$ implies

   $$\sum_{k=1}^{n_h} p^k \geq \bar{z}$$

   so that $\pi = 1$; declaring $p^h > \tau^h$ will not improve on this outcome; declaring $p^h < \tau^h$ may result in $\pi = 0$ which will reduce utility.

2. Suppose $\tau^h - z^h + \Delta^h < 0$. Declaring $p^h = \tau^h$ implies

   $$\sum_{k=1}^{n_h} p^k < \bar{z}$$

   and declaring $p^h < \tau^h$ will not improve on this outcome; declaring $p^h > \tau^h$ may result in $\pi = 1$ which will reduce utility.

Therefore declaring $p^h = \tau^h$ is a weakly dominant strategy.

Finally notice that the problem remains essentially unchanged if the term $\max\left(\Delta^h,0\right)$ in (C.148) is replaced by $\kappa^h\left([p]^{-h}\right)$ where $\kappa^h(\cdot)$ is an arbitrary function and $[p]^{-h}$ is the list of announced valuations $(p^1,p^2,\ldots)$ with the hth component deleted, as in (10.1).

INDEX

D

T

U